T5-CFT-474

JOURNAL FOR THE STUDY OF THE NEW TESTAMENT SUPPLEMENT SERIES

110

Sheffield Academic Press
Sheffield

The Davidic Messiah in Luke–Acts

The Promise and its Fulfillment in Lukan Christology

Mark L. Strauss

Journal for the Study of the New Testament Supplement Series 110

Published by Sheffield Academic Press Ltd
Mansion House
19 Kingfield Road
Sheffield, S11 9AS
England

Typeset by Sheffield Academic Press
and
Printed on acid-free paper in Great Britain
by Bookcraft
Midsomer Norton, Somerset

British Library Cataloguing in Publication Data

A catalogue record for this book is available
from the British Library

ISBN 1-85075-522-1

CONTENTS

PREFACE

The nature of Lukan Christology has been much debated in recent years, with various scholars claiming the pre-eminence of such categories as Lord, Prophet (like Moses), Christ, or Isaianic Servant. In the face of such diverse views, others have rejected any unity in Luke's presentation, claiming instead that the author borrows freely and inconsistently from a variety of traditional perspectives.

The present work is an examination of one major theme within Luke's christology, Jesus as the coming king from the line of David. Much of the work is dedicated to establishing the importance and significance of this royal-messianic theme within Luke's christological purpose. Even the casual reader of Luke–Acts will recognize, however, that royal messianism is only one among many Lukan motifs. Themes such as Jesus' status as saviour, prophet, servant, Son of God, and Lord are also prominent. A major part of the work is therefore dedicated to reaching a synthesis between this and other christological motifs. On the basis of the conclusions reached, Luke's christological presentation may be seen to be both consistent and unified, playing an integral part in his wider purpose in Luke–Acts.

This study is a revised and somewhat abbreviated version of a thesis submitted for the degree of PhD at the University of Aberdeen in 1992. The most significant alteration to the original is a thorough revision of Chapter 2, which now contains a brief overview rather than a detailed study of the Davidic promise tradition in first-century Judaism. At other points footnotes were omitted and discussion abbreviated. These changes were meant to bring the work to a more managable size without loss to the thesis argument.

This work could not have been completed without the support and encouragement of family and friends. I would like to thank the post-graduate community at Aberdeen, who were a continual source of both intellectual stimulation and spiritual support. My wife and I also owe a great debt to our friends at Deeside Christian Fellowship. Throughout our stay in Aberdeen they welcomed us into their hearts and homes and truly became our second family.

Special thanks also go to my advisor, Dr Max Turner, whose careful reading and insightful guidance helped me to avoid many errors and inconsistencies which would otherwise have entered the work. I am also most grateful to Professor I. Howard Marshall and Professor C.K. Barrett, who provided many helpful suggestions and who encouraged the publication of this work.

Most of all, I want to thank my family, my parents and especially my wife Roxanne, whose love and support sustained me throughout this endeavour.

This work is dedicated to the memory of my father, Dr Richard L. Strauss, who entered the presence of the Lord on 11 September 1993. His great love for God's Word and sincere and faithful devotion to his Master have had a profound and eternal impact on my life.

ABBREVIATIONS

ANQ	*Andover Newton Quarterly*
ANRW	*Aufstieg und Niedergang der römischen Welt*
APOT	R.H. Charles (ed.), *Apocrypha and Pseudepigrapha of the Old Testament*
ARW	*Archiv für Religionswissenschaft*
ASTI	*Annual of the Swedish Theological Institute*
ATR	*Anglican Theological Review*
BAGD	W. Bauer, W.F. Arndt, F.W. Gingrich and F.W. Danker, *Greek–English Lexicon of the New Testament*
BDB	F. Brown, S.R. Driver and C.A. Briggs, *Hebrew and English Lexicon of the Old Testament*
BDF	F. Blass, A. Debrunner and R.W. Funk, *A Greek Grammar of the New Testament*
Bib	*Biblica*
BJRL	*Bulletin of the John Rylands University Library of Manchester*
BK	*Bibel und Kirche*
BSac	*Bibliotheca Sacra*
BTB	*Biblical Theology Bulletin*
BZ	*Biblische Zeitschrift*
CBQ	*Catholic Biblical Quarterly*
ConBNT	Coniectanea biblica, New Testament
CTM	*Concordia Theological Monthly*
EvQ	*Evangelical Quarterly*
EvT	*Evangelische Theologie*
ExpTim	*Expository Times*
HTR	*Harvard Theological Review*
HUCM	Hebrew Union College Monographs
Int	*Interpretation*
JBL	*Journal of Biblical Literature*
JETS	*Journal of the Evangelical Theological Society*
JJS	*Journal of Jewish Studies*
JSNT	*Journal for the Study of the New Testament*
JSOT	*Journal for the Study of the Old Testament*
JSS	*Journal of Semitic Studies*
JTS	*Journal of Theological Studies*
LTP	*Laval théologique et philosophique*

MNTC	Moffatt NT Commentary
Neot	*Neotestamentica*
NovT	*Novum Testamentum*
NRT	*La nouvelle revue théologique*
NTS	*New Testament Studies*
OTS	*Oudtestamentische Studiën*
RB	*Revue biblique*
RevExp	*Review and Expositor*
RevQ	*Revue de Qumran*
RSR	*Recherches de science religieuse*
ScEccl	*Sciences ecclésiastiques*
SE	*Studia Evangelica*
SEÅ	*Svensk exegetisk årsbok*
Sem	*Semitica*
SJT	*Scottish Journal of Theology*
ST	*Studia theologica*
Str–B	H. Strack and P. Billerbeck, *Kommentar zum Neuen Testament aus Talmud und Midrasch*
TDNT	G. Kittel and G. Friedrich (eds.), *Theological Dictionary of the New Testament*
TLZ	*Theologische Literaturzeitung*
TQ	*Theologische Quartalschrift*
TTZ	*Trierer theologische Zeitschrift*
TU	Texte und Untersuchungen
TynBul	*Tyndale Bulletin*
TZ	*Theologische Zeitschrift*
VT	*Vetus Testamentum*
VTSup	*Vetus Testamentum*, Supplements
ZAW	*Zeitschrift für die alttestamentliche Wissenschaft*
ZKG	*Zeitschrift für Kirchengeschichte*
ZNW	*Zeitschrift für die neutestamentliche Wissenschaft*
ZTK	*Zeitschrift für Theologie und Kirche*

Part I

INTRODUCTION AND SETTING

Chapter 1

INTRODUCTION

1. *'Proof from Prophecy' and Lukan Purpose*

Since the publication in 1957 of Paul Schubert's seminal essay, 'The Structure and Significance of Luke 24', it has been widely recognized that what Schubert describes as 'proof from prophecy' is one of Luke's primary interests throughout his two-volume work.[1] Schubert's essay picks up and develops a line laid down by H.J. Cadbury in *The Making of Luke–Acts,* namely that Luke–Acts is pervaded with the theme of divine control and purpose—a purpose set forth beforehand in the Scriptures.[2] Schubert focuses especially on Luke 24, which he views as the climax of Luke's Gospel. He examines the three resurrection scenes in Luke 24: the discovery of the empty tomb, the Emmaus account and Jesus' appearance to the eleven and 'those with them'. While each of these scenes contains a traditional core, Luke links them together with the same redactional climax, which Schubert designates 'proof from prophecy' that Jesus is the Christ.[3] This theme is 'the structural and material element which provides the literary and theological unity and climax of the gospel', and which assures the reader 'that the attested events of the life, death and resurrection of Jesus as the Christ are guaranteed beyond doubt, by the long-foretold and on-going prophecies which unfold in history the "will and plan" of God (see Acts 2.23; 4.28; 13.36; 20.27)'.[4]

While substantially agreeing with Schubert that a promise-fulfillment motif plays a central role in Luke's christological use of the Old

1. P. Schubert, 'The Structure and Significance of Luke 24', in *Neutestamentliche Studien für Rudolf Bultmann* (1957), pp. 165-86, cf. esp. p. 176.

2. H.J. Cadbury, *The Making of Luke–Acts* (2nd edn, 1958), pp. 303-305. For Schubert's debt to Cadbury see 'Structure and Significance', p. 165 n. 1.

3. Schubert, 'Structure and Significance', pp. 173-77.

4. Schubert, 'Structure and Significance', p. 176.

Testament, Darrell Bock challenges his designation 'proof from prophecy', suggesting instead the description 'proclamation from prophecy and pattern'.[1] 'Proclamation' because Luke's use of the Old Testament for Christology is not primarily in terms of a defensive apologetic, but rather involves the direct and positive proclamation of Jesus. The church is 'on the offensive concerning Jesus'.[2] Bock insists on 'pattern' as well as prophecy because Luke sees the Scriptures fulfilled in Jesus not merely in terms of the fulfillment of Old Testament prophecy, but also in terms of the reintroduction and fulfillment of Old Testament patterns (i.e. typology) that point to the presence of God's saving work.[3] While Bock is surely correct in his inclusion of typology and his emphasis on positive proclamation, proclamation *per se* does not necessarily rule out 'defensive' and apologetic interests on Luke's part. By positively proclaiming the significance of Jesus' words and deeds in the context of Old Testament prophecy, Luke would both reassure believers in their faith and defend the church's claims against external attacks.[4] That *apologia* is part of Luke's proclamation is suggested by Acts 9.20-22 where Paul 'proclaims' Jesus in the synagogues, 'confounding the Jews...by proving that this one is the Christ'.

The present work is an examination of one Old Testament theme within Luke's 'proclamation from prophecy and pattern' motif. This theme is the fulfillment of the promises to David through Jesus the messiah. Justification for the study is the lack of a comprehensive and satisfying treatment of the topic. This need may be demonstrated by a survey of recent research.

2. *Recent Research on the Davidic Messiah in Luke–Acts*

The majority of work on the theme of the Davidic messiah in the New Testament has centered on the christological *Hoheitstitel* 'son of David',

1. D.L. Bock, *Proclamation from Prophecy and Pattern: Lucan Old Testament Christology* (1987). Bock's work is primarily a challenge to M. Rese, *Alttestamentliche Motive in der Christologie des Lukas* (1969), who argued that promise and fulfillment was *not* a major motif in Luke's christological use of the Old Testament. In my opinion, Bock has conclusively answered Rese on this point.

2. Bock, *Proclamation*, p. 275.

3. Bock, *Proclamation*, esp. pp. 274-75.

4. Without explicitly saying so, Bock, *Proclamation*, pp. 277-78, 279, seems to allow for an apologetic purpose of sorts when he suggests that Luke is writing for a church suffering doubt caused by the pressure of persecution.

with primary focus on the pre-synoptic tradition. These works have dealt especially with three areas: (1) the entrance and significance of the title in earliest Christianity;[1] (2) the interpretation of the traditional *Davidssohnfrage* pericope of Mk 12.35-37; and (3) the relationship of the healing son of David to the figure of Solomon.[2] More relevant to the present work are those studies which focus on the redactional interest of the Evangelists themselves. While various works have examined the 'son of David' title in Matthew[3] and Mark,[4] Luke's seeming lack of interest in the *title* has resulted in relatively few studies on Davidic messianism in Luke–Acts. Some scholars have concluded that Luke has little interest in this theme. On the contrary, the present work will seek to show that Jesus' royal Davidic status is a leading motif in Luke's work.

The most important *traditionsgeschichtliche* study of Davidic messiahship in the New Testament in general, and Luke–Acts in particular, is C. Burger's *Jesus als Davidssohn: eine traditionsgeschichtliche Untersuchung* (1970). After a brief chapter on Jewish background, Burger traces the Davidic promise tradition from the early pre-Pauline credo incorporated in Rom. 1.3, 4, through the New Testament corpus, with chapters dealing, respectively, with Christian confessional formulas, Mark (separate discussions of pre-Markan and Markan material), Matthew, Luke–Acts, John and Revelation. Burger's primary thesis

1. See especially W. Wrede, 'Jesus als Davidssohn', in *Vorträge und Studien* (1907), pp. 147-77; F. Hahn, *Christologische Hoheitstitel: Ihre Geschichte im frühen Christentum* (1963), ET: *The Titles of Jesus in Christology* (1969), pp. 240-78; D.C. Duling, 'Traditions of the Promises to David and His Sons in Early Judaism and Primitive Christianity' (PhD Diss.; University of Chicago, 1970). Duling's basic argument appears in abbreviated form in his article, 'The Promises to David and their Entrance into Christianity: Nailing Down a Likely Hypothesis', *NTS* 19 (1973), pp. 55-77. See also the works cited in Chapter 2, section 3a.

2. For these latter two, see the discussion and works cited in Chapter 2, section 3c.

3. In addition to the commentaries, cf. J.M. Gibbs, 'Purpose and Pattern in Matthew's Use of the Title Son of David', *NTS* 10 (1963-64), pp. 446-64; A. Suhl, 'Der Davidssohn im Matthäus-Evangelium', *ZNW* 59 (1968), pp. 57-81; J.D. Kingsbury, 'The Title 'Son of David' in Matthew's Gospel', *JBL* 95 (1976), pp. 591-601; D.C. Duling, 'The Therapeutic Son of David: An Element in Matthew's Christological Apologetic', *NTS* 24 (1977–78), pp. 392-410.

4. In addition to the commentaries and Burger's work cited below, see V.K. Robbins, 'The Healing of Blind Barimaeus (10:46-52) in Marcan Theology', *JBL* 92 (1973), pp. 224-43; J.D. Kingsbury, *The Christology of Mark's Gospel* (1983).

throughout is that Christian belief in Jesus' Davidic messianic status arose at a relatively late date in the Hellenistic-Jewish church, rather than in the early Palestinian communities. It was Mark himself who added the 'son of David' cry to an originally unmessianic Bartimaeus account (Mk 10.46-52) and who transformed the *Davidssohnfrage* (Mk 12.35-37)—originally a denial of the Davidic descent of the messiah (so Wrede, *contra* Hahn)—into an affirmation of the two-stage Christology his community affirmed (Jesus was both son of David *and* Son of God).[1] Matthew picked up the title from Mark's Bartimaeus account and redactionally introduced it throughout the Gospel (Mt. 20.29-34; 9.27-31; 12.22-24; 15.21-28; 21.9), thus greatly expanding Mark's portrait and raising 'son of David' to an *Hoheitstitel*.[2] In short, Matthew's portrait of Jesus as the Davidic messiah obtained nothing from Palestinian traditions, but drew entirely from Mark's presentation and a few Hellenistic-Jewish Christian traditions.

In his chapter on Luke–Acts, Burger claims that throughout his two-volume work, Luke maintains a consistent theological perspective on the Davidic promises. While Jesus is indeed a descendant of David, he receives his royal authority not in Jerusalem but at his exaltation to God's right hand. Davidic messiahship thus *plays no role in Jesus' earthly ministry*. While Luke tends to follow his Markan material quite closely, his minor changes may be seen to reflect this theological interest. Whereas Mark uses the 'son of David' cry in the Bartimaeus account to prepare for Jesus' royal entrance to Jerusalem (Mk 11.1-11), Luke follows his version (Lk. 18.35-43) with the Zacchaeus story, and so obscures this Markan connection. The emphasis thus shifts from an acclamation of the Davidic messiah to one miracle among many in Luke's travel narrative. Unlike Matthew, Luke places no special emphasis on the son of David title in Jesus' earthly ministry.[3] In his version of the approach to Jerusalem (Lk. 19.28-40), Luke stresses the non-political character of the entrance: he omits the reference to the kingdom of David; he adds a reference to 'peace in heaven and glory in the highest'; and he presents the story as a descent from the Mount of Olives rather than an entrance into Jerusalem. In addition, various contextual factors point to Luke's view of a delay of the parousia and a

1. C. Burger, *Jesus als Davidssohn: Eine traditionsgeschichtliche Untersuchung* (FRLANT, 98; Göttingen: Vandenhoeck & Ruprecht, 1970).

2. Burger, *Jesus als Davidssohn*, pp. 72-91.

3. Burger, *Jesus als Davidssohn*, pp. 107-12.

non-political kingdom.[1] Though Luke takes the *Davidssohnfrage* over almost unchanged from Mark (Lk. 20.41-44), his presentation in Acts resolves the question left open in the Gospel. Jesus can be David's Lord as well as his son because he has been exalted as Lord at God's right hand.[2] In his study of the Lukan birth narrative, Burger reaches source conclusions in line with his study of Matthew. The Evangelist himself is responsible for the references to Jesus' Davidic sonship. Only in the Benedictus (Lk. 1.68-79) was a traditional piece used, but this came from *Baptist* rather than Christian circles. The story of Jesus' Bethlehem birth (Lk. 2.1-20), though traditional, was supplemented by Luke with references to the virgin birth and thc Davidic sonship of Jesus. The annunciation to Mary (Lk. 1.26-38), with its reference to Jesus' Davidic reign, is wholly the work of the Evangelist. By the 'throne of his father David' (v. 32) Luke does not mean an earthly kingdom, but the enthronement of the son of David developed in Acts 2.30-36.[3]

This Lukan theme of Jesus' exaltation as his Davidic enthronement is prominent in speeches in Acts (2.25-36; 13.23, 32-37 and 15.16-18). The perspective in all three speeches is the same: Jesus did not fulfill the promises to David in his earthly life, but in his resurrection and exaltation to the right hand of God. While Jesus is anointed (Lk. 3.22; 4.18) and proclaimed as Son of God (Lk. 9.35) during his ministry, he is not yet enthroned. The title 'king' applied to him in his earthly life is proleptic.[4]

Burger's study as a whole is comprehensive and well-argued, and is justifiably considered the standard work in the field. The work's greatest strengths are its witness to the diversity of perspectives within the early church, especially with regard to the contributions of the individual Evangelists. Various weaknesses, however, may be noted. For one thing, many of Burger's conclusions are based on a rigid distinction between Palestinian and Hellenistic communities (as set forth by Bousset,

1. Burger, *Jesus als Davidssohn*, pp. 112-14.

2. Burger, *Jesus als Davidssohn*, pp. 114-16. Burger also examines the Lukan genealogy, concluding that since Luke shows no interest either in its Adam-Christ typology or its 7 × 11 structure, he must have received the whole of it from the tradition. It is probably the creation of two Greek-speaking authors: the first developed a genealogy from David through Nathan, intentionally avoiding the ungodly line of kings; the second used the book of Chronicles to take the genealogy from David to Adam. Luke then incorporated it into his work to serve as proof of Jesus' Davidic descent (pp. 116-23).

3. Burger, *Jesus als Davidssohn*, pp. 127-37.

4. Burger, *Jesus als Davidssohn*, pp. 137-42.

Bultmann, Hahn *et al.*). It is now widely accepted that such a strict distinction is somewhat artificial, and that from the earliest period the predominantly Aramaic-speaking communities of Palestine were in touch with Hellenistic ideas and contained Greek-speaking members.[1] This raises doubts concerning Burger's methodology, particularly when he attempts to eliminate Davidic material from the early Palestinian tradition. Even if a rigid distinction between communities were allowed, Burger's arguments in favor of a Hellenistic origin are frequently strained and unconvincing, particularly in relation to the birth narratives and the Markan material. Indeed, Burger's consistent attempt to separate claims of Jesus' Davidic descent from the earliest period is puzzling in light of two of his other points. First, in Burger's background study, the sources he examines to confirm the widespread Jewish expectation for a coming Davidic king are almost all Palestinian, suggesting (though he does not say so) that this expectation was particularly prominent among Palestinian Jews. Secondly, he consistently claims that 'son of David' was a theological rather than a genealogical statement, and was first ascribed to Jesus because he was considered to be the messiah. When these two points are brought together, it seems that the early *Palestinian* church would be the community *most* interested in affirming Jesus' Davidic descent. Yet, according to Burger, this community had no interest in this designation. It was the Hellenistic-Jewish church which first confessed Jesus as the son of David. One wonders whether Burger's insistence on the non-Palestinian origins of the son of David material is not influenced by a dogmatic desire to separate the church's claims from the historical Jesus.

Other criticisms of Burger relate more directly to the present work. By concentrating solely on explicitly Davidic passages, Burger is not able to deal sufficiently with related themes, such as Jesus' messiahship in general, his divine sonship, his kingship, or his role as savior. Since these themes are all closely related to Davidic messiahship, the need remains for a more comprehensive study of royal messianism. In the present work these wider issues will be examined by focusing on one New Testament author (Luke). While a response to Burger's individual

1. Cf. M. Hengel, *Judaism and Hellenism: Studies in their Encounter in Palestine During the Early Hellenistic Period* (1974), I, esp. pp. 104-106; *idem*, *Between Jesus and Paul* (1983), esp. pp. 1-47; I.H. Marshall, 'Palestinian and Hellenistic Christianity: Some Critical Comments', *NTS* 19 (1972–73), pp. 271-87, esp. pp. 273-74, and the literature cited there.

conclusions on Luke–Acts must await later chapters, the following points will indicate my general direction. First, while Burger is surely right that Luke's redaction depicts Jesus' exaltation as a Davidic-enthronement, he does not sufficiently relate this conclusion to Luke's wider purpose in Luke–Acts, nor does he suggest a community situation(s) which Luke may be addressing. More specifically, there is little consideration of how the Davidic theme relates to the church's preaching to the Jews or to Luke's attitude toward Judaism. The need remains for an examination of the Davidic promise theme in the wider context of Lukan purpose and theology. In addition, while Jesus' heavenly enthronement is certainly a central theme in Luke–Acts, it must be asked whether Burger's claim that Jesus does not function as the Davidic messiah during his earthly ministry is adequately founded.

Many scholars have followed Burger's conclusion that for Luke, Davidic messiahship for Luke is essentially an exaltation category. An example may be found in the work of E. Kränkl, who examines the salvation-historical place of Jesus in the speeches in Acts.[1] Kränkl concludes that at the centre of Luke's Christology is Jesus' exaltation and enthronement at the right hand of God, and this enthronement is viewed by Luke as the reception of the Davidic throne promised in Lk. 1.32-33.[2] Luke's presentation of Jesus as David's son no longer describes the appearance and status of the earthly Jesus (as in Rom. 1.3-4, Mark and Matthew), but his heavenly dignity. Jesus' descent from David predestines him for the throne at God's side and is the salvation-historical condition of his installation as Son of God.[3]

Though Burger's work is the most comprehensive examination of this theme, many other works have dealt in some way with Davidic messiahship in Luke–Acts. In a short article, F.F. Bruce examines passages in Luke–Acts which relate to the Davidic messiah.[4] Bruce's primary purpose is not to determine the significance of Davidic messiahship for Luke but to point out the importance of *testimonia* drawn from the Davidic promises (Pss. 2.7; 16.10; 110.1; Isa. 55.3, etc.) in the exegetical

1. E. Kränkl, *Jesus der Knecht Gottes: Die heilsgeschichtliche Stellung Jesu in den Reden der Apostelgeschichte* (1972).

2. Kränkl, *Knecht Gottes*, pp. 85-87; 207-208.

3. Kränkl, *Knecht Gottes*, pp. 86-87, following Burger, *Jesus als Davidssohn*, p. 174.

4. F.F. Bruce, 'The Davidic Messiah in Luke–Acts', in *Biblical and Near Eastern Studies* (1978), pp. 7-17.

activity of the early church. Two of his subsidary points, however, raise important questions which must be dealt with in the present work. (1) The first is the paucity of Davidic material between the birth narrative and the speeches in Acts. Bruce points to the surprising fact that in spite of the dominance of the theme in the nativity, no mention is made of Jesus' Davidic descent throughout the Gospel, the only exception being the incidental reference by the blind man of Jericho. Then, 'like an underground stream...the Davidic motif emerges into the light of day again when we come to the apostolic preaching in Luke's second volume'.[1] The dearth of Davidic references in such a large body of material demands explanation. (2) A second point is the centrality of this theme in three key speeches in Acts. Specifically with reference to the Pentecost speech, he offers the observation that while the 'Davidic-Messiah group of *testimonia* is by no means the only one found in the speeches in the early chapters of Acts...Luke may have reasons of his own for putting it in the forefront of the apostolic preaching'.[2] It is part of my purpose to determine what these reasons were.

In an article on 'The Davidic-Royal Motif in the Gospels', S.E. Johnson seeks to establish the *Sitz im Leben* of various pericope and a plausible line of development from the historical Jesus onward.[3] In his section on Luke–Acts, he points out that, while the Davidic-royal motif is prominent in the nativity and in Acts, 'there is hardly anything in the gospel to suggest that Jesus was regarded as an earthly, political Messiah'.[4] If, as has often been suggested, the reason for this is Luke's desire to minimize the political element for apologetic reasons, how do we account for the strong Davidic expectations in the birth narrative and Acts? Picking up on a point made by P.S. Minear,[5] he suggests that, since Luke does not precisely discriminate among christological titles and images, one

1. Bruce, 'Davidic Messiah', p. 9. Another exception—not noted by Bruce—is the genealogy, which also affirms Jesus' Davidic descent.

2. Bruce, 'Davidic Messiah', p. 11.

3. S.E. Johnson, 'The Davidic-Royal Motif in the Gospels', *JBL* 87 (1968), pp. 136-50. Johnson goes so far as to date various pericope on the basis of historical events in the first century (blind Bartimaeus, *c.* AD 70–73; feeding of the five thousand, *c.* AD 46–66). He also makes the rather implausible suggestion that, in the struggle for authority in the church, the family of Jesus claimed leadership by virtue of their Davidic lineage.

4. Johnson, 'Davidic-Royal Motif', p. 144.

5. P.S. Minear, 'Luke's Use of the Birth Stories', in *Studies in Luke–Acts* (1966), esp. pp. 117-19, 125-26.

need not suppose he senses the political dynamite of the royal-Davidic language.[1] Johnson next turns to the Jewish background of Davidic messianism, pointing to the similarity between Luke's nativity, the *Psalms of Solomon*, and the writings of Qumran. Though the *Psalms of Solomon* contain the theme of the destruction of the Gentiles, they are less activistic than other writings of this time and portray the messiah as one who is endowed with the Holy Spirit and who trusts in God rather than horse, rider and bow. At Qumran, the Davidic 'branch' does not lead armies to victory but appears as a man of peace after the battle. Johnson concludes that Luke was willing to utilize the traditions he did in the birth narrative because they originated within a circle of Palestinian Christians who viewed the Davidic promises with the special emphases of the *Psalms of Solomon*, and so were not inclined to be political activists.[2]

Two of Johnson's points may be questioned: first, whether Luke's Gospel proper is as non-royal as he suggests (a question we will examine in detail), and secondly, whether the *Psalms of Solomon* would *dis*-incline anyone to political activism. It seems any messiah who 'smashes the arrogance of sinners like a potter's jar', 'shatters their substance with an iron rod' and 'destroys unlawful nations with the word of his mouth' (*Pss. Sol.* 17. 22-23; cf. 17.35-36), is a political (and military!) force to be reckoned with. While Johnson's conclusions appear to be inadequate, he raises the important question of why Luke, if he views Jesus' messiahship as essentially non-political, provides such a strong Davidic and nationalistic-sounding introduction to his two-volume work.

In a good summary article, A. George addresses the issue of the royalty of Jesus in Luke–Acts.[3] He argues that Luke places great stress on the royalty of Jesus, using the messianic language of Hellenistic Judaism to mark the fulfillment of the promises to David. Luke's Hellenistic readers could comprehend this message through their knowledge of the Septuagint, and, depending on their cultural background, through Hellenistic titles like κύριος, σωτήρ and ἀρχηγός. Luke takes special care to demonstrate the *uniqueness* of Jesus' royalty, evidenced by his humble origins, his suffering and death, and the divine transcendence of his royalty over that of all earthly kings.[4] In the birth narrative

1. Johnson, 'Davidic-Royal Motif', p. 145.

2. Johnson, 'Davidic-Royal Motif', pp. 146-48.

3. A. George, 'La royauté de Jésus', in *Etudes sur l'œuvre de Luc* (1978), pp. 257-82. Cf. J. Navone, *Themes of St Luke* (1970), ch. 8.

4. George, *Etudes*, pp. 257-72, esp. pp. 271-72.

Jesus is presented as the messianic king promised to Israel. Yet he fulfills the Old Testament promises in a new and surprising way—in the obscurity of his birth, in his poverty, his service, his universal dominion and his mysterious participation in the holiness of God, the only Lord. Significantly, only one text points explicitly to Jesus' future status (Lk. 1.32-33); all others reveal Jesus as the present messiah (Lk. 1.43, 69; 2.11, 26): 'These two chapters, in effect, are much more explicit concerning the mystery of Jesus than the rest of the Gospel.' They are meant not so much to describe the time before salvation, but to provide a revelation of Jesus' royalty in its fullness, perceived in the light of Easter.[1] In the prelude to Jesus' ministry (Lk. 3.1-4.13), Luke discreetly introduces features of Jesus' royal identity. The question of John the Baptist (Lk. 3.15-16) and the enthronement language of Ps. 2.7 (Lk. 3.22; George follows the Western text) give the baptism of Jesus a messianic interpretation. This is reinforced with the Davidic genealogy (3.23-38) and the temptation account (4.1-13), where Jesus refuses Satan's offer of earthly kingship. In this section, then, Jesus' kingship is inaugurated by the word of God (Lk. 3.22), but it is not yet fulfilled.[2] After the nativity and the prologue of 3.1–4.13, little is said of Jesus' royalty until the re-emergence of the theme in the last days of Jesus' ministry. With the 'son of David' cry in Lk. 18.38-39, the parable of pounds (19.11-27) and the royal entrance to Jerusalem (19.29-38), Jesus is portrayed as the legitimate king of Israel. Yet he will receive his kingdom not in Jerusalem but in a 'distant land' from whence he will return to judge his servants and adversaries. Already Jesus' rejection by Jerusalem is in view (Lk. 19.14, 27, 42-44). In the passion account he is tried and crucified as a royal pretender. Throughout this section Jesus' royalty is contrasted with the kingdoms of the world and is marked by a growing lack of comprehension by both Jews and Gentiles. With the Easter revelations of Luke 24 and the apostolic proclamation in Acts, the suffering role of the Christ and the true nature of his kingship is revealed. The ascension of Jesus completes the revelation in two ways: it represents his royal enthronement as Christ and Lord at the right hand of God (Acts 2.30-36), and it prefigures the eschatological manifestion of that kingship at his glorious return (Acts 3.18-20).[3]

George points to the seeming incoherence in the revelation of Jesus'

1. George, *Etudes*, p. 273.
2. George, *Etudes*, pp. 273-74.
3. George, *Etudes*, pp. 274-81.

royalty. How can Jesus be proclaimed 'Christ the Lord' at his birth (Lk. 2.11), confessed the 'Christ of God' and 'king' during his ministry (Lk. 9.20; 19.38), 'made Lord and Christ' at his exaltation-enthronement (Acts 3.36), and return as the 'Christ appointed for you' (Acts 3.20)? While these statements are no doubt partly a result of diverse sources, it must be asked whether there is not some internal unity in Luke's perspective. George suggests progressive stages in the manifestion of Jesus' kingship. By virtue of his descent from David and divine sonship, Jesus is king already from the beginning. Yet this royalty is manifested and recognized only little by little in the development of salvation-history. Only Jesus hears the divine voice at the baptism (Lk. 3.22); only he knows the temptation by Satan to seize ahead of time his royal authority (4.5-7). It is first Peter, then the disciples in general, who recognize Jesus' messiahship during his ministry (9.20; 19.38). After Easter it is only believers who recognize his heavenly enthronement. Finally, at his return at the end of time his kingship will be fully manifested (Acts 3.20; Lk. 19.15-27). Though 'real' from the first moment of his existence, the royal lordship of Jesus is accomplished in stages until its final manifestation in the kingdom of God.[1]

By examining royal messianism in general, George's article represents a positive correction to Burger's more limited approach. He correctly demonstrates that royal messianism in Luke–Acts extends beyond explicitly Davidic passages and that various royal terms and titles are closely integrated by Luke. Many of his individual conclusions will be confirmed in the present work. George's concept of 'stages' in the revelation of Jesus' kingship also represents an improvement on the purely 'proleptic' view of Jesus' messiahship. As we shall see, there is a sense in which Jesus is already acting with messianic authority and performing the scripturally ordained deeds of the Christ during his earthly ministry. Indeed there may be more royal messianism in the Nazareth Sermon and Jesus' ministry than George notes. On the other side, however, George probably does not make enough of the uniqueness of the status attained by Jesus at his exaltation-enthronement. Being 'made Christ and Lord' (Acts 2.36) suggests more than just a wider *manifestation* of a royalty which Jesus already possessed: it is not merely a greater degree of revelation, but a supreme status of authority and dominion to which Jesus is now appointed.

1. George, *Etudes*, pp. 281-82.

A.R.C. Leaney is another scholar who stresses the importance of Jesus' royalty in Luke–Acts. In his commentary on the Gospel, Leaney claims that Luke's purpose in his two-volume work is 'to make, explain, and defend the claim that Jesus was a king'.[1] In line with this purpose, the main theme of his theology is 'the reign of Christ, how it is established and how it must be maintained'. From birth Jesus is destined to inherit the throne of David, and throughout his ministry he exercises his kingly power, raising the dead, healing and forgiving sins. He enters Jerusalem as a king and on the eve of his death he bequeaths a kingdom to his apostles. In Acts, they will wield this royal authority delegated to them. Jesus' kingdom is attained through suffering, and at his resurrection and ascension he enters his glory. 'This entrance into glory is deliberately chosen by Luke as the keystone of his theological arch'—in preference to the future coming in glory emphasized by Mark and Matthew. While Luke envisages a final manifestation of the kingdom in the future, he places all the stress on Jesus' present heavenly glory as reigning king.[2] Leaney's results are significant and rightly stress the importance of Jesus' kingship in Luke's Christology. It is particularly significant, as we shall see, that Luke introduces the theme in sections which are introductory and programmatic for his work as a whole. While Leaney connects this motif particularly to Luke's desire to demonstrate the non-political nature of Jesus' kingship (and hence the political innocence of Christianity),[3] the present work will link it more strongly to his promise-fulfillment motif. The reality and nature of Jesus' royalty and present heavenly reign confirm that he is indeed the messianic king promised in Scripture.

Other works on Lukan Christology deal to a greater or lesser extent with Davidic messianism in Luke–Acts. A number of these suggest the importance of royal-Davidic categories, but subordinate them to other titles or designations.[4] In his work on the *Grundzüge* of Lukan

1. A.R.C. Leaney, *The Gospel According to St Luke* (2nd edn, 1966), p. 7.

2. Leaney, *Luke*, pp. 34-37

3. Leaney, *Luke*, p. 7: 'Luke writes as if to say in effect, "We Christians do indeed claim that our Lord was a king, but it is impossible to understand—and very easy to misunderstand—what we mean by his kingship and his kingdom unless you hear the story from the very beginning."'

4. In addition to the studies cited below, see the discussion of D.P. Moessner's work in Chapter 6 sections 3b and 4. Moessner believes royal-Davidic messiahship is of little importance in Luke-Acts when compared to a prophet like Moses Christology.

Christology, G. Voss devotes a chapter to 'Jesus, the messianic king'.[1] While Voss acknowledges the foundational christological significance of Lk. 1.28-37 in its 're-awakening' of the Davidic covenant, the essential content of this covenant is not the Davidic descent of Yahweh's agent, but the message of 'God with us' inherent in it. God appears to his people, leading and redeeming them through his chosen agents (the patriarchs, Moses, the judges, David). Such a perspective is evident in Acts 10.38, where it is said of Jesus that God 'anointed him' and 'was with him'. Jesus as the 'Christ'—the anointed one—may thus be seen as the basis of all other christological statements and titles since it expresses this sense of God's intervention through his chosen agent.[2] From this foundation Voss argues that Jesus' messiahship does not rest on his legitimate descent from David but on his unique sonship to God. (The Spirit-conceived virgin birth confirms this uniqueness). Indeed, Luke intentionally *avoids* designating Jesus as a descendant of David: he is not the *son* of David, but a *new* David, the shoot from the root of *Jesse* (Isa. 11.1).[3] In a sense, then, Luke subordinates Jesus' royal-messiahship to his divine sonship. It is by virtue of his special relationship with and obedience to the Father that Jesus is messiah and king.[4] In addition to these points, Voss solves the difficult question of how Jesus can fulfill the messianic role prior to his exaltation-enthronement by asserting that Jesus' *baptism* represents his enthronement into his kingly office. It is from this point forward that Jesus, by the power of the Holy Spirit, begins to fulfill the commission prophesied about him.[5] A number of Voss's points will be dealt with in subsequent discussion. Here it may be pointed out that it is unlikely that Luke denigrates Jesus' Davidic descent, as Voss suggests, or that he draws such a dichotomy between Davidic and divine sonship.[6] In addition, while the baptism as a royal-enthronement is an appealing solution to the difficulty of Jesus'

1. G. Voss, *Die Christologie der lukanischen Schriften in Grundzügen* (1965), pp. 61-97.

2. Voss, *Christologie*, pp. 61-65.

3. Voss, *Christologie*, pp. 65-72. The basis of this interpretation is Voss's understanding of Isa. 7.14, a passage Luke alludes to (according to Voss) in Lk. 1.31. For more on this issue see the excursus following Chapter 3 below, '"Son of David" or "New David"'.

4. Voss, *Christologie*, pp. 61-97; esp. pp. 78-81, 94-97.

5. Voss, *Christologie*, p. 92. Voss bases this view partly on his acceptance of the Western text (D) of Lk. 3.22, which follows Ps. 2.7.

6. On the question of 'son of David' or 'new David' see the excursus below.

'messianic' activity prior to his exaltation, it is doubtful whether Luke's statements elsewhere can sustain this interpretation.

In his work on Lukan theology and purpose, E. Franklin claims that Luke's aim in writing is to strengthen and confirm faith in Jesus as the present Lord.[1] While χριστός is an important title for Luke, describing Jesus as God's instrument in fulfilling the Old Testament promises, Luke subordinates it to κύριος, since the former 'was not able to do full justice to the exaltation'.[2] χριστός is for Luke 'a secondary term, used nearly always in an *argumentum ad hominem,* expressing the conviction that Jesus is truly God's decisive instrument, and that the details of his career prove this rather than confound it'.[3] Franklin rightly points to the apologetic value Luke gives to χριστός with reference to the salvation-historical status of Jesus. He also correctly notes the importance of κύριος in Luke–Acts; there is little doubt this is Luke's favourite title to express his faith (and the faith of his church) in Jesus the exalted one. At the same time it is questionable whether it is correct to say that χριστός is a 'secondary term' which Luke subordinates to κύριος. In subsequent discussion of Acts 2 and other passages, it will be suggested that Luke uses 'Lord' *primarily* as an expression of Jesus' *authority,* while 'Christ' expresses his salvation-historical *status.* The two terms thus serve different, but parallel, functions. In his exaltation status Jesus is the messianic king now given authority (= lordship) over all. The two titles *together* express the significance of Jesus' exaltation glory. It is important to note that in three key texts expressing Jesus' salvation-historical significance (Lk. 2.11; Acts 2.36; 10.36) κύριος appears together with χριστός, suggesting that the two titles are complementary (in these contexts); together they express the *status and authority* of Jesus. Franklin's own presentation unintentionally suggests this parallel importance of the titles. In defining κύριος in Acts 2.36, he claims the title does not reflect divine status, but expresses the authority of one who is the instrument of, and, wholly subordinate to, the Father.[4] Franklin thus presents Jesus' lordship as essentially a *messianic* lordship. The juxtaposition of κύριος and χριστός in Acts 2.36 designates Jesus

1. E. Franklin, *Christ the Lord: A Study in the Purpose and Theology of Luke–Acts* (1975), p. 48.

2. Franklin, *Christ the Lord*, p. 56. Franklin bases this conclusion upon an inadequate interpretation of Lk. 22.66-71. See Chapter 6 section 6bi below.

3. Franklin, *Christ the Lord*, pp. 55-57.

4. Franklin, *Christ the Lord*, p. 54.

as the messiah (status) who reigns as Lord (authority). This distinction is not a rigid one, of course, and particularly in the context of preaching to Gentiles, κύριος often carries the sense of status as well as authority. The point is that, in the proclamation to the Jews (i.e. in the context of Luke's 'proclamation from prophecy' motif), the two titles complement one another; χριστός is not subordinated to κύριος.

In Darrell Bock's work on Lukan Old Testament Christology, he too emphasizes the supremacy of lordship over messiahship, but in a different manner than Franklin. Bock places strong emphasis on the Davidic promises as a key theme in Luke's promise-fulfillment scheme. In the infancy material, Luke presents Jesus as the Davidic messiah who is also the victorious servant of the Lord. This 'foundational christological category' of messiah-servant continues throughout the Gospel. In the accounts of the baptism, the Nazareth sermon, the transfiguration, the approach to Jerusalem and other passages, Jesus is portrayed as both Davidic messiah and Isaianic servant. In Jesus' last days in Jerusalem, however, a 'more than messiah' tension begins to emerge in such texts as Lk. 20.42-43 and 21.27, which refer to the messianic figures of Lord and Son of man. This tension is resolved in Acts when Jesus is openly declared to be Lord (Acts 2.36; 10.43).

> By Acts 10, there is little doubt that Jesus as the Messiah-Servant is actually more than a regal messianic figure. He is Lord of all as he uniquely exercises many divine prerogatives with God, functioning as mediator of His salvation in His presence at His right hand.[1]

In short, Bock proposes that 'The christological presentation of Luke consciously takes the reader from seeing Jesus as the regal Messiah-Servant to seeing him as Lord of all.'[2]

As we shall see, Bock is to be commended in his recognition that the Davidic promises play a key introductory role in Luke's birth narrative, and that Luke connects this portrait to the Isaianic servant. In addition, he rightly points to the strong link made in these chapters between χριστός and Davidic messiahship, a link suggesting that the Davidic portrait established in the nativity continues implicitly in the Gospel narrative. While these points are fundamental to the present work, Bock's further claim that there is a *decisive shift* in Luke's Christology from messiahship to lordship must be questioned. The following

1. Bock, *Proclamation*, p. 265; cf. pp. 79-82, 132, 183-87, 234-40.
2. Bock, *Proclamation*, 278; cf. pp. 236, 240, 262, 270.

points—developed in more detail in subsequent discussion—represent some important difficulties with Bock's conclusions.

First, what does Bock mean by 'more than messiah'? More than *which* messiah? If he means 'more than (= different from) the traditional *Jewish expectation* of the Davidic messiah', then it is true that one of Luke's central purposes is to show that Jewish expectations concerning the messiah were inadequate and incomplete. Luke already subtly begins this 'more than the expected messiah' motif in the birth narrative with the messiah's humble birth, his unique sonship to God (by virtue of the virgin birth) and the division of Israel his coming will cause. This theme continues throughout the Gospel, climaxing initially in Luke 24 and finally in Acts. Yet it seems what Bock actually means by 'more than messiah' is more than *Luke's* understanding of this Old Testament figure. In other words, for Luke the Old Testament portrait of the royal-messiah is not adequate to describe Jesus; so this category is exceeded by that of 'Lord' in a divine sense. It must be questioned, however, whether Luke actually views 'messiah' as an inadequate category. Though it is true he broadens the messianic description of Jesus to include scriptural passages which the Jews did not traditionally apply to the Davidic messiah, it may be argued that for Luke these passages refer to, and have always referred to, the Davidic messiah. It was because the Jews were 'foolish and slow of heart' that they missed them. Since Luke's conception of the messiah exceeds that of the Jews, his apologetic may better be regarded as 'the truth about the messiah', rather than '*more* than messiah'.

It is also questionable whether 'Lord' carries the *unique* and *climactic* revelatory significance that Bock ascribes to it.[1] Already in Lk. 2.11 Jesus is identified as *both* Christ and Lord (Lk. 2.11), the same two titles applied to him in the exaltation declaration of Acts 2.36. Bock responds to this objection by claiming that, while Jesus is introduced in the birth narrative as 'Christ', 'Son of God' and 'Lord', only 'Lord' is *not* defined through the use of an Old Testament allusion or text.[2] 'The Lucan meaning of *that term only emerges later* in his work when Lord is explicitly tied to Old Testament passages about David's Lord and the

1. On Luke's use of κύριος already during Jesus' ministry see Franklin, *Christ the Lord*, pp. 49-55. For Bock's response to this argument see *Proclamation*, pp. 268-69.

2. Bock, *Proclamation*, p. 266.

confessing of Jesus as Lord'.[1] Yet the withholding of the full content of a title until Acts is not unique to κύριος; it applies also to χριστός (and other christological titles). While Jesus is said to be χριστός already in Lk. 2.11, the suffering role of the messiah is the surprising revelation of Lk. 24.26, and his reception of the messianic throne *in the heavenly sphere* is the startling declaration of Acts 2.30-36. As mentioned above, in Acts 2.36 'Christ' and 'Lord' stand parallel to one another, suggesting they are integrally related in the context of Jesus' exaltation glory. One is not subordinated to the other.[2] It should also be noted that in this passage Luke reveals Jesus to be more than the traditional expectations of the Davidic messiah, but not more than what Scripture said he (the Davidic messiah) would be, that is, exalted to the right hand of God as the messianic Lord (Ps. 110.1). Again we have not a 'more than messiah' scheme but a 'more than the expected messiah'.

Thirdly, the sermon of Paul in Acts 13 does not fit Bock's view of a *climactic* role for κύριος over χριστός in Luke's narrative. If Luke presents a progressive revelation of Jesus' identity from messiah to Lord—climaxing in Acts 10—why would he then return to a thoroughly royal-Davidic portrait of Jesus in Acts 13 (in the inaugural speech of the most important character in Acts![3]). It could perhaps be suggested that a new cycle of 'messiah to Lord' begins with the Pauline material in Acts 13; but this does not really work, since Acts 13–28 does not climax with a 'more than messiah' motif. In any case, such a two-cycle theory would not fit Bock's thesis, since he views Luke's Old Testament Christology as ceasing after Acts 13. It seems, then, that a 'more than messiah' scheme, with lordship surpassing messiahship, does not adequately describe Luke's use of the Davidic promise motif.

Many more works could be cited which touch in some way on the theme of Davidic messiahship in Luke–Acts.[4] This brief survey, however, has highlighted the main questions which will be addressed in the subsequent discussion: (1) How does Luke view Jesus as fulfilling the

1. Bock, *Proclamation*, p. 266; cf. pp. 78-82.

2. For more on κύριος in Acts 2.36 see the discussion of this passage in Chapter 4.

3. See Chapter 4 section 3a.

4. Noteworthy in this regard is R.C. Tannehill's literary-critical analysis of Luke–Acts, *The Narrative Unity of Luke Acts: A Literary Interpretation* (vol. I, *The Gospel According to Luke*, 1986; vol. II, *The Acts of the Apostles*, 1990). Tannehill repeatedly stresses the importance of royal-messianic categories for Luke (cf. especially I, pp. 25-26, 38-39, 58-60, 63, 223, 268-70; II, pp. 38-39, 164-75, 351-52).

Davidic promises? Is it only in his exaltation-enthronement, or also in his death? resurrection? earthly ministry? (2) If the latter, how do we account for the relative paucity of explicitly royal-messianic material in the Gospel proper? (3) Does Luke subordinate this Old Testament category to any other, either from the beginning of his Gospel, or in his subsequent narrative development? (4) How does the seemingly nationalistic-sounding material in the birth narrative relate to Luke's perspective on these promises elsewhere? (5) More generally, how does Luke relate this theme to other theological emphases: his Christology in general, his eschatology, soteriology and ecclesiology? (6) Finally, how does this theme relate to Luke's overall purpose(s) in Luke–Acts? Are there clues here to his community situation?

3. *Methodology*

The methodology of the present study is eclectic, combining redaction- and narrative-critical approaches. The complex literary nature of Luke–Acts makes this the preferred approach. As P. Schubert pointed out over thirty years ago:

> Especially in the study of Luke–Acts it has become more and more obvious that textual and 'source' criticism, structural and literary analysis, and exegesis must be pursued together, since both methods and findings in all these aspects of the interpretive task constantly bear on one another.[1]

Since Schubert's day, narrative and literary approaches have developed considerably in the context of biblical studies, and have yielded helpful insights when applied to Luke–Acts.[2] Proponents of narrative analysis rightly criticize the excesses of a redaction-critical approach which focuses too exclusively on 'Lukan' redactional alterations of putative sources and not enough on the literary unity (the 'story') of Luke–Acts.

Some scholars, however, have gone to the opposite extreme, wholly

1. Schubert, 'Structure and Significance', p. 166.

2. See for example C.H. Talbert, *Literary Patterns, Theological Themes and the Genre of Luke–Acts* (1974); L.T. Johnson, *The Literary Function of Possessions in Luke–Acts* (1977); D.L. Tiede, *Prophecy and History in Luke–Acts* (1980); R.J. Karris, *Luke: Artist and Theologian. Luke's Passion Account as Literature* (1985); J.B. Tyson, *The Death of Jesus in Luke–Acts* (1986); Tannehill, *Narrative Unity*; W.S. Kurz, 'Narrative Approaches to Luke–Acts', *Bib* 68 (1987), pp. 195-220; D.P. Moessner, *Lord of the Banquet: The Literary and Theological Significance of the Lukan Travel Narrative* (1989).

rejecting synoptic comparison in favour of a purely literary approach.[1] Yet a complete rejection of source and redaction analysis may also produce skewed results. There is no doubt that Luke used sources and that these sources may be discerned (to some degree) through comparison with Mark and Matthew. It will therefore be of some benefit in determining Luke's literary and theological *Tendenzen* to examine his alterations of these sources. Though the two-source theory has been under attack in recent years, I consider that two of its fundamental assertions have weathered the storm and will be assumed to be valid in the present work. First is Markan priority, that is, that both Matthew and Luke used Mark, or a document very much like Mark, as a source.[2] Second is the independence of Matthew and Luke.[3] Luke is not dependent on Matthew as a literary source (or vice versa), but used a common source, or sources (= 'Q'). As used here, the designation 'Q' does not necessarily refer to a single written document, but more generally to the source or sources (whether written or oral) Luke shares in common with Matthew. Since Markan priority and Matthean–Lukan independence remain widely accepted among New Testament scholars, they will be assumed in the present work.

1. See for example Moessner, *Lord of the Banquet*, pp. 3-7.

2. See especially J.A. Fitzmyer, 'The Priority of Mark and the "Q" Source in Luke', in *Jesus and Man's Hope* (1970), I, pp. 131-70; G.M. Styler, 'The Priority of Mark', in C.F.D. Moule, *The Birth of the New Testament* (3rd edn, 1981), pp. 285-316; C.M. Tuckett, *The Revival of the Griesbach Hypothesis* (1983); F. Neirynck, 'La matière marcienne dans l'Evangile de Luc', in *L'Evangile de Luc* (*The Gospel of Luke*) (1989), pp. 67-111; *idem*, *The Minor Agreements of Matthew and Luke against Mark* (1974); W.D. Davies and D.C. Allison, *A Critical and Exegetical Commentary on the Gospel According to Saint Matthew* (1988), I, pp. 97-114, and the literature cited there. Cf. the bibliography in J.A. Fitzmyer, *The Gospel According to Luke I–IX* (1981), pp. 99-100.

3. Fitzmyer, *Luke I–IX*, pp. 73-75; H. Bigg, 'The Q Debate since 1955', *Themelios* 6 (1981), pp. 18-28; Davies and Allison, *Matthew*, pp. 115-21, and the literature cited there (p. 115 n. 68). The most significant recent challenge to Matthean–Lukan independence has come from M.D. Goulder, 'On Putting Q to the Test', *NTS* 24 (1978), pp. 218-34; *idem*, 'The Order of a Crank', in *Synoptic Studies* (1984), pp. 111-30; *idem*, *Luke: A New Paradigm*, 2 vols. (1989). For a response to Goulder see C. M. Tucket, 'On the Relationship between Matthew and Luke', *NTS* 30 (1984), pp. 130-42 and the works cited above. On Goulder's latest work, see the reviews of R.F. O'Toole, *CBQ* 53 (1991), pp. 525-26 and F.W. Danker, *JBL* 110 (1991), pp. 162-64, and the comments of G.N. Stanton, *A Gospel for a New People: Studies in Matthew* (1992), pp. 32-36.

While a holistic literary approach will be given precedence throughout the present work, the methodological focus will shift depending on the degree of certainty concerning the nature and extent Luke's sources. In the nativity and Acts, where Luke's source material is extremely difficult to isolate (and source analysis is likely to be skewed by subjectivity),[1] conclusions will be derived *primarily* from a more general literary analysis.[2] In the body of the Gospel, however, where parallels are found in Mark and Matthew ('Q'), more attention will be given to Luke's treatment of his sources.[3]

1. On the difficulty of identifying sources in Acts see especially J. Dupont, *The Sources of the Book of Acts: The Present Position* (1964), esp. pp. 88, 166-67. C.H. Talbert calls the question of sources in Luke 1–2 'well nigh impossible to answer' ('Prophecies of Future Greatness: The Contribution of Greco-Roman Biographies to an Understanding of Luke 1.5–4.15', in *The Divine Helmsman: Studies on God's Control of Human Events* [1980], p. 129). H. Schürmann, *Das Lukasevangelium I: Kommentar zu Kap. 1,1–9,50* (1969), I, pp. 143-44, writes, 'Die traditionsgeschichte von Lk. 1–2 liegt trotz aller scharfsinnigen Untersuchungen immer noch im Dunkel sich widersprechender Hypothesen'.

2. For definitions of the conventional literary categories adopted here (setting, character, plot, etc.) see S. Chatman, *Story and Discourse: Narrative Structure in Film and Literature* (1978); N.R. Petersen, *Literary Criticism for New Testament Critics* (1978); M.H. Abrams, *A Glossary of Literary Terms* (4th edn, 1981); D. Rhoads and D. Michie, *Mark as Story: An Introduction to the Narrative of a Gospel* (1982); J.D. Kingsbury, *Matthew as Story* (1986), pp. 1-40. As a result of the methodological eclecticism of the present work, the usual literary-critical distinction between the *author* (the person who composed the work) and the *narrator* (the imaginary story-teller) cannot be sustained.

3. A similar methodological approach is taken by J.T. Carroll, *Response to the End of History: Eschatology and Situation in Luke–Acts* (1988), p. 32: 'The position that will guide this examination of Luke–Acts is that the gospel and Acts must be approached differently, insofar as tradition-redaction analysis is concerned. In the gospel, Luke's treatment of his sources (where extant, or recoverable ['Q'] with some precision) will be scrutinized closely and accorded due weight. In Acts (as also in Luke 1–2), the absence of any reliably reconstructed sources requires that tradition-redaction analysis take a back seat to the literary analysis of the finished product... The literary function of a passage in the context of Luke–Acts as a whole will be a governing concern at every phase of the study–both for the assessment of Luke's theological perspective and for the formulation of a hypothesis concerning Luke's situation'.

4. *Plan of the Study*

In Chapter 2 the setting of the Davidic promise tradition in first-century Judaism and early Christianity will be surveyed to determine the concepts and constructs available to Luke. Chapters 3 and 4 will deal, respectively, with the birth narrative and the speeches in Acts, those sections of Luke–Acts which are most strongly royal-Davidic. The purpose of these chapters is to determine the prominence of this theme in Luke–Acts and to gain a general idea of how Luke conceives of these promises as fulfilled in Jesus. In light of these findings, Chapters 5 and 6 will return to Luke's Gospel narrative—a section less explicitly Davidic messianic—to determine whether, in fact, royal-messianic categories play any significant role there. In Chapter 7 conclusions from the previous chapters will be summarized and suggestions made with regard to Lukan purpose and theology, specifically dealing with questions of Christology, eschatology, soteriology and ecclesiology.

A few further points of definition are in order. Since I will repeatedly refer to 'Luke's christological purpose' in relation to individual passages, or Luke–Acts as a whole, it is necessary to draw a distinction between (1) Luke's Christology—his total conception of who Jesus is (to which we have only limited access)—and (2) his christological purpose in Luke–Acts—the particular message concerning Jesus he wishes to pass on to his readers. The latter, which is the primary concern of this work, will necessarily be restricted by Luke's purpose in writing and by the constraints of space and sources. When Christology and christological purpose are confused, Luke's view of Jesus has sometimes been considered 'low' or inferior by comparison with other New Testament writers, since he says little or nothing about Jesus' pre-existence, his divine status, or his atoning work. Yet it may not have been within his christological purpose to deal with these questions. Luke (and his readers) may or may not believe these things; Luke may even imply or presuppose them in his presentation; but it seems clear it was not within his purpose to directly address them. Since Luke does speak a great deal about Jesus' messiahship, this theme is likely to be an integral part of his christological purpose, and the task ahead is to determine the function of Davidic messianism within this purpose.[1]

1. For more on this issue and the possibility of a very high *implicit* Christology in Luke–Acts, see the conclusions reached in Chapter 7 section 2a.

Chapter 2

SETTING: THE DAVIDIC PROMISE TRADITION IN FIRST-CENTURY JUDAISM AND EARLY CHRISTIANITY*

1. *Origin and Sources of the Davidic Promise Tradition: The Old Testament Background*

a. *Primary Statements*

The Davidic promise tradition has its origin in the legitimization formulas of the Davidic dynasty. The primary statement of the promise appears in the oracle of Nathan in 2 Sam. 7.5-16 (cf. 1 Chron. 17.4-14) and its poetic counterpart in the royal Psalm 89 (cf. Ps. 132.1-18; 2 Sam. 23.1-7).[1] Key components of the promise tradition appear in both texts, including: (1) the promise of continuity for David's seed (Ps. 89.5, 30, 37; 2 Sam. 7.12); (2) the promise of Yahweh's perpetual faithfulness (אמונה) and mercy (חסד) (Ps. 89.5, 25, 29; 2 Sam. 7.15) in spite of his chastisement for the sins of David's son(s) (Ps. 89.31-33; 2 Sam. 7.14); (3) the promise of a unique father–son relationship (Ps. 89.27-28; 2 Sam. 7.14); and (4) the promise of an eternal throne for David (Ps. 89.5, 30, 37; 2 Sam. 7.13, 16). (5) In 2 Samuel 7 there is the promise that Solomon will build the temple (v. 13). This promise will be taken up by subsequent generations when the temple lies in ruins (in Zechariah and the rabbinic writings), or when the present temple cultus is viewed as corrupt (at Qumran, where the 'temple' becomes the community; cf. 4QFlor). (6) A sixth aspect of the promise is peace and security for Israel in the Land. This, in turn, implies a united kingdom and the abolition of foreign

* The present chapter is an abbreviated version of Chapter 2 of my Aberdeen dissertation. Due to the constraints of space, what in the original work was a detailed study of the Davidic promise tradition in first-century Judaism has been reduced t[illegible] summary of the data. The reader wishing to pursue the conclusions reac[illegible] further should consult the original work.

1. On the relationship of these texts see A. Caquot, 'La prophétie [illegible] ses échos lyriques', *VTSup* 9 (1963), pp. 213-24.

domination. In Ps. 89.22-26, 'David' is promised strength and victory against his adversaries (vv. 22-24). Yahweh will exalt his horn (= make him strong) and will set his (left) hand on the sea, and his right hand on the rivers (vv. 25-26), i.e. he will extend Israel's borders to their rightful place (cf. Exod. 23.31; Ps. 72.8; Zech. 9.10). In 2 Sam. 7.10-11 Yahweh promises:

> I will appoint a place for my people Israel and will plant them, that they may live in their own place and not be disturbed again, nor will the wicked afflict them any more as formerly...and I will give you rest from all your enemies.

The Deuteronomistic promise of a place of rest and security for Israel following the exodus (Deut. 3.20; 12.9-10; Josh. 1.15) and her 'planting' in the land (Exod. 15.17)[1] is here expanded and applied to the Davidic dynasty. The Davidic promise thus becomes an extension and individualization of Yahweh's covenant relationship to the nation Israel.[2]

The promise tradition is affirmed and expanded in other royal psalms (Pss. 2, 18, 20, 21, 45, 72, 101, 110, 132, 139, 144)[3] and Davidic legitimation formulas (esp. Gen. 49.8-12; Num. 24.17-19). God's faithfulness to his 'covenant' (ברית; Pss. 89.4, 29; 132.12) with David assures the perpetuity of David's line (Pss. 18.15; 45.6, 16-17; 132.10-12, 17). The king's divine sonship is affirmed (Ps. 2.7; cf. 110.3[4]) together with his enthronement on Mount Zion (Pss. 2.4-6; 110.2), his reign in justice and righteousness (Pss. 45.7; 72.1-4, 7), his victory over enemies through Yahweh's power (Pss. 2.1-9; 18.31-42; 20.1-9; 21.1-13; 45.5; 72.9-11; 110.1-2, 5-6) and material prosperity in the Land (Ps. 72.16). New

1. Cf. Pss. 44.2-3; 80.8-11, 15; Jer. 24.6; 32.41; Ezek. 17.23; Amos 9.15; Isa. 60.21.

2. See E. O'Doherty, 'The Organic Development of Messianic Revelation', *CBQ* 19 (1957), pp. 16-24.

3. The royal psalms were presumably composed for court occasions (births, enthronements, marriages, etc.) during the Davidic dynasty and served to legitimate its authority. For a summary and bibliography of the royal psalms see O. Eissfeldt, *The Old Testament: An Introduction* (1965), pp. 102-104. Since scholars differ on the *Sitz im Leben* of these psalms, there is no unanimity concerning their number.

4. The enigmatic phrase 'from the womb of the dawn' in Ps. 110.3 may, like Ps. 2.7, indicate divine sonship. See S. Mowinckel, *He That Cometh* (1956), pp. 62, 67, 75. It is interesting to note that the LXX appears to link the two psalms when it translates the phrase as 'out of the womb, before dawn, I begot thee' (Ps. 109.3 LXX). See E. Schweizer, 'The Concept of the Davidic "Son of God" in Acts and its Old Testament Background', in *Studies in Luke–Acts* (1966), p. 189.

features introduced include worldwide dominion (Pss. 2.8; 72.8-11), a privileged position at Yahweh's right hand (Ps. 110.1), and a perpetual Melchizedekian priesthood (Ps. 110.4).

b. *Isaiah and the Prophets*

Some scholars assert that there are no true messianic prophecies before the Babylonian exile and the collapse of the Davidic dynasty.[1] Only after the monarchy had fallen could the prophets predict that God would raise up a Davidic king to restore and renew the nation. Yet there is evidence in the eighth-century prophets that the division of the kingdom after Solomon, the disillusionment with the corruption of the monarchy, and the subsequent collapse of the northern kingdom resulted in hope for a return to the glories of the united kingdom with a new 'David' on the throne (Isa. 9.1-7 [MT 8.23–9.6]; 11.1-5; Mic. 5.1-5 [MT 4.14–5.5]; Hos. 3.5; Amos 9.11). While the court prophecy of an earlier period merely affirmed the legitimacy of the Davidic dynasty and the royal institutions, the eighth-century prophets began to announce a period of judgment and woe, after which a restoration would take place.

In the southern kingdom, the spiritual failures of the Davidic kings brought this hope to its most profound expression in the prophecies of Isaiah ben-Amoz. Two passages, Isa. 9.1-7 (MT 8.23–9.6) and 11.1-16, are closely related to the royal psalms since they speak in exalted language concerning a coming Davidic king. While it is possible that both passages were composed at the birth or enthronement of an actual Davidic monarch,[2] it seems better to view them as originally 'messianic', that is, as expressing hope in an ideal king yet to come.[3] While Isa. 9.1-7

1. So for example, Mowinckel, *He That Cometh*, pp. 122-86.

2. If an enthronement, the birth language represents the adoption of the king by Yahweh, as in Psalm 2.7. Cf. A. Alt, 'Jesaja 8, 23-9, 6: Beifreiungsmacht und Kronungstag', in *Kleine Schriften zur Geschichte des Volkes Israel* (1959), II, pp. 206-25; J. Becker, *Messianic Expectation in the Old Testament* (1980), pp. 45-46; Duling, 'Traditions', pp. 113-16; J.L. McKenzie, 'Royal Messianism', *CBQ* 19 (1957), pp. 41-42; M.B. Crook, 'A Suggested Occasion for Isaiah 9.2-7 and 11.1-9', *JBL* 68 (1949), pp. 213-24; J. Klausner, *The Messianic Idea in Israel: From its Beginning to the Completion of the Mishna* (1955; German original, 1903), pp. 56-58.

3. So G. von Rad, *Old Testament Theology* (1962), II, pp. 169-75; *idem*, 'The Royal Ritual in Judah', in *The Problem of the Hexateuch and Other Essays* (1966), p. 230; O'Doherty, 'Organic Development', p. 19; O. Kaiser, *Isaiah 1–12* (1983), pp. 125-30. Von Rad sees in these passages a revolutionary break-through by the prophet. Both Isaiah and Micah reject the current Davidic kings and look toward the

appears to have had little influence on later messianic thought, Isa. 11.1ff. became the framework upon which the most exalted hopes of Second Temple Judaism were built.

Isaiah's image of a 'shoot' or sprout from the stump of Jesse (11.1) was picked up by the exilic and post-exilic prophets and became a favourite metaphor for the coming Davidic king.[1] In common with the royal psalms, the king is portrayed as a righteous judge who shows mercy to the downtrodden and destroys the wicked (11.4-5). The king's permanent possession of the Spirit (11.2) draws its precedent from 1 Sam. 16.13 (cf. 1 Sam. 10.6, 9-10), where, following David's anointing by Samuel, it is said that 'the Spirit of Yahweh came mightily upon David *from that day forward'*. Distinctive features of the prophecy—and those repeatedly taken up in post-exilic Judaism—include the king's extraordinary powers of wisdom and discernment by virtue of his Spirit-endowment (11.2-3) and the spectacular way he destroys the wicked 'with the rod of his mouth' and 'the breath of his lips' (11.4). The Davidic shoot here takes on prophetic as well as royal traits.

With the collapse of the Davidic monarchy and the Babylonian exile, expectation for the restoration of the dynasty became a common—though not universal—feature within the more general hope for Israel's renewal. Both Jeremiah and Ezekiel affirm that God will one day raise up a Davidic 'shoot' (צמח, Jer. 23.5-6; 33.14-26) or a new 'David' (Ezek. 34.23-24; 37.24-25), to reign over a restored and united kingdom.

2. *Post-Exilic and Second Temple Judaism*

a. *Waning Messianic Hopes?*

Though the Davidic hopes expressed in the restoration theologies of Jeremiah and Ezekiel did not disappear after the Exile, the political realities of the Persian period served to undermine them. With the loss of political sovereignty after the fall of Jerusalem in 586 BC, the royalty was deprived of its status and influence in the community. The Persian authorities, while allowing the re-establishment of the temple cult under the leadership of the high priest, granted only limited political autonomy to the returnees. Though there was a resurgence of Davidic expectation

restoration of the Davidic empire with a 'new David' on the throne.

1. The term used in Zechariah and Jeremiah is צמח, which does not appear in Isa. 11.1, but may have been taken from Isa. 4.2: 'In that day the branch (צמח) of Yahweh will be beautiful.'

centering on the Davidid Zerubbabel and the rebuilding of the temple (cf. Hag. 2.22-23; Zech. 3.1-10; 4.6-10; 6.9-14), these hopes inevitably diminished when Zerubbabel passed from the scene. The role and authority of the high priest grew as his functions increasingly filled the administrative void left by the Davidic king. This in turn led to a more prominent role for priestly figures in eschatological expectation; in some writings an eschatological high priest, or 'priestly messiah', appears beside a royal one.[1] This is not to say that the covenant to David was forgotten, or that hopes for a Davidic king disappeared completely, but increasingly, as the hierocratic administration took on greater authority, Davidic hopes were set aside or postponed to an indefinite future.[2]

Evidence for this may be found in the Wisdom of Ben Sirach (*c.* 180 BC) and in 1 Maccabees. While Sirach confirms the eternal nature of the Davidic covenant (Sir. 47.11, 19-22),[3] he shows no interest in its fulfillment in an individual messiah.[4] This probably resulted from his confidence in a priestly-led theocratic kingdom (Sir. 17.17), with the high priest, rather than the Davidic king, as the mediator between God and the nation.[5] A similar lack of interest in a Davidic deliverer appears in 1 Maccabees, motivated no doubt by Hasmonean claims to royal

1. This is evident in the messianic expectations of Qumran (see discussion below) and in the *Testaments of the Twelve Patriarchs.* For the two messiah view in Second Temple Judaism see G.R. Beasley-Murray, 'The Two Messiahs in the Testaments of Twelve Patriarchs', *JTS* 48 (1947), pp. 1-12; J. Liver, 'The Doctrine of the Two Messiahs in Sectarian Literature in the Time of the Second Commonwealth', *HTR* 52 (1959), pp. 149-85; K.G. Kuhn, 'The Two Messiahs of Aaron and Israel', in *The Scrolls and the New Testament* (1958), pp. 54-64.

2. See E. Schürer, *The History of the Jewish People in the Age of Jesus Christ (175 BC–AD 135)* (rev. edn, 1973–87), II, p. 498.

3. P.W. Skehan and A.A. Di Lella, *The Wisdom of Ben Sira* (1987), p. 528. *Contra* J.J. Collins, 'Messianism in the Maccabean Period', in *Judaisms and their Messiahs at the Turn of the Christian Era* (1987), p. 98; A. Caquot, 'Ben Sira et le Messianisme', *Sem* 16 (1966), p. 55, who claim that 47.11 does not necessarily imply that the dynasty will last forever.

4. Ben Sirach does, however, express belief in Elijah's eschatological coming, alluding to Mal. 4.5-6 (= MT 3.23-24) in 48.10. While this has sometimes been said to show that he believed Elijah to be 'the messiah', it would be more accurate to say that Elijah appears as eschatological prophet who prepares the nation for the salvation that Yahweh himself will bring. In line with Sirach's theocratic emphasis, no stress is laid on a *royal* mediator.

5. Collins, 'Messianism in the Maccabean Period', p. 98; Klausner, *Messianic Idea*, p. 255.

authority. Like Sirach, the author affirms the traditional hope for the eternal duration of the Davidic line (1 Macc. 2.57)[1] but assigns its restoration to the eschatological future.

b. *Renewed Davidic Expectations in the First Century* BC

This waning of messianic expectations appears to have reversed in the late Hasmonean and early Roman periods, when the failures of the priestly leadership brought about a renewal of Davidic hopes. Growing disenchantment with the Hellenizing tendencies and abuse of royal power of the later Hasmoneans, and the subsequent subjugation by Rome, renewed hopes for a new Davidic king who would act as God's agent to judge corrupt rulers and priests, to purge the nation of foreign influence and domination, and to bring in an era of justice, peace and prosperity.

i. *The Psalms of Solomon.* The *Psalms of Solomon*, an anti-Hasmonean and anti-Roman collection composed in the latter half of the first century BC, represents the strongest expression of this hope in the Second Temple period.[2] The psalms are written from the perspective of a group of Jewish pietists who cry out against certain 'sinners' (the Hasmonean priest-kings) who have arrogantly usurped the Davidic throne and have defiled the temple of God (1.6-8; 2.3-5; 8.8-13; 17.5-9, 19-22).[3] In

1. Cf. Collins, 'Messianism in the Maccabean Period', p. 104. *Contra* J.A. Goldstein, *I Maccabees* (1976), pp. 240-41; *idem*, 'How the Authors of 1 and 2 Maccabees Treated the "Messianic" Promises', in *Judaisms and their Messiahs at the Turn of the Christian Era* (1987), pp. 75, 92 n. 34, who claims that in 2.57 the author is asserting that David's dynasty lasted 'for ages' (εἰς αἰῶνας), but has now been replaced by the Hasmoneans.

2. For issues related to date, provenance, original language, manuscript history, and bibliography, see R.B. Wright, 'The Psalms of Solomon', in J.H. Charlesworth (ed.), *The Old Testament Pseudepigrapha* (1985), II, pp. 639-50, and the works cited there.

3. Since Wellhausen, the psalms have traditionally been ascribed to Pharisaic circles. See J. Wellhausen, *Die Pharisäer und die Sadduzäer* (1874), pp. 112-13; H.S. Ryle and M.R. James, *ΨΑΛΜΟΙ ΣΟΛΟΜΩΝΤΟΣ, Psalms of the Pharisees. Commonly Called The Psalms of Solomon* (1891), pp. xliv-lii; G.B. Gray, 'The Psalms of Solomon', *APOT*, II, p. 630; J. Schüpphaus, *Die Psalmen Salomos: Ein Zeugnis jerusalemer Theologie und Frömmigkeit in der Mitte des vorchristlichen Jahrhunderts* (1977), pp. 5-11, 138-53. Others suggest an Essene origin. See for example J. O'Dell, 'The Religious Background of the Psalms of Solomon', *RevQ* 3 (1961–62), pp. 241-57; O. Eissfeldt, *Old Testament*, pp. 610-13; A. Dupont-Sommer,

response to their sins, God has sent a foreign conqueror, 'a man alien to our race' (17.8), who defeated the city, killed and expelled its citizens, and laid waste the land (2.6-8; 2.3; 7.2; 8.14-22; 17.11-20).[1] There is a general consensus that these allusions best fit the subjugation of Jerusalem by the Roman general Pompey in 63 BC, and that the psalms (at least those with historical allusions) were written sometime after this event.

In *Pss. Sol.* 17.21ff., the psalmist beseeches the Lord to 'raise up' for them their king, the 'son of David', to rule over 'your servant Israel'. The characteristics and functions of the Davidic king are drawn from the Old Testament Davidic promise tradition, and especially from Isa. 11.2-5.[2] The king will be 'powerful in the Holy Spirit' (v. 37; cf. Isa. 11.2) and will judge and rule in wisdom and understanding, strength and righteousness (vv. 22, 23, 26, 29, 32, 37, 38, 40, 43; Isa. 11.2-5; cf. Jer. 23.5-6). His task will be to 'destroy the unrighteous rulers' (v. 22; cf. vv. 23, 36; Num. 24.17), to overthrow the unlawful nations and to purge Jerusalem (vv. 22, 24, 25, 28, 30, 45). Like the Davidic warrior-king of Ps. 2, he will smash the arrogance of sinners like a potter's jar, shattering their substance with an iron rod (vv. 23-24; Ps. 2.9; cf. Isa. 11.4; Pss. 89.24; 110.5-6). Though he rules the Gentile nations with wisdom and compassion (vv. 29, 30, 34), there is little universalism here. Foreigners are expelled from Israel (v. 28) and return only to pay tribute and to see God's glory (v. 31). Salvation and blessing belong to Israel. The king will gather a holy people (v. 26; cf. Isa. 11.12); he will faithfully and righteously shepherd the Lord's flock, championing the cause of the weak (vv. 40-41; cf. Isa. 11.4a; Ezek. 34.23; 37.24; Mic. 5.4, MT 5.3). He will restore the nation's boundaries, and redistribute the land according to the original tribal divisions (vv. 26, 28, 44; cf. Isa. 49.6; Ezek. 45.8; 47.13, 21).

The Essene Writings from Qumran (1961), p. 196. In light of our incomplete knowledge of both parties during this period, it is probably best to stop short of an exact identification, classifying the psalms more generally as arising from the Jerusalem *Hasidim* ('pious ones'), the movement from which (it is generally believed) both parties emerged.

1. Verse divisions and translations from Wright, 'Psalms of Solomon', *OTP*, II, pp. 665-69. Wright's verse divisions are aligned with A. Rahlfs (ed.), *Septuaginta* (1935; 1979), which appear in parentheses in *APOT*. Wright says these are the same as those of Ryle and James, but this is mistaken. The verse divisions in Ryle and James agree with *APOT* (non-parenthesis), not with Rahlfs.

2. See M.-A. Chevallier, *L'Esprit et le Messie dans le Bas-Judaïsme et le Nouveau Testament* (1958), p. 12, for a list of parallels.

Though a human figure, the king bears divine attributes. He is sinless (v. 36), and condemns sinners 'by the thoughts of their hearts' (v. 25; cf. Isa. 11.3; Lk. 1.51), allowing no unrighteousness to dwell in the land (v. 27). Most striking are the psalmist's three allusions to Isa. 11.4: the Davidic king destroys unlawful nations 'with the word of his mouth' (v. 24); he 'strikes the earth with the word of his mouth forever' (v. 35); and he 'drives out sinners by the strength of his word' (v. 36). Though a warrior-king, the messiah's weapons are not horse, rider and bow (v. 33) but God's word and Spirit. Though great in power and authority, he is subordinated to, and wholly dependent on, Yahweh himself (vv. 30, 32, 34, 39).

Two titles applied to the messianic king are particularly significant on account of their originality. *Pss. Sol.* 17.21 is the earliest witness of the designation 'son of David'—the most common title for the messiah in the rabbinic literature.[1] The title χριστὸς κύριος ('anointed lord', or 'lord messiah') in 17.30 is attested elsewhere only in Lam. 4.20 (LXX), where it is a mistranslation of the Hebrew משיח יהוה, 'Yahweh's anointed', and in Lk. 2.11.[2] While most commentators consider the title in *Pss. Sol.* 17.21, like Lam. 4.20, to be a mistranslation of the Hebrew,[3] R.R. Hann and G.B. Wright argue convincingly that the phrase is an accurate translation, and that the Hebrew original was actually משיח אדון, 'anointed lord'.[4] 'My lord' (אדני; κύριος μου), is a common designation for the king in Samuel and Kings,[5] and the phrase 'anointed lord', though original to the *Psalms of Solomon*, has parallels in the 'anointed priest' of Lev. 4.3, 5, 16; 6.15, the 'anointed prince' (משיח נגיד) of Dan. 9.25-26, and the later rabbinic designation 'king messiah'. It is not

1. *Contra* Duling, 'Traditions', pp. 227-28, who suggests that the Hebrew *Vorlage* of the psalms read 'shoot', and that 'son' emerged in the Greek translation under Christian influence

2. See the discussion of Luke's use of the title in Lk. 2.11 in Chapter 3 below.

3. Wellhausen, *Die Pharisäer*, p. 132; Gray, *APOT*, II, p. 650; Rahlfs, *Septuaginta*, II, p. 488; Schüpphaus, *Die Psalmen Salomos*, p. 71.

4. R.R. Hann, 'Christos Kyrios in PsSol 17.32: "The Lord's Anointed" Reconsidered', *NTS* 31 (1985), pp. 620-27; Wright, 'Psalms of Solomon', *OTP*, II, p. 643, 667-68 n. z. This is also suggested as a possibility by Ryle and James, *ΨΑΛΜΟΙ ΣΟΛΟΜΩΝΤΟΣ*, p. 142.

5. According to BDB, 11, אדני appears 75 times in Samuel and Kings with reference to the king. Cf. the vocative in Jer. 22.18; Jer. 34.5: הוי אדון, 'Alas, lord!' (of Jehoiakim and Zedekiah).

unlikely, therefore, that the reading χριστὸς κύριος is an accurate translation of the original.

ii. *The Qumran Scrolls*. Like the *Psalms of Solomon,* the Qumran scrolls reflect opposition to the Hasmoneans and the Romans, and strong expectation for a coming Davidic king. In the priest-led community at Qumran, however, expectation centered on *two* 'messiahs', one royal (Davidic) and one priestly (Aaronic) (see 1QS 9.11; 1QSa 2.11-21; 1 QSb; 4QTestim), with precedence given to the priestly figure.[1] While this priestly dominance appears to have characterized Qumran messianism during its 'classic' period (from *c.* 110 BC onward),[2] various Cave 4 documents suggest an *increase in royal-Davidic expectation* in the sect's later years (*c.* 4 BC to AD 68).[3] As in the community which

1. For important works on Qumran messianism see the bibliography in J.A. Fitzmyer, *The Dead Sea Scrolls: Major Publications and Tools for Study* (rev. edn, 1990).

2. Though the historical development of Qumran messianism is greatly debated, there is a general consensus that dyarchic messianism characterized the sect during this period. In his seminal work, J. Starcky discerned four stages of messianic development corresponding to the four periods of Qumran occupation identified by archaeologists and paleographers ('Les quatre étapes du messianisme à Qumran', *RB* 70 [1963], pp. 481-505). Starcky discerned (1) an initial non-messianic 'Maccabean' period—the time of the rise of the teacher of righteousness (*c.* 152–110); (2) a 'Hasmonean' period (*c.* 110–63 BC), characterized by dyarchic messianism; (3) a 'Pompeian' period (*c.* 63–37 BC), representing a shift in expectation to a *single* 'messiah of Aaron *and* Israel' (cf. CD 12.23–13.1, 14.19, 19.10-11 [ms. B]; cf. CD 7.18-20); and, (4) a 'Herodian' period (*c.* 4 BC to AD 68), which began with the return of the sectarians after a three decade long abandonment of the site, and which was characterized by a return to dyarchic messianism, together with a revival of traditional Davidic expectation. With the exception of his controversial third stage, Starcky's framework has been widely accepted. For alternative explanations of the stage three evidence (from the Damascus Document), see R. Brown, 'J. Starcky's Theory of Qumran Messianic Development', *CBQ* 28 (1966), pp. 51-57; A.S. van der Woude, *Die messianischen Vorstellung* (1957), p. 29; A. Caquot, 'Le messianisme Qumrânien', in *Qumrân, sa piété, sa théologie et son milieu* (1978), pp. 231-24, esp. 237-43; and J.H. Charlesworth, 'From Jewish Messianology to Christian Christology', in *Judaisms and their Messiahs at the Turn of the Christian Era* (1987), p. 232.

3. There is widespread agreement on this point. See Liver, 'Doctrine of the Two Messiahs', pp. 184-85; J.T. Milik, *Ten Years of Discovery in the Wilderness of Judaea* (1959), p. 96; Starcky, 'Les quatre étapes', p. 504; Brown, 'J. Starcky's Theory', p. 52; J.A. Fitzmyer, 'The Aramaic "Elect of God" Text from Qumran

produced the *Psalms of Solomon,* the domination of Palestine by Rome appears to have increased hope for a king from the line of David who would rule justly and establish God's righteousness.

The five most important documents are: 4QFlor (= 4Q174), whose first thirteen lines contain a *pesher* on 2 Sam. 7.10-14; 4QPBless (= 4Q252), a fragment containing an interpretation of Jacob's blessing on Judah (Gen. 49.10); 4QpIsa[a] (= 4Q161), an Isaiah commentary containing a quotation and commentary on Isa. 11.1-3; 4Q504, a collection of prayers including a general affirmation of the Davidic covenant (4Q504 4); and 4Q285, a fragment related to the War Scroll (1QM) describing an eschatological battle between the forces of good and evil.[1] These texts draw their Davidic titles and functions from a range of Old Testament passages, including Isa. 11.1-5; 2 Sam. 7.11-14; Num. 24.17; Gen. 49.11; Jer. 23.5-6; 33.15-17; Ezek. 34.23-24; 37.24-25; Amos 9.11. All the foundational elements of the promise tradition are present—God's faithfulness to his covenant promises, the raising up of David's 'seed', the reign of this Davidic heir forever on the Davidic throne, his domination of the pagan nations, and a father–son relationship with God.

Cave 4', in *Essays on the Semitic Background of the New Testament* (1971), p. 139; Duling, 'Traditions', p. 183; *idem*, 'The Promises to David and their Entrance into Christianity—Nailing Down a Likely Hypothesis', *NTS* 19 (1973), pp. 55-77 (64); A. Caquot, 'Le messianisme Qumrânien', pp. 243-46; G.R. Beasley-Murray, *Jesus and the Kingdom of God* (1986), p. 54; *et al. Contra* M. de Jonge, *TDNT*, IX, p. 520; and Charlesworth, 'From Messianology to Christology', p. 233, who denies evidence of clear development or consistent content in Qumran messianology. Charlesworth's statement is made primarily with reference to the differences between the Community Rule and the Damascus Rule; he does not comment on the Cave 4 documents which refer more explicitly to Davidic expectations.

1. 4QPBless and 4QpIsa[a] were published by J.M. Allegro in 'Further Messianic References in Qumran Literature', *JBL* 75 (1956), pp. 182-87. 4QFlor was published by Allegro in 'Fragments of a Qumran Scroll of Eschatological *Midrashim*', *JBL* 77 (1958), pp. 350-54. See now the comprehensive monograph by G.J. Brooke, *Exegesis at Qumran: 4QFlorilegium in its Jewish Context* (1985). 4Q285 was rediscovered by Robert Eisenman and announced in the *New York Times,* 8 November 1991, sec. A. The debate is still raging over whether the Davidic prince of this controversial text slays the king of the Kitians or is himself slain. In my opinion the evidence points strongly toward the former. See G. Vermes, 'The Oxford Forum for Qumran Research Seminar on the Rule of War from Cave 4 (4Q285)', *JJS* 43 (1992), pp. 85-90; M. Bockmuehl, 'A "Slain Messiah" in 4Q Serekh Milhamah (4Q285)?', *TynBul* 43 (1992), pp. 155-69; M.G. Abegg Jr, 'Messianic Hope and 4Q285: A Reassessment', *JBL* 113 (1994), pp. 81-91.

This last, while mentioned in the quotation from 2 Samuel 7 in 4QFlor, is not interpreted or developed further. In line with the promise tradition, the messiah is designated as a 'prince' (4Q285; cf. 1QSb 5.20-29; CD 7.20; 1QM 5.1; 19.11) and 'shepherd' (4Q504 4), as well as the 'shoot', 'hut' and 'seed' of David (4QFlor; 4QPBless; 4QpIsa[a]). Unique to Qumran are the titles 'messiah of Israel' (1QS 9.11; 1QSa 2.11-21) and 'messiah of righteousness' (4QPBless). We see here, as in the *Psalms of Solomon,* the emerging use of משיח in the absolute. No longer is it exclusively 'Yahweh's anointed' or 'his anointed', but '*the* anointed (for Israel)' and '*the* anointed (who is righteous)'.

The task of the messiah is primarily an executive one. In common with the *Psalms of Solomon,* he acts as God's agent to defeat Israel's enemies and to rule and judge righteously. Unlike his seemingly passive role in Jeremiah and Ezekiel where Israel is saved 'in his days', or where the messiah appears on the scene *after* the eschatological conflict, in 4QFlor he is explicitly named as a deliverer 'who will stand up to save Israel'. He is a warrior-king after the model of Isa. 11.1-5 who slays the ungodly with the breath of his lips, who judges with his sword, and whose mighty scepter ravages the earth and rules the nations (4QpIsa[a]; 1QSb 5.24-26; 4Q285). Yet, unlike the Hasmoneans, he never acts as a despot, but is wholly submissive to the will of God. His loins are girded with righteousness; he upholds the Law and learns at the feet of the priests: 'As they teach him, so shall he judge' (4QpIsa[a] fr. D). He is the 'messiah of righteousness', bearing the Spirit of God and acting as Yahweh's agent to establish the kingdom and renew the covenant. As in the *Psalms of Solomon,* nothing is said of the details of his reign or of its duration. The emphasis, rather, is on the reality of the renewal God will achieve through his chosen agent.

c. *Apocalyptic Literature*

Though arising in diverse settings and circumstances, it is broadly true that the Jewish apocalypses are 'crisis' literature, 'intended for a group in crisis with the purpose of exhortation and/or consolation by means of divine authority'.[1] In those apocalypses characterized by visions and an interest in the development of history, the writer seeks to assure his

1. D. Hellholm, in 'The Problem of Apocalyptic Genre and the Apocalypse of John', in *SBL 1982 Seminar Papers* (1982), p. 168; cited by J.J. Collins, *The Apocalyptic Imagination* (1984), p. 31. But see Collins's clarification that a 'group in crisis' does not apply to all apocalypses, though all address some underlying problem.

readers that God is in control, and that he will bring history to its proper conclusion, judging and destroying the wicked and bringing salvation and blessing to the righteous.[1] In some works, God alone is the deliverer; in others, a messianic agent(s) appears. When a 'messiah' does appear, he is often described with allusions to the Davidic promise tradition.

Two works are particularly relevant to this discussion, *1 Enoch* and *4 Ezra*. *First (Ethiopic Apocalypse of) Enoch* is a composite, though interrelated, corpus representing various periods and writers (*c*. second century BC–first century AD).[2] The most important messianic texts appear in the *Similitudes* (chs. 37–71), now commonly dated pre-AD 70.[3] The messianic deliverer—identified variously as the 'elect one', the 'son of man', the 'righteous one' and the Lord's 'anointed'—appears as a pre-existent heavenly figure who will act as God's agent to save the righteous, destroy the wicked and reign forever in righteousness upon his throne.[4] While this portrait is based primarily on the Danielic 'son of man',[5] the author also draws allusions from royal-Davidic texts, especially Isaiah 11.[6] *1 En*. 49.3 cites almost verbatim Isa. 11.2 when it attributes the spirit of wisdom, insight, understanding and might to the 'elect one'. Spirit endowment appears again in 62.2, where the elect one slays sinners 'with the word of his mouth' (cf. Isa. 11.4). An allusion to Psalm 2 appears in 48.10, where judgment is directed against all who

1. On the two main types of apocalypses, see Collins, *Apocalyptic Imagination*, p. 5.

2. For a brief introduction see E. Isaac, '1 (Ethiopic Apocalypse of) Enoch', in Charlesworth (ed.), *OTP*, I, pp. 5-12. On the various messianic perspectives in the work see G.W.E. Nickelsburg, 'Salvation without and with a Messiah: Developing Beliefs in Writings Ascribed to Enoch', in *Judaisms and their Messiahs at the Turn of the Christian Era* (1987), p. 56.

3. While in the past, suspicion of late or Christian authorship has caused many scholars to avoid using the *Similitudes* as a witness to Second Temple Judaism, there is a growing consensus that they are Jewish, Palestinian, and pre-AD 70 in date. See Charlesworth, *OTP*, p. 89; *idem*, 'From Messianology to Christology', pp. 237, 260-61 n. 29, who lists among the specialists adhering to this position E. Isaac, G. Nickelsburg, M.E. Stone, M. Black, J. VanderKam, J.C. Greenfield and D.W. Suter.

4. See especially *1 Enoch*, pp. 45-55, 61-63.

5. Danielic images permeate the *Similitudes*. They are particularly evident in chs. 46 (the revelation of the son of man), ch. 47 (the vision of the heavenly throne room; cf. Dan. 7.9-10), and ch. 52 (the allegory of the metal mountains; cf. Dan. 2.31ff.).

6. Nickelsburg, 'Salvation', pp. 58-64; M. Black, *The Book of Enoch or I Enoch: A New English Edition* (1985), p. 189.

have 'denied the Lord of the spirits and *his anointed*' (cf. Ps. 2.2).

The merging of Danielic and royal-Davidic imagery also appears in the late first-century apocalypse *4 Ezra*.[1] In the eagle vision of *4 Ezra* 11.1–12.39, the messiah is identified as a lion (cf. Gen. 49.6-10; 1QSb 5.29; Rev. 5.5) who reproves and destroys the eagle (the Roman empire), and who delivers the 'remnant' of the people (12.34). He is said to arise 'from the posterity of David', having been 'kept' by the Most High until the end of days (12.32). A statement of Davidic descent is thus placed side by side with one implying pre-existence (cf. 7.28; 13.26, 52; 14.9). In ch. 13 the messiah is identified as a man who emerges from the sea, flies on the clouds of heaven, and reproves and destroys the wicked with a stream of fire (= 'the Law') from his mouth (13.3-11; 26-38). The passage draws its images from Isaiah 11, Psalm 2 and Daniel 2 and 7 and is reminiscent of the 'divine warrior' traditions of the Old Testament.[2] The messiah's judgment recalls *Pss. Sol.* 17, and, like that passage, draws its images primarily from Isa. 11.4 (cf. Ps. 2.9).

While a messianic agent sometimes plays a prominent and executive role in the apocalypses, the overwhelming concern is with the salvation God is about to accomplish. The writers forcefully stress that *God is in control and he will bring history to its proper conclusion, saving and delivering his people.* This emphasis accounts for the original idea that the messiah is 'hidden' or 'kept' by God, ready to be revealed at the end of time. Present tribulation and distress can be endured because God

1. *4 Ezra* is the Jewish work comprising chs. 3–14 of the work called 2 Esdras in English versions of the Apocrypha. Chapters 1–2 and 15–16, sometimes called 5 Ezra and 6 Ezra respectively, are later Christian interpolations. Though composed after the destruction of Jerusalem (*c.* 100 AD), the work is relevant to the present work since it is roughly contemporary with Luke and the author utilizes traditional messianic material. On the date, provenance and original language see M.E. Stone, *Fourth Ezra: A Commentary on the Book of Fourth Ezra* (1990), pp. 9-11; B.M. Metzger, 'The Fourth Book of Ezra', in Charlesworth, *OTP*, I, pp. 516-24. On the work's messianic perspective see M.E. Stone, 'The Concept of the Messiah in IV Ezra', in *Religions in Antiquity* (1968), pp. 295-312; *idem*, 'The Question of the Messiah in 4 Ezra', in *Judaisms and their Messiahs at the Turn of the Christian Era* (1987), pp. 209-24; *idem*, 'Excursus on the Redeemer Figure', in *Fourth Ezra*, pp. 206-13 (these articles overlap considerably); J.H. Charlesworth, 'The Concept of the Messiah in the Pseudepigrapha', *ANRW* II 19.1 (1979), pp. 188-218 (202-206); Klausner, *Messianic Idea*, pp. 349-65.

2. For divine warrior imagery and its significance in the passage see Stone, *Fourth Ezra*, p. 212.

has already foreseen and prepared for the deliverance of the righteous. While traditional features like Davidic descent are sometimes picked up (cf. *4 Ezra* 12.32), the authors more often draw on the Davidic promise traditions which emphasize the warring, saving and judging role of the king (esp. Isa. 11; Ps. 2). In short, it is the fact of God's deliverance, rather than the person of the deliverer, which is of utmost concern.

d. *Early Christian Witnesses*

Despite their potentially polemic nature, early Christian sources must be given due weight when seeking Jewish messianic expectations of the first century. The Gospels depict the Jews of first-century Palestine in high expectation for the Davidic messiah:

(1) Luke portrays pious Jews in Jerusalem anxiously awaiting the coming of the 'Lord's Christ' (χριστὸς κυρίου), the 'horn of salvation from the house of David' (Lk. 1.69; 2.26). (2) When John the Baptist appears on the scene, the Jewish people are said to be in a state of expectation, wondering whether he might be *the* Christ (Lk. 3.15; cf. Jn 1.20). (3) Matthew says that when Herod questioned the chief priests and scribes in Jerusalem, they affirmed that the Christ was to be born in Bethlehem of Judea (Mt. 2.4). (4) In John, speculation that Jesus might be the Christ raises the objection, 'The Christ is not coming from Galilee, is he? Has not the Scripture said that the Christ comes from the seed of David, and from Bethlehem the place where David was' (Jn 7.41-42). (5) In the *Davidssohnfrage,* the synoptic Jesus affirms that '*the scribes say* that the Christ is the son of David' (Mk 12.35, //s), and the blind man outside Jericho addresses Jesus by this title (Mk 10.47, 48). (6) At his trial Jesus is questioned by the Sanhedrin as to whether he is 'the Christ, the son of the Blessed', and is mocked on the cross as 'the Christ, the king of Israel' (Mk 14.61; 15.32; cf. Mt. 26.63; 27.40-42; Lk. 22.67-70; 23.35-37).

Other eschatological figures are also expected. In the Synoptics, Herod Antipas is disturbed by Jewish speculation that Jesus may be Elijah or another prophet raised from the dead (Mk 6.15; Mt. 16.14; Lk. 9.8, 19). Jesus' disciples affirm that the scribes say that Elijah must come before the resurrection (Mk 9.11; cf. Mt. 17.10; 11.14). Elijah is also expected by the Jews in the Fourth Gospel, where the Baptist is questioned whether he is the Christ, or Elijah, or the prophet (Jn 1.25). 'The prophet', also mentioned in Jn 7.40, is probably a reference to the prophet like Moses of Deut. 18.15.[1] Evidence for this appears in Jn 6.14, where, after the wilderness feeding the crowds intend to make Jesus king because he is 'the prophet who is to come into the world'. John may here be in contact with Qumranian, or perhaps Samaritan traditions (cf. Jn 4.25). The Samaritans expected not a Davidic messiah but the Taheb (= 'the one who returns'), evidently a Mosaic figure. In short, the Gospels portray a diversity of eschatological figures and hopes, but with a strong and persistent stream of royal-Davidic expectations. The Davidic messiah is expected to be God's instrument of deliverance against Israel's enemies (Lk. 1.71). In light of the previous discussion, there seems no reason to doubt the general veracity of this picture.

e. *Early Rabbinic Thought*

It is significant that, among the diverse expectations of post-exilic Judaism, it is the hope for the promised Davidic heir which survived the destruction of Jerusalem and became an integral part of the eschatology of rabbinic Judaism. This suggests that the rabbinic material lies in a continuing stream of tradition with the *Psalms of Solomon* and other Second Temple literature.

i. *Synagogue Prayers: The* Shemoneh Esreh. A critical link in this tradition appears in the *Shemoneh Esreh,* or 'Eighteen Benedictions', the most important prayer in Judaism (also known as the *Tefillah*, התפלה = 'the Prayer').[2] The fifteenth blessings of the Babylonian recension beseeches God to:

> 15. Cause the shoot of David to shoot forth quickly, and raise up his horn by thy salvation. For we wait on thy salvation all the day. *Blessed art thou, Lord, who causest the horn of salvation to shoot forth.*[3]

While the prayers for the rebuilding of Jerusalem in Benediction 14 and for the restoration of temple worship in Benediction 17 suggest that the Babylonian recension of the *Tefillah* did not reach its final form till after the destruction of Jerusalem in AD 70, parallels elsewhere suggest its underlying structure and language are much older. The hymn of

1. See H.M. Teeple, *The Mosaic Eschatological Prophet* (1957).
2. Schürer, *History* (revised), II, p. 456.
3. Translation from Schürer, *History* (revised), II, p. 458. The Hebrew text appears in W. Staerk, *Altjüdische Liturgische Gebete* (1910), p. 18.

praise from the Hebrew text of Sirach (Sir. 51.12 i-xvi, ms B)[1]—probably to be dated in the second- or early first-century BC[2]—contains a number of remarkable parallels to the *Tefillah.*[3] Distichs vii and viii praise God for 'rebuilding his city and his sanctuary' and for making 'a horn to sprout for the house of David'. The fact that references to the Temple and the Davidic messiah appear together and in the same order as the *Tefillah* suggests dependence of some kind; and it is not unlikely that the common tradition was an earlier version of the *Shemoneh Esreh.* Similarly striking is a parallel in Lk. 1.69, where it is said that God 'has raised up a *horn of salvation* for us in the house of David his servant'. The phrase 'horn of salvation' appears in the Old Testament only at 2 Sam. 22.3 (= Ps. 18.2), and there it refers not to the Davidic shoot but to the power of Yahweh. Since it is unlikely that the author of the fifteenth Benediction borrowed the phrase from early Christianity, the application of 'horn of salvation' to the Davidic messiah in Lk. 1.69 probably depends either on the fifteenth Benediction itself or on a tradition related to it. This again suggests a pre-Christian date for the strong Davidic expectations found in the *Shemoneh Esreh.*

ii. *The Targums and Rabbinic Literature.* Rabbinic and targumic traditions are notoriously difficult to date, and it is uncritical merely to assume that the messianic expectations expressed in the targums, the *midrashim* or the Talmud *necessarily* reflect Second Temple views. On the other hand, rabbinic expectations which parallel those of earlier texts are likely to represent trajectories emerging from the Second Temple period.

While the references to the Davidic messiah in the targums do not

1. See A.A. Di Lella, *The Hebrew Text of Sirach* (1966).

2. The reference to the sons of Zadok as the rightful heirs to the priesthood parallels statements at Qumran, and it has been proposed that the sectarians themselves added the hymn to Sirach. Whether or not this is the case, the reference suggests that the hymn was composed either (1) before the Maccabees, when the Zadokite priests were still in office, or (2) during the Hasmonean dynasty, as polemic against the non-Zadokite Hasmonean priest-kings. See Di Lella, *Sirach*, pp. 104-105.

3. Parallels include: God as 'shield of Abraham' (Sir. 51.12 x = *Shemoneh Esreh* 1); as 'redeemer of Israel' (Sir. 51.12 v = *Shem. Esr.* 8); as 'gatherer of the dispersed of Israel' (Sir. 51.12 v = *Shem. Esr.* 10); as 'builder of his city and sanctuary' (Sir. 51.12 vii = *Shem. Esr.* 14); and as he 'who makes a horn to sprout from the house of David' (Sir. 51.12 viii = *Shem. Esr.* 15); Schürer, *History* (revised), II, p. 459 n. 159.

reveal absolute consistency or unanimity of viewpoint, it is possible to delineate a general portrait.[1] The messiah is a human king, a descendant of David[2] born in Bethlehem[3] who serves as God's agent of deliverance.[4] Endowed with the power and Spirit of God, he will destroy Israel's enemies,[5] gather the dispersion and reunite the kingdom.[6] The nation's frontiers will be restored.[7] He will rebuild Jerusalem and the temple.[8] In his day peace, security and prosperity will be established in the land and throughout the world.[9] The messiah will have universal dominion.[10] He will be a righteous ruler, dispensing justice and equity to the poor and oppressed.[11] The Holy Spirit will rest on him and he will have the gift of prophecy.[12] Though warrior, king and judge, he is wholly dependent on God.[13] It is God who inaugurates the new era. 'Messiah' (משיחא) and 'king messiah' (מלכא משיחא) are the favourite

1. See especially S. H. Levey, *The Messiah: An Aramaic Interpretation* (1974).

2. *Targ. Neb.* Hos. 2.2; 'Shoot' of David: *Targ. Neb.* Jer. 23.5; 33.15; *Targ. Ket.* Ps. 132.17; descendant of Jesse: *Targ. Neb.* Isa. 11.1; 14.29. Cf. *Targ. Neb.* Jer. 30.9; Hos 3.5; *Targ. Ket.* Esth. 1.1.

3. *Targ. Neb.* Mic. 5.1.

4. *Targ. Neb.* 2 Sam. 22.32; Hab. 3.18; *Targ. Ket.* Ps. 18.32; Ps. 21.1-8; 80.16-18; Lam. 4.22.

5. *Targ. Onq.*, *Frg. Targ.* and *Targ. Ps.-J.* on Num. 24.17-24; *Frg. Targ.* and *Targ. Ps.-J.* on Gen. 49.11; *Targ. Neb.* Isa. 10.27; 11.4; 14.29; 42.1; 52.15; 53.7, 11-12; Jer. 23.6; Zech. 4.7; 10.4; *Targ. Ket.* Ps. 45.4-6. Cf. *Pes. R.* 37 (163a); *Gen. Rab.* 98.8 on 49.10; 99.8 on 49.10.

6. *Targ. Neb.* Isa. 11.11-12; 42.7; 53.8; Hos. 2.2;14.8; Mic. 4.6-7; 5.3; *Targ. Ket.* Cant. 1.8; 7.13-14. Cf. *Qoh. R.* 1.7 on 1.7; *Gen. R.* 98.9 on 49.11 (van der Woude, *TDNT*, IX, p. 526).

7. Str–B, IV, p. 899; *b. B. Bat.* 56a; *Gen. R.* 44 on 15.18; *Num. R.* 14.1 on 7.48.

8. *Targ. Neb.* Isa. 53.5; Zech. 6.12-13; *Targ. Ket.* 1.17. For rabbinic material cf. Str–B, IV, pp. 883, 919-20, for Jerusalem (*Exod. R.* 52.5 on 39.32) and Str–B, I, pp. 1003-1004, IV, pp. 884, 929-30, for the temple (*Pes. K.* 21 (145a); *Gen. R.* on 49.10.

9. *Targ. Neb.* Isa. 9.5-6; 11.6-9; 16.5; Hos. 3.5; 14.8; Jer. 23.6; 33.16ff.; *Targ. Ket.* Ps. 72.6-7, 16.

10. *Frag. Targ.* Gen. 49.10; *Targ. Ps. Jn.* Gen. 49.10; *Targ. Neb.* Isa. 16.1; 53.3; Amos 9.11; Zech. 4.7; *Targ. Neb.* Mic. 5.3; *Targ. Ket.* Ps. 45.13ff.; 72.8-11.

11. *Targ. Neb.* Isa. 9.6; 11.3-4; 16.5; 28.6; Jer. 23.5; 33.15; *Targ. Ket.* Ps. 45.8; 72.1-4, 12-15; cf. *b. Sanh.* 93b.

12. *Targ. Neb.* Isa. 11.2; 42.1; *Targ. Ket.* Ps. 45.3.

13. *Targ. Neb.* Hab 3.18 and *passim*.

targumic titles for the eschatological deliverer.[1] 'Messiah, the son of David' appears occasionally.[2]

The *midrashim* and the talmudic literature agree with this general portrait but tend to place even more emphasis on the person of the messiah, so that he becomes the central figure in eschatological hopes.[3] 'Son of David' (בן דוד) is the favourite designation of the rabbis, appearing often in sayings attributed to Tannaites.[4] 'David' is also used, but with less frequency.[5] Though it is not always expressly stated that the messiah must be of Davidic lineage, 'it became the dominant conviction that only a descendant of David could exercise Messianic rule'.[6]

In line with some apocalypses (cf. *4 Ezra* 7.29-32; 12.34; *2 Apoc. Bar.* 30.1; 40.3) the rabbis generally view the messianic era as an interim period, preceding the resurrection, the judgment and the age to come.[7] As in the apocalypses, the messianic era is often preceded by a time of tribulation and suffering, the 'messianic woes' or 'birth pangs of the messiah'.[8] Messianic speculation in the rabbis centers on four main themes: (1) the name of the messiah;[9] (2) the conditions of his coming;[10]

1. The former in the 'official' targums, the latter in the *Targum of the Writings* (*Targ. Ket.*) and the Palestinian targums.

2. *Targ. Neb.* Jer. 30.9; Hos. 3.5; *Targ. Ket.* Esth 1.1.

3. See Klausner, *Messianic Idea,* 459.

4. For example: R. José ben Qisma (*c.* AD 110) in *b. Sanh.* 98a; R. Johanan ben Torta (*c.* AD 130) in *y. Ta'an* 4.8; R. Jehuda ben Il'ai and R. Nehemia (*c.* AD 150) in *b. Sanh.* 97a. Cf. Klausner, *Messianic Idea*, pp. 461-62; E. Lohse, *TDNT*, VIII, 481; Str–B 1.525; G. Dalman, *The Words of Jesus* (1902), pp. 316-19.

5. *b. Hag.* 14a; *b. Meg.* 17b; *y. Ber.* 2.3-4; cf. Str–B, I, p. 65; II, p. 337; J. Neusner, *Messiah in Context* (1984), p. 93; E. Lohse, *TDNT*, VIII, p. 481. In *b. Sanh.* 98 there are references to the messiah as David *redivivus* as well as statements refuting this view.

6. E. Lohse, *TDNT*, VIII, p. 481; *idem*, 'Der König aus Davids Geschlecht: Bemerkungen zur messianischen Erwartung der Synagoge', in *Abraham Unser Vater* (1963), p. 341. The key phrase here is 'dominant conviction'; particularly in the earlier period it could not be said to be the 'universal conviction'. On Akiba's attribution of messiahship to bar Koseba (Kohkba), see below.

7. The terminology is loose, however, and at times the two ages seem to be equated. R. Akiba taught that the messianic age was a part of the present aeon (*Gen. R.* 44.22-23). See Klausner, *Messianic Idea*, pp. 408-26; Str–B, IV, pp. 816-44; III, pp. 828-30; M. de Jonge, *TDNT*, IX, p. 525; H. Sasse, *TDNT*, I, pp. 204-207.

8. *m. Sota* 9.15; Klausner, *Messianic Idea*, pp. 440-50; Str–B, I, p. 950; IV, pp. 981-86; Schürer, *History* (revised), II, pp. 514-15.

9. *b. Sanh.* 98b; *Midr. Lam.* on 1.16; Str–B, I, pp. 64-66; A.S. van der Woude,

(3) the time of his coming;[1] (4) and the length of the messianic age.[2]

In short, while the rabbinic literature expands and embellishes its messianic images with apocalyptic and other traditions, its descriptions agree in general with the portraits of the coming Davidic king found in the writings of the Second Temple period, and especially the *Psalms of Solomon.* Though the messiah plays a greater role in the end-time events, it is still the fact of Israel's salvation—the establishment of the messianic kingdom—rather than the person of the messiah which is of central importance.

f. *Summary and Conclusions*

While an earlier generation of scholars tended to assume that 'Judaism' was a single monolithic entity with a common set of beliefs, and that all first-century Jews were awaiting '*the* messiah', more recent research has focused on the diversity of eschatological expectations in the Second Temple period.[3] The present chapter has confirmed the validity of this new direction in the context of one strand of expectation, that of the coming king from the line of David. From its roots in the legitimization formulas of the Davidic dynasty, the Davidic promise tradition was picked up and utilized in a variety of ways by the different 'Judaisms' of the Second Temple period.

The roots of this phenomenon may be traced to the eighth century prophecies of Isaiah ben-Amoz. In the context of the destruction of the northern kingdom and the corruption of the southern monarchy, Isaiah draws on the covenant promises to David to prophesy the coming of a new David who will destroy the wicked, protect the poor and oppressed and establish an eternal era of peace, justice and righteousness. Unlike the corrupt kings of the present dynasty, this 'shoot from Jesse' will be wholly dependent on God's Spirit to guide him. In the context of the (coming) Babylonian exile, Jeremiah and Ezekiel predict that God will

TDNT, IX, p. 525. As in the targums, the messiah's name is said to have been created before the world was made. Cf. *b. Ber.* 49a; *Gen. R.* 1; *b. Pesah* 5a.

10. *b. Sanh.* 97b-98; *b. Shabb.* 118b; cf. Neusner, *Messiah in Context*, pp. 96-98; Klausner, *Messianic Idea*, pp. 408-19.

1. *b. Sanh.* 96b-97a; cf. Schürer, *History* (revised), II, pp. 523-24; Klausner, *Messianic Idea*, pp. 420-21.

2. *b. Sanh.* 99a; *Sifre* 134a; cf. Str–B, IV, pp. 977-1015; Klausner, *Messianic Idea,* 408-426.

3. See *Judaisms and their Messiahs at the Turn of the Christian Era* (eds. J. Neusner *et al.*, 1987).

bring forth a righteous 'shoot' for David who will reunite the nation and shepherd and lead God's people. In the post-exilic period, Zechariah and Haggai recall the promise that David's son will build a house for Yahweh to embolden the Davidid Zerubbabel and the people to return to the task of building the temple.

In the middle and late Second Temple period, the Davidic promise tradition is used especially to challenge the claims of royal pretenders to the throne, first the Hasmoneans and then the Herodian dynasty. The author(s) of the *Psalms of Solomon* draw extensively on the promise tradition, focusing on three main aspects: the Davidic descent of the deliverer, the eternal nature of the Davidic throne and the destruction of the wicked resulting in security for Israel in the land. The Hasmoneans have fallen because they were non-Davidic usurpers. The Romans, the instruments of God's judgment, will themselves be judged since they have oppressed and murdered God's people. When the son of David comes, he will return the nation to its God-ordained leadership and bring in an eternal era of peace and prosperity. The Qumran sectarians also focus on God-ordained leadership—which in their perspective is dyarchic (cf. *Testaments of the Twelve Patriarchs*). Priestly and royal messiahs respectively oversee the religious and lay aspects of the community. As a priest-led community, the role of the royal messiah is sometimes minimalized. In some of the later scrolls, however, this emphasis appears to shift and special prominence is given to the Davidic figure. As in the *Psalms of Solomon,* he is an authentic Davidid—in contrast to the Hasmoneans and the Herodians—who appears as an active agent of deliverance. The same features of the promise tradition are emphasized: Davidic descent, continuing mercy for David's house, an eternal throne and the destruction of Israel's enemies.

While acknowledging the diversity within first-century eschatological expectation, this survey has also noted the growing influence of royal-Davidic expectations in first-century Judaism. The primary reason for this appears to have been the loss of political sovereignty and the domination by Rome, leading to an increasing emphasis on the coming king as the agent of liberation.

Some scholars, by contrast, have taken the evidence of messianic diversity during this period to a more radical conclusion, suggesting that the whole idea of the 'Jewish messiah' is a myth—a construct of the early Christians to explain the enigmatic identity of Jesus. W.S. Green claims that the scant and inconsistent use of the designation 'messiah' in early Judaism indicates that the term 'is all signifier with no signified... notable primarily for its indeterminacy'.[1] It was the early Christians, in their attempts to demonstrate the continuity between Christianity and Judaism, who applied diverse Old Testament 'prophecies' to Jesus and thereby created a promise-fulfillment motif:

> By naming Jesus *christos* and depicting him as foretold and expected... early Christian writers gave the figure of the messiah a diachronic dimension. They situated the messiah's origin not in the present but in Israelite antiquity and thus established the Hebrew scriptures as a sequence of auguries.[2]

Whatever the truth concerning the motivations of the early Christians, Green's conclusions on the Jewish context must be challenged. While it is correct to say that 'the messiah' was not a universally recognized and *precisely* defined symbol, the evidence of the *Psalms of Solomon,* the Qumran scrolls, early Christian statements, the first-century apocalypses, and tannaitic rabbinism, all suggest that Jews of the first century were beginning to use the term in the absolute with reference to a coming deliverer, and that in general (though there are exceptions) this deliverer was viewed as a Davidic figure.

This being the case, Green's further implication that it was the early Christians who created the so-called 'messianic hope' must also be challenged—at least in the royal Davidic strand we have examined. Though first-century perspectives vary in detail, the present survey has confirmed a widespread tradition that God would soon raise up a Davidic king who would save and deliver his people. It was this tradition of expectation that the Christians picked up and applied to Jesus.

Despite diversity on many points, there are three features that are common to all the documents examined. The first is the messianic agent's dependence on, and obedience to Yahweh—his Lord. It is God himself who accomplishes salvation, either alone or through his chosen agent. Secondly, though some works focus more than others on the activity of the messianic agent, throughout it is the *fact of salvation,* rather than the person of the savior, which is the *ultimate* concern.[3]

1. W.S. Green, 'Messiah in Judaism: Rethinking the Question', in *Judaisms and Their Messiahs at the Turn of the Christian Era* (1987), 2-4.

2. Green, 'Messiah in Judaism', p. 5.

3. As Charlesworth, *OTP*, p. 118, observes (with reference to the Pseudepigrapha), the authors 'seem to be attending more to the dawning of *God's* final act in history than to the figure or mediator God would choose to inaugurate this act. They were

Even in the *Psalms of Solomon,* where it is clear that the deliverer *must* be a Davidid, it is still the overthrow of the Romans, the salvation of Israel, and the establishment of God's righteous kingdom, which is the ultimate concern. It is in this context one must evaluate the claim of Rabbi Akiba that Bar Koseba—seemingly a non-Davidid—was the messiah.[1] This is often introduced as proof that Davidic descent was not an *essential* qualification for messiahship. While this is basically true, the emphasis should be placed on the positive side: the *most important* qualification for messiahship was the concomitant destruction of the wicked, the securing of Israel's borders and the establishment of the kingdom.[2] When it seemed Koseba would achieve this aim, Akiba willingly acclaimed him 'king messiah'. Davidic descent in this case took a back seat to divine deliverance. While it was not always expected that there would be a messiah, or that the messiah would *himself* accomplish the deliverance, it was unthinkable that God would reveal his anointed one, then fail to save his people! Indeed, it has sometimes been suggested that the two-messiah conception of later rabbinism resulted from speculation following the failure of Bar Koseba.[3] What would happen if the messiah (ben-Joseph/Ephraim) came, but deliverance did not follow? The answer: a second messiah (ben-David) would immediately follow and *he* would deliver God's people. Though expectation for a messiah was not an essential component of eschatological salvation, a messiah who did not bring ultimate salvation was unthinkable.

This emphasis on ultimate salvation brings up a third component common to all the works examined, and that is the *nature* of the salvation achieved. Though the king's coming is an 'eschatological' event, that is, an event marking the end of the present era and the beginning of

hence more eschatologically oriented than messianically focused'. Mowinckel, *He That Cometh*, p. 8, says, 'An eschatology without a Messiah is conceivable, but not a Messiah apart from a future hope'.

1. In *y. Ta'an.* 4.8 [68d, pp. 48-51]) Akiba is said to have hailed bar Koseba as 'king messiah', and to have applied the 'star' prophecy of Num. 24.17 to him. To this R. Johanan ben Torta is said to have answered: 'Akiba, grass will grow out of thy jaw-bone, and still the son of David will not come.' Cf. van der Woude, *TDNT*, IX, p. 523.

2. Van der Woude, *TDNT*, IX, p. 523, correctly points out that 'expectation of the Messianic kingdom determined expectation of the redeemer and not *vice versa.* As one viewed the coming kingdom, so one viewed God's Messiah.'

3. Str–B, II, p. 294; Klausner, *Messianic Idea*, p. 493; Levey, *The Messiah*, p. 16.

an ideal age of peace, prosperity and security, the kingdom he establishes is essentially an earthly one. This does not mean it is 'secular', nor even 'temporal'—it may be expected to continue forever. It is rather an earthly and 'spiritual' kingdom in the true Old Testament sense. 'Spiritual' in that every aspect of life will be wholly devoted to Yahweh's glory; where, as the prophet puts it, even the cooking pots will be 'holy to Yahweh of Hosts' (Zech. 14.20-21). 'Earthly' in that Israel will be secure and established *within her borders*. Whether dominion over the rest of the world is expressly stated or not, Israel will never again fear foreign domination. All the world will honor and respect the nation, knowing that Yahweh himself has saved her and dwells among her; Jerusalem will be the center of the earth.

3. *The Davidic Promises in Early (Pre-Lukan) Christianity*

Subsequent chapters will examine how Luke interprets and utilizes the Davidic promise tradition in his two volume work. It is necessary, therefore, to survey not only the Jewish background, but also the early Christian understanding of this theme. What follows is not a comprehensive examination of this theme in the New Testament and early Christianity, but a general overview of the Christian traditions and perspectives available to Luke and his audience.

a. *Early Traditions*

Already in the earliest New Testament documents the designation χριστός is so closely associated with Jesus that it is treated as his second name. While this nominal use is probably related to the gospel's entrance into non-Jewish circles (where χριστός would lose much of its significance), the fact that this term was chosen over others suggests that at a very early period believers were confessing Jesus as 'the messiah'.[1] It is a matter of considerable debate, however, why the early Christians

1. For a different view see A.E. Harvey, *Jesus and the Constraints of History* (1982), pp. 120-53, who suggests that Jesus was first given the *name* χριστός (during his earthly ministry) and that this was only later interpreted with the title ὁ χριστός. According to Harvey it was the people's recognition that Jesus was particularly endowed with the Spirit that prompted them to identify him as the 'anointed' (χριστός) prophet of Isa. 61.1. Cf. W.C. van Unnik, 'Jesus the Christ', *NTS* (1961–62), pp. 113-16. Green, 'Messiah in Judaism', p. 4, like Harvey, says that the nominal use of χριστός came first, since this is how the term is used in the Pauline epistles and in Mark.

gave this title to Jesus and exactly what it signified.[1] There were almost certainly a range of factors. The following are suggestive.

(1) It is highly likely that there was at least some royal or 'messianic' speculation surrounding Jesus' ministry. R.A. Horsley and J.S. Hanson have demonstrated from Josephus and the early rabbinic literature how willing the first-century Palestinian peasantry were to follow and proclaim as 'king' a charismatic leader.[2] Even if we leave out of the discussion those passages in which Jesus explicitly or implicitly accepts the title χριστός, there is still much that is implicitly royal in his ministry: (a) It is universally recognized that Jesus' proclamation of the kingdom of God was central to his message. Since the literature of the era often linked an eschatological king to the establishment of God's final rule,[3] this alone could have produced messianic acclamation from the populace. (b) Many of Jesus' words and actions had royal connotations, including his entry to Jerusalem riding on a donkey (Mk 14.7-11 //s), his cleansing of the temple (Mk 11.15-17 //s), and his claim that he would rebuild the temple after three days (Mk 14.57-58; 15.29; Mt. 26.61; 27.40; Jn 2.19; Acts 6.14).[4] While some of these may be viewed as 'royal' in a general sense, the last, at least, would have strongly *Davidic* implications (cf. 2 Sam. 7.13; Zech. 6.12-13 and the rabbinic literature cited above).[5] (c) The request of James and John for chief seats in the kingdom (Mk 10.35-37 //s)—a passage with strong claims for authenticity[6]—indicates royal speculation among the disciples (cf. Acts 1.6).

(2) Messianic expectations could also have been aroused if Jesus was believed to be a descendant of David. Despite the objections of W. Wrede, C. Burger and others that 'son of David' is merely a *theologumenon* without historical basis, Cullmann, Michaelis, Hahn, Brown

1. For good discussions of this topic see van Unnik, 'Jesus the Christ', pp. 101-16; M. de Jonge, 'The Earliest Christian Use of *Christos*: Some Suggestions', *NTS* 32 (1986), pp. 321-43; and the survey of literature in Duling, 'Traditions', pp. 5-84.

2. R.A. Horsley with J. S. Hanson, *Bandits, Prophets, and Messiahs: Popular Movements in the Time of Jesus* (1985), esp. ch. 3, 'Royal Pretenders and Popular Messianic Movements'; also R.A. Horsley, 'Popular Messianic Movements around the Time of Jesus', *CBQ* 46 (1984), pp. 471-95.

3. Cf. *Pss. Sol.* 17; *Shem. Esr.* 11, 15 (Palestinian recension: 11, 14); etc.

4. By the 'criteria of multiple attestation' this statement has good support as an authentic logion.

5. On this whole issue see O. Betz, *What Do we Know About Jesus?* (1967), pp. 87-92.

6. Cf. V. Taylor, *The Gospel According to St Mark* (2nd edn, 1966), p. 439.

et al. have argued convincingly that Jesus' family possessed (or believed they possessed) a Davidic lineage.[1] If there was already speculation in the air concerning Jesus as a potential deliverer, his Davidic descent could only have fueled this expectation.

(3) Jesus' expression of a special father–son relationship with God may also have prompted royal-messianic speculation.[2] Though the survey above has suggested that divine sonship was the *least* utilized aspect of the David promise tradition in Second Temple Judaism, its appearance in 4QFlor (and perhaps elsewhere[3]) indicates that it was not actively suppressed prior to the rise of Christianity.[4] Its neglect was no doubt due to its lack of apologetic or polemic value. While features like the king's Davidic descent and his role in the destruction of the wicked were utilized when opposing non-Davidids on the throne, or when stressing God's ultimate salvation of Israel, his father–son relationship with God had little use in such contexts. It is not unlikely, therefore, that Jesus' self-expressions awakened dormant traditions that the Davidic deliverer would be called God's son.

(4) If Jesus was viewed as one particularly endowed with the Spirit of God, this may also have aroused royal-messianic speculation. As we have seen, Isa. 11.1-4, with its description of the king's special Spirit-endowment, was widely utilized in Second Temple expectations. *Pss. Sol.* 17.37 says of the coming Davidic king that he will be 'powerful in the

1. For the authenticity of Jesus' Davidic descent see especially O. Cullmann, *The Christology of the New Testament* (2nd edn, 1963), pp. 127-33; W. Michaelis, 'Die Davidssohnschaft Jesu als historisches und dogmatisches Problem', in *Der historische Jesus und der kerygmatische Christus* (1963), pp. 317-30; Hahn, *Titles*, pp. 240ff.; R.E. Brown, *The Birth of the Messiah* (1977), pp. 505-12. Against the view of Burger, Wrede and others that 'son of David' is a *theologomenon* rather than a genealogical statement, it must be said that since Davidic descent was not an *essential* element of messianic expectation, there is no reason the church would have felt it necessary to create a Davidic lineage for Jesus.

2. Cf. especially J. Jeremias, *The Prayers of Jesus* (1967), pp. 11-65; *idem, New Testament Theology* (1971), pp. 61-68; I.H. Marshall, 'The Divine Sonship of Jesus', *Int* 21 (1967), pp. 87-103.

3. Cf. 1QSa 2.11-12; 4QpsDan A^{a} (=4Q243); Ps. 109.3 LXX; *4 Ezra* 7.28, 29; 13.32, 37, 52; 14.9; *T. Levi* 4.2.

4. The interpretion of *Targ. Neb.* 2 Sam. 7.14 ('I shall be to him *as* a father, and he will be *like* a son before me') and *Targ. Ket.* Ps. 2.7 ('I will tell the decree of the Lord: he said, 'You are *as dear to me* as a son is to a father...') are probably anti-Christian polemic.

Holy Spirit'.[1] At the same time, prophets could also be described as 'anointed ones' endowed with the Spirit (Isa. 61.1; CD 2.12; cf. 1QM 11.7), so such an attribution would not *necessarily* refer to the coming king.

(5) Whatever the nature of the speculation during Jesus' life, there is little doubt that he was viewed as a threat by the authorities and that he was crucified as a royal pretender.[2] The probable authenticity of the *titulus* 'King of the Jews' on the cross suggests, first, that Jesus was accused before Pilate of sedition (i.e. of royal claims), and secondly, that he responded to the charge of kingship either positively or in silence. While Jesus' death at first shattered the disciples' messianic expectations, his resurrection was viewed as vindication of his person and work.[3] Any royal-messianic claims attributed to him prior to his death would be seen as confirmed by the resurrection.

(6) At this point the 'raising up' language of the Davidic promise tradition probably played a key role in the early church's interpretation of the resurrection. The disciples now confessed that God had fulfilled his promises to David by 'raising' Jesus from the dead (2 Sam. 7.12; Jer. 23.5; 30.8-9; Amos 9.11; *Pss. Sol.* 17.23; etc.), and exalting him to his heavenly throne (Ps. 110.1). He had vindicated his anointed.[4]

The earliest evidence that Jesus' resurrection was linked to the Davidic promise tradition appears in Rom. 1.3-4, where the apostle Paul summarizes the 'gospel of God' which was promised beforehand in the scriptures:

1. Cf. especially, Chevallier, *L'Esprit et le Messie, passim.* For the suggestion that Jesus was first called χριστός because he was viewed as one 'anointed' with God's Spirit (cf. Lk. 3.22; 4.1, 14; Acts 10.38), see van Unnik, 'Jesus the Christ', pp. 113-14, who points to the connection between anointing and Spirit-endowment in 1 Sam. 16.13; cf. Josephus, *Ant.* 6.166-68 (of David); CD 2.12 (of the prophets); and 2 Cor. 1.22-23 (of Christian believers).

2. Cf. especially N.A. Dahl, 'The Crucified Messiah', in *The Crucified Messiah and Other Essays* (1974), pp. 10-36.

3. Cf. B. Lindars, *New Testament Apologetic* (1961), pp. 251-52.

4. This point is made by many commentators. See E. Lövestam, *Son and Saviour: A Study of Acts 13, 32-37* (1961), pp. 8-10; Schweizer, 'Davidic "Son of God"', p. 190; Betz, *What Do we Know About Jesus?*, p. 97; Duling, 'Promises to David', pp. 70-77; *idem*, 'Traditions', pp. 261ff.; J.H. Hayes, 'The Resurrection As Enthronement and the Earliest Church Christologies', *Int* 22 (1968), pp. 337, 342.

περὶ τοῦ υἱοῦ αὐτοῦ
τοῦ γενομένου ἐκ σπέρματος Δαυὶδ κατὰ σάρκα,
τοῦ ὁρισθέντος υἱοῦ θεοῦ ἐν δυνάμει κατὰ πνεῦμα ἁγιωσύνης
ἐξ ἀναστάσεως νεκρῶν,
Ἰησοῦ Χριστοῦ τοῦ κυρίου ἡμῶν.

It is almost universally recognized that these verses contain a very early pre-Pauline confessional formula.[1] Its original form, however, is a matter of much dispute. Most would agree that Paul added the introduction, περὶ τοῦ υἱοῦ αὐτοῦ, as well as the final phrase Ἰησοῦ Χριστοῦ τοῦ κυρίου ἡμῶν. More in dispute is ἐν δυνάμει[2] and the two κατά clauses. I would agree with those who take κατὰ σάρκα as a later addition, introduced either by Paul himself,[3] or at a pre-Pauline stage of

1. For the many arguments in favour of the formula's pre-Pauline origin see E. Schweizer, 'Röm 1, 3-4 und der Gegensatz von Fleisch und Geist vor und bei Paulus', *Neot* (1963), p. 180; P. Beasley-Murray, 'Romans 1.3-4: An Early Confession of Faith in the Lordship of Jesus', *TynBul* 31 (1980), pp. 147-48; J.D.G. Dunn, 'Jesus–Flesh and Spirit: An Exposition of Romans 1.3-4', *JTS* 24 (1973), pp. 40-41; R.P. Menzies, *The Development of Early Christian Pneumatology* (1991), p. 287; and the literature cited there. For an opposing view (and a good summary of the evidence) see V. Poythress, 'Is Romans 1.3-4 a Pauline Confession after All?' *ExpTim* 87 (1975–76), pp. 180-83, who suggests that the confession was composed by Paul using a number of traditional expressions.

2. Some regard ἐν δυνάμει as a Pauline addition, intended to soften the adoptionistic implications of τοῦ ὁρισθέντος υἱοῦ θεοῦ. So Schweizer, 'Röm 1, 3-4', p. 180; R.H. Fuller, *The Foundations of New Testament Christology* (1965), p. 165; W. Kramer, *Christ, Lord, Son of God* (1966), p. 110 (tentatively). Others consider it original to the formula. So Hahn, *Titles*, p. 247; P. Beasley-Murray, 'Romans 1.3-4', p. 148, *et al.*

3. So R. Bultmann, *Theology of the New Testament* (1951), I, p. 49; N.A. Dahl, 'The Messiahship of Jesus in Paul', in *Crucified Messiah*, p. 43; E. Linnemann, 'Tradition und Interpretation in Röm. 1, 3-4', *EvT* 31 (1971), pp. 273-74; Menzies, *Development*, pp. 290-94.

The most serious challenge to this view has come from E. Schweizer, 'Röm 1, 3-4', pp. 180-89; *idem, Erniedrigung und Erhöhung bei Jesus und seinen Nachfolgern* (1962), pp. 91-92, who claims that both κατά clauses are pre-Pauline. He argues that in the Pauline contrast between σάρξ and πνεῦμα, the former always refers to moral inadequacy or inferiority. In Rom 1.3-4, by contrast, σάρξ refers to Jesus' earthly and physical existence. Schweizer is followed by many scholars, including Hahn, *Titles*, pp. 247-50; Fuller, *Foundations*, pp. 165-66, 187; Kramer, *Christ, Lord, Son of God*, p. 109; Burger, *Jesus als Davidssohn*, pp. 25-26; Beasley-Murray, 'Romans 1.3-4', p. 149; *et al.* The force of Schweizer's argument is diminished, if, as suggested by Linnemann, κατὰ σάρκα and πνεῦμα ἁγιωσύνης were added at transmission.[1] It is unlikely that whoever first introduced the element of Davidic descent would then diminish its significance by clarifying it as merely κατὰ σάρκα.[2] In light of the Semitic nature of πνεῦμα ἁγιωσύνης, and since elsewhere Paul always uses πνεῦμα ἅγιον, this second phrase is probably pre-Pauline,[3] though whether it was part of the original formula is uncertain. Linnemann raises the plausible suggestion that the phrase was originally a genitive, modifying ἐν δυνάμει (instrumental): '...appointed Son of God by the power of the Spirit of holiness (πνεύματος ἁγιωσύνης)'.[4] As we shall see, this would bring the original confession closer to its parallel in Lk. 1.32, 35. Though any reconstruction is hypothetical, the original confession may have read:

> Jesus Christ,
> born of the seed of David,
> decreed (or, appointed) Son of God by the power of the Spirit of holiness
> from the resurrection of the dead.

The juxtaposition of Davidic descent and divine sonship is striking, recalling the Nathan oracle of 2 Sam. 7.12, 14, where Yahweh promises that he will 'raise up' David's 'seed' after him, and will have a father–

different stages of transmission (see below). The somewhat unusual use of the κατά clauses would have resulted when Paul added κατὰ σάρκα to an already existing construct.

1. So H. Schlier, 'Zu Röm 1, 3-4', in *Neues Testament und Geschichte* (1972), pp. 207-18; R. Jewett, *Paul's Anthropological Terms* (1971), pp. 136-39. Cf. O. Michel, *Der Brief an die Römer* (12th edn, 1963), p. 38; M. Hengel, *The Son of God* (1976), p. 60.

2. As Jewett, *Paul's Anthropological Terms*, p. 136, asks, '...why would the congregation which emphasized the Davidic origin of Jesus as the Messiah wish at the same time to stigmatize it as obsolete and corruptible with the phrase κατὰ σάρκα?'

3. So most commentators: Schweizer, 'Röm 1, 3-4', p. 180; Hahn, *Titles*, p. 249; Burger, *Jesus als Davidssohn*, p. 25; Kramer, *Christ, Lord, Son of God*, p. 108; Betz, *What Do we Know About Jesus?*, p. 95; Dunn, 'Jesus–Flesh and Spirit', p. 60; P. Pokorny, *The Genesis of Christology* (1987), pp. 65, 73 n. 25; Beasley-Murray, 'Romans 1.3-4', p. 149; Schlier, 'Zu Röm 1, 3-4', p. 211; Linnemann, 'Tradition', pp. 272-75. *Contra* Menzies, *Development*, pp. 289-90.

4. Linnemann, 'Tradition', pp. 273-75. δύναμις τοῦ ἁγίου πνεύματος appears in Acts 1.8 and Rom. 15.13, and δύναμις τοῦ πνεύματος in Lk. 4.14. Linnemann suggests that Paul created the flesh-spirit contrast by introducing κατά σάρκα and changing the genitive πνεύματος ἁγιωσύνης to an accusative κατά clause.

son relationship with him. The text also recalls Psalm 2, where the Davidic king repeats the 'decree' of Yahweh (חק, probably the Davidic covenant): 'You are my son, today I have begotten you' (cf. Ps. 89.27-28). L.C. Allen suggests that ὁρίζω in Rom. 1.4 (and elsewhere in the New Testament) is an allusion to the 'decree' of Ps. 2.7.[1] This is plausible since the conceptual framework of the confession clearly parallels that of Ps. 2.7, representing a two-step proof of Jesus' Davidic messiahship. As a descendant of David, Jesus was a legitimate heir to the throne of David—the messiah-designate. At his resurrection, he was 'decreed' or 'appointed' to be the messianic Son of God.

I prefer the designation 'two-step proof of messiahship' to the 'two-*stage* Christology' suggested by Schweizer, Hahn, Burger and others,[2] for the following reasons: (1) The statement of Jesus' Davidic descent is meant first and foremost to affirm his qualification for the messianic office, and hence for his exaltation as the messianic Son of God, not to *contrast* what Jesus *was* (seed of David) and what he *became* (Son of God). The primacy of a 'two-stage Christology' is only valid if κατὰ σάρκα was an original part of the formula, which is unlikely. (2) It is sometimes suggested that the use of ὁρίζω confirms that the formula was originally 'adoptionistic', indicating that Jesus first became Son of God at his resurrection. Against this it should be noted that Paul himself does not understand the verb in this way (cf. Gal. 4.4; Rom. 8.3), since he retained it when he passed on the formula. This suggests that ὁρίζω *could* be understood as a 'decree' of sonship, or perhaps an 'appointment' to a more glorified state of sonship, rather than an adoption. Since the hymn's formulators likely borrowed ὁρίζω from the traditional language of Ps. 2.7 (in a Semitic context), we must examine the early Christian interpretation of this psalm to determine *their* understanding of the term. It is significant that every New Testament writer who cites or alludes to Ps. 2.7 treats it not as an adoption to sonship but as a confirmation, vindication or glorification of an already existing status (Acts 13.33; Heb. 1.5; 5.5; cf. Mk 1.11 //s; 9.7 //s).

1. L.C. Allen, 'The Old Testament Background of (Προ)ὁρίζειν in the New Testament', *NTS* 17 (1970–71), pp. 104-108. If an allusion is present here, it would have been made in an Aramaic *Vorlage* of the formula. The LXX renders the Hebrew חק, 'decree', of Ps. 2.7 with πρόσταγμα, not with a cognate of ὁρίζω. Allen suggests a similar Ps. 2.7 source for (προ)ὁρίζω in Acts 10.42; 17.31; 4.28; 2.23; Lk. 22.22; 1 Cor. 2.7-8; Rom. 8.29 and Eph. 1.5.

2. Schweizer, 'Röm 1, 3-4', p. 187; *idem*, *TDNT*, VIII, pp. 366-67; Hahn, *Titles*, pp. 246-51; Burger, *Jesus als Davidssohn*, p. 27.

The only possible exception is Mark 1.11, which is sometimes interpreted as an appointment or adoption.[1] It seems more likely, however, that in Mark's view the divine voice confirmed a status Jesus already possessed.[2] Since the church had a strong tradition that Jesus had spoken of God as his father and himself as the son (see discussion above), the best solution seems to be that the early post-resurrection church took up Jesus' self-designation and linked it with the enthronement language of Ps. 2.7. While Jesus was already God's son during his earthly ministry, at his resurrection he was appointed or installed in his full functional status as the enthroned and glorified Son of God.[3] There is no evidence that the early church viewed Jesus as first entering into his sonship at his resurrection.

Returning to Rom. 1.3-4, it is evident that the Davidic promise tradition provided an important exegetical key for comprehending Jesus' death and resurrection in the context of Israel's salvation history. The 'raising up' language of the promise tradition was viewed as a prophecy of the resurrection and exaltation of Jesus as the messianic Son of God. As O. Betz writes:

> The disciples believed that through Jesus, son of David at the end-time, God had fulfilled his promise to set an eternally ruling Davidic king on the throne. Nathan's prophecy helped them to see the resurrection of Jesus as being also an exaltation, an installation in the kingly dignity of the Messiah; thus the christological meaning of Easter became clear.[4]

Though the introduction to the confession was probably composed by Paul, its affirmation that this 'gospel of God' was 'promised beforehand

1. Cf. M. Dibelius, *From Tradition to Gospel* (1934; 1971), pp. 271-72; Bultmann, *History*, pp. 247-48; Rhoads and Michie, *Mark as Story*, p. 74; E. Schweizer, *The Good News According to Mark* (1971), p. 41.

2. See E. Haenchen, *Der Weg Jesu: Eine Erklärung des Markus-Evangeliums und der kanonischen Parallelen* (1966), p. 54; R.A. Guelich, *Mark 1–8.26* (1989), p. 34; W.L. Lane, *The Gospel According to Mark* (1974), pp. 57-58; Kingsbury, *Christology of Mark's Gospel*, p. 67.

3. See especially Marshall, 'Divine Sonship', pp. 87-103; *idem, The Origins of New Testament Christology* (1976), pp. 119-20. While Hahn, *Titles*, pp. 307-16, claims that Jesus' reference to himself as the 'Son' had a different origin than the church's title 'Son of God', Marshall argues convincingly that Jesus' manner of referring to himself formed the source for the church's thought. It was because the church remembered Jesus' claims to be God's son that they applied Ps. 2 and other 'messianic' passages to him.

4. Betz, *What Do we Know About Jesus?*, p. 94.

through the prophets in the holy scriptures' (Rom. 1.2) fits the formula's purpose perfectly; 'the history of God's relationship with Israel has found its fulfillment in Jesus. He is the promised son of David.'[1]

If the formula in 2 Tim. 2.8 is not directly dependent on Rom. 1.3-4, it provides further evidence for the view that the resurrection is the vindication of the Davidic messiah. The author writes, μνημόμευε Ἰησοῦν Χριστὸν

> ἐγηγερμένον ἐκ νεκρῶν,
> ἐκ σπέρματος Δαυίδ,
> κατὰ τὸ εὐαγγέλιόν μου.

In common with Rom. 1.3-4, the confession presents a legitimation-vindication formula: Jesus is the Davidic heir vindicated by God at the resurrection. There is no reference to an appointment to divine sonship and so no allusion to Ps. 2.7. The order in Rom. 1.3-4 is also reversed, with the statement of the resurrection preceding that of Davidic descent. This, together with the absence of a flesh–spirit antithesis, makes the formula even more clearly a two-step proof of messiahship, rather than a two-stage (adoptionistic) Christology. Jesus' resurrection and his Davidic descent confirm that he is who the church confesses him to be—the Davidic messiah.

As we shall see, the material Luke presents in the speeches of Acts confirms that he was aware of traditions similar to Rom. 1.3-4 and 2 Tim. 2.8. In Paul's sermon at Pisidian-Antioch (Acts 13.17-33), the apostle presents Jesus as the 'seed' of David raised up as saviour in fulfillment of the promises made to the fathers. As in Rom. 1.3-4, the resurrection marks the decisive turning point in the salvation event, when Jesus is declared (or appointed) by God to be his Son (Ps. 2.7). In the Pentecost sermon of Acts 2.14-36,[2] Peter demonstrates that in Jesus' resurrection (Ps. 16.8-11) and heavenly enthonement (Ps. 110.1), God has fulfilled the 'oath' he swore to David to seat his descendant upon his throne forever (Ps. 132.11). All Israel should now know for certain that God has made this Jesus both Lord and Christ. As in Rom. 1.3-4 and Acts 13.32ff., the resurrection is presented here as prophesied in scripture and as divine vindication of Jesus as the Davidic heir. This much, at least, is traditional for Luke. The use of Ps. 110.1 with reference

1. E. Schweizer, *Jesus* (1968), pp. 70-71.

2. On the antiquity of the traditions in Acts 2.22-36 see Lindars, *New Testament Apologetic*, pp. 36-59; Hayes, 'Resurrection as Enthronement', pp. 338-40.

to the exaltation of the risen Christ is also traditional, being one of the most frequently alluded to Old Testament texts in the New Testament.[1] Only in Acts 2.36, however, is this exaltation-formula explicitly linked to Jesus' *Davidic* enthronement and hence designated as the fulfillment of God's promises to David. While the formulas in Rom. 1.3-4 and 2 Tim. 2.8 (cf. Acts 13.30-34) refer to the *resurrection* as God's vindication of the Davidic heir, they do not refer to his exaltation-enthronement at the right hand of God. *Luke alone explicitly identifies Jesus' exaltation at God's right hand as a Davidic enthronement.*[2] Though this idea seems to be implied in other texts (and so is probably traditional), in Luke it becomes a key component of his exaltation Christology. As we shall see, this is one of his special, if not wholly original, contributions to early Christian interpretation of the Davidic promise tradition.

The perspective in these passages, that Jesus' resurrection and exaltation represent divine vindication that he is the Christ and the Son of God, is almost certainly the earliest post-resurrection Christology. Here I would follow the majority of scholars against the views of Hahn, Fuller, Robinson *et al.*, who suggest that Jesus was first confessed only as the vindicated prophet (like Moses) who would return to *become* the Son of man or the messiah.[3] It is more likely that Jesus was viewed from the resurrection onward as the vindicated and exalted Christ, who would soon return to establish his kingdom on earth.[4]

The statement in Acts 2.36 that at his exaltation-enthronement Jesus was 'made Christ' has caused many commentators to suggest that we

1. Mk 14.62 //s; 'Mk' 16.19; Acts 2.33-36; 5.30, 31; 7.55-56; Rom. 8.34; 1 Cor. 15.25; Eph. 1.20; 2.6; Col. 3.1; Heb. 1.3, 13; 8.1; 10.12-13; 12.2; 1 Pet. 3.22; Rev. 3.21; by implication in Mk 10.35-37 //s. Cf. *1 Clem.* 36.5-6; Pol. *Phil.* 2.1; *Barn.* 12.10-11; *Apoc. Pet.* 6; *Sib. Or.* 2.243. For details see D.M. Hay, *Glory at the Right Hand* (1973), esp. pp. 45-46; W.R.G. Loader, 'Christ at the Right Hand–Ps. cx. 1 in the New Testament', *NTS* 24 (1977–78), pp. 199-217.

2. Cf. Leaney, *Luke*, p. 34: 'Luke alone, with his story of the Ascension, makes historically actual the enthronement of the divinely chosen king for whom Judaism had been looking throughout history'.

3. So with various nuances Hahn, *Titles*, esp. 28ff.; Fuller, *Foundations*, pp. 143-51, 173-14; J.A.T. Robinson, 'The Most Primitive Christology of All?', *JTS* 7 (1956), pp. 177-89.

4. See for example J. Weiss, *Earliest Christianity* (1959; original German ed., 1914), I, pp. 118-19; Hayes, 'Resurrection as Enthronement', pp. 333-45. Bultmann, *Theology*, I, pp. 43-44, says Jesus was viewed as the one resurrected to be messiah, who would return as the Son of man.

have here the remnants of an early Christian view that Jesus became the messiah at his resurrection. Brown and others have suggested that for the earliest believers the resurrection alone was *the* 'christological moment'—that is, the moment at which Jesus *became* the messiah—and that the church subsequently read this title back into Jesus' earthly life, conception and eventually pre-existence.[1] While this suggestion is certainly possible, the language of Acts 2.36 does not prove it. As we have seen, משיח/χριστός was not so established as a title in first century Judaism that it had lost its significance as the 'Lord's anointed', i.e. one chosen by God to be his instrument (generally the king; cf. *Pss. Sol.* 18.5, 7; Lk. 2.26). Since the emphasis was on divine choice and empowerment, the term could mean either the one who *will* accomplish Yahweh's task (cf. Isa. 45.1) or the one who *has* accomplished his task. In other words, the lexemes משיח and χριστός could mean either 'messiah-designate' or 'messiah-enthroned'. That Acts 2.36 carries the latter sense does not mean that the earliest communities never used the former. If, as suggested above, there was 'messianic' speculation surrounding the events of Jesus' ministry, it would be surprising indeed if the early post-resurrection believers never referred to Jesus as the Lord's anointed in his earthly ministry. It is perhaps significant that the very early formula, 'Christ died for us (or, our sins),' suggests that Jesus suffered not just to become the Christ, but *as* the Christ.[2] It is also significant that Luke is willing to use the term with *both* meanings in different contexts. In Lk. 2.11, 9.20, 22.67 and 24.26, χριστός means the messiah-designate. In Acts 2.36, 3.20, and elsewhere, it refers to the messiah-enthroned. This cannot be attributed merely to Luke's clumsy handling of his sources; it must rather indicate his awareness that the term can carry two different nuances.[3]

b. *Paul*

Paul probably uses the confessional formula in Rom. 1.3-4 to demonstrate to the Roman community that they share a common faith.[4] In his hands, however, the formula takes on new significance. Whether or not

1. Brown, *Birth*, pp. 29-32.
2. Cf. Rom. 5.6; 14.15; 1 Cor. 8.11; 2 Cor. 5.14-15; 1 Thess. 5.9-10. For an evaluation of the formula see Kramer, *Christ, Lord, Son of God*, pp. 19-44; Pokorny, *Genesis*, pp. 68-72.
3. For more on this issue see Chapter 3 section 3a and Chapter 4 section 2c.
4. So most commentators.

the apostle added κατὰ σάρκα, his introductory phrase περὶ τοῦ υἱοῦ αὐτοῦ clearly shifts the emphasis from the confirmation of Jesus' Davidic messiahship to the sending of the pre-existent Son. Though 'seed of David according to the flesh' still serves to legitimize Jesus' messianic status, it also characterizes the humble incarnation of the pre-existent one (Gal. 4.4; Rom. 8.3; Phil. 2.7). This relative lack of interest in Davidic messiahship is characteristic of the Pauline tradition. Apart from the confessional formula in 2 Tim. 2.8, there is only the incidental reference in Rom. 15.12, where Isa. 11.10 is cited to defend the Gentile mission: 'There shall come the root of Jesse...in him shall the Gentiles hope.' While Paul knows that the crucified χριστός is a stumbling block for Jews (1 Cor. 1.23), he makes no effort to prove to his readers that Jesus is ὁ χριστός expected by the Jews.[1] He assumes, rather than defends, Jesus' Davidic descent and messianic office.[2]

c. *The Gospel of Mark*

Mark also confirms that Jesus is the messianic son of David, but indicates that this designation is insufficient to describe Jesus' essential dignity. Three passages refer directly or indirectly to Jesus' Davidic descent: the healing of blind Bartimaeus, the entrance into Jerusalem and Jesus' question concerning David's son (the *Davidssohnfrage*). Since all three occur in the closing days of Jesus' ministry, they are clearly related to one another in Mark's christological purpose.

By introducing the account of the healing of blind Bartimaeus (Mk 10.46-52) immediately before Jesus' entrance into Jerusalem, Mark uses the blind man's cry, 'son of David, have mercy on me!' to define Jesus' status as the Davidic messiah. He thus prepares the reader for the (less explicit) cry of the crowd of pilgrims approaching Jerusalem: 'Blessed be the coming kingdom of our father David.' Jesus enters the

1. M. de Jonge, 'Earliest Christian Use', p. 321. On the use of χριστός in Paul with reference to the messiah, see Dahl, 'Messiahship of Jesus', pp. 37-47; Kramer, *Christ, Lord, Son of God*, pp. 203-14. In addition to the titular use in Rom. 9.5, Dahl detects 'messianic connotations' in Rom. 15.7; 1 Cor. 1.23; 10.4; 15.22; 2 Cor. 5.10; 11.2-3; Gal. 3.16; Phil. 1.15, 17; 3.7. 'But in no case in Paul can *Christos* be translated with "Messiah"' (pp. 40, 171 nn. 11, 12).

2. One of Paul's few allusions to a promise tradition text, 2 Cor. 6.18, applies 2 Sam. 7.14 to believers in general: 'And I will be a father to you, and you shall be sons and daughters to me,' says the Lord Almighty'. The passage recalls Gal. 4.4-6, where Christ's sonship is the basis of believer's adoption as sons. It thus provides indirect proof that Paul *assumes* the fulfillment of the Davidic promises in Jesus.

city and cleanses the temple as the longed for and prophesied Davidic messiah.[1]

Whether the son of David designation is a late addition to the story, added either by the Hellenistic-Jewish church[2] or by Mark himself,[3] is a more difficult question. Chief evidence brought forward for a secondary addition is the supposedly Christian content of the title, since, according to Hahn's oft-repeated dictum, 'the messianic king of Judaism was not expected to be a doer of miraculous deeds'.[4] While this may be the case specifically with regard to *miracles,* the coming Davidic king *was* expected to help and deliver the poor and oppressed in Israel (cf. Isa. 11.4; *Pss. Sol.* 17.40-41; *T. Jud.* 24.6; *4 Ezra* 12.34). Psalm 72.12 says of the ideal Davidic king that 'he will deliver the needy when he cries for help (!), the afflicted also, and him who has no helper. He will have compassion on the poor and needy, and the lives of the needy he will save.'[5] The cry for mercy by Bartimaeus hardly seems 'strange'[6] when seen in this light. In addition, as we have seen, the king *was* expected to have extraordinary and supernatural powers and abilities by virtue of his Spirit-endowment. Finally, there appears to have been a general expectation for healing associated with the messianic period (cf. Isa. 29.18-19; 35.5-6).[7] Together these arguments render the request for healing at

1. So with various nuances Burger, *Jesus als Davidssohn*, pp. 42-46, 49-63; Robbins, 'Healing of Blind Bartimaeus', pp. 224-43; L.W. Hurtado, *Mark* (1989), p. 175; Kingsbury, *Christology of Mark's Gospel*, pp. 102-108. Many commentators also point to a discipleship motif in the episode. For example, Robbins suggests the passage is transitional, linking Mark's section on suffering discipleship, where Jesus teaches about the suffering and rising Son of man (10.46–12.44), with his Jerusalem ministry, where he acts as the authoritative son of David (10.46–12.44). The two sections revolve around the common theme of discipleship; the disciples move from following 'in the way of the Son of man' toward Jerusalem to following 'in the way of the son of David' into Jerusalem.

2. So Hahn, *Titles*, pp. 253-57.

3. So Burger, *Jesus als Davidssohn*, pp. 59-63 and Robbins, 'Healing', pp. 234-36.

4. Hahn, *Titles*, pp. 253-54; cf. 189-90. Burger (p. 46) and Robbins (p. 234 n. 65; cf. p. 242) both refer to Hahn. Cf. Klausner, *Messianic Idea,* 506: '...the Messiah...is never mentioned anywhere in the Tannaitic literature as a wonder-worker *per se*.'

5. It is perhaps significant that in both the LXX and the MT the psalm is associated with Solomon, the *son of David.*

6. So Burger, *Jesus als Davidssohn*, p. 44 ('*befremdlich*').

7. Cf. Klausner, *Messianic Idea*, pp. 502ff. It will be part of Luke's purpose to

least plausible in a Palestinian context. This also makes it unnecessary to appeal to traditions supposedly relating Jesus to a Solomon-like (= 'son of David') healer or exorcist.[1] Though such traditions may indeed have exerted an influence on the Jesus-tradition, the blind man's cry for *mercy* is not incompatible with expectations for the coming Davidic king; and *Pss. Sol.* 17.21 confirms that 'son of David' was used for this figure in some Jewish circles.[2]

While Mark affirms the messiah's vocation as dispenser of mercy and justice, he emphatically rejects the traditional characterization of the messiah as a warrior-king (*Pss. Sol.* 17.22-24 etc.). According to Mark's story, Jesus accomplishes salvation not through conquest and destruction but as the healing son of David and the humble and suffering Son of man (Mk 10.32-34, 45). This becomes evident in the *Davidssohnfrage* (Mk 12.35-37), where Mark confirms that 'son of David', though a valid designation for Jesus, is insufficient in itself to describe him.[3]

The origin and original significance of the pericope is a matter of much dispute, and a bewildering array of interpretations have been suggested.[4] It is unlikely that the saying ever was a denial of the

bring together the two strands of eschatological healing and the role of the Davidic king. See Chapter 5.

1. See for example L.R. Fisher, 'Can This Be the Son of David?', in *Jesus and the Historian* (1968), pp. 82-97; E. Lövestam, 'Jésus Fils de David chez les Synoptiques', *ST* 28 (1974), pp. 97-109; K. Berger, 'Die königlichen Messiastraditionen des Neuen Testament', *NTS* 20 (1974), pp. 1-44. For a good survey and critique of this view see D.C. Duling, 'Solomon, Exorcism and the Son of David', *HTR* 68 (1975), pp. 235-52.

2. The 'Markan' features in the story noted by Robbins and Burger only confirm that it is Mark who is telling the story in his own way, not that he has introduced the title. The fact that Mark shows no interest in the title elsewhere suggests, rather, that he did *not* introduce it here.

3. See especially Kingsbury, *Christology*, pp. 108-14.

4. Four major views may be discerned: (1) The saying (which is authentic) is merely a *Vexierfrage* to silence Jesus' opponents; no theological point is being made. So R.P. Gagg, 'Jesus und die Davidssohnfrage', *TZ* 7 (1951), pp. 18-30. (2) The passage represents *a denial of the Davidic descent of the messiah,* originating either: (a) with Jesus himself to defend his messiahship in spite of his non-Davidic descent, so J. Klausner, *Jesus of Nazareth* (1926); or, (b) within the early community, (i) among a limited circle of disciples, so R. Bultmann, *History of the Synoptic Tradition* (1963), pp. 66, 145-46; *idem, Theology*, I, p. 28; or (ii) to defend Jesus' non-Davidic messiahship, so Suhl, 'Der Davidssohn', pp. 57-59; G. Schneider, 'Zur Vorgeschichte des christologischen Prädikats "Sohn Davids"', *TTZ* 80 (1971), pp. 247-53, 252;

messiah's Davidic descent, particularly since none of the Synoptists show concern that it could be mis-interpreted this way (all three present the account without substantial alteration). For all three Jesus is both son of David and messiah.[1] In Mark's version, Jesus is teaching in the temple when he asks: 'How can the scribes say that the Christ is the son of David?' In Ps. 110.1 David himself, inspired by the Holy Spirit, calls the messiah 'Lord' (Mk 12.35-37). The point is that since David addresses the messiah as his superior, the messiah must be more than simply David's son. The implication for Mark's readers is that Jesus' identity exceeds Jewish expectations concerning the messianic 'son of David'. Though the pericope offers no answer to Jesus' question, it serves as one step in the progressive revelation of Jesus' identity—a revelation

Burger, *Jesus als Davidssohn*, p. 57, *et al.* (see the list in Burger). (3) The passage was *a denial that the son of David is necessarily the messiah;* so B. Chilton, 'Jesus *ben David:* reflections on the *Davidssohnfrage', JSNT* 14 (1982), pp. 88-112, who argues that the saying (which is authentic) identifies Jesus with the compassionate and healing son of David, but distances this figure from popular messianic expectation. (4) The saying was *a qualified acceptance of the son of David title, but subordinated it to another title or status,* originating either with Jesus or in the early church. In this view, the saying was intended: (a) to oppose political implications of Davidic messiahship, so Taylor, *St Mark*, p. 492, and (more strongly) Cullmann, *Christology*, pp. 131-33; (b) as a rabbinic-type *haggadah* question proving the messiah is *both* David's son and David's Lord, so D. Daube, *The New Testament and Rabbinic Judaism* (1956), pp. 158-69; J. Jeremias, *Jesus' Promise to the Nations* (1958), pp. 52-53; *idem*, *New Testament Theology*, p. 259; cf. J. Fitzmyer, 'The Son of David Tradition and Matthew 22.41-46 and Parallels', *Concilium* 2, 10 (1966), pp. 40-46; E. Lövestam, 'Die Davidssohnfrage', *Svensk Exegetisk Arsbok*, 27 (1962), pp. 81-82; (c) to emphasize Jesus is more than the son of David, he is the *Son of man* of Dan. 7.13, so F. Neugebauer, 'Die Davidssohnfrage (Mark 12.35-7 parr.) und der Menschensohn', *NTS* 21 (1974), pp. 81-108; J. Schniewind, *Das Evangelium nach Markus* (10th edn, 1963), pp. 164-65; (d) to emphasize Jesus is more than son of David, he is *the Son of God* (cf. Rom. 1.3-4), so Betz, *What Do we Know About Jesus?*, pp. 102-103; *et al.* or (e) against Pharisaic ideas about the Davidic messiah, so G. Schneider, 'Die Davidssohnfrage (Mk 12.35-37)', *Biblica* 53 (1972), pp. 84-85; (f) as a Hellenistic-Jewish Christian argument representing a two-stage Christology—Jesus was son of David who is exalted as Lord (= messiah; cf. Rom. 1.3-4), so Hahn, *Titles*, p. 253. (Obviously, these views overlap, and various scholars borrow from more than one perspective).

1. *Contra* Wrede, 'Jesus als Davidssohn', pp. 168, 175; Suhl, 'Der Davidssohn', p. 60; *idem, Die Funktion der alttestamentlichen Zitate und Anspielungen im Markusevangelium* (1965), p. 93; W.H. Kelber, *The Kingdom in Mark* (1974), pp. 95-96, who all say that *Mark* understood the passage as a denial.

which begins at his baptism and climaxes with the cry of the centurion at the cross, 'Truly this man was the Son of God!' While some commentators suggest that the category that exceeds Davidic sonship is that of 'Lord'[1] or 'Son of man',[2] Mark's emphasis on divine sonship throughout his work suggests that this is what he has in mind.[3] Jesus is more than the son of David, he is the Son of God.

d. *Birth Traditions*

That Davidic messianism continued to play a role in the post-Markan churches is evident from the traditions incorporated in the Matthean and Lukan genealogies and birth narratives.[4] Here again, however, we are confronted with the difficulty of identifying and dating sources. We are on most certain ground with those traditions which appear independently in Matthew and Luke. Fitzmyer and Brown list a number of these, three of which are clearly Davidic: Joseph's descent from the house of David (Lk. 1.27, 32; 2.4; Mt. 1.16, 20), Jesus' identification as a son of David (Lk. 1.32; Mt. 1.1) and Jesus' birth in Bethlehem (Lk. 2.4-7; Mt. 2.1).[5] Less explicitly Davidic are the prediction of a virgin birth in an allusion to Isa. 7.14 (Mt. 1.23; Lk. 1.27, 31[6]), the identification of Jesus as the expected 'Christ' (Mt. 1.16, 17; 2.4; Lk. 2.11, 2.26), and his role as 'saviour' (Lk. 2.11; Mt. 1.21). From this we can draw the general conclusion that in some Christian communities in the mid to late first century, there was a continuing interest in confessing and defending Jesus' legitimate Davidic origins.

1. E. Lohmeyer, *Gottesknecht und Davidssohn* (1953), p. 75; E. Lohse, *TDNT*, VIII, pp. 484-85; Lane, *Mark*, pp. 437-38; *et al.*

2. Neugebauer, 'Davidssohnfrage', pp. 89-95; Bultmann, *History*, pp. 136-37.

3. So Burger, *Jesus als Davidssohn*, pp. 65-66; Kingsbury, *Christology*, pp. 110-14; Hurtado, *Mark*, p. 203; and many others. See Kingsbury for a good defense of this position. On the significance of Jesus' divine sonship in Mark see also N.B. Stonehouse, *The Witness of the Synoptic Gospels to Christ* (1944; rpt. 1979), pp. 12-21, 80; P. Vielhauer, 'Erwägungen zur Christologie des Markusevangeliums', in *Aufsätze zum Neuen Testament* (1964), pp. 199-214; R.A. Martin, *Mark: Evangelist and Theologian* (1973), pp. 126-32, and the works cited by Kingsbury, *Christology*, p. 14 n. 52. Taylor, *Mark*, p. 120, writes 'Beyond question this title represents the most fundamental element of Mark's Christology'.

4. On the traditional nature of the Lukan genealogy see Chapter 5 section 2c.

5. Brown, *Birth*, pp. 34-35; Fitzmyer, *Luke I–IX*, p. 307.

6. It is uncertain whether there is an allusion to Isa. 7.14 in Lk. 1.31. See the discussion of this passage in Chapter 3.

e. *Conclusion*

This brief summary has been intended to give a general perspective of the Christian traditions relating to the Davidic messiah which were available to Luke. In the early confessional material and in the traditions in Acts, a pattern of promise-fulfillment emerges. Jesus is the descendant of David who, though crucified by godless men, was vindicated by God at his resurrection. According to the pattern of 2 Sam. 7.14, Pss. 2.7 and 110.1, the Davidic heir is 'raised up', declared to be God's son and exalted to his right hand. It seems evident from this that the early church used the language of the Davidic promise tradition to interpret and proclaim the salvation-historical significance of Jesus' death, resurrection and exaltation. At the same time, the explicit link between Jesus' vindication as Davidic messiah and his exaltation-enthronement is made only in Acts 2.36.

In the letters of Paul, the Markan church, and in other New Testament writings,[1] emphasis on Jesus' Davidic messianic identity recedes and other christological categories predominate. This shift no doubt reflects the changing needs and situations of various Christian communities. Evidently in some circles there was no pressing need or interest in defending Jesus' Davidic messiahship.

As with other Second Temple Jewish communities, the early Christians took up and utilized those traditions related to the coming Davidic king which were most meaningful and appropriate to them. In their case the interest lay in the messiah's Davidic descent, his role as saviour, and his status as Son of God. For obvious reasons, they did not utilize those traditions which characterized the messianic king as a warrior wreaking

1. One example must suffice: Like Paul, the author of Hebrews probably assumes Jesus' Davidic sonship, but lays no emphasis on it. It is Jesus' status as eternal Son and eschatological high priest which are his primary concerns. In Heb. 1.5 and 5.5 he cites the promise tradition texts of 2 Sam. 7.14 and Ps. 2.7 to demonstrate the high status of the pre-existent Son of God over the angels. Only secondarily and perhaps by assumption do these texts confirm that Jesus has fulfilled the promises made to David. While Jesus' Davidic lineage may be implied in the reference to his descent from Judah (Heb. 7.14; cf. Gen. 49.10), this point is made to demonstrate Jesus' non-Levitical priesthood 'according to the order of Melchizedek' (Heb. 5.6, 10; 6.20; 7.11, 17), not to affirm his legitimate right to the throne of David. As the author encourages his readers to leave behind the old covenant of Law as a mere shadow of heavenly things (10.1; 8.5; 9.23), so he leaves behind the traditional portrait of Davidic kingship in favour of an exaltation Christology of the eternal and pre-existent Son.

destruction on Israel's enemies and restoring the nation's independence in the land (except, perhaps, with reference to the parousia?[1]). As Christian communities broke away from the synagogue, the need to respond to such traditions would probably have decreased. On the other hand, if Christians were in continuing dialogue with Jews, these issues might be raised in apologetic discussion. How could Jesus be the Davidic king if he did not fulfill the role expected of him? It was obvious to all he had not overthrown the Romans and returned political sovereignty to the nation; he had not extended the nation's borders to their rightful place 'from the sea to the rivers'; perhaps most significantly he had not re-established the Davidic throne in Jerusalem. Indeed, his apparently 'unmessianic' life and untimely death would seem to nullify any messianic claims he may have made.

The following chapters will examine how Luke deals with the Old Testament promises to David. It will be suggested that his presentation addresses some of these very questions left unanswered in previous writings and traditions. Luke shows how Jesus' seemingly unmessianic life and untimely death were in fact part of the plan and will of God and fulfilled the Old Testament promises related to the (Davidic) messiah. He also seeks to demonstrate the legitimacy of Jesus' Davidic descent, his Davidic enthronement in the heavenly sphere, and the reality of the salvation which he has achieved. If these points are confirmed, they will provide important data to be taken into account in the continuing search for the overall purpose, theology and *Sitz im Leben* of Luke's two-volume work.

1. Here we are on uncertain ground since the synoptic tradition always links Jesus' return with the coming Son of man, not with the Davidic king. In Revelation, on the other hand, Jesus is identified as 'the Lion of the tribe of Judah' and 'the root and offspring of David' who is coming quickly (Rev. 5.5; 22.12, 16; cf. 3.7).

Part II

Promise and Fulfillment: The Davidic Messiah in the Nativity and in Acts

Chapter 3

THE FULFILLMENT OF THE PROMISE ANNOUNCED: THE LUKAN BIRTH NARRATIVE

1. *Introduction*

The theme of the Old Testament promises to David arises explicitly three times in Luke's birth narrative. At the Annunciation (1.26-38) Mary, who is engaged to a descendant of David, is told by the angel Gabriel that her child will reign forever on the throne of David. In the Benedictus (1.68-79) Zechariah, the father of John the Baptist, prophesies that God has raised up a horn of salvation in the house of David, who will deliver his people from their enemies. Finally, in the story of Jesus' birth (2.1-20), Joseph is again referred to as a descendant of David and it is Bethlehem, the 'city of David' where the child is born. There are also implicit allusions in the Nunc Dimittis and in the account of the boy Jesus in the temple.

This chapter is comprised of two parts. The purpose of the first is to establish the importance of the birth narrative in the structure and theology of Luke–Acts. Once this has been demonstated, the main christological passages will be examined to determine the role of the Davidic promise tradition in the narrative. If the birth narrative is found to be an integral introductory and programmatic section for the whole of Luke–Acts, and if the key christological presentation of this section is royal-Davidic, this will have important implications for the Christology of Luke–Acts as a whole.

2. *The Significance of the Birth Narrative in the Context of Luke–Acts*

In his ground-breaking examination of Lukan theology, *Die Mitte der Zeit*,[1] Hans Conzelmann largely ignored the birth-stories in the

1. H. Conzelmann, *Die Mitte der Zeit* (5th edn, 1964); ET: *The Theology of St*

development of his theory of three stages of salvation history. While contending in his introduction that his study 'is concerned with the whole of Luke's writings as they stand', he summarily dismissed the birth narrative from his investigation, going so far as to state that 'the authenticity of these first two chapters is questionable'.[1] Conzelmann has been justly criticized for this exclusion, and subsequent writers have confirmed both the authenticity of the birth narrative and its importance for the structure and theology of Luke–Acts as a whole.[2] The following points confirm this importance.

a. *Lukan Language and Style*

The question of sources within the birth narrative is notoriously difficult and source theories range from those who consider Luke to have created all but the barest pieces of tradition to those who see written sources behind most of the material.[3] From the material Luke shares in common with Matthew, it is clear that he has utilized traditional material in these stories.[4] It is equally clear, however, that the narrative as a whole is Luke's work and that he has woven whatever sources he had into a coherent narrative. The analyses of Lukan style and vocabulary by A. Plummer, J.C. Hawkins, R. Morgenthaler and P.S. Minear have all confirmed the strongly 'Lukan' nature of the birth narrative.[5] Indeed, it

Luke (1961). The fifth German edition (the ET is based on the second) was consulted where appropriate.

1. Conzelmann, *Theology*, pp. 9, 118.

2. Some scholars have held that Conzelmann's three-stage scheme is correct but when properly examined, the infancy narrative fits well within this scheme. So H.H. Oliver 'The Lucan Birth Stories and the Purpose of Luke–Acts', *NTS* 10 (1963–64), pp. 202-26; W.B. Tatum, 'The Epoch of Israel: Luke i-ii and the Theological Plan of Luke–Acts', *NTS* 13 (1966–67), pp. 184-95; G. Voss, 'Die Christusverkündigung der Kindheitsgeschichte im Rahmen des Lukasevangeliums', *BK* 21 (1966), pp. 112-15. Others use the birth stories to dispute Conzelmann's theological perspective. So P.S. Minear, 'Luke's Use', pp. 111-30; J.-P. Audet, 'Autour de la théologie de Luc I–II', *ScEccl* 11 (1959), pp. 409-18; H.S. Songer, 'Luke's Portrayal of the Origins of Jesus', *RevExp* 64 (1967), pp. 453-63.

3. For a summary of various source theories see Brown, *Birth*, pp. 244-47 and I.H. Marshall, *The Gospel of Luke* (1978), pp. 47-49.

4. See the list of common traditions in Fitzmyer, *Luke I–IX*, p. 307; Brown, *Birth*, pp. 34-35.

5. J.C. Hawkins, *Horae Synopticae* (1899), pp. 13-23; A. Plummer, *A Critical and Exegetical Commentary on the Gospel According to St. Luke* (1906), pp. lix-lxx; R. Morgenthaler, *Statistik des neutestamentlichen Wortschatzes* (1982), esp. pp. 51,

is generally concluded that these two chapters show greater evidence of Luke's hand than the rest of the Gospel.[1] Though this does not mean that Luke is freely composing,[2] it does confirm that he has taken special care to make his sources his own.

b. *Characteristic Lukan Themes and Common Theological Perspectives*

In addition to Lukan style and vocabulary, the birth narrative exhibits many characteristic Lukan themes. It is a particularly Lukan motif that the dawn of God's eschatological salvation is marked by joy and rejoicing and the giving of praise and glory to God.[3] The verb 'rejoice' (χαίρω) occurs twelve times in the Gospel and seven in Acts, and the noun 'joy' (χαρά) eight times in the Gospel and four in Acts. By comparison, in Mark the verb and the noun occur only once each, while Matthew uses each six times. Luke's redactional interest in the theme is evident in Lk. 19.37, where he introduces the verb into Markan material. Phrases such as to 'praise God' (αἰνεῖν τὸν θεόν) and to 'glorify God' (δοξάζειν τὸν θεόν) are also characteristic of Luke. He introduces the former into Markan material at 19.37, and the latter at 5.25 and 18.43. Repeatedly, Luke's Gospel stories conclude with the recipients of God's benefits praising and giving glory to God (Lk. 5.25-26; 7.16; 13.13; 17.15, 18; 18.43). This theme continues in Acts (Acts 2.47) where praise accompanies both healings (Acts 3.8-9; 4.21) and the salvation of the Gentiles (Acts 11.18; 13.48; 21.20). Nowhere is the theme more prominent, however, than in the birth narrative. In the very first scene, the angel tells Zechariah that 'you will have joy and gladness,

62-63, 181, 187; Minear, 'Luke's Use', pp. 113-14.

1. Hawkins, *Horae Synopticae*, p. 23, writes that characteristic Lukan expressions 'are used more abundantly in the first two chapters than in the rest of the gospel'. Plummer, *St. Luke*, p. lxix, concludes a section on the integrity of the Gospel with the statement that 'the peculiarities and characteristics of Luke's style and diction...run through our Gospel from end to end...In the first two chapters they are perhaps somewhat more frequent than elsewhere'; cf. J.M. Creed, *The Gospel According to St. Luke* (1950), p. lxxxii.

2. H.J. Cadbury's famous remark on Lukan style is appropriate here: 'His own style is more obvious at some times than at others, but it is never so totally wanting as to prove alien origins for a passage, and is never so persuasive as to exclude the possibility that a written source existed, although the source be no longer capable of detection by any residual difference of style' (*The Making of Luke–Acts*, p. 67).

3. Cf. Plummer, *St. Luke*, p. xlvi; I.H. Marshall, *Luke: Historian and Theologian* (1970), pp. 202-203.

and many will rejoice at his [John's] birth' (1.14). This prophecy is fulfilled in 1.57 when at the birth the neighbors of Elizabeth rejoice with her. Joy and praise are especially associated with the birth of Jesus. When Mary greets Elizabeth, the baby John leaps for joy in her womb (1.41, 44). The four hymns of the narrative continue this joyful spirit. Mary 'exalts the Lord' and rejoices in 'God my saviour' (1.46-47). Zechariah 'blesses' the Lord God because He has visited and accomplished redemption for his people (1.64, 68), and Simeon 'blesses God' at the birth of the Lord's Christ (2.28). The use of εὐλογέω with God as object occurs elsewhere in the Gospels only at Lk. 24.53, where the disciples return to Jerusalem with joy, continually 'blessing God' in the temple. Finally, the host of angels who appear to the shepherds praise God with the anthem 'glory to God in the highest' (2.13-14), and the shepherds themselves echo this praise by 'glorifying and praising God for all they had heard and seen' (2.20). Though much of this material may be traditional, Luke uses it to introduce a theme which will be prominent throughout Luke–Acts: God is to be praised for the joyful time of redemption has arrived.

Luke's historiographic purpose set forth in the prologue (1.1-4) and evident throughout Luke–Acts is also present in the birth narrative. Compare, for example, the precise dating for the beginning of Jesus' ministry (3.1-2) to that of his birth during the time of the census (2.1-3; cf. 1.5).

The same may be said for the centrality of Jerusalem, another well-established Lukan theme.[1] The birth narrative begins in the temple, the center of Jewish worship in Jerusalem and ends with two journeys to Jerusalem, the presentation of the baby Jesus in the temple (2.21-38) and the Passover visit when he is twelve (2.41-52). It is possible that these two journeys are symbolic of Jesus' journey to Jerusalem in Luke's central section (Lk. 9.51-19.28), which culminates in his passion (cf. Lk. 2.22, 34-35; 2.49; 19.45).

Many commentators have noted Luke's special interest in prayer

1. Cf. C.C. McCown, 'The Geography of Luke's Central Section', *JBL* 57 (1938), pp. 51-66; Conzelmann, *Theology*, pp. 73-94; W.C. Robinson, *Der Weg des Herrn: Studien zur Geschichte und Eschatologie im Lukas-Evangelium* (1964); E. Lohse, *TDNT*, VII, pp. 331-32; Marshall, *Historian*, pp. 148-156; Fitzmyer, *Luke I–IX*, pp. 164-71, 261; P. Simpson, 'The Drama of the City of God: Jerusalem in St. Luke's Gospel', *Scripture* 15 (1963), pp. 65-80; M. Bachmann, *Jerusalem und der Tempel* (1980).

throughout the Gospel and Acts.[1] Luke repeatedly introduces references to Jesus' prayers into Markan material (Lk. 3.21; 5.16; 6.12; 9.18; 9.28-29; 11.1). The material unique to Luke also describes Jesus' prayers (22.31-32; 23.46; cf. 23.34) as well as his teaching on prayer (11.5-8; 18.1-8; 21.36), and there are frequent references to the prayers of the church in Acts.[2] In the birth narrative, too, prayer is a prominent theme. The reader is told that while Zechariah is performing his priestly service in the temple, the 'whole multitude of the people were in prayer outside' (1.10). (πᾶς τὸ πλῆθος τοῦ λαοῦ is thoroughly Lukan in style; cf. Lk. 6.17; 8.37; 19.37; 23.1, 27; etc.). Gabriel then announces to Zechariah that Elizabeth will bear a son because 'your *petition* has been heard' (1.13). Finally, the piety of Anna the prophetess is described by Luke in terms of her service, fasting and *prayer* (2.38).

Closely related to (and naturally overlapping with) these Lukan interests are theological perspectives which the nativity shares with the rest of Luke–Acts. The twin themes of Gentile salvation and Jewish rejection of the gospel which are so prominent in Acts, and which bring the book to its climax (Acts 28.25-28), are foreshadowed already in the two oracles of Simeon. In the Nunc Dimittis, Simeon declares that the salvation which God has prepared will be 'a light of revelation to the Gentiles' (2.31; Isa. 42.6; 49.6; cf. Acts 13.47; 26.23). To Mary he then predicts that the child Jesus 'is appointed for the fall and rise of many in Israel, and for a sign to be opposed...' (2.34). Luke's two-volume work thus begins and ends with this important theme.

As will be demonstrated in detail in this chapter and the next, there are also important *christological* similarities between the nativity and Acts. The most prominent of these are the emphases on Jesus as the one who fulfills the promises to David (Lk. 1.32-33, 69; Acts 2.29-31; 13.23-37) and on the important christological titles χριστός and κύριος (Lk. 1.43; 2.11; Acts 2.36; 10.36).

Two theological issues which have received much attention in relation to the role of the nativity in Luke–Acts are the significance of the Holy Spirit and the relationship of John the Baptist to Jesus. Though the precise *role* of the Spirit in Luke–Acts is a matter of much discussion

1. See for example, Plummer, *St. Luke*, pp. xlv-xlvi; W. Ott, *Gebet und Heil: Die Bedeutung der Gebetsparänese in der lukanischen Theologie* (1965); Marshall, *Historian*, pp. 203-204; Fitzmyer, *Luke I–IX*, pp. 244-47.

2. Acts 1.14, 24; 2.42; 3.1; 4.24-31; 7.59-60; 9.11; 10.4, 9; 12.5, 12; 13.3; 14.23; 16.25; 20.36; 21.5.

and debate,[1] its centrality as a Lukan theme is well established.[2] Compared to the six in Mark and twelve in Matthew, Luke has seventeen (or possibly eighteen, cf. 1.80) references to the Spirit in his Gospel and fifty-seven in Acts.[3] Of the Gospel references, seven (or eight) occur in the birth narrative. Gabriel prophesies that John will be 'filled with the Holy Spirit from his mother's womb' (1.15; cf. 1.41-44), and Elizabeth and Zechariah are 'filled with the Spirit' when they break into prophetic utterance (1.41, 67). This use of πίμπλημι with the Holy Spirit is characteristic of Luke, appearing frequently in Acts (Acts 2.4; 4.8, 31; 9.17; 13.9, 52). The Spirit also rests upon righteous Simeon, granting charismatic guidance and revelation (2.25-27). In line with the step parallelism between Jesus and John throughout the narrative (see below), Jesus is not just filled with the Spirit but actually Spirit-conceived (1.35).[4]

W.B. Tatum agrees that the role of the Spirit in the birth narrative is thoroughly Lukan, but seeks to link this role to Conzelmann's three-period view of salvation history.[5] The Old Testament Spirit of prophecy which comes upon Elizabeth, Zechariah, Simeon and John places the nativity wholly in the period of Israel, while Jesus' unique Spirit conception distinguishes him from it. During Jesus' life, then, he alone bears the Spirit, setting this period apart as 'the middle of time'. Finally, in the period of the church, the Spirit of prophecy is poured out on *all*

1. For surveys of research and bibliography see F. Bovon, *Luc le théologien* (1978), pp. 210-54; M. Turner, 'Jesus and the Spirit in Lucan Perspective', *TynBul* 32 (1981), pp. 3-42; Menzies, *Development*, pp. 18-47. Menzies' thesis is the most significant recent contribution to the field. He contends that Luke intentionally avoids attributing soteriological functions or miracle-working to the Spirit since in Luke's view the Spirit is essentially the Spirit of prophecy. For a response to Menzies with regard to the role of the Spirit in Jesus' miracles see M. Turner, 'The Spirit and the Power of Jesus' Miracles in the Lucan Conception', *NovT* 33 (1991), pp. 124-52.

2. This point is made by many commentators. See Fitzmyer, *Luke I–IX*, p. 227; G.W.H. Lampe, 'The Holy Spirit in the Writings of Luke', in *Studies in the Gospels* (1957), pp. 159-200, calls Luke's description of the activity of the Spirit 'the essential theme of his writings'.

3. According to Fitzmyer, *Luke I–IX*, p. 227.

4. Menzies, *Development*, pp. 122-30, claims that while Luke retains the traditional reference to Jesus' Spirit-conception (cf. Mt. 1.18) in order to continue the step parallelism between Jesus and John, he diminishes its force by clarifying that the conception itself was through the 'power of the Most High'. Only indirectly is Jesus conceived by the Spirit. See the discussion of this passage below.

5. Tatum, 'Epoch of Israel', pp. 184-95.

believers—distinguishing this period both from the period of Jesus and the period of Israel.

While it is certainly true that the Spirit's role in the nativity is a prophetic one of preparation,[1] there is also a strong element of fulfillment which moves beyond an exclusive depiction of the period of Israel. There was a widespread tradition in Second Temple Judaism that, because of the nation's sins, the Spirit of prophecy had been withdrawn from Israel since the last prophets, and that it would be poured out on the restored Israel at the end.[2] This would suggest that Luke is here portraying the dawn of the eschatological restoration of the Spirit to the righteous remnant of Israel.[3] This 'fulfillment' motif is also indicated by the nature of the prophetic utterances: When Zechariah breaks into his Spirit-inspired hymn, he rejoices that 'the Lord God...has visited us and accomplished redemption for his people' (1.68-69). Simeon, too, blesses God 'for my eyes have seen your salvation'. The prophetic Spirit does not just promise the future redemption of Israel, he announces the arrival of the time of salvation. The role of the Spirit in these two chapters thus serves as a preview to the prophetic role of the Spirit in Acts and forms a bridge or transition from the age of promise to the age of fulfillment.[4] As I.H. Marshall writes:

> Here [in the birth narrative] the manifestations of the Spirit which dominate the life of the early church in Acts are seen to begin right from the commencement of the new age which dawned with the birth of Jesus. From the outset the activity of the Spirit is the characteristic of the new age.[5]

1. Cf. Fitzmyer, *Luke I–IX*, p. 229.
2. For references see M. Turner, 'Holy Spirit', in *Dictionary of Jesus and the Gospels* (1992), p. 342; Menzies, *Development*, pp. 92-111.
3. As Turner, 'Holy Spirit', p. 343 points out, it is exclusively those awaiting the messianic salvation of Israel that experience the Spirit.
4. With this statement I am taking a view of Lukan salvation history closer to that of E.E. Ellis *et al.* than to Conzelmann. Ellis, *The Gospel of Luke* (1974), p. 16, writes: 'Luke's structure of redemptive history consists in the time of promise ('the law and the prophets') followed by the time of fulfillment ('the kingdom of God'). The latter begins with the mission of Jesus and the Church...but it is consummated only at the *parousia*. Therefore Luke's scheme may be represented as follows: the time of promise, the manifestation of the kingdom in the present age, the future manifestation of the kingdom in 'the age to come' (18.30). Cf. Acts 17.30-31'. Cf. I.H. Marshall, 'Luke and his "Gospel"', in *Das Evangelium und die Evangelien* (1983), pp. 299-300.
5. Marshall, *Historian*, p. 91; cf. Oliver, 'Lucan Birth Stories', p. 224; J. Nolland, *Luke 1–9:20* (1989), p. 54.

The significance of the nativity as a *transition* from the Old Testament age of promise to the ministry of Jesus is especially evident in Luke's portrait of John the Baptist. In both the nativity and the rest of Luke–Acts, Luke gives special prominence to John as the forerunner and herald of the messiah.[1] In addition to presenting John as a foil for Jesus in the birth narrative, Luke refers to John nine times in Acts (1.5, 22; 10.37; 11.16; 13.24, 25; 18.25; 19.3, 4).[2] John's function, as predicted in the nativity and presented in the rest of Luke–Acts, is to prepare the people for the Lord, to call men to repentance and to offer the forgiveness of sins (Lk. 1.16-17, 76; 3.3; 7.27; Acts 13.24; 19.4). Malachi 3.1 is cited with reference to John's role both in the nativity (1.76) and elsewhere in the Gospel (7.27). The widely discussed parallels between Jesus and John in the nativity[3] serve not only to relate the two to the dawn of eschatological salvation, but also to demonstrate Jesus' superior position and role. While John is 'great before the Lord' (1.15), Jesus is 'great' without qualification (1.32). John, who is filled with the Holy Spirit from his mother's womb, is called 'the prophet of the Most High' (1.76); but Jesus, the Spirit-conceived Christ, is '*the Son* of the Most High' (1.32). John's birth to a barren woman is miraculous, as are similar births in the Old Testament; but Jesus' birth to a virgin through the direct intervention of the Spirit is unique and unprecedented. John's role will be to prepare the way for the Lord (1.76); but Jesus is himself χριστὸς κύριος (2.11; cf. 1.43), who will reign forever on the throne of David (1.32-33). This subordination of John to Jesus is continued in the Gospel

1. In my opinion, the view of H. Conzelmann (*Theology*, pp. 19-27, 101-102, 112) that Luke intentionally separates the ministry of John from that of Jesus, placing the former exclusively in the 'epoch of Israel' has been decisively answered by his critics. For full discussion see J.A. Fitzmyer, 'The Lucan Picture of John the Baptist as Precursor of the Lord', in *Luke the Theologian* (1989), pp. 86-116, esp. pp. 102-110; Minear, 'Luke's Use', pp. 122, 123; W. Wink, *John the Baptist in the Gospel Tradition* (1968), pp. 51-57; W.G. Kümmel, '"Das Gesetz und die Propheten gehen bis Johannes": Lukas 16, 16 im Zusammenhang der heilsgeschichtlichen Theologie der Lukasschriften', in *Verborum Veritas* (1970), pp. 89-102; Marshall, *Historian*, pp. 145-47; H. Flender, *St. Luke: Theologian of Redemptive History* (1967), pp. 21-22; 122-28; Robinson, *Der Weg des Herrn*.

2. Fitzmyer, 'Lucan Picture', p. 102.

3. On these parallels see A. George, 'Le parallèle entre Jean-Baptiste et Jésus en Lc 1-2', in *Etudes sur l'œuvre de Luc* (1978), pp. 43-65; Oliver, 'Lucan Birth Stories', pp. 216-19; Brown, *Birth*, pp. 248-53, 282-85, 292-301, 408-10; Fitzmyer, *Luke I–IX*, pp. 313-16.

and Acts. Luke 3.15-17 confirms that while John functions as the eschatological forerunner, he denies all messianic claims. This is repeated in the sermon in Acts 13, where Paul cites the Baptist as affirming that 'I am not (the one)', i.e. the saviour from the seed of David (13.23-25). While John is the forerunner, Jesus is the greater, for he is the Christ.

It is evident that the portrait of John in the birth narrative agrees with his role elsewhere in Luke–Acts.[1] Luke uses the circumstances surrounding John's birth to announce the arrival of the time of salvation; he then parallels the history of Jesus with that of John to define John's role as the eschatological forerunner and to highlight Jesus' messiahship. John's role (like the role of the nativity as a whole) serves as a bridge between the old and the new era—the times of promise and fulfillment.[2]

Many more Lukan themes and motifs could be mentioned which are prominent in the birth narrative.[3] Enough has been said, however, to confirm that the birth narrative is thoroughly Lukan in theme, style and theology. The above discussion has also revealed another point significant for the present work, namely, that Luke uses these stories to introduce, define and foreshadow themes which will become prominent in the rest of his two-volume work.[4] This is true not only for the Gospel, but especially for Acts. As demonstrated above, the connection of the

1. *Contra* Conzelmann, *Theology*, p. 20 n. 3, 22 n. 2; p. 23 n. 2, 24, who repeatedly claims that the nativity contradicts Luke's view of John in the Gospel since it portrays him as closely related to Jesus. While Conzelmann is correct that the nativity contradicts *his* interpretation of John's role in Luke's Gospel, the scholars cited above have decisively refuted this interpretation. The clear direction of contemporary scholarship is to view John as a transitional figure, bridging the two ages, and hence to view his role in the nativity as perfectly in line with that of the rest of the Gospel.

2. Cf. Marshall, *Historian*, p. 146. Fitzmyer, *Luke the Theologian*, p. 107, sums up this perspective well: '...John is to be taken as a transitional figure, acting as the caesura between the Period of Israel and the Period of Jesus. He basically belongs to the Period of Israel because of his circumcision and incorporation into the Israel of God; but he is a figure of the period chosen by God to inaugurate the Period of Jesus, when salvation would be accomplished.'

3. Cf. Minear, 'Luke's Use', pp. 115-18, who lists, among others (1) the use of speeches, citations and hymns as 'programmatic entrances' or 'proleptic anticipations of what is to follow', (2) the reliance on epiphany and angels, and (3) similar portrayals of the responses of individuals to God's redemption.

4. Tiede, *Prophecy and History*, p. 24, says that Luke 1–2 constitutes 'an extended prologue or preface, an overture to the larger work in which critical themes are sounded'. Cf. Bock, *Proclamation*, p. 55; Brown, *Birth*, p. 242.

birth stories with Acts is evident in such areas as the prediction of Gentile salvation and Jewish rejection (Lk. 2.32, 34), the prophetic role of the Spirit (Lk. 1.15, 41, 67, 80; 2.25-27; Acts 2.17), and the christological statements that Jesus fulfills the promises to David (Lk. 1.32-33, 69; Acts 2.29-31; 13.23-37) and is both χριστός and κύριος (Lk. 1.43; 2.11; Acts 2.36; 10.36).[1] These similarities further confirm the unity of Luke–Acts and demonstrate that *the nativity is meant to introduce not only the Gospel but the whole of Luke's two-volume work.*

c. *The Role of the Nativity in the Structure of Luke–Acts*

Having confirmed the thoroughly Lukan character of the birth narrative and its thematic and theological unity with the rest of Luke–Acts, we may raise the question of its role in the Lukan writings as a whole. Why did Luke include these stories rather than beginning, as Mark did, with the baptism of John? Is he simply answering the questions of curious Christians concerning Jesus' origins?

The first thing which strikes the reader of the birth narrative is its thoroughly Semitic style and language. Whether this style is a result of translation Greek from a Semitic source or whether it is an intentional imitation of the LXX (imitation translation Greek) is a much disputed question and is probably irresolvable with any certainty.[2] In either case,

1. On the close relationship between the nativity and Acts, see Brown, *Birth*, p. 243. Brown also lists: (1) the frequency of angelic appearances, and (2) the similarity of the parallelisms between John the Baptist and Jesus in the Gospel, and Peter and Paul in Acts. Though these two certainly reveal Luke's artistic hand at work and thus help to affirm the authenticity of the nativity, it is doubtful whether they are consciously used by him to point forward from the nativity to his second volume.

2. See the survey of the issue and various views in S. Farris, *The Hymns of Luke's Infancy Narratives* (1985), pp. 31-66; Brown, *Birth*, p. 246; Fitzmyer, *Luke I–IX*, p. 312. The possibility of an Aramaic rather than an Hebrew original has now been generally abandoned. Some key proponents of the view that the narrative is translation Greek include C.C. Torrey, E. Burrows, P. Winter and R. Laurentin. Those who have argued for imitation translation Greek (LXX) include A. von Harnack, J.H. Moulton, H.F.D. Sparks, N. Turner, M. Goulder and M. Sanderson. The most significant recent study is that of Farris, who uses the criteria for determining Semitic sources behind Greek documents developed by R.A. Martin. Farris concludes rather tentatively that Luke has drawn on source material which was not simply Semitic Greek but was actually composed in one of the Semitic languages (*Hymns*, p. 62). In the end, however, one must concede the near impossibility of distinguishing between a document translated from Hebrew or Aramaic and one which intentionally uses the same terms, phrases and grammatical constructions which would occur in such a translation.

it is certain that it is *intentional* on Luke's part. The fine Greek literary style of the prologue (Lk. 1.1-4) reveals that Luke could have re-worked whatever sources he had into a different style had he so desired. Instead, he chose to retain (or compose) the Semitic style of the nativity and thus give the narrative a strong Old Testament flavour. Luke artistically plunges the reader from the Greek milieu of the prologue into the Semitic world of the Old Testament. Typological parallels to the Old Testament abound: Elizabeth's conception out of barrenness recalls the barrenness of Sarah (Gen. 18), Rebekah (Gen. 25.21) and Rachel (Gen. 30.22-23) as well as the mothers of Samson (Judg. 13) and Samuel (1 Sam. 1); the annunciations to Zechariah and Mary recall similar Old Testament birth announcements (Gen. 16.7-13; 17.1-21; 18.1-15; Judg. 13.2-23).[1] The first scene of the nativity begins in the temple in Jerusalem, the center of Jewish religious life. The characters we meet are models of Jewish piety. Elizabeth and Zechariah are 'righteous in the sight of God, walking blamelessly in all the commandments and requirements of the Lord' (1.6); Simeon is 'righteous and devout, looking for the consolation of Israel' (2.24; cf. 2.36). Jewish names, terms and practices abound. Tribes and divisions of tribes are clarified (1.5; 2.36); Old Testament figures are recalled (1.5, 17, 27, 32, 55, 69, 73; 2.4, 11, 22; cf. 1.70, 72). Zechariah performs his priestly service, burning incense in the temple. Joseph and Mary do 'all according to the law of Moses', circumcising Jesus and presenting him to the Lord with the prescribed sacrifice (2.21-25). This is the world of faithful and devout Jews, anxiously awaiting the fulfillment of God's promise in the person of the Christ.

But the setting is more than a repetition and recollection of the promises of the Old Testament. It portrays the promise *at the dawn of its fulfillment*. The role of the nativity is not only to introduce themes which will be important later in Luke–Acts; it also forms a bridge between the Old Testament age of promise and the age of fulfillment, structurally setting the stage for the theme of promise-fulfillment which will run as a connecting thread throughout the whole of Luke–Acts. It becomes significant, then, that *Luke here defines the promise primarily in terms of the Davidic promise*. Jesus is the horn of salvation God raises up in the house of David to bring deliverance to his people Israel, to be a light to the Gentiles and to reign over the house of Jacob forever

1. On these parallels see Brown, *Birth*, pp. 156, 292-301; Fitzmyer, *Luke I–IX*, pp. 313-15, 335. See especially Brown's chart on p. 156.

(1.32-33; 68-75; 2.4, 11, 26, 29-32). That this Davidic theme represents the controlling Christology of the nativity may be confirmed by an examination of Luke's christological presentation in these first two chapters.

3. *The Davidic Messiah in Luke's Narrative Development*

a. *The Annunciation, Luke 1.26-38*

The angelic Annunciation to Mary contains not only the first reference to the Davidic promise in the nativity, but also *the first explicitly christological statement in Luke's two volume work.*[1] The narrator's introduction in vv. 26-27 serves two purposes. First, it links the pericope with the annunciation to Zechariah in the preceeding passage: the time reference 'in the sixth month' refers to the sixth month of Elizabeth's pregnancy and again it is Gabriel (cf. v. 19) who brings the message from God. Secondly, the introduction shows Luke's two main interests in the story: (1) Gabriel appears '*to a virgin*'; (2) Mary is 'engaged to a man whose name was Joseph, *of the house of David* (ἐξ οἴκου Δαυίδ[2])'. The reader is thus prepared for both the divine conception and the Davidic-messianic role of the child.[3]

1. Though Gabriel had previously informed Zechariah that John would 'go before *him* in the spirit and power of Elijah (Mal. 3.23-24)...to make ready a people prepared for the Lord' (Lk. 1.17), the 'him' is not specified and contextually would refer to the Lord God (v. 16). The parallels to the stories of John and Jesus certainly suggest that John 'goes before' Jesus, who is also called 'the Lord' (1.43; 2.11), but Luke here retains the vagueness of the Malachi text and does not specify who the Lord is. From a literary perspective, therefore, the statements of 1.17 are not explicitly christological, even if they may attain christological significance later in Luke's work.

2. The phrase is a stereotyped Old Testament one to describe David's descendants (1 Sam. 20.16; 1 Kgs 12.19;13.2; 2 Chron. 23.3). Luke uses it again in 1.69 and 2.4. Though Origen understood the phrase to refer to Mary and John Chrysostom took it as a reference to both Mary and Joseph, it stands grammatically closer to Joseph and almost certainly refers only to him (Brown, *Birth*, p. 287).

3. The apparent contradiction between a virgin birth and Jesus' Davidic descent through Joseph is no problem for Luke (or for Matthew) who places the two side by side. E.E. Ellis, *The Gospel of Luke* (1966, 1974), pp. 71, 84, says his presentation is probably not a result of the forced interpolation of the virgin birth into an original story but is rooted in the realism of Semitic thinking whereby Luke recognized Joseph's fatherhood both legally and realistically. The fact that Joseph is not Jesus' natural father is thus not viewed by Luke as inconsistent with Jesus' Davidic descent. See excursus below.

As mentioned above, the Annunciation contains parallels to the angelic announcement to Zechariah (1.8-23; cf. Mt. 1.20-21) and has elements in common with Old Testament birth announcements (cf. Gen. 16.7-13; 17.1-21; 18.1-15; Judg. 13.2-23). Typical of these announcements, the angel's appearance and greeting result in a troubled response by Mary (Lk. 1.28-29). In v. 30 Gabriel tells Mary not to be afraid since she has found favour with God—favour which will be manifested in the birth of a son. The description of the birth in v. 31 is verbally similar to Gen. 16.11 and Isa. 7.14 (cf. Judg. 13.3, 5), and may be a conscious allusion to the latter with the name 'Immanuel' changed to 'Jesus'.[1]

In vv. 32-33 the child is described:

> He will be great, and will be called the Son of the Most High;
> and the Lord God will give him the throne of his father David;
> and he will reign over the house of Jacob forever;
> and his kingdom will have no end.

Though no Old Testament text is explicitly cited, the verse represents a classic statement of the Davidic promise as epitomized in 2 Samuel 7 and Psalm 89 (see chart below). Three key elements of the promise are present: Davidic descent, father–son relationship with God (2 Sam. 7.14; Pss. 2.7; 89.26-27; 4QFlor 1.10-11), and an eternal reign, throne and kingdom (Gen. 49.10; 2 Sam. 7.13, 16; Isa. 9.7; 16.5; Ezek. 37.25; Pss. 89.4-5, 29-30; 132.11-12).

Luke 1.32-33	*2 Samuel 7*	*Psalm 89*
v. 32 'He will be great,	'And I will make you a great name…' (v. 9)	'I also shall make him firstborn, the highest of the kings of the earth' (v. 27)
and will be called the Son of the Most High;	'I will be a father to him and he will be a son to me;' (v. 14)	'He will cry to me, 'You are my Father, my God, and the rock of my salvation' (v. 26)

1. Ellis, *Gospel of Luke*, p. 31. While the actual language of the verse is as close to Gen. 16.11 LXX as to Isa. 7.14 LXX (see the comparison in Bock, *Proclamation*, pp. 61-62), the description of Mary as a παρθένος (Lk. 1.27, 34; cf. Isa. 7.14 LXX), the reference to the οἶκος Δαυίδ (Lk. 1.27; Isa. 7.13 LXX), and the greeting 'the Lord is *with you* ' (Lk. 1.28; cf. Isa. 7.14, 'Immanuel')—all in a context of Davidic expectations—suggest that Luke indeed had Isa. 7.14 in mind

and the Lord God will give him the throne of his father David;	'I will raise up your seed after you...and I will establish the throne of his kingdom forever...your throne shall be established forever' (vv. 12-16).	'I will establish his seed forever and his throne as the days of heaven' (v. 29).
v. 33 and he will reign over the house of Jacob forever; and his kingdom will have no end'.	'I will establish his kingdom...and I will establish the throne of his kingdom forever...And your house and your kingdom shall endure before me forever' (vv. 12-16).	'His seed shall endure forever, and his throne as the sun before me' (v. 36).

It is particularly significant that, in the first mention of Jesus in the Gospel, he is described in this way. This point should be stressed: the first thing the narrator tells the reader about Jesus—the main character in his story—is that *through him God will fulfill his promises to David.* This indicates, at the least, that this Davidic-messianic motif has a prominent place in Luke's christological presentation.

Two further points should be made. First, it is clear from this passage that for Luke *Davidic* messiahship is co-referential with *royal* messiahship. Jesus' enthronement as king will be upon the throne of his father David. Such a statement may seem a truism, but this is not really the case. In Jewish expectation royal traits are sometimes ascribed to non-Davidic messianic figures like a priestly messiah, a new Moses or the Son of man. The point is that *for Luke,* Jesus' royal dignity is defined here as essentially Davidic. The consequence of this is that a comprehensive study of Jesus as David's son and heir must necessarily include references to Jesus' royal dignity and kingly authority.

Another significant point is that Luke presents the promise in its Old Testament form with little modification. It is not yet suggested that Jesus' assumption of the throne of David will occur at his ascension-exaltation nor that suffering and humiliation will be an integral part of his messianic role. The statement rather retains the earthly and national implications of the original promise. This Old Testament and Jewish 'flavour' is evident in the references to the θρόνος Δαυίδ, the οἶκος Ἰακώβ and the Semitic sounding υἱὸς ὑψίστου. Luke *intentionally* stays close to the Old Testament 'promise' context he has established in the nativity as a whole.[1]

The only significant modification to the Davidic promise tradition of the Old Testament comes in the following verses in relation to the virgin birth and Jesus' sonship to God (vv. 34-35). Upon hearing the announcement that she is to bear a child who will reign as Davidic king, Mary asks the angel how this is possible since she does not know a man. The angel responds:

> The Holy Spirit will come upon you;
> and the power of the Most High will overshadow you;
> and for that reason the offspring shall be called holy,[2] the Son of God.

The general force of the statement is clear enough: 'The conception and birth of Jesus for the fulfillment of his divine destiny will be entirely the work of God.'[3] The real difficulty is not its meaning, but its background. Though presented in Old Testament language, there is no real parallel in Judaism to the divine generation of a son of God by the Spirit.[4] The conjunction διό in the third clause stresses the causal connection between the conception and the designation 'Son of God'. It is because of the Spirit's unique role in the conception of the child that he will be called (= 'will be'[5]) Son of God. The closest parallels in the

1. That the Old Testament sounding language (whether traditional or not) is intentional on Luke's part is suggested by the facts that (1) Luke will pick up the reference to the 'throne of David' again in a climactic christological reference in Acts 2.30; and, (2) ὁ ὕψιστος (used in the LXX as a translation of אל עליון), appears almost exclusively in Luke in the New Testament: Lk. 1.35, 76; 6.35; 8.28; Acts 7.48. Elsewhere only at Mk 5.7 (par. to Lk. 8.28) and Heb. 7.1; cf. Sir. 4.10; 4Q243 2.1 (= 4Qps Dan A^{a}). Cf. Fitzmyer, *Luke I–IX*, p. 347; *idem*, 'The Contribution of Qumran Aramaic to the Study of the New Testament', *NTS* 20 (1973–74), pp. 382-407, esp. 391-94; Marshall, *Gospel of Luke*, p. 67.

2. The grammatical function of the adjective ἅγιον is disputed. It could serve (1) as translated above—as predicate of the verb κληθήσεται, (2) as the predicate of a verbless clause ('the offspring will be holy, he will be called Son of God'), or (3) substantivally as the subject of the verb κληθήσεται ('the holy one born will be called the Son of God'). The first view is favoured by most commentators and is the most likely. In Lk 4.34 and Acts 3.14 ἅγιος is used as a title for Jesus (cf. Acts 4.27, 30); in the former it is closely linked to the titles Son of God and Christ (v. 41).

3. C.F. Evans, *Saint Luke* (1990), p. 163.

4. Pagan source theories also offer few convincing parallels and are now generally rejected by scholars. See the commentaries.

5. The verb κληθήσεται 'brings to expression what is, so that it means no less

Old Testament and Judaism are passages which refer to the Spirit's role in the creation of the cosmos (Gen. 1.2; Ps. 33.6) or in the creation of individuals (Job 33.4; Ps. 104.30; *2 Apoc. Bar.* 21.4; Jdt. 16.14). Cf. Ezek. 37.14, where Yahweh puts his Spirit within Israel to bring new life from the dead. This creative action, however, is never linked to the designation 'son of God'. The Israelite conception of the nation as a son is generally conceived in terms of election or adoption (Exod. 4.22), and the king was the son of God because of his special relationship to God and because he embodied the nation's sonship (2 Sam. 7.14 etc.). The 'begetting' language of Ps. 2.7 is metaphorical, referring to a new relationship entered into at the king's enthronement; there is no reference to the Spirit. There is also the disputed text at Qumran (1QSa 2.11-12) which may refer to God's 'begetting' of the messiah,[1] but again the Spirit is not the specified agent. While, as we have seen, the Old Testament speaks of the Spirit coming upon men, including David (1 Sam. 16.13) and the coming Davidic king (Isa. 11.1-4), this is never associated with human conception. The verse thus appears to be an *original application* of the creative role of the Spirit, perhaps linking it to the idea of the begetting of the king as in Ps. 2.7.

The most important parallel to Lk. 1.32, 35 is Rom. 1.3-4, where Jesus is the descendant of David 'decreed' Son of God at the resurrection.[2] It is often suggested from this that Lk. 1.35 represents one step in the gradual reading back of the 'christological moment' from Jesus' parousia to his resurrection, transfiguration, baptism, conception and eventually pre-existence.[3] A more nuanced statement of this view (and more

than "he will be"' (cf. Mt. 5.9) (Brown, *Birth*, p. 289).

1. For the literature on this greatly debated text see Fitzmyer, *Major Publications*, pp. 164-67.

2. Brown, *Birth*, pp. 312-16; Schürmann, *Lukasevangelium*, I, pp. 54-55; Turner, 'Jesus and the Spirit', pp. 34-35; Fitzmyer, *Luke I–IX*, pp. 340-41; F. Bovon, *Das Evangelium nach Lukas* (1989), p. 77. Another interesting parallel is the tantalizing but opaque reference in an Aramaic fragment from Qumran, 4QpsDan A[a] (= 4Q243), where an individual is described as 'great upon the earth' and is called 'son of God' and 'son of the Most High'. There is also reference to the establishment of a kingdom and a perpetual (עלם) reign. Fitzmyer suggests that the text is probably apocalyptic and that a Davidic king may be in view. Certainty is not possible because of the fragmentary nature of the text. The fragment shows, at the very least, that the titles 'Son of the Most High' and 'Son of God' in Lk. 1.32 and 1.35 do not *necessarily* go back to different sources. See Fitzmyer, 'Contribution', pp. 391-94.

3. See Brown, *Birth*, p. 313; Hahn, *Titles*, pp. 243, 267 n. 29, 295-98.

appropriate, in my opinion) is that early Christians gradually *recognized* that what was true of Jesus after his resurrection must also have been true still earlier.[1] Though vv. 32 and 35 do not seem to be directly dependent on Rom. 1.3-4, the parallels are significant, since both texts juxtapose Davidic descent and divine sonship and both relate the Holy Spirit and δύναμις to the attribution of Jesus as Son of God. Since Davidic descent and Jesus' status as Son of God are both linked to Jesus' earthly life, there is clearly no 'two-stage Christology' here but rather a proof of Jesus' messiahship.[2] Jesus' Davidic descent is not exceeded or superseded by his divine sonship; rather, his messiahship is confirmed by both his Davidic descent and his sonship to God. (It will be recalled that a similar conclusion was reached above concerning the *original* meaning of the confession in Rom. 1.3-4.) While Rom. 1.3-4 and Lk. 1.32-35 are clearly concerned with two different 'christological moments', it is not clear whether this is a result of a 'reading back' of Jesus' resurrection status as Son of God into an earlier period, or whether it indicates two stages of Jesus' divine sonship. That this latter is *Luke's* view is clear from the fact that he includes all four 'christological moments' without any contradiction: Jesus is conceived by the Spirit as Son of God at conception (Lk. 1.35); empowered and anointed by the Spirit as the Son at his baptism (Lk. 3.21-22); revealed to his disciples as Son of God at the transfiguration (Lk. 9.35); and vindicated before all as Son of God at his resurrection (Acts 13.33; through the Spirit's power in Rom. 1.3-4). The precise view of the pre-Lukan community is uncertain.

Though the Lukan vocabulary in v. 35 suggests his editorial activity, it is difficult to determine whether the verse is uniquely his or whether he has re-formulated previous traditions. The virgin birth as well as Jesus' conception by the Spirit are clearly traditional, appearing also in Mt. 1.18-25. Further, though Matthew does not specifically associate Jesus' divine

1. Cf. Fitzmyer, *Luke I–IX*, p. 340, and Brown's clarification of his position in *Birth*, p. 134 n. 6; *idem*, 'Gospel Infancy Research from 1976 to 1986: Part II (Luke)', *CBQ* 48 (1986), p. 678.

2. Brown, *Birth*, pp. 315-16; Bovon, *Evangelium nach Lukas*, 1, p. 77: '...die Thematik des Verses ist weder die der zwei Naturen noch die der zwei christologischen Stufen, sondern die der wahren Natur des Messias und seines Reichs. Wir stehen damit innerhalb der Polemik gegen das Judentum...' It should be added, however, that though there is a hint that the Jewish conception is inadequate, neither the true nature of the messiah nor of his kingdom has yet been revealed. Luke's narrative development of this theme has just begun.

sonship with his conception, he does seem to take Jesus' birth as a 'christological moment'. Jesus is 'the Christ' and 'Immanuel' already from birth (Mt. 1.23; 2.4). This raises questions, at least, as to whether it was Luke who first connected the Son of God title with Jesus' birth.

More certainty is possible concerning Luke's *primary interest* in the passage. Elsewhere Luke shows no interest in Jesus' virgin birth or his conception by the Spirit. The references in Acts to Jesus' endowment with the Spirit point rather to his 'Spirit-anointing' at his baptism (Acts 4.27; 10.38). Though Jesus' wondrous conception confirms that God was working out his salvation-historical purpose from the beginning of Jesus' life, this point is not developed further in Luke–Acts. Luke's *primary* interest in v. 35 is in the grounding of Jesus' *divine sonship* in the creative power of God. The verse appears to play two functions in the Lukan narrative: (1) First (and less significantly), it is a prelude to the Passover visit to Jerusalem of the twelve-year-old Jesus (Lk. 2.41-51). By identifying Jesus as the Son of God already from his conception, Luke prepares the reader for the boy Jesus' affirmation of his unique and filial relationship with God (Lk. 2.49). (2) More importantly, v. 35 defines and clarifies the nature of the messianic sonship introduced in v. 32. While the Jewish conception considered the Davidic king to be Son of God by virtue of his *role* as God's representative, Luke grounds this sonship not in Jesus' role but in his *origin.* Luke seems to be consciously opposing the view that Jesus' divine sonship is merely 'functional'—a special relationship with God by virtue of his role as king.[1] He is rather the Son of God from the point of conception, before he has taken on any of the functions of kingship.

Though v. 35 exceeds traditional Jewish expectations, it does not leave the context of the Davidic promises.[2] Rather, the close contextual link between vv. 32 and 35 indicates that Jesus' divine sonship serves as

1. Hahn, *Titles*, pp. 243-44, 267 n. 29, argues that the passage goes back to two different sources which reflected contradictory christologies. In v. 32, Jesus is called 'Son of the Most High' in a context of Davidic expectations (Jewish 'adoptionistic' sense) while in v. 35 he is called 'Son of God' by virtue of miraculous procreation (a Hellenistic sense). Cf. G. Schneider, 'Lk. 1, 34.35 als redaktionelle Einheit', *BZ* 15 (1971), pp. 255-59. Though the passage clearly displays two different ideas in relation to the Son of God title, these are not necessarily contradictory. A development on traditional Jewish *messiology* (which the passage certainly displays) does not mean the existence of two contradictory *christologies.* In any case Luke clearly did not see the two as contradictory since he has placed them side by side.

2. See especially Tannehill, *Narrative Unity*, I, p. 25.

proof that he is indeed the heir to the throne. Through his unique conception by the power and Spirit of God, Jesus is revealed to be the *Davidic Son of God* (cf. 2 Sam. 7.14; Ps. 2.7).

In summary, the first mention of Jesus in Luke's Gospel introduces him as the Son of the Most High and heir to the Davidic throne. Luke does this in v. 32 with thoroughly Jewish terminology which shows that for him the new age that is dawning is inextricably linked to the old. The promises to David are to be fulfilled through this child. In verse 35, then, Luke clarifies the meaning of the Davidic messiah's father–son relationship with God by linking Jesus' divine sonship to his conception by the Spirit, thus connecting this sonship to his divine origin rather than merely to his *role* as king.

In light of the particular interest of this passage in Jesus' status as Son of God, a comment is appropriate here on Luke's use of the title elsewhere in Luke–Acts. While Luke picks up traditional elements of Jesus' divine sonship, such as his submission to the will of his Father, his unique and intimate relationship with God and the mystery which surrounds his identity, he shows a special redactional interest in the *messianic* significance of the title.[1] As just noted, this is already evident in Lk. 1.32-35, where Jesus' divine sonship is linked particularly to his status as the Davidic heir to the throne of Israel. There are other examples. Twice Luke explicitly clarifies the Son of God title with χριστός. In Lk. 4.41 he records that, following Jesus' exorcisms, demons came out of many, crying, 'You are the Son of God!' The passage echoes the demonic recognition of Jesus' identity in Mk 1.23 (// Lk. 4.34: 'the Holy One of God') and Mk 3.11-12 ('You are the Son of God') (cf. Mk 5.7 and //s). Luke is alone, however, in clarifying that the Son of God title reveals that the demons 'knew him to be *the Christ*'. A similar interpretation is found in Acts 9.20, 22. Following the account of Paul's conversion, Luke records that Paul proclaimed Jesus in the synagogues saying, 'He is the Son of God' (Acts 9.20). Two verses later, Paul is said to have been 'confounding the Jews...by proving that Jesus was the Christ'. Proclaiming Jesus as the *Son of God* is made parallel to the proof that he is the *Christ.* Luke also brings over traditional passages which link Jesus' divine sonship to his messianic identity, including the baptism (Lk. 3.22 //s), the temptation (Lk. 4.2-13; Mt. 4.1-11), the transfiguration

1. For a good survey of the data see A. George, 'Jésus Fils de Dieu', in *Etudes sur l'œuvre de Luc* (1978), pp. 215-36, esp. 234-36.

(Lk. 9.35 //s) and the question before the Sanhedrin (Lk. 9.66-71).[1] In the first of these, Luke intentionally brings out the messianic significance of the account through his redaction in Lk. 3.15 (see Chapter 5 section 2a). A connection between divine sonship and kingship is also evident in Jesus' statement at the last supper that '*my Father* has conferred on me a *kingdom* (or 'royal rule': βασιλείαν) (Lk. 22.29)'.[2] This reference, in turn, may be related to the parable of the vineyard (Lk. 20.9-19, //s), where the 'beloved son' (= Jesus) is murdered by the wicked tenant farmers (= the Jewish leaders). Though Luke's form of the parable differs little in significant detail from Mark's version,[3] Jesus' statement in Lk. 22.29 provides an interpretive addition: the 'inheritance' (20.14) of the murdered son is seen more clearly as his vindication and appointment of kingly power following his suffering and death.

To this Gospel evidence may be added the sermon in Acts 13, where Paul cites Ps. 2.7, 'you are my Son, today I have begotten you' (Acts 13.33), to prove that in 'raising up' Jesus God has fulfilled his covenant promises to David (cf. 13.23). Again Jesus' divine sonship is linked to his messiahship, and specifically to his Davidic messiahship. It is evident from these examples that, while Luke may see deep relational significance in the title Son of God, he has a particular interest in linking it to Jesus' status as χριστός and heir to the throne of David.

There is little of a christological nature between the Annunciation (1.26-38) and the Benedictus (1.67-79). The only exception is Elizabeth's unusual description of Mary as 'the mother of my Lord' (1.43).[4] The

1. See Chapters 5 and 6 for discussion of these texts.

2. Tannehill, *Narrative Unity*, I, p. 26; George, *Etudes*, p. 230.

3. One alteration is worth noting: Luke adds an allusion to the judgment of those who fall on the stone, or who are crushed by it (v. 18; cf. Dan. 2.34, 44-45; Isa. 8.14-15) to the 'rejected stone' allusion from Ps. 118.22-23 (v. 17; Mk 12.10; Mt. 21.42). This image is in line with Simeon's oracle concerning Jesus as the cause of many rising and falling in Israel, and a sign to be opposed (Lk. 2.34) (see discussion below).

4. The phrase may echo 2 Sam. 24.21 (LXX) where Araunah refers to David as ὁ κύριός μου ὁ βασιλεύς at the surprise visit from the king. David's response that he wishes to build an altar to the Lord (τῷ κυρίῳ) shows that it is not unusual to find κύριος used of Yahweh and of the king in the same context. R. Laurentin, *Structure et Théologie de Luc 1-11* (1964), pp. 79-81, suggests that the phrase alludes to 2 Sam. 6.9, 'how can the ark of the Lord come to me?', and uses this as part of his argument that Mary is portrayed throughout the nativity as the ark of the covenant. Evidence for this is Mary's three-month stay with Elizabeth (1.56) which parallels the

context immediately following the description of Jesus in 1.32-33 suggests that κύριος here has a 'messianic' sense somewhat equivalent to 'the mother of *my king*'.[1] Further evidence for this is Luke's use of κύριος in the near context at 2.11. There the shepherds are told that the saviour who has been born in Bethlehem is χριστὸς κύριος. Whether appositional or epexegetical (see discussion below), the title there specifically links Jesus' lordship to his messiahship. Though Fitzmyer is correct that the significance of κύριος in Lukan theology as a whole must be considered in interpreting this reference,[2] it is of even greater importance to follow Luke's narrative development and not read ideas into a passage which Luke has not yet presented or clarified. Elizabeth's statement is best taken as an acclamation that the child born to Mary is destined to be her ruler, and by implication, to rule over God's people Israel. At the same time the personal nature of the statement ('*my* Lord') suggests that the passage foreshadows the acclamation of allegiance of Luke and his community.[3]

Though in the Magnificat (1.46-55) Mary praises 'God my Saviour' for his mercy and help, she makes no explicitly christological or Davidic statements.[4] The song is rather a personal hymn of thanksgiving, similar in many respects to Hannah's in 1 Sam. 2.1-10, and continuing Luke's theme that God is fulfilling his Old Testament promises to the nation

three-month sojourn of the ark in the house of Obed-edom (2 Sam. 6.11). It seems unlikely, however, that Luke would be drawing so subtle an allusion here. For criticism of Laurentin see Brown, *Birth*, pp. 327-28, 344-45; Fitzmyer, *Luke I–IX*, pp. 364-65.

1. So Schürmann, *Lukasevangelium*, I, p. 68 n. 183. The meaning 'mother of the messiah' is proposed by many commentators: Plummer, *St. Luke*, p. 29; Creed, *St. Luke*, p. 22; W. Manson, *The Gospel of Luke* (1930), p. 11; Marshall, *Gospel of Luke*, p. 81; Cf. Lk. 20.41-44; Acts 2.34. Schürmann points to Dan. 4.16, where Daniel addresses Nebuchadnezzar as 'my Lord' (MT: מָרְאִי; LXX (= 4.19): βασιλεῦ; Theodotion: κύριε), and to *b. Sanh.* 98a, where 'Lord' is used in an address to the messiah. See G. Dalman, *The Words of Jesus*, pp. 324-27.

2. Fitzmyer, *Luke I–IX*, p. 365.

3. On this conception see Franklin, *Christ the Lord*, esp. pp. 49-55.

4. Verse 55, which speaks of God remembering his mercy (ἔλεος): καθὼς ἐλάλησεν πρὸς τοὺς πατέρας ἡμῶν, τῷ 'Αβραὰμ καὶ τῷ σπέρματι αὐτοῦ εἰς τὸν αἰωνα, is strikingly similar to the closing words of the song of David in 2 Sam. 22.51 (LXX): καὶ ποιῶν ἔλεος τῷ χριστῷ αὐτοῦ, τῷ Δαυὶδ καὶ τῷ σπέρματι αὐτοῦ ἕως αἰῶνος. (Cf. the similarity of v. 51 to Ps. 88.11 LXX, in a psalm which praises God for the Davidic covenant.) It has been suggested that this is an implicit recollection of the Davidic promises; but the absence of any mention of David makes this questionable.

Israel. What *is* clear from these verses is that Luke views the promises to Abraham, to the fathers and to David as part of the same unified plan and purpose of God. After being told that she will give birth to the Davidic king (1.32-33), Mary responds by praising God for remembering his mercy to Abraham and his descendants forever (vv. 54-55). The coming of the Davidic messiah is thus seen to fulfill the promises made to Abraham and the fathers. This theme is continued in the Benedictus. God's raising up 'a horn of salvation in the house of David' (v. 69) is 'to show mercy toward the fathers, and to remember his holy covenant, the oath which he swore to Abraham our father' (vv. 72-73). Luke sees the mercy to the fathers, the covenant with Abraham and the promises to David as a unity, all pointing to fulfillment in Jesus. Yet when he speaks of the *means* by which God has fulfilled these promises, it is most frequently in relation to *the promise given to David* (cf. Lk. 1.32-35, 69; 2.1-11; Acts 2.30-31; 13.16-37; 15.15-17). I would suggest, therefore, that *Luke places the fulfillment of the promise to David at the heart of his promise-fulfillment scheme*—not in isolation, but as the epitome and summation of the promises, oaths and covenants which God made to his people.

b. *The Benedictus, Luke 1.68-79*

The next allusion to the promises to David occurs in the Benedictus of Zechariah (1.67-76). The hymn is composed of two quite distinct sections. Up to v. 75 the finite verbs are aorists and the hymn is a *beraka* or praise hymn to God. From v. 76 the tense shifts to the future and Zechariah addresses the infant John directly. This section has been described as a *genathliakon,* or birth ode. Because of this change in style, many have argued that these two sections have different origins, and various source theories have been proposed.[1] Whether or not this is the case, in its present Lukan context the hymn forms a unified composition and may be shown to play an integral part in Luke's narrative development. Several themes introduced already by Luke are picked up

1. Three views predominate: (1) The hymn is a compilation of two original hymns, the first of Jewish origin (vv. 68-75), and the second of Christian or Baptist origin (vv. 76-79). (2) The hymn is an original unity (a Jewish or Jewish-Christian messianic psalm) to which Luke (or another Christian) has added the mention of John's activity in vv. 76-77. (3) The hymn is a unity (including vv. 76-77) which has undergone some Lukan redaction. For discussion and proponents of each view, and bibliography, see Farris, *Hymns*, pp. 15-30, 128-33.

and developed in the hymn; others which will become important in the subsequent narrative are introduced for the first time. An examination of five of these will illuminate the theological and christological import of the hymn for Luke.

(1) As elsewhere in the birth narrative, it is *the actions of God* which are stressed.[1] Zechariah opens his hymn by blessing the *Lord God* for visiting his people, accomplishing redemption, and raising up the horn of salvation (vv. 68-69). Further, it is God himself who speaks through the prophets, shows mercy to the fathers, and grants deliverance from enemies (vv. 70-75). The reference to the dawn of salvation as a divine 'visitation' appears twice in the hymn, first with reference to the Lord God in v. 68 and again in the description of the ἀνατολή 'from on high' in verse 78. The verb ἐπισκέπτομαι is common in the LXX (= פקד) with reference to God's action in caring for and saving his people (Exod 3.16, 4.31; Ruth 1.6; Pss. 80.14; 106.4). It is used in this Hebraic sense only by Luke in the New Testament (1.78; 7.16; Acts 15.14), and in a quotation from Psalm 8 in Heb. 2.6. Luke will pick up this 'visitation' theme again in the Gospel narrative at 7.16 and will bring it to something of a climax at 19.41-44, where Jesus predicts the destruction of Jerusalem, 'because you did not know the time of your visitation (ἐπισκοπή)' (19.44). A tragic climax thus awaits Israel's rejection of her visitation.[2] In the hymn, however, there is no hint yet of this rejection. The scene is one full of hope and expectation. Israel's salvation is at her doorstep; the promise for the deliverer is about to be fulfilled.

(2) As promised to Mary in the Annunciation, *the agent of this deliverance is the coming Davidic king,* the horn of salvation 'from David's house'. This Davidic emphasis may already be implied in the hymn's opening statement of praise: Εὐλογητὸς κύριος ὁ θεὸς τοῦ Ἰσραήλ. While this blessing formula has parallels in the psalms

1. This theme runs as a connecting thread throughout the birth narrative: In the Annunciation, the Lord God gives the messiah the throne of David (1.32). In the Magnificat, it is 'God my saviour' who exalts the humble and brings down the proud (1.48-55). The Nunc Dimittis speaks of the Lord preparing salvation in the presence of all peoples (2.31).

2. Incidentally, this theme of visitation points to the danger in distinguishing too sharply between tradition and redaction—between 'Lukan' and 'non-Lukan'—in the search for Luke's purpose and theology. Though the verses which contain the theme of visitation (vv. 68, 78) are almost universally considered to be traditional, Luke has used his traditions to compose a unified symphony of meaning. *The sources have influenced the redactor as much as the redactor has altered the sources.*

(Pss. 40.14; 71.18; 88.53; 105.48 LXX; cf. 1 Chron. 16.36), these all serve as closing benedictions rather than as initial invocations of praise. Two more likely sources for the allusion are 1 Kgs 1.48 LXX and 1 Kgs 8.15 LXX.[1] Both are initial invocations of praise and both occur in contexts related to the heir to the Davidic throne. The first is a statement of David cited by Jonathan ben-Abiathar concerning the appointment of Solomon to the throne: Εὐλογητὸς κύριος ὁ θεὸς Ἰσραήλ, ὃς ἔδωκεν σήμερον ἐκ τοῦ σπέρματός μου καθήμενον ἐπὶ τοῦ θρόνου μου...The second is spoken by Solomon at the dedication of the temple: Εὐλογητὸς κύριος ὁ θεὸς Ἰσραὴλ σήμερον, ὃς ἐλάλησεν ἐν τῷ στόματι αὐτοῦ περὶ Δαυὶδ τοῦ πατρός μου καὶ ἐν ταῖς χερσὶν αὐτοῦ ἐπλήρωσεν...This latter is even closer to the Davidic promise theme since it occurs in the context of the initial fulfillment of the promise for the building of the temple in 2 Sam. 7.13. In addition, a number of allusions to the promise context of 2 Sam. 7.1-16 are made by Solomon (compare 2 Sam. 7.2, 4, 5, 8 with 1 Kgs 8.16-21). The similarity of these two passages to Lk. 1.68 suggests that Luke may view Zechariah's initial blessing as already setting the stage for the Davidic statement of v. 69. Whether or not this is the case, Zechariah's next words identify the reason for his praise as the 'raising up' of the Davidic messiah. God is to be praised:

> For he has visited and accomplished redemption for his people,
> And has raised up a horn of salvation for us in the house of David his servant.

'Horn' (κέρας = Heb. קרן) in the Old Testament denotes power or strength, an image probably derived from the horns of powerful animals.[2] The lifting or exalting of a horn denotes an increase in power. When used of the actions of men it indicates arrogance; it is for God to exalt or trample down the horn (i.e. the strength of men).[3] The 'horn' of the Davidic king is said to be exalted by Yahweh in 1 Sam. 2.10 and Ps. 89.25. Here in Lk. 1.69, however, the horn is not exalted but is 'raised up' (ἐγείρω), a term which in the LXX generally indicates the action of

1. Farris, *Hymns*, p. 95; Bock, *Proclamation*, pp. 70-71; R. Deichgräber, *Gotteshymnus und Christushymnus* (1967), pp. 40-43. Three of the psalms also suggest a Davidic context: Pss. 71 (LXX) and 88 (LXX) are full of Davidic references and Ps. 40 (LXX) is called a 'Psalm of David'.

2. Deut. 33.17; Ps. 148.14; 1 Sam. 2.1-10; Dan. 7.7-8; *1 En.* 90.9; *Shem. Esr.* 15; Rev. 5.6; 12.3; W. Foerster, *TDNT*, III, pp. 69-671; Marshall, *Gospel of Luke*, p. 91; Fitzmyer, *Luke I–IX*, p. 383.

3. Ps. 74.4, 5 (LXX); W. Foerster, *TDNT*, III, p. 670.

God in raising up *people* to accomplish his purpose (judges: Judg. 2.16, 18; 3.9, 15; kings: 1 Kgs 11.14, 23; Jer. 51.11 [28.11]). This is closer to the unusual image in Ps. 132.17 (LXX 131.17), where it is said that a horn will 'sprout'[1] for David (a merging of Davidic 'horn' and 'shoot' imagery). That a personification of the horn is intended in Lk. 1.69 is confirmed by the next phrase of the hymn: the 'horn' is raised up 'in the house of David'. As we have seen, the expression has striking parallels in *Shemoneh Esreh* 15 and in Sir. 15.12 vii.[2] From a narrative perspective, Luke's reference is clearly meant to reflect contemporary Jewish expectation for the coming Davidic king.

Because of its vocabulary and style, v. 70 appears to be a Lukan insertion.[3] If so, its purpose is to stress the Lukan theme of promise-fulfillment, especially with reference to the Davidic statement of v. 69.[4] Burger suggests that the verse is used to interrupt the flow of thought and so downplay the nationalistic tone of v. 71. Luke wants to stress that 'the salvation from David's descendant has nothing to do with earthly-political expectation'.[5] This suggestion is unlikely. If Luke wanted to downplay the political aspects of the Davidic promises he could have omitted v. 71 completely. The introduction of v. 70 does little to diminish its force, and may indeed increase it. Verse 70 emphasizes that the verses both before and after are in line with Old Testament prophecy.

Verse 71 defines the salvation God will accomplish through the Davidic horn:[6] 'salvation from our enemies and from the hand of all who hate us'. The language is reminiscent of Ps. 105.10 LXX (cf. 2 Sam. 22.18 = Ps. 17.18 LXX) and suggests contemporary Jewish hopes of

1. ἐξανατελῶ, MT = אצמיח; cf. Ezek. 29.21.
2. See Chapter 2 section 2e.
3. See the evidence in Fitzmyer, *Luke I–IX*, p. 384; Schürmann, *Lukasevangelium*, I, p. 87; Nolland, *Luke 1–9:20*, pp. 86-87.
4. Cf. Fitzmyer, *Luke I-IX*, p. 384; Schürmann, *Lukasevangelium*, I, p. 87.
5. Burger, *Jesus als Davidssohn*, pp. 131, 132.
6. Fitzmyer, *Luke I–IX*, p. 384, calls the phrase 'an abstract appositive to the "horn of salvation"'. Marshall, *Gospel of Luke*, p. 91, says it is 'a very loosely attached description of the salvation resulting from God's action, σωτηρίαν being in apposition to the content of vs. 68-69'. Cf. Schürmann, *Lukasevangelium*, I, p. 87 n. 41: 'Lose angefügte Apposition, wohl nicht nur κ. σωτηρίας, sondern alle Aussagen von VV 69b-70 explizierend.' Whether appositional to κέρας σωτηρίας or more generally to vv. 68-69 or 69-70, the phrase serves to clarify the nature of the salvation which God accomplishes through the Davidic messiah.

political and national deliverance (cf. *Pss. Sol.* 17; 4QpIsa[a] D 1–8; 1QSb 5.20-29; 1QM *passim; Shem. Esr.* 7, 10, 12; etc.). The idea is repeated in v. 74, where God is said to grant deliverance 'from the hand of our enemies'. Again strong nationalistic overtones are evident. As indicated in Chapter 2, Israel's salvation always included ethical and spiritual renewal as well as physical deliverance. This becomes clear later in the hymn, where the 'knowledge of salvation' which John brings is accomplished 'through the forgiveness of sins'. While such terminology would no doubt be pregnant with Christian meaning for Luke and his audience,[1] it is significant that in these verses Luke continues to define the role of the coming Davidic king in language reminiscent of the political and national deliverance of the Old Testament and Judaism.

(3) In vv. 72-75 the focus shifts to *the Abrahamic covenant.* Again Luke returns to a theme introduced earlier (1.55). The purpose (or result[2]) of God's salvation is 'to deal faithfully with our fathers (i.e. to deal with ἔλεος/חסד),[3] and to remember his holy covenant'. The two clauses are roughly synonymous. The covenant is described in v. 73 as 'the oath (ὅρκος) which he swore to Abraham' (Gen. 17.4; 22.16-18; 26.3; Deut. 7.8). Though the looseness of the syntax allows various interpretations, the infinitival construction in vv. 73b-75 is probably meant to present the content of the oath made to Abraham:[4] 'To grant to us, having been delivered from the hand of our enemies, to serve him without fear in holiness and righteousness before him all our days.' The general sense is clear: God's salvation accomplished through his 'horn' is faithful to the covenant promises he made to the fathers and has as its

1. The expression, 'forgiveness of sins' is a favourite of Luke's, who has 8 of the 11 New Testament appearances of the phrase.

2. Brown, *Birth*, p. 372, argues that the two non-articular infinitives form a result clause here, reflecting a Semitic construction; but as Farris, *Hymns*, p. 137, suggests, with God as the subject there is little difference between the two.

3. ποιῆσαι ἔλεος μετά is a Semitic expression reflecting the Hebrew עשׂה חסד עם (cf. Gen. 24.12; Judg. 1.24; 8.35; 1 Sam. 20.8; 2 Sam. 3.8; cf. Lk. 10.37; Acts 24.17). In the present context it almost certainly means 'to deal faithfully with' rather than 'to show mercy to'. Cf. Judg. 1.24 for this meaning (Marshall, *Gospel of Luke*, p. 92; BDF §206). It should be recalled that eternal חסד was an integral part of God's covenant promise to David (2 Sam. 7.15; Ps. 89.25, 29). See Chapter 2 section 1a.

4. So most commentators: Plummer, *St. Luke*, pp. 41-42; Creed, *St. Luke*, p. 26; Schürmann, *Lukasevangelium*, I, p. 88; Brown, *Birth*, p. 372; Marshall, *Gospel of Luke*, p. 92; Fitzmyer, *Luke I–IX*, p. 385; Farris, *Hymns*, p. 137.

goal free and unhindered worship for his people. Though the patriarchs are in view here, the general covenant language is not far from the Davidic promise with which the hymn began (cf. the covenant language with reference to David in Pss. 89.4, 29; 132.11-12; 1 Kgs 9.4-5).[1] As mentioned above, Luke views the promises and covenants of God as a unity.

(4) The mid-point of the hymn marks a syntactical (from aorist to future tenses) and semantic shift as Zechariah turns and addresses *John, the forerunner*:

> And you, child, will be called the prophet of the Most High;
> For you will go on before the Lord to prepare his ways;
> To give to his people the knowledge of salvation
> By the forgiveness of their sins (vv. 76-77).

The role of John here echoes 1.17 as well as his description in the Gospel and Acts (3.4; 7.27; Acts 13.24; cf. Isa. 40.3; Mal. 3.1, 23). John will 'go before' the Lord (1.17, 76; 7.27) preparing his way (1.76; 3.4; 7.27; cf. Mal. 3.1; Isa. 40.3-4) and preparing a people to meet him (1.17). According to 1.17 he will 'turn back' (ἐπιστρέφω)[2] the sons of Israel, a role closely related to his preaching of 'repentance' (3.3, 8; Acts 13.24) 'for the forgiveness of sins' (1.77; 3.3). His coming heralds the time of God's salvation (1.77; 3.6; cf. Isa. 40.5). Again Luke builds on a theme he has introduced earlier, and one which will be developed further in the subsequent narrative: while Jesus is the messiah, John is the forerunner. As in 1.17, the 'Lord' John will go before is left unspecified. While there the context indicates that κύριος ὁ θεός (1.16) is meant, the introduction of the personified 'horn of salvation' in v. 69 may point here to Jesus (cf. 1.31-35, 43).[3] Luke characteristically uses κύριος (sometimes

1. Brown, *Birth*, p. 389. It may be significant that David himself is called 'patriarch' in Acts 2.29.

2. The term is commonly used in the sense of 'to repent' in Luke–Acts: Lk. 22.32; Acts 3.19; 9.35; 11.21; 14.15; 15.19; 26.18; 26.20; 28.27; cf. Tannehill, *Narrative Unity*, I, p. 23.

3. So most commentators (for Luke, though not necessarily for his source): Leaney, *Luke*, p. 90; Schürmann, *Lukasevangelium*, I, pp. 90-91; Fitzmyer, *Luke I–IX*, pp. 385, 386; Marshall, *Gospel of Luke*, p. 93 ('for Christian readers'); Farris, *Hymns*, p. 139. Others argue that on the basis of 1.16-17, Yahweh must be meant: G. Schneider, *Das Evangelium nach Lukas* (1977), II, p. 62; Plummer, *St. Luke*, p. 42. Nolland, *Luke 1–9:20*, p. 89, speaks of 'a happy ambiguity about the reference'.

ambiguously) for both Jesus and God.[1] On the other hand, the reference to the 'visitation' of the Lord God in v. 68 indicates that God visits his people through Jesus his messianic agent. Either meaning would therefore be appropriate in the context.

(5) In v. 78, the knowledge of salvation which John will bring is said to be offered because of God's compassionate mercies (διὰ σπλάγχνα ἐλέους θεοῦ ἡμῶν).[2] The phrase forms a transition to the closing section of the hymn, leaving the description of John and introducing a new christological theme: *Jesus as the* ἀνατολή, *the 'dawn' from on high.* God's compassionate mercies will result in a divine visitation: ἐν οἷς ἐπισκέψεται ἡμᾶς ἀνατολὴ ἐξ ὕψους. The idea of a visitation links this section to the beginning of the hymn and suggests a return to the Davidic theme present there. 'From on high' (ἐξ ὕψους) signifies the abode of God (Eph. 3.18; 4.8), raising the possibility of the pre-existence of the 'messianic' figure described here. This is not essential, however, since the verse may simply refer to one who is sent from God 'Most High'. The meaning of ἀνατολή has been a matter of much discussion. The word itself signifies a 'rising' and may refer to the rising of a heavenly body (e.g. 'sunrise'; and so also to the area of sunrise = 'east'; Lk. 13.39; Mt. 2.1, 2; frequently in the LXX[3]) or to the growing of a plant (thus 'shoot' or 'branch'). The term appears in the LXX as the translation of the Hebrew צמח 'shoot' (Jer. 23.5; Zech. 3.8; 6.12; cf. Isa. 4.2), a title which came to designate the messianic king in Second Temple Judaism.[4] Ps. 132.17 and Ezek. 29.21 use the cognate verbs (צמח; ἀνατέλλειν) with reference to the 'horn' which will 'sprout' for

1. The title is used of Jesus in Lk. 1.43, 76 (?); 2.11; 7.13, 19; 10.1, 39, 41; 11.39; 12.42; 13.15; 17.5, 6; 18.6; 19.8, 31, 34; 20.42, 44; 22.61; 24.3, 34. The use of the title in narrative to refer to Jesus is distinctive of Luke (Marshall, *Gospel of Luke*, p. 81).

2. The phrase διὰ σπλάγχνα ἐλέους θεορῦ ἡμῶν may be taken with the preceeding statement about John (connected to προπορεύσῃ, σωτηρίας, ἄφεσιν or to the whole of vv. 77-78; so Plummer, *St. Luke*, p. 43; Brown, *Birth*, p. 373) or as introducing the final clause (full stop after v. 77; so Fitzmyer, *Luke I–IX*, p. 386), but is probably best taken as transitional, loosely connected to the whole previous statement (vv. 77-78) and introducing the reason for the divine visitation of v. 78 (so Marshall, *Gospel of Luke*, p. 94; Farris, *Hymns*, p. 141).

3. Primarily as 'east' (Gen. 2.3; 10.30, etc.) and as 'rising' of the sun (Num. 2.3; 3.38; Judg. 5.31, etc.).

4. Cf. 4QPBless 3; 4QFlor 1.11; *Shem. Esr.* 15; *Targ. Neb.* Isa. 4.2; Jer. 23.5; 33.15; Zech. 3.8; 6.12; Str–B, II, p. 113.

David (Ezekiel: for Israel), and both *Shem. Esr.* 15 and Sir. 51.12 vii (as noted above) pick up this 'sprouting horn' imagery. The linking of these two concepts may point to a similar connection between the ἀνατολή of v. 78 and the 'horn' from the house of David in v. 69. The translation in v. 78 could thus be, 'the shoot (i.e. the Davidic messiah) will visit us from on high'.

The near context, however, indicates that ἀνατολή should be understood as a light metaphor.[1] According to v. 79, the role of the ἀνατολή will be: ἐπιφᾶναι τοῖς ἐν σκότει καὶ σκιᾷ θανάτου καθημένοις, τοῦ κατευθῦναι τοὺς πόδας ἡμῶν εἰς ὁδὸν εἰρήνης.[2] Though no Old Testament passage is directly cited, a number of allusions are present (Isa. 9.2; 42.7; 49.6; Ps. 107.10). The wording of the first phrase is closest to Ps. 106.10 (LXX): καθημένους ἐν σκότει καὶ σκιᾷ θανάτου... But as the image of light shining on those in darkness is not present there, the picture as a whole is tied more closely to Isa. 9.2 and Isa. 42.7. Isaiah 9.2 (MT 9.1) provides a close verbal parallel to the first phrase (especially in the non-LXX rendering in Mt. 4.15-16[3]) but does not refer to a leading or guiding of those in darkness—an image that *does* occur in Isa. 42.7. This latter passage also concerns more

1. So Plummer, *St. Luke*, p. 43; Creed, *St. Luke*, p. 27; Brown, *Birth*, pp. 373-74; 389-91; Schürmann, *Lukasevangelium*, I, p. 92.

2. P. Vielhauer, 'Das Benedictus des Zacharias', in *Aufsätze zum Neuen Testament* (1965), pp. 35-36, considers this second phrase to refer to John. He argues that because both are articular, the infinitives 'to guide' (v. 79) and 'to give' (v. 77) should be linked, with John being the subject of both. In this view, vv. 78-79a would be a parenthesis, with 79b returning to the description of John's ministry. This view is unlikely. There is no indication of a change in subject in v. 79b and the two infinitive phrases in the verse are most naturally seen as parallel to one another, with the second epexegetic of the first. The subject of both is ἀνατολή. So Farris, *Hymns*, pp. 194-95 n. 106; Schürmann, *Lukasevangelium*, I, p. 92; Marshall, *Gospel of Luke*, p. 95; Brown, *Birth*, p. 374.

3. Matthew's text reads ὁ λαὸς ὁ καθήμενος ἐν σκότει φῶς εἶδεν μέγα, καὶ τοῖς καθημένοις ἐν χώρᾳ καὶ σκιᾷ θανάτου φῶς ἀνέτειλεν αὐτοῖς. The LXX essentially follows the MT except that it renders the perfect tense verbs ראו and נגה respectively as an imperative, ἴδετε, and a future, λάμψει. Matthew differs from the LXX by rendering both participial clauses with κάθημαι instead of πορεύομαι and κατοικέω respectively and in his use of the ἀνατέλλω instead of λάμπω for his finite verb. Marshall, *Gospel of Luke*, p. 95, points out that the use of ἀνατέλλω in Matthew (LXX has λάμπω) provides a link to the present passage and may indicate the existence of an exegetical tradition. Cf. C.H. Dodd, *According to the Scriptures* (1952), p. 80.

specifically the actions of an individual (Isa. 42.1: 'my servant'), who will act as a light for the nations (cf. Isa. 49.6). This accords with Lk. 1.78, which seems to portray the ἀνατολή as an individual who provides light for those living in darkness. Thus through an amalgamation of Old Testament allusions, v. 79 suggests that ἀνατολή should be rendered 'dawn', 'sunrise' or 'rising light'.

That this meaning is relevant to the present context is clear from several LXX passages where the cognate verb ἀνατέλλω is used in the metaphor of a rising light in an eschatological setting similar to Lk. 1.78-79. In a context which speaks of the coming of Elijah the prophet (cf. Lk. 1.17) before the day of the Lord (Mal. 3.1; 3.22 LXX), Mal. 3.20 (LXX) promises that 'to those who fear my name the sun of righteousness will rise (ἀνατελεῖ) with healing in its wings'. Similarly, Isa. 60.1 (LXX) says 'Shine, shine, O Jerusalem, for your light is come and the glory of the Lord has risen (ἀνατέταλκεν) over you...and kings shall walk in your light and nations in your brightness'. Cf. Isa. 58.8 (LXX): 'Then your [the house of Jacob's] light will break out like the dawn and your healing will quickly spring forth (ἀνατελεῖ).'

Many scholars have suggested that in view of the Septuagintal use of ἀνατολή for both 'shoot' and 'rising light', the word here carries a double meaning.[1] This is linguistically improbable. Just because a word is polysemous does not mean that both senses are combined in any single occurrence of the term. Since there is no indication that Luke is making a pun, ἀνατολή probably means *either* 'shoot' *or* 'rising light'. And the context clearly indicates the latter.[2]

On the other hand, it is not unlikely that ἀνατολή is understood by Luke as a light metaphor *with royal-messianic reference*. Several Old Testament passages describe the coming of the Davidic king with light imagery. In Isa. 9.1ff., a passage alluded to in v. 79, the light which shines on those in darkness heralds the birth of the child who will reign forever on the throne of David. Similarly, Num. 24.17, which speaks of

1. So Bock, *Proclamation*, p. 73: 'Thus it seems that ἀνατολή is intended to convey a double meaning, pointing not only to light, but also to the messianic Branch.' Farris, *Hymns*, p. 140, writes: 'The metaphor may well be somewhat mixed, combining as it does the image of the "sprout" and "rising light"' (Farris elsewhere [pp. 34-35] suggests the conclusion reached below); cf. Marshall, *Gospel of Luke*, pp. 94-95; Fitzmyer, *Luke I–IX*, p. 387.

2. If the passage read something like 'the ἀνατολή will "sprout up" to shine upon those who sit in darkness…', this would suggest both senses were intended.

a star coming forth from Jacob and a scepter (or, 'comet') rising (LXX: ἀνατελεῖ) from Israel, was widely interpreted as 'messianic' (sometimes Davidic) in Second Temple Judaism.[1] This suggests that in some circles the coming Davidic king was conceived metaphorically as a light to the fearful benighted. This is also supported by later rabbinic evidence which links the messiah to light.[2] *T. Jud.* 24.1-6 (whether of Jewish or Christian provenance) is particularly relevant here as it draws a connection between Num. 24.17 and the Davidic shoot:

> And after these things a star will arise to you from Jacob in peace, And a man shall arise from my seed like the sun of righteousness...This is the branch (βλαστός) of God Most High.[3]

Justin Martyr in the second century draws a similar connection. In his first *Apology* (I, 32.12) he mis-quotes Isa. 11.1, combining its Davidic shoot imagery with the rising star of Num. 24.17:

> And indeed Isaiah, another prophet, prophesying the same thing in other words, spoke thus: 'A star shall rise (ἀνατελεῖ) out of Jacob, and a blossom (ἄνθος) shall spring from the root of Jesse; and in his arm shall the nations hope.'[4]

There is also a connection between the Davidic messiah and light imagery in Rev. 22.16, where Jesus announces, 'I am the root and offspring of David, the bright morning star.' Together this evidence suggests that rising light and 'shoot' imagery were closely linked together in the Davidic messianism of first-century Judaism and early Christianity.

Impetus for the use of the noun ἀνατολή to refer to this Davidic

1. 4QTestim 12; CD 7.18; 1QM 11.6; *T. Levi* 18.3; *T. Jud.* 24.1-6. Cf. *Targ. Onq.* Num. 24.17; *Targ. Ps.-J.* Num. 24.17; *Frg. Targ.* Num. 24.17; Str–B, I, pp. 76-77. Also in early Christianity: Mt. 2.2; Rev. 22.16; Justin Martyr, *Apologia* I, 32.12; Origen, *Contra Celsum* 1.59. Origen takes the 'star' as the star which appeared at Jesus' birth and the 'man' who rises from Israel (so LXX) as Jesus.

2. Str–B, I, pp. 67, 151, 161-62. Rabbinic texts frequently speak of the 'light' of the messiah and of the messianic age. Light is specifically associated with the messiah in *Pesiq. R.* 36 (161[a]); 37 (164[a]); *Pes. R. Kah.* 149[a]; and *Lev. R.* 31 (129[a]) (citing Ps. 132.17). In *Gen. R.* 1 and *Midr. Lam.* 1.16 'light' is said to be one of messiah's names (taken from Isa. 60.1 and Dan. 2.22).

3. Translated from the critical Greek text of M. de Jonge *et al. The Testaments of the Twelve Patriarchs* (1978), pp. 76-77.

4. Translated from the Greek edition of A.W.F. Blunt (ed.), *The Apologies of Justin Martyr* (1911), p. 52.

messianic 'rising light' probably came from its use in the LXX as a translation for the shoot in Jer. 23.5; Zech. 3.8; 6.12.[1] Such a mis-interpretation of these LXX passages is found in the Hellenistic Jew Philo, who cites Zech. 6.12 (LXX) and interprets ἀνατολή as a light metaphor.[2] Similarly, Justin Martyr repeatedly refers to this same passage each time interpreting ἀνατολή as a light, rather than a plant metaphor.[3] As ἀνατολή became a common designation for the coming Davidic king, it lost its original (and unusual) meaning of 'shoot' in these passages, and was interpreted with its more common meaning 'dawn' or 'rising light'.

It seems probable, then, that though Luke interprets ἀνατολή as a light metaphor, he understands its referent as the coming Davidic king. This fits the narrative context best, since an allusion to Isa. 9.2 (MT 9.1) immediately follows in 79a. Further support for this, of course, is the fact that the title is introduced in a hymn where Jesus has already been defined as the *Davidic* horn of salvation (v. 69).[4]

In summary, though Luke has probably drawn the Benedictus (at least partially) from traditional sources, he uses it to carry his narrative forward. Several themes introduced already are picked up and developed, including God's initiative in bringing salvation, Jesus as the Davidic deliverer, God's faithfulness to the Abrahamic covenant, and John the forerunner. Further, a new christological theme is introduced, the messiah as the ἀνατολή from on high, a light shining on those in darkness. This theme will be picked up again in the Nunc Dimittis (1.32)

1. For the suggestion that the Hebrew צמח was associated with light imagery already in a Semitic context see G. Box, *The Virgin Birth of Jesus* (1916), pp. 46-48; Farris, *Hymns*, p. 34.

2. Philo, *Conf. Ling.* 60-63. Philo cites Zech. 6.12 ('a man whose name is ἀνατολή) and says this would be a strange description if it referred to a being composed of soul and body. Thus it must refer to 'that Incorporeal one, who differs not a whit from the divine image', that is, the Divine Logos (cf. 41-42).

3. Justin Martyr, *Dialogue with Trypho* 106.4; 121.2; 126.1 (cf. 100.4). In 106.4 he cites Zech. 6.12 ('behold a man, ἀνατολή is his name') and Num. 24.17 together as proof that Jesus 'should arise like a star from the seed of Abraham'.

4. Whether Luke drew this understanding from Judaism or early Christianity is difficult to determine since representatives from both connect the Davidic messiah to light and interpret ἀνατολή in its LXX 'shoot' contexts as a rising light. It is not impossible, of course, that this interpretation of ἀνατολή is a new and creative metaphor introduced by Luke (or by his canticle source) on the basis of the Old Testament and Jewish connections described above.

and elsewhere in Luke–Acts, particularly in the context of Gentile salvation (Acts 13.47; 26.23; cf. Isa. 42.1; 49.6). The central focus of the Benedictus is the same as that of the Annunciation and the Magnificat: God has acted decisively to save and deliver Israel. Through various Old Testament allusions, this salvation is shown to be rooted in Israel's past and to be a direct fulfillment of God's promises to her. Though dealing generally with God's faithfulness to Abraham and the fathers (vv. 72-73), the central *christological* emphasis of the hymn is on the promises to David. The hymn begins with the horn of salvation who is raised up in the house of David and ends with the Davidic ἀνατολή, the eschatological rising light (cf. Num. 24.17; Isa. 9.1-7; Isa. 42.1; 49.6), who will shine on those sitting in darkness and the shadow of death. Though the references to salvation and forgiveness of sins would no doubt be pregnant with Christian meaning for Luke's readers, Luke intentionally stays close to the Old Testament and Jewish language of promise. Zechariah the pious priest of Jerusalem praises God at the birth of his son—the forerunner of the 'Lord'—for his faithfulness to his covenant promises, faithfulness manifested in the raising up the Davidic messiah to save and deliver the nation from the hand of her enemies.

c. *The Birth of Jesus, Luke 2.1-20*

The story of the birth of Jesus follows the Benedictus and the statement concerning the child John's growth and development (1.80). Again one finds a story which repeatedly alludes to Jesus as the coming Davidic king. In v. 4 the reader is told that as a result of the census, Joseph went up from Galilee to 'the city of David (εἰς πόλιν Δαυίδ) which is called Bethlehem, because he was from the house and family of David'. This description of Bethlehem is repeated in v. 11, when it is announced to the shepherds ὅτι ἐτέχθη ὑμῖν σήμερον σωτὴρ ὅς ἐστιν χριστὸς κύριος ἐν πόλει Δαυίδ.

i. *The birth story, vv. 1-7.* Luke begins his account with the reason for Joseph and Mary's trip to Bethlehem and Jesus' subsequent birth there. At least part of his purpose here is to explain why Jesus, whose family is from Nazareth, nevertheless was born in Bethlehem. The purpose of the trip is the worldwide census decreed by Caesar Augustus requiring all to register in their own cities.[1] Since Joseph is 'from the house and family

1. The complex historical questions related to the census are beyond the scope of this investigation. For a discussion of the problems, various possible solutions, and

of David' (ἐξ οἴκου καὶ πατριᾶς Δαυίδ), he goes up from Nazareth to Judea, to Bethlehem the city of David. The general sense of πατριά in Greek is the family as derived from the father, but it can have the more general meanings of 'house' or even 'tribe' or 'nation' (Acts 3.25; Eph. 3.14-15). The context suggests that the two terms are used co-referentially, both referring to Joseph's Davidic descent. Schrenk proposes that since 'house of David' implies 'house of the ruler' (2 Sam. 3.6, 10; 1 Kgs 13.2, etc.), πατριά is added to make it clear that the reference is simply to ancestral descent.[1] Another possibility is that Luke is here using a source which used the Hebraic expression 'father's house' (בית־אב; pl. בית־אבות), often rendered as οἶκος πατριᾶς in the LXX.[2] In either case, the emphasis is on Joseph's Davidic descent, which legitimizes Jesus' claim to the Davidic throne.

Bethlehem is closely associated with David in the Old Testament. It was his birthplace and original home (1 Sam. 17.12ff.; 17.58), a place where he returned for family occasions (1 Sam. 20.6, 28-29) and retained an affection for later in his life (2 Sam. 23.15).[3] Apart from the key prophecy of Mic. 5.2 (MT 5.1), little importance is given to the town in the Old Testament or in Second Temple Judaism. Only a few targumic and rabbinic sources designate Bethlehem as the place of the messiah's origin.[4] Various reasons for this have been suggested. Origen claimed that later Jewish scholars suppressed the expectation that the messiah would be born at Bethlehem.[5] Bousset, Gressmann, and Burger suggest instead that the tradition was an isolated one.[6] Burger claims that in Judaism the appearance of the Davidic shoot is expected in

bibliographies see Schürmann, *Lukasevangelium*, I, pp. 100-101; Brown, *Birth*, pp. 547-56; Marshall, *Gospel of Luke*, pp. 99-104; Fitzmyer, *Luke I–IX*, pp. 399-406, 415-17; Nolland, *Luke 1–9.20*, pp. 94-96, 99-102.

1. Schrenk, *TDNT*, V, pp. 1016-17; cf. Plummer, *St. Luke*, p. 52.
2. Schrenk, *TDNT*, V, pp. 1016-17.
3. Plummer, *St. Luke*, p. 52.
4. Mic. 5.1 is given a messianic interpretation in *Targ. Neb.* Mic. 5.1 and *Pirqe R. El.* 3 (2^b), the latter as part of an argument that the messiah was created before the world. In two rabbinic texts, *y. Ber.* 2.4 (5^a, 12) and *Midr. Lam.* 1.16 (58^b), Bethlehem is cited as the place of messiah's birth without reference to Mic. 5.1; see Str–B, I, pp. 82-83.
5. Origen, *Contra Celsum*, p. 1.51.
6. W. Bousset and H. Gressman, *Die Religion des Judentums im späthellenistischen Zeitalter* (1926), p. 226; Burger, *Jesus als Davidssohn*, p. 24.

Jerusalem, not in Bethlehem.[1] This, however, is a somewhat misleading statement. Jewish expectations related to Jerusalem center on the messiah's activities, not on his origin. Indeed, I know of no Second Temple text which even speaks of the Davidic messiah's birth, let alone locates it either in Jerusalem or Bethlehem. The real problem, therefore, is not so much the rarity of references to Bethlehem *per se,* but the rarity of references to the messiah's birthplace at all. The most that can be said is that, from the *rather meagre sources presently available,* the tradition of the Bethlehem birthplace appears to be a relatively isolated one, though the dearth of material makes such a conclusion extremely tentative. The evidence of the rabbinic and targumic sources, and the independent references in Mt. 2.4-6 and Jn 7.41-42, together indicate that at least *some* first-century Jews expected the coming Davidic king to be born in Bethlehem.

Luke's description of Bethlehem as the 'city of David' is unusual since the town is never so designated in the Old Testament or in Judaism. The 'city of David' refers instead to Mount Zion in Jerusalem (2 Sam. 5.7, 9 = 1 Chron. 11.5, 7; 2 Sam. 6.10, 12, 16; 1 Kgs 2.10, etc.), formerly the stronghold of the Jebusites. In 2 Sam. 5.7, 9 David captures the stronghold and makes it his own, hence it became his city—'the city of David'. Why, then, would Luke apply the designation to Bethlehem? Brown's suggestion that he is consciously associating Bethlehem with Jerusalem is unlikely.[2] A better explanation is that Luke wishes to stress the Davidic connection to Bethlehem, the traditional location of Jesus' birth (cf. Mt. 2.1). If this is the case, Luke is here using πόλις Δαυίδ more as a descriptive phrase than a title, somewhat similar to John's τῆς κώμης ὅπου ἦν Δαυίδ (Jn 7.42).[3] The phrase εἰς πόλιν Δαυὶδ ἥτις καλεῖται Βηθλέεμ could thus be rendered 'to the city associated with David, which is called Bethlehem'.[4] Luke's purpose is to associate the birthplace of Jesus with that of David and again *to stress the*

1. Burger, *Jesus als Davidssohn*, pp. 24, 136.

2. Brown, *Birth*, pp. 422-23. See discussion below.

3. The structure of the phrase may point in this direction since the name Bethlehem seems to clarify what is meant by πόλις Δαυίδ. In addition, Luke's use of an anarthrous construction may point to a descriptive rather than a titular sense. This latter point is speculative since the title occurs as a designation for Jerusalem both with and without the article in the LXX (cf. 2 Sam. 5.7, 9; 6.10, 12 [articular]; 2 Sam. 6.16; 1 Kgs 2.10 [anarthrous]).

4. Leaney's (*Luke*, p. 93) translation, 'a city of David', points in this direction but would be too indefinite in the present context.

Davidic connection in Jesus' messianic identity.

Whereas Matthew emphasizes Jesus' Bethlehem birth because it fulfills the prophecy of Mic. 5.2 (Mt. 2.5-6), Luke wishes to stress the Davidic link. This is not to suggest that Matthew does not connect Bethlehem with David,[1] nor that Luke is unaware of the prophecy of Micah 5.2. The issue is one of emphasis. Matthew seeks to show that Jesus fulfills a specific Old Testament prophecy, while Luke first and foremost links Jesus' birthplace to his Davidic messianic identity.

Some scholars, by contrast, have claimed that Luke's whole presentation is modeled around the conceptual framework of Micah 4–5.[2] Brown says that the flow of people and nations to Jerusalem in Micah resembles the movement of the whole world affected by the census of Augustus. Also, in Micah's prophecy, mention is twice made of a woman who is in labor (4.10; 5.3), an image resembling Luke's birth motif. The 'time' (Mic. 5.3) when this woman (identified in 4.10 as the 'Daughter of Zion') gives birth may be in view in the reference to 'this day' in Luke's announcement to the shepherds (Lk. 2.11).[3]

These allusions are somewhat far-fetched. The eschatological 'movement of peoples' associated with the nations streaming to the mountain of Yahweh in Mic. 4.1-2 is a very different image than Luke's census account. Further, Luke's birth motif is a necessary characteristic of his story, with or without an allusion to Micah. The emphasis in Micah on the travail of labor (4.10; 5.3) is not present in Luke, who states only the bare fact of the birth. Finally, verse 11 gives no indication that 'today' (σήμερον) refers to the eschatological day of salvation; more likely it is literal, referring to the actual day of Jesus' birth.[4]

This is not to say that Mic. 5.2 could not have formed the framework for the pre-Lukan birth tradition, nor that Luke was unaware of the passage, but only that he is not consciously imitating Micah's prophecy. While Luke no doubt views Jesus' Bethlehem birth as the fulfillment of Mic. 5.2, it is the Davidic significance of the prophecy, rather than the conceptual framework of Mic. 4.1-5.4, which is his primary concern. In this respect we do have a similarity between Luke and Micah, since both

1. Matthew's birth narrative is permeated with Davidic themes and his quote of Mic. 5.2 concerning the ruler from Judah 'who will shepherd my people Israel' (Mt. 2.6) would certainly recall David the shepherd king.

2. Brown, *Birth*, pp. 421-24; cf. Laurentin, *Structure*, pp. 86-88.

3. Brown, *Birth*, p. 422.

4. Marshall, *Gospel of Luke*, p. 109.

follow the pattern of David's life, and both focus on the ruler who will arise from the house of David. While David was born in Bethlehem (1 Sam. 17.12ff; 17.58), it was Jerusalem which formed the background for the key conflicts and victories in his life. In Micah, though the ruler comes from Bethlehem (Mic. 5.2), Yahweh's triumph through him is centered in Jerusalem/Zion and returns dominion to her (Mic. 4.8). Similarly in Luke, after Jesus' birth in Bethlehem his parents 'go up' to Jerusalem to present him to the Lord (2.22). From this point on, Bethlehem is forgotten and all the emphasis shifts to Jerusalem, where Jesus' ministry climaxes in conflict and ultimate victory.[1]

While Luke's brief description of the birth of Jesus (vv. 6-7) raises more questions than it answers, there is little doubt that the child's humble birth stands in contrast to his exalted descriptions in Lk. 1.32, 35, 69, and 78-79.[2] The reader cannot but be struck by the paradox of the longed-for and expected king from the line of David laid in a 'manger' (φάτνη) because there was no room in the 'guest-room' (κατάλυμα).[3] That Luke considers the reference to the manger important is evident from the fact that he twice repeats it elsewhere in the story (vv. 12, 16). Brown claims that the description is wholly positive. The shepherds coming to the manger symbolically indicate that Israel, who formerly did not know 'the manger (φάτνη) of her lord' (Isa. 1.3

1. Brown, *Birth*, pp. 422-23, on the contrary, sees a shift away from the Micah passage by Luke, who places all the emphasis on Bethlehem: 'But while Micah focuses on the triumph of Jerusalem/Zion through the ruler from Bethlehem, Luke shifts the total attention to Bethlehem.' He draws evidence for this shift from the 'city of David' designation (normally given to Jerusalem), and from the fact that Joseph 'goes up' to Bethlehem (ascent language normally associated with Jerusalem). He concludes that Luke probably shifted Micah's reference to 'the mountain of the house of the Lord' from Jerusalem/Zion to Bethlehem, since that is where the shepherds must go to see the Lord (2.11-12) (Brown, *Birth*, pp. 422-23). Brown's conclusion here takes account only of the birth story rather than the whole presentation of Luke–Acts. For Luke, the conflict and triumph of Jesus does not occur in Bethlehem but in Jerusalem. There is thus no shift from Jerusalem to Bethlehem, rather (as in Micah) the ruler comes from Bethlehem, but his key actions take place in Jerusalem. We have already seen Luke's reason for the city of David ascription to Bethlehem. The ascent language is more likely a literal description of the ascent into the hill country of Judea (1.39) than symbolic language for Jerusalem.

2. For the many possible interpretations of the scene see the commentaries.

3. Cf. Schürmann, *Lukasevangelium*, I, pp. 104-105; Marshall, *Gospel of Luke*, p. 107; E. Schweizer, *The Good News According to Luke* (1984), p. 49.

LXX), has now begun to return to her master.[1] This interpretation seems strained, particularly since it does not account for the sense of mild exclusion and deprivation in the concluding phrase, διότι οὐκ ἦν αὐτοῖς τόπος ἐν τῷ καταλύματι. Though not necessarily a portrait of abject poverty or rejection, the common peasant scene begins to raise questions over the exalted descriptions of the coming king presented earlier.

ii. *The Angelic Annunciation to the Shepherds*. Following the description of the birth, Luke turns to the story of the shepherds. While not an explicit allusion to Mic. 5.4 (there it is the ruler who is the shepherd), the references to the shepherds after the double mention of David in v. 4 may perhaps recall David's role as a shepherd.[2] Luke's primary interest in the story, however, is in the angelic annunciation and its christological significance.

The angel announces to the shepherds: ὅτι ἐτέχθη ὑμῖν σήμερον σωτὴρ ὅς ἐστιν χριστὸς κύριος ἐν πόλει Δαυίδ. The σωτήρ title, which Luke has already applied to God (1.47), occurs elsewhere in Luke only in Acts 5.31 and 13.23—both times with reference to Jesus.[3] The use of the cognates σωτηρία and σῴζω, together with related concepts, however, shows that salvation is a key Lukan theme.[4] The reference in the present context would recall both the 'horn of salvation' raised up to bring 'salvation from our enemies' (1.69, 71) and the phrase 'God my saviour' in 1.47. Jesus is saviour because it is through him that God 'our saviour' delivers his people. Yahweh himself visits and saves men through the person of Jesus. The narrative development to this point suggests that this salvation will include both physical and ethical dimensions—a presentation in line with Jewish expectations. The Davidic king was expected to act as Yahweh's agent to deliver the nation from

1. Brown, *Birth*, pp. 419-20. Brown also suggests that the couple's location outside the κατάλυμα is a positive allusion to Jer. 14.8 (they no longer live as aliens 'in lodgings') and that the swaddling of the child (cf. Wis. 7.4-5) is a sign that the messiah is being properly received and cared for by his people. Cf. Fitzmyer, *Luke I–IX*, pp. 394-95. For criticism of this view as 'far-fetched' see Evans, *Saint Luke*, p. 200.

2. Schürmann, *Lukasevangelium*, I, p. 108.

3. The term is rare elsewhere in the New Testament. Referring to Jesus: Eph. 5.23; Phil. 3.20; 2 Tim. 1.10; Tit. 1.4; 2.13; 3.6; 2 Pet. 1.1, 11; 2.20; 3.2, 18; 1 Jn 4.14. Referring to God: 1 Tim. 1.1; 2.3; 4.10; Tit. 1.3; 2.10; 3.4; Jude 25.

4. On salvation as a central theme of Luke–Acts see especially Marshall, *Historian*, esp. pp. 88-102.

her enemies and to oversee spiritual and ethical renewal (cf. *Pss. Sol.* 17.21-43; 18.5-9; 4QFlor 1.10-13; 1QSb 5.21-29; 4 Ezra 11.1–12.39; etc.). 4QFlor 1.13 says that he will 'arise to save Israel'. By placing the title together with the description of Jesus as χριστὸς κύριος (see below), Luke closely links Jesus' messiahship to his saving role. A similar connection will be made in Acts 13.23, where Jesus is the Davidic *saviour* God has brought to Israel.

The angel identifies this saviour from David's house as χριστὸς κύριος. The context of the phrase—a report of a child born in πόλις Δαυίδ to a Davidic descendant—makes it clear that χριστός here refers to the *Davidic* messiah, the king destined to reign over the house of Jacob forever (1.32-33). This has important definitional significance for Luke. While it must not be ruled out that elsewhere χριστός carries a more general sense for Luke, it is significant that in the first use of the title in his two-volume work he defines it in Davidic terms. This conclusion necessarily expands the scope of the present study since Luke's understanding of how Jesus fulfills the Davidic promises will be closely linked to his presentation of Jesus as ὁ χριστός.

It has been suggested, not without reason, that χριστός is Luke's most important christological title.[1] Luke introduces the title at key points in his narrative (e.g. 24.26; Acts 2.36) and has a tendency to link other 'royal' titles to this one (κύριος, Lk. 2.11; Acts 2.36; υἱὸς θεοῦ, Lk. 4.41; 22.66-71; Acts 9.20-22; υἱὸς Δαυίδ, 20.41; βασιλεύς, 23.2, 35-38; cf. Acts 17.7). Two aspects of Luke's use of the title are particularly relevant for the present work. The first is the special emphasis he places on the title's Old Testament and Jewish roots—particularly with reference to the king arising from the seed of David. This emphasis is present both here and in Lk. 2.25-26, where pious Simeon's hope is the hope of all who are righteous in Israel: to see the 'Lord's anointed' (χριστὸς κυρίου)—the messianic deliverer—and so experience 'the consolation of Israel'. This connection to the title's Jewish roots continues in the rest of the Gospel, where Luke consistently uses χριστός as a title;[2] he thus avoids the tendency, well established by his time (cf. Mk 1.1), to use it as a second name for Jesus (a use which naturally moves away from the title's Jewish origins). It is only in Acts that Luke

1. So Fitzmyer, *Luke I–IX*, p. 197; cf. Evans, *Saint Luke*, p. 73.

2. The title occurs in the Gospel at Lk. 2.11, 26; 3.15; 4.41; 9.20; 20.41; 22.67; 23.2, 35, 39; 24.26, 46. The title retains the sense of the 'Lord's anointed' in 2.26; 9.20 and 23.35.

adopts this nominal use,[1] though even here he frequently retains the titular sense.[2] In this way Luke places the title at the very heart of his promise-fulfillment scheme.

Secondly, while Luke links the title closely to its Old Testament and Jewish roots and seeks to show that in his person and work Jesus was the fulfillment of Old Testament hopes and promises, at the same time he makes it clear that popular Jewish expectations concerning the Christ were inadequate and insufficient. Jesus fulfills the promised role of the Christ in a surprising and unexpected way. As we shall see, this paradox of continuity and discontinuity with Jewish hopes is a key theme in Luke's Christology. Though only hinted at and foreshadowed in the birth narrative, this theme will be developed in the later Gospel narrative and in Acts.

Though χριστός clearly signifies the royal-messiah, the meaning of the double title χριστὸς κύριος is a more difficult question. The anarthrous phrase is an unusual one, occurring nowhere else in the New Testament and elsewhere only in Lam. 4.20 (LXX) and *Pss. Sol.* 17.32. As we have seen, the former is a mistranslation of the Hebrew construct case and should read χριστὸς κυρίου, while the latter is probably original, perhaps a translation of the Hebrew משיח אדון.[3] Some have argued that the text in Luke, like that in Lam. 4.20, should read χριστὸς κυρίου, having been altered either through a mistranslation of an original Hebrew construct case or through a copyist's error.[4] This is possible since there is some weak textual evidence for the reading χριστὸς κυρίου (it$^{\beta, r1}$ syr$^{h, pal}$ Diatessaron Ephraem) and since Luke uses this same phrase in 2.26. On the other hand, there is strong textual support for the reading χριστὸς κύριος. The phrase is certainly possible for Luke since in Acts 2.36 he writes that God has made Jesus both Lord and Christ (καὶ κύριος καὶ χριστός) (cf. Lk. 23.2).[5] In addition, Luke has already referred to Jesus as Lord in the nativity through Elizabeth's statement (1.43) and (perhaps) by implication in

1. Acts 2.38; 3.6; 4.10, 33; 8.12 [37]; 9.34; 10.36, 48; 11.17; 15.26; 16.18; 17.3 [?]; 20.21; 24.24; 28.31.

2. Acts 2.31, 36; 3.18, 20 [?]; 4.26; 5.42; 8.5; 9.22; 17.3; 18.5, 28; 26.23.

3. See Chapter 2 section 2bi.

4. So Vielhauer, *Aufsätze*, p. 40; Creed, *St. Luke*, p. 35; P. Winter, 'Lukanische Miszellen', *ZNW* 49 (1958), pp. 67-75; D.L. Jones, 'The Title *Christos* in Luke–Acts', *CBQ* 32 (1970), pp. 75-76. Jones gives a list of other proponents.

5. Cf. W. Grundmann, *TDNT*, IX, p. 533 n. 276; Hahn, *Titles*, p. 260.

1.76. This would indicate that for Luke, χριστὸς κύριος is an appropriate title for Jesus in the present context.

What then is the meaning of the phrase? At least four distinct interpretations have been proposed. (1) It is grammatically possible that χριστός functions as an adjective to the noun κύριος, giving the meaning '(the) anointed Lord'. (2) Another possibility is that χριστός is used as a personal name and κύριος as a title ('Christ [personal name] the Lord').[1] The phrase would then be little different from 'Jesus the Lord'. (3) Considering Luke's tendency to use χριστός in its titular sense, however, it is more likely that both terms function as titles ('Christ, [the] Lord') and κύριος is either appositional or epexegetical. If appositional, both titles would carry the implication of kingship. If epexegetical, κύριος may express the sovereignty and dominion which the messiah possesses, or may be a Lukan explanation of χριστός for non-Jewish readers.[2] (4) A fourth possibility is that the two terms reflect a single compound title and should be translated something like 'Messiah-Yahweh', with implications of an epiphany.[3]

Though this last view offers an intriguing possibility, there is little in the context to suggest such a meaning, and it is unlikely that a Greek reader would immediately take it as such—unless, of course, the double title was a common designation for Jesus in Luke's community. This is unlikely, however, since it does not occur elsewhere in the Lukan corpus nor in the rest of the New Testament. The thoroughly Davidic messianic context suggests instead that κύριος here (as in 1.43) refers to messianic lordship—the authority and dominion which the Christ deserves and possesses. As suggested in Chapter 2 with reference to *Pss. Sol.* 17.32, χριστὸς κύριος does not *necessarily* go outside the realm of Jewish thought, since it could represent the messianic title משיח אדון. Our study of Acts 2.36 in Chapter 4 will provide further evidence for this understanding. There Jesus is acclaimed both Christ and Lord—the messiah who has the position of lordship.

1. So Evans, *Saint Luke*, pp. 204-206.

2. The latter is suggested by Schürmann, *Lukasevangelium*, I, pp. 111-12. This meaning is almost identical to the appositional sense since again both titles would imply kingship.

3. Marshall, *Historian*, p. 101; *idem, Gospel of Luke*, p. 110, following H. Sahlin, *Der Messias und das Gottesvolk* (1945), pp. 214-18. Marshall points to *T. Levi* 2.11: 'And by thee and Judah shall the Lord appear among men, saving every race of men' (cf. *T. Sim.* 6.5; *T. Levi* 5.2).

In summary, the third major christological section of the nativity presents the same Davidic messianic theme present in the first two. Jesus is χριστὸς κύριος, the Davidic Christ born to a descendant of David in Bethlehem, the city of David. As the messiah, his chief role will be to bring salvation to God's people, salvation which no doubt will include both spiritual and physical dimensions. Exactly how this salvation will be worked out in Jesus' life, death and resurrection is not yet suggested.

d. *The Presentation in the Temple, Luke 2.22-38*

Though there is no mention of David in the story of Jesus' presentation at the temple, the repetition of various themes introduced earlier suggests that Luke is here staying close to the Davidic messianic theme which permeates the nativity. In vv. 25-26, the aged Simeon is said to be awaiting the 'Lord's Christ' (ὁ χριστὸς κυρίου). In the light of Luke's description of Jesus in 1.32-33 and 2.11, χριστὸς κυρίου must here mean the anointed king—the Davidic messiah. In the hymn which follows, the Nunc Dimittis, Simeon asks to depart in peace (cf. 1.79; 2.14) 'for my eyes have seen your salvation'. The phrase would recall for Luke's readers both the κέρας σωτηρίας from the house of David (Lk. 1.69) and the child born in Bethlehem, the σωτὴρ ὅς ἐστιν χριστὸς κύριος (Lk. 2.11). The use of the neuter adjective σωτήριον (cf. Isa. 40.5) instead of the feminine noun σωτηρία may serve to emphasize that it is not just the salvation but the salvation-bringer himself who is in view.[1] Finally, in the third couplet of the hymn, this salvation which God has prepared is presented as 'a light of revelation to the Gentiles'. As the messianic ἀνατολή from on high would shine on those living in darkness (Lk. 1.78-79), so now the 'Lord's Christ' is portrayed as a light of revelation to the Gentiles. We thus have a repetition of three ideas introduced earlier in the nativity, all of which are closely related to Jesus' Davidic messiahship.

A new aspect is here added to the fulfillment theme of the nativity. The salvation which God has prepared is described as φῶς εἰς ἀποκάλυψιν ἐθνῶν, καὶ δόξαν λαοῦ σου Ἰσραήλ. The first phrase is an allusion to Isa. 42.6 and 49.6, while the second recalls Isa. 46.13. 'Light' and 'glory' are probably parallel to one another and in apposition to σωτήριον in v. 30.[2] Up to this point in the narrative the benefits of

1. Marshall, *Gospel of Luke*, p. 120; Farris, *Hymns*, p. 147.

2. So Creed, *St. Luke*, p. 41; Farris, *Hymns*, p. 149. Others take 'glory' as appositional to 'revelation', and both governed by 'light'. The light would thus be for

salvation have been spoken of only for Israel. Now it is revealed that the salvation which the messiah will bring is not only for the glory of Israel, but will also shine the revelatory light of salvation on the Gentiles.

These scriptural allusions point to another key feature of the presentation account: the story is permeated with Isaianic images.[1] 'Israel's consolation' (παράκλησις τοῦ Ἰσραήλ) which Simeon anxiously awaits (v. 25) is a major theme of Isaiah 40-55 (Isa. 40.1; 49.13; 51.3; 52.9; 57.18; 61.2).[2] The Nunc Dimittis is also full of Isaianic allusions. In addition to the allusions to Isa. 42.6 and 49.6 in v. 32, the second couplet, ὅτι εἶδον οἱ ὀφθαλμοί μου τὸ σωτήριόν σου ὃ ἡτοίμασας κατὰ πρόσωπον πάντων τῶν λαῶν (vv. 30-31), bears similarities to Isa. 52.10 and Isa. 40.5 (LXX), which speak of salvation being revealed to all the world.[3] Finally, in v. 38 the prophetess Anna speaks with all those awaiting the 'redemption of Jerusalem' (cf. Isa. 52.9). While it would be going too far to say with Bock that 'in this section, Luke unveils a παῖς theology',[4] it is clear that Luke here begins to define the salvation Jesus will bring in Isaianic categories. And the sensitive reader of Luke's narrative might recall that the enigmatic 'servant' plays a key role in this salvation. Indeed, in Isa. 42.6 and Isa. 49.6 it is the servant who is 'a light to the nations'. As we shall see, these Isaianic categories will have

'a revelation for the Gentiles and for the glory of Israel' (so Brown, *Birth*, p. 440; Fitzmyer, *Luke I–IX*, p. 428). Against this position is the observation that in the Old Testament passages which form the background to this verse 'light' is closely associated with the Gentiles (Isa. 42.6; 49.6; 51.5 [LXX]). Similarly, glory is associated with Israel in this same section of Isaiah. Isa. 46.13 speaks of salvation in Zion for 'Israel my glory'. Cf. Isa. 60.1 for a similar parallelism of light and glory.

1. Again the reader is struck by the smooth merging of tradition and redaction in the Lukan story. Though the Nunc Dimittis is generally considered traditional for Luke, its Isaianic images overflow into the surrounding context as the author crafts his narrative into a unified composition.

2. In rabbinic tradition this terminology was used of the messianic hope and the messiah was sometimes given the name of *Menahem,* 'Consoler' (Str–B, I, pp. 66; II, pp. 124-26). Cf. Bock, *Proclamation*, pp. 85-86.

3. Isa. 40.5 LXX reads καὶ ὄψεται πᾶσα σὰρξ τὸ σωτήριον τοῦ θεοῦ. In the MT, the object of the phrase 'will see' is omitted, with no mention of salvation. The implied object is 'the glory of the Lord'. 'Salvation' has probably been added to the LXX translation through the influence of Isa. 52.10 or Ps. 98.2. Luke will cite Isa. 40.5 LXX in Lk. 3.6 with reference to the actions of John the Baptist. Cf. Bock, *Proclamation*, p. 86.

4. Bock, *Proclamation*, p. 87. Cf. p. 88: 'Here [in the nativity] the two themes of the promised Davidic heir and the victorious Servant are most influential for Luke.'

great importance for Luke in the subsequent Gospel narrative and in Acts.

The second oracle of Simeon introduces a new and ominous twist in the story. Following his oracle of praise in vv. 29-32, Simeon turns and addresses Mary: 'Behold this (child) is appointed for the fall and rise of many in Israel and for a sign provoking opposition (σημεῖον ἀντιλεγόμενον).' The statement marks a sudden change in tone. *For the first time in the narrative, opposition, conflict and division are associated with the coming of Jesus.* This will have profound significance for the subsequent narrative. The idea of rising and falling probably reflects a stone metaphor and refers to two responses to Jesus among those in Israel.[1] To some, the stone is stumbled over (Isa. 8.14-15); to others, it becomes a foundation stone to build upon (Isa. 28.16; Ps. 118.22). Luke will use this double stone image again in Lk. 20.17-18, citing Ps. 118.22 (cf. Mt. 21.42). The metaphor is traditional for Luke and was an important one for the early church, both to explain the rejection of Israel (cf. Rom. 9.30-32, citing Isa. 28.16) and to describe the foundation of the church (Eph. 2.20). Both images are found in 1 Pet. 2.6-8, which cites all three relevant Old Testament passages: Isa. 28.16, Ps. 118.22 and Isa. 8.14. If the reference to 'falling' in Lk. 2.34 is an allusion to Isa. 8.15 ('then they will fall and be broken'), the next phrase—that the child will be for a sign to be opposed—may allude to the same context. In Isa. 8.18, Isaiah and his children are said to be 'for signs and wonders in Israel'. This 'sign' imagery occurs repeatedly in the Isaianic oracles addressed to the house of David. In Isa. 7.14 the birth of the child to be called Immanuel is said to be a sign from the Lord. In addition, in Isa. 11.10 it is said that 'the nations will resort to the root of Jesse, who will stand as a *sign* (or, 'standard')[2] for the peoples'. Though the Hebrew word used here (נס) is different than that of Isa. 7.14 and Isa. 8.18 (אות), the LXX translates both as σημεῖον.[3] It is tempting, in light of the Davidic emphasis throughout the nativity, to suggest that the 'sign to be opposed' in v. 34 is the Davidic σημεῖον of Isa. 11.10. But it is probably going beyond the evidence to assume such

1. So Brown, *Birth*, p. 461; Plummer, *St. Luke*, p. 70; Schürmann, *Lukasevangelium*, I, p. 128; J. Jeremias, *TDNT*, VI, pp. 541-42. Marshall, however, prefers to see the rising and falling as a reference to a single group, who in their response to the messiah fall before they rise (*Gospel of Luke*, p. 122).

2. BDB, p. 651.

3. Brown, *Birth*, p. 461 n. 49.

an allusion would be apparent to the reader. The important point for Luke is that the appearance of the 'Lord's Christ' will result not only in acceptance and salvation, but also in resistance and opposition. This clearly moves beyond the portrait of the coming Davidic king in Judaism. While in Jewish expectation the messianic king often faces opposition and war from the Gentile nations, here it is 'many *in Israel*' who will fall, and who stand in opposition to the 'sign'. A clear note of warning is sounded in the story.

In summary, Simeon's oracles implicitly continue the Davidic messianic theme of the nativity by returning to various themes introduced earlier (the coming of the Christ; messianic salvation; the messiah as light). In addition, several new thoughts are introduced. The first is that the salvation brought by the messiah will be a light of revelation to the Gentiles as well as to the Jews. This idea of universal salvation is drawn from Isa. 42.6 and 49.65, and the presentation story as a whole is permeated with Isaianic motifs. Another new theme is the ominous prediction of Jewish rejection as well as acceptance. Though some will 'rise' in Israel, others will 'fall'; Jesus will be a 'sign' provoking opposition. This heralds a sudden change in tone. Up to this point, all responses to the messiah's birth have been positive ones of joy and rejoicing. With Simeon's second oracle it is revealed that some in Israel will respond to their messiah with opposition and rejection. As hinted at previously in the narrative, Jesus' royal-messianic identity moves beyond the bounds of contemporary Jewish expectation.

e. *The Boy Jesus in the Temple, Luke 2.41-51*

The last christological passage to be dealt with is the Jerusalem Passover visit of the twelve-year-old Jesus (Lk. 2.41-52). Properly speaking, the story is not part of the *infancy* narrative since it occurs many years after the events of Lk. 1–2.39.[1] It rather forms a transition to the adult ministry of Jesus and introduces an aspect of Jesus' divine sonship (unique relationship to the Father) which will be developed in more detail in the rest of the Gospel. This transitional role is evident in the passage's connection to both what precedes and what follows. Though structurally linked to the rest of the nativity in its closing statement concerning Jesus' growth and development (2.52; cf. 2.40), the story

1. See the discussions of Brown, *Birth*, pp. 479-80 and Fitzmyer, *Luke I–IX*, pp. 434-35. There are aspects of this story which both link it and separate it from the rest of the nativity.

contains the beginning of Jesus' self-revelation through his own words and deeds, rather than—as in the rest of the nativity—prophetic declarations of who he is (and will become) by others. Though structurally linked to *both* the nativity and the rest of the Gospel, the passage will be dealt with here since it, like the birth stories, contains material unique to Luke which prepares the reader for the account of Jesus' public ministry.

There is general agreement that the story is traditional for Luke (at least in its basic outline). The motif of a hero who shows unusual intelligence even as a child is common in Greek and Hellenistic biography and occurs in Hellenistic-Jewish writers like Philo and Josephus.[1] Its presence in *Jub*. 11.16 in relation to the fourteen-year-old Abraham's decision to forsake idols shows the motif is not limited to Hellenistic-Jewish circles. In its present form, Luke's story has two major themes: 'on the one hand, the surprising intelligence of the young Jesus (47); on the other hand, his awareness that God, as his real Father, has claims upon him, to which his parents have to take second place (49)'.[2] While most commentators emphasize the latter, there are indications that Luke, as final redactor, had a special interest in the former. Structurally, H.J. de Jonge suggests that the story is 'concentric symmetry', climaxing in the center with the statement of Jesus' amazing intelligence (vv. 46b-47).[3] This is not to say that Jesus' statement of allegiance to his Father in v. 49 does not form a second climax; yet while an earlier form of the story (without v. 47) may have stressed *only* this point, the present form clearly indicates an earlier climax in the wisdom motif of vv. 46b-47. If v. 47 is a Lukan addition, as many commentators suggest,[4] then Luke

1. Cf. the references in Bultmann, *History*, pp. 300-301; Creed, *St. Luke*, p. 44; H.J. de Jonge, 'Sonship, Wisdom, Infancy: Luke II.41-51a', *NTS* 24 (1978), pp. 317-54, esp. 339-42.

2. De Jonge, 'Sonship', p. 315.

3. De Jonge, 'Sonship', pp. 337-39, presents the following outline:

A. *Parodos:* Mary, Joseph and Jesus go to Jerusalem (ἀναβαινόντων, 41-2);
B. Jesus stays in Jerusalem, which is not noticed (43);
C. his parents seek and find him (44-6a);
X. Jesus among the doctors (46b-47);
C′. his parents, annoyed, reproach him (48);
B′. Jesus' reaction, which is not understood (49-50);
A′: *Exodos:* Jesus, Mary and Joseph return to Nazareth (κατέβη, 51a).

4. See especially the analysis of B.M.F. van Iersel, 'The Finding of Jesus in the Temple: Some Observations on the Original Form of Luke ii 40-51a', *NovT* 4 (1960), pp. 161-73, who suggests that vv. 44 and 47 are Lukan additions to an earlier story.

has not only introduced the motif of wisdom into the story, but has also intentionally structured the story to climax with this motif (if de Jonge's structural analysis is correct). On the other hand, it cannot be concluded with certainty that Luke himself added v. 47.[1] While the presence of Lukan vocabulary suggests that Luke has re-worked the story as a whole, this does not mean that he was the first to introduce the motif of wisdom. More convincing evidence for Luke's special interest in the boy Jesus' amazing intelligence are his transitional statements in vv. 40 and 52. In both, it is emphasized that Jesus was filled with (v. 40), or grew in (v. 52) *wisdom*. Luke thus makes a statement about Jesus' wisdom, tells a story which highlights this characteristic, then concludes with his continued increase in wisdom. Luke's own introduction and conclusion should thus warn against over-emphasizing the second climax of the pericope (allegiance to his Father) and ignoring the first (amazing wisdom). Both were clearly important for Luke and, in fact, his redactional comments serve to emphasize the former.[2]

Various allusions have been suggested for the wisdom motif, including the description of Samuel in 1 Sam. 2.21, 26 (cf. 1 Sam. 3.1; Prov. 3.1-4)[3] and the young Sirach in Sir. 51.13-17.[4] Neither of these parallels is wholly appropriate, however; the former does not even mention Samuel's wisdom[5] and the latter speaks of Sirach's early and eager desire to seek wisdom, rather than his possession of it. Luke's point is that Jesus already possessed wisdom at an early age, and continued to increase in it even more.[6] A better parallel is to be found in the Second Temple descriptions of the eschatological deliverer as one particularly endowed with wisdom: the coming Davidic king (*Pss. Sol.* 17.37; 4QIsa[a] fr. C 10-11; cf. 1QSb 5.25); the 'elect one' (*1 En.* 49.3); the 'new priest'

Cf. de Jonge, 'Sonship', pp. 342-45; Nolland, *Luke 1-9:20*, p. 130.

1. Cf. Schürmann, *Lukasevangelium*, I, pp. 134-35, and the careful comments of de Jonge, 'Sonship', pp. 344-45.

2. Notice, too, that Luke's redactional comment in v. 51, that Jesus submitted himself to the will of his parents, actually tones down—albeit very slightly—the second climax.

3. U. Wilckens, *TDNT*, VII, p. 514.

4. G. Stählin, *TDNT*, VI, p. 713.

5. This is not to say that Luke's statements in vv. 40 and 52 may not have been partially modelled on 1 Sam. 2.26 ('growth in stature and favour'). But the wisdom motif could not have been taken from this passage and so must have come from somewhere else.

6. De Jonge, 'Sonship', p. 348.

(*T. Levi* 18.7; cf. 2.3).[1] As we have seen, the direct or indirect source of these statements is the prophecy of the coming Davidic king in Isa. 11.1-3. The LXX reads (parallels to Lk. 2.40 in bold type):

καὶ ἐξελεύσεται ῥάβδος ἐκ τῆς ῥίζης Ἰεσσαί,
καὶ ἄνθος ἐκ τῆς ῥίζης ἀναβήσεται.
καὶ ἀναπαύσεται **ἐπ' αὐτὸν** πνεῦμα **τοῦ θεοῦ**,
πνεῦμα **σοφίας** καὶ συνέσεως,
πνεῦμα βουλῆς καὶ ἰσχύος,
πνεῦμα γνώσεως καὶ ευσεβείας, **ἐμπλήσει αὐτὸν** πνεῦμα φόβου θεοῦ.

There is a clear similarity in thought to Lk. 2.40 (cf. vv. 47, 52), where Jesus is said to be πληρούμενον σοφίᾳ, καὶ χάρις θεοῦ ἦν ἐπ' αὐτό. This is especially so in the LXX (diff. MT), which speaks in Isa. 11.3 of the spirit 'filling' him. Luke may have substituted χάρις for πνεῦμα (cf. Isa. 11.2), since he has not yet described the descent of the Spirit upon Jesus at his baptism (Lk. 3.22).[2] The close relationship for Luke between God's Spirit and his grace as divine power in the life of an individual is evident in Acts 4.31-33, where the disciples are 'all filled with the Holy Spirit...and abundant grace was upon them'.

It seems justified, therefore, to conclude with de Jonge that: 'Luke ii. 41-51 is a biographical rendering of the traditional conception that the messiah would be endowed by God with wisdom and understanding (σοφία, 40; σύνεσις, 47)'.[3] I would add that the strongly Davidic messianic character of the birth stories which precede this episode further suggests that Luke has the royal-Davidic context of Isaiah 11 (cf. *Pss. Sol.* 17) in view and wishes to emphasize the Spirit-endowed wisdom of the *Davidic* messiah. At the same time, Luke uses the pericope to begin developing the conception of Jesus' unique relationship to God as his Father—an idea which (as we have seen) does not necessarily leave the realm of the Davidic promises.

4. *Conclusion*

This examination of the Davidic promises in the Lukan birth narrative has demonstrated conclusively that Davidic messiahship represents the controlling Christology of Luke's introductory section.[4] Of the five

1. Cf. de Jonge, 'Sonship',
2. Compare Lk. 1.80, where it is said that John ἐκραταιοῦτο πνεύματι.
3. De Jonge, 'Sonship', 349.
4. Bock, *Proclamation*, pp. 55, 80, reaches this same conclusion: 'An examination

major christological sections—the Annunciation (1.26-38), the Benedictus (1.68-76), the Birth Story (2.1-20), the Presentation in the Temple (2.8-20) and the Passover visit to Jerusalem (2.41-52)[1]—the first three are explicitly Davidic-messianic, and the fourth and fifth are implicitly so.[2]

In addition to establishing a controlling Christology, the present chapter has demonstrated that Luke uses the infancy narrative as an introduction to and preparation for his presentation in the rest of Luke–Acts.[3] This might suggest that Davidic messiahship is programmatic and definitional for Luke's christological purpose in Luke–Acts. Jesus is *introduced and defined* as the one who will fulfill the Old Testament promise made to David.

At the same time, *how* Jesus will fulfill this promise is barely suggested. Rather, statements concerning Jesus are couched in strongly Old Testament and Jewish terminology and concepts. While Jesus' wondrous Spirit-conception as Son of God (1.35), his humble birth (2.7) and the opposition his coming will provoke (2.34) all begin to hint that Jesus' messiahship will exceed traditional expectations, these are adumbrations only. In general, the narrative stays remarkably close to the language of the promise. In Lk. 1.32-35 Jesus is introduced as the Son of the Most High, appointed by the Lord God to reign over the house of

of what is here [in the nativity] explicitly declared about Jesus reveals one clear theme. Jesus is the awaited Davidic ruler.'

1. There is also Elizabeth's statement in 1.43 but this can hardly be called a 'christological section'.

2. An objection may be raised at this point as to whether Luke actually has a special literary interest in this Davidic theme or whether (since Matthew's birth narrative is also strongly royal-Davidic: Mt. 1.1, 16, 17, 20; cf. 2.1, 2, 4-6), he is merely repeating material taken over from his sources. While Luke's sources almost certainly contained references to Jesus' Davidic descent and messiahship, nevertheless it is significant that: (1) as demonstrated above, the birth narrative is introductory and programmatic for Luke, confirming that the themes introduced here are important to him; (2) Luke has artistically chosen, edited and re-worked his sources into a continuous and unified narrative; (3) within this continuity, Luke repeatedly returns to the Davidic messianic theme; and finally (4), as will be demonstrated in Chapter 4, Luke picks up this theme again in the speeches in Acts that are programmatic for his Christology as a whole.

3. This is especially so if, as Brown, Fitzmyer and others suggest, the nativity was added by Luke after the Gospel (or even the whole of Luke–Acts) was completed. This would indicate that Luke had already clearly defined his purpose and determined those themes which he most wanted to stress. See Fitzmyer, *Luke I–IX*, p. 311; Brown, *Birth*, pp. 242-43.

Jacob forever on the throne of his father David. He is the 'horn of salvation' and 'dawn from on high' raised up in the house of David to bring salvation from enemies to his people and to permit free and unhindered worship of the Lord God (1.68-79). Through the use of this 'promise' language, Luke has created an air of anticipation for his readers. How does this nationalistic and political sounding language apply to the crucified, resurrected and ascended Jesus? If Jesus is not now reigning on an earthly Davidic throne in Jerusalem, how can he be the Christ, the one to fulfill the promise set forth in Luke 1.32-33? Through the dominance of the Davidic messianic theme in the nativity, Luke has implicitly set this question before his readers. This suggests that the nature of Jesus' messiahship is an important concern for the Lukan community and may indicate a context within that community of apologetic dialogue with the Jews. In the subsequent Gospel narrative and in Acts, Luke will answer these questions.

The following chapter will examine the Davidic promise theme in Acts. The reason for skipping the Gospel narrative and moving directly to Acts is threefold. First, several of the key speeches in Acts, like the nativity, are strongly royal-Davidic in their emphasis. To confirm Luke's overall understanding and interpretation of this theme it will be helpful to move directly to its climax. Secondly, (and related to this) as suggested above (section 2) a number of themes introduced in the birth narrative are brought to narrative conclusion in Acts, including Jesus' status as 'Christ' and 'Lord', his Davidic enthronement at the right hand of God and Gentile acceptance and Jewish rejection of the Gospel. By moving directly to Acts, Luke's total perspective on these themes can be better appreciated. Finally, since the speeches in Acts are generally considered to be examples *par excellence* of Lukan theology and purpose, this study should confirm or disprove the primacy of the royal-messianic theme in Luke's 'proclamation from prophecy' motif.

Excursus

'SON OF DAVID' OR 'NEW DAVID'?

As we have seen, Luke's presentation in the birth narrative confirms his special interest in Jesus' Davidic descent. It is surprising, therefore, when G. Voss claims that Luke intentionally avoids designating Jesus as a descendant of David.[1] This is part of his argument that Luke's perspective on Jesus' Davidic descent is based on a particular interpretation of Isa. 7.14, which Luke probably alludes to in Lk. 1.31.[2] According to Voss, the reference to the 'young woman' (Heb: עלמה; Gk: παρθένος) in Isa. 7.14 refers more to marital freedom—and so to illegitimacy—than to sexual virginity. It is thus the sign-character of the prophecy, rather than its miraculous nature, which is central. Since Ahaz, who represents the sinful Davidic line of kings, has forsaken God, the prophet predicts that God will break the normal throne-succession and will raise up a new David, an 'illegitimate' 'sprout from the root of *Jesse*' (Isa. 11.1). The name of the child, 'God with us' (Immanuel), shows that God holds to his promises to save his people; but since the ruling Davidic house has lost its saving function, God will begin a new work, raising up a new shoot from Jesse.[3] Voss claims that Luke takes up this interpretation of Isa. 7.14 and so presents Jesus as a new David rather than a Davidic descendant. He points to the following evidence: (1) Luke avoids designating Jesus as a descendant of David; it is Joseph, rather than Mary, who in 1.27 and 2.4 is from David's line. Voss follows M. Dibelius in claiming that Luke's source in 1.27 originally referred to *Mary's* Davidic descent, and that Luke has intentionally altered this to refer to Joseph.[4] He thus changes a natural descent from David into a

1. Voss, *Christologie*, p. 68.
2. See above, Chapter 3 section 3a.
3. Voss, *Christologie*, pp. 67-68.
4. Voss, *Christologie*, p. 68. The phrase would thus originally have read, 'to a virgin of the seed of David, whose name was Mary'.

legal one. This same view is expressed in the genealogy, where Jesus is '*supposedly* (ὡς ἐνομίζετο) the son of Joseph...the son of David'. Voss also sees significance in Luke's use of ἐν instead of ἐκ in Lk. 1.69. Jesus the 'horn of salvation' is said to be raised up 'in' David's house, not 'from' or 'out of' that house. In addition, Luke never uses the late-Jewish designation 'shoot' of David, and only the blind man outside Jericho (18.38-39) calls Jesus 'son of David'. How can the messiah be called the son of David when David himself in Ps. 110.1 calls him 'Lord' (Lk. 20.41-44)? Thus, while affirming Jesus' legal right to David's throne, Voss claims that Luke rejects his natural descent from David. (2) Luke's genealogy, which traces Jesus' descent through Nathan, instead of through the kingly line of Solomon, shows his opposition to the kingly line. (3) Jesus is born not in Jerusalem, where David reigned, but in Bethlehem, where he was born. This points to David's origin instead of a royal succession coming through his sons. (4) Finally, Voss considers the expression ἀνατολὴ ἐξ ὕψους in Lk. 1.78, to be an allusion combining the messianic 'branch' (cf. Zech. 6.12 LXX) with the 'star' rising from Jacob (Num. 24.17). In Luke's case, however, the star rises not from Jacob, but ἐξ ὕψους, from the heavenly heights, the presence of God himself. Luke thus rejects an earthly origin of Jesus in favour of a heavenly one.[1]

In drawing these conclusions, Voss makes a distinction between legal and natural descent, which was clearly not an issue for Luke. While it is true that Jesus is only 'in the minds of the people'[2] (ὡς ἐνομίζετο) the *physical* son of Joseph (3.23; cf. 4.22), this does not make him any less a legitimate Davidic descendant or heir to the Davidic throne. ὡς ἐνομίζετο rather reminds the reader of the virgin birth and, like Jesus' statement in Lk. 2.49, points to God as his true heavenly Father to whom he owes highest allegiance; it does not deny that Joseph is his legitimate earthly father.[3] Dibelius' proposal that Lk. 1.27 originally referred to *Mary's* Davidic descent is speculative and unlikely. The emphasis

1. Voss, *Christologie*, pp. 69-72. Earlier in his presentation, Voss notes that Luke adds the title 'king' to the Markan entry account but drops the mention of David (p. 61).

2. Fitzmyer's translation (*Luke I–IX*, pp. 488, 499).

3. Cf. Marshall, *Gospel of Luke*, p. 157: 'There is no inconsistency in Luke's mind between the account of the virgin birth and the naming of Joseph as one of the parents of Jesus. From the legal point of view, Joseph was the earthly father of Jesus, and there was no other way of reckoning his descent. There is no evidence that the compilers of the genealogies thought otherwise'.

throughout the synoptic tradition is on Joseph's Davidic descent; there is no reason to suppose that the reference in 1.27 was originally to Mary.[1]

That Luke does not distinguish between legal and natural descent when referring to Jesus' Davidic descent is clear from his choice of language. He sees no discrepancy in referring to David as 'his father David' (1.32), and even using such physical-sounding language as 'from the fruit of his (David's) loins (ἐκ καρποῦ τῆς ὀσφύος αὐτοῦ)' (Acts 2.30) and 'from the seed (ἀπὸ τοῦ σπέρματος) of this man' (Acts 13.23). If Luke wanted to downplay Jesus' natural descent from David he surely would not have referred to him as coming from David's seed and David's loins!

Neither is there evidence that Luke intentionally avoids the son of David title; he takes over both Markan passages in which the title occurs (Lk. 18.35-43; 20.41-44). As we shall see (Chapter 6 section 5e), the traditional *Davidssohnfrage* in Lk. 20.41-44 is not meant to deny Jesus' Davidic descent, as Voss seems to suggest, but is used by Luke to show that Jesus is *both* David's son and David's lord. Further, whatever is to be made of Luke's genealogy, it *does* trace Jesus' descent through David (Lk. 3.31; see Chapter 5 section 2c). Why would Luke include a genealogy at all if not to show the importance and legitimacy of Jesus' descent? Voss confuses a separate issue when he points to Jesus' descent through the non-kingly line of Nathan. While this may be an intentional rejection of the sinful line of Solomonic kings, it does not deny Davidic descent in favour of a 'new David' descended from Jesse. The genealogy still goes back to David!

Jesus is thus presented as a legitimate *son* of David, not simply as a 'new David'. This is in line with contemporary Jewish expectations, which merged and mixed these two concepts. Jewish hope in both cases centered on a figure who would return the nation to the glory and splendour of the Davidic era and bring in a new age of peace, security and prosperity. Whether this Davidic figure is called 'David's seed', 'shoot', 'son of David' or simply 'David', the expectations are roughly the same. The model and prototype is David himself, the greatest of Israel's kings. In light of this, Jesus' birth in Bethlehem cannot be said to argue in favour of a 'new David' and against a 'son of David'. Matthew frequently refers to Jesus as son of David and at the same time affirms

1. Burger, *Jesus als Davidssohn*, p. 133, further argues that it is inconceivable that Luke would suppress a tradition which could have spared him the trouble of connecting the virgin birth with the genealogy of Joseph.

his Bethlehem birth. Nor is ἀνατολὴ ἐξ ὕψους in Lk. 1.78 a significant argument for Voss's view. Though probably alluding indirectly to Num. 24.17 and other passages, the phrase in no way sets Jesus' coming from God in contrast to his earthly lineage. In fact, Jesus' descent from David is affirmed earlier in the *Benedictus* (Lk. 1.69). There is no evidence in this latter passage that Luke has altered an original ἐκ to ἐν to downplay Jesus' Davidic descent. While it is fitting to refer to one's descent as ἐξ οἴκου καὶ πατριᾶς Δαυίδ (Lk. 2.4), the phrase with ἐγείρω in 1.69 makes ἐν οἴκῳ Δαυίδ the better construction in this case. It is more natural to say that one is raised up 'in' a house, than 'from' or 'out of' a house.

We may conclude that for Luke Jesus' Davidic descent is just as authentic and real whether he is a legal or a natural son of Joseph.[1] The virgin birth in no way abrogates this position and status. Luke's genealogy proves that Jesus is truly David's son and heir to his father's throne.

1. Ellis, *Gospel of Luke*, pp. 71, 84, points out that this is in line with Semitic thought patterns, which would regard Jesus' relationship to Joseph as 'real', as well as legal, sonship.

Chapter 4

THE FULFILLMENT OF THE PROMISE ACHIEVED: THE SPEECHES OF ACTS

1. *Introduction*

It is widely accepted that the missionary speeches in Acts provide special insight into the christological perspective and purpose of Luke.[1] The words of G.W.H. Lampe over thirty years ago are still appropriate today:

> Whether, however, we ought to consider the missionary speeches...as Lk's own composition—his summaries of the gospel as he understood it—; whether they represent the authentic thought and language of the actual individuals, Peter, Stephen and Paul; or whether they embody an accurate tradition of the sort of thing said by all primitive missionaries—the common form of the early kerygma—, the fact remains that Lk. has embodied them in his work in order to teach his readers what the Christian gospel means. They are obviously intended to play a large part in the achievement of the purpose of Luke–Acts...It would seem improbable that the interests of an evangelist would be so little theological and so powerfully and scientifically historical as to allow him to reproduce for his readers versions of the gospel which he himself believed to be inadequate but which he retained because he knew them to be historically appropriate on the lips of his characters.[2]

The purpose in this chapter, like that of the birth narrative, is two-fold: (1) First, to establish the *importance* of the Davidic promise tradition in the narrative of Acts. As pointed out above, the importance of the speeches as a whole in relation to Lukan theology is well established. The following discussion will demonstrate that two of these speeches, those in Acts 2 and 13, are of particular Lukan importance. As the

1. This is the view of most scholars, whether the speeches are considered to contain much traditional material, or whether they are viewed primarily as Lukan compositions.

2. G.W.H. Lampe, 'The Lucan Portrait of Christ', *NTS* 2 (1955–56), p. 161.

inaugural addresses of Luke's two main characters, Peter and Paul, they represent exemplary models of Luke's view of the apostolic and Pauline kerygma to Jews (and in Acts 13 to Godfearers). These speeches thus have a purpose parallel to the nativity. As the first two chapters of the Gospel introduced Jesus' identity to characters symbolic of the pious of Israel awaiting their messiah, so these speeches proclaim who Jesus is and what he has accomplished to the rest of Israel. Both the nativity and the speeches in Acts 2 and 13 will be shown to be christologically introductory and programmatic for Luke's promise-fulfillment motif. It is highly significant, therefore, that both are strongly Davidic messianic. In addition to these two proclamatory addresses, the address of James at the Council of Jerusalem, with its key citation of Amos 9.11-12, will be shown to have special Lukan significance.

(2) The second goal of the chapter is to examine *how* Luke conceives of the Davidic promises as fulfilled in Jesus. This will be accomplished by an examination of Luke's christological purpose in the passages in Acts where the Davidic-promise theme appears.

2. *Peter's Pentecost Speech, Acts 2.14-41*

a. *The Significance of the Speech in the Narrative of Acts*

The account of the outpouring of the Spirit on the Day of Pentecost (Acts 2.1-13) forms the contextual background for Peter's first speech in Acts. A number of factors point to the importance of this address in Luke's narrative.

(1) First is the position of the speech in the context of Acts. Though Peter has already given a short address concerning the replacement of Judas (1.16-22), the Pentecost speech is the first missionary proclamation of the apostles. Since the key theme of Acts is the advancement of the gospel message from Jerusalem outward (1.8), the reader is looking for an example of the content of this proclamation. By its very position, the speech is likely to be a summation of Luke's interpretation of the proclamation of the gospel to Israel.

(2) Second is the association of the speech with the outpouring of the Spirit at Pentecost. The great significance of the Spirit in Lukan theology has been noted already.[1] The Pentecost event of Acts 2.1-13 and the speech which follows describe the initiatory activity of the Spirit in relation to the church. This climactic event, anticipated at the end of

1. See Chapter 3 section 2b.

Luke's Gospel and the beginning of Acts (Lk. 24.49; Acts 1.5), is of decisive importance in Luke's scheme. The Spirit in Acts will be not only the guide and power behind the church but represents the very presence of God (Acts 5.9; 8.39) and of Jesus (Acts 16.7). It is likely, therefore, that the speech which accompanies the event of the initial outpouring of the Spirit is of great significance for Luke's purpose.

(3) Finally, it is significant that Peter is the one who delivers the speech. For Luke, Peter will be the leading character of the first twelve chapters of Acts. He is portrayed as the leader of the apostolic band and what he says here and elsewhere is viewed by Luke as representing the apostolic preaching as a whole (2.14, 37; 5.29; cf. 1.15ff.; 3.6; 3.12ff.; 4.8ff.; 5.3ff.; 5.15; 8.12ff.; 9.32ff.; 10.1ff.; 11.1ff.; 12.3ff.).

The speech of Acts 2 may therefore be seen as representing for Luke the apostolic kerygma *par excellence,* and is likely to be introductory and programmatic for his proclamatory message throughout Acts. A similar conclusion is reached by many scholars. J. Roloff says that 'In the framework of Acts, Peter's Pentecost Sermon has programmatic significance',[1] and L. Goppelt claims that Acts 2 'systematically summarizes at the very outset the content of Acts just as the Nazareth pericope summarizes in a similar fashion the content of Luke's Gospel'.[2] R.F. Zehnle writes that 'Acts 2 is the "keynote address" of Acts, a summary statement of the theological viewpoint of the author from which the subsequent unfolding of the book is to be understood'.[3] Similar statements are to be found in many writers.[4]

b. *Overview, Structure and Unity of the Speech*

i. *Overview*. The speech of Peter is prompted by the amazed and mocking reaction of the Jerusalem crowds when they hear the Spirit-inspired *glossalalia* of the disciples on the Day of Pentecost. Peter responds by citing Joel 2.28-32 (3.1-5a MT)[5] to demonstate that the tongue-speaking is the fulfillment of Joel's prophecy that in the last

1. J. Roloff, *Die Apostelgeschichte* (1981), p. 48.
2. L. Goppelt, *Apostolic and Post-Apostolic Times* (1970), p. 22.
3. R.F. Zehnle, *Peter's Pentecost Discourse* (1971), p. 17; cf. pp. 61-70, 95-130.
4. Cf. for example O. Betz, 'The Kerygma of Luke', *Int* 22 (1968), p. 133; Robinson, 'Most Primitive Christology?', p. 185, says that 'Acts 2 comes to us as the most finished and polished specimen of the apostolic preaching, placed as it were in the shop window of the Jerusalem Church and of Luke's narrative.'
5. See Bock, *Proclamation*, pp. 156-63, for a discussion of the citation's possible sources, textual variants, and alterations from the LXX.

days[1] God would pour out his Spirit on all mankind, resulting in prophetic utterances by God's people (vv. 14-21). The remainder of the speech is a kerygmatic summary of the life, death, resurrection and exaltation of Jesus (vv. 22-36), followed by a response from the hearers (v. 37) and a call to repentance (vv. 38-40). The climax is reached in v. 36, where Peter proclaims: 'Therefore let all the house of Israel know assuredly that God has made him both Lord and Christ—this Jesus whom you crucified.' This declaration results in a response of dismay from the hearers, who cry out, 'Brethren, what shall we do?' Peter responds with a call to repentance and baptism in the name of Jesus Christ, 'and you shall receive the gift of the Holy Spirit'. Those who repent and acknowledge Jesus as Lord and Christ thus become part of the eschatological people of God and receive the gift of the Spirit, the sign of the new age. The success of Peter's sermon is extraordinary. In v. 41 Luke reports that more than three thousand receive Peter's word and are baptized.

ii. *Structure*. The speech itself may be conveniently divided into three parts: (1) the Pentecost event as fulfillment of the prophecy of Joel 2.28-32 (vv. 14-21); (2) the kerygma of Jesus' life, death, resurrection and exaltation as enabling the fulfillment of the Joel prophecy (vv. 22-36); and (3) Peter's call for repentance following the response of the crowd in v. 37 (vv. 38-41). While some commentators divide the middle section into two because of the renewed address to the hearers in verse 29,[2] this is not appropriate since the resurrection argument which begins in vv. 24-28 is not actually completed until v. 32. A better division may be between

1. The substitution of ἐν ταῖς ἐσχάταις ἡμέραις (cf. Isa. 2.2) for the LXX μετὰ ταῦτα emphasizes that the coming of the Spirit is associated with the last days. E. Haenchen, *The Acts of the Apostles* (1971), p. 179, contends on dogmatic grounds that the text of B (μετὰ ταῦτα) should be preferred since in Lukan theology the last days do not begin as soon as the Spirit has been poured out. Most commentators have rejected this view, taking the B text as an assimilation to the LXX. So G. Schneider, *Die Apostelgeschichte* (1980), I, p. 68; R. Pesch, *Die Apostelgeschichte* (1986), I, pp. 119-20; I.H. Marshall, *The Acts of the Apostles* (1980), p. 73; Roloff, *Apostelgeschichte*, p. 53; A. Weiser, *Apostelgeschichte Kapitel 1-12* (1982), pp. 91-92. Weiser (p. 92) says that Luke does not wish to say with the Joel text that *now* the end times have begun; rather the whole period since the time of Jesus' activity constitutes the end times.

2. So for example Schneider, *Apostelgeschichte*, I, pp. 263-64; Pesch, *Apostelgeschichte*, I, p. 116.

vv. 32 and 33, since this marks the transition from the resurrection argument from Ps. 16.8-11 (vv. 24-32) to the exaltation-enthronement argument from Ps. 110.1 (vv. 33-35). On the other hand, since both sections climax together at v. 36 it seems best to view vv. 22-36 as a single unit.

iii. *Unity*. While portions of a pre-Lukan Pentecost speech may perhaps be perceived behind the narrative, in its Lukan context the speech forms a unified whole. This unity may be seen in vv. 33, 36, and 38-40, which link the latter two sections to the first. In v. 33, following the scriptural proof of the resurrection from Psalms 16 and 132, Peter links Jesus' exaltation at the right hand of God directly to the pouring out of the Spirit and the quote from Joel 2.28-32 (3.1-5a MT, LXX). Further, Luke's inclusion of the extended quotation from Joel is almost certainly to reach the final statement of Joel 2.32a (3.5a): πᾶς ὃς ἂν ἐπικαλέσηται τὸ ὄνομα κυρίου σωθήσεται (Acts 2.21). At the climax of the speech, then, Jesus is declared to be κύριος and χριστός (v. 36), and Peter calls the hearers to repentance, urging them to be baptized ἐπὶ τῷ ὀνόματι Ἰησοῦ Χριστοῦ for the forgiveness of their sins and to receive the gift of the Spirit (vv. 38-40). Both the reference to Jesus as 'Lord' and baptism in his 'name' recall Joel 3.5a (MT) and the salvation which comes from calling on the name of the Lord. Finally, in v. 39 Peter alludes again to the quotation of Joel at the point where he left off in v. 21: 'For the promise is to you and to your children, and for all that are far off, everyone whom the Lord our God calls to him' (v. 39; cf. Joel 3.5b LXX: οὓς κύριος προσκέκληται). Thus in both the second and third sections of the speech, reference is made back to the outpouring of the Spirit described in 2.1-13 and interpreted by Peter in vv. 14-21.

While these connecting links indicate that the discourse as a whole is structured around the Pentecostal outpouring of the Spirit, the main body of the speech (and its climax) is christological, explaining the scriptural significance of Jesus' death, resurrection and exaltation. The chief concern of the discussion which follows is to determine the main christological thrust of the passage. It will be demonstrated that both the resurrection argument of vv. 22-32 and the exaltation argument of vv. 33-35 focus on the theme of God's fulfillment of promises made to David. Finally, it will be asked whether there may not be a Moses-typology alluded to in v. 33 with reference to Jesus' exaltation and pouring out of the Spirit.

a. *Christological Themes and Purpose*

i. *The Death and Resurrection of the Davidic Christ (vv. 22-32).* Verses 22-24 summarize Jesus' life and wrongful death and set the stage for the resurrection argument which follows. Though Jesus was a man attested by God through miracles, wonders and signs,[1] he was rejected and put to death by his people, who used the Gentiles as their instruments.[2] As elsewhere in Luke–Acts, Jesus' death is presented as a paradox: though the Gentiles and people of Israel acted wrongly in crucifying Jesus, nevertheless it was part of God's purpose and plan that this should happen (v. 23; cf. Lk. 22.22; 24.26-27, 46; Acts 3.18; 4.25-28; 17.3; 26.23).[3]

Though godless men put Jesus to death, God vindicated him by raising him from the dead (v. 24).[4] The resurrection is described as God 'loosing the (birth)pangs of death' (λύσας τὰς ὠδῖνας τοῦ θανάτου). The expression αἱ ὠδῖνες τοῦ θανάτου is a Septuagintism, appearing in 2 Sam. 22.6, Ps. 17.5 LXX and Ps. 114.3 LXX as a translation of חבל מות, 'cords of death'. Presumably the LXX translator misread the Hebrew חבלי as חֵבֶל, ('pain', usually 'birthpang'), instead of correctly as חֶבֶל, 'cord'. Thus a loosening of the 'cords' (= power) of death becomes a releasing of the '(birth)pangs' of death.[5] How Luke understands the unusual phrase is a matter of much debate: (1) Some commentators suggest that death is here metaphorically portrayed as a woman in

1. Luke may here be drawing a conscious allusion to the apocalyptic signs of v. 19 (τέρατα ἐν τῷ οὐρανῷ ἄνω καὶ σημεῖα ἐπὶ τῆς κάτω; note the additions of σημεῖα and κάτω in v. 19 to the LXX text). This would suggest that for Luke, the precursors of the signs which will herald the coming of the Day of the Lord were present in the miracles of Jesus. Alternatively, the signs in v. 19 may refer to the Pentecost event itself and/or the miracles which the apostles will perform later in Acts (cf. 2.43). It is possible, of course, that Luke has all three in view.

2. διὰ χειρὸς ἀνόμων. Ἄνομος is used especially of the Romans in Jewish writings (Haenchen, *Acts*, p. 180 n. 11).

3. Pesch, *Apostelgeschichte*, I, p. 121, writes: 'Lukas markiert seine Theologie vom Plan Gottes, der sich im gläubigen Handeln der Menschen realisiert und sich trotz ihrer Verweigerung durchsetzt.'

4. This *Kontrastschema*—the sinful actions of men in putting Jesus to death contrasted with God's righteous actions in raising him—is common in Acts (3.13-15; 4.10; 5.30-31; 10.38-40) and will recur in a Davidic context in 13.27-30.

5. So Haenchen, *Acts*, p. 180; Schneider, *Apostelgeschichte*, I, p. 272; Roloff, *Apostelgeschichte*, p. 56; many others. For alternatives to an LXX mistranslation see the views of Bock and Bratcher below.

labour unable to hold back the birth of the messiah.[1] God releases (= brings to an end) death's travail when she gives up Jesus. (2) Since ὠδίν sometimes means pain in general (Exod. 15.14; Deut. 2.25; Job 21.17) rather than specifically birthpang (1 Sam. 4.19; Job 39.2), others interpret the phrase to mean a release of Jesus from the pain or anguish of death.[2] (3) Haenchen, followed by Pesch, suggests that the 'death-pangs' are here regarded as a 'mysterious expression for the power of death'.[3] Jesus' resurrection releases him from death's *power.* Bratcher reaches a similar interpretation by arguing that ὠδῖνες is an accurate translation of חֶבֶל, and here means 'cords' or 'bonds'.[4] (4) Since the context of all three Old Testament passages contains the ideas of distress in the face of death *and* of death as encircling power, Bock thinks the LXX translator has consciously mixed his metaphors, bringing in both elements in the phrase. The New Testament image would thus be one of Jesus' release from death's pain in a context where death is viewed as encircling cords (a combination of views 2 and 3).[5]

A solution to this question is difficult since all four interpretations are grammatically unusual. Since ὠδίν *can* mean pain in general, and since neither Luke's context nor the LXX passages in which the phrase occur seem to indicate birth pain, there seems no reason to posit the metaphor of a woman in travail. While it is unlikely that the phrase itself means *both* release from pain and release from death, the fact that Luke concludes v. 24 with the phrase καθότι οὐκ ἦν δυνατὸν κρατεῖσθαι αὐτὸν ὑπ' αὐτοῦ, suggests he has the LXX context of death as an encircling power in view. It seems likely, then, that Luke uses the phrase—which itself means release from pain—to recall its wider LXX context[6] and so introduce the twin themes that Jesus is freed from his

1. So Lövestam, *Son and Saviour*, pp. 43-45; BAGD, p. 483; Marshall, *Acts*, pp. 75, 76; G. Bertram, *TDNT*, IX, p. 673; and many others.

2. So Schneider, *Apostelgeschichte*, I, p. 272 n. 77, and many English translations (NASB, NIV, Phillips, Jerusalem Bible, etc.).

3. Haenchen, *Acts*, p. 180; Pesch, *Apostelgeschichte*, I, pp. 121-22. Strangely, Haenchen still considers the phrase to be a mistranslation of the Hebrew.

4. R.G. Bratcher, 'Having Loosed the Pangs of Death', *The Bible Translator* 10 (1959), pp. 18-20. He draws this conclusion because of the LXX context, which contains the thought of active peril or danger, and from the implausibility of other interpretations in Acts 2.24. The problem is this meaning of ὠδῖνες is unattested elsewhere.

5. Bock, *Proclamation*, pp. 171-72.

6. That Luke has introduced this unusual phrase in this context at all suggests that he is aware of its LXX context. If he had simply found it in his source (and was

anguish when death is compelled to release him.

The statement of death's inability to hold Jesus sets the stage for the resurrection argument which follows (vv. 25-31). In these verses Peter presents Ps. 16.8-11 (LXX 15.8-11) as proof that the resurrection of the Christ was prophesied beforehand in Scripture. David is assumed to be the author of the psalm, but David spoke concerning another: Δαυὶδ γὰρ λέγει εἰς αὐτόν. What Peter means by εἰς αὐτόν becomes clear in the verses which follow. Not only was David speaking *about* the messiah, but he was speaking prophetically in the voice of the messiah. While in Acts 13.35 Paul will cite only v. 10b of the psalm, here Peter cites vv. 8-11.[1] Luke probably includes vv. 8-9a to demonstrate the intimacy of Jesus' fellowship with God throughout his life, and especially in his hour of death (cf. Lk. 23.46).[2] The statement thus provides an indirect link to the divine attestation of Jesus' ministry in v. 22. The 'ways of life' in v. 11 (Acts 2.28) are probably understood as Jesus' path to resurrection life, but may also refer to the way to eternal life which Jesus, the ἀρχηγὸς ζωῆς (Acts 3.15), opened up.[3] Verses 9b-10 form the key to the resurrection argument (Acts 2.26b-28):

> Moreover my flesh will abide in hope,
> Because you will not abandon my soul to Hades,
> Nor give your holy one to see corruption.

A renewed address to the hearers follows in v. 29 as Peter begins to develop his argument from the psalm. Because the tomb of David 'the patriarch'[4] is known to his hearers, Peter can speak confidently (μετὰ

unaware of its Old Testament significance), he would probably have altered it.

1. Pesch, *Apostelgeschichte*, I, p. 122, thinks the original pre-Lukan Pentecost speech included only the citation of Ps. 16.10. Luke expanded the citation to refer to Jesus' whole life, death and resurrection.

2. So Haenchen, *Acts*, p. 181; Schneider, *Apostelgeschichte*, I, p. 273; Pesch, *Apostelgeschichte*, I, p. 122.

3. So Schneider, *Apostelgeschichte*, I, pp. 273-74. It is somewhat surprising that Luke does not include the last two phrases of the psalm, since v. 11c refers to the pleasures available at God's 'right hand' and so would have provided a connection to Ps. 110.1 in Acts 2.34-35. Perhaps Luke avoids the phrase since his concern at this point is with the resurrection rather than the exaltation.

4. The designation πατριάρχης for David is unusual since the term is generally restricted in the New Testament to Abraham, Isaac, Jacob and Jacob's twelve sons (Acts 7.8-9; Heb. 7.4). Since the term is usually used to denote the founder or ancestor of a family, it may here designate David as the founder of the royal dynasty. If this is the case and the term is more than a designation of respect (as Haenchen,

παρρησίας) that he is both dead and buried. The unexpressed implication is that since David's tomb remains undisturbed, his body *did* undergo decay, so he cannot have fulfilled the prophecy spoken in Psalm 16. And if David did not fulfill the psalm, someone else must have. Peter offers the solution in v. 30: knowing that God had promised to seat one of his descendants on his throne, David spoke prophetically of the resurrection of the Christ. With this statement, *Luke interprets Psalm 16 in light of God's promise to David.* The resurrection and (by implication) the death of the Christ were predicted in Ps. 16.8-11 and are part of the fulfillment of the promise to seat one of David's descendants on his throne. The promise statement in v. 30 is an allusion from Ps. 132.11 (LXX 131.11), but draws generally from the promise tradition (cf. 2 Sam. 7.12-16; Ps. 89):

Acts 2.30	Ps. 131.11 (LXX)
ὅρκῳ **ὤμοσεν** αὐτῷ ὁ θεὸς ἐκ **καρποῦ** τῆς ὀσφύος[1] αὐτοῦ καθίσαι ἐπὶ τὸν **θρόνον** αὐτοῦ	**ὤμοσεν** κύριος τῷ Δαυίδ ἀλήθειαν καὶ οὐ μὴ ἀθετήσει αὐτήν **Ἐκ καρποῦ** τῆς κοιλίας σου θήσομαι ἐπὶ τὸν **θρόνον** σου.

The use of καθίσαι instead of the LXX θήσομαι points forward to the citation of Ps. 110.1 in v. 34,[2] indicating that the enthronement at God's right hand is understood by Luke as the fulfillment of God's promise to David to seat one of his descendants upon his throne. Most commentators see the antecedent of σοῦ in the phrase ἐπι τὸν θρόνον σου to be God.[3] Though the idea that the throne is ultimately God's is certainly correct,[4] Luke's primary reference here is to *David's* throne:

Acts, p. 182, suggests), then Luke is preparing his readers for the reference to the Davidic promise in the next verse. Though David did not fulfill the promise of Ps. 16, he started a dynasty through which it was fulfilled.

1. The use of ὀσφῦς ('loins') instead of the LXX κοιλία may be due to Luke himself, since he uses κοιλία only of the womb (but see the ms. variant in Lk. 15.16), or it may be from a source which considered ὀσφῦς the better translation for the Hebrew בטן in the context of the Psalm.

2. It may be significant that Psalm 132 speaks in v. 10 of the 'anointed' of God and in v. 7 has a key word ('footstool') in common with Ps. 110.1.

3. So Pesch, *Apostelgeschichte*, I, p. 123; Haenchen, *Acts*, p. 182; Schneider, *Apostelgeschichte*, I, p. 274 n. 104.

4. David's throne was ultimately God's because it was bestowed on him by Yahweh (1 Chron. 17.14; 28.5; 29.23; 2 Chron. 9.8; 13.8). Note especially 1 Chron. 29.23: 'Then Solomon sat on the throne of Yahweh of David his Father.' Cf. Hay, *Glory at the Right Hand*, p. 20.

(1) In the psalm, the reference is clearly to David's throne and it is likely that Luke has the context of the psalm in view. (2) The closest antecedent to 'his throne' in verse 30 is τῆς ὀσφύος αὐτοῦ 'his (David's) loins'. (3) In Luke 1.32 Gabriel promises Mary that the Lord God will give Jesus 'the throne of his father David'.

In Luke's scheme, this prophecy is fulfilled at Jesus' exaltation to God's right hand, viewed as an assumption of the promised throne of David (see discussion of vv. 33-36 below). From this exalted position he now reigns over all (cf. Acts 10.36). While this portrayal goes beyond the Old Testament conception of the Davidic throne in Jerusalem, this does not mean Luke leaves the context of the Davidic promises. Rather, he defines the 'throne' promise in relation to Jesus' ascension and session at God's right hand.

J. Dupont considers Luke's use of Ps. 131.11 (LXX) here to be not christological but historical, merely providing source material from David's life.[1] But this is not the case. The allusion speaks of God's promise to one day seat a descendant of David upon his throne. The interpretation of Ps. 110.1 which follows reveals this as a prophecy which has found its fulfillment in the exaltation-enthronement of Jesus. The use of the psalm must therefore be seen as christological and in the same prophecy-fulfillment vein as Psalms 16 and 110.

At this point, however, we are getting ahead of Peter's argument in the speech. Though he alludes to Jesus' exaltation by citing Ps. 132.11, his interest at this point is still in the resurrection. Since David was not speaking of himself: 'he looked ahead and spoke of the resurrection of the Christ, that he was neither abandoned to Hades, nor did his flesh see corruption' (v. 31). David's prediction that he would not undergo decay did not concern himself but his promised heir—the Davidic messiah. The role of Psalm 16 in the argument is not, as some assert, to prove that the resurrection of Jesus actually occurred. Peter presupposes this both in vv. 24 and 32. The only evidence he offers for the resurrection is the fact that the apostles are witnesses to it (v. 32b). The purpose of Psalm 16, rather, is *to prove that scripture predicted that the Christ, David's greater son, would rise from the dead.*

The link to the resurrection of Jesus follows in v. 32. Here Peter brings the argument back to where it started in v. 24: 'This Jesus God raised up, of which we are all witnesses' (v. 32). Up to v. 24 he had

1. J. Dupont, 'Messianic Interpretation of the Psalms in the Acts of the Apostles', in *The Salvation of the Gentiles* (1979), pp. 105-106.

demonstrated only that Jesus was a man attested by God who was murdered by the Jews, but whom God had raised from the dead. With verses 25-31, he shows that David predicted the resurrection of the Christ. The (unspoken) conclusion which verse 32 reaches is that since Jesus was resurrected from the dead he must be the Christ.[1]

To sum up Peter's argument from the statement of the resurrection (v. 24) to this point: (1) Speaking in the first person, David predicted that the Lord's 'holy one' would not see corruption (vv 25-29). (2) The death and burial of David, and the presence of his tomb in Jerusalem show that he has not fulfilled this prophecy (v. 29). (3) David must therefore have been speaking of another. The natural conclusion is that David, knowing that God had promised to place one of his descendants on his throne, spoke prophetically of the resurrection of the Christ (v. 30; the 'holy one' of v. 27). (4) David therefore predicted that the Christ would rise from the dead (v. 31). (5) The apostles are witnesses to the fact that God raised this man Jesus from the dead (v. 31). (6) The unexpressed conclusion: Jesus is the Christ. Peter postpones stating this conclusion, however, until verse 36. This is because he wishes to prove not just that Jesus was the Davidic messiah, but that he has already been exalted to the Davidic throne. In the climax of the sermon in verse 36, he will proclaim both conclusions together, that Jesus is both the Christ and the reigning Lord.

ii. *The Exaltation-Enthronement of the Messianic Lord (vv. 33-35).* The first half of Peter's kerygmatic summary therefore presents Jesus as the Davidic Christ whose resurrection was prophesied by David. The next statement by Peter carries forward this conclusion, with a reference back to the Pentecost event:

> Therefore having been exalted at[2] the right hand of God, and having received from the Father the promise of the Holy Spirit, he has poured out this which you see and hear (v. 33).

1. Cf. Dupont, *Salvation of the Gentiles*, p. 109.

2. The question of whether the dative here is instrumental or local is disputed. The only other place in the New Testament where τῇ δεξιᾷ occurs without a preposition is in Acts 5.31 where the same difficulty arises. If Acts 2.33 is an allusion to Ps. 118.16 (δεξιὰ κυρίου ὕψωσέν με), then the dative would probably be instrumental, translated 'exalted *by* the right hand of God'. So F.F. Bruce, *The Acts of the Apostles* (3rd edn, 1990), p. 126; Dupont, *Salvation of the Gentiles*, pp. 125-26; Voss, *Christologie*, p. 133. This view is supported in the verse by the appearance of

The exaltation is presented as a separate act which naturally followed the resurrection,[1] and the smooth transition suggests that Luke is still operating in the context of the Davidic promises.[2] The particle οὖν in v. 33 is inferential. It is because Jesus is the heir to the Davidic throne, as his resurrection confirms, that he is exalted to the right hand of God and given the gift of the Spirit, through which he now implements the Davidic reign. This interpretation is confirmed by the link noted above between the promise statement of v. 30 ('to seat one of his descendants upon his throne') and the enthronement language which follows in vv. 34-35. Both the resurrection and the exaltation lead to Jesus' enthronement as messianic king and represent the fulfillment of the promises to David.[3]

Peter offers the outpouring of the Spirit as indirect proof of the exaltation and so links his christological conclusion to the Pentecost event. The Spirit-inspired *glossalalia* which the hearers are experiencing[4] is a result of Jesus' exaltation to the right hand of God. With this reference Luke alludes back not only to the Pentecost event and its interpretation in 2.14-21 but also to the words of Jesus in Lk. 24.49 and Acts 1.4, where the pouring out of the Spirit is likewise referred to as the 'promise of the Father' (ἐπαγγελία τοῦ πατρός).

the verb ὑψόω in common with Psalm 118 and the passive construction (ὑψωθείς τῇ δεξιᾷ). On the other hand, the existence of the local use of δεξιά in the citation of Ps. 110.1 which follows would indicate that Luke is here anticipating that statement. This influence, along with the possible influence of the phrase τερπνότητες ἐν τῇ δεξιᾷ σου εἰς τέλος from Ps. 16.11 (the verse which Luke stopped short of in his citation of Ps. 16.8-10), makes it probable that Luke intends the local sense here. So Lindars, *New Testament Apologetic,* 42ff.; R.F. O'Toole, 'Acts 2.30 and the Davidic Covenant of Pentecost', *JBL* 102 (1983), p. 256; Haenchen, *Acts*, p. 183 n. 1, and most modern commentators. See below concerning the possible influence of Psalm 68 in this verse.

1. On the Lukan distinction between the resurrection and the exaltation see Roloff, *Apostelgeschichte*, pp. 51, 58-59; Weiser, *Apostelgeschichte 1-12*, p. 93; Schneider, *Apostelgeschichte*, I, p. 275. For a summary of various views on Luke's understanding of the resurrection, ascension and exaltation see R.F. O'Toole, 'Luke's Understanding of Jesus' Resurrection-Ascension-Exaltation', *BTB* 9 (1979), pp. 106-14.

2. Cf. O'Toole, 'Acts 2.30', pp. 255-56; Burger, *Jesus als Davidssohn*, pp. 146-47; Tannehill, *Narrative Unity*, II, pp. 38-39.

3. Cf. Tannehill, *Narrative Unity*, II, p. 38.

4. Notice the present tense in the phrase ὃ ὑμεῖς βλέπετε καὶ ἀκούετε. Luke suggests that the glossalalia is still going on around the hearers.

Just as Ps. 16.8-11 confirms that Scripture predicted the messiah would be raised from the dead, so now Ps. 110.1 is cited to prove that he would be exalted to heaven. Just as it was not David who rose from the dead, neither was it David who ascended into heaven (v. 34), for David himself said:

> The Lord said to my Lord,
> Sit at my right hand,
> Till I make your enemies a stool for your feet (Ps. 110.1).

Peter takes the psalm as an address by Yahweh to David's Lord, the messiah, who is invited to sit at Yahweh's right hand. The argument is similar to that of Psalm 16. Just as the existence of David's sealed tomb proves that he did not rise from the dead, so his description of another as 'my Lord' proves that he did not ascend to heaven. He must therefore have been speaking of the ascension of the Christ. The argument runs as follows: (1) Having been raised from the dead, Jesus was exalted to the right hand of God and received the Holy Spirit promised by the Father. (2) This exaltation is confirmed by the out-pouring of the Spirit which the hearers are experiencing. (3) Since David is still in his tomb, and since he is addressing another in Ps. 110.1, it was not he who ascended. In Psalm 110, therefore, he was speaking of the exaltation of the Christ. (4) The conclusion which must be reached is that Jesus is the exalted Lord at God's right hand.

This conclusion along with the unstated conclusion of the resurrection argument from Psalm 16 (vv. 25-32) are proclaimed together as the sermon reaches its climax in v. 36:

> Let all the house of Israel therefore know assuredly that God has made him both Lord and Christ—this Jesus whom you crucified.

The inferential οὖν draws the natural conclusion from the preceding argument and ἀσφαλῶς speaks of its certainty. The meaning of χριστός is clear: vv. 25-32 have demonstrated that Jesus is the Davidic Christ who David prophesied would rise from the dead. The exact significance of κύριος is less certain. Though Luke's use of the title for both Jesus and God may at times imply Jesus' equality or identity with God, the present context seems to suggest (primarily, at least) *messianic* lordship, that is, the universal authority that Jesus the Christ possesses by virtue of his status at God's right hand. Various contextual factors point in this direction: (1) First, as we have seen, this perspective fits Luke's narrative development to this point. The purpose of vv. 25-32 was to show that David prophesied in Psalm 16 that the Christ would rise from the dead. Since Jesus has risen, he must be the Christ. The purpose of vv. 32-35, then, is to demonstrate that David also prophesied in Psalm 110 that the Christ would be exalted to God's right hand. Since Jesus was exalted, then he must be not only the Christ but also the Lord, that is, the Christ *now reigning* on David's throne. The allusion to Ps. 132.11 in Acts 2.30 clearly interprets Jesus' exaltation as a Davidic (= messianic) enthronement. (2) Further, κύριος in v. 36 is drawn *primarily* from the quotation of Ps. 110.1 in vv. 34-35 (for the link to Joel 3.5a see below), where it clearly carries a messianic sense.[1] David prophesied that the Lord God would say to 'my Lord', the messiah, 'Sit at my right hand...' (3) Finally, this meaning best fits Luke's narrative setting, where a reference to Jesus' equality with the Lord God would be contextually strange. The speech is presented as an address to the Jews of Jerusalem on the Day of Pentecost. Peter presents proof from Scripture that through his resurrection and ascension Jesus has fulfilled the prophecies of Psalms 16, 132 and 110, all three of which he interprets in the context of the promise to David for his coming heir. The conclusion the hearers are meant to reach is that Jesus is the resurrected, exalted and enthroned Davidic messiah. When Peter reaches the climax of the speech in v. 36 and declares that God has made this Jesus both χριστός and κύριος, the hearers are 'pierced to the heart' because they have crucified their long-awaited king, the Davidic messiah. The whole tenor of the passage suggests a messianic sense for κύριος.

Against this view, Bock argues that the main thrust of Peter's argument is to identify Jesus as the 'Lord' who is called upon to be saved in the Joel quote (Joel 3.5a; Acts 2.21), and so to affirm 'that Jesus is κύριος in the same way that God is, because he sits at God's side doing his work'. Luke thus affirms that 'Jesus' name, task, and authority *are equal* to those of God' (emphasis his).[2] Though a very high Christology is certainly indicated by Jesus' role as the mediator of God's salvation and—even more striking—as the mediator of God's Spirit,[3] the nature

1. Cf. Marshall, *Acts*, pp. 79-80.

2. Bock, *Proclamation*, pp. 184, 185. This is part of Bock's 'more than messiah' motif: 'Jesus is more than a regal Messiah, as his task and position show. He is Lord, a title which shows Jesus in his task and person to be equal with God and thus able to be substituted for him both in task and name' (p. 184). See the discussion of Bock's 'more than messiah' motif in Chapter 1.

3. Cf. especially M.M.B. Turner, 'The Spirit of Christ and Christology', in

of this mediation is not clear. Does Peter here identify Jesus as God's co-regent, sharing equally in his status and functions, or his vice-regent, ruling and acting as his representative? While the former may indeed be in Luke's mind and perhaps implicit in the identification of Jesus as the 'Lord' of Joel 3.5a, it does not seem to have been *Luke's primary christological purpose* to make this point.[1] As we have seen, Luke's emphasis rather lies on Jesus' status as the messianic king, now enthroned at God's right hand.

Returning to the climax of the sermon in v. 36, it must be asked what Luke means when he says God has 'made' Jesus both Lord and Christ. It has already been noted that while the phrase may be drawn from earlier tradition, it in no way contradicts Luke's perspective.[2] Luke presents Jesus' messiahship as achieved in various stages.[3] From birth Jesus is the Lord's anointed because he is the divinely elected saviour of Israel. He is the messiah-designate. At his baptism he is anointed by the Spirit and empowered for his messianic task—a task which, as we shall see, begins already during his earthly ministry. Only at his exaltation-enthronement, however, is Jesus installed in the full authority as reigning

Christ the Lord (1982), pp. 168-90. Turner points out that in the Old Testament and Judaism, the Spirit is considered the vitality and self-expression of God himself. He suggests that the church's belief that Jesus was now the mediator of God's Spirit was a key factor in their attribution of divinity to him: 'To speak of Jesus directing God's Spirit...would surely be tantamount to calling him God' (p. 183). While Jesus' mediation of the Spirit thus implies a very high, perhaps even a divine Christology, it is not Luke's *main christological purpose* in the speech to make this point. This is evident from the fact that the speech does not reach its climax in v. 33 but in v. 36, where Jesus is proclaimed Lord and Christ. Roloff, *Apostelgeschichte*, p. 59, reaches a similar conclusion, pointing out that Luke's choice of scriptural proof in v. 34 is determined by his christological purpose: 'Weil der eigentliche Zielpunkt der Rede jedoch nicht in der Aussage über den Geist, sondern in der Entfaltung des christologischen Kerygmas liegt, darum verzichtet Lukas auf einen Schriftbeweis für die Geistausgießung—er wäre von Ps. 68,19 (vgl. Eph 4,8) her durchaus möglich gewesen—, sondern bringt statt dessen mit Ps. 110,1 den klassischen Schriftbeweis für die Erhöhung Jesu (vgl. Mk 12,36; Hebr 1,13; 1.Kor 15,25; Eph 1,20; Kol 3,1).' (For more on the possibility of an allusion to Ps. 67.19 LXX see discussion below.)

1. See the distinction made in Chapter 1 between Luke's Christology and his christological purpose in individual passages.

2. It is unlikely Luke would introduce a statement—no matter how old or 'apostolic'—which contradicted his own perspective. *Contra* Haenchen, *Acts*, p. 187; Hahn, *Titles*, pp. 106ff., 170, 377.

3. Cf. George, *Etudes*, pp. 281-82; Tannehill, *Narrative Unity*, II, p. 39.

Christ and Lord. An analogy may be drawn here to David, who was chosen by God and anointed by Samuel long before he was enthroned as king. In 1 Sam. 16.1 God tells Samuel: 'Fill your horn with oil and go; I will send you to Jesse the Bethlehemite, for I have selected a king for myself among his sons.' In God's eyes, David was already king, even though he had not yet been anointed or enthroned. Similarly, though Jesus was already Christ and Lord by God's divine choice during his earthly ministry, at his resurrection-exaltation he became the reigning Christ and Lord of all.[1] This status has now been revealed to Israel (v. 36a) and it is for her to respond in repentance and acceptance.

iii. *A Moses–Sinai Typology?* A number of scholars have proposed that the Pentecost event, together with the ascension statement in v. 33, are meant to recall the giving of the Law at Sinai and hence to portray Jesus as a new Moses.[2] Three main arguments are brought forward for this view: (1) the association of the Day of Pentecost with the giving of the Law at Sinai in first-century Judaism; (2) literary parallels between Luke's Pentecost account and Jewish Sinai traditions; and, (3) an alleged allusion in Acts 2.33 to Ps. 67.19 (LXX), a passage which was interpreted by the rabbis with reference to Moses' ascension to heaven to receive the Torah in order to give it to men (*Targ. Ket.* Ps. 68.19; cf. Eph. 4.8). Jesus' ascension would thus be viewed as parallel to that of Moses, and the gift of the Spirit as the sign of the new covenant which replaces the old.[3]

1. Marshall, *Acts*, p. 80, points out that in Luke's presentation it was because Jesus was already the messiah that he was raised from the dead (Acts 2.22ff.; 2.31; 10.38ff.), and it was one who was already called Lord who was summoned to sit at God's right hand (2.34).

2. See especially W.L. Knox, *The Acts of the Apostles* (1948), pp. 85-86; J. Dupont, 'La nouvelle Pentecôte (Ac 2, 1-11)', pp. 193-98, and 'Ascension du Christ et don de l'Esprit d'après Ac 2.33', pp. 199-209, both in *Nouvelles Etudes sur les Actes des Apôtres* (1984); *idem,* 'The First Christian Pentecost', in *The Salvation of the Gentiles* (1979), pp. 39-45; R. Le Déaut, 'Pentecost and Jewish Tradition', *Doctrine and Life* 20 (1970), pp. 250-67; G. Kretschmar, 'Himmelfahrt und Pfingsten', *ZKG* 66 (1954-55), pp. 209-53. Cf. J. Potin, *La fête de la Pentecôte* (1971), pp. 301-302; J. Kremer, *Pfingstbericht und Pfingstgeschehen* (1973); B. Noack, 'The Day of Pentecost in Jubilees, Qumran and Acts', *ASTI* 1 (1962), pp. 73-79. See also the works noted by O'Toole, 'Acts 2.30', p. 247 n. 12; Menzies, *Development*, pp. 229-44, and those cited below.

3. Cf. F.H. Chase, *The Credibility of the Book of the Acts of the Apostles* (1902),

In my opinion, these arguments have been decisively answered by various scholars, including R. Menzies, E. Lohse, R.F. O'Toole, I.H. Marshal and D. Bock.[1] (1) While later rabbinic writers associate Pentecost with the giving of the Law at Sinai, there is little evidence that this connection was widespread (if present at all) in first-century Judaism. Menzies is surely correct when he concludes that 'it is... illegitimate to assume that the mere mention of τὴν ἡμέραν τῆς πεντηκοστῆς (Acts 2.1) would have evoked images of Moses, Sinai or the covenant renewal ceremony in the minds of Luke's readers'.[2] (2) While there is indeed some imagery common to Luke's account and the Sinai traditions found in Philo and Josephus, these are not unique to Sinai but are common to theophanic language in general.[3] There are as many features of the Sinai traditions absent from the Acts account as present (including the dark cloud, lightning flashes, smoke and the sound as a trumpet blast). (3) Finally, while the general conceptual framework of the targum on Ps. 68.19 (ascending-receiving-giving) makes it conceivable that a tradition related to this psalm was present in the pre-Lukan version of the Acts account, its echo in the present text is faint indeed. Bock demonstrates that such an allusion can be achieved only through a radical reconstruction of the text,[4] and O'Toole points to a number of Old Testament Passages with as much or more verbal

p. 151; H.J. Cadbury, 'The Speeches in Acts', in *The Beginnings of Christianity*, V, pp. 408-409; Knox, *Acts*, pp. 80ff.; Kretschmar, 'Himmelfahrt', pp. 216, 218; Le Déaut, 'Jewish Tradition', pp. 260-62; Lindars, *New Testament Apologetic*, pp. 51-59; Turner, 'Spirit of Christ', pp. 176-79; Dupont, *Nouvelles Etudes,* 199-209; *idem*, *Salvation of the Gentiles*, pp. 35, 112-13. Dupont had earlier rejected this view in 'Les problèmes du Livre des Actes entre 1940 et 1950', reprinted in *Etudes sur les Actes des Apôtres* (1967), p. 100. For a history of this interpretation see Dupont, *Nouvelles Etudes*, pp. 202-207.

1. E. Lohse, *TDNT*, VI, pp. 48-49; Menzies, *Development*, pp. 231-39; O'Toole, 'Acts 2.30', pp. 245-58; I.H. Marshall, 'The Significance of Pentecost', *SJT* 30 (1977), pp. 348-49; Bock, *Proclamation*, p. 182. See also a detailed defense of this position in my Aberdeen thesis, 'The Davidic Messiah in Luke–Acts', pp. 157ff.

2. Menzies, *Development,* 235. He probably goes too far, however, when he states emphatically that 'Pentecost was not celebrated as a festival commemorating the giving of the law at Sinai at the time of Luke's writing.'

3. Menzies, *Development*, pp. 236-39; cf. Kremer, *Pfingstbericht*, pp. 245-48; Schneider, *Apostelgeschichte*, I, pp. 246-47. Menzies cites parallels from *4 Ezra* 13, *1 Enoch* 14, 2 Samuel 22, Isaiah 66, and other texts. On the language miracle parallels in the later rabbinic material see the criticism of Menzies, *Development*, pp. 239-241.

4. Bock, *Proclamation*, p. 182.

similarity to Acts 2.33 than Ps. 68.19, including Ps. 117.16a (LXX); Isa. 52.13 and Ps. 88.20, 24-25, 28-30 (LXX).[1] In short, though it is *possible* that a pre-Lukan version of the speech contained an allusion to Ps. 67.19 (LXX), there is little evidence that Luke is either conscious of it or that he wishes to emphasize it for his readers.[2] This conclusion is strengthened by the absence of contextual references either to Moses or to the Sinai event.

b. *Conclusion*

In summary, in his Pentecost speech Peter uses scriptural proof to demonstrate that Jesus is the messianic king, now enthroned in heaven. Since neither Ps. 16.8-11 nor Ps. 110.1 concern David himself, they must be understood as prophecies concerning the resurrection and ascension-exaltation of Jesus the Christ. Together they represent the fulfillment of God's oath to David to seat his descendant upon the throne of his kingdom forever (Ps. 132.11). Through his death, resurrection and exaltation, Jesus has been vindicated and enthroned as the Davidic messiah, the king of Israel. In this exalted status, he pours out salvation blessings upon his people. All who repent receive forgiveness of sins and the gift of the Holy Spirit (v. 38; cf. 5.31). While elsewhere Luke will develop a Moses typology and draw on Sinai allusions (cf. Lk. 9.28-36; Acts 3.22; 7.17-53),[3] here the theme of Jesus as the Davidic messiah predominates throughout.

1. O'Toole, 'Acts 2.30', pp. 245-58, esp. 248ff. Psalm 88 is particularly significant, since (1) it is a royal Davidic psalm, and so would fit the Davidic context of Acts 2; (2) it contains the verb ὑψόω (Acts 2.33) six times (Ps. 88.20, 24-25, 28-30); (3) both the Pentecost speech (v. 30) and Psalm 88 (vv. 4, 36, 50 LXX) speak of God's oath sworn (ὀμνύω) to David: and (4) Luke will allude to Ps. 88.21 (LXX) again in Acts 13.22 where, in a sermon parallel to this one, Paul seeks to show that Jesus' resurrection fulfills the promises to Abraham and David.

2. Note the cautious conclusion of Marshall, *Acts*, p. 79: 'it is possible that the present verse contains an implicit contrast between the gift of the law to men (which, as noted above, was associated with Pentecost in the second-century) and the gift of the Spirit, but it must be emphasized that this view is somewhat speculative and it is doubtful whether Luke himself had detected the allusion...the important fact is that the bestowal of the Spirit offers further testimony that Jesus is the Messiah'.

3. See the discussions of this theme in Chapter 6 sections 2c and 4a.

3. *Paul's Sermon at Pisidian-Antioch, Acts 13.16-41*

a. *The Significance of the Sermon in the Narrative of Acts*
As Luke provided an example of the apostolic proclamation in Peter's Pentecost speech, so now with the sermon of Paul at Pisidian-Antioch he provides an example of the Pauline missionary preaching. A number of factors point to the importance of this sermon in Luke's narrative.

(1) The sermon represents the *first missionary proclamation of the Apostle Paul.* As Peter was the leading character of the first half of Acts, so Paul becomes the dominant figure in the remaining chapters (chs. 13-28). As Peter's Pentecost speech represented an example of the apostolic kerygma, so Paul's sermon in Pisidian-Antioch depicts a model of his missionary proclamation to Jews and God-fearers: (a) It is in the context of this sermon that Paul becomes the leading character in Acts. Though Luke introduced Paul (Saul) into his narrative in 7.58; 8.1-2 and in the account of his conversion in 9.1-31, it is here that he brings him into the spotlight as the great diaspora missionary and the leading figure in Acts. That this narrative shift occurs with the apostle's missionary activity in Pisidian-Antioch is seen by Luke's description of the missionaries in 13.13 as οἱ περὶ Παῦλον and by the sudden change in the order from *Barnabas* and Saul (13.2, 7) to *Paul* and Barnabas (13.43). (b) The sermon is Paul's first speech on this *first* (and therefore introductory) missionary journey. Paul's missionary activity will become the dominant theme in the last half of Acts. As he sets out on this first journey, the reader is looking for an example of the message he carries. (c) The sermon and the incidents which surround it are given center stage in this first journey. The sermon's importance in the context of this journey is brought out by the manner in which Luke develops his narrative in Acts 13. Following the account of the missionary tour of Cyprus (vv. 4-12), Luke's story moves quickly to the Sabbath synagogue setting of Pisidian-Antioch. The only details of the (normally long and arduous) journey from Paphos to Antioch are brief notes concerning the stop in Perga and the return of John Mark to Jerusalem (v. 13). The account then slows dramatically as Luke takes 40 verses to relate the events in the synagogue and their consequences. The sermon alone takes 26 verses, over a third of the entire account of the journey (75 verses total). Luke clearly views the sermon along with its narrative setting as the high point of Paul's first missionary journey.

(2) The sermon represents the *only example in Acts of a diaspora*

synagogue sermon. Luke frequently mentions Paul's teaching in synagogues (9.20; 13.5, 14; 14.1; 17.1-2, 10, 17; 18.4, 19, 26; 19.8) describing it as his normal pattern of evangelism (17.1-2). For Luke the sermon must therefore represent a model of the message Paul brought to the synagogues of the diaspora.[1] That Luke wishes the speech to reflect *Paul's* gospel message is clear from Pauline characteristics present in the sermon, including the emphasis on God's choice of Israel (vv. 17; cf. Rom. 9-11) and the statement of justification apart from the Law of Moses (v. 39). Though it is a matter of debate whether these statements represent authentic Pauline material or merely Lukan imitation,[2] it is certain that in using them Luke wished *to represent the Pauline kerygma.*

(3) In this sermon *Luke picks up and develops various themes introduced earlier.* Jesus is presented as the 'saviour' (v. 23; cf. Lk. 2.11; Acts 5.31) who fulfills the promises to David (vv. 23, 32-37; cf. Lk. 1.32; Acts 2.24-36). John the Baptist is the forerunner who denies messianic claims (vv. 24-25; Lk. 3.15-16).[3] Jesus' death is a paradox; though sinful men wrongly condemned and crucified him (vv. 27-29; cf. Acts 2.23; 10.39), their actions were in fulfillment of Scripture (vv. 27, 29; cf. Lk. 18.31; 24.25-27; 44; Acts 26.22-23). The *Kontrastschema* common elsewhere in Acts (2.24; 3.13-15; 4.10; 5.30-31; 10.38-40) also appears; though evil men put Jesus to death, 'God raised him from the dead' (v. 30).

(4) Finally, the sermon and its consequences on the following Sabbath (13.46-51) introduce a theme of major significance for the rest of Acts: the widespread rejection of the message by the Jews and the subsequent turning to the Gentiles (Acts 18.6; 19.9; 26.20; 28.28). It is with this theme that the narrative of Acts will climax in ch. 28.[4]

These points indicate that this sermon, like the speech in Acts 2, has

1. Cf. M.F.-J. Buss, *Die Missionspredigt des Apostels Paulus im Pisidischen Antiochien* (1980), p. 17; Tannehill, *Narrative Unity*, II, p. 164. Buss also points to the sermon's location in the *center* of the Lukan report of the first missionary journey, and Luke's choice of the important Roman colony of Pisidian-Antioch as the location of the sermon.

2. For opposing viewpoints see P. Vielhauer, 'On the 'Paulinism' of Acts', in *Studies in Luke–Acts* (1966), pp. 33-50, esp. 41-43, and F.F. Bruce, 'Justification by Faith in the Non-Pauline Writings of the New Testament', *EvQ* 24 (1952), pp. 66-77.

3. See Chapter 3 sections 2b and 3b above.

4. Cf. especially J. Dupont, 'La conclusion des Acts et son rapport à l'ensemble de l'ouvrage de Luc', in *Nouvelles études sur les Actes des Apôtres* (1984), pp. 457-511.

introductory and programmatic importance for Luke. After noting the important role of the sermon in the context of Acts, M.F.-J. Buss concludes that: 'All the aforementioned facts demonstrate the programmatic character of the Antioch speech'.[1] (p. 17). Similarly, J.B. Tyson writes that Acts 13.13-52 'may, in fact, serve as a programmatic introduction to Paul's ministry as Luke 4.16-30 served for Jesus' ministry...'[2] It becomes highly significant, then, that here again the main christological theme is Jesus' fulfillment of the promises to David. Luke's probable use of sources[3] does not diminish the importance of this point. Even if Luke drew on a source (or sources) for the bulk of his material, it is significant that he has chosen from these sources a homily based on the promises to David.[4] Whatever its source(s), the sermon forms a unity in its Acts context.[5] This unity will be confirmed as we examine the sermon's literary form and structure.

b. *Literary Form and Structure*

It is generally recognized that the Old Testament promises to David, especially as set forth in 2 Sam. 7.6-16, form the conceptual framework for the sermon. Paul begins his message with a brief historical survey designed to move the sermon forward to the statement concerning God's choice of David as king (vv. 16b-22). From here he moves directly to Jesus as the promised offspring of David raised up by God to be a saviour for Israel (v. 23). The rest of the sermon stays with this theme, portraying Jesus' (life, death and) resurrection as the fulfillment of the promise to David (vv. 26-33a), offering scriptural proof for this assertion (vv. 33b-37), and calling the hearers to repentance on the basis of this conclusion (vv. 38-41).

1. Buss, *Missionspredigt*, p. 17.
2. Tyson, *The Death of Jesus in Luke–Acts*, p. 39.
3. Luke's use of sources is suggested by the diverse types of material in the speech (historical survey, christological kerygma, etc.), by the presence of Jewish exegetical techniques (see discussion below) and by the traditional use of Old Testament citations (from a testimony collection?). For a survey of the many tradition- and form-critical proposals for the sermon see Buss, *Missionspredigt*, pp. 12-17.
4. Even if the sermon is taken as 'the gist' of an authentic Pauline sermon given at the time and location indicated in the narrative, it is significant that Luke has chosen to present an extended account of this particular sermon rather than one given by Paul elsewhere (in Cyprus, perhaps, or elsewhere in Galatia).
5. Buss, *Missionspredigt*, pp. 24-31, *et passim,* argues extensively for the unity of the sermon in its Lukan context.

i. *Literary Form.* A number of scholars have proposed that the sermon follows a pattern found in the homiletic midrashim of rabbinic Judaism.[1] If this is the case, Luke (or the author of his source) may have written following the pattern of the synagogue homily, or his source may have been an authentic synagogue sermon. Though neither authenticity nor source questions are of primary concern in the present work, an understanding of the pattern by which the theme of the sermon is developed is essential for an understanding of Luke's intended meaning. It will therefore be profitable to turn briefly to this question of literary form.

In his work, *Jewish Hermeneutics in the Synoptic Gospels and Acts,* J.W. Doeve proposed that the sermon was an early Christian midrash based on 2 Sam. 7.6-16, originally in an Hebraic language.[2] E. Lövestam picked up Doeve's suggestion and pointed further to the similar midrashic presentation based on 2 Samuel 7 in 4QFlorilegium.[3] Other scholars have followed the lead of these writers, including D. Goldsmith,[4] J.W. Bowker,[5] M. Dumais[6] and others.[7]

1. On these homiletic midrashim see J. Mann, *The Bible as Read and Preached in the Old Synagogue* (vol. I, 1940; vol. II, 1966); H. Thyen, *Der Stil der jüdisch-hellenistischen Homilie* (1955); P. Borgen, *Bread From Heaven* (1965). On the meaning of midrash see A.G. Wright, 'The Literary Genre Midrash', *CBQ* 28 (1966), pp. 105-38, 417-57; R.T. France and David Wenham (eds.), *Gospel Perspectives.* III. *Studies in Midrash and Historiography* (1983), *passim.*

2. J.W. Doeve, *Jewish Hermeneutics in the Synoptic Gospels and Acts* (1954), pp. 168-76. According to Doeve, midrashic techniques in the speech include the numerous allusions to 2 Sam. 7.6-16, an appeal to both the Writings (Ps. 2.7 in v. 33) and the Prophets (Isa. 55.3 in v. 34) and the use of a word from one passage (חסדי in Isa. 55.3) to explain a word from another (חסיד in Ps. 16.10). Against Cadbury and Lake, *Beginnings*, II, p. 337, Doeve says this verbal connection is based on the Hebrew text rather than the LXX (p. 176).

3. Lövestam, *Son and Saviour*, p. 7.

4. D. Goldsmith, 'Acts 13.33-37: A *Pesher* on II Samuel 7', *JBL* 87 (1968), pp. 321-24. Goldsmith compares the Old Testament citations in Acts 13.33-37 to 4QFlor, suggesting that this section of the Acts speech reflects a Christian *pesher* on the Nathan oracle.

5. J.W. Bowker, 'Speeches in Acts: A Study in Proem and Yelammedenu Form', *NTS* 14 (1967–68), pp. 96-111.

6. M. Dumais, *Le langage de l'evangélisation, l'annonce missionaire en milieu juif (Acts 13,16-41)* (1976), pp. 67-114.

7. L. Hartmann, 'Davids son: A propa Acta 13, 16-41', *SEÅ* 18-19 (1964), pp. 117-34; E.E. Ellis, 'Midrashic Features in the Speeches in Acts', in *Prophecy and Hermeneutic in Early Christianity* (1978), pp. 198-208; Pesch, *Apostelgeschichte*, II,

Bowker's article is the most specific of these works, relating the sermon in Acts 13 to the pattern of the synagogue 'proem' homily. The typical synagogue service began with readings from the Pentateuch (the seder) and the Prophets (the haftarah). Since the hearers often did not understand Hebrew, the scripture was then explained with an accompanying targum and with a homily. Bowker focuses especially on one type of homily, the proem. It began with the reading of an introductory text (the proem or petihta) not taken from either the seder or the haftarah readings. This text was meant to form a bridge between the two readings and was required to have at least a one-word linguistic connection with haftarah. Following the reading of the proem, the preacher expounded its meaning by quoting a series of texts which carried the theme forward, a process called haruzin ('stringing pearls'). This haruzin eventually led back to that day's seder, either by citing a text from the seder reading itself, or by citing a different text which in some way pointed to the seder.[1] Bowker argues that the Acts 13 sermon reflects this pattern. He proposes 1 Sam. 13.14 as the proem text (cited in Acts 13.22), with a seder from Deut. 4.25-46 (vv. 37-38 are implied in the historical summary in Acts 13.17-19) and a haftarah from 2 Sam. 7.6-16 (implied throughout the sermon). Though Bowker admits that the structure of the speech does not fit the pattern exactly, he concludes that there is enough evidence to warrant its classification as an early form of proem homily.[2]

M. Dumais comes to similar conclusions. After a detailed discussion of the characteristics of the homiletic midrashim, he concludes that the sermon in Acts 13 is a midrash on 2 Samuel 7 with many traits characteristic of Jewish homily and of the pesher interpretation found at Qumran.[3] Differing from Bowker, Dumais considers the sermon to be

pp. 31-43. Hartmann's work is an extended synoptic comparison of Acts 13.17-41 and 2 Sam. 7.6-16.

1. Bowker, 'Speeches in Acts', pp. 99-100.

2. The sermon cannot be a true proem homily since in Acts 13 the proem text is not introductory, but follows the historical survey of vv. 17-21. The purpose of vv. 17-21, according to Bowker, is to link the seder reading to the proem text (Bowker, 'Speeches in Acts', p. 104). See the criticism of Buss, *Missionspredigt*, pp. 22-24, who points to the uncertain knowledge of Jewish homilies and the differences between Acts 13 and Bowker's proem pattern. Buss overstates his case, however, when he asserts that the lack of unedited rabbinic sources dooms to failure all attempts to find synagogue sermons in the New Testament (p. 23).

3. Dumais, *Langage*, pp. 67-114; esp. 87, 114.

based solely on the haftarah reading (2 Sam. 7.6-16) without reference to the seder.[1]

The work of these scholars reveals remarkable similarity between the sermon in Acts 13 and the pattern of the homiletic midrashim. It is at least plausible, therefore, that Luke's source was a synagogue homily. In any case, that Luke is aware of the basic pattern of the synagogue service is evident not only from the development of the sermon itself but also from its narrative introduction (the reading of the Law and Prophets and the offer to Paul and Barnabas to speak). In examining the structure of the sermon, it will therefore be profitable to compare the exegetical methods and techniques found in the homiletic midrashim with those utilized in the sermon.

ii. *Structure*. Externally, the speech is structured around three major addresses: Paul's initial address to his audience (v. 16); a renewed address at the beginning of his description of the life, death and resurrection of Jesus (v. 26); and a final shorter address at the beginning of the concluding paraenetic section (v. 38). In addition to this external framework, there are a number of internal structural characteristics which bear similarities to the homiletic midrashim.

(1) As mentioned above, the sermon centers on the Old Testament promises to David and implicit allusions to 2 Samuel 7 are present throughout. This type of Old Testament exegesis (frequent allusions to a 'base text' without actually citing that text) is common in homiletic midrashim.[2] Parallels and allusions to 2 Sam. 7.6-16 are presented below.[3]

1. Dumais, *Langage*, pp. 108-109. Dumais points to the pattern of synagogue sermons in the first century and to internal support from Acts 13 to support this contention.

2. M. Gertner, 'Midrashim in the New Testament', *JSS* 7 (1962), pp. 267-92, distinguishes between overt and covert (or 'invisible') midrash. In the former, the base text is quoted and the interpretation is given separately and explicitly. The latter is presented either as a concise paraphrase or as an expanded paraphrastic composition.

3. Rather than the full MT and LXX readings, the 2 Samuel 7 passages have been given in English translation (following the MT reading) with key MT and LXX words given where appropriate.

Comparative chart of 2 Samuel 7.6-16 and Acts 13.16-38

Parallel	*Acts 13*	*2 Samuel 7*
Historical Survey:		
Exodus from Egypt	13.17 ὁ θεὸς τοῦ λαοῦ τούτου Ἰσραὴλ... ἐξήγαγεν αὐτοὺς ἐξ αὐτῆς (Αἰγύπτου),	2 Sam. 7.6b: '...since the day I brought up (LXX: ἀνήγαγον) the sons of Israel from Egypt...'
The land given (or promised) as an inheritance and place of rest for the nation	13.19 κατεκληρονόμησεν τὴν γῆν αὐτῶν...	2 Sam. 7.10 (as a future promise): 'And I will appoint a place for my people Israel...that they may dwell in their own place and be disturbed no more...'
Raising up Judges	13.20 καὶ μετὰ ταῦτα ἔδωκεν κριτὰς...	2 Sam. 7.11: 'from the time that I appointed judges (LXX: κριτάς; MT: שפטים) over my people Israel'.[1]
Rejection of Saul	13.21...καὶ ἔδωκεν αὐτοῖς ὁ θεὸς τὸν Σαοὺλ...καὶ μεταστήσας αὐτὸν...	2 Sam. 7.15: 'Saul, whom I removed from before you' (no mention of Saul in LXX: 'those whom I removed').
Choice of David	13.22b ἤγειρεν τὸν Δαυὶδ αὐτοῖς εἰς βασιλέα, ᾧ καὶ εἶπεν μαρτυρήσας, **Εὗρον Δαυὶδ** τὸν τοῦ Ἰεσσαί, **ἄνδρα κατὰ τὴν καρδίαν μου**, ὃς ποιήσει πάντα τὰ θελήματά μου (Ps. 89.21; 1 Sam. 13.14; Is 44.28?).	2 Sam. 7.8: 'Thus says the Lord of hosts, "I took you from the pasture...that you should be ruler over my people Israel."' (Cf. 2 Sam. 7.3: 'And Nathan said to the king, "Go, do all that is in your heart; for the Lord is with you."')

1. Cf. 2 Sam. 7.7b: '...one of the tribes (LXX: φυλήν, MT: שבטי; but cf. 1 Chron. 17.6 [MT]: 'judges'—שפטי) of Israel, whom I commanded to shepherd my people...'

The Promise to David: God's promise to raise up a descendant for David	13.23 τούτου ὁ θεὸς ἀπὸ τοῦ σπέρματος κατ' ἐπαγγελίαν ἤγαγεν τῷ Ἰσραὴλ σωτῆρα Ἰησοῦν,	2 Sam. 7.12 'I will raise up your seed (LXX: ἀναστήσω τὸ σπέρμα σου; MT: והקימתי את־זרעך) after you, who shall come forth from your loins, and I will establish his kingdom.'
Concerns a descendant who is 'raised up'	13.33 ὅτι ταύτην ὁ θεὸς ἐκπεπλήρωκεν τοῖς τέκνοις ἡμῖν ἀναστήσας Ἰησοῦν (cf. vv. 34, 37).	2 Sam. 7.12: 'I will raise up your seed…'
Promise of father–son relationship	13.33 **Υἱός μου εἶ σύ, ἐγὼ σήμερον γεγέννηκά σε** (Ps. 2.7).	2 Sam. 7.14: 'I will be his father, and he shall be my son.'
Promise of steadfast love and a kingdom made 'sure'	13:34b…Δώσω **ὑμῖν τὰ ὅσια Δαυὶδ τὰ πιστά** (Isa. 55.3 LXX; MT: חסדי דוד הנאמנים) 13.35…Οὐ δώσεις τὸν ὅσιόν σου ἰδεῖν διαφθοράν (Ps. 15.10 LXX; MT: חסידיך).	2 Sam. 7.15 'But I will not take my steadfast love (MT: חסדי; LXX: ἔλεός μου) from him…'; 2 Sam. 7.16: 'And your house and your kingdom shall be made sure (MT: ונאמן; LXX: πιστωήσεται) forever before me; your throne shall be established forever'.
Contingent on David's death	13.36 Δαυὶδ μὲν γὰρ ἰδίᾳ γενεᾷ ὑπηρετήσας τῇ τοῦ θεοῦ βουλῇ ἐκοιμήθη καὶ προσετέθη πρὸς τοὺς πατέρας αὐτοῦ καὶ εἶδεν διαφθοράν,	2 Sam. 7.12 'When your days are fulfilled and you lie down (κοιμηθήσῃ) with your fathers…'

The chart indicates the numerous parallels between the sermon and Nathan's oracle. In addition to the many parallels in content, there are a number of verbal connections, especially in the Old Testament citations: τοῦ σπέρματος (v. 23)—τὸ σπέρμα σου (2 Sam. 7.12); υἱός μου (v. 33, citing Ps. 2.7)—ἔσται μοι εἰς υἱόν (2 Sam. 7.14); τὰ πιστά (v. 34, citing Isa. 55.3)—πιστωθήσεται (2 Sam. 7.15); τὰ ὅσια (v. 34, citing Isa. 55.3)—חסדי (2 Sam. 7.15 [MT only, LXX ἔλεός μου]); ἐκοιμήθη... πρὸς τοὺς πατέρας αὐτοῦ (v. 36)—κοιμηθησῃ μετὰ τῶν πατέρων σου (2 Sam. 7.12).

(3) Another structural characteristic of the sermon is the presence of

key word-groups which thematically relate the two main parts of the sermon and form a connecting thread running through it.[1] The first of these is ἐπαγγελία, which occurs in vv. 23 and 32 and serves to link the climactic statements of the first and second sections of the sermon together with a common 'promise-fulfillment' theme. Another key word-group is the 'elevation' language represented by the verbs ἐγείρω and ἀνίστημι (vv. 22, 23, 30, 33, 34, 37; cf. v. 23, ἄγω).[2] Again, these terms serve to link the first section to the second and to carry the theme of the sermon forward. As the chart above demonstrates, this 'raising up' language is linked closely with the Davidic promise tradition.

Based on these features, an outline of the sermon may be developed around the three addresses to the audience (vv. 16b; 26; 38), dividing the sermon into two major sections (vv. 16b-25; 26-37) with a concluding application to the hearers (vv. 38-41).[3] The two main sections build to a similar climax: the promise made to David and to the fathers is fulfilled in Jesus (vv. 23 and 32-33). Both conclude with proof of this claim: the former with the historical testimony of John the Baptist (vv. 24-25), the latter with proof from Scripture (vv. 32-37). This outline is presented below:

1. Dumais, *Langage*, pp. 60-65 calls these words *mots-vedettes,* or 'bold-type' words.

2. Dumais, *Langage*, pp. 63-65. Dumais includes words in both groups of *mots-vedettes* which in my opinion are incidental to the narrative, rather than crucial for the carrying forward of the theme. He relates the similar -αγγελω ending verbs (εὐαγγελίζω in v. 32; καταγγέλλω in v. 38) with the 'promise language' and the description of the 'making great' (ὑψόω) of the nation Israel in Egypt (v. 17) with the 'raising up' language. While Luke may perhaps use these related words for stylistic effect, they do not have the same thematic significance as those noted above.

3. Similar outlines centered on the three addresses are suggested by others. See O. Glombitza, 'Akta XIII. 15-41. Analyse einer lukanischen Predigt vor Juden', *NTS* 5 (1958–59), p. 316; G. Stählin, *Die Apostelgeschichte* (1936; 1962), p. 181; Dumais, *Langage*, pp. 56-60; Pesch, *Apostelgeschichte*, II, p. 30. U. Wilckens, *Die Missionsreden der Apostelgeschichte* (3rd edn, 1974), pp. 50-54, outlines the sermon in six parts, making the statement concerning John the Baptist (vv. 24-25) a distinct section and dividing the closing application into two parts: vv. 15-23; 24-25; 26-31; 32-37; 38-39; 40-41. Buss, *Missionspredigt*, pp. 30-31, suggests a similar five-part outline but places the Baptist section with the address in v. 26 and brings together the four-verse conclusion into a single section: vv. 16a-23; 24-26; 27-31; 32-37; 38-41. Both are inadequate in that they separate the Scripture proofs of vv. 32-37 from their context in relation to the death and resurrection of Jesus (vv. 26-31). They also fail to adequately explain the role of the Baptist passage in relation to the rest of the sermon.

The Historical Survey through David the King to Jesus: 'Promise', vv. 16b-23
- The address to the hearers, v. 16b
- The historical survey to David, vv. 17-22
- *Climax:* The fulfillment of the promise to David in Jesus, v. 23
- John the Baptist's testimony to Jesus, vv. 24-25

The Application of the Message to the Hearers: 'Fulfillment', vv. 26-41
- The renewed address, v. 26
- The kerygma of the death and resurrection of Jesus, vv. 27-31
- *Climax:* The fulfillment of the promise in Jesus, vv. 32-33a
- Scripture proof for the fulfillment of the promise in Jesus, vv. 33b-37
  - Ps. 2.7 in v. 33b
  - Isa. 55.3 in v. 34
  - Ps. 16.10 in vv. 35-37

The offer of forgiveness and justification and the warning against rejection, vv. 38-41
- Third address to the hearers, v. 38a
- Forgiveness of sins and justification available through Jesus, vv. 38-39
- Warning against rejection, vv. 40-41

The literary form and structure of the sermon thus confirms that while the sermon is thoroughly 'Lukan', that is, it carries forward themes crucial to Luke's narrative development, it is also thoroughly Jewish in form and content. It fits perfectly into its narrative context as a synagogue sermon preached by Paul to Jews and God-fearers. The study has also confirmed that the fulfillment of the promises to David is the focal point of the sermon. How and in what sense these promises are fulfilled may be determined by an examination of the development of this theme in Luke's narrative.

c. *The Promise and its Fulfillment in Jesus the Saviour*

i. *The Historical Survey through David to Jesus: 'Promise', vv. 16b-23.* Following the request from the synagogue officials for a 'word of encouragement' (v. 15),[1] Paul addresses the audience of both Jews and God-fearers (v. 16b). He begins with a survey of Israel's history from the patriarchs to David.[2] That the purpose of this survey is to reach David is clear from the summary nature of the events leading up to the time of Saul and David. In four verses (62 words in Greek) Paul

1. Glombitza's suggestion ('Akta XIII. 15-41', pp. 308ff.) that λόγος παρακλήσεως is a technical term for a messianic interpretation of Scripture is appealing, but probably reads too much into the phrase.

2. Cf. Psalm 78, which surveys Yahweh's dealings with Israel from the days of Egypt to David. Cf. Bruce, 'Davidic Messiah', p. 11.

summarizes the history of Israel up to Samuel in seven great events: the choice of the fathers (v. 17), the sojourn in Egypt (v. 17), the exodus (v. 17), the wilderness period (v. 18), the conquest of Canaan (v. 19), the distribution of the land (v. 19) and the period of the judges (v. 20). The emphasis is on God's sovereign choice and providential care for his people.[1] From the mention of Samuel the prophet (v. 20), the summary slows with a relatively detailed description of Saul (v. 21) culminating in his removal by God (v. 22a). The survey reaches its goal in v. 22:

> ...and having removed him, he raised up David to be their king, of whom also he testified (saying), 'I have found David the son of Jesse, a man after my heart, who will do all my will.'

The verse is a composite of Old Testament allusions.[2] The words εὗρον Δαυίδ occur in Ps. 88.21 (LXX), a passage which, like this one, emphasizes the divine choice of David (cf. Ps. 88.20 LXX). The phrase ἄνδρα κατὰ τὴν καρδίαν μου comes from 1 Sam. 13.14 (Bowker's suggested proem text). The final phrase, ὃς ποιήσει πάντα τὰ θελήματά μου, is similar in its wording to Isa. 44.28 LXX, a reference to Cyrus. M. Wilcox suggests a more likely (Davidic) context, in the targum of 1 Sam. 13.14, which replaces the MT phrase 'a man after his heart' with 'a man doing his will'.[3] This view is appealing in that it draws both phrases in the second half of the verse from the same Old Testament text. The problem is the targum does not have the word 'all', which *does* occur in Isa. 44.28 LXX. The most likely solution is that the phrase arose in a Semitic context related to *Targ. Neb.* 1 Sam. 13.14 but was assimilated to the LXX wording of Isa. 44.28 when it was translated into Greek.

In any case, the historical survey clearly reaches its culmination in

1. This fact may tip the scale in favour of the variant reading ἐτροφοφόρησεν ('he cared for [them]') over ἐτροποφόρησεν ('he bore with [them]') in v. 18. The manuscript evidence is evenly balanced and the LXX text to which the passage probably alludes (Deut. 1.31) presents the same two variants (the Hebrew term can mean either 'endure' or 'care for'). Cf. Pesch, *Apostelgeschichte*, II, p. 35; B. Metzger, *A Textual Commenary on the Greek New Testament* (1975), pp. 405-406.

2. That the verse was part of 'testimony collection' is suggested by various scholars. See for example M. Wilcox, *The Semitisms of Acts* (1965), p. 23; Haenchen, *Acts*, pp. 3-4. *1 Clem.* 18.1, which like Acts 13.22 combines Ps. 88.20 LXX with 1 Sam. 13.14, lends some support to this possiblity: (Εὗρον) ἄνδρα κατὰ τὴν καρδίαν μου Δαυὶδ τὸν τοῦ Ἰεσσαί, ἐν ἐλέει αἰωνίῳ ἔχρισα αὐτόν.

3. Wilcox, *Semitisms*, p. 21.

God's raising up of David. This paves the way for the climax of this first section in v. 23, where Paul proclaims Jesus to be the fulfillment of God's promise to David:

> From the seed of this one, according to promise,
> God has brought[1] to Israel a saviour, Jesus.

Though neither the content nor the recipient of the 'promise' is stated, the reference to David's 'seed' shows that the Davidic promise is meant.[2] That Jesus is brought 'to Israel' demonstrates the continuity between this action of God and those described in vv. 17-22. His arrival is the culmination of God's choice of and providential care for Israel.

Jesus is here called 'saviour', a title given to him already in the angelic announcement in Lk. 2.11 and in Peter's speech before the Council in Acts 5.31. The contexts of both Lk. 2.11 (cf. Lk. 1.69, 71, 77; 2.30) and the present verse indicate that for Luke the key function of the Davidic messiah will be to 'save'. In the Gospel, the verb σῴζω is used of Jesus' healing activity (Lk. 8.36, 48; 17.19; 18.42) as well as his raising the dead (8.50). That this 'saving' can mean more than physical deliverance is indicated by the fact that the formula 'your faith has saved you' appears not only in healing contexts (Lk. 8.48; 17.19; 18.42; cf. 8.50), but also in Lk. 7.50, where it refers to the forgiveness of sins (v. 48). In the Zacchaeus account, too, where the reference is clearly to spiritual salvation, Jesus announces that 'today salvation has come to this house', and that 'the Son of man has come...to save' (Lk. 19.9-10). More will be said in Chapters 5 and 6 on Jesus' role as mediator of eschatological salvation during his earthly ministry. Here it is sufficient to point out that since in the Gospel Luke presents Jesus' saving activity as present already (in some sense) during his lifetime, the statement that God 'has brought to Israel a saviour' (v. 23) envisages his earthly ministry as well as his post-resurrection saving activity. This would suggest that Luke views Jesus as fulfilling the Davidic promise already during his earthly ministry.

1. ἤγαγεν. Though the variant ἔγειρε is appealing in view of the use of the 'raising up' language to describe David in the previous verse and Jesus in vv. 30, 33, 34, and 37, ἤγαγεν has better manuscript evidence and represents the harder reading. The copyist who altered the text no doubt considered God's 'bringing' Jesus to Israel as a saviour equivalent to his 'raising up' of Jesus. As we shall see, this was probably Luke's view as well.

2. Pesch, *Apostelgeschichte*, II, p. 36, says the fact that the promise is presupposed argues for the hypothesis of a sermon connected to the reading from the prophets (2 Samuel 7).

The short digression[1] concerning John the Baptist which follows provides indirect proof of Jesus' messianic identity.[2] Paul says that as John's ministry was drawing to an end, he emphatically stated that he was not the Christ but testified concerning the greater one 'coming after me' (cf. Lk. 3.15-16; Jn 1.20, 26-27; 3.28-30). Though it is possible this statement was meant to refute some who claimed messianic status for John,[3] Luke's primary purpose is more positive. John testified that he was not the one; rather the Christ would come 'after me' (v. 25). Since historically Jesus came after John (v. 24), Jesus must be the Christ.[4] Verses 24-25 thus serve as an historical testimony to the identity of Jesus. Their purpose is similiar to vv. 33-37. As the Old Testament quotes in these latter verses offer *scriptural* proof for Jesus' Davidic messiahship, so John's prophetic testimony in vv. 24-25 offers historical proof (see outline above).

ii. *The Application of the Message to the Hearers: 'Fulfillment', vv. 26-31*. The second section of the sermon begins with a renewed address to the hearers. Again, both Jews and God-fearers are addressed. The mention of ὁ λόγος τῆς σωτηρίας links the verse back to v. 23 and the salvation brought by Ἰησοῦς ὁ σωτήρ, the seed of David. That this salvation is sent ἡμῖν shows that the time of fulfillment has arrived and that those

1. So Marshall, *Acts*, p. 224, Haenchen, *Acts*, pp. 415-16, calls it an 'excursus'; Schneider, *Apostelgeschichte*, II, pp. 133-34, a 'parenthesis'.

2. So Haenchen, *Acts*, pp. 415-16; Marshall, *Acts*, pp. 224-25. Wilckens, *Missionsreden*, pp. 102, 106, following H. Conzelmann's perspective on John, claims Luke has inserted vv. 24-25 to separate John from the period of Jesus. This suggestion is unlikely. The purpose of the sermon up to this point has been to show that Jesus' arrival is the culmination and fulfillment of God's activity on behalf of Israel. It is reading an alien theological perspective into the sermon to say that now, with the statement concerning John, Luke wishes to separate Jesus from that history. It is significant that the spheres of ministry of Jesus and John are said to be the same. Just as Jesus is sent τῷ Ἰσραήλ as a saviour, so John's proclamation is παντὶ τῷ λαῷ Ἰσραήλ. As indicated in Chapter 3, Luke views John as a transitional figure between the times of promise and fulfillment. For a more detailed response to Conzelmann's view see Buss, *Missionspredigt*, pp. 25, 50-65, esp. 64-65. Buss states that Conzelmann's threefold scheme is not applicable to the sermon since Paul is here seeking to demonstrate that the Jesus event belongs to the period of Israel.

3. So Haenchen, *Acts*, pp. 415-16.

4. A similar point is made by Paul in Acts 19.4: 'John baptised with the baptism of repentance telling the people to believe in him who was *coming after him*, that is, in Jesus.'

present are the intended recipients of the messianic salvation-blessings.

The content of this 'word of salvation' is developed in the kerygmatic summary which follows (vv. 27-31). Events mentioned include Jesus' condemnation (v. 27), death (v. 28), burial (v. 29), resurrection (v. 30) and resurrection appearances (v. 31).[1] J. Doeve suggests that the course of thought of vv. 27-29 is determined by Ps. 2.1-2. Noting correctly that the sermon as a whole is developed from 2 Sam. 7.6-16, he points to the connection between the citation of Ps. 2.7 in v. 33 ('you are my son') and the father–son relationship spoken about in 2 Sam. 7.14a. Since Ps. 2.7 is cited in v. 33, the previous section concerning the death of Jesus (vv. 27-29) is likely to be an interpretation of Ps. 2.1-2, which speaks of the opposition to the 'Lord's anointed'. This conclusion is confirmed for Doeve by the fact that in Acts 4.24-30, Luke presents Ps. 2.1-2 as a prophecy concerning the death of Jesus.[2] Though it is true that Acts 4.24-30 speaks of the opposition to and death of the Davidic messiah, there are no explicit allusions to Psalm 2 in the present passage until the citation of Ps. 2.7 in v. 33.[3] It is unlikely, therefore, that Luke has Ps. 2.1-2 specifically in mind. Nevertheless, Doeve's discussion does indicate that Luke is here working from the same conceptual framework as in Acts 4.24-30. The condemnation and death of Jesus is presented as the fulfillment of Scripture, and contextually this death is the death of the Davidic heir (cf. vv. 22-23; 32-37). Jesus' crucifixion is again presented by Luke as the *God-ordained opposition to the Davidic messiah predicted beforehand in Scripture.*

In vv. 32-33a the sermon reaches its second climax. Turning to the hearers again, Paul states:

> And we proclaim (εὐαγγελιζόμεθα) to you the promise made to the fathers, that God has fulfilled this (promise) to us the children,[4] having raised up (ἀναστήσας) Jesus…

1. It is significant that this summary contains all the events named in the traditional statement of the gospel message in 1 Cor. 15.3-5, including the insistence that these events were 'according to scripture' (cf. vv. 27, 29) (cf. Pesch, *Apostelgeschichte*, II, p. 39).
2. Doeve, *Jewish Hermeneutics*, pp. 172-73.
3. The only word in common with Ps. 2.1-2 is ἄρχοντες, but while it is (probably) applied to Gentile leaders in Acts 4.27, here it refers to the Jewish leaders (cf. Acts 3.17).
4. For the legitimacy of the reading ἡμῖν and the questionable nature of αὐτῶν see Metzger, *Textual Commentary*, pp. 410-11.

The statement clearly describes God's 'raising up' of Jesus as the *means* by which the promise to David is fulfilled. The sense of this 'raising up', however, is a matter of much debate. Though the majority of commentators consider ἀναστήσας Ἰησοῦν to refer to the resurrection, a minority view takes it as the raising up of Jesus onto the scene of history.[1] In this latter view, vv. 32-33 summarize the whole historical appearance of Jesus, offering Ps. 2.7 (v. 33) as scriptural proof. Verses 34-37 then move to the resurrection, with proof from Isa. 55.3 and Ps. 16.10. Not only did God fulfill his promise to David by 'raising' Jesus onto the scene, but he confirmed that fulfillment by 'raising' him from the dead. (1) One argument for this position is the absence in v. 33 (in contrast to vv. 30 and 34) of the qualifier ἐκ νεκρῶν. This omission, along with the introductory ὅτι δέ in v. 34, may indicate a change in meaning. God fulfilled his promise to David in that (ὅτι, v. 33) he raised up Jesus *and* in that (ὅτι δέ, v. 34) he raised him *from the dead*. (2) Further support for this view is the use of ἀναστήσας elsewhere in Acts (3.22, 26; 7.37) to refer to Jesus' appearance onto the scene of history.[2] Luke does not seem to distinguish ἐγείρω and ἀνίστημι semantically, using both for the resurrection (ἐγείρω: Lk. 9.22; 24.6, 34; Acts 3.15; 4.10; 5.30; 10.40; 13.37; ἀνίστημι: Lk. 24.7, 46; Acts 2.24, 32; 10.41; 13.34; 17.3, 31) and both for historical appearance (ἐγείρω: Lk. 1.69; 7.16; Acts 13.22; ἀνίστημι: Acts 3.22, 26; 7.18, 37). If a pun is intended in v. 34, it is not surprising that Luke would use ἀνίστημι with two of its common meanings in subsequent verses (cf. vv. 22 and 37, where he uses ἐγείρω in the same two ways). (3) The use of ἐγείρω

1. So Rese, *Alttestamentliche Motive*, pp. 82-86; F.F. Bruce, *The Book of Acts* (2nd edn, 1988), pp. 259-60; *idem, Acts*, p. 309; *idem,* 'Davidic Messiah', p. 12; R.N. Longenecker, 'The Acts of the Apostles', in *The Expositors Bible Commentary* (ed. Frank E. Gaebelein; 1981), IX, p. 428; H.H. Wendt, *Die Apostelgeschichte* (9th edn, 1913), p. 213; Lampe, 'Holy Spirit', p. 174.

2. Rese, *Alttestamentliche Motive*, pp. 83-84. Rese adds to these arguments two additional ones: (1) the use of Ps. 2.7 for the resurrection is unprecedented, and (2) also in Acts 17.18, 'Jesus and the resurrection' is the content of Paul's preaching. The latter argument proves little since in either view a statement concerning Jesus' appearance (vv. 23-29) is followed by his resurrection. The former argument is also of questionable validity. Though Ps. 2.7 is nowhere else cited explicitly of the resurrection, it is used (beside 2 Sam. 7.14!) in Heb. 1.5 (cf. 5.5) with reference to the exaltation. Similarly, though the psalm is not explicitly cited in the resurrection statement of Rom 1.3-4, its conceptual framework appears to be present (see Chapter 2 section 3a).

in Lk. 1.69 offers a Davidic-context parallel to this one. Zechariah says that God has raised up (ἤγειρεν) the horn of salvation in David's house—almost certainly a reference to God's bringing Jesus, the Davidic messiah, *onto the scene of history.* (4) Perhaps the strongest argument for this view is the parallel to vv. 22-23. After raising up (ἤγειρεν) David to be king (v. 22), God fulfilled his promise to him by bringing Jesus to Israel (v. 23). Since the fulfillment of the promise is here applied to Jesus' whole life and ministry, it is likely that the 'raising up' of v. 33 has this same general reference. If this is the case, then the citation of Ps. 2.7 in v. 33 is scriptural proof not specifically for the resurrection, but for God's declaration of Jesus' divine sonship in general.[1]

Others argue that ἀναστήσας must be a reference to the resurrection:[2] (1) The lack of qualifier (ἐκ νεκρῶν) for ἀναστήσας is not decisive against this view since elsewhere in Acts ἀνίστημι is used of the resurrection without qualification (2.24, 32). (Though there is contextual qualification). (2) The context both before and after (vv. 31, 34) speaks of the resurrection.[3] (3) The combination of ἀνίστημι (or ἐγείρω) with Jesus (of Nazareth) occurs frequently in Luke–Acts with reference to the resurrection (Acts 2.24, 32; 4.10; 5.30; 10.40; 13.30). On the other hand, when these verbs are used with the significance of 'raise onto the scene', a title always follows (Lk. 1.69: 'a horn of salvation'; Acts 3.22, 7.37: 'a prophet'; 3.26: 'his servant'; 13.22: 'David...to be king').[4] (4) The pre-Pauline confession in Rom. 1.3-4 suggests that the early church linked Ps. 2.7 to Jesus' resurrection. (5) Since in Acts 4.25-27 Luke presents Ps. 2.1-2 as a prophecy concerning the opposition to and death of the Davidic messiah, it is likely that he would interpret v. 7

1. Bruce, *Book*, p. 260, suggests it is a reference to the baptism. Bock's proposal (*Proclamation*, pp. 244-49) that ἀναστήσας Ἰησοῦν refers to the resurrection but that Ps. 2.7 does not (it is rather a general statement of the fulfillment of the promise referring back to v. 32a) is to be rejected since the ὡς clause of v. 33 clearly connects ἀναστήσας with the scripture citation which follows.

2. This view is held by most commentators, including J. Dupont, 'Filius meus es tu. L'interpétation de Ps. II,7 dans le Nouveau Testament', *RSR* 35 (1948), pp. 522-43, esp. 528-35; Lövestam, *Son and Saviour*, pp. 8-11; Haenchen, *Acts*, p. 411; Wilckens, *Missionsreden*, p. 51 n. 3; Schweizer, 'Davidic "Son of God"', p. 190; Burger, *Jesus als Davidssohn*, p. 140; Dumais, *Langage*, pp. 179-80; Buss, *Missionspredigt*, p. 89; Schneider, *Apostelgeschichte*, II, p. 137; Roloff, *Apostelgeschichte*, p. 207; Pesch, *Apostelgeschichte*, II, p. 38.

3. Lövestam, *Son and Saviour*, p. 9.

4. Dupont, 'Filius meus es tu', p. 530.

of the same psalm with reference to his resurrection-vindication. The resurrection interpretation better reflects the temporal order of the prophetic psalm.

I would suggest that the best solution is a modified version of the first view, which draws on elements of the second. While taking Ps. 2.7 as a prophecy fulfilled at the resurrection (as in view 2), Luke introduces the verse primarily to prove that Jesus is the Son of God, and hence the messiah, who fulfills the promises to David in his whole life, death and resurrection (as in view 1). In line with his statement in v. 23 (cf. Lk. 1.69), Luke probably uses ἀναστήσας to refer to the whole Jesus event.[1] Jesus' whole life, death and resurrection were κατ' ἐπαγγελίαν (v. 23), that is, they were part of the fulfillment of God's promise to David. While this fulfillment begins with Jesus' coming onto the scene of history, it also encompasses the resurrection—the climax of his 'raising up'. The citation of Ps. 2.7 in v. 33 serves a two-fold purpose. First and foremost, it provides scriptural proof for the claim of vv. 23 and 33 that Jesus is the messiah raised up from David's seed in fulfillment of God's promise to the fathers. Since Jesus is the Son of God (Ps. 2.7b), he is also the messiah. The citation of Ps. 2.7b (υἱός μου εἶ σύ) thus plays a role similar to the allusion in Luke's baptism narrative (σύ εἶ ὁ υἱός μου), where it confirms Jesus' messianic identity (Lk. 3.22; cf. 9.35; see discussions of these passages in Chapters 5 and 6 below). The second purpose of the quote is to introduce the resurrection argument which follows. The second phrase (Ps. 2.7c: ἐγὼ σήμερον γεγέννηκά σε) moves the argument forward by setting the stage for the statement of the resurrection (v. 34a) and its scriptural proofs from Isa. 55.3 and Ps. 16.10 (vv. 34b, 35). The 'today' is probably taken by Luke as the day of the resurrection and the begetting language a reference to the new resurrection life bestowed on Jesus by the Father. If one were to ask Luke *when* Ps. 2.7 was fulfilled (as a prophetic psalm), he would probably respond 'at the resurrection'. However, as the allusions to the Ps. 2.7b in Lk. 3.22 and 9.35 confirm, Luke understands the verse in the sense, '*because* you are my son (and hence, the *messiah*), I have begotten you to new resurrection life'. As in Lk. 3.22 and 9.35, the statement of sonship is meant first and foremost *to confirm Jesus' messianic identity*. The allusion thus fits perfectly as scriptural proof of

1. Cf. Lake and Cadbury, *Beginnings*, IV, pp. 154-55: 'In this case ἀναστήσας is not exactly a reference to the Resurrection, but to the whole career of Jesus, including the Resurrection and the Glorification.'

the general 'raising up' of Jesus to be the saviour of Israel. Secondarily, it sets up the resurrection argument which follows by confirming that the resurrection marked the climax and culmination of this fulfillment.

This explanation solves various problems of the other two views: (1) It takes account of the parallels in Lk. 1.69 and in vv. 22 and 23. Just as God raised up David to be king (v. 22), and just as God brought Jesus to Israel as a saviour in fulfillment of the promise to David (v. 23), so also he 'raised up' Jesus in fulfillment of God's promise to the fathers (v. 33). The latter two statements are roughly equivalent. (2) This view also agrees with Luke's use of Ps. 2.7 elsewhere in Luke–Acts and suggests his awareness of the early Christian application of the psalm to the resurrection and/or exaltation.[1] It also fits with the temporal order of the prophetic psalm as suggested by Acts 4.25-26. From conception Jesus is the Son of God (Lk. 1.35), so God declares this to be the case at the baptism (Lk. 3.22) and the transfiguration (9.35). At Jesus' death and resurrection, then, the prophetic psalm itself was fulfilled: Ps. 2.1-2 when Jesus was put to death by the Gentiles and the people of Israel (Acts 4.25-28); Ps. 2.7 when he was vindicated at his resurrection as the Son of God and messiah. (3) This view also fits well with the grammatical structure of the passage. The particle ὡς in v. 33b introduces Ps. 2.7 as scriptural proof of the raising up of Jesus to be Israel's saviour. The ὅτι δέ of v. 34 is parallel to the ὅτι of v. 33; it takes up the resurrection allusion in Ps. 2.7c, carrying the argument forward with a play on words on the 'raising up' language of v. 33. δέ is adversative and explanatory, introducing a new and more specific line of thought:[2] '...that (ὅτι) God has fulfilled the promise...having raised up Jesus (as the messiah)... indeed (or, 'even') that (ὅτι δέ) he raised him *from the dead*...' (4) This view also makes better sense of the three Old Testament quotations,

1. See the discussion in Chapter 2 section 3a. For attempts to link the psalm's birth motif to the resurrection see Lövestam, *Son and Saviour*, pp. 43-47, who discusses Acts 2.24 (where I rejected a birth motif), *4 Ezra* 4.40-42, Col. 1.18, Rev. 1.5, Heb. 1.6 (exaltation), Rom 1.4 (no birth image, but a connection to Ps. 2.7). See Bock, *Proclamation*, pp. 246-48, for opposition to Lövestam. Whether the birth image of Ps. 2.7 was specifically developed in relation to Jesus' resurrection, Rom. 1.4 and Heb. 1.5 suggest that the psalm itself was linked to Jesus' resurrection and/or exaltation.

2. BDF, p. 232 (§447, 8); cf. Rom. 3.22. Bock, *Proclamation*, 248, suggests that δέ is here parenthetical (BDF, p. 232, §447, 7), and that v. 34a is a parenthetic explanation of the citation of Ps. 2.7. This is unlikely, however, since the ὅτι clauses are parallel.

Pss. 2.7, 16.10 and Isa. 55.3. Ps. 2.7 confirms that Jesus is the promised messiah who fulfills the promises to David; Ps. 16.10 provides scriptural proof that the messiah was to be raised from the dead (see below); and Isa. 55.3 demonstrates that the salvation blessings which result are given to God's people (see below). If Ps. 2.7 was intended primarily as scriptural proof of the resurrection, it would serve the same purpose as Ps. 16.10.

Moving forward in the argument, the opening phrase of v. 34 thus offers an elaboration on the 'raising up' statement of v. 33. Jesus was not only raised up to be Israel's saviour but he was also raised *from the dead incorruptible.* Scripture proof related to this assertion is now introduced: οὕτως εἴρηκεν ὅτι δώσω ὑμῖν τὰ ὅσια Δαυὶδ τὰ πιστά. The citation is taken from Isa. 55.3 LXX.[1] A brief examination of the significance of the phrase in the MT and the LXX will help to illuminate its meaning in the present context. The MT reads, 'I will make with you an everlasting covenant, the faithful mercies of David.' God here renews the eternal Davidic covenant (ברית עולם) with his people, assuring them that the sure mercies (חסדי הנאמנים) promised to David are still valid towards them (cf. 2 Sam. 7.15,חסד, 16, נאמן). Since there is no expectation for Davidic renewal elsewhere in Isaiah 40-55, many commentators consider these verses to represent the transfer of the blessings of the Davidic covenant from the dynasty to the people in general.[2] Though

1. Instead of δώσω ὑμῖν the LXX reads διαθήσομαι ὑμῖν διαθήκην αἰώνιον. Various reasons for this alteration have been suggested: (1) The alteration is meant to provide a verbal connection with the word δώσεις in the quotation of Ps. 16.10. But a verbal connection already exists between these passages (τὰ ὅσια—τὸν ὅσιον), making this alteration unnecessary (though still possible). (2) The verb may be a verbal assimilation from the near context in Isa. 55.4 LXX which says 'he gave him (ἔδωκα αὐτον) as a witness to the peoples'. (3) Rese, *Alttestamentliche Motive*, p. 87, suggests that the omission was made by Luke because he prefers to speak of the Abrahamic rather than the Davidic covenant (Lk. 1.72; Acts 3.25; 7.8). This is possible since Luke seems to prefer 'promise' language for David (never using διαθήκη of him) and 'covenant' language for Abraham. If this is the case, Luke's reason for distinguishing the two terms is probably for clarity of expression rather than for any theological purpose since, as we have seen, he views the covenants and promises of God as a unity (cf. Lk. 1.69-73) (see the final comments of Chapter 3 section 3a above). Whatever the reason for the alteration, Lövestam, *Son and Saviour*, pp. 54-55, 80, points out that the original meaning of Isa. 55.3 is retained since God's covenant was not a binding agreement between two equal partners, but rather a covenant promise conferred ('given') by God upon his people Israel.

2. So O. Eissfeldt, 'The Promises of Grace to David in Isaiah 55.1-5', in

the dynasty is at an end, God remains faithful to his chosen people. Others see here a continued expectation for the renewal of the Davidic dynasty.[1] The issue is a difficult one. While the absence of Davidic references elsewhere renders it at least debatable whether the author expected the re-establishment of the Davidic line, it is even more difficult to comprehend how he could have viewed the renewal of the Davidic covenant *without* the restoration of the throne and dynasty.[2] After all, of the six aspects of the covenant promise of 2 Samuel 7 (see Chapter 2 section 1a), five are directly related to the figure of the king. If the author merely wanted to affirm God's eternal faithfulness to his covenant people, why not appeal to the Abrahamic or Noachic covenants (as he does in Isa. 54.7-10)?[3] To invoke and radically reinterpret the Davidic covenant when, in fact, he envisaged no hope for its actual fulfillment would only confuse the issue. The evidence would thus seem to favour the latter view.

The LXX altered the verse in an unusual way, translating חסד with ὅσιος rather than ἔλεος, its normal Greek equivalent. This resulted in the plural construction τὰ ὅσια Δαυὶδ τὰ πιστά ('the holy things of David which are faithful') rather than τὰ ἐλέη Δαυὶδ τὰ πιστά ('the faithful mercies of David'). It has been suggested that the translators confused the substantive חֶסֶד ('favour', 'loving kindness') with the adjective חָסִיד ('holy', 'pious'—generally rendered ὅσιος);[4] but the

Israel's Prophetic Heritage (1962), pp. 196-207; von Rad, *Old Testament Theology*, II, p. 240; R.N. Whybray, *Isaiah 40–66* (1975), pp. 191-92; C. Westermann, *Isaiah 40–66* (1969), pp. 283-84.

1. So Mowinckel, *He That Cometh*, p. 166; J. Eaton, *Festal Drama in Deutero-Isaiah* (1979), p. 119; J. Skinner, *The Book of the Prophet Isaiah* (1929), II, pp. 159-60; G.A.F. Knight, *Deutero-Isaiah* (1965), pp. 257-59.

2. As Bock, *Proclamation*, p. 250, correctly notes, 'One can include the nation and talk about the fulfillment of the Davidic promise, but can one exclude the line and still talk about this covenant promise?' Bock also points out that the reference to the exploits and example of David in Isa. 55.4 is inexplicable unless a true parallel is being invoked.

3. B.W. Anderson, 'Exodus and Covenant in Second Isaiah and Prophetic Tradition', in *Magnalia Dei: The Mighty Acts of God* (1976), pp. 339-60, argues that the author of Deutero-Isaiah invokes the unconditional and eternal covenants with Noah (Isa. 54.7-10; cf. Gen. 9.16), David, and perhaps antecedently with Abraham, so as to avoid the conditional nature of the Mosaic covenant. This may be the case, but it is still inconceivable how the author could affirm the continuing reliability of the Davidic covenant without the renewal of the Davidic throne.

4. So J. Dupont, 'TA 'OΣIA ΔAYIΔ TA ΠIΣTA (Actes 13,34 = Isaïe 55,3)',

alteration may have been intentional. Both Dupont and Lövestam refer to the only other use of the plural ὅσια in the LXX, Deut. 29.18. In this passage the word is used in a sense similar to that found in Greek inscriptions from Cnidus, where it applies to favours expected from a deity. In both Deut. 29.18 and Isa. 55.3, the LXX may therefore have borrowed an expression from Greek religious language to speak of divine benefits bestowed by God.[1] If this is the case, the meaning of the LXX is not much different from the MT, speaking in a covenant context of the divine benefits promised to David and partaken of by God's people. Though the interpretations of the LXX and MT are therefore relatively straightforward, a confusing array of interpretations have been suggested for the meaning of the phrase in its context in Acts.[2] These views may be divided into four general categories:

(1) The phrase refers to David's holiness or piety. In this view, proposed by H.H. Wendt, τὰ ὅσια in v. 34 and τὸν ὅσιον in v. 35 correspond to each other and both are explained by v. 36, which says that David 'served the will of God in his generation'. David is thus judged in Acts as having been ὅσιος by virtue of his acts of piety. Because of his death, however, David's piety only lasted for his generation; whereas the oracle says that τὰ ὅσια are πιστά, or unalterably firm. For this to be realized, the holy one must have an imperishable life, which Jesus obtained at his resurrection.[3] One problem with this view is its failure to

in *Etudes sur les Actes des Apôtres* (1967), pp. 339-41, 343-44.

1. Dupont, *Etudes sur les Actes*, pp. 343-44; Lövestam, *Son and Saviour*, pp. 75-76. Other factors which may have influenced the LXX translators decision to use ὅσια include the close association of חֶסֶד and חָסִיד in the Old Testament, the association of both words (and their Greek equivalents) with the idea of covenant, and the similarity of sound between ὅσιος and חֶסֶד (so Lövestam, *Son and Saviour*, pp. 74-79).

2. For summaries of various interpretations of the phrase (from somewhat different perspectives) see the discussions of Lövestam, *Son and Saviour*, pp. 50-54; Dupont, *Etudes sur les Actes*, pp. 338-42; Bock, *Proclamation*, pp. 252-53. The issue is made more complicated by some interpretations which explain the significance of the verse without specifically stating what or who τὰ ὅσια Δαυὶδ are. Further confusion results from the lack of clear definition for such terms as 'Heilsgüter' ('salvation blessings') and 'messianic blessings', which sometimes seem to mean the promises made to David (from 2 Samuel 7) and sometimes the salvation blessings which the messiah brings (forgiveness of sins, resurrection life, etc.).

3. Wendt, *Apostelgeschichte*, pp. 213-15. A. Loisy, *Les Actes des Apôtres* (1920), pp. 534-35, takes a similar view but describes τὰ ὅσια Δαυὶδ τὰ πιστά as the 'true' holiness of David which, when connected to Ps. 16.11, is shown to be equivalent to the 'incorruptibility' of the holy one, a reference to the resurrection of

take into account the Old Testament context of the passage, which speaks of God's action toward David, not David's active piety. In addition, this view does not adequately explain how τὰ ὅσια are given 'to you'.

(2) The phrase refers to the messiah or the messiah's resurrection. Lake and Cadbury proposed that the phrase was unintelligible by itself; its meaning is defined by the citation of Ps. 16.10 in the following verse. According to this view, the author or preacher is here following the rabbinic method of interpreting by analogy, whereby a clear passage (Ps. 16.10 in v. 35) is brought forward to explain an obscure one (Isa. 55.3 in v. 34). Since ὅσιος in v. 35 refers to the 'holy one' who was resurrected, τὰ ὅσια must also be a reference to the resurrection.[1] The reasoning of Lake and Cadbury is here inconsistent. In v. 35 ὅσιος refers not to the resurrection itself but to the messiah who is resurrected. On the basis of the rabbinic method they propose, these authors should have concluded that τὰ ὅσια referred to the *messiah,* and the whole phrase, δωσω ὑμῖν τὰ ὅσια Δαυὶδ τὰ πιστά, to the resurrection. This latter interpretation seems to be held by Haenchen, who says that the Isaiah text implies: 'I will give you Christians the scion of David together with the immortal life of the Resurrection.'[2] The key problem with both these views is the neuter plural τὰ ὅσια, which makes it unlikely that the referent here is a person (the 'holy one' of Ps. 16.10).

(3) The phrase refers to salvation blessings. After a detailed examination, J. Dupont concludes that τὰ ὅσια are 'la sainteté (τήν ὁσιότητα), considérée dans ses manifestations concrètes, purification des péchés, justification, dispositions saintes qui confèrent à toute la vie chrétienne une signification cultuelle.'[3] Dupont reasons primarily along three lines: (a) The statement that David did the will of God (v. 36; cf. v. 22) shows that he was ὅσιος (v. 34), which may be defined as a life of pious service to God. Yet David was ὅσιος only in his generation, it remained for Jesus, ὁ ὅσιος who did not undergo corruption, to fulfill the

the Christ. 'David's holiness of which Isaiah speaks is the immortal glory of the resurrected Christ' (p. 535).

1. Lake and Cadbury, *Beginnings*, IV, p. 155.

2. Haenchen, *Acts*, p. 412. Another view similarly developed on rabbinic principles is proposed by Doeve, *Jewish Hermeneutics*, pp. 174-75, who bases his argument on the Hebrew text rather than the Greek, as did Lake and Cadbury.

3. Dupont, *Etudes sur les Actes*, p. 357.

promise.[1] (b) The emphasis throughout the sermon is on the fulfillment of the promise and the present application to the hearers (cf. vv. 26; 32-33; 38). Stress must therefore be placed on 'to you' in the phrase δώσω ὑμῖν τὰ ὅσια Δαυὶδ τὰ πιστά.[2] (c) Preceded by δώσω ὑμῖν, and followed by τὸν ὅσιον, τὰ ὅσια must therefore refer to the piety that is bestowed on believers by God; that is, the salvation blessings that come through Jesus, the Christ. These blessing are defined in vv. 38-39 as forgiveness of sins and justification apart from the law. The citation of Isa. 55.3, then, does not directly concern the resurrection; rather the context of vv. 34-37 as a whole demonstrates that Christ's incorruptible resurrection life is prerequisite and basis of the gift of τὰ ὅσια Δαυίδ.

Dupont's discussion is valuable in many respects, especially in pointing to the importance of the application to the hearers (ὑμῖν) in the context of the sermon. He also rightly points out that the purpose of the argument in vv. 34-37 is not merely to prove the resurrection, but to stress Jesus' incorruptible resurrection life and its salvific significance.[3] But there are several significant problems with his view. First, the phrase which introduces the quote (ἀνέστησεν αὐτὸν ἐκ νεκρῶν...οὕτως εἴρηκεν ὅτι...), suggests that the clause *does* directly relate to the resurrection. Secondly, by taking τὰ ὅσια as David's active piety, he (like Wendt) goes against the Old Testament context which refers to God's favor towards David. Finally, Dupont does not take enough account of the fact that it is τὰ ὅσια *Δαυίδ*, the holy things *of David,* which are bestowed by God. His explanation that this is the holiness of the other, immortal 'David' (Jesus) is not convincing.[4] It is difficult to see how he gets from David's piety to the salvation benefits provided by the death and resurrection of Jesus.

(4) The phrase refers to the covenant promises to David.[5] In this view, which is adopted here, τὰ ὅσια are the 'divine blessings' promised to David in 2 Sam. 7.5-16 and developed elsewhere in the Old Testament (cf. Pss. 89, 132).[6] The plural construction τὰ ὅσια is appropriate since

1. Dupont, *Etudes sur les Actes*, pp. 344-50.
2. Dupont, *Etudes sur les Actes*, pp. 351-54.
3. Dupont, *Etudes sur les Actes*, p. 359.
4. Dupont, *Etudes sur les Actes*, pp. 356, 359.
5. This is basically the view of Lövestam, *Son and Saviour*, pp. 71-81 (cf. Pesch, *Apostelgeschichte*, II, p. 39). Near the end of his discussion, however, Lövestam seems to alter this somewhat by applying τὰ ὅσια Δαυίδ specifically to the person of the messiah rather than to the Davidic promises as a whole (p. 79 n. 4).
6. W. Bauer, BAGD, p. 585, also sees the reference here to the promises to

these blessings are multi-faceted, comprising the covenant promises of an heir, perpetual favour from God (for that heir), an eternal house, throne and kingdom, and rest and protection from enemies. The descriptive adjective πιστά presents these covenant promises as faithful or enduring and bears verbal correspondence to 2 Sam. 7.16: David's house and kingdom will be made sure (πιστωθήσεται) forever. This view is immediately appealing for two reasons. First, it agrees with the Old Testament context of Isa. 55.3, evident (with slightly different nuances) both in the MT and the LXX. In spite of the unusual rendering of חסדי by τὰ ὅσια in the LXX, the covenant context and the mention of David make it clear that the LXX has the Davidic promises in view. Secondly, this position agrees with the overall development of the sermon, which is seeking to show that Jesus has fulfilled the promises to David.

In its Old Testament context, Isa. 55.3 is a renewal of the promise to David, emphasizing its enduring quality (an 'eternal covenant' concerning 'faithful mercies') and its present application to Israel ('I will make a covenant with *you*'). This is exactly how Luke takes it. He first states that not only did Jesus rise from the dead, but he rose *incorruptible*. This, he points out, is in accord with the nature of the promises to David (τὰ ὅσια Δαυίδ) which are eternal and absolutely reliable (πιστά).[1] Thus the key emphasis is on the adjective πιστός, the reliability and

David but describes the significance of the quotation somewhat differently. He says Isa. 55.3 is meant to show that the quote which immediately follows (Ps. 16.10) could not refer to David but to Christ alone. According to Isa. 55.3, the promises to David have solemnly been transferred 'to you'. Since David served not you but his own generation (v. 36), the promises to God cannot refer to him, so must refer to his messianic descendant. One problem with this view is that by stressing only ὑμῖν, the relationship between the resurrection statement (v. 34a) and the quotation is ignored. In addition, it is strange that a statement meant to clarify the significance of Ps. 16.10 would be placed *before* it. It would seem there must be some further significance behind the quotation.

1. As we have seen, eternalness and reliability were an integral part of the Davidic promise tradition throughout its history in Judaism. The phrase עד־עולם (= εἰς [τὸν] αἰῶνα) is found three times in 2 Sam. 7.13-16, and this idea is picked up elsewhere in the Old Testament (Ps. 89.30 MT) and in later Judaism (Sir. 47.11; 1 Macc 2.57; *Pss. Sol.* 17.4; 4QPBless). Reliability is seen in God's promise that his lovingkindness will not depart from the Davidic heir (2 Sam. 7.15; cf. Ps. 89.29 MT; Sir. 47.19-22) and is implied in the descriptions of the promise as a divine decree (Ps. 2.7), an oath (Ps. 89.4 MT; 132.11; *Pss. Sol.* 17.4) and a covenant (2 Sam. 23.5; Ps. 89.4-5, 29 MT; 132.12; Isa. 55.3; 2 Chron. 13.5; 21.7; Sir. 47.11; 4QPBless). Cf. Lövestam, *Son and Saviour*, pp. 72-75.

enduring nature of the promises. A secondary emphasis is on the fact that these promises are given 'to you'. This aspect, like that of eternalness and reliability, was an integral part of the promise tradition.[1] Through David's heir all of God's people receive salvation blessings. This is not to say, as in Dupont's view, that τὰ ὅσια 'given' in v. 34 are equivalent to the salvation blessings of vv. 38-39 (forgiveness of sins and justification). Rather, it is the blessings of the *Davidic promises as a whole* which are given, i.e. the messiah together with his eternal house, throne and kingdom. It is then the messiah, the saviour of Israel (v. 23), who brings the salvation blessings of forgiveness of sins and justification (vv. 38-39) to God's people. Seen in this light, the quotation has a double function: to demonstrate the eternal nature of the Davidic promises and to show the application to the hearers brought about by the fulfillment of the promise in Jesus. Its use is both descriptive and prophetic.

That this is the best interpretation of the quotation is clear not only from its agreement with the Old Testament context and with the flow of the sermon, but also because it enables the verse to be interpreted on its own merit, without dependence upon the quotation from Ps. 16.10 which follows. Though it is true that this interpretation requires a certain amount of contextual pre-understanding on Luke's part and on that of his audience, his emphasis on the Davidic promises elsewhere shows that this pre-understanding is likely. The fact that Luke presents the quotation in such an abbreviated form likewise suggests the presence here of a stereotypical phrase which he assumes will be familiar to his audience.

From the statement of the eternal nature of the promise, v. 35 moves on to the person of the messiah and how his resurrection fulfills this promise of permanence. The verbal connection between the plural τὰ ὅσια (v. 34) and the singular τὸν ὅσιόν (v. 35) agrees perfectly with this narrowing of the topic. The resurrected messiah, the 'holy one' who will not see corruption, is thus one of the 'holy things' promised to David. The conjunction διότι introduces an explanation of the relationship between the resurrection to incorruptible life (v. 34a) and the eternal nature of the Davidic covenant (v. 34b).

The argument from Psalm 16 is similar to that of Acts 2. Both passages cite Ps. 16.10 (16.8-11 in Acts 2), where David prophesies that God would not allow his 'holy one' to undergo decay (2.25-28, 31; 13.35).

1. 2 Sam. 7.10; Jer. 23.6; Ezek. 34.22ff.; 37.25ff.; 4QFlor; *Pss. Sol.* 17.21ff.; etc. Cf. Lövestam, *Son and Saviour*, 81.

Both then imply that David has not fulfilled this prophecy since he died and underwent decay (2.29; 13.36).[1] In spite of these agreements, there is an important difference in nuance between the two passages. In Acts 2.25-32, the purpose of the argument is to demonstrate that Jesus is the Davidic messiah. Peter claims that the resurrection David predicted in Ps. 16.10 was not his own but the messiah's. Since Jesus was resurrected, he must be the messiah. In Acts 13.35-37 the purpose is to show that Jesus' resurrection proves that he has fulfilled the promise to David of an eternal reign. While David served the will of God[2] during his own generation,[3] his reign did not last forever, as his death and bodily decay prove (v. 36). Jesus, however, was resurrected to incorruptible life (v. 37) so his reign will last forever (cf. Lk. 1.33).

In conclusion, the argument throughout this complex of Old Testament prophecies stays close to the Davidic promise tradition. It is significant that each of the Old Testament texts takes up a different aspect of the tradition. As demonstrated in Chapter 2, the promise of 2 Sam. 7.5-16 stressed the 'raising up' of David's seed, his father–son relationship with God, the assurance of God's perpetual חסד, the eternal duration of David's house, throne and kingdom, and rest and security for God's people. Verse 33 with its citation of Ps. 2.7 clearly picks up the first two aspects of this promise. Jesus is the descendant of David raised up and declared by God to be his son. Isaiah 55.3 indicates the perpetuity of God's חסד toward David, and confirms the bestowal of these salvation blessings on God's people. Psalm 16.10 indicates Jesus' incorruptibility and, by implication, the eternal duration of his reign and

1. That David underwent decay is implied in Acts 2.29 and explicitly stated in 13.37.

2. So Dupont, *Etudes sur les Actes*, pp. 345-46; Bruce, *Book*, p. 258; Marshall, *Acts*, p. 227. The phrase τῇ τοῦ θεοῦ βουλῇ could also be taken with the verb ἐκοιμήθη: 'fell asleep by the will of God' (so Haenchen, *Acts*, p. 412; Schneider, *Apostelgeschichte*, II, p. 139; Pesch, *Apostelgeschichte*, II, p. 39). In either case the significance of ἰδίᾳ γενεᾷ ὑπηρετήσας remains the same: David served only his own generation.

3. In my opinion, both Wendt and Dupont place the wrong emphasis on the phrase ἰδίᾳ γενεᾷ ὑπηρετήσας τῇ τοῦ θεοῦ βουλῇ. The purpose of this statement is not to associate the 'holy one' with David. This would produce a contradiction, since God promised that his holy one would not see corruption; but David did see corruption! Rather, the purpose of the phrase is to show that David's reign was temporal. While he faithfully served God in his own generation, his reign was limited to his lifetime and so did not fulfill the promise of an eternal kingdom.

kingdom. Since Jesus is begotten to incorruptible life, the kingdom he initiates will be eternal.

d. *The Conclusion of the Sermon and the Events of the Following Sabbath*

i. *An Offer of Salvation and a Warning of Rejection, vv. 38-41*. Paul concludes his sermon with an offer of salvation and a warning against rejection. Because Jesus is the reigning Davidic messiah, through him forgiveness of sins (v. 38; cf. 2.38; 3.19; 5.30f.; 10.43; 13.38; 26.18) and justification apart from the Law is offered to all who believe (v. 39). The description of salvation as being 'justified' (δικαιωθῆναι) is unique in Luke–Acts and is clearly intended to recall the proclamation of Paul.[1] As is typical of Luke, the means by which Jesus' death and resurrection provide salvation is not developed. The reason for this is not necessarily an inadequate understanding on Luke's part of the sacrificial significance of Jesus' death. It may simply confirm that Luke's narrative purpose in the sermon is primarily christological rather than soteriological (see Chapter 7 section 2bii). Paul demonstrates that Jesus has fulfilled the Davidic promises; and the key role of the Davidic messiah is to bring salvation to Israel (v. 23; cf. Lk. 1.69; 2.11; Acts 5.31) and to the ends of the earth (v. 47; cf. Lk. 2.32). The important point of vv. 38-39 is not *how* Jesus saves, but *that* he saves. Twice it is stressed that *through him* (v. 38, διὰ τούτου; v. 39, ἐν τούτῳ) salvation has come. With the coming of Jesus the saviour, the promise to Israel has been fulfilled, the time of salvation has arrived. The nation need only lay hold of it.

In light of the urgency of the hour, Paul balances the offer of salvation with a warning against rejection. He tells his listeners to beware lest they fulfill the words of Hab. 1.5 predicting the destruction of those who scoff at the new work which God is accomplishing 'in your days'. The offer of justification to 'all who believe' (v. 39), together with this warning against rejection, foreshadow the events of the following week (vv. 44-48), where the rejection by the Jews (v. 45) is followed by the turning of the missionaries to the Gentiles (v. 46) (see below). That πᾶς ὁ πιστεύων is meant to include the Gentiles (at least for the implied reader) is

1. Cf. Pesch, *Apostelgeschichte*, II, pp. 40, 42, for comments on the relationship of the teaching of Paul here to that of his letters. Vielhauer's suggestion ('On the "Paulinism" of Acts', p. 42) that Luke poorly imitates Paul by presenting a *partial* justification by faith which supplements justification by the Law is reading too much into the text (so Haenchen, *Acts*, p. 412 n. 4, and most commentators).

suggested by the appearance of the same phrase in Peter's speech in Acts 10.43, where it refers to Gentile inclusion in the blessings of salvation.

The meeting breaks up with requests for Paul and Barnabas to return the following Sabbath (v. 42) and with many Jews and 'devout proselytes'[1] showing interest and receiving encouragement from Paul and Barnabas.

ii. *The Events of the Following Sabbath, vv. 44-48.* The account of the following Sabbath (vv. 44-48) is integrally linked to Paul's sermon. The story forms the climax to the events at Pisidian-Antioch and sets the stage for Paul's missionary activity throughout the rest of Acts. The enormous turnout (πᾶσα ἡ πόλις [!], v. 44) to hear Paul and Barnabas provokes the jealousy of the Jews who begin contradicting Paul's words and 'blaspheming' (v. 45). In response, Paul and Barnabas boldly announce that, because of this repudiation, 'we are turning to the Gentiles'. They quote Isa. 49.6 LXX as their justification: 'I have appointed you as a light for the Gentiles, that you may be for salvation to the end of the earth.' Hearing this the Gentiles respond with rejoicing and acceptance, and 'the word of the Lord' spreads through the whole region (vv. 48-49). The episode initiates a pattern which will be repeated throughout Acts. When the Jews reject the Gospel, Paul turns to the Gentiles (13.46; 18.6; 19.9; 28.25-28). The importance of the theme is evident from the fact that Acts climaxes with a passage closely parallel to the present one (Acts 28.25-28).[2]

This pattern raises the fundamental question of the relationship between Jewish rejection and Gentile reception of the gospel. Though a detailed examination of this question is beyond the scope of the present work, I would agree in general with the view of J. Dupont over against those of J. Jervell on the one side, and H. Conzelmann, E. Haenchen, J.T. Sanders, *et al.*[3] on the other. These latter suggest that for Luke the

1. προσήλυτων may be a gloss since σεβόμενος generally denotes God-fearing Gentiles who did not become full converts (suggested by Haenchen, *Acts*, p. 413 n. 5). On the other, since the story will climax a week later with the reception of the gospel by Gentiles (vv. 48-49), it would be strange for Luke to mention Gentile converts at this stage. σεβόμενος in this case would mean simply 'devout'.

2. For various parallels see J. Dupont, 'Je t'ai établi lumière des nations (*Ac 13, 14.43-52)',* in *Nouvelles Etudes sur les Actes des Apôtres* (1984), p. 344.

3. Conzelmann, *Theology*, pp. 162-63; Haenchen, *Acts*, pp. 100-103; J.T. Sanders, *The Jews in Luke–Acts* (1987); J.C. O'Neill, *The Theology of Acts in its Historical Setting* (1970), p. 90.

Gentile mission arises as a result of Israel's rejection of the Gospel. Because of her obduracy, Israel is rejected by God and her role in salvation-history is replaced by the Gentiles. The church becomes the 'new Israel'. Jervell disputes this perspective, pointing to the phenomenal success of the gospel among the Jews in Acts.[1] He claims that the Gentile mission is not triggered by Israel's rejection, but the reverse. The promises to Israel are fulfilled in the Jews who accept Jesus. It is through their ministry, then, that the Gentiles gain a share in the kingdom as an 'associate people' of God. Israel's restoration is the presupposition of the Gentile mission.

Dupont and others take a mediating position.[2] Though there is widespread Jewish rejection of the gospel (as Scripture predicted there would be, Acts 13.40-41; 28.26-27), this rejection is not universal, nor does it indicate God's blanket rejection of Israel. This is evident from the fact that in Acts many Jews believe (so correctly Jervell[3]). These conversions are particularly numerous in Jerusalem (Acts 2.41, 47; 4.4; 6.1, 7; 21.20), but they also occur throughout Paul's ministry (13.43; 14.1; 17.4, 12; 18.8; 28.24). In the present sermon, Luke has just noted that many Jews and proselytes followed Paul and Barnabas and were urged 'to continue in the grace of God' (13.43). Nor can it be said that Jewish rejection is *the decisive reason* for the Gentile mission. Luke makes it clear throughout his two-volume work that all along it was part of God's plan to bring the gospel to the Gentiles (Lk. 2.32; 3.6; Acts 13.47).[4] The apostles are entrusted with the gospel for all nations (Lk. 24.45-48; Acts 1.8), and Paul is commissioned specifically as a missionary to the Gentiles (Acts 9.15; 10.34ff.; 15.6-11). In the present sermon, Paul's citation of Isa. 49.6 in v. 47 confirms that Scripture prophesied the missionaries' role as 'a light for the Gentiles'.[5] Though it is true that Paul's decision to turn to the Gentiles frequently follows Jewish rejection (Acts 13.46; 18.6; 28.28), that rejection is not the fundamental motivation for the Gentile mission. Rather, Paul's pattern reflects the God-ordained *order* of mission: to the Jew first, then to the

1. J. Jervell, *Luke and the People of God* (1972).
2. See especially Dupont, *Nouvelles Etudes*, pp. 343-49, 457-511.
3. Jervell, *People of God*, pp. 44-49.
4. Tannehill, *Narrative Unity*, II, p. 173.
5. Dupont, *Nouvelles Etudes*, p. 346: 'Si l'évangélisation des païens a été ordonnée par Dieu dans un oracle prophétique, comment peut-on la faire dépendre du refus opposé par les Juifs au message du salut?'

Gentile. Paul's words in Acts 13.46 make this clear: 'it was necessary that the word of God should be spoken to you *first*...' Only after the message has been brought to the Jews are the missionaries free to turn to the Gentiles. This is why, despite Paul's claim that '*from now on* I go to the Gentiles' (Acts 18.6), he continues to preach to the Jews. In each city Paul must fulfill the God-ordained order of evangelism.

Jervell claims that Paul and Barnabas interpret Isa. 49.6 in terms of the mission of Israel. As the restored Israel, the Jewish missionaries have been appointed as a 'light for the Gentiles'.[1] It is more likely, however, that Luke understands the phrase christologically.[2] The missionaries fulfill the role of the 'servant' of Isaiah 42 and 49 as representatives of Jesus the messiah. In Lk. 2.30 (cf. 1.79) it is Jesus himself who is a light of revelation to the Gentiles (cf. Isa. 42.6; 49.6; 9.6). Similarly, in Acts 26.23 Paul affirms that Scripture predicted that having been the first to rise from the dead, the Christ 'would announce light both to the people and to the Gentiles'. As the resurrected and exalted messiah, Jesus proclaims 'light' through his chosen envoys. This is why, in the same context, Paul describes his commissioning in terms which again recall the role of the servant (Isa. 42.7). Already in Acts 1.8 Jesus has told the disciples that 'you shall be my witnesses in Jerusalem...and to the ends of the earth' (cf. Lk. 24.47). The phrase ἕως ἐσψάτου τῆς γῆς is an allusion to Isa. 49.6; it is as *Jesus' witnesses* that the church fulfills the scripture-ordained task of bringing salvation to the Gentiles. Though for Luke Jesus is the Isaianic 'servant' who fulfills the role of 'servant' Israel,[3] his disciples are *his* representatives, not (first and foremost) the representatives of a restored Israel; they continue the light-giving task of Jesus himself.[4]

In summary, while the rejection of the gospel by Israel is neither universal nor final, it is a central theme of Acts. Introduced in the present sermon, it will be repeatedly played out throughout the book, ultimately forming its climax. When Israel rejects her messiah, the missionaries turn to the Gentiles who joyfully receive the message. This is no alteration in God's plan, however, but was prophesied beforehand in Scripture. Indeed, Luke takes special care to link the theme of Gentile

1. Jervell, *People of God*, p. 61.
2. Dupont, *Nouvelles Etudes*, p. 348.
3. See Chapter 5 sections 2d and 3b and Chapter 6 section 6c.
4. For more evidence for this christological interpetation see Dupont, *Nouvelles Etudes*, pp. 347-49.

salvation closely to the fulfillment of the promise through *Israel's* messiah. Already in the Jewish 'promise' context of the birth narrative, Simeon announces that the salvation brought by the 'Lord's Christ' will be both the glory of Israel and 'a light of revelation to the Gentiles' (Lk. 2.32; cf. 1.79). God's plan is being worked out both in the 'fall and rise of many in Israel' (Lk. 1.34) and in the offer of salvation to the Gentiles.

e. *Summary and Conclusions*

The sermon of Paul in Acts 13.16-41, like Peter's speech in Acts 2.14-36, centers on the fufillment of the Davidic promises through Jesus the messiah. While Acts 2 uses the context of the pouring out of the Spirit at Pentecost to demonstrate Jesus' exaltation-enthronement at the right hand of God, this sermon emphasizes his divine sonship and incorruptible life in relation to his resurrection. Paul begins with a summary of Israel's history culminating in God's choice of David to be king. This provides the springboard for a presentation of Jesus as the seed of David, the saviour of Israel. A summary of the role of John the Baptist in relation to Jesus forms a transition from the promise made to David (vv. 17-23) to its fulfillment in the events of Jesus' life, death and resurrection (vv. 26-37). This kerygmatic summary reaches its climax in the statement that God has fulfilled his promise to the fathers having 'raised up' Jesus. This 'raising up' has a double significance. Not only has God raised up Jesus as a saviour in Israel, but he has raised him from the dead incorruptible. The citation from Ps. 2.7 serves as divine attestation of Jesus' messianic identity (cf. Lk. 3.22; 9.35), and sets the stage for the resurrection argument which follows. At the resurrection Jesus was declared to be the Son of God (Ps. 2.7) and entered into incorruptible life (Ps. 16.10). This was in accord with Isa. 55.3, which promised that the Davidic covenant would endure forever and that its benefits would be given to God's people. The resurrection thus marks the climax of the fulfillment of the promise, as God establishes 'the throne of his kingdom forever' (2 Sam. 7.13; cf. Lk. 1.32).

In light of Luke's emphasis on the resurrection, C. Burger claims that Luke views the Davidic promise as fulfilled *exclusively* in this event; the promise plays no role in verses 24ff., which report the life and death of Jesus. 'Just as in the Third Gospel Jesus is not conceived of as son of David in his earthly activity. Luke understands the Davidic sonship differently than Matthew.'[1] While a full response to Burger must await

1. Burger, *Jesus als Davidssohn*, p. 140.

the conclusions concerning Luke's Gospel presentation (Chapters 5 and 6), his claim concerning the present sermon must be challenged. I have argued that the 'raising up' in v. 33 refers to the whole Jesus event from birth to exaltation-enthronement. If this is the case, then Luke clearly views Jesus' earthly ministry as integral to his fulfillment of the promises to David. Even if v. 33 refers to the resurrection, however, Burger's conclusion cannot be sustained. As we have seen, v. 23, which describes Jesus as the saviour brought by God to Israel, refers (at least in part) to Jesus' earthly ministry. This is verified by vv. 24-25, which show that John testified that the one coming after him would be the Christ. The promise is being fulfilled in that the seed of David has arrived in Israel. This presentation continues in vv. 27-31, where Jesus is presented as the Christ whose suffering was predicted beforehand in Scripture. The fact that Jesus suffers *as* the Christ shows that the promise is already being fulfilled in his life and passion. While Jesus' vindication through his resurrection and exaltation-enthronement forms the climax of the fulfillment, Jesus' role as the saviour of Israel, and hence as the fulfillment of the promises made to her, begins already during his earthly ministry.

Paul's concluding warning (vv. 40-41), together with the events of the following Sabbath (vv. 44-48), mark a sudden change in tone as the 'scoffers' within Israel reject the work God is accomplishing in their days (v. 41; Hab. 1.5). The strongly Jewish setting, form and content of the sermon all serve to bring out the stark contrast between God's faithfulness to his covenant people and Israel's rejection of her promised salvation. Jesus is *Israel's* messiah, the fulfillment of God's covenant promises to the fathers. While some in Israel accept the message, many others reject it and the missionaries turn to the Gentiles. Israel is divided. While a remnant believes, the majority turn away and become the scoffers of Hab. 1.5 (Acts 13.41) and the blind and deaf of Isa. 6.9-10 (Acts 28.26-27). While some might say that God's promise to Israel has failed, this is not the case. Luke has already affirmed that all along it was God's plan that his Christ would be a 'sign' to be opposed, the cause of both rising and falling in Israel (Lk. 2.34). All along it was intended that he would be a light for the Gentiles and that the message would go to the ends of the earth (Lk. 2.32; 24.46-47; Acts 1.8). The sermon and its narrative setting together confirm that the Christian proclamation is no new and aberrant religion but rather the climax of God's dealings with Israel and the fulfillment of his promises to her.

This conclusion raises a subsidiary but important point which has been emerging from this study. Luke's extraordinary knowledge of the LXX,[1] his use of Jewish exegetical techniques and his familiarity with contemporary synagogue practice all raise questions concerning the traditional view of the Luke's work as the 'Gentile Gospel' written to a predominantly Greek audience. Though it is true that the author is thoroughly conversant with Greek literary and historiographic conventions, he is also 'at home in the synagogue'.[2] Whether Luke is a Jew, a proselyte or a God-fearer, and whether his community is made up predominantly of Jewish or Gentile Christians, these points suggest that he and his audience are closer to their Jewish roots than has sometimes been assumed. Indeed, there is much to commend Tiede's claim that 'the polemics, scriptural arguments, and "proofs" which are rehearsed in Luke–Acts are part of an *intra-family* struggle...over who is really the faithful "Israel"'.[3] This point will be taken up again in Chapter 7, when conclusions will be drawn concerning Luke's community situation and overall purpose in Luke–Acts.

4. *James' Address at the Council of Jerusalem, Acts 15.13-21*

a. *The Significance of the Address in the Narrative of Acts*

In his address before the Council of Jerusalem, James cites Amos 9.11-12 as part of his argument that the entrance of Gentiles into the church is the will and plan of God. The address, together with its Old Testament citation, forms an important high point in Luke's narrative. Though not of the same christological import as the speeches of Peter and Paul in Acts 2 and 13, it has important ecclesiological significance for Luke. This may be demonstrated by the following points:

(1) *The Council of Jerusalem with its discussion of the relation of Gentiles to the Law of Moses forms the structural and theological centre of Acts.*[4] Since the main theme of Acts is the expansion of the church from Jerusalem to the ends of the earth (Acts 1.8), the issue of

1. See J. A. Sanders, 'Isaiah in Luke', *Int* 30 (1982), p. 146.

2. Tiede, *Prophecy and History,* 8. Tiede notes that 'The author of Luke–Acts lived within the world of the hellenistic synagogue where the scriptures provided an ancient heritage, a theological vocabulary, and a set of rituals that distinguished and identified the Jews.'

3. Tiede, *Prophecy and History*, p. 7.

4. Marshall, *Acts*, p. 242; J. Dupont, 'Un peuple d'entre les nations (Acts 15.14)' *NTS* 31 (1985), pp. 321-35.

Gentile salvation forms an important part of this theme. As we have seen, the development of this (sub-)theme begins in Luke's Gospel (cf. Lk. 1.32) and slowly builds in Acts with the gradual assimilation of Gentiles into the church. In Lk. 24.47 and Acts 1.8, Jesus himself announces that the message of salvation is not just for the Jews but for all the nations. The application of the promise to the Gentiles may be hinted at in Peter's Pentecost speech (2.39; cf. 3.25) and begins implicitly with the story of the conversion of the Ethiopian eunuch (8.26-38). With the detailed account of the conversion of Cornelius and his household (10.1-11.18), the theme is explicitly developed. In 10.34-35 Peter states, 'Truly I understand that God shows no partiality, but in every nation any one who fears him and does what is right is acceptable to him.' Finally, with Paul's first missionary journey (chs. 13-14) the Gentile mission begins in earnest. Upon returning from the journey, Paul and Barnabas relate to the church at Antioch how God 'had opened a door of faith to the Gentiles' (14.27). This provides the backdrop for the question raised in ch. 15 of the requirements for Gentile salvation (vv. 1, 5).

Luke begins his narrative by relating how certain men came down from Judea to Antioch and began teaching the (Gentile) brethren, saying, 'unless you are circumcised according to the custom of Moses, you cannot be saved'. The dissension and debate which follows prompts the church at Antioch to send Paul, Barnabas and 'certain others' to Jerusalem to present the issue before the elders and apostles there. The decision reached by James and approved by the council indicates that Gentiles not be required to be circumcised or keep the Law, but that they should abstain from 'idolatrous pollutions, from fornication, from things strangled, and from blood'.[1] From the point of view of the Lukan narrative, the Council of Jerusalem settles this issue once and for all. Nowhere else in Acts are Jewish Christians presented as demanding of Gentile believers circumcision or adherence to the Law. This chapter thus forms a center point in the narrative of Acts. Gentile conversions are related in the passages leading up to it, and the rest of Acts will be devoted to the Pauline missionary movement. With ch. 15 Luke justifies

1. The complex textual and interpretive issues surrounding the apostolic decree and the nature of the requirements imposed on Gentile believers are beyond the scope of the present study. For discussion and bibliography on the textual questions see Metzger, *Textual Commentary*, pp. 429-434. On the interpretation of the decree see the extensive bibliographies in Schneider, *Apostelgeschichte*, II, pp. 169-71, and Pesch, *Apostelgeschichte*, II, pp. 68-69.

the entrance of Gentiles into the church by showing that this movement was initiated and preordained by God and that it gained the full approval of the apostles and elders of the church in Jerusalem.

(2) *James' address is the climactic and deciding section of the narrative of ch. 15.* Though Luke includes Peter's arguments before the council (vv. 7-11) and mentions that Barnabas and Paul also spoke (v. 12), it is James who presents the final arguments and who renders the decision. His judgment (v. 19: διὸ ἐγὼ κρίνω) is final and his authority is not questioned by those present. Drawing on the portrait of James in chs. 15 and 21, J. Jervell has demonstrated his important role as a character in Acts.[1] Since Luke sees no need to introduce who James is or how he assumed leadership in the church, it is clear that, 'For Luke's readers James is an undisputed authority, an uncontestable figure so well-known that it is unnecessary for Luke even to make the slightest mention of his credentials.'[2] While some of the implications that Jervell draws from this conclusion may be questioned,[3] it is clear that, when James sums up the debate and renders a decision, he speaks with the highest authority.

(3) *The citation of Amos 9.11-12 forms the crux of James' argument.* James' argument may be divided into two parts, a summary of Peter's address in vv. 7-11 (v. 14) and a scriptural argument from Amos 9.11-12. While Peter offers the experiential proof that God has chosen to bring Gentiles into the church (vv. 7-11),[4] James offers the scriptural

1. J. Jervell, 'James: The Defender of Paul', in *Luke and the People of God* (1972), pp. 185-207.

2. Jervell, *People of God*, p. 187.

3. Jervell, *People of God*, p. 192, claims that Luke uses James to legitimize Paul's faithfulness to the Law. This occurs in 15.14-21, where it is not Paul but James who exempts the Gentiles from the Law, and in 21.15-26, where James indicates that the accusations that Paul teaches against the Law are false. This proves to Jervell that, though Luke's readers greatly respect James, they have little confidence in Paul or any ecclesiastical practices that could be traced to him. Against this view, there is little evidence in Acts either that Luke's readers distrust Paul or that Luke views him as a defender of the Law. Jervell's denial that Paul's statement in 13.38-39 is critical of the Law is unconvincing (pp. 196-99).

4. In vv. 7-11 Peter draws on his experience in the Cornelius episode to show that God himself had determined that the Gentiles should hear the gospel and believe (15.7). The bestowal of the Spirit on the Gentiles proves that God makes no distinctions (vv. 8-9), and that both Jews and Gentiles are saved by faith through the grace of the Lord Jesus (vv. 9-11).

proof. The conclusion James draws (v. 19) from all this is that Gentile converts ought not to be troubled concerning the issues raised at the Council (circumcision and keeping the Law, v. 5). J.W. Bowker argues that James' address follows the pattern of the rabbinic 'yelammedenu' homily, in which a legal (halakic) question is asked and answered.[1] According to Bowker, James' answer is a classic yelammedenu-type response to the halakic question, 'Is it necesssary for proselytes to be circumcised and keep the law of Moses?' He further conjectures that this response was part of a much fuller yelammedenu *homily*. For so important a question, James' response would almost certainly have originally centered on a Torah text, with corroboration from prophetic texts: 'This suggests that what has survived in Acts is a fragment of a longer discourse...'[2] Though Bowker's argument is somewhat conjectural, it seems probable that a longer discourse lies behind the account in Acts. If so, it is significant that, in abbreviating this report, Luke has retained an Old Testament text which supports Gentile salvation *from the perspective of the fulfillment of the Davidic promises.*

(4) *Amos 9.11-12 is pivotal in relation to Luke's ecclesiological purpose in Acts.* This point is extensively developed by P.-A. Paulo in an examination of the ecclesiological significance of the two Amos citations in Acts.[3] Paulo looks first at the apologetic citations in Acts, discerning in Luke's use of these citations a cyclical progression in two circuits (Acts 1-8; 13-28). Each of these circuits follows a similar progression of thought: from the mystery of the person of Jesus to the condition of Israelite unbelief, to the condition of non-Israelite belief.[4] While the

1. Bowker, 'Speeches in Acts: A Study in Proem and Yelammedenu Form', *NTS* 14 (1967–68), pp. 99-100, 107-109. The term 'yelammedenu' is derived from the request for instruction *yelammedenu rabbenu,* 'let our teacher instruct us'. Bowker offers the following evidence that this is a yelammedenu address: (1) the Pharisaic nature of the question (v. 5) (halakic questions were a particular Pharisaic concern); (2) the use of the word ἀπεκρίθη in James' response; (3) James' appeal to both the past and to Scripture (the two classic grounds for establishing halakah); and (4) the issuing of a *taqqanah,* an amendment or alleviation of Torah to a specific group of people in particular circumstances. This last point helps to explain the enigmatic v. 21: the alleviation is not so drastic since the full law of Moses is still maintained in every synagogue Sabbath to Sabbath (p. 108).

2. Bowker, 'Speeches in Acts', p. 109.

3. P.-A. Paulo, *Le problème ecclésial des Actes à la lumière de deux prophéties d'Amos* (1985).

4. Paulo, *Le problème ecclésial*, pp. 19-31. Paulo examines only explicit

majority of the apologetic citations are christological, five are primarily ecclesiological and are used by Luke to answer the key ecclesiological problem of Acts: how to account for the paradox of Jewish rejection and Gentile acceptance of the gospel?[1] Three of these five are used to explain the present blindness of Israel (Amos 5.25-27 at Acts 7.42-43; Hab. 1.5 at 13.38-41; Isa. 6.9-10 at 28.26-27) and two to show the situation of the church opposite Israel (Isa. 66.1-2 at 7.49-50; Amos 9.11-12 at 15.16-18). Paulo argues that of these five, the two Amos citations form the 'two great axes' of the solution.[2] Amos 5.25-27 (cited by Stephen in Acts 7.42-43) explains the origin and consequence of the blindness of Israel, and Amos 9.11-12 (cited by James in Acts 15) explains the reason for Gentile entrance into the church: just as Amos prophesied, the Davidic restoration results in the 'rest of mankind' seeking the Lord.[3] In spite of the limitations in the scope of his work,[4] Paulo's conclusion concerning the importance of the citation of Amos 9.11-12 in Luke's narrative is significant. It is natural that Luke would place the Old Testament citation which he considered most appropriate in relation to Gentile entrance into the church at the point in his narrative where this issue reaches its climax.

citations, not allusions, and only those which begin with an introductory formula. By his count there are 18: 16 in discourses and 2 in narrative sections.

1. Paulo, *Le problème ecclésial*, pp. 31-51.

2. The importance of these two citations is proven for Paulo by the facts that: (1) both are introduced by the formula καθὼς γέγραπται (which Paulo argues is the most important introductory formula in Acts; pp. 28-36, 47); (2) the other three ecclesiological citations may be seen as subordinate to these two (pp. 47-48); and (3) the two Amos passages are cited together at Qumran (CD 7.14-16; cf. 4QFlor 1.12-13; pp. 48-49).

3. Paulo, *Le problème ecclésial*, pp. 45-49.

4. Paulo himself admits that he is not studying the ecclesiology of Acts, but only the ecclesiology from the perspective of the two Amos prophecies (p. 15). Even his study of the apologetic citations is limited by this perspective. By examining only citations with introductory formulas, he does not take account of Old Testament allusions or even citations without formulas (e.g. he does not deal with the important citation of Ps. 118.22 in Acts 4.11). This leaves important gaps in his analysis. In addition to this problem, his 'circuits' seem to be somewhat artificial. It is doubtful whether Luke viewed the progressive development of the Old Testament citations independently of the development of the narrative as a whole.

b. *The Citation of Amos 9.11-12 and its Narrative Significance*
James begins his address by referring back to Peter's statements in vv. 7-11: 'Simeon has related how God first visited to take out from the Gentiles a people for his name' (v. 14). The contrast between λαός and ἔθνη is striking since in the Old Testament the nations or Gentiles (ἔθνη) generally stand in contrast to the people (λαός) of Israel (cf. LXX: Exod. 19.5; 23.22; Deut. 7.6; 14.2; 26.18-19).[1] Here, God takes a people *from among* the Gentiles.[2] The fact that this people are τῷ ὀνόματι αὐτοῦ points forward to the citation of Amos which speaks of 'the Gentiles who are called by my name' (v. 17; Amos 9.12). James follows with scriptural proof from Amos 9 to demonstrate that it was part of God's plan that the Gentiles should seek him. The introductory formula links Amos 9.11-12 to the statement concerning the Gentiles in the previous verse: καὶ τούτῳ συμφωνοῦσιν οἱ λόγοι τῶν προφητῶν, καθὼς γέγραπται. The citation of Amos 9.11-12 (Acts 15.16-18) follows:

> 'After these things I will return,
> And I will rebuild the hut (σκηνή) of David that has fallen,
> And its ruins I will rebuild,
> And I will restore it,
> That the rest of mankind may seek the Lord,
> And all the Gentiles who are called by my name,'
> Says the Lord who makes these things known from of old.

The text as a whole follows the LXX, though the citation of v. 11 seems to be a free paraphrase. Instead of μετὰ ταῦτα, the LXX begins the quote with ἐν τῇ ἡμέρᾳ ἐκείνῃ. It has been suggested that this

1. Bruce, *Book*, p. 293; J. Dupont, 'ΛΑΟΣ 'ΕΞ 'ΕΘΝΩΝ (Ac 15, 14)', in *Etudes sur les Actes des Apôtres* (1967), pp. 361-65.

2. Because Luke seldom uses λαός with reference to Gentiles (only here and in 18.10), its significance in this passage is a matter of dispute. Jervell, *People of God*, pp. 50-55, argues that the term has no theological value but refers merely to 'a quantity of people'. This is part of his argument that the Gentiles are an 'associate' people beside the chosen people Israel. For a similar view see C. Perrot, 'Les décisions de l'assemblé de Jérusalem', *RSR* 69 (1981), pp. 195-208, who argues that the absence of the article indicates that James thinks here of a people of God associated with Israel (p. 202). Dupont, 'Un peuple', pp. 321-35, esp. 329, on the other hand, claims the word retains its full 'theological' force of 'the people of God', and that there can be only one people of God. S.G. Wilson, *The Gentiles and the Gentile Mission in Luke–Acts* (1973), p. 225, suggests that the use here and in 18.10 may simply be due to Luke's linguistic imprecision.

alteration was introduced to separate the time of the fulfillment of the prophecy from the period of the church.[1] In this view, the adverb πρῶτον in v. 14 is set in contrast with μετὰ ταῦτα in v. 16 and the sense of the two verses is: God *first* (πρῶτον) visited the Gentiles (v. 14)...*after this* (μετὰ ταῦτα) he will return and rebuild the tent of David (v. 16). James is thus made to envision a still future restoration of the Davidic dynasty at which time the Gentiles will *again* seek the Lord. Support for this view is said to be the introduction of the non-LXX verb ἀναστρέψω ('I will return'), which suggests that the prophecy will be fulfilled at the second coming of Christ.[2]

One problem with this view is the fact that ἀναστρέφω is never used of the second coming of Christ in the New Testament. The use here may just as likely mean to turn back to, or to turn towards again. A more significant problem is that this interpretation weakens the proof-value of the Old Testament prophecy for the question at stake.[3] While it is at least conceivable that a *future* restoration would motivate the church to begin letting in Gentiles *now,* it is far more likely that James would cite a verse which relates directly to the present situation. Indeed, the introductory formula implies that Amos 9.11-12 is a prophecy which applies to the *present* entrance of Gentiles into the church. It is 'to this', i.e. the salvation of the Gentiles in v. 15, that the words of Amos agree. The alteration from ἐν τῇ ἡμέρᾳ ἐκείνῃ to μετὰ ταῦτα is probably instead a reference to the context of Amos 9. Beginning in Amos 7, the author depicts a series of judgments that would devastate and disperse Israel. In the final verses of the book (Amos 9.11-15), there is a message of hope that a renewal will occur after this period of judgment.[4] It is likely that

1. This view is developed by W.M. Aldrich, 'The Interpretation of Acts 15.13-18', *BSac* 111 (1954), pp. 317-23, esp. 320ff.; A. MacRae, 'The Scientific Approach to the Old Testament', *BSac* 110 (1953), pp. 309-11, esp. 311ff.; C. Zimmerman, 'To This Agree the Words of the Prophets, *Grace Journal* 4 (1963), pp. 28-40; J.E. Rosscup, 'The Interpretation of Acts 15.13-18' (ThD dissertation; Dallas Theological Seminary, 1966).

2. Aldrich, 'Interpretation', p. 322.

3. Cf. W.C. Kaiser, Jr., 'The Davidic Promise and the Inclusion of the Gentiles (Amos 9.9-15 and Acts 15.13-18): A Test Passage for Theological Systems', *JETS* 20 (1977), p. 105.

4. The disputed question of whether these final verses were an original part of Amos is not relevant to the present discussion. Their presence in Acts 15 and at Qumran, and the lack of any Old Testament manuscript evidence for their absence, make it clear that by the New Testament era they were considered authentic.

Luke has this context in view. James is thus saying, 'After these things, that is, after the judgments described in Amos, God will return (ἀναστρέψω) to re-establish the house of David.'[1]

Amos describes this restoration as the raising up of the 'fallen hut of David'. The LXX σκηνή renders the MT סֻכָּה which normally signifies a booth or hut made of branches (cf. Lev. 23.40, 42; Deut. 16.13). The idea here seems to be that the dynasty or kingdom of David, normally designated 'the house of David' (בית דויד = LXX οἶκος Δαυιδ, cf. 2 Sam. 7.5, 11; 1 Kgs 11.38; Isa. 7.2, 13), is now merely a hut.[2] סֻכָּה/σκηνή thus expresses the present humble state and fragility of the dynasty. Though it is now lowly and fallen (or 'falling'[3]), God will raise up and rebuild the Davidic dynasty. In the last two phrases of v. 11 the metaphor changes from a 'fallen hut' to a house or building whose walls are rebuilt and restored.

The important question for the present study is how Luke understands the phrase. What does he consider the 'hut of David' to refer to? Four views are prominent: (1) The rebuilt hut of David is the restored Israel made up of Jews who have accepted Jesus as their messiah. J. Jervell takes this position, arguing that the Amos citation demonstrates that God promised he would first rebuild and restore Israel, and, as a result, the Gentiles would seek the Lord.[4] Jervell says this interpretation retains

1. Kaiser, 'Davidic Promise', p. 106. Another possibility, suggested by many scholars, is that the phrase is an allusion to Jer. 12.15 LXX: 'And it will be after (μετά) I have cast them out, I will return (ἐπιστρέψω), and have mercy on them...' (cf. Zech. 1.16). A direct allusion is improbable, however, since the only word in common is μετά (but see the D text of Acts 15.16 which reads ἐπιστρέψω). Paulo, *Le problème ecclésial*, pp. 78-79, proposes a third possible reason for the use of ἀναστρέψω. He points out that in Acts 7.42-43, where the other Amos citation (5.25-27) occurs, the word ἔστρεψεν is used with reference to God's turning away from his people. Luke's point here, therefore, is that the same God who turned away from his unfaithful people in the wilderness announces that he will turn again to them. Though this view is appealing, the distance between the two contexts renders it dubious.

2. E. Hammershaimb, *The Book of Amos* (1970), p. 140.

3. The Hebrew participle נֹפֶלֶת may mean 'falling', 'about to fall' (impending) or already fallen. Hammershaimb, *Amos*, p. 140, says that the reference to a rebuilding shows that 'fallen' is meant. On the other hand, a dilapidated ('falling' or 'about to fall') hut would also require rebuilding (so Kaiser, 'Davidic Promise', p. 101). Whatever the original sense, the LXX translates with a perfect participle, giving the sense 'fallen'.

4. Jervell, *People of God*, pp. 51-54, 92-93; Longenecker, 'Acts', pp. 446-47.

the connection between vv. 16 and 17. Since v. 17 speaks of 'the rest of mankind' and 'the Gentiles' seeking the Lord, it is natural that the first half of the quote would allude to the Jews. This is in line with the previous context, which is concerned with the relationship between believing Jews and converted Gentiles (cf. vv. 7, 14). Thus, 'the quotation fits admirably with his [Luke's] scheme of "Jew first" and, as a result, the Gentiles, the rest of men.'[1] What distinguishes this perspective from view '2' below is Jervell's insistence that restored Israel remains a group distinct from the Gentiles within the church, the people of God.[2]

(2) A similar view, taken by the majority of commentators, agrees that the rebuilt hut of David refers to the restoration of the true Israel. In this case, however, the following verse (v. 17) refers to the incorporation of the Gentiles into *this same people of God.* The necessary implication is that the rebuilt hut of David refers to the church as a whole, made up first of Jews and then of both Jews and Gentiles (the 'true Israel').[3] G. Lohfink writes, 'Im Sinne des Lukas muß man wohl sogar so formulieren: *das wahre Israel ist erst dann erreicht, wenn die Heiden in die Gemeinschaft des Gottesvolkes eingebracht worden sind.*'[4]

(3) Haenchen claims the reference is not to the restoration of the Davidic kingdom, nor to an image of the true Israel, but to 'the story of Jesus, culminating in the Resurrection, in which the promise made to David has been fulfilled: the Jesus event that will cause the Gentiles to seek the Lord'.[5]

(4) A fourth perspective combines views '2' and '3': The rebuilt hut refers to the whole plan of God accomplished through Jesus' resurrection-exaltation *and* the establishment of the church.[6] Paulo

1. Jervell, *People of God*, pp. 52-53.

2. Jervell, *People of God*, p. 190.

3. G. Lohfink, *Die Sammlung Israels* (1975), p. 59; Roloff, *Apostelgeschichte*, p. 232; Weiser, *Apostelgeschichte 13-28*, p. 382; Pesch, *Apostelgeschichte*, II, p. 80; Marshall, *Acts*, p. 252.

4. Lohfink, *Die Sammlung Israels*, p. 60.

5. Haenchen, *Acts*, p. 448; cf. Schneider, *Apostelgeschichte*, II, p. 182; Burger, *Jesus als Davidssohn*, p. 141.

6. This is the view of Bruce in the first edition of his NIC commentary on Acts (1954): 'James's application of the prophecy finds the fulfillment of the first part (the rebuilding of the tabernacle of David) in the resurrection and exaltation of Christ, the Son of David, and the reconstitution of His disciples as the new Israel...' (p. 310). In the first edition of his Greek commentary (*The Acts of the Apostles* [1951]), he seemed to take view '2': 'The Church is the legitimate continuation and fulfillment of the old

seems to take this view when he writes, 'Inauguré par la résurrection de Jésus, le relèvement de la maison de David se poursuit dans la communauté du salut, l'ἐκκλησία des croyants.'[1]

A solution to this question is difficult because of the lack of evidence in the text. The primary emphasis in the passage is on the latter half of the quote, the entrance of the Gentiles, and no interpretation is offered for the first half. Contextual and Lukan theological factors must therefore be considered. Jervell's point that there is a distinction between vv. 16 and 17 seems to be valid. The rebuilt hut of David is distinct from the Gentile mission, making it unlikely that the reference is to the church made up of Jews and Gentiles. Proponents of view '2' would counter that the reference is to the *Jewish origin* of the church at Pentecost, after which Gentiles join the restored people of God. But there seems to be a completeness in the rebuilding prior to the entrance in the Gentiles. It is after the house has been rebuilt that the Gentiles will seek the Lord. On the other hand, Jervell's view is not entirely convincing. The primary emphasis of the context is not on the relationship of Jews and Gentiles, as he argues, but on the initiative of God. This is the point made by both Peter (vv. 7-9) and James (vv. 14-18). The argument of the passage as a whole is that since God has chosen the Gentiles and provided for and confirmed their salvation, it is not for the church to place restrictions on them. It is God's actions in rebuilding the hut of David which enable (v. 17: ὅπως ἄν) the Gentiles to seek the Lord. If it is asked what actions of God Luke normally stresses as the presupposition for the Gentile mission, it would have to be the death and resurrection of Jesus. In Acts 26.23 Paul says, '...that the Christ must suffer, and that by being the first to rise from the dead he would announce light both to our people and to the Gentiles'[2] (cf. Lk. 1.30-32; Acts 2.38-39; 10.43; 11.17-18; 13.39). While it is true that God uses Paul and other Jewish

Church of Israel' (p. 297). In the revision of the former work, however, he drops the reference to the church and so moves closer to the view adopted below: 'It has already been emphasized in Acts that, by the resurrection and exaltation of Jesus, the Son of David, God has fulfilled his dynastic promises to David (cf. Peter's argument in 2:25-36 and Paul's in 13:23, pp. 32-37). This may be what is understood here as the raising up of David's fallen tent' (Bruce, *Book*, p. 294).

1. Paulo, *Le problème ecclésial*, p. 85; cf. 79ff. Elsewhere, Paulo seems to favour view '2' (cf. pp. 101-102, 134-35).

2. Translation from Bruce, *Book*, p. 469. Both occurrences of 'that' render the Greek εἰ, which here is practically equivalent to ὅτι (so Haenchen, *Acts*, p. 684 n. 2; p. 687 n. 5, citing H.J. Cadbury; cf. Bruce, *Book*, p. 469 n. 36).

missionaries to bring the message to the Gentiles (Acts 13.47), it is the work of Christ, not the restoration of Israel, which opens the way for the Gentiles to seek the Lord.[1]

The best solution, therefore, would seem to be a modified version of view '3': Luke takes the promised rebuilding of τὴν σκηνὴν Δαυίδ as a reference to the restoration of the Davidic dynasty accomplished through the life, death, resurrection and exaltation of Jesus. This interpretation is in line with the play on the word 'house' in 2 Samuel 7. When David seeks to build a house for the Lord (vv. 1-3), Nathan responds that instead Yahweh will build a house for David (v. 11). The context reveals that this 'house' is a reference to an eternal dynasty (house, throne and kingdom, v. 16).[2] As we have seen, this promise is viewed by Luke as accomplished in the life, death, resurrection and exaltation of Jesus (Acts 2.25-36; 13.23, 32-37). It is through these events that the fallen hut (the dynasty) of David is re-established. The raising up of the hut of David is thus 'a brief but direct reference to the total program of God announced to David in 2 Samuel 7'.[3]

To be sure, the distinction between this view and the others is a fine one. My point is that it is not the church or the nation Israel but the Davidic dynasty (or 'kingly reign') that is here said to be re-built. When Christ re-established the Davidic reign, both Jews and Gentiles were offered a place in the messianic community of salvation. They may be participants of the kingdom which Jesus initiates, but they are not

1. This is not to question that Luke views the gospel as for the Jew first (Lk. 24.47; Acts 1.8; 10.36; 13.46), but only Jervell's assumption that Jewish acceptance of the Gospel (the restoration of Israel) is the necessary presupposition for the Gentile mission. Nor, as we have seen, is Jewish rejection the reason for the Gentile mission. All along the Gentile mission was part of the plan and purpose of God (Lk. 24.47; Acts 2.39; 13.47; 15.16-18) (so rightly Jervell, *People of God*, pp. 60ff.).

2. This interpretation is also in line with Luke's use of οἶκος Δαυίδ in the birth narrative (Lk. 1.27, 69), where it refers to the 'family' or 'dynastic line' of David.

3. Kaiser, 'Davidic Promise', p. 108. In Kaiser's interpretation, this Davidic promise includes not just a Davidic heir and an eternal kingdom but also a mandate for all mankind. He takes this interpretation from 2 Sam. 7.19b, which he translates as a reference to a 'charter for humanity'. The Davidic promises are therefore 'nothing less than an updated and supplemented Edenic and Abrahamic promise which at once embraced 'all the nations of the earth'—i.e. 'humanity'—if they would but believe in that Man of promise, the 'Seed'. God's intention was to bless the whole earth through David' ('Davidic Promise', pp. 100, 108). See his article 'The Blessing of David: The Charter for Humanity', in *The Law and the Prophets* (1974), pp. 310-18.

themselves the Davidic dynasty. This interpretation agrees both with the context of Amos 9 (which refers to the restoration of the Davidic dynasty) and with Luke's overall perspective.

Further support for this position is the interpretation of Amos 9.11 in 4QFlor 1.12, where the raising up of the fallen 'hut of David' refers to a messianic figure—the 'shoot of David' (4QFlor 1.11)—rather than a messianic community.[1] This reveals that an individual messianic interpretation of the verse was present in first-century Judaism.[2]

The result of the re-establishment of the Davidic dynasty is presented in the second half of the quote (Amos 9.12; vv. 17-18). The text follows the LXX, which differs significantly from the MT.[3] As indicated above, ὅπως ἄν suggests that the rebuilding of the fallen tent of David enables the rest of mankind and all Gentiles 'called by my name' to seek the Lord. In the Old Testament, to be called by God's name placed the object or person so designated under divine ownership.[4] In v. 17 it

1. See 4QFlor 1.10-13. Though the relative pronoun in the phrase, '...this is the fallen hut of David *that* (or, who) will stand up to save Israel', could refer either to a person or a thing (the community?), the parallel with the Davidic 'shoot' in line 11, as well as the role of the hut in 'saving' Israel, indicates a messianic figure (or perhaps a dynasty) is in view. For the Hebrew text see Allegro, 'Fragments', p. 350. Another interpretation of the passage appears in CD 7.16, where the 'hut' is interpreted as the books of the Law. The sectarians were often inconsistent in their interpretations of Scripture (see Brooke, *Exegesis at Qumran*, pp. 139, 241 n. 147).

2. Cf. T. Holtz, *Untersuchung über die alttestamentlichen Zitate bei Lukas* (1968), pp. 152-53.

3. The LXX reads 'that the rest of mankind may seek (the Lord)' instead of the MT 'that they may possess the remnant of Edom'. Presumably, the LXX translators read יִדְרְשׁוּ ('they will seek') for יִירְשׁוּ ('they will possess') and אָדָם ('humankind') for אֱדוֹם ('Edom'), omitting אֶת־ before שְׁאֵרִית. Codex A, as well as Acts 15.17, adds the object τὸν κύριον (Hammershaimb, *Amos*, pp. 140-41). Haenchen, *Acts*, p. 448, argues that the idea of conquest in the MT shows that the argument depends on the LXX. The Hebrew text would be useless for James' argument, and would even contradict it. It is therefore Luke, not James, who is speaking. Various alternatives, however, are possible: (1) The LXX may be based on a Hebrew text no longer extant, which James is here citing. The significant textual variations found in Acts, Qumran, the LXX and the MT show that a variety of textual traditions existed; (2) it is possible that James spoke in Greek, citing the LXX; (3) the MT reading could itself support James' point if 'possessing' is taken in the positive sense of the nations sharing in the blessings of the messianic age. Cf. Kaiser, 'Davidic Promise', pp. 102-103; Bruce, *Book*, p. 294; Marshall, *Acts*, pp. 252-53.

4. Kaiser, 'Davidic Promise', p. 103. Cf. Deut. 28.10; 2 Sam. 12.28; 1 Kgs 8.43; Isa. 4.1; Jer. 14.9; 15.16; 2 Chron. 7.14.

probably refers to those Gentiles chosen and called by God (cf. v. 7; 2.39). The addition of the concluding clause γνωστὰ ἀπ' αἰῶνος alters the meaning of the LXX phrase from what God accomplished to what he revealed (cf. Isa. 45.21). That he revealed these things in ages past proves again that the entrance of the Gentiles into the church was part of the plan and purpose of God.

c. *Conclusion*

In his important address before the Council of Jerusalem, James cites Amos 9.11-12 to demonstrate that the entrance of Gentiles into the church was part of the purpose and plan of God. The prophecy of the rebuilding of the hut of David draws on the promise to David that his house, throne and kingdom would be established forever (cf. 2 Sam. 7.16). Luke probably understands the rebuilding of David's hut in this same way—as a reference to the the re-establishment of the Davidic dynasty accomplished through the death, resurrection and exaltation of Jesus. Again the Old Testament promises to David play an important role in Luke's narrative. The restoration of the Davidic reign predicted in Amos 9.11-12 and accomplished in the resurrection-exaltation of Jesus is presented by James as scriptural justification for the Gentile mission and as the means by which 'the rest of mankind' may seek the Lord.

5. *Conclusion*

Our study of these three passages has achieved an important result: three of the most *theologically* important characters in Acts all deliver keynote addresses which are strongly Davidic-messianic. In his inaugural Pentecost speech (Acts 2.14-40), Peter uses Ps. 16.8-11 and Ps. 132.11 to demonstrate that Jesus' resurrection proves he is the Davidic messiah. He then draws on Ps. 110.1-2 to show that, by virtue of Jesus' exaltation at the right hand of God, he is not only the messiah, but also the already-enthroned messianic Lord. Those who will repent are offered forgiveness of sins and the promised gift of the Spirit. In Paul's sermon at Pisidian-Antioch (Acts 13.16-41, 46-47)—a model of his diaspora proclamation to Jews and God-fearers—the apostle summarizes the history of Israel to the point of the promise made to David and its fulfillment in Jesus, the saviour. He then shows that, through Jesus' life, death and especially his resurrection, he has fulfilled these promises and so offers the salvation blessings of forgiveness of sins and justification to Israel and—in light of the events of the following Sabbath—to the Gentiles. Finally, in his address and decisive judgment before the Council of Jerusalem, James shows that the entrance of the Gentiles into the church was part of the plan and purpose of God. Proof for this is provided from Amos 9.11-12, where the prophet predicted that God would raise up the fallen 'hut of David'—the Davidic dynasty—so that the rest of mankind could seek the Lord. In the latter two discourses, Jesus' status as Davidic messiah is closely linked to the entrance of Gentiles into the church. When these results are viewed together with those obtained for the birth narrative, the prominence and importance of this Davidic-messianic theme is evident. Luke places this description of Jesus at the heart of his promise-fulfillment motif.

At the same time, it must be noted that Luke does not exclude other Old Testament christological motifs. Peter's speech in Acts 3.12-26, for example, presents a mixed Christology, identifying Jesus as the messiah whose role is that of the Isaianic servant and the eschatological prophet like Moses. The Stephen-speech in Acts 7 contains no royal-messianic motifs but develops a strong Jesus–Moses typology. As in Acts 3.22, Jesus is identified as the eschatological prophet like Moses predicted in Deut. 18.15. Further, in the account of Philip and the Ethiopian in Acts 8.26-40, Jesus is identified with the 'suffering servant' of Isa. 53.7-8. Thus, while Luke tends to introduce the royal-Davidic motif in those passages which are introductory and programmatic for his narrative purpose, it is evident that his Old Testament christological interest extends beyond a single category. It will be part of the purpose of the following chapters to determine how these motifs are integrated in Luke's overall christological presentation.

In Chapters 5 and 6 Luke's christological purpose in his Gospel presentation will be examined. Two main questions will be addressed. First, if the Davidic messianic theme is so important in the nativity and Acts, why does it (seemingly) play a much smaller role in the Gospel proper? Second, how (if at all) does Luke integrate other christological motifs with his royal-messianic one?

Part III

The Davidic Messiah in the Gospel Narrative

INTRODUCTION TO PART III

The title of Part III may appear at first sight a misnomer since there is little in Luke's Gospel narrative that is *explicitly* Davidic messianic. After the birth narrative, David is referred to in only four Gospel passages (7 times: Lk. 3.31; 6.3; 18.38, 39; 20.41, 42, 44). One of these is unrelated to the Davidic promise tradition (6.3); two more are taken over from Luke's Markan source (18.38, 39; 20.41, 42, 44); and the fourth occurs in Luke's genealogy (3.31) which seems to exhibit little specific interest in David (but see Chapter 5 section 2c below). This creates something of a christological puzzle for the Lukan writings as a whole. As we have seen, the nativity and three key speeches in Acts are strongly royal-messianic in emphasis. If this theme is central in these introductory and programmatic sections, why is it relatively rare in the Gospel proper?

One possible solution is that in the nativity and in the speeches of Acts Luke has drawn Davidic material from his sources with little concern for its relationship to the christological purpose of his Gospel narrative. But if Luke–Acts is viewed as a single two-volume work with a unified theological perspective, one would expect a Christology in the Gospel that is more in line with that in the nativity and Acts. The more common explanation is that while Luke links Jesus' Davidic kingship to his exaltation-enthronement, he avoids associating it with his earthly ministry.[1] Some say that Luke portrays Jesus' earthly life as prophetic, rather than royal activity; only at the resurrection is the messiahship promised to Jesus in the birth narrative actualized.[2] Though not denying the

1. See especially Burger, *Jesus als Davidssohn*, pp. 140-41 (see also Chapter 4 section 3e above)

2. See I. de la Potterie, 'L'onction du Christ', *NRT* 80 (1958), pp. 225-52, 239; W. Grundmann, *TDNT*, IX, p. 534. Many works emphasize Jesus' prophetic identity in Luke–Acts. See for example Moessner, *Lord of the Banquet*, especially pp. 46-79; P.F. Feiler, 'Jesus the Prophet' (PhD dissertation, Yale, 1986); R.J. Dillon, *From Eyewitnesses to Ministers of the Word: Tradition and Composition in Luke 24*

application of the royal-messianic titles to Jesus already during his earthly ministry, the use of these titles is said to be proleptic and anticipatory.

While there is an element of truth in this last statement, I would suggest that a better solution may lie (1) in the nature of Luke's Gospel sources, and (2) in Luke's christological purpose in his Gospel narrative. First, it seems likely that Luke used all the explicitly 'Davidic' material he found in his Gospel sources. He takes over the only two 'son of David' passages found in Mark (the healing of the blind beggar, Mk 10.46-52 = Lk. 18.35-43; and the *Davidssohnfrage,* Mk 12.35-37 = Lk. 20.41-44), and there is little evidence that the theme was present in 'Q'.[1] Though it is of course impossible to establish whether Luke's *Sondergut* contained Davidic-messianic references which he did not use, the nature of the material he does use suggests his special sources contained little of an explicitly messianic nature. The relative paucity of Davidic material, then, may be due to Luke's careful handling of his sources rather than to an intentional avoidance of royal-Davidic categories in his Gospel narrative. This suggestion will require testing in the course of exegesis.

Secondly, as the study of the nativity in Chapter 3 has shown, in this introductory and programmatic section Luke defines Jesus' messiahship in specifically Davidic terms (cf. Lk. 1.32-33; 2.11). Though this, of course, does not mean that χριστός cannot carry other meanings elsewhere in Luke–Acts, there is no indication that in the Gospel proper

(1978); T.R. Carruth, 'The Jesus-as-Prophet Motif in Luke–Acts' (PhD dissertation; Baylor, 1973); G.R. Green, 'The Portrayal of Jesus as Prophet in Luke–Acts' (PhD dissertation; Southern Baptist Theological Seminary, 1975); M. Karimattam, 'Jesus the Prophet: A Study of the Prophet Motif in the Christology of Luke–Acts' (PhD dissertation; Pontifical Biblical Institute, Rome, 1978); G. Nebe, *Prophetische Züge im Bilde Jesu bei Lukas* (1989). J. Drury, 'Luke', in *The Literary Guide to the Bible* (1987), pp. 421-22, writes: 'For Luke Jesus is a prophet, not incidentally, but first and foremost: "a prophet mighty in deed and word before God and all the people", as the two on the road to Emmaus call him (24.19)'.

1. Though Matthew uses the 'son of David' title with some frequency (9 times: Mt. 1.1, 20; 9.27; 12.23; 15.22; 20.30, 31; 21.9, 15; cf. 22.42, 43), it is generally accepted that this is due to his editorial activity and that the title did not occur in the 'Q' material. Since methodologically I am following the majority of scholars in affirming Matthean–Lukan independence, there is no evidence that Luke consciously avoided the title. All that can be said for certain is that he does not introduce it into passages where it did not originally appear; and this may best be attributed to his method of handling his sources rather than to an aversion to this theme.

Luke withdraws or sets aside the royal-Davidic significance he has established in the birth narrative. While Luke expands and broadens this category, he does not abandon it. The following chapters, then, are an examination of how Luke develops the theme of messiahship in the Gospel narrative. It will be argued that though the exaltation-enthronement plays a central role in Luke's christological portrait, Luke is also intent to show that Jesus' whole life and ministry had royal-messianic significance. The basic thesis is twofold: first, that the nature and significance of Jesus' messiahship is a leading theme—perhaps *the* leading theme—of Luke's Gospel,[1] and secondly, that royal-Davidic categories continue to play a prominent role in the development of this theme.

In Chapter 5 the programmatic Nazareth sermon will be examined in its wider context to determine how Luke christologically defines Jesus' ministry. Chapter 6 will turn to Jesus' journey to Jerusalem and the climax of his ministry there. It will be argued that Luke does not abandon his royal-messianic portrait, but rather expands and broadens it—particularly with the use of Isaianic imagery—to demonstrate that through his whole life, death, resurrection and exaltation Jesus accomplishes the messianic task prophesied in Scripture and so fulfills the promises made to the fathers.

1. Cf. Ellis, *Gospel of Luke*, p. 10; Leaney, *Luke*, pp. 7, 34-37.

Chapter 5

THE INAUGURATION OF MESSIAH'S MINISTRY: THE NAZARETH SERMON IN CONTEXT

1. *Introduction*

It is almost universally recognized that Jesus' inaugural sermon in Nazareth (Lk. 4.16-30) has programmatic significance for Luke.[1] If this is so, a correct understanding of Luke's theological presentation here is essential for a proper understanding of the nature and significance of Jesus' ministry as a whole. The present chapter is comprised of three parts. In the first, the context leading up to and following the Nazareth sermon will be examined in order to determine how Luke presents the inauguration of Jesus' public ministry. This will provide important clues concerning the nature of Jesus' self-revelation in the Nazareth sermon. Next, the sermon itself will be examined with a special emphasis on resolving the seemingly conflicting royal and prophetic features. Finally, the results of the second part will be used to demonstrate the role of the messiah according to the Nazareth sermon and suggest how this role is worked out in the subsequent Gospel narrative.

2. *The Royal-Messianic Context of the Nazareth Sermon*

The Nazareth Sermon is set in the context of the inauguration of Jesus' public ministry (3.1-4.44). It is preceded by the preaching and baptismal ministry of John (3.1-20), Jesus' baptism (3.21-22), the genealogy (3.23-38), the temptation (4.1-13) and a summary of Jesus' teaching ministry in Galilee (4.14-15), and is followed by Jesus' activity in Capernaum (4.21-43) and another summary concerning Jesus' synagogue teaching

1. Similar statements are found in almost every article and monograph on the sermon. As Sanders, *The Jews in Luke–Acts*, p. 165, dryly remarks: 'This scene is 'programmatic' for Luke–Acts, as one grows almost tired of reading in the literature on the passage…'

(4.44). It is in this wider context that the sermon must be viewed. The following discussion will seek to show that Luke's redaction in this section points to the inauguration of a royal-messianic ministry.

a. *John the Baptist and 'the Christ', Luke 3.15-17*

In common with the other Gospels, Luke begins the account of Jesus' adult ministry with a description of the role and message of John the Baptist (Lk. 3.1-18). Luke alters his source by omitting the description of John's clothing and diet (cf. Mk 1.67) and adding an example of the Baptist's ethical teaching (vv. 10-14).[1] His most significant addition for the present discussion is his editorial comment in v. 15:[2]

> Προσδοκῶντος δὲ τοῦ λαοῦ καὶ διαλογιζομένων πάντων ἐν ταῖς καρδίαις αὐτῶν περὶ τοῦ Ἰωάννου, *μήποτε αὐτὸς εἴη ὁ χριστός*.

Luke thus introduces John's statement of self-subordination in vv. 16-17 with a description of the people's messianic expectation. In this way he *makes more explicit* what is implied in Mark (1.7-8) and 'Q' (Mt. 3.11-12): by subordinating himself and his baptism to the baptism and judgment of the 'mightier one' who is coming (vv. 16-17), John disavows his own messiahship and affirms that *Jesus who comes after him is the Christ* (cf. Acts 13.25).[3] Luke thus continues the parallelism/contrast between Jesus and John begun in the nativity. While John's role is only that of forerunner, *Jesus is the messiah.* Luke's redaction has important implications for the subsequent narrative. First, it gives the account of Jesus' baptism which follows (vv. 21-22) a stronger royal-messianic flavour. The people's expectation concerning 'the Christ' together with John's denial sets the narrative stage for the messiah's

1. Fitzmyer, *Luke I–IX*, p. 464 considers vv. 10-14 to be special Lukan material ('L'). Plummer, *St. Luke*, p. 90, and Schürmann, *Lukasevangelium*, I, p. 169, on the other hand, take it as 'Q' material which Matthew has dropped.

2. Luke's hand is suggested by (1) the rare New Testament optative εἴη (28 optatives in Luke–Acts; 2 in Mark, 0 in Matthew); and (2) the use of the verb προσδοκάω: 11 times in Luke–Acts; 5 elsewhere in the New Testament.

3. There is a similiar—and even more explicit—denial of messiahship by John the Baptist in Jn 1.19-28, esp. v. 20 (cf. Acts 13.25). Though this shows the traditional nature of John's denial, it does not diminish the significance of the point just made, since Luke has still intentionally edited his sources to include this tradition. This suggests that the Lukan community—and the traditions available to it—were concerned with this aspect of John's role. This is confirmed by Luke's inclusion of this tradition again in Acts 13.25.

appearance. Secondly, if the Spirit's descent at the baptism is viewed as a messianic anointing and empowering to office, this emphasis will colour the whole period of Jesus' preparation and the inauguration of his ministry, especially the temptation narrative and the programmatic Nazareth sermon in 4.16-30.

It is significant that this first use of χριστός after the birth narrative assumes that within Israel the title is a universally recognized designation for a specific figure. 'All the people' wonder if this might be *the* Christ. From the perspective of narrative development, the reader must look back to the birth narrative to see how Luke intends the title to be understood. Since he defines it there in a thoroughly royal-Davidic context, it is likely that this is its intended meaning here.

John contrasts his water baptism with that of the 'coming one', who will baptize ἐν πνεύματι ἁγίῳ καὶ πυρί ('Q': Mt. 3.11; Mark omits 'and fire'). In its original context John's saying probably envisioned not two baptisms (Spirit for salvation, fire for judgment), but a single eschatological deluge of Spirit-and-fire which judges the wicked and purifies the righteous—an idea which has parallels in the Old Testament and Judaism (cf. Isa. 4.4).[1] The messiah of *4 Ezra* 13.8-11 (cf. 13.27, 37-38) judges and destroys the wicked with a stream of fiery breath issuing from his mouth. 'Divine warrior' imagery (cf. Ps. 18.9; Isa. 30.27-28, etc.) here converges with allusions to the Spirit-endowed Davidic king of Isa. 11.1-4 (cf. *1 En*. 49.2-3; 62.1-2; *Pss. Sol*. 17.22-25, 30, 35-37; 18.7).[2] For Luke the prophecy finds its primary fulfillment in the Pentecost event (Acts 1.5; and subsequent 'Spirit-baptisms' in Acts: 11.16), where the sound of rushing 'wind' and the 'tongues of fire' herald the eschatological 'baptism' with the Spirit (Acts 2.2, 3). Jesus the messiah pours out the eschatological Spirit, empowering his disciples to accomplish the messianic task. In common with the Jewish background, Luke probably understands the 'fire' in terms of the purging and judging role of the

1. Turner, 'Holy Spirit', p. 344. A flood or stream of fire which judges and/or purifies appears in many texts, including Dan. 7.10; 1QH 3.20-36; *1 En*. 67.13, *T. Isaac* 5.21-25; cf. 1 Cor. 3.10-15; *T. Abr*. 12-13. 1QS 3.7-9 and 4.21 speak of God cleansing man of his sins with the Holy Spirit (cf. 1QS 3.7-9). For details and more texts related to water, fire and רוּחַ/πνεῦμα ('Spirit, 'breath', 'wind), in the context of judgment and purification see J.D.G. Dunn, 'Spirit-and-Fire Baptism', *NovT* 14 (1972), pp. 81-92; Davies and Allison, *Matthew*, I, pp. 316-18; Marshall, *Gospel of Luke*, p. 147; Fitzmyer, *Luke I–IX*, pp. 473-74; Nolland, *Luke 1-9.20*, p. 153.

2. See Chapter 2 section 2c above.

Spirit (cf. Acts 5.6, 9). It is in this context that Jesus' saying in Lk. 12.49-53 should be interpreted. The 'fire' Jesus longs to cast upon the earth following his own 'baptism' (12.49-50) probably refers to the judging message of the kingdom—mediated by the Spirit—which separates the righteous from the wicked and causes strife and division among men (12.51-53).[1] While ultimate fulfillment awaits the consummation when Jesus will judge the world in righteousness (Acts 10.42; 17.31; cf. Lk. 17.24-37; 18.7-8; 21.25-28, 36), Jesus' present mediation of the Spirit is already separating the chaff from the wheat—causing the rise and fall of many in Israel (Lk. 2.34).[2] As is characteristic of Luke, the emphasis lies on Jesus' *present* heavenly reign and his saving and judging work mediated by the Spirit through his chosen envoys.

b. *The Baptismal Anointing, Lk. 3.21-22*

i. *Luke 3.21-22 as Jesus' Spirit-anointing*. For Luke, the anointing described in Lk. 4.18 almost certainly refers back to the descent of the Spirit upon Jesus at his baptism (Lk. 3.21-22).[3] It is significant that following the baptism account, while all three Synoptics mention the Spirit's role in directing Jesus into the wilderness to be tempted (Mk 1.12; Mt. 4.1; Lk. 4.1), Luke alone says that he returned from the Jordan 'full of the Holy Spirit' (Lk. 4.1). Following his temptation, then, Jesus returns to Galilee 'in the power of the Spirit' (4.14, Luke only). A few sentences later, Jesus enters the Nazareth synagogue and cites Isa. 61.1-2 to define his ministry: Πνεῦμα κυρίου επ' ἐμέ, οὗ εἵνεκεν *ἔχρισέν* με...(v. 18). The narrative link between the descent of the Spirit at the baptism and the 'Spirit-anointing' described by Jesus in Lk. 4.18 (Isa. 61.1) is unmistakable.

The significance of the baptism account as an anointing is further confirmed by the kerygmatic statement in Acts 10.36-42 (cf. Acts 4.25-27). If the descent of the Spirit at the baptism is taken as Jesus' anointing, chronologically vv. 37-38 fit Luke's Gospel narrative perfectly. John's preaching and baptizing ministry (v. 37; Lk. 3.2-20) are

1. Cf. Ellis, *Gospel of Luke*, pp. 182-83.

2. For Luke the prophecy may also encompass Jesus' Spirit-empowerment to accomplish the messianic task of saving and judging during his ministry.

3. With the exception of Heb. 1.9 (an Old Testament quotation), Luke is the only New Testament writer who refers to the anointing of Jesus. See R.C. Tannehill, 'The Mission of Jesus according to Luke iv.16-30', in *Jesus in Nazareth* (1972), pp. 51-75, 69.

followed by Jesus' Spirit-anointing (v. 38a; Lk. 3.21, 22) and the beginning of his preaching and healing ministry (v. 38b)—a ministry defined and inaugurated in the Nazareth sermon (Lk. 4.16-30).[1]

In the Old Testament and in Judaism the Davidic messiah was closely related to the Spirit. Isaiah 11.2 says that 'The Spirit of the Lord will rest upon him...' (cf. *Pss. Sol.* 17.37; 18.7; 1QSb 5.25; 4QpIsa[a] 3.15-29; cf. also *1 En.* 49.2-3; 62.1-2). It may be significant that in referring to the descent of the Spirit upon Jesus (Lk. 3.22), Luke alters Mark's εἰς αὐτόν to ἐπ' αὐτόν, the preposition used in Isa. 11.2 (though this may be a stylistic change). As the Spirit of Yahweh came upon David (LXX: ἐπὶ Δαυίδ) to empower him from the moment of his anointing (1 Sam. 16.13), and as the Davidic messiah was prophesied in Isa. 11.2 to be the bearer of the Spirit, so Jesus at his baptism is anointed by the Spirit and commissioned for his messianic task.

It must be added that the coming Davidic king was not the only Old Testament figure said to bear the Spirit of God. The Isaianic servant (Isa. 42.1; cf. Isa. 61.1), judges (Judg. 3.10; 6.34; etc.), and prophets (2 Chron. 15.1; 20.14; Neh. 9.30; cf. Lk. 1.15) are described as receiving the Spirit.[2] Nor was the king the only Old Testament figure to be anointed; priests (Lev. 4.3, 5, 16; 8.12)[3] and perhaps also prophets (1 Kgs 19.16; cf. CD 2.12; 6.1; 1QM 11.7) were similarly commissioned. Could Jesus' baptismal anointing be merely a prophetic anointing, or does Luke attribute royal significance to it?

ii. *Allusions in the Divine Voice.* It was suggested above that Luke's redaction in 3.15b emphasizes the royal-messianic significance of the baptism. Is there other evidence in the baptism pericope which would point in this direction? Luke's redaction in 3.21-22 tends to downplay the actual baptism of Jesus and emphasizes instead Jesus' prayer and the events surrounding the descent of the Spirit and the voice from heaven.[4]

1. On the close relationship between Acts 10.35-38 and the Nazareth sermon see Turner, 'Jesus and the Spirit', pp. 22-23, who points out that the wording of Acts 10.36-38 is modelled on Luke 4.16-30 and is used to interpret it.

2. Nolland, *Luke 1-9.20*, p. 162.

3. Priestly anointing is implied in the Qumran designation 'messiah of Aaron' and may also appear in 11QMelch 18 (if the reference here is to Melchizedek—see the discussion of this passage in section 3bi [5] below).

4. In Mark's account, Jesus' baptism is a main clause with a finite verb ('And it came about Jesus came from Nazareth of Galilee and he was baptized by John in the Jordan...'). Luke's construction is more complex. His main clause is ἐγένετο

If the Spirit's descent suggests the moment of Jesus' anointing, how is the divine voice to be understood?

Luke's version of the voice from heaven is identical to Mark's: σύ εἶ ὁ υἱός μου ὁ ἀγαπητός, ἐν σοὶ εὐδόκησα.[1] In its original context, the saying seems to have been a mixed allusion, and various Old Testament texts have been proposed to explain it. The first part, σὺ εἶ ὁ υἱός μου, probably alludes to Ps. 2.7: υἱός μου εἶ σύ, ἐγὼ σήμερον γεγέννηκά σε (LXX). This would suggest a royal-messianic context for the saying. The final phrase (ἐν σοὶ εὐδόκησα), together with the reference to the descent of the Spirit, seems to reflect Isa. 42.1, suggesting Isaianic servant imagery: 'Behold my servant, whom I uphold, my chosen, *in whom my soul delights* (MT: רצתה נפשׁי); I have put my Spirit upon him'. Many scholars consider the original saying to reflect both passages, and so to merge royal and 'servant' ideas. Others argue for

followed by three infinitive phrases referring to the heavenly events ('And it came about...the heaven *opened* and the Holy Spirit *descended* in bodily form as a dove and a voice *came* from heaven...'). The baptism of the people, Jesus' baptism and his prayer are all subordinated to this main clause: ἐγένετο δὲ ἐν τῷ βαπτισθῆναι ἅπαντα τὸν λαὸν καὶ Ἰησοῦ βαπτισθέντος καὶ προσευχομένου...('And it came about when all the people were baptized, and when Jesus also had been baptized and was praying...'). The aorist tenses of the infinitive βαπτισθῆναι and the genitive absolute participle βαπτισθέντος contrast with the present tense of the second genitive absolute προσευχομένου. Jesus' baptism is thus not only distinguished from the baptism of the people, but both are separated notionally from Jesus' prayer and the subsequent opening of the heavens, descent of the Spirit and divine voice. Luke further distinguishes the (present) heavenly events from the (past) earthly baptism by replacing Mark's 'coming up out of the water' with the statement of Jesus' prayer. See BDF §404.2; Nolland, *Luke 1-9.20*, p. 160; Marshall, *Gospel of Luke*, p. 152; Creed, *St. Luke*, p. 57; cf. Plummer, *St. Luke*, pp. 98-99. This grammatical construction suggests that Luke views the descent of the Spirit, rather than the baptism itself as the moment of Jesus' anointing.

Tannehill, 'Mission of Jesus', p. 69, further suggests that the absence of any reference to John as the one who baptized Jesus in Lk. 3.21-22, may be due to Luke's desire to avoid any confusion as to who it was who anointed Jesus. For Luke Jesus was anointed by God, in conformity with Isa. 61.1.

1. The Western reading (which I would reject) continues the quote of Ps. 2.7: ...ἐγὼ σήμερον γεγέννηκά σε. For arguments against this reading see Marshall, *Gospel of Luke*, pp. 154-55; Fitzmyer, *Luke I–IX*, p. 485; Schürmann, *Lukasevangelium*, I, pp. 193-94; Nolland, *Luke 1-9.20*, p. 162; Metzger, *Textual Commentary*, p. 136; Bock, *Proclamation*, pp. 100-101; and the very detailed investigation in C.E. Wood, 'The Use of the Second Psalm in Jewish and Christian Tradition of Exegesis' (PhD dissertation; St. Andrews, 1975).

purely messianic[1] or purely servant imagery.[2] The origin of the term ἀγαπητός is more difficult and a range of allusions have been suggested, including (among others[3]): (1) Gen. 22.2, 12, 16 (LXX: ὁ υἱός σου ὁ ἀγαπητός), developing an Isaac typology;[4] (2) Ps. 2.7, following a tradition expressed in the targum of Ps. 2.7 (חביב = ἀγαπητός) and so continuing the royal imagery;[5] (4) Exod. 4.22-23, developing an Israel typology;[6] or, (4) Isa. 41.8 (LXX; cf. 44.2), drawing a parallel between the nation Israel and the Isaianic servant.[7]

1. Those who take the Western reading of Luke's text as original would naturally follow this view. E. Schweizer, *TDNT*, VIII, p. 368, accepts the non-Western reading but suggests that ἐν σοὶ εὐδόκησα is not an allusion to Isa. 42.1 but rather refers to 2 Sam. 22.20, which speaks of God's deliverance of David 'because he delighted in me' (LXX: ὅτι εὐδόκησεν ἐν ἐμοί). This would keep the saying as a whole in the realm of Davidic messiahship.

2. J. Jeremias, *New Testament Theology*, I, pp. 53-55; *idem*, *TDNT*, V, pp. 701-702, and others have argued that, in its original form, the allusion referred only to Isa. 42.1, and the supposed allusion to Ps. 2.7 is a verbal coincidence brought about by the later Hellenistic substitution of υἱός for an original, ambiguous παῖς ('servant' or 'son') (cf. Cullmann, *Christology*, p. 66; Hahn, *Titles*, pp. 337-41). For a thorough response to this position see I.H. Marshall, 'Son of God or Servant of Yahweh?—A Reconsideration of Mark 1.11', *NTS* 15 (1968–69), pp. 326-36.

This view, of course, applies only to the original form of the saying. Since Luke's source clearly read υἱός (cf. Mk 1.11), not παῖς, it is unlikely he would have seen only servant imagery. A similar response may be made to the view of P. Bretscher, 'Exodus 4.22-23 and the Voice from Heaven', *JBL* 87 (1968), pp. 301-11, who says that the sonship context of Exod. 4.22-23 best explains the allusion. He argues that an original πρωτότοκος has been altered to ἀγαπητός (the two being parallel in Judaism) to avoid nationalistic overtones. Again, however, since Luke's text already read ἀγαπητός he would not have detected such an allusion.

3. For others see Davies and Allison, *Matthew*, pp. 340-41, who note *Asc. Isa.* 1.4; 3.13; etc.; *T. Benj.* 11; Jud. 9.4; *3 Macc.* 6.11 (cf. 6.28); *Par. Jer.* 7.24; *m. 'Abot* 3.15; *Gk. Apoc. Ezra* 5.12; 6.3, 16; 7.1, 13; *2 En.* 24.2; *T. Isaac* 2.7; 6.23, 33; *T. Jacob* 1.13; cf. 4.3; 7.17.

4. Cf. *T. Abr.* 4, 7, 15; *T. Levi* 18.6; Rom. 8.32. See E. Best, *The Temptation and the Passion: The Markan Soteriology* (1965), pp. 169-72; cf. Marshall, 'Son of God', p. 334.

5. E. Schweizer, *TDNT*, VIII, p. 368.

6. See n. 2 above.

7. So Bock, *Proclamation*, pp. 103-105. Isa. 41.8 LXX reads: Σὺ δέ, Ἰσραήλ, παῖς μου Ἰακωβ, ὃν ἐξελεξάμην, σπέρμα Ἀβραάμ, ὃν ἠγάπησα...Bock suggests that this verse links together the themes of servanthood, election and love in relation to the nation Israel. The allusion therefore brings out the parallel implied in the Isaiah context between the nation (Isa. 41.8) and the 'servant' (Isa. 42.1) and so

Since Luke brings the saying over unchanged from his source, it must be asked which, if any, of these allusions he has detected. A link between ἀγαπητός and a specific Old Testament passage is the most doubtful of the possible allusions. The fact that in Lk. 9.35 Luke alters his source from ἀγαπητός to ἐκλελεγμέμος should caution against placing too great an emphasis on the former's significance here. While it is conceivable that Luke has detected an allusion to Gen. 22.2, 12, 16 (LXX), there is little evidence here or elsewhere that he is developing an Isaac typology.[1] Similarly, though doubtless for Luke, ἀγαπητός would be an appropriate term to describe God's relationship with Israel, the Isaianic servant or the Davidic messiah, it is precarious to conclude on the basis of a single word, brought over from the tradition, that Luke has a specific passage in view.

Since Luke cites Ps. 2.7 in Acts 13.33, he is likely to have detected this allusion. The thoroughly Davidic messianic context of Acts 13.16-41 further suggests that he would understand it royal-messianically.[2] Whether Luke has detected an allusion to Isa. 42.1 is a more difficult question. The juxtaposition of a statement of God's pleasure and the endowment of his Spirit certainly recalls Isa. 42.1, and Luke's redaction in 9.35 may also point in this direction.[3] Yet the LXX text of Isa. 42.1 is quite different from the wording of the MT, referring to '*Jacob* my servant' and '*Israel* my chosen', and translating the Hebrew רצה with προσδέχομαι instead of εὐδοκέω: '...my soul has *accepted* him'. If

suggests 'that behind the election of and God's pleasure for his Servant there is a love relationship'.

1. For further criticism of this Isaac typology see Bock, *Proclamation*, p. 102.

2. De la Potterie, 'L'onction du Christ', p. 236, argues that Luke would not recognize an allusion to Ps. 2.7 here since in Acts 13.33 he applies the text to Jesus' *glorification*, not his baptism. Against this view it may be argued that Luke distinguishes between Jesus' royal anointing (baptism) and his royal enthronement (ascension-exaltation). While in Acts 13.33 Paul *quotes* Ps. 2.7 as *fulfilled* at the resurrection, Luke alludes to the verse here not as a fulfillment text but as divine affirmation of Jesus' messianic identity. See the discussion of this passage in Chapter 4 above.

3. Luke's alteration from ἀγαπητός to ἐκλελεγμέμος (cf. Isa. 42.1) in 9.35, though perhaps significant, cannot be pressed too far. The only phrase Lk. 9.35 has in common with Isa. 42.1 (LXX) is 'my chosen one' and even these are not identical, since the LXX has the substantival adjective ἐκλεκτός, while Luke has the participle ἐκλελεγμέμος. Only if Luke had already seen an allusion to Isa. 42.1 in Lk. 3.22 can 9.35 be considered an assimilation to this same passage.

Luke knew only the LXX reading, it is questionable whether he would have seen an allusion here. On the other hand, it is certainly possible that Luke knew a Greek translation closer to the MT, like that found in later Greek versions and in Mt. 12.18.[1]

The range of uncertainties calls for caution. Since Luke brings the statement over unchanged from his Markan source, it is of questionable validity to assume that he has detected multiple allusions, and then to draw far-reaching conclusions about his christological presentation from these allusions. I would suggest tentatively that Luke has detected allusions to Ps. 2.7 and probably also to Isa. 42.1, and so views the divine voice as containing both royal and 'servant' imagery.[2] This suggestion will be tested in subsequent discussion.

iii. *The χριστός Title and Jesus' Baptismal Anointing*. Further indication that Luke views Jesus' baptismal 'anointing' as royal-messianic is suggested by his etymological interest in the χριστός title.[3] This interest is most evident in Acts 4.25-26, where Ps. 2.1-2—a royal Davidic text for Luke (cf. Acts 13.33)—is cited with reference to the opposition 'against the Lord and against *his Christ*' (κατὰ τοῦ κυρίου καὶ κατὰ *τοῦ χριστοῦ αὐτοῦ*). In an apparent allusion to Isa. 61.1 (Lk. 4.18),

1. Theodotion and Symmachus both use εὐδοκέω to translate the Hebrew רצה ('be pleased with', 'accept favourably', BDB, p. 953) as does Matthew in Mt. 12.18-21 (Marshall, 'Son of God', p. 335). On the complex nature of Matthew's text, which differs considerably from the MT as well as the LXX, see K. Stendahl, *The School of Saint Matthew and its Use of the Old Testament* (2nd edn, 1968), p. 115, and R.H. Gundry, *The Use of the Old Testament in St. Matthew's Gospel* (1967), pp. 110-16.

2. It is likely that both Matthew and Mark detect both images here. Matthew's introduction of ἀγαπητός in his citation of Isa. 42.1 at Mt. 12.18 is almost certainly an assimilation to the baptism, linking the two passages together. As noted above, Matthew also translates the Hebrew רצה with εὐδοκέω, in line with the baptismal voice. For a contrary view see M.D. Hooker, *Jesus and the Servant* (1959), pp. 68-73.

3. See van Unnik, 'Jesus the Christ', pp. 113-14. *Contra* Hahn, *Titles*, p. 404 n. 209 and de la Potterie, 'L'onction du Christ', pp. 225-52, esp. 238-42, who deny a connection between the χριστός title and Jesus' baptismal anointing. With reference to Acts 4.25-27, de la Potterie denies that the 'anointing' of v. 26 (which refers to the baptism) is linked to the χριστός title in the psalm citation (v. 26). He concludes, 'Les deux thèmes, celui du Christ' (= Oint) et celui de l'onction' reçue par Jésus, suivent dans saint Luc un développement parallèle, indépendamment l'un de l'autre' (pp. 241-42).

v. 27 takes up the etymology of the title by referring to 'Jesus, *whom you anointed*'.[1] Similarly, in the kerygmatic summary of Acts 10.35-43 Peter speaks of the peace that comes through Jesus Christ (v. 36), then elaborates in v. 38 by describing 'how God *anointed Jesus of Nazareth* with the Spirit and with power...' This description suggests a titular significance for χριστός in v. 36 ('Jesus *the Christ*') and so links the title to Jesus' anointing.[2] Further evidence of this significance for Luke may be found in his distinctive use of the titles 'Christ of God' (Lk. 9.20; 23.35) and the 'Lord's Christ' (Lk. 2.26; cf. 'his Christ', Acts 3.18), which imply the Old Testament idea of 'Yahweh's anointed'. Together these points suggest that the baptismal 'anointing' (Lk. 3.21) referred to in Lk. 4.18 (Isa. 61.1) points the reader toward the χριστός title and the royal-messianic significance attributed to it in the birth narrative (Lk. 2.11, 26).

In summary, whatever additional significance Luke may attribute to the baptismal anointing by the Spirit in Lk. 3.21-22 (cf. Lk. 4.18), a royal-anointing is certainly in view. This is indicated by: (1) Luke's Davidic-messianic interpretation of χριστός in the birth narrative, *together with* (a) Luke's redaction in favour of the title in 3.15b; and (b) the Lukan connection between the title and Jesus' baptismal anointing (Acts 4.18; 10.36-38); (2) the royal-messianic implications of eschatological baptism 'by Spirit and fire' (Isa. 11.4; *4 Ezra* 13.8-11, 27, 37-38); (3) the relationship of the Spirit to the coming Davidic king in Judaism; and (4) the allusion to Ps. 2.7 in the divine voice (cf. Acts 13.33; Acts 4.25-26).[3]

1. Turner, 'Jesus and the Spirit', pp. 25-26, says Acts 4.25-27 probably has nothing to do with anointing with the Spirit. It is rather a pre-Lukan tradition and is an archaism underscoring *God's* appointment of the one men rejected. But whatever its pre-Lukan significance, the references in Lk. 4.18 and Acts 10.38 suggest that Luke would have taken it as a reference to the baptismal anointing by the Spirit.

2. That Acts 10.35ff. refers back to the anointing described in Lk. 4.18 is evident from the many verbal parallels between the two passages. It seems likely that Peter's words here are modelled on Lk. 4.16-30. See Turner, 'Jesus and the Spirit', pp. 22-23.

3. No consensus has been reached on the significance of the dove imagery related to the descent of the Spirit (Davies and Allison, *Matthew*, pp. 331-34, list sixteen suggested interpretations!). I would tend to agree with those who see the background in Gen. 1.2, and so signifying Jesus as the bringer of the new creation. Apart from making the imagery more concrete (σωματικῷ εἴδει), Luke gives few clues as to how he interprets it.

c. *The Genealogy, Luke 3.23-38*

While Matthew places a genealogy of Jesus at the beginning of his Gospel, Luke includes his after Jesus' baptism, at the beginning of his public ministry. The reason for this position is uncertain. Some have suggested that if Luke added the birth narrative after the completion of the Gospel, this would be the most natural place for it, following the first mention of Jesus' name in the original narrative (3.23).[1] The problem with this view (on its own) is the obvious fact that Luke could have moved the genealogy had he so desired. Others have suggested that Luke intentionally placed the genealogy between the baptism (3.21-22) and temptation (4.1-13)—two passages where Jesus is designated Son of God—in order to contrast Adam's (and perhaps, mankind's) divine sonship to Jesus' own. It will be argued below that it is unlikely that this is Luke's *primary* motivation. It is more likely that the genealogy was placed (or, retained) here as one of a series of proofs concerning Jesus' messianic claim. As the baptism confirms the divine approval of Jesus' messianic task, and the temptation proves his obedience to the will of the Father to complete that task, so the genealogy establishes the legitimacy of his messianic (i.e. Davidic) ancestry.

Since the list begins with Joseph, the genealogy almost certainly represents the legitimacy of Joseph's ancestry rather than Mary's. This is confirmed by the fact that elsewhere it is Joseph's Davidic descent which Luke stresses (Lk. 1.27; 2.4).

There has been much debate concerning the origin and sources of the genealogy.[2] This debate has often centered on the LXX version of most

1. This view is promoted especially by advocates of the Proto-Luke hypothesis, some of whom consider the original Gospel to have begun at 3.1. So B.H. Streeter, *The Four Gospels* (1953), p. 209.

2. See especially G. Kuhn, 'Die Geschlechtsregister Jesu bei Lukas und Matthäus nach ihrer Herkunft untersucht', *ZNW* 22 (1923), pp. 206-28; J. Jeremias, *Jerusalem in the Time of Jesus* (1969), pp. 290-97; Burger, *Jesus als Davidssohn*, pp. 116-23; M.D. Johnson, *The Purpose of the Biblical Genealogies with Special Reference to the Setting of the Genealogies of Jesus* (2nd edn, 1988); Brown, *Birth*, pp. 84-94; J. Masson, *Jésus fils de David dans les généalogies de Saint Matthieu et de Saint Luc* (1982); Goulder, *Luke: A New Paradigm*, pp. 283-91. Neither the genealogy's historicity nor its relationship to Matthew's is our primary concern (except where these issues relate to Lukan purpose). On these issues see the commentaries and the works cited above. Our concern, rather, is to determine whether the genealogy is the work of Luke or a previous editor and what role it plays in Luke's narrative.

(but not all—see below) of the names and the presence of Καϊνάμ in v. 36, a name which appears in the LXX (as Καϊνάν, Gen. 11.12; 10.24; 1 Chron. 1.18 LXX A), but not in the MT.[1] Though many scholars confidently assert from this that the author of the genealogy was a Hellenistic (Jewish?) Christian working from the LXX, this is weak evidence on which to make such a claim. Names would naturally be assimilated to the LXX form as the genealogy was passed down in a Greek-speaking community. Further, if it is asked where the LXX translators themselves found the name Καϊνάμ, the most likely answer is in a Semitic text different than our MT. Uncertainty concerning the nature of the pre-Masoretic textual tradition as well as the translation history of the LXX should caution against asserting too quickly a Greek or Septuagintal *origin* for these names. Another problem in the genealogy is the presence of the patriarchal names Levi, Simeon, Judah and Joseph in vv. 29b-30a, since there is no evidence for the pre-exilic use of these as personal names in Israel.[2] While this issue raises difficult questions concerning the historicity of the genealogy, it does not provide answers to the questions of whether the list has a Greek or Semitic origin, who first compiled it or the nature of its transmission history. Conclusions on these issues must remain speculative.

Firmer ground may be found concerning the question of whether Luke himself composed the genealogy. Though the many textual variants raise questions about the extent of the genealogy, there seems to be an underlying structure consisting of 77 names falling into 11 groups of 7. Evidence of this structure is the presence of prominent names such as Abraham, Enoch and David at the end of each of these groups of seven (or 'weeks'). Such a pattern may reflect the division of world history into eleven weeks, followed by the 12th week of the messianic era. Jesus' coming is thus seen as the end of the 11th week, the climax of world history. Similar schematizations of world history occur in pseudepigraphic and rabbinic works, including *1 En.* 91ff.; *2 Apoc. Bar.* 53–74; *Apoc. Abr.* 30–31; 4 Ezra 14.11 and *b. Sanh.* 97b.[3] If this scheme is correct, the genealogy may originally have stood in reverse order, starting with Adam and descending to a climax in Jesus (a descending,

1. See especially Burger, *Jesus als Davidssohn*, pp. 116-23.

2. Jeremias, *Jerusalem*, p. 296. A possible exception is the presence of the name Joseph in 1 Chron. 25.2—though this list is also frequently considered anachronistic.

3. Many commentators point to these parallels. See especially Goulder, *Luke: A New Paradigm*, pp. 283-91.

rather than ascending, order is the normal pattern for genealogies of this length, cf. Mt. 1.1-16).[1] Two additional factors point to this conclusion. First, in the present Lukan form, the list contains 78 names, so either Jesus or God would not be included in the 11 × 7 framework.[2] That the latter (τοῦ θεοῦ) is a Lukan addition is suggested by the absence in Jewish writings of a genealogy beginning or ending with God.[3]

While it is thus likely that an 11 × 7 scheme formed the original framework of the genealogy, Luke does not seem to have been aware of it. Unlike Matthew, who explicitly points to a numerical system (Mt. 1.17), Luke does not mention one. Further, by reversing the order (probably because he began with a statement about Jesus in v. 23) and adding τοῦ θεοῦ, Luke actually obscures the pattern.[4] This suggests that Luke received the full genealogy (with the exception of τοῦ θεοῦ) from a source, rather than composing it himself or extending an existing genealogy from Abraham to Adam (see below).[5] Further evidence

1. 'Descending' = proceeding in the direction of one's descendants. This is the general rule for long genealogies, though there are exceptions (cf. 1 Chron. 6.33-38).

2. Goulder, *Luke: A New Paradigm*, pp. 238-91, argues that the 11 × 7 framework (with God at the end) is Luke's own construction and it is Jesus' name which is not part of the scheme. Luke's intention is thus to end with Joseph and so make Jesus the beginning of the 12th week (the messianic era). The difficulty with this is that the Lukan list proceeds in the opposite direction, ending not with Jesus, but with God. It is unlikely, therefore, that Luke views Jesus as the beginning of the 12th week. By reversing the order, Luke inadvertantly obscures the scheme.

3. Johnson, *Purpose*, p. 237. At the same time, the idea of God as the father of Adam is found in the Hellenistic Jew Philo (*Virt.* 204-205). This shows that such an idea is not necessarily alien to Hellenistic Jewish thought. On Philo's text cf. Nolland, *Luke 1-9:20*, p. 173 and discussion below.

4. Similar conclusions are reached by Marshall, *Gospel of Luke*, p. 160, and Nolland, *Luke 1-9.20*, p. 168.

5. The latter is the view of Kuhn, 'Geschlechtsregister', p. 216, and others. Goulder, *Luke: A New Paradigm*, pp. 288-89, argues for Lukan composition throughout. The evidence he adduces includes: (1) God as the father of Adam is not Jewish; (2) Cainam is in the LXX, but not the MT; (3) Admin is non-Jewish; (4) Nathan replaces Solomon, whom Luke elsewhere shows hostility towards (Acts 7.44-48); (5) Luke elsewhere shows closest connection with pseudepigraphic writings (as with his location of paradise, Lk. 23.43) so that the scheme of weeks is best attributed to him; (6) the idea of a full final week to come would fit Luke's eschatological thought; (7) Goulder attributes similar creation of ancestral names from the Old Testament to Luke in ch. 1 with Zechariah and Elizabeth. While it is likely that Luke added τοῦ θεοῦ, the rest of Goulder's arguments are extremely shaky. As mentioned above, Cainam's name was not *necessarily* taken from the LXX. Even if it was, this

against Lukan composition are the presence of non-LXX forms of various names,[1] and a number of other differences between Luke's genealogy and the genealogy in 1 Chronicles 1–3 LXX (which Luke is said to have followed).[2] This makes it unlikely that Luke has created his list on the basis of the LXX. We may conclude that Luke received the full genealogy from a source.[3]

Much has been made of the fact that while Matthew's genealogy begins with Abraham, Luke's goes back to Adam. Some suggest this reflects Luke's universalistic outlook in contrast to Matthew's Jewish one. Others claim Luke here portrays Jesus as the 'last Adam' (cf. Rom. 5.12-21; 1 Cor. 15.21-22, 45-49).[4] While both these may be factors in Luke's presentation, it is doubtful that either constitutes his primary interest. Since Luke is unlikely to have known Matthew's genealogy,[5]

would only suggest a Hellenistic-Jewish (or perhaps Hellenistic), not necessarily a Lukan, origin. Though Admin is not attested in the LXX (actually an argument against Lukan composition since Goulder thinks he borrows his names from that source!), to classify it as 'non-Jewish' is speculative. It may be either an abbreviation or a corruption of Amminadab or another name. The fourth argument of a supposed polemic against Solomon in Acts is actually directed against the temple. In any case, this argument is countered by the fact that Luke does not attribute any significance to Nathan's line elsewhere. Arguments '(5)' and '(6)' could apply equally well to almost any educated Christian of Luke's day. Finally, Goulder's claim that the names Zechariah and Elizabeth in Luke 1 reflect a Lukan pattern of creating names based on the Old Testament must be rejected as pure speculation.

1. Luke has 'Ιωβήδ (v. 32; cf. Mt. 1.5) for the LXX 'Ωβήδ (1 Chron. 2.12; Ruth 4.17, 21-22; but cf. LXX A: 'Ιωβήδ); Σάλα (v. 32) for the LXX Σαλμών (1 Chron. 2.11; cf. Mt. 1.4; Ruth 4.20-21 = Σαλμάν); and Καϊνάμ (twice, vv. 36, 37) for the LXX Καϊνάν (Gen. 11.12; 10.24; 1 Chron. 1.18, ms. A; Gen. 5.9; 1 Chron. 1.1).

2. (1) Zerubbabel's descent in Luke is through Nathan (Lk. 3.27-31), whereas in 1 Chron. 3.10-19 it is through Solomon (cf. Mt. 1.7-13; Jeremias, *Jerusalem*, pp. 295-96); (2) Luke gives Zerubbabel's son as 'Ρησά, who is not mentioned as one of his sons in 1 Chron. 3.19-20; (3) Luke has two names, 'Αδμίν and 'Αρνί for the one 'Αράμ in 1 Chron. 2.10 LXX. Burger's (*Jesus als Davidssohn*, p. 118) appeal to the mention of both 'Ράμ (cf. MT = רָם) and 'Αράμ in some LXX manuscripts to explain this alteration is not convincing.

3. So Burger, *Jesus als Davidssohn*, p. 117; Brown, *Birth*, pp. 93-94; Marshall, *Gospel of Luke*, p. 161; Nolland, *Luke 1-9:20*, p. 168.

4. Cf. Ellis, *Gospel of Luke*, p. 93; J. Jeremias, *TDNT*, I, pp. 141-43. For further arguments against this view see Johnson, *Purpose*, pp. 233-35.

5. *Contra* Goulder, *Luke: A New Paradigm*, p. 289, who says, 'He knew that Matthew's genealogy was in part the evangelist's own creation, and he wanted to follow the same idea on a larger scale, and to a more ambitious plan.'

there is no evidence that he has consciously *extended* an Abrahamic genealogy back to Adam. As concluded above, the evidence rather suggests that he received from the tradition a genealogy already extending back to Adam. Nor is Jesus as the 'last Adam' a prominent Lukan theme.[1] While Luke's placement of the temptation narrative—which shows Jesus successfully overcoming temptation to which Adam succumbed—may subtly suggest that Jesus (the true Son of God, 3.22; 4.3, 9) has succeeded where Adam (the original 'son of God', v. 38) failed, this cannot be Luke's *primary* interest in the genealogy. If it were, one would have to conclude that Luke introduces the genealogy at this point mainly to show that Adam, like Jesus, was a son of God (even if a failed one). But this is clearly not Luke's most important motivation. Nor can it be concluded that the purpose of the genealogy is to clarify the divine voice at the baptism (Lk. 3.22) by showing that Jesus is the Son of God by virtue of his common descent from Adam—the original son of God.[2] This would imply that Jesus' divine sonship is no different from that of other men, a perspective clearly contrary to Luke's own (cf. Lk. 1.35). It seems one should not read too much into Luke's addition of τοῦ θεοῦ following Adam's name. While it is possible that Luke presents a subtle Jesus–Adam contrast, it is more likely that the phrase should be taken at face value: Adam had no earthly father since his origin was in God himself.[3] While the idea of universal sonship to God (cf. Acts 17.28b-29: γένος τοῦ θεοῦ) and its relationship to Jesus' divine sonship may represent a minor or sub-point, the genealogy's main purpose is to confirm Jesus' identity: as a son of Adam his person and work have saving significance for the whole of mankind; as son of Abraham his mission is part of God's salvation-historical work through the nation Israel (cf. Luke 1-2); and as son of David he is heir to the throne of David—a throne which is promised universal dominion and eternal duration.

Luke's narrative development up to this point suggests that this last

1. Cf. Johnson, *Purpose*, pp. 234-35.

2. Johnson, *Purpose*, pp. 237-39. While Johnson is right that Luke links the Son of God title closely to its Old Testament and Jewish roots, this is far from saying that Jesus is Son of God *because* of his human descent from Adam.

3. See the similar statement of Philo in *Virt.* 204-205: τοῦ δὲ πατὴρ [μὲν] θνητὸς οὐδείς, ὁ δὲ ἀΐδιος θεός ('his father was no mortal, but the eternal God'). The only real difference is Philo seems to view Adam's situation as unique, while elsewhere (Acts 17.28b-29) Luke affirms the universal status of mankind as the offspring of God (cf. Nolland, *Luke 1-9:20*, p. 173).

point—the establishment of Jesus' *Davidic* descent—is Luke's most important interest. While Jesus' relationship to Israel is clearly emphasized in the birth narrative and the temptation (see below) and Abraham is twice described as the father of Israel (both in the hymns: Lk. 1.55, 73; cf. 1.72), concerning Jesus' individual ancestry it is Davidic descent which is most prominent (Lk. 1.27, 32, 69; 2.4, 11). Luke shows particular interest both in Joseph's Davidic descent (1.27; 2.4) and in the Davidic ancestry of the coming messiah (1.32, 69; 2.4, 11).[1] This would confirm the suggestion made at the beginning of this section: Luke places the genealogy at this point in his narrative to show that the mission Jesus is embarking upon is a *royal-messianic* one. Further evidence for this is the fact that Luke presents the genealogy after the baptism of Jesus, a passage which Luke intentionally redacts in favour of messiahship. It goes without saying that a genealogy descending through David, the primary purpose of which is to confirm Jesus' messianic identity, portrays him as the Davidic messiah.

Is there significance in the fact that Luke traces Jesus' Davidic descent through Nathan, the third son of David (2 Sam. 5.14; 1 Chron. 3.5; 14.4), while Matthew traces his through Solomon? Johnson points out Jewish and Christian confusion between Nathan the son of David and Nathan the prophet, and claims that Luke's intention is to present Jesus as a prophetic figure.[2] This is highly speculative and unlikely. The

1. Fitzmyer, *Luke I–IX*, p. 499, makes a similar point: 'Joseph has been identified in the infancy narrative as "of the house of David" (1.27; cf. 2.4). Now the genealogy explains this Davidic connection.' He does not further develop this point, however, and, in my opinion, makes too much of the Son of God motif suggested by 3.38 (p. 198), as also does Nolland, *Luke 1-9.20*, pp. 173-74.

2. Johnson, *Purpose*, pp. 240-52. In his second edition, Johnson, *Purpose*, p. xxvii, backs up a bit in the face of criticism, suggesting that, 'In view of the paucity of sources, this question must necessarily remain open.' E.L. Abel, 'The Genealogies of Jesus 'Ο ΧΡΙΣΤΟΣ', *NTS* 20 (1974), pp. 203-10, adopts Johnson's identification of Nathan as the prophet and seeks to show that the offices of prophet and messiah were linked in the first century. At the same time he rejects Johnson's perspective that Luke himself either created or detected this prophetic allusion (p. 209). While Abel's article points to the multiplicity of messianic figures—including prophetic ones—in the first century, he presents little evidence for the merging of prophetic and royal figures. In fact, much of the data he brings forward concerns priestly figures, which he seems to assume would bear prophetic characteristics (p. 208). In addition to this criticism, Abel's opening *assumption* that Luke presents a prophet-messiah in contrast to Matthew's royal one (pp. 205-206) is too simplistic a description of Luke's messiology. See discussion below, section 3b.

sources Johnson cites are almost all late and, as Fitzmyer points out, 'there is no evidence that such an identification existed in pre-Christian Judaism or in the pre-Lucan Christian community'.[1] In any case, nothing in the context lays emphasis on this name, nor does Luke show any interest here or elsewhere in a prophetic *ancestry* for Jesus. It is Jesus' Davidic descent that is central. It is more likely, perhaps, that Luke's genealogy intentionally avoids the kingly line passing through Solomon and Jehoiakim, since Jeremiah prophesied that no descendant of Jehoiakim (Jer. 36.30), or of his son Jechoniah (Jer. 22.24-30) would sit on the throne of David.[2] Whether Luke himself understood the genealogy in this way is uncertain since he does not explain the significance of the Nathan line, and, as argued above, probably received the full list from the tradition before him. What may be said is that Luke *could* have used the LXX to follow the kingly line had he so desired. The inclusion of Zerubbabel and Shealtiel in his list would have made this simple enough (cf. 1 Chron. 3.1-19 LXX). Since Luke retains the descent through Nathan, he may see some significance in the avoidance of the failed line through Jehoiakim.

In summary, Luke brings his genealogy over from the tradition and places it at this point in his narrative primarily to serve as further proof of Jesus' royal-messianic identity. Jesus' ancestry confirms his legitimate right to the throne of his father David.

d. *The Temptation, Luke 4.1-13*

The obedience of the Son to the will of the Father is the main theme of the temptation account (4.1-13), where Satan repeatedly tempts Jesus to exploit his position as the Son of God for his own gain.[3] The scene is

1. Fitzmyer, *Luke I–IX*, p. 497. Cf. Brown, *Birth*, p. 92 n. 75; Marshall, *Gospel of Luke*, p. 161; Nolland, *Luke 1-9.20*, p. 172.

2. Cf. Evans, *Saint Luke*, p. 252; Nolland, *Luke 1-9.20*, p. 170. Scripture is aware already of some special role for the house of Nathan (Zech. 12.12).

3. See Marshall, *Gospel of Luke*, pp. 170-71. The absence of the statement 'if you are the Son of God…' in the second temptation does not mean that it is unrelated to Jesus' divine sonship (it is precisely as the Son that Jesus is the heir to the kingdom; cf. Lk. 20.14; 22.29). Rather, the nature of the temptation—usurping the Father's authority and worshiping another—is acting contrary to the normal rights of sonship and so such an introduction would be inappropriate. The first and third temptations (first and second in Matthew), on the other hand, tempt Jesus to act in accordance with the normally legitimate rights of sonship (physical sustenance and protection).

antitypical of the experience of Israel in the wilderness.[1] While God's son Israel (Exod. 4.22-23) failed when tested in the wilderness, Jesus the true Son remains obedient and emerges victorious. Jesus' forty days of temptation in the wilderness are analogous to Israel's forty years, and the three Old Testament passages Jesus cites (Deut. 8.3; 6.13, 16) are all related to Israel's failures in the wilderness. The interpretive key to the account lies in Deut. 8.2-3, where Moses recalls how 'the Lord your God led you in the wilderness these forty years, that he might humble you, testing you to know what was in your heart...'[2] (1) Israel was tested with hunger so that she would learn dependence on God (Deut. 8.3) but failed to do so; Jesus depends wholly on God for his sustenance, quoting Deut. 8.3 (Lk. 4.4; Mt. 4.3, 4). (2) Israel was commanded to worship God alone (Deut. 6.13-15) but turned to idolatry (Deut. 9.12; Judg. 3.5-7); Jesus rejects the devil's offer of the kingdoms of the world in exchange for his worship, quoting Deut. 6.13 (Lk. 4.5-7; Mt. 4.8-9). (3) Israel doubted God's power and put him to the test at Massah/Meribah (Deut. 6.16; Exod. 17.1-7); Jesus refuses to throw himself from the temple and so test the Lord God, citing Deut. 6.16 (Lk. 4.9-12).[3] As the messianic king and Son of God (2 Sam. 7.14; Ps. 2.7; 89.27; 4QFlor), Jesus represents the nation and fulfills the task of eschatological Israel in the wilderness. This was almost certainly the significance of the traditional ('Q') temptation pericope, and it seems likely that both Matthew and Luke understood it in this way.

In light of this 'Israel-in-the-wilderness' background, it is particularly significant that the ministry of John is introduced in Lk. 3.4-6 with the 'new exodus' announcement from Isa. 40.3-5.[4] John announces the preparation of a 'way' in the wilderness for the coming of the Lord. In the episodes which follow, Jesus ὁ χριστός arrives on the scene, he is anointed and empowered by the Holy Spirit at the baptism, and is led 'full of the Holy Spirit' into the wilderness where he fulfills the role of the eschatological Israel. Such an interpretation would fit well with the

1. See especially B. Gerhardsson, *The Testing of God's Son* (1966); Davies and Allison, *Matthew*, p. 352; Marshall, *Gospel of Luke*, p. 166; Evans, *Saint Luke*, pp. 255-56; Fitzmyer, *Luke I–IX*, pp. 510-12. There may also be an Adam–Jesus typology (so Nolland, *Luke 1-9.20*, p. 182; Ellis, *Gospel of Luke*, p. 94; cf. Lk. 3.38), but this would be secondary. Fitzmyer (p. 512) calls a new-Adam interpretation 'highly eisegetical'.

2. See Davies and Allison, *Matthew*, p. 352; Evans, *Saint Luke*, p. 255.

3. See Evans, *Saint Luke*, p. 255.

4. For more on this see Chapter 6 section 4c.

suggestion that the divine voice at the Baptism identifies Jesus not only as the messianic king but also as the Isaianic 'servant' who fulfills the role of 'servant Israel'. As we shall see, the servant plays a pivotal role in Isaiah's description of the new exodus deliverance of God's people. This whole area of the Isaianic new exodus and its relationship to Luke–Acts will be dealt with in detail in Chapter 6. There it will be argued that it is precisely in Jesus' role as Davidic king and Isaianic servant that Jesus, like Moses before him (and hence, as the prophet-like-Moses), leads an eschatological new exodus of God's people to their promised salvation.

While the accounts in both Matthew and Luke probably contain this new exodus motif, in Luke the devil's offer of world authority and glory takes on special significance since Jesus has already been promised an eternal throne and kingdom (1.32-33; cf. 22.29). The offer is thus more clearly seen as a short cut, a way to avoid suffering and death, on the 'way' to the kingly authority and glory promised to Jesus (Lk. 1.32-33; 22.29) and attained at his exaltation-enthronement (Lk. 24.26; Acts 2.30-36). When viewed from the perspective of Luke–Acts as a whole, the account may be seen to carry forward the theme that Jesus rightly receives the kingdom by following the God-ordained path of obedience and suffering.

e. *Jesus' Kingdom Proclamation and Demonic Recognition of 'the Christ', Luke 4.14-15, 40-43*

Luke's wider context links Jesus' announcement in Nazareth to his proclamation of the kingdom of God, and this proclamation, in turn, is closely linked to Jesus' royal messiahship. Luke's introduction in 4.14-15 serves a similar function to Mk 1.14-15. Both report Jesus' return to Galilee and give a short summary of his activity. The difference is Luke's summary does not give the content of Jesus' message, because Luke wishes to supply this in the Nazareth Sermon. In a sense, then, Luke's '*Today* this scripture has been fulfilled in your hearing' (v. 21) in Jesus' sermon is equivalent to Mark's 'the time is fulfilled, and the kingdom of God is at hand...' (Mk 1.14). That Luke considers the Nazareth sermon to represent Jesus' kingdom proclamation is evident from Lk. 4.43, where Jesus announces, 'I must preach (εὐαγγελίσασθαι) the kingdom of God to the other cities *also*, for I was sent (ἀπεστάλην) for this purpose.' Luke's statement follows immediately the events in Nazareth (4.16-30) and Jesus' healing ministry in Capernaum (4.31-43)—healings which represent the beginning of the fulfillment of Isa. 61.1-2.[1] From a narrative perspective, being 'sent to proclaim good news of the kingdom' must refer back to the Nazareth sermon and to Jesus' announcement that he has been anointed by the Spirit to perform the tasks described in Isa. 61.1-2. Luke establishes a link between the passages by replacing Mark's κηρύσσω with εὐαγγελίζομαι and ἐξέρχομαι with ἀποστέλλω, almost certainly under the influence of the same two verbs in Lk. 4.18 (Isa. 61.1).[2]

The content of Jesus' kingdom proclamation for Luke, then, is not (first and foremost) that the kingdom is 'near' or 'at hand' (Mk 1.14) but that scripture is now being fulfilled in Jesus' person and work (4.21). One might go so far as to say that the shift is from the coming of the kingdom to the presence of the king.[3]

With this in mind, Luke's redaction in 4.41 becomes particularly significant. He brings Mk 3.11-12 forward and combines it with Mk 1.34. When Jesus exorcises demons, they come out crying, 'You are the Son of God!' (cf. Mk 3.11-12), whereupon Jesus commands them to silence. While in Mark this is because 'they knew who he was', Luke clarifies that 'they knew him to be *the Christ*'. Mark's account suggests that the demons recognize Jesus' divine sonship (Mk 3.11-12; 5.7) or perhaps his status as the 'holy one of God' (Mk 1.24); Luke stresses instead his messiahship. Further, the intentional juxtaposition of divine sonship and messiahship (cf. Acts 9.20) suggests not messiahship in general, but *royal-Davidic* messiahship. This is true both in the Old Testament and Judaism (2 Sam. 7.14; Ps. 2.2, 7; 89.26-27; 4QFlor), and elsewhere in Luke (Lk. 1.32; Acts 13.22-23, 33; see Chapter 3 section 3a).

This conclusion has implications for the wider context. First, by clarifying the Son of God title with χριστός at this point in the narrative, Luke emphasizes the royal connotations of the (traditional) Son of God statements just presented in the baptism (3.22) and temptation (4.3, 9). This helps to explain why Luke brings Mk 3.11-12 forward at this point

1. On the close link between the Nazareth sermon and the subsequent events in Capernaum see especially U. Busse, *Das Nazareth-Manifest* (1978), pp. 13-14.

2. On the Isaianic background to Luke's use of εὐαγγελίζομαι see Chapter 5 section 3biv(4).

3. As we shall see, this close association of the kingdom with Jesus is characteristic of Luke. Though Luke identifies Jesus as 'Christ' rather than 'king' in 3.16; 4.41, it is evident from the birth narrative (1.32; 2.11) and from Lk. 23.2, 3, 35-38 and Acts 17.7 of that he considers χριστός to be a royal title.

in the narrative: he wishes to state again Jesus' status as the 'Son of God' so that he can clarify this sonship with χριστός. In addition, since this verse serves as a christological climax to this first section of healings and exorcisms (4.31-41), it provides further evidence regarding Jesus' self-revelation in the Nazareth Sermon. Though as yet only demons recognize Jesus' true identity, Luke affirms that it is as the messianic Son of God (i.e. the Davidic messiah) that Jesus is fulfilling the mission announced in Lk. 4.18-19.

f. *Conclusion*

In summary, Luke's redaction and narrative presentation in the account of the beginning of Jesus' public ministry (Lk. 3-4) indicates the inauguration of a royal-messianic ministry. This conclusion will have important implications concerning the nature of Jesus' announcement in the Nazareth sermon. It is to the sermon itself, therefore, that we now turn.

3. *The Nazareth Sermon, Luke 4.16-30*[1]

a. *Introduction*

i. *Overview*. It seems likely that Lk. 4.16-30 represents the same event as that recorded in Mk 6.1-6 (cf. Mt. 13.53-58).[2] The basic components of Mk 6.1-4 are present in Luke: Jesus comes to his own town where he teaches in the synagogue on the Sabbath; the people are amazed at his words and deeds but take offense because of his local origin; Jesus responds by citing a proverb about a prophet's rejection in his home town. That Luke intends his account to replace Mk 1.1-6 is confirmed by his omission of that episode when he reaches it in the Markan order.

Despite these general similarities, there are important differences between the two accounts. Luke's story is much longer and differs considerably both in detail and in emphasis. Mark simply states that Jesus taught in the synagogue; Luke gives the content of his teaching (vv. 18-21; cf. vv. 23-27). In Mark, the emphasis is on the astonishment and

1. Much scholarly activity has centered on the Nazareth pericope in recent years. For a survey of recent research and a bibliography of works since 1972 see C.J. Schreck, 'The Nazareth Pericope, Luke 4, 16-30 in Recent Study', in *L'Evangile de Luc–The Gospel of Luke* (1989), pp. 399-471. The most thorough recent study of the pericope is G.K.-S. Shin, *Die Ausrufung des endgültigen Jubeljahres durch Jesus in Nazareth* (1989).

2. *Contra* Lane, *Mark*, p. 201 n. 2, who suggests two visits to Nazareth.

subsequent offense caused by Jesus' wisdom and mighty works (v. 2), and the resulting pronouncement by Jesus in v. 4: 'A prophet is not without honor, except in his own country...' In Luke, the episode contains two distinct parts. In the first half (4.16-22a), Jesus attends the synagogue service at his home town Nazareth, where he stands up to read Isa. 61.1-2a (with a line inserted from Isa. 58.6d LXX),[1] concluding with the announcement of the 'acceptable year of the Lord' (v. 2a), but significantly stopping short of the announcement of the day of God's vengeance (v. 2b). Isaiah 61 has clear connections to the Jewish year of jubilee (Lev. 25; cf. Exod. 21.2-6; 23.10-12; Deut. 15.1-18; 31.9-13),[2] and in 11Q Melchizedek is linked to jubilee and interpreted eschatologically.[3] The inclusion of the line from Isa. 58.6 ('to set free the oppressed') in Lk. 4.18d heightens the idea of release and so emphasizes the jubilary nature of Isa. 61.1;[4] but it is uncertain whether it was Luke

1. ἀποστεῖλαι τεθραυσμένους ἐν ἀφέσει (LXX: ἀπόστελλε). In addition to containing this line (and stopping short at v. 2c), Luke's text differs from the LXX in his use of κηρῦξαι instead of καλέσαι in 4.19, and in his omission of the fourth of the six colons: ἰάσασθαι τοὺς συντετριμμένους τῇ καρδίᾳ. The former may perhaps reflect awareness of the Hebrew text since the same Hebrew term (לקרא) is rendered in the LXX by κηρῦξαι in verse 1c and καλέσαι in v. 2a. Bo Reicke, 'Jesus in Nazareth–Luke 4,14-30', in *Das Wort und die Wörter* (1973), pp. 48-49, argues for the inclusion of the omitted line (present in some manuscripts) on the basis of structural considerations. Against Reicke, the external evidence slightly favours the omission of the line and internal evidence suggests a scribal addition from the LXX. See Shin, *Ausrufung*, p. 21.

2. On the connection between Isaiah 61 and the jubilee year see W. Zimmerli, 'Das "Gnadenjahr des Herrn"', in *Archäologie und Altes Testament* (1970), 321ff. The key point of contact is the phrase לקרא דרור ('to proclaim release', Isa. 61.1; Lev. 25.10; Jer. 34.8, 15, 17), which occurs in the Old Testament only with reference to the jubilee release (though sometimes metaphorically). Since דרור occurs in no other context, it was probably viewed as a technical term for the jubilee release.

3. For the text and interpretation see A.S. van der Woude, 'Melchisedek als himmlische Erlösergestalt in den neugefundenen eschatologischen Midraschim aus Qumran Höhle XI', *OTS* 14 (1965), pp. 354-73; M. de Jonge and A.S. van der Woude, '11Q Melchizedek and the New Testament', *NTS* 12 (1965–66), pp. 301-26. Cf. J.A. Fitzmyer, 'Further Light on Melchizedek from Qumran Cave 11', *JBL* 86 (1967), pp. 25-41; M. Miller, 'The Function of Isa. 61.1-2 in 11Q Melchizedek', *JBL* 88 (1969), pp. 467-69.

For eschatological interpretations of jubilee elsewhere in Jewish literature see R.B. Sloan, *The Favorable Year of the Lord: A Study of Jubilary Theology in the Gospel of Luke* (1977), p. 23 nn. 32-36.

4. Isa. 58.6 had a history of sabbatical and jubilary interpretation in Judaism.

who added the line, or whether he was aware of the jubilary significance of the passage.[1] What *is* clear is that—like 11QMelch—he interprets the text eschatologically and similarly applies it to release from those afflicted by Satan (cf. Lk. 7.21-22; 11.20ff.; 13.16; Acts 10.38; 'Belial' and his hosts in 11QMelch).

This first half of the pericope reaches a climax when Jesus sits down and dramatically announces that, '*Today* this Scripture has been fulfilled in your hearing' (v. 21). He thus claims to be the one anointed by God to perform the tasks inaugurating the eschatological time of fulfillment: preaching the good news to the poor; proclaiming release to captives and recovery of sight to the blind, setting free the oppressed; and proclaiming the acceptable (δεκτός) year of the Lord (vv. 18-19; Isa. 61.1-2; 58.6). The clear implication is that as the messianic herald, Jesus not only announces, but also brings to fulfillment God's eschatological salvation.

The second half of the episode (vv. 23-30) witnesses a dramatic shift as the initial favourable reaction of the townspeople (v. 22ab) turns first to skepticism, when they consider Jesus' humble origins (v. 22bc),[2] and

See details in Sloan, *Favorable Year*, pp. 39-40. On the possible jubilary significance of the Nazareth sermon and its influence on Luke's theology elsewhere see Sloan, *Favorable Year, passim*, esp. pp. 32-89; A. Strobel, 'Die Ausrufung des Jobeljahres in der Nazarethpredigt Jesu: zur apokalyptischen Tradition Lk. 4. 16-30', in *Jesus in Nazareth* (1972), pp. 38-50; J.A. Sanders, 'From Isaiah 61 to Luke 4', in *Christianity, Judaism and Other Greco-Roman Cults* (1975), I, pp. 75-106; U. Busse, *Die Wunder des Propheten Jesus* (1977); S.P. Kealy, A Jubilee Spirituality', *Doctrine and Life* 33 (1983), pp. 584-92; B.J. Koet, *Five Studies on the Interpretation of Scriptures in Luke–Acts* (1989), pp. 31-32; and the survey of recent research in Schreck, 'Nazareth Pericope', pp. 450-53.

1. See the reserve expressed by Turner, 'Jesus and the Spirit', p. 21, and Tannehill, *Narrative Unity*, I, p. 68. Both rightly criticize Sloan for making jubilary release central not only for the Nazareth sermon but for the whole of the Gospel. In my opinion, while Luke probably attaches jubilary significance to the text, it is not the controlling motif of his Gospel, but is one of many metaphors he uses to describe the eschatological time of salvation Jesus has inaugurated. See the similar conclusions concerning the Isaianic 'new exodus' in Chapter 6.

2. This seems to be a better interpretation than a wholly favourable or a wholly negative response in v. 22. Though the exact tone of the phrase 'Is not this Joseph's son?' is difficult to ascertain, Jesus' strong words in vv. 23-27 suggest that the mood of the crowd shifts to skepticism and (mild?) offense at this point (v. 22c; cf. Mk 6.3)—sparked by Jesus' astonishing claims (vv. 18-21) which seem at odds with his humble local origins. Betz, 'Kerygma of Luke', p. 135, says: 'The countrymen of

finally to rage, when Jesus announces that God's blessings extend to outsiders (vv. 28-30). In v. 23, Jesus discerns the thoughts of the people, citing a proverb and a demand for signs: 'Doubtless you will quote to me this proverb, "Physician, heal yourself;[1] what we have heard you did at Capernaum, do here also in your own country."' Two strands of thought are present here: unbelief and rejection by Jesus' home town (πατρίς), on the one hand, and benefits received by those outside (i.e. those in Capernaum) on the other. Verse 24 picks up and emphasizes the former. Jesus explains the unbelief and rejection at Nazareth as the common fate of prophets: 'Truly I say to you, no prophet is acceptable (δεκτός) in his own country (πατρίς)' (cf. Mk 6.4).[2] The verse probably foreshadows not only Jesus' rejection and attempted murder in the

Jesus were pleased with the message, but they could not accept the messenger.' J. Jeremias, *Jesus' Promise to the Nations*, pp. 44-45, on the other hand, follows B. Violet in the suggestion that the message is what offends and already in 22a the mood of the crowd is openly hostile. He argues that μαρτυρέω in v. 22a carries a negative sense ('bear witness against') and that it is Jesus' audacious claims and his mutilation of scripture (in omitting the 'day of vengeance' from Isa. 61.1-2) which spark the rage of the crowd. This, however, seems to be an unnatural reading of the text. For the many critics of Jeremias' perspective see the survey in Schreck, 'Nazareth Pericope', pp. 427-36. Rather than hostility from the outset (Jeremias, Violet, *et al.*), or a wholly favourable reaction in v. 22 (Fitzmyer, *Luke I–IX*, p. 535; Koet, *Five Studies*, p. 40, and many others—see Schreck), it seems best to view the crowd's response as building from favourable surprise (v. 22ab) to skepticism and mild offense (v. 22c), to open rage (vv. 28-30). The surprise expressed in v. 22b (θαυμάζω) thus forms a transition from the favourable reaction in v. 22a, to the skepticism of v. 22c. See the similar conclusion in Shin, *Ausrufung,* 197-204.

1. On the proverb's historical background see J.L. Nolland, 'Classical and Rabbinic Parallels to 'Physician, Heal Yourself' (Lk. iv 23)', *NovT* 21 (1979), pp. 193-209; S.J. Noorda, ''Cure Yourself Doctor!' (Luke 4, 23): Classical Parallels to an Alleged Saying of Jesus', in *Logia, Les Paroles de Jésus. The Sayings of Jesus* (1982), pp. 459-67.

2. Koet, *Five Studies*, pp. 43-44, follows the suggestion of J. Bajard that δεκτός here carries the sense of 'favourable', 'pleasing' and is linked to the 'acceptable' (δεκτός) year in v. 19 (so also Sanders, 'From Isaiah 61', pp. 98-99; 104-105). While some connection between the two terms is almost certainly intended, Koet is probably wrong when he sees v. 24 (like v. 19) referring to the benefits which come from *God* (active sense, 'no prophet brings benefits to his πατρίς', instead of passive, 'no prophet is acceptable in his πατρίς'). This is an unnatural reading of v. 24. It is better, rather, to see a contrast between what man accepts (δεκτός, v. 24), which is of no consequence, and what God accepts (δεκτός, v. 19), which is all that matters in the eschaton (Sanders, 'From Isaiah 61', pp. 98-99).

following verses (vv. 28-30), but also his coming rejection by Israel. The ambiguous πατρίς (= Nazareth) thus takes on symbolic significance (= Israel).

The significance of vv. 25-27 is a more difficult question.[1] First, are the stories of Elijah and Elisha meant to provide examples of prophets rejected by Israel (illustrating v. 24),[2] or is the emphasis on the recipients and non-recipients of God's blessings (parallel in thought to v. 23—outsiders receive, insiders lose out)? Since there is no mention of the rejection of Elijah and Elisha, the latter is more likely: just as outsiders benefited from the ministries of Elijah and Elisha, so outsiders will receive the blessings of Jesus' ministry. This brings up the further question of whether these verses foreshadow the Gentile mission in Acts,[3] or whether they point only to Jesus' ministry to sinners and tax collectors—'outsiders' within Israel. Finally, if the former, does God's choice of the Gentiles imply his rejection of Israel?[4]

A key point in all three analogies (Jesus in relation to Nazareth and Capernaum, v. 23; a prophet in relation to his πατρίς, v. 24; Elijah and Elisha in relation to Israel and Gentiles, vv. 25-27) is the contrast between 'outsiders', who receive God's blessings, and 'insiders', who do not. In the context of Jesus' public ministry—which the Nazareth sermon introduces—this contrast would primarily concern the 'outsiders' within Israel (sinners, tax collectors and non-Jews). On the other hand, the mention of Gentiles in vv. 25-27 would almost certainly suggest to Luke and his readers the Gentile mission. While many Jews were rejecting the gospel (cf. Simeon's oracle, Lk. 2.34), the Gentiles were receiving the benefits (cf. Lk. 2.32).

While these verses thus foreshadow (1) the rejection of God's messenger by many in Israel, and (2) God's offer of salvation to those outside (primarily the 'outcasts' in the Gospel, but probably also the Gentiles), they cannot be said to announce God's rejection of Israel.[5]

1. For various views on the relationship of vv. 25-27 to v. 23 and v. 24 see Nolland, *Luke 1-9.20*, pp. 200-201; Schreck, 'Nazareth Pericope', pp. 443-49.

2. So recently R.J. Miller, 'Elijah, John, and Jesus in the Gospel of Luke', *NTS* 34 (1988), pp. 611-22, esp. 615.

3. So most commentators.

4. See especially Sanders, *The Jews in Luke–Acts*, pp. 165-68; *idem*, 'The Prophetic Use of the Scriptures in Luke–Acts', in *Early Jewish and Christian Exegesis* (1987), pp. 191-98.

5. Schreck, 'Nazareth Pericope', p. 447. Schreck rightly points out that though all three analogies share in common the 'insiders' rejection of God's messenger, 'It

This would be unthinkable in the context of Jesus' announcement of Israel's eschatological year of jubilee.[1] The primary emphasis lies in the universal offer of salvation; it is God's grace and sovereign choice which brings the gospel to those formerly 'outside'.

ii. *Sources*. The significant differences between the accounts of Mark and Luke raise complex source questions, and a variety of source theories have been proposed.[2] Though Luke's account is frequently considered a redactional expansion of Mark,[3] it seems more likely that Luke possessed an alternate version of the episode which he preferred to Mark's.[4] While vv. 16, 22 and 24 portray the same general scene as

is essential to stress…that rejection by Nazareth, the prophet's πατρίς, and Israel neither implies nor entails reciprocal rejection by Jesus, the prophet, or Elijah and Elisha'. Cf. R.L. Brawley, *Luke–Acts and the Jews* (1987), p. 26. Koet, *Five Studies*, pp. 42-55, points out that in the Old Testament story of Elijah (and Elisha), as well as in the depiction of Elijah in later Judaism, the prophet's main role is the restoration of the covenant between Yahweh and Israel. Through their ministry to Gentiles, these prophets sought to bring Israel back to the knowledge of the Lord. While this seems a valid point, Koet's additional claim (p. 50) that the pericope does not serve as a prefigurement of the Gentile mission is unjustified. How are Jews provoked to repentance if not through the salvation of the Gentiles?

1. Cf. Koet, *Five Studies*, p. 52.
2. See the survey of recent views in Schreck, 'Nazareth Pericope', pp. 403-27.
3. Views vary considerably from those who see Luke's additions to Mark as primarily traditional to those who argue for free Lukan composition. The most widely held view is that vv. 17-21 and 28-30 represent free Lukan composition over Mark's basic framework (seen in vv. 16, 22, 24), to which a few fragments of tradition have been added (usually v. 23 and perhaps vv. 25-27). So Bultmann, *History*, p. 32; Creed, *St. Luke*, p. 65; Tannehill, 'Mission of Jesus', p. 52; Schneider, *Evangelium nach Lukas*, pp. 106-107; J. Drury, *Tradition and Design in Luke's Gospel* (1976), p. 66; M. Dömer, *Das Heil Gottes* (1978), pp. 52, 57-58; Fitzmyer, *Luke I–IX*, pp. 526-27. For other recent advocates see Schreck, 'Nazareth Pericope', pp. 404-407.
4. So with various nuances H. Schürmann, 'Der 'Bericht vom Anfang': Ein Rekonstruktionsversuch auf Grund von Lk. 4, 14-16', in *Studia Evangelica* 2 (1964); *idem*, 'Zur Traditionsgeschichte der Nazareth-Perikope Lk. 4, 16-30', in *Mélanges bibliques* (1970), pp. 187-205; *idem*, *Lukasevangelium*, I, pp. 225-44 (vv. 16-30 from 'Q'); P.D. Miller, 'An Exposition of Luke 4.16-21', in *Int* 29 (1975), pp. 417-21, 418; Marshall, *Gospel of Luke*, pp. 179-80; Schweizer, *Luke*, pp. 84-92; J.W. Prior, 'John 4.44 and the "Patris" of Jesus', *CBQ* 49 (1987), pp. 254-63, 256; Bock, *Proclamation*, pp. 110, 317 n. 59. For others see Schreck, 'Nazareth Pericope', pp. 407-11. Many authors suggest sources in addition to Mark, but are unclear whether these entail a connected narrative (a sermon in Nazareth?) or isolated

Mk 6.1-4, there is little verbal agreement, suggesting Luke is working with a different strand of tradition. Especially significant in this respect is the presence of Ναζαρά in v. 16 and ἀμήν in v. 24—two terms uncharacteristic of Luke's style[1] yet absent from Mk 6.1 and 4. If Luke was working *only* from his Markan source in these verses, it is strange that he would introduce such 'non-Lukan' terms.[2] At the same time, the presence of Lukan style and vocabulary throughout the pericope[3] suggests that Luke has worked over his source(s) and made it his own.

Whether Luke's account arose primarily from an independent version of the episode or a re-working of Mark (and other traditions?), as stated above there is almost universal agreement that the passage has programmatic significance for Luke.[4] Luke intentionally brings it forward to the head of Jesus' ministry and uses it to introduce key themes which will unfold in the subsequent narrative.[5] The first half defines the nature

traditions which Luke added to Mark's account (as in the previous view).

1. Ναζαρά occurs elsewhere in the New Testament only in Mt. 4.13. Luke normally uses Ναζαρέθ. Similarly, Luke tends to avoid ἀμήν, using it only six times in his Gospel (13 times in Mark; 31 in Matthew; 25 in John). Sometimes he substitutes ἀληθῶς (Lk. 9.27, 12.44; 21.3; cf. 11.51), other times he omits it altogether (7.9, 28; 10.12, 24; 12.59; 15.7; 22.18, 34).

2. For evidence of other non-Lukan vocabulary and style throughout the pericope see Schürmann, 'Zur Traditionsgeschichte', pp. 191-200; *idem*, *Lukasevangelium*, I, pp. 225-44; Jeremias, *Die Sprache des Lukasevangeliums* (1980), pp. 121-28. On the other hand, Schürmann's suggestion, 'Der 'Bericht vom Anfang'', *passim,* that the Nazareth pericope occurred at this point in Q as part of the 'report of the beginning' (Lk. 3.3-17; 4.1-13, 14-44 and Matthean //s) is probably to be rejected. J. Delobel, 'La rédaction de Lc., IV,14-16a et le 'Bericht vom Anfang', in *L'Evangile de Luc–The Gospel of Luke* (1989), pp. 203-23, has argued persuasively that Lk. 4.14-15—the key to Schürmann's argument—almost certainly arose from Lukan redaction of Mk 1.14-15, rather than from Q. Most scholars have accepted Delobel's critique of Schürmann (cf. Delobel's *Notes Additionnelles*, pp. 306-12 and Schreck, 'Nazareth Sermon', pp. 412-13, both in *L'Evangile de Luc*).

3. See especially Tannehill, 'Mission of Jesus', pp. 53-73.

4. Cf. C.H. Talbert, *Luke and the Gnostics* (1966), p. 35: 'Regardless of how one settles the issue of Luke's sources for 4.16-30, verses 17-21 are clearly Lucan. If 4.16-30 is considered a variation of Mark 6.1-6, then verses 17-21 are a Lucan addition to Mark. If 4.16-30 is regarded as L tradition, then the very preference is an indication of the Lucan mind.'

5. That Luke has moved the episode forward to this place is further suggested by the mention in v. 23 of deeds done in Capernaum before a Capernaum visit is related. Luke adjusts for this by the general statement of Jesus' preaching ministry in v. 15. Various scholars, on the other hand, have suggested that v. 23 is meant to be prophetic

and significance of Jesus' preaching and healing ministry; the second foreshadows the rejection by his own people and acceptance by those outside.[1]

b. *Isaiah 61.1-2 (58.6) and Jesus' Self-Revelation*

If there is a general consensus on the programmatic nature of the pericope, there is less agreement concerning its interpretation, especially with regard to the nature of Jesus' self-revelation in vv. 18-21 and the significance of his rejection in vv. 22b-30 (as discussed above). On the former question, the 'anointing' described in v. 18 (Isa. 61.1) has been variously interpreted as: (1) a prophetic anointing, and so portraying Jesus as a prophet,[2] or more specifically as *the* eschatological prophet (like Moses);[3] (2) a priestly anointing, and so presenting him as a priestly-messiah;[4] (3) a royal-messianic anointing, and so the Davidic messiah;[5] or, (4) an anointing as the 'servant of Yahweh'.[6] The interpretation of the Isaiah quotation is of crucial importance since it is in this

('Doubtless you *will* quote to me…') for the incidents which occur in the following episode (4.31ff.). Cf. Conzelmann, *Theology*, pp. 32-33; Voss, *Christologie*, p. 157; Tannehill, 'Mission of Jesus', pp. 54-55, 63; Busse, *Nazareth-Manifest*, p. 50. This interpretation, however, seems too forced, requiring an unnatural reading of v. 23.

1. On the structural and literary unity of the pericope in its Lukan context see Busse, *Nazareth Manifest*, pp. 13-67; Koet, *Five Studies*, pp. 26-29.

2. De la Potterie, 'L'onction du Christ', pp. 225-52; Nolland, *Luke 1-9.20*, p. 196. Cf. Fitzmyer, *Luke I–IX*, p. 529 (either prophetic or heraldic).

3. Hahn, *Titles*, pp. 381-82; Voss, *Christologie*, pp. 155-70; Busse, *Wunder*, pp. 372ff., 381-411; P. Stuhlmacher, *Das paulinische Evangelium* (1968), I, pp. 218-22; II, pp. 142-47; Turner, 'Jesus and the Spirit', pp. 18-28. Cf. Marshall, *Gospel of Luke*, p. 178; *idem, Historian*, pp. 125-28 (the eschatological prophet, who is to be identified with the messiah and the servant of Yahweh). According to Turner, the 'prophet like Moses' view had been earlier suggested as a possibility by W. Grundmann, *Das Evangelium nach Lukas* (2nd edn, 1961), p. 121 and G.W.H. Lampe, *The Seal of the Spirit* (2nd edn, 1967), p. 177.

4. G. Friedrich, 'Beobachtungen zur messianischen Hohepriestererwartung in den Synoptikern', *ZTK* 53 (1956), pp. 265-311, 285f.; W.H. Brownlee, 'Messianic Motifs of Qumran and the New Testament', *NTS* 3 (1956-57), pp. 205-206.

5. F. Schnider, *Jesus der Prophet* (1973), pp. 163-67; Schürmann, *Lukasevangelium*, I, p. 229; Leaney, *Luke*, p. 118; Tannehill, 'Mission of Jesus', p. 69; *idem, Narrative Unity*, I, p. 63; Dömer, *Heil Gottes*, pp. 63ff. Cf. van Unnik, 'Jesus the Christ', pp. 113-16.

6. Ellis, *Gospel of Luke*, p. 97. Cf. Bock, *Proclamation*, pp. 105-11 (Davidic-messiah servant); Marshall, *Gospel of Luke*, p. 178; *idem, Historian*, pp. 125-28 (eschatological prophet viewed as messiah and servant).

context that Jesus' subsequent ministry is introduced and defined.

The difference of opinion concerning Jesus' self-revelation is not surprising when one examines the content of the sermon. Though set in a royal messianic context (as demonstrated above) and containing a number of royal features, the sermon also portrays Jesus in prophetic terms. Schürmann recognizes these seemingly disparate images and suggests that in Luke's source (the *Bericht vom Anfang* in Q), v. 18 originally referred to a prophetic anointing, but that Luke has reinterpreted it as royal messianic.[1] This suggestion, however, implies that Jesus' self-revelation is out of place in Luke's wider context. I would propose that a better solution lies in Luke's interpretation of Isaiah 61 in the context of Isaiah's wider portrait of God's eschatological salvation. In the following discussion, the prophetic *and* royal features of the sermon will first be demonstrated. Then a synthesis of these seemingly conflicting portraits will be sought by examining Luke's likely understanding of the messianic redeemer in the wider context of Isaianic eschatological salvation.

i. *Prophetic Features in the Sermon.* The following evidence has been brought forward to demonstrate that the Nazareth sermon portrays Jesus as a prophetic figure:

(1) This is the most natural interpretation of the first-person language of Isaiah 61, which (it is said) depicts the call of the prophet himself.[2] This interpretation occurs in the targum of this passage and in other rabbinic literature.[3]

(2) Charismatic power in proclamation and miracle working (Isa. 61.1) are primarily *prophetic* rather than royal-messianic gifts.[4]

(3) Though references to prophetic anointing are rare in the Old Testament (1 Kgs 19.16; Ps. 105.15 [?]; 1 Chron. 16.22 [?]), at Qumran the term 'anointed ones' is used collectively of the prophets (CD 2.12; 6.1; cf. 1QM 11.7 [the teacher of righteousness?]). Prophetic anointing

1. Schürmann, *Lukasevangelium*, I, p. 229 n. 59; *idem*, 'Zur Traditionsgeschichte', pp. 190-91.

2. See Westermann, *Isaiah 40–66*, pp. 364-67; Whybray, *Isaiah 40–66*, p. 240.

3. B.D. Chilton, *The Isaiah Targum* (1987), p. 118; Sanders, 'From Isaiah 61', pp. 85-88; de la Potterie, 'L'onction du Christ', pp. 230-31; Nolland, *Luke 1-9.20*, p. 196.

4. De la Potterie, 'L'onction du Christ', pp. 230-31.

was thus not unknown in pre-Christian Palestinian Judaism.[1]

(4) The second half of the pericope (vv. 22b-30) describes Jesus' rejection in prophetic terms.[2] In addition to the proverb in v. 24 and the mention of the prophets Elijah and Elisha (vv. 25-27), vv. 28-30 may allude to the death of 'false prophets' (Deut. 13.1-12), or to the murder attempt against Jeremiah (Jer. 11.21).[3]

(5) This prophetic portrait is in line with Luke's description of Jesus elsewhere (Lk. 7.16, 39; 13.33-34; 24.19; Acts 3.22-23; 7.37) and with his statements concerning the suffering of the prophets (Lk. 4.24; 11.47-52; 13.33-34; 16.31; Acts 7.52).[4] Jesus is referred to by others as a great prophet (Lk. 7.16; 24.19) and twice (indirectly) attributes this designation to himself (Lk. 4.24; 13.33-34). Of course for Luke, Jesus is more than an ordinary prophet.[5] The eschatological context and the unique status Jesus claims for himself in the present passage (v. 21) indicate that this is no general prophetic call, but that of an eschatological figure. Hopes for an eschatological prophet in Judaism centered especially on the figures of Elijah and Moses. While Jesus' actions in the Gospel are sometimes analogous to those of Elijah and other prophets, for Luke it is John the Baptist who fulfills the role of the eschatological Elijah

1. Fitzmyer, *Luke I–IX*, pp. 529-30, 537; Nolland, *Luke 1-9:20*, p. 196.

2. De la Potterie, 'L'onction du Christ', pp. 231-34; Turner, 'Jesus and the Spirit', p. 26; Schürmann, 'Zur Traditionsgeschichte', pp. 190-91.

3. Cf. Schürmann, 'Traditionsgeschichte', pp. 190, 199. Schnider, *Jesus der Prophet*, pp. 163-67, downplays this prophetic significance, claiming that v. 24 does not emphasize Jesus' rejection *as a prophet,* but prepares for his radical rejection in vv. 28-29. Nor do vv. 25-27 compare Jesus to Elijah and Elisha *as prophets.* Rather, the comparison is between the actions of these men, who did not do miracles in their homeland, with those of Jesus, who likewise rejects the demand to perform miracles in his home town. While it is true that the emphasis of vv. 25-27 is on the recipients and non-recipients of God's blessings, rather than on the prophetic vocations of Elijah and Elisha, v. 24 cannot be so easily dismissed. Though Luke found this verse in the tradition, his choice to retain it shows his agreement with it, and both here and in 13.33-34 he compares Jesus' suffering fate to that of the prophets. There is little doubt, then, that v. 24 and (probably) vv. 28-30, portray Jesus' rejection in Nazareth (and by implication, his rejection in Israel) in prophetic terms.

4. De la Potterie, 'L'onction du Christ', pp. 226-29; Nolland, *Luke 1-9:20*, pp. 196, 200. On Jesus' role as a prophet in Luke's Gospel see also P.S. Minear, *To Heal and to Reveal* (1976), pp. 102-47; Johnson, *Literary Function of Possessions*, pp. 38-126; and the works cited in the introduction to Part III above.

5. Even John the Baptist, whom Luke repeatedly subordinates to Jesus, is the last and greatest of the prophets—indeed 'more than a prophet' (Lk. 7.26, 28).

(Lk. 1.17, 76; 3.3-6; 7.27).[1] On the other hand, Luke twice identifies Jesus as the 'prophet like Moses', explicitly in Acts 3.22ff. and implicitly in 7.37 (cf. Lk. 7.11-35; 9.28-36; 24.19; Acts 7.22ff.).[2] Jewish expectations concerning this figure arose primarily from the prophecy of Deut. 18.15, and centered not so much on a *Moses redivivus* as a prophet *like Moses*. Hahn points out that while typical elements of the Elijah figure included the preaching of repentance and the proclamation of the judgment of God, in the case of the prophet like Moses emphasis was laid on miracle and authoritative teaching.[3] It is not unlikely, then, that this figure is implicitly in view in the present passage. Possible evidence for this may be found in the two passages in Acts where the title occurs. In Acts 3.12-26, a context where Jesus is twice referred to as χριστός (vv. 18, 20), Peter cites Deut. 18.15: 'Moses said, "The Lord God shall raise up for you a prophet like me from your brethren; to him you shall give heed in everything he says to you."' For Luke, then, the prophet like Moses is also ὁ χριστός, and is associated with Jesus' preaching and teaching ministry (and his continuing testimony through the apostles)—a ministry defined and inaugurated in the Nazareth sermon. Luke's second reference to this figure in Acts 7 also has thematic links to the Nazareth sermon. In Stephen's narration of the Moses story (vv. 17ff.), Deut. 18.15 is again cited, implicitly associating Jesus with this eschatological figure (v. 37). At the conclusion of the sermon, Stephen accuses his audience of first murdering the prophets who announced the coming of the righteous (or 'innocent') one, and then betraying and murdering the righteous one himself (v. 52). Since vv. 35-38 of the sermon probably reflect a Jesus–Moses typology and the prophet like Moses of v. 37

1. Turner, 'Jesus and the Spirit', p. 27. I would agree with the assessment of Marshall, *Historian*, pp. 146-47, that though Luke does not identify John with Elijah in a literal sense (Elijah himself appears in 9.30!), he considers him to be the Elijah-like figure spoken about in Malachi. This accounts for Luke's omissions of material found in Mk 1.6 and 9.9-13, without dismissing the clear statements of Lk. 1.17, 76; 3.3-6; 7.27.

2. Turner, 'Jesus and the Spirit', pp. 26-28. Turner points to typological parallels between Moses and Jesus in Acts 7; verbal parallels between the description of Jesus in Lk. 24.19 and Moses in Acts 7.22; Lukan redaction in the transfiguration account; and, the association of the designation 'a great prophet' in Lk. 7.16 with the description of Jesus as the one who fulfills Isa. 61.1 in 7.22. On the background to this figure see Teeple, *Mosaic Eschatological Prophet* (1957); Hahn, *Titles*, pp. 352-406.

3. Hahn, *Titles*, p. 365.

is the only christological figure explicitly referred to, it seems likely that 'righteous one' of v. 52 at least implicitly refers back to this figure. Stephen accuses his audience of first murdering God's prophets through the ages, and finally of murdering God's final agent, the eschatological prophet himself. This depiction of Jesus as suffering the fate of the prophets parallels the portrait of Lk. 4.24 (cf. 13.33-34) and suggests that the function of eschatological prophet may be implicitly in view in Lk. 4.16-30.[1]

In summary, on the basis of Luke's presentation in the second half of the pericope and elsewhere in Luke–Acts, it seems likely that the Nazareth sermon presents Jesus as a prophet, and implicitly as the eschatological prophet like Moses who will act as God's agent in bringing in the time of eschatological salvation.

ii. *Royal characteristics of Luke 4.18-19 (Isaiah 61.1-2; 58.6)*. Though Isa. 61.1-2 is frequently considered to represent a prophet's call, a number of scholars have pointed to distinctly regal features in the herald's[2] announcement.[3]

(1) Apart from Isa. 61.1-2, the two features of anointing and Spirit-endowment are found in the Old Testament only in connection with the king (1 Sam. 16.12-13; 2 Sam. 23.1-2; cf. *Pss. Sol.* 17.32, 37; 18.5, 7).[4]

1. De Jonge and van der Woude, '11Q Melchizedek', p. 307, suggest that the figure who fulfills Isaiah 61 in 11QMelch may in fact be the eschatological prophet like Moses. 4QTestim (= 4Q175) quotes Deut. 18.18-19 before Num. 14.15-17 and Deut. 33.8-11, thereby joining a prophet to the expected king and high priest. Though 11QMelch is seen against a different Old Testament background, 'it is quite possible that the "anointed by the the [*sic*] Spirit" mentioned here is the same as the "prophet like Moses" in 4Q Test'. Though of course possible, this suggestion is too speculative to serve as proof of such a connection in 11QMelch.

2. The designations 'herald' or 'prophet-herald' will henceforth be used to describe the figure represented in Isaiah 61 without implying by this any particular view concerning the tradition history of the passage or the historical identity of the speaker.

3. Cf. Eaton, *Festal Drama*, pp. 90-91; H. Ringgren, *The Messiah in the Old Testament* (1956), pp. 33-34; H. Gressmann, *Der Messias* (1929), pp. 204-205; Sloan, *Favorable Year*, pp. 54-67; M. Noth, *Gesammelte Studien zum Alten Testament* (1960), p. 332 n. 49; W.J. Houston, '"Today in Your Very Hearing": Some Comments on the Christological Use of the Old Testament', in *The Glory of Christ in the New Testament* (1987), pp. 37-47.

4. Eaton, *Festal Drama*, p. 90; Houston, '"Today in Your Very Hearing"', pp. 45ff.

Though it is true that the king's anointing and his Spirit-endowment are two separate things, and that an anointing *by* the Spirit appears only in Isa. 61.1 (and its interpretations in Judaism; cf. 11QMelch 6-9), the two acts are closely related in a text like 1 Sam. 16.13: it is by virtue of David's divine election and anointing that he receives the Spirit. This is not to suggest that a prophetic or a priestly figure could not be both anointed and endowed with the Spirit; but the juxtaposition of these ideas is most closely associated with kingship.

(2) It has been noted frequently that the figure in Isa. 61.1-2 not only announces the arrival of God's eschatological salvation but also brings it about. W.J. Houston writes:

> To proclaim 'freedom to captives, amnesty to prisoners' is a performative speech-act in the political realm: it is done by one who has the political authority to affect it. In a word it is one who announces his investiture with Yahweh's ruling power (v. 1a) who here speaks.[1]

That this is the intended meaning in the Nazareth sermon is evident from the inclusion of the line from Isa. 58.6 (whether added by Luke or another): 'To set at liberty those who are oppressed.'[2] The herald *both announces and brings to fulfillment* the release of the oppressed from their captivity. Manumission is a particularly royal prerogative.

(3) If Luke interpreted Isaiah 61 specifically in terms of jubilary release (which is uncertain[3]), this might also carry royal connotations. When the monarchy was in place, it was the king's responsibility to announce the sabbath/jubilee release (cf. Jer. 34.8-22).[4] Whether or not Luke drew this jubilee connection, the establishment of social justice indicated in Isa. 61.1-3 points most naturally to the executive power of the king. During the monarchical period, it was the king who served as Yahweh's

1. Houston, 'Today in Your Very Hearing', p. 45. Cf. Shin, *Ausrufung*, p. 138.

2. Cf. Bock, *Proclamation*, p. 109, who points out that the inclusion of the line from Isa. 58.6 emphasizes the messianic nature of Jesus' announcement: '*This figure does not merely bring a message and healing, but effects salvation*' (emphasis his).

3. See section 3a above.

4. See especially Sloan, *Favorable Year*, pp. 58-67, who points out that Josiah's activities in 2 Chron. 34.14-33—assembling the people, reading the law, and covenant renewal—were almost certainly an attempt to revive the ancient Sabbath year law of Deut. 31.9-13. By way of precedent, then, it is the king who announces the Sabbath or jubilee year. See also Jer. 34.8, 15, 17, the only occurence outside Lev. 25.10 and Isa. 61.1 of the jubilee language לקרא דרור ('proclaim release'). Jeremiah here rebukes king Zedekiah and induces him to enact the Sabbath/jubilee law of slave release. Jubilee-like release is here linked to a *royal* decree.

agent to 'establish judgment and righteousness' (עשׂה משפט וצדקה; 2 Sam. 8.15-18, David; 1 Kgs 10.9, Solomon; cf. 1 Kgs 3.28; 6.12),[1] and this role was picked up in messianic expectations. As we have seen, one of the main tasks of the coming Davidic king would be to rule wisely and to establish judgment and righteousness in the land (Isa. 9.6; 11.1-5; Jer. 23.5-6; 33.15; Ezek 21.27; *Pss. Sol.* 17.22, 26, 29, 32, 37, 40; 4QpIsa[a] fr. D 1-8; 1QSb 5.24-26; *T. Judah* 24.1, 6; cf. *1 En.* 61.8-9; 62.1-12). In Isa. 11.4 the Spirit-endowed king is said to 'judge the poor in righteousness, and decide for the meek of the earth with fairness'.

(4) Sloan and others have pointed out that the herald's announcement in Isaiah 61.1ff. is strikingly similar in 'conventional content' to accession to the throne speeches of the ancient Near East.[2] Points in common include: divine sanction for the king's rule (Isa. 61.1); benefits for the poor and oppressed (vv. 1-2); prisoner amnesty (v. 1); natural abundance and material prosperity (vv. 5-7); the establishment of justice and righteousness (vv. 8-11). Houston notes, too, that apart from Isa. 49.1-6 (a 'servant' text, see discussion below) the nearest formal parallel to Isa. 61.1-3 is 2 Sam. 23.1-7, the last words of David. Though these parallels do not prove that *Luke* interpreted Isa. 61.1-2 in a royal manner, they do indicate the text's distinctly royal 'flavour'.

(5) Finally, 11Q Melchizedek interprets Isa. 61.1 eschatologically and appears to identify the 'herald' of Isa. 61.1 with the heavenly redeemer Melchizedek—a royal-priestly figure.[3] This would suggest that the sectarians identified royal as well as prophetic features in the text

1. Houston, 'Today in Your Very Hearing', p. 46; Sloan, *Favorable Year*, pp. 62-65.

2. Sloan, *Favorable Year*, pp. 54-58; Houston, 'Today in Your Very Hearing', p. 46; Ringgren, *Messiah*, pp. 22-23. Ringgren and Sloan cite texts found in J.B. Pritchard (ed.), *Ancient Near Eastern Texts Relating to the Old Testament* (1950).

3. The reference is disputed. Sanders, 'From Isaiah 61', p. 91, identifies the מבשר as Melchizedek (cf. Fitzmyer, 'Further Light on Melchizedek', pp. 31, 40), while de Jonge and van der Woude, '11Q Melchizedek', pp. 306-308, and F.L. Horton, *The Melchizedek Tradition* (1976), p. 78, consider him to be a second prophetic figure (the eschatological prophet of 1QS 9.11?). Since in lines 5-6 it appears to be *Melchizedek* who will 'proclaim liberty to them' (וקרא להמה דרר [jubilee language]; Isa. 61.1; Lev. 25.10; Jer. 34.8), i.e. who will fulfill the role of the prophet-herald of Isa. 61.1, it seems likely that he is also the 'herald' (מבשר) (Isa. 52.7) and the 'anointed one of the Spirit' (Isa. 61.1) who 'announces salvation' (Isa. 52.7) in lines 15-19.

(though not necessarily Davidic).[1] Though the targum interprets Isaiah 61.1 with reference to the prophet himself, Sanders points out that the text seems intentionally to *eliminate* messianic overtones, perhaps providing indirect witness to earlier messianic interpretations.[2]

In summary, while some of these features are not exclusively royal, they are all qualities associated with kingship. It is not unlikely, therefore, that a first-century reader of Isaiah 61 would recognize royal as well as prophetic features in the text. Since, as we have seen, Luke presents the events leading up to the Nazareth sermon as the prelude to a *royal-messianic* ministry, it seems likely that he has interpreted the sermon as Jesus' inaugural kingly address.[3] How, then, does this presentation correspond with the *prophetic* features of the sermon recognized above? I would suggest that the answer lies in Luke's reading of Isaiah as a unity and his association of the complementary portraits of the prophet-herald of Isaiah 61, the 'servant' of Isaiah 40–55 and the expected Davidic king of Isaiah 9 and 11.

iii. *The First-Century Unity of Isaiah*. There is a growing trend in Isaianic research to focus on the book's redactional unity.[4] While past

1. That the 'herald' of 11QMelch has royal features is also suggested by the end of line 18, which appears to refer to Daniel and so probably identifies the 'herald' and 'anointed one' as the 'anointed prince' (משיח נגיד) of Dan. 9.25. G. Vermes, *The Dead Sea Scrolls in English* (3rd edn, 1987), p. 301, reconstructs the text: 'and *the messenger* (מבשר) is the Anointed one of the Spirit, concerning whom Dan[iel] said, [*Until an anointed one, a prince*...]' (Dan. 9.25) (cf. Fitzmyer, 'Further Light on Melchizedek', pp. 27, 30, 40). An allusion to Dan. 9.25 fits the context well since the 'seventy weeks of years' of Dan. 9.24-27 are alluded to in line 7. See Fitzmyer, 'Further Light on Melchizedek', p. 29.

2. The targum refers the passage to the prophet himself (v. 1); speaks of 'appointing' instead of 'anointing' (v. 1); and translates 'to proclaim the year of acceptance *of* Jehovah' as 'to proclaim the year of acceptance *before* the Lord' (translating ל with Aramaic קדם and so emphasizing that the herald-prophet proceeds from God's presence to proclaim *God's* message) (v. 2) (Sanders, 'From Isaiah 61', pp. 85-86). Sanders (p. 86) also points to rabbinic statements which eliminate the idea of anointing and which stress that the passage refers to the prophet alone and none other—probably reflecting anti-Christian *Tendenz* as one tradition of Jewish interpretation.

3. Cf. Sloan, *Favorable Year*, p. 54.

4. See especially M.A. Sweeney, *Isaiah 1–4 and the Post-Exilic Understanding of the Isaianic Tradition* (1988); R.E. Clements, 'The Unity of the Book of Isaiah', *Int* 36 (1982), pp. 117-29; *idem*, 'Beyond Tradition-History: Deutero-Isaianic

research tended to study the major sections of the work in isolation, viewing the final redactors as mere compilers ('scissors and paste men'), more recent research has focused on the thematic and structural relationships between these various sections.[1] While these studies are primarily concerned with the composition and theology of the book's various redactors, they have also served to bring out the sometimes forgotten point that in its canonical form, the work is a unified whole, and merits examination from that perspective. Childs refers to this redactional unity when he writes:

> In light of the present shape of the book of Isaiah the question must be seriously raised if the material of Second Isaiah in fact ever circulated in Israel apart from its being connected to an earlier form of First Isaiah. Certainly the force of much of the imagery of both Second and Third Isaiah is missed unless the connection with First Isaiah is recognized. The schema of before and after, of prophecy and fulfillment, provides a major bracket which unites the witnesses.[2]

Childs's comments not only indicate the importance of examining Isaiah for signs of internal unity, but also raise an issue important to the present study: the literary unity of the work in first-century Judaism and

Development of First Isaiah's Themes', *JSOT* 31 (1985), pp. 95-113; *idem,* 'Patterns in the Prophetic Canon: Healing the Blind and the Lame', in *Canon, Theology and Old Testament Interpretation* (1988), pp. 189-200; R. Rendtorff, 'Zur Komposition des Buches Jesajas', *VT* 34 (1984), pp. 295-320; *idem, The Old Testament: An Introduction* (1986), pp. 190ff.; P.R. Ackroyd, 'Isaiah I–XII: Presentation of a Prophet', VTSup 29 (1974), pp. 16-48. For a summary of recent work in this area see J. Vermeylen, 'L'unité du livre d'Isaïe', in *The Book of Isaiah. Le Livre D'Isaïe* (1989), pp. 11-53.

1. For an example of this kind of work see Clement, 'Beyond Tradition-History', pp. 100-101. Clement says that if one starts with the generally accepted assumption that Isaiah 40–55 originated in the sixth century BC, three broad possibilities concerning their relationship to chs. 1–39 present themselves: (1) Though the author of these chapters had nothing to do with the original Isaiah, a later scribe for unknown reasons brought together the two works. (2) Though written independently, a later scribe recognized the suitability of chs. 40–55 as a sequel to chs. 1–39 and so brought the two together. Further material was then added which developed the sense of interconnectedness still further. (3) From the outset, chs. 40–55 were intended to develop and enlarge upon the prophetic saying from Isaiah of Jerusalem. Clements accepts this last possibility and seeks to show its validity by examining the development of various themes throughout the work.

2. B. S. Childs, *Introduction to the Old Testament as Scripture* (1979), pp. 328-30.

Christianity. Though the questions of when and how the book received its present canonical form may be debated, it seems certain that Jewish and Christian readers of the first century viewed and interpreted the work as a unified whole. It is significant that the Isaiah Scroll from Qumran (1QIs[a]), the earliest complete Hebrew manuscript of an Old Testament text of this size, presents the book basically in the form in which we know it.[1] A first-century Christian reader would almost certainly have approached the book as a single composition containing the inspired prophecies of Isaiah ben Amoz concerning God's eschatological salvation and the coming of the Christ.

iv. *Luke and Isaiah*. Though it cannot be merely assumed that every New Testament writer had copies of the Law, the Prophets and the Writings at his disposal, there is good evidence that Luke knew Isaiah well and used it as a unified literary work.[2] In his examination of Luke's use of the Old Testament, T. Holtz concluded that the three Old Testament books which had the most influence on Luke were the Twelve Prophets, Isaiah and the Psalms, and that, at least in the case of Isaiah and the Minor Prophets, Luke had access to a version similar to the LXX A-text.[3] Concerning Isaiah, Holtz writes: 'It appears certain to me that Luke had an Isaiah scroll in his possession or at least at hand during the writing of his work.'[4] D. Seccombe cites Holtz approvingly

1. Cf. Clements, 'Beyond Tradition-History', p. 95.

2. Evidence for unity comes from the fact that Luke explicitly identifies passages from all three sections of the book—Isa. 6.9-10; Isa. 40.3-5; Isa. 53.8-9 and Isa. 61.1-2—as coming from the pen of the prophet Isaiah (Acts 8.28, 30; Lk. 3.4; Acts 28.25; Lk. 4.17).

3. Holtz, *Untersuchung*, esp. pp. 166-73. Cf. the earlier work of W.K.L. Clarke, 'The Use of the Septuagint in Acts', in F.J. Jackson and K. Lake, *Beginnings*, II, pp. 66-105, who proposed that the Old Testament quotations in Acts were primarily derived from the LXX A-type text. More controversial are Holtz's assertions (1) that Luke had no other text form available to him; (2) that he seldom introduces theological alterations to his quotations and (3) that he had no text of the Pentateuch at his disposal. For evaluations of Holtz's contribution see Rese, *Alttestamentliche Motive*, pp. 211-26; Bovon, *Luc le théologien*, pp. 107-12; Bock, *Proclamation*, pp. 14-16.

4. Holtz, *Untersuchung*, p. 41. On Luke's intimate knowledge of the Greek Old Testament see also Sanders, 'Isaiah in Luke', pp. 144-55. Sanders rejects Holtz's claim that Luke did not know the Pentateuch or the Deuteronomistic history (Deuteronomy to 4 Kgs), stating that Holtz's conclusions on this point 'are simply wrong' (p. 146 n. 4).

and points to a number of facts which indicate Luke's special interest in Isaiah: (1) In addition to numerous allusions and short citations, Luke has four extended citations of Isaiah (Lk. 3.4-6 = Isa. 40.3-5; Lk. 4.18-19 = Isa. 61.1-2; Acts 8.28-33 = Isa. 53.7-8; Acts 28.25-27 = Isa. 6.9-10). In the first, he seems intentionally to extend the quote beyond his source ('Q'; cf. Mt. 3.3) to reach Isaiah's statement 'all flesh shall see the salvation of God' (Lk. 3.6; Isa. 40.5). Significant also are (2) Luke's interest in the *book* of Isaiah (Lk. 3.4, βίβλος; 4.17, 20, βιβλίον; Luke only in both cases) and (3) the fact that though most quotations in Luke–Acts occur in the course of speeches, those from Isaiah in Luke 3 and Acts 8 are part of Luke's telling of the story. (4) Particularly significant in the case of the latter is the Ethiopian's question concerning whether the prophet was speaking of himself or another (Acts 8.34). The question has a modern ring to it, revealing Luke's critical awareness of the key interpretive question related to the passage.[1]

Luke's familiarity with Isaiah as a unified literary work is further suggested by his special interest in various Isaianic themes—themes which recur frequently in both Isaiah and Luke: (1) As in the Nazareth sermon, Jesus' answer to John the Baptist in Lk. 7.18-23 alludes to Isa. 61.1 and other Isaianic passages to describe the dawn of the eschatological age as a time when the blind will see, the deaf will hear, the lame will walk, the dead will be raised and good news will be proclaimed to the poor (Isa. 61.1-2; 29.18-19; 35.5-7; 26.18-19).[2] Though Luke received this passage from the tradition ('Q', cf. Mt. 11.2-6), the programmatic place he gives Isa. 61.1-2 in the Nazareth sermon shows his special interest in this Isaianic theme. Luke's interest in Jesus' miraculous deeds as proof of his identity and confirmation that the time of salvation has arrived recurs in summaries of Jesus' activity in Acts (Acts 2.22; 10.38). The verbal parallels between Acts 10.35-38 and the Nazareth sermon are well established.[3] The words λόγον ὃν ἀπέστειλεν in v. 36, while based on Ps. 106.20 LXX, recall ἀπέσταλκέν με of Lk. 4.18 (Isa. 61.1); and

1. D. Seccombe, 'Luke and Isaiah', *NTS* 27 (1981), pp. 252-59.

2. See Jeremias, *New Testament Theology*, I, pp. 103-105. The cleansing of leprosy (Lk. 7.22) is not mentioned in Isaiah and (together with raising the dead) may be linked to the miracles of Elijah and Elisha (cf. Lk. 4.25-27; and compare Lk. 7.11-17 with 1 Kgs 17.17-24) (Tannehill, *Narrative Unity*, I, p. 79 n. 7). Jeremias (p. 105) says Jesus' addition of these to the Isaiah lists suggest his fulfillment goes far beyond all promises, hopes and expectations.

3. See Turner's list in 'Jesus and the Spirit', pp. 22-23.

εὐαγγελιζόμενος εἰρήνην, while derived from Isa. 52.7, echoes εὐαγγελίσασθαι πτωχοῖς (Lk. 4.18; 7.22; Isa. 61.1).[1] In v. 38, Peter describes how Jesus of Nazareth was anointed by God with the Holy Spirit and 'went about doing good, and healing all who were oppressed by the devil...' Spirit-anointing, preaching, healing and exorcism are thus brought together in a manner parallel to the Nazareth sermon. This suggests that, for Luke, the Isaianic theme of freeing the captives (Isa. 42.7; 49.9; 58.6; 61.1)—emphasized by the line from Isa. 58.6 in Lk. 4.18—refers especially to Jesus' exorcisms and release from the power of Satan (cf. Lk. 4.31-37, 41). Jesus' preaching, healing and exorcisms are thus set in the context of Isaianic eschatological salvation.[2]

(2) Closely related to healing and release of prisoners for both Luke and Isaiah are the themes of light and darkness, blindness and sight.[3] The salvation available through the coming of Jesus is described by Luke as a light shining on those in darkness (Lk. 1.79; Isa. 9.1-2; 42.6-7), a light of revelation to the Gentiles (Lk. 2.32; Acts 13.47; Isa. 42.6; 49.6), and sight for the blind (Lk. 4.18; 7.22; Isa. 29.18; 35.5; 61.1 LXX; cf. Acts 26.18, 23). The present rejection of the gospel by many in Israel is also explained in Isaianic terms. In Acts 28.26-27, Paul describes the spiritual blindness and deafness which prevents Israel from believing in terms of Israel's spiritual state in Isaiah's day (Isa. 6.9, 10).

(3) Other references to the time of eschatological salvation are drawn from Isaiah. As we have seen, Simeon awaits the 'consolation of Israel' (Lk. 2.25; παράκλησιν τοῦ Ἰσραήλ) and Anna speaks of the child Jesus to all who seek the 'redemption of Jerusalem' (Lk. 2.36; cf. Isa. 52.9). The use of παράκλησις to describe the time of Israel's salvation is characteristic of LXX Isaiah (Isa. 35.4; 40.1, 11; 49.10, 13; 51.3, 12; 57.18; 61.2; 66.10-13).[4] The universalism of the gospel is also depicted in Isaianic terms. Jesus' coming results not only in the 'glory of Israel' (Lk. 2.32; Isa. 46.13) but also in light for the Gentiles (Lk. 2.32;

1. Turner, 'Jesus and the Spirit', p. 22. The same connection between Isa. 52.7 and 61.1 is made in 11QMelch.

2. The same may be said for the apostolic healings in Acts. Compare Acts 3.2, 8 with Isa. 35.6 LXX.

3. For the prominence of this theme in Isaiah and its relation to the redactional unity of the book see Clements, 'Beyond Tradition-History', pp. 101-104, *idem*, 'Patterns', pp. 189-200.

4. Seccombe, 'Luke and Isaiah', p. 255; G.W. Grogan, 'The Light and the Stone: A Christological Study in Luke and Isaiah', in *Christ the Lord* (1982), pp. 151-67, 152; Schmitz and Stählin, *TDNT*, V, p. 792.

Acts 13.47; 26.22-23; Isa. 9.1-2; 42.6; 49.6). Jesus' commission in Acts 1.8 to be witnesses ἕως ἐσχάτου τῆς γῆς is drawn from the servant's mission in Isa. 49.6.[1]

(4) The key Lukan verb εὐαγγελίζομαι, which the author prefers to Mark's substantive εὐαγγέλιον, is probably to be traced to Isaiah.[2] Though the verb appears in other Old Testament books, only in Isaiah is it employed in a significant theological manner (cf. Isa. 40.9; 52.7; 61.1 LXX).[3] The probable influence of Isa. 61.1 LXX (Lk. 4.18-19) in the summary of Jesus' kingdom preaching in Lk. 4.43 has been noted above;[4] and it is not unlikely that Luke's use in general is dependent upon Isaiah.[5] Seccombe points to significant parallels between the use of the verb in Isaiah and in Luke: in both, the recipients of the 'good news' are Israel (Isa. 40.9; Lk. 2.10; 3.18; Acts 10.36) and the poor (Isa. 61.1; Lk. 4.18; 6.20; 7.22), and the content of the message is God's reign (Isa. 40.9-10; Lk. 4.43) and peace (Isa. 52.7; Lk. 2.14; Acts 10.36).[6]

More connections between Luke and Isaiah will be presented in subsequent discussion. Here I would suggest that Luke's many allusions to Isaiah, as well as his emphasis on the Isaianic themes of Spirit-anointing, eschatological healing, emancipation of prisoners, blindness and sight, and light and darkness all indicate a special interest in and use of Isaiah's

1. See Chapter 4 section 3dii.

2. While the substantive appears only twice in Luke–Acts (Acts 15.7; 20.24), the verb occurs ten times in the Gospel (Lk. 1.19; 2.10; 3.18; 4.18, 43; 7.22; 8.1; 9.6; 16.16; 20.1) and fifteen times in Acts (Acts 5.42; 8.4, 12, 25, 35, 40; 10.36; 11.20; 13.32; 14.7, 15, 21; 15.35; 16.10; 17.18). In contrast Mark uses the noun eight times (Mk 1.1, 14, 15; 8.35; 10.29; 13.10; 14.9; 16.15) and never the verb, while in Matthew the verb appears only once (Mt. 11.5) and the noun four times (Mt. 4.23; 9.35; 24.14; 26.13). Though Stuhlmacher, *Das paulinische Evangelium*, I, pp. 210-22, is undoubtedly correct that εὐαγγελίζομαι *may* be used neutrally without the implication of *good* news, Luke uses it in an almost technical sense to refer to the proclamation of the gospel—the good news that God has acted to save mankind: whether that gospel is proclaimed by John the Baptist, Jesus, or the apostles. Cf. Marshall, *Historian*, p. 124; *contra* Conzelmann, *Theology*, p. 23 n. 1, pp. 221-22.

3. So Seccombe, 'Luke and Isaiah', p. 254.

4. See section 2e above. Stuhlmacher, *Das paulinische Evangelium*, I, pp. 233-34, claims the use of the verb in the New Testament is traceable to Isa. 61.1, and Tannehill, 'Mission of Jesus', p. 69 n. 54, suggests Luke's preference may be linked to the same passage.

5. Cf. Marshall, *Historian*, pp. 123-24. The verb occurs in important summaries of Jesus' ministry in Lk. 8.1; 20.1; Acts 10.36; cf. Lk. 7.22; 16.16.

6. Seccombe, 'Luke and Isaiah', p. 254.

work. Though the use of Isaiah's prophecy to describe the deeds of Jesus was part of the gospel tradition prior to Luke, it is clear Luke gives it special interest and prominence. This knowledge of Isaiah would seem to extend beyond Luke's use of 'testimonia' or of sources containing Isaianic allusions. Seccombe comes to similar conclusions and states that 'in approaching quotations from and allusions to Isaiah there is a presumption in favour of Luke's awareness of their context and wider meaning within Isaiah as a whole'.[1] With this point in mind, we turn to Isaiah's descriptions of the prophet-herald, the servant and the coming Davidic king.

v. *Isaiah 61 and the Servant Songs of Isaiah 40–55.* Many commentators have noted the striking similarities between Isaiah 61 and the so-called 'servant songs'[2] of Isaiah 40–55 (Isa. 42.1-7; 49.1-9; 50.4-11;[3] 52.13-53.12).[4] Indeed, Isaiah 61 has been variously described as another

1. Seccombe, 'Luke and Isaiah', p. 259.

2. The designation *Ebed-Lieder*, 'Servant Songs', was first set out by B. Duhm in his ground breaking commentary on Isaiah, *Das Buch Jesaia* (5th edn, 1968). Though Israel as a nation is frequently referred to as Yahweh's 'servant' in Isaiah 40–55, Duhm pointed out that in four passages, 42.1-4; 49.1-6; 50.4-9; 52.13–53.12, there seems to be reference to an individual 'servant of Yahweh'. The literature on the unity, extent and significance of these servant songs is voluminous, and views concerning the servant's identity range from the nation Israel (or a remnant thereof) to the prophet himself, to a messianic figure of some sort. For surveys see especially C.R. North, *The Suffering Servant in Deutero-Isaiah: An Historical and Critical Study* (1948); H.H. Rowley, 'The Servant of the Lord in the Light of Three Decades of Criticism', in *The Servant of the Lord and Other Essays on the Old Testament* (1952), pp. 1-57.

3. The extent of these first three songs is disputed with some commentators judging them as 42.1-4; 49.1-6; 50.4-9. This is a form-critical question which has little bearing on the canonical reading of the text here under discussion. The early Christians surely did not anticipate Duhm in 1892 by isolating these songs from their larger Isaianic contexts. On the other hand, in view of the individual description of the 'servant' in these passages, it is likely they would have viewed this individual as distinct from Israel—as Luke clearly does (Lk. 22.37; Acts 8.32-35).

4. See especially W.A.M. Beuken, 'Servant and Herald of Good Tidings: Isaiah 61 as an Interpretation of Isaiah 40–55', *The Book of Isaiah. Le Livre D'Isaïe* (1989), pp. 411-42. Beuken's comparison extends beyond the servant songs to the whole of Isaiah 40–55.

servant song,[1] a midrash on the servant idea,[2] or the prophet (identified as Trito-Isaiah) taking on the role of the servant for himself,[3] or for his community.[4] In the first servant song, as in Isaiah 61, an individual is empowered by the Spirit to carry out his task (42.1; 61.1). He announces release of prisoners (61.1; 42.7; cf. 49.9) and brings justice and comfort to the oppressed and faint of spirit (61.1-3; 42.3-4). The second song, like Isaiah 61, speaks the time of Yahweh's favour (49.8; 61.2), when comfort will be provided for the oppressed and afflicted (49.13; 61.3). Both passages speak of a rebuilding and restoration of the land (cf. 61.4; 49.8), and in both there is a response of joy and praise (49.13; 62.10; cf. 61.3).[5]

The supposition that later Judaism read Isaiah 61 in the context of the servant songs finds support in the LXX of 61.1, which rendered the unusual Hebrew phrase in verse 1, ולאסורים פקח־קוח (lit.: '...and to prisoners, complete opening' [generally of eyes, or ears][6]), as καὶ τυφλοῖς ἀνάβλεψιν ('and to the blind, recovery of sight'; Isa. 61.1e). The translator probably dealt with the mixed Hebrew idiom by alluding to Isa. 42.7 (42.18, 22; 43.8; cf. Isa. 29.18; 35.5), which had already brought together the ideas of sight to the blind and the release of prisoners.[7] Like the servant of Isa. 42.7 (Israel in the LXX), the herald in Isa. 61.1 LXX (cf. Lk. 4.18) releases prisoners and opens blind eyes.

At Qumran, too, texts from Isaiah 61 and Isaiah 40–55 are found in close connection to one another. As we have seen, in 11Q Melch the 'herald' (מבשר) of Isa. 52.7 is identified with the anointed one of

1. See W.W. Cannon, 'Isaiah 6.[1-3] an Ebed-Jahweh Poem', *ZAW* 47 (1929), pp. 284-88. Other proponents are cited by North, *Suffering Servant*, pp. 137-38.

2. Sanders, 'From Isaiah 61', p. 80, following Zimmerli and others, says that the passage is an exilic sermon based on both Lev. 25.10 and Deutero-Isaianic traditions, especially Isaiah 42 and 49.

3. Westermann, *Isaiah 40–66*, pp. 365-67; Whybray, *Isaiah 40–66*, p. 240. The servant for Westermann and Whybray is Deutero-Isaiah himself. Cf. Beuken, 'Servant and Herald', pp. 438ff.

4. E. Achtemeier, *The Community and Message of Isaiah 56–66* (1982), pp. 88-90. In addition, Achtemeier points out that both use images of grazing sheep (cf. 49.9; 61.5) and of a marriage (cf. 49.18; 61.11).

5. Achtemeier, *Community and Message*, pp. 88-89; Beuken, 'Servant and Herald', *passim*.

6. See Sanders, 'From Isaiah 61', pp. 81-82.

7. Cf. Sanders, 'From Isaiah 61', pp. 82-83; R.T. France, *Jesus and the Old Testament*, pp. 252-53; Bock, *Proclamation*, p. 316 n. 54; Shin, *Ausrufung*, p. 121.

Isa. 61.1-2 who 'proclaims' (לבשר) good news to the poor. In 1 QS 8.5b-7a terminology from Isa. 42.1, 3; 43.10, 12; 60.21; and 61.3 occurs in a context where atoning value seems to be attributed to the suffering of the council of the community (under the influence of Isaiah 53?).[1] While it is debated whether the Qumran community interpreted the 'servant' messianically or even identified 'him' as a specific figure, they clearly drew verbal links between the language of Isaiah 40–55 and the anointed figure of Isaiah 61.

It should also be noted that the servant like the herald bears both royal and prophetic traits.[2] The prophetic features have been frequently noted. The servant (Israel?)[3] of the second song is appointed 'from the womb' to bring Israel back to the Lord (Isa. 49.1, 5), a description which parallels the prophetic call of Jeremiah (Jer. 1.5). In the third song, Yahweh gives him 'the tongue of those who are taught' and opens his ear to listen (50.4)—both prophetic images. Royal features are also prominent:[4] (1) The chief tasks of the servant are to bring forth 'judgment' (Isa. 42.1, 3, 4) and to release prisoners (42.7; 49.9; cf. Isa. 61.1ff.). Yahweh has made his mouth 'a sharp sword' (49.2),

1. Cf. S.H.T. Page, 'The Suffering Servant between the Testaments', *NTS* 31 (1985), p. 485; F.F. Bruce, *Biblical Exegesis in the Qumran Texts* (1960), p. 60.

2. Cf. J.J.M. Roberts, 'Isaiah in Old Testament Theology', *Int* 30 (1982), p. 141: 'The role of the servant seems to combine elements drawn from both royal and prophetic experience.'

3. Most commentators consider 'Israel' in 49.3 to be an interpretive gloss (see Whybray, *Isaiah 40–66*, p. 138; Westermann, *Isaiah 40–66*, p. 209), though this is debated.

4. Cf. E. Burrows, 'The Servant of Yahweh in Isaiah: an Interpretation', in *The Gospel of the Infancy and other Biblical Essays* (1941), pp. 59-80; I. Engnell, 'The Ebed Yahweh Songs and the Suffering Messiah in 'Deutero-Isaiah'', *BJRL* 31 (1948), pp. 54-93; J. Morgenstern, 'The Suffering Servant, a New Solution', *VT* 11 (1961), pp. 292-320; Gressmann, *Messias*, pp. 337ff.; H.H. Rowley, 'The Suffering Servant and the Davidic Messiah', in *The Servant of the Lord and Other Essays on the Old Testament* (1952), pp. 86-87. See also the literature cited by Rowley (pp. 86-87) and Zimmerli, *TDNT*, V, p. 667 n. 70. Many scholars link the servant's suffering to the ritual humilation of the king at the (hypothetical) New Year's enthronement of Yahweh festival. See especially Eaton, *Festal Drama, passim,* who suggests that Deutero-Isaiah drew from royal festal traditions to depict the humiliation and restoration of the Davidic dynasty through the Babylonian exile. In his view, the servant represents not an individual king but the dynasty in general, and the main message of the book is the coming restoration of the nation together with, and symbolized by, her Davidic rulers.

suggesting 'messianic' judgment (cf. Isa. 11.4). As we have seen, judgment and manumission are tasks normally assigned to one with regal or governmental power (as a king, priest or judge). While an individual who is *both* prophet and judge may perhaps exercise such a role (cf. Deborah [Judg. 4.5] and Samuel [1 Sam. 3.20; 7.6, 15]), it is not generally a prophetic function.[1] (2) The titles 'servant' and 'chosen one' assigned to the figure of Isa. 42.1, though used for a wide variety of figures in the Old Testament, are both closely associated with David. In Ps. 89.20-21 (MT) the two titles occur together with reference to David in a passage with strong messianic connotations. (3) Though the servant of the second song is first said to be despised and a servant of rulers, he will afterward be acknowledged and worshipped by kings and princes 'for the Lord's sake' (Isa. 49.7). The idea of obeisance offered by rulers to the servant suggests royal imagery, where vassal kings come to submit themselves before their superior in an act of loyalty. (4) The dual picture of the servant as identified with the nation Israel (Isa. 49.3; Isa. 42.1 LXX) but also distinct from her (Isa. 49.5-7 etc.), may also suggest royal imagery. The combination of individual and collective attributes points most closely to the figure of the king, who served as representative of the nation before God but was at the same time a distinct figure.[2]

In summary, in spite of some differences in emphasis,[3] it is not unlikely that a first-century reader of Isaiah would associate the herald of Isaiah 61 with the servant of Isaiah 40–55 and would recognize both as (in some sense) royal figures.[4] This is not to suggest that 'servant' was a

1. Cf. North, *Suffering Servant*, pp. 139-41.

2. See F.F. Bruce, *This Is That: The New Testament Development of Some Old Testament Themes* (1968), pp. 88-89.

3. See Westermann, *Isaiah 40–66*, pp. 365-67; Whybray, *Isaiah 40–66*, pp. 38-43, 239ff.; Beuken, 'Servant and Herald', *passim.* These and other commentators consider Isaiah 61 to be a development and reinterpretation of themes found in Second Isaiah. Such a conclusion begins with the modern critical assumption that Isaiah is a composite work. These differences would surely be insignificant to a writer like Luke who reads Isaiah as a unity and affirms that all Scripture points to the Christ (cf. Lk. 24.27).

4. This close association of the servant and the herald renders invalid Fitzmyer's contention (*Luke I–IX*, p. 529) that the servant cannot be in view in Lk. 4.18-19 since the Isaianic passages quoted (61.1-2; 58.6) are not part of a servant song. In reading Isaiah as a unity Luke is unlikely to have distinguished the servant songs from their wider contexts, nor to have viewed Isaiah 40–55 independently of chs. 56–66.

messianic title in Judaism or early Christianity, but only that the figure described in these 'servant songs' could easily be identified with the anointed one of Isaiah 61.

vi. *The Herald, the Servant and the Davidic King (Isaiah 9, 11).* With these points in mind, it is significant that the coming Davidic king portrayed in Isa. 9.1-7 and 11.1-5, 10 bears striking similarities to both the herald of Isa. 61.1ff. and (especially) the servant of Isa. 40-55.[1] The ideal king, like the servant and the herald, is endowed with the Spirit of God (Isa. 11.2; 42.1; 61.1). Though not explicitly stated, as king he is undoubtedly an anointed figure (cf. 1 Sam. 16.13; 2 Sam. 23.1-2; Ps. 2.2), chosen by God for his appointed task (cf. Isa. 61.1; Isa. 42.1). He is a wise counselor (Isa. 9.5; 11.2) whose task, like that of the servant, is to establish judgment (Isa. 9.6; 42.1, 3, 4; cf. Isa. 11.3-5; 61.1) and righteousness (Isa. 9.6; 11.4-5; 42.6, 21; cf. 9.3-4; 41.2, 10, 26; 45.8, 13; 61.3). He will bring comfort and gladness to the poor and to those who are oppressed (Isa. 8.23-9.3; 11.4; 42.1, 3; 50.4; 61.2-3; cf. the theme of 'comfort' throughout Isa. 40–55: 40.1; 49.13; 51.3, 12; 52.9; cf. 66.13). He will be a light to the nations (Isa. 8.23–9.1; 42.6-7; 49.6; cf. 11.10; 42.1, 16; 51.4), dispelling 'darkness' by releasing prisoners and freeing the oppressed (9.1, 3; 42.7; 49.9; 61.1). In addition, his reign will be marked by a new exodus of Yahweh's people (Isa. 11.11-16), a theme which recurs frequently in relation to eschatological salvation in Isaiah, especially in chs. 40–55.[2]

Again the LXX provides an important link between these passages. While the MT of Isa. 11.10 says of the root of Jesse that 'to him the nations shall seek' (דרש), the LXX reads ἐπ'αὐτῷ ἔθνη ἐλπιοῦσιν ('in him the nations shall hope'). Similarly, while the MT of Isa. 42.4 says of the servant that 'the coastlands will wait for his law', the LXX again reads ἐπὶ τῷ ὀνόματι αὐτοῦ ἔθνη ἐλπιοῦσιν ('in his name the nations shall hope'; cf. Mt. 12.21). The close parallel, in both cases diverging from the MT, suggests a common tradition in some way linking the servant of Isaiah 42 to the coming Davidic king of Isaiah 11. Though there is little evidence that the equation 'servant = Davidic messiah' was a common one in post-exilic Judaism,[3] the conceptual links for such an

1. Cf. C.A. Evans, 'The Unity and Parallel Structure of Isaiah', *VT* 38 (1988), pp. 137-38.

2. See Chapter 6 section 4b.

3. For a balanced treatment of this greatly disputed issue see Page, 'Suffering

equation were ready-at-hand to be taken up by Jesus, the early church, or by Luke himself.[1]

vii. *Conclusions: Jesus the Messiah as Prophet, Servant and King*. In light of these many parallels, I would suggest that Luke read Isaiah as a unity and considered both the prophet-herald of Isaiah 61 and the servant of Isaiah 40–55 to represent an expanding Isaianic description of the Davidic messiah introduced already in Isaiah 9, 11. It may be argued

Servant', pp. 481-97. Page concludes that, while there are strands of evidence which suggest that a messianic interpretation of the servant, and even the suffering servant, may have been known in some circles, 'It is unlikely that the concept of a messiah who would atone for sin through his suffering was developed in the intertestamental period, but there is good reason to think that some initial steps had been taken in that direction' (p. 493). I would go a step further and add that nowhere in the literature is there explicit identification of the servant with the coming Davidic king. The strongest evidence for a pre-Christian 'messianic' interpretation of the servant are (1) allusions to the servant songs with reference to the 'elect one' of the *Similitudes* of *1 En*; (2) the targum of Isaiah, which identifies the servant with the messiah in Isa. 42.1 (some mss.), 43.10, 52.13 and 53.10, but surprisingly transfers his suffering to the Jewish nation (52.14; 53.3, 4, 8, 10), the temple (53.5), the Gentiles (53.3, 7, 8) or to the wicked generally (53.9); and (3) Justin's *Dialogue with Trypho* (mid-second century AD), where Trypho concedes that the messiah was to suffer (cf. 36.1; 39.7; 89.2; 90.1). Since it is doubtful that the Jews would begin to interpret Isaiah 53 messianically after the Christians had adopted it as a christological proof text, the views expressed in these writings may go back to pre-Christian traditions. On the other hand, it should be noted that the latter two writings arose when a range of messianic figures and concepts had begun to coalesce on the figure of the *Davidic* messiah. While earlier traditions may have individualized the servant and attributed certain 'messianic' features to 'him', there is little evidence that he was identified as the Davidic king. While the *Similitudes* of *1 En.* describe the messianic deliverer with allusions to both Davidic and 'servant' traditions, this figure is not identified as a Davidid, nor is he expected to suffer. It is perhaps significant the some of the most negative conclusions on this issue come from H.H. Rowley, who explicitly delimits his study to a comparision of the suffering servant and the *Davidic* messiah ('The Suffering Servant and the Davidic Messiah', pp. 61-88). He concludes (perhaps too dogmatically) that 'There is no serious evidence...of the bringing together of the concepts of the Suffering Servant and the Davidic Messiah before the Christian era...' (p. 85). For general bibliography on this issue see Schürer, *History* (revised), III, pp. 547-49.

1. For a good defence of the view that Jesus himself drew this connection between the servant and the messiah see France, *Jesus and the Old Testament*, pp. 110-135. *Contra* M.D. Hooker, *Jesus and the Servant, passim.*

that this is imposing a particular reading of Isaiah onto Luke's work, but this is not really the case. It is rather seeking a valid explanation for something Luke has already done—namely the merging of various 'messianic' portraits which at first sight may seem contradictory. It must be kept in mind that it is *Luke* who narrates his story by first introducing Jesus as the expected Davidic messiah in his birth narrative and then presenting his role as that of the prophet-herald of Isa. 61.1-2 (Lk. 4.18-21). Further, it is Luke who elsewhere explicitly identifies Jesus with the figure of Isa. 52.13–53.12 (Lk. 22.37; Acts 8.32-35; cf. Acts 3.13) and who uses 'light', 'comfort' and 'redemption' imagery from Isaiah 40–55 to describe the time of eschatological salvation inaugurated by the arrival of the Davidic messiah (Lk. 1.79; 2.25, 30, 32, 38; see below). The merging of these various images finds its most obvious justification in the reading of Isaiah as a unified work promising the coming of God's final deliverer and the inauguration of his eschatological salvation. For Luke, Jesus is the messianic saviour whose portrait is painted throughout Isaiah, as well as in all the Scriptures (cf. Lk. 24.25-27). The Davidic messiah functions as servant and prophet-herald. On the other hand, it is not correct to say that Luke intentionally merges previously separate messianic figures. Rather for Luke, Isaiah gives various descriptions of the one messiah. All the Scriptures speak of the Christ.

This perspective of the Davidic messiah as the Isaianic eschatological saviour finds support elsewhere in Luke–Acts:

(1) Luke's frequent use of imagery related to Isaianic eschatological salvation has already been noted. It should be added, however, that these allusions are frequently associated with Jesus' royal-messiahship. This is especially so in the birth narrative: In the Benedictus, Zechariah identifies Jesus as both the horn of salvation from the house of David (Lk. 1.69) and the ἀνατολή who will 'shine on those sitting in darkness' (Lk. 1.78f.)—an allusion combining Isa. 8.23-9.1 and 42.6-7. This 'light' metaphor is picked up again in the account of Jesus' presentation in the temple, where, as the 'Lord's Christ' (Lk. 2.26), Jesus is Yahweh's 'salvation' (Lk. 2.30; Isa. 49.6; 51.5), a light of revelation to the Gentiles (Lk. 2.32; Isa. 42.6; 49.6) and the glory of Israel (Lk. 2.32; Isa. 46.13). As mentioned above, the salvation he brings is similarly described in Isaianic terms, as Israel's consolation (Lk. 2.25; Isa. 40.1; 49.13; 52.9) and the redemption of Jerusalem (Lk. 2.38; Isa. 52.9). For Luke, therefore, Jesus' royal messiahship is linked to Isaianic eschatological salvation and especially to the promise of light for the Gentiles

and consolation and glory for Israel. As we have seen, this connection also appears in Acts. In Acts 13.47, following a sermon in which Jesus is presented throughout as the Davidic messiah, Paul cites Isa. 49.6 to describe the role of the missionaries as a fulfillment of the servant's role. As a continuation and extension of Jesus' ministry, the missionaries bring the light of the messiah's salvation to the Gentiles. Similarly, in the citation of Amos 9.11-12 in Acts 15.16-18 it is the raising up of the hut of David which results in the salvation of the Gentiles. Repeatedly, then, Luke links the Gentile mission to Jesus' Davidic messiahship in the same way that Isaiah LXX links the role of the coming Davidic king (Isa. 9.1, 2; 11.10) and the servant (Isa. 42.6; 49.6) to the universality of God's salvation.

(2) A merging of royal-messianic and Isaianic images may also be seen in the question of John the Baptist in Lk. 7.18-23 ('Q': Mt. 11.2-6). John's inquiry whether Jesus is 'the coming one' has been interpreted by some as a reference to the eschatological prophet.[1] Yet whatever the significance of ὁ ἐρχόμενος in the tradition prior to Luke, Luke's presentation elsewhere suggests that the Davidic messiah is at least partially in view. Not only do Jewish expectations in Luke–Acts focus on the royal messiah (Lk. 1.68-69; 2.25-26; 3.15; 22.67), but repeatedly it is the Davidic messiah who is said to 'come after' John. In Lk. 3.15, Luke's redaction points to ὁ χριστός as the 'stronger one' John proclaims 'is coming', and in Acts 13.22-25 it is the 'seed of David' (v. 23) John announced would 'come after' him (v. 25). This emphasis begins already in the birth narrative, where John's ministry prepares the way for the 'horn of salvation from David's house' (Lk. 1.68-79) and where the expectations of Simeon center on 'the Lord's Christ' (Lk. 2.25-26). Similarly, in Lk. 19.38 the one 'who *comes* in the name of the Lord' (Ps. 118.26) is explicitly named by Luke as '*the king* who comes...' (ὁ ἐρχόμενος ὁ βασιλεύς, cf. Zech. 9.9), i.e. the royal messiah.[2] In Luke

1. Cf. Stuhlmacher, *Das paulinische Evangelium*, I, pp. 218-19; II, pp. 142-47; Hahn, *Titles*, p. 380; Cullmann, *Christology*, p. 26; Rese, *Alttestamentliche Motive*, pp. 166-68, 206; Fuller, *Foundations*, p. 171. Turner, 'Jesus and the Spirit', pp. 27-28, points more specifically to the eschatological prophet like Moses. Marshall, *Historian*, pp. 126-28, says it reflects the task of the messiah understood in terms of the functions of the Mosaic prophet. Fitzmyer, *Luke I–IX*, pp. 664, 666-68, says John's question concerns 'the messenger of Yahweh', *Elias redivivus,* and that Jesus' answer is a rejection of this role.

2. Though denying that ὁ ἐρχόμενος originally referred to the kingly-messiah, Schürmann, *Lukasevangelium*, I, p. 409 n. 5, suggests on the basis of Lk. 19.38 that Luke may have understood it in this way. Cf. J. Schneider, *TDNT*, II, p. 670.

7.18-23, then, Jesus confirms that he is the coming Davidic king by pointing to his fulfillment of the signs of eschatological salvation promised in Isaiah (Isa. 61.1-2; 29.18-19; 35.5-7; 26.18-19).

(3) The prophetic features characteristic of the herald and the servant, and associated with Jesus in the Gospel and Acts, in no way negate this royal interpretation, since, for Luke, the Davidic messiah is both prophet and king. Luke's portrait is thus similar to Isa. 11.1-2, where the coming Davidic king is said to have charismatic gifts of wisdom, counsel and understanding.[1] Significant, too, in this regard are Luke's statements concerning David. In Acts 2.30 he explicitly identifies David as a prophet, and in Acts 1.16 and 4.25, David's psalms are attributed to the Holy Spirit speaking 'through the mouth' of David, a description elsewhere applied to the utterances of the prophets (Lk. 1.70; Acts 3.18, 21). This portrait of David as a prophet also appears in contemporary Jewish literature.[2] If David was a prophet it is not surprising that his greater son would also bear prophetic gifts. Isa. 61.1-2 then serves as an ideal text to introduce Jesus' ministry, as it merges royal and prophetic features so characteristic of Luke's total portrait of Jesus. As the Davidic messiah, Jesus functions as eschatological prophet.

(4) E. Kränkl and others have pointed out that Luke does not use the term παῖς in a technical sense, nor exclusively with reference to the Isaianic servant. Rather, in line with the descriptive use of παῖς/עבד in the Old Testament and in Judaism, the term may refer to great men of God in the past (Acts 4.25, David; cf. Isa. 37.35 etc.), to the nation Israel (Lk. 1.54; cf. Isa. 41.8-10 etc.), or to the coming messiah (Acts 3.13, 26, 4.27, 30). As such, it is not a christological title *per se* but indicates one who functions as God's instrument to accomplish his divine will.[3] This

1. Cf. George, *Etudes*, p. 273, who says that for Luke, the messiah is the prophet *par excellence*—along the lines of Isa. 11.1-2.

2. See J.A. Fitzmyer, 'David, "Being Therefore a Prophet..." (Acts 2.30)', *CBQ* 34 (1972), pp. 332-39. Though David is nowhere explicitly called a prophet in the Old Testament, Josephus says that, following his anointing by Samuel, 'divine power' and the 'divine Spirit' departed from Saul and came to David and he began to prophesy. The text then describes how David's music exorcised Saul's demons (*Ant.* 6.166-68). At Qumran David's Psalms are ascribed to his prophetic gift (11QPs[a] 27.2-11). See J.A. Sanders, *The Dead Sea Psalms Scrolls* (1967), pp. 134-37. Cf. van Unnik, 'Jesus the Christ', p. 114; de Jonge, 'Earliest Christian Use', pp. 334-35; *idem*, *Christology in Context* (1988), p. 167.

3. See Kränkl, *Knecht Gottes*, p. 172. Kränkl claims 'servant of God' describes a *heilsgeschichtlich* function rather than a messianic privilege.

point is well taken, and should caution against assuming too quickly that an occurrence of παῖς in the New Testament *necessarily* indicates the Isaianic servant. On the other hand, some writers go further and suggest that Luke's infrequent and varied use of the term reveals his lack of interest in the figure depicted in Isaiah 52.13ff.[1] Yet it is not the use of the title but the presence of allusions which are determinative for this identification. Though it is disputed whether Luke attributes atoning significance to the suffering of the servant (and consequently, to Jesus' suffering and death),[2] it is beyond dispute that he identifies Jesus with this figure. This connection is explicit in Luke 22.37 (Isa. 53.12) and

1. Cf. D.L. Jones, 'The Title 'Servant' in Luke–Acts', in *Luke–Acts, New Perspectives from the Society of Biblical Literature Seminar* (1984), pp. 148-65, 154-55, 158-59. Jones follows H.J. Cadbury, 'The Titles of Jesus in Acts', in *Beginnings*, V, pp. 354-75; Hooker, *Jesus and the Servant*, esp. pp. 107-12; and O'Neill, *The Theology of Acts*, pp. 133-39 (not in 2nd edition: 1970) in downplaying the significance of the servant in Luke's work. He argues that Luke's use of παῖς for both Jesus and David in Acts 4.25ff., and for Israel and David in Lk. 1.54, 69 shows that he understands the title in a general sense, and that no particular reference to Deutero-Isaiah is intended. Though it is probably true that παῖς is used descriptively rather than as a title, this in no way precludes an Isaianic identification in any particular context. It is the context of Acts 3.13 which suggests an allusion to Isa. 52.13, and it is the close proximity of this passage to Acts 4.27—together with the allusion to Isa. 61.1 in the latter—which suggests that Luke may have identified the two. Jones (p. 153) further argues that since the functions of the servant are ascribed to Paul in Acts 26.18 (Isa. 42.7) and Paul and Barnabas in Acts 13.47 (Isa. 49.6), it is unlikely that Luke intended an exclusive identification of Jesus with the figure of the suffering servant. Yet surely Luke sees the missionaries as continuing the mission of *Jesus* following his resurrection (cf. Acts 1.1-2, 8). It is as Jesus' emissaries that they are a light to the Gentiles. See Chapter 4 section 3dii.

2. The question centers especially on whether Luke interprets these 'servant' passages (Isa. 53.7-9, 12; Lk. 22.37; Acts 8.32-33) atomistically without reference to their setting, or whether he views them in their larger Isaianic context, which speaks of the 'servant' making himself a sin offering, justifying the 'many' by bearing their sins and iniquities (Isa. 53.4-6, 8, 10-12). The former view is taken by Cadbury, 'The Titles of Jesus in Acts', *Beginnings*, V, pp. 369-70; Hooker, *Jesus and the Servant*, pp. 113-14; Jones, 'The Title 'Servant' in Luke–Acts', p. 150, and others. Though it is clear that Luke does not *emphasize* the atoning significance of Jesus' death, this does not mean he denies it (cf. Acts 20.28), or that he intentionally replaces a *theologia crucis* with a *theologia gloriae*. See F. Bovon, 'Le salut dans les écrits de Luc', in *L'oeuvre de Luc* (1987), pp. 165-79, and Fitzmyer, *Luke the Theologian*, pp. 203-33; and the conclusions reached in Chapter 7 below.

Acts 8.32-33 (Isa. 53.7-9) and implicit in Lk. 11.21-22,[1] Acts 3.13[2] and throughout the passion narrative (see Chapter 6 section 6c).

In conclusion, Jesus' self-revelation from Isa. 61.1-2 in no way represents a prophetic call out of step with the royal-messianic presentation of the birth narrative. Nor does it represent a 'shift' from a royal to a prophetic Christology. Rather, by reading Isaiah as a unity, Luke links the roles associated with both the servant and the prophet-herald with the person of the Davidic king. Without abandoning his royal-messianic presentation, Luke's description of Jesus thus broadens beyond features generally associated with the coming Davidic king in Judaism. This will be shown to have important christological and apologetic significance for Luke. By linking royal messiahship to proclamatory and miracle-working activity in the context of Isaiah, Luke is able to show that Jesus' deeds were in line with the role of the Davidic messiah prophesied in Scripture. With this suggestion in mind, we return to the wider question of Luke's christological purpose in the Nazareth sermon and how this purpose is worked out in the subsequent Gospel narrative.

1. While both the Markan and Lukan versions of the binding of the strong man suggest the influence of Isa. 49.24-25, Luke's version changes the imagery from household burglary to victory in battle and so moves closer to the Isaianic allusion. It also speaks of the stronger one in victory 'dividing his spoils' (τὰ σκῦλα αὐτοῦ διαδίδωσιν), adding a second allusion to Isa. 53.12, where the servant through suffering is exalted and 'divides the booty of the strong' (τῶν ἰσχυρῶν μεριεῖ σκῦλα, LXX). If Luke has both Old Testament contexts in view, he is here presenting Jesus as the Isaianic servant who acts as Yahweh's agent to defeat the forces of Satan and so bring benefits to God's people. Cf. Evans, *Saint Luke*, pp. 492-93; Marshall, *Gospel of Luke*, pp. 476-78; Seccombe, 'Isaiah and Luke', pp. 256-57.

2. The reference to Jesus as the servant of God (τὸν παῖδα αὐτοῦ) whom he glorified (ἐδόξαζεν), reflects Isa. 52.13 LXX and the fourth servant song. This is confirmed by the context which speaks of Jesus' rejection by the nation and delivering up (παρεδώκατε, cf. Isa. 53.11) to death, despite his innocence (δίκαιον, cf. Isa. 53.11; Acts 7.52; 22.14). It is significant that the speech goes on to identify Jesus as 'his Christ' (v. 18; probably an allusion to Ps. 2.7), and as the prophet like Moses of Deut. 18.15 (v. 22). Luke's prophet-servant-king Christology thus appears in a nutshell. For evidence of the Ps. 2.7 allusion, see Lake and Cadbury, *Beginnings*, IV, p. 37; Wendt, *Apostelgeschichte*, p. 105; Bruce, *Acts*, p. 143; Wilckens, *Missionsreden*, p. 159.

4. *The Role of the Christ in the Nazareth Sermon and in the Gospel Narrative*

As a programmatic introduction to Jesus' ministry, the two parts of the Nazareth sermon introduce two messianic themes which will be of central importance for Luke: (1) the nature of Jesus' messianic ministry, and (2) the divine necessity of his death. Introduced in the sermon, these themes may be seen to reach climaxes, respectively, in the confession of Peter and in the account of the Emmaus disciples.

a. *The Words and Deeds of the Christ (Luke 4.18-21)—Climaxing in the Confession of Peter (Luke 9.20)*

In the first half of the sermon (vv. 18-21), Jesus announces the arrival of the time of salvation and the inauguration of a preaching and healing ministry. Anointed and empowered by the Spirit, he will preach the gospel to the poor, release spiritual captives, give sight to the blind, and proclaim the acceptable year of the Lord. Though these activities were not generally associated with the coming Davidic king in Judaism, through his redaction in the context of the inauguration of Jesus' ministry (see section 2 above), and by linking Jesus' Davidic messiahship to the wider context of Isaianic eschatological salvation, Luke demonstrates that Jesus' words and deeds fulfill the scripturally ordained role of the Christ.

Luke's emphasis on the deeds of Jesus as proof of his messianic identity appears again in the question of John in Lk. 7.18ff. ('Q'; Mt. 11.2-6) and in summaries of Jesus' ministry in Acts (Acts 2.22; 10.38). Though doubts concerning Jesus have arisen in John's mind, Jesus assures him that through his words and deeds he is fulfilling the Isaianic signs of eschatological salvation, proving that he is indeed ὁ ἐρχόμενος.

This theme reaches a climax in the the confession of Peter in Lk. 9.20. Luke's omission of the whole of Mk 6.45–8.26 (the so-called 'great omission') brings two passages, the question of Herod the tetrarch (9.7-9) and the feeding of the five thousand (9.10-17), into the immediate context of Peter's confession. Whatever other reason(s) Luke may have had for omitting this material,[1] structurally it presents Peter's confession as the answer to Herod's question concerning the identity of Jesus.

1. See the discussions in Schürmann, *Lukasevangelium*, I, pp. 525-27; Marshall, *Gospel of Luke*, p. 364; Fitzmyer, *Luke I–IX*, pp. 770-71.

In Lk. 9.7-9 (// Mk 6.14-16), Luke follows Mark concerning Herod's awareness of the activities of Jesus and his disciples (preaching and healing, v. 6) and the popular speculation about who Jesus is. Their narratives differ in Herod's perplexity (only in Luke) and in his evaluation of Jesus. While in Mark Herod concludes that Jesus is John raised from the dead, in Luke he assumes that John is dead and so wonders who Jesus could be: 'John I beheaded; but who is this about whom I hear such things?' (v. 9). Luke's alteration thus emphasizes the inadequacy of the answers given by the people concerning Jesus' identity (John the Baptist, Elijah, a prophet of old)[1] and so prepares the reader for *a positive answer* concerning Jesus' identity.[2] The answer will be provided 11 verses later with Peter's confession that Jesus is the 'Christ of God' (Lk. 9.18-21). By omitting Mk 6.45–8.26, Luke draws these two passages together and emphasizes the connection between the inadequate expectation of the people recorded in Lk. 9.8 (cf. Mk 6.15) and the almost verbatim answer of the disciples to Jesus' question, 'Who do the crowds say that I am?' (Lk. 9.18-19; cf. Mk 8.28). Redactionally, Luke emphasizes the connection by changing Mark's εἶς τῶν προφητῶν to προφήτης τις τῶν ἀρχαίων ἀνέστη (Lk. 9.19; cf. Mk 8.28) to conform with his redaction in 9.8 (cf. Mk 6.15).

It has been suggested that the story of the feeding of the five thousand (Lk. 9.10-17 //s) was meant to recall Moses and the feeding of the people with manna in the desert (Exod. 16; Num. 11; cf. Jn 6.14-40), Elisha's feeding of a hundred men with barley loaves and grain (2 Kgs 4.42-44), or God's eschatological promises to feed his people (Isa. 25.6; 65.13-14). Parallels have also been drawn to the synoptic account of the institution of the Lord's Supper (Mk 14.22-25; Lk. 22.15-20). Any or all of these may have been factors in Luke's understanding. He would certainly have seen profound eschatological and christological significance in the event. Fitzmyer states: 'The bounty that is displayed in the miracle linked to such preaching [of the kingdom of God] clearly identifies Jesus as a person in whom God's message, activity, power, and creative presence are revealed.'[3] While this is no doubt true, Fitzmyer seems to

1. Cf. Marshall, *Gospel of Luke*, p. 355. It is significant that all three inadequate answers are prophetic figures. See discussion below on Luke 24.

2. This emphasis on Herod's question is heightened by Luke's omission of the detailed description of the arrest and execution of John presented by Mark (Mk 6.17-29; cf. Mt. 14.3-12).

3. Fitzmyer, *Luke I–IX*, pp. 763-64

move in the wrong direction when he concludes that the incident provides the first *answer* to the question, 'Who is this?' raised by Herod in 9.9.[1] While it is certainly true that this miracle, like the earlier Lukan miracles, is part of Luke's revelation of Jesus, the lack of a christological title or of Lukan redaction in favour of a specific figure makes it unlikely that Luke views this passage as providing the definitive answer to Herod's question. Though the incident clearly points to Jesus as a unique eschatological individual, on par with, and even superior to, Moses, Elisha, and the prophets, it is not clear how this miracle reveals his specific identity any better than the miracles Luke has already presented—especially in light of the absence of reference to nature miracles in 4.18-19 and 7.22. It seems better, with Marshall, to conclude that—like the Herod passage before it—the incident poses again the *question,* 'Who is this?'[2] It thus serves a similar purpose to the stilling of the storm in Lk. 8.22-25. Following Jesus' miraculous intervention over the powers of nature, the amazed disciples exclaim, 'Who then is this, that he commands even the winds and the water, and they obey him?' (v. 25; cf. Lk. 8.25). Both passages—like Herod's question in 9.9—raise the question of Jesus' identity, and both provide clues for the disciples' understanding. In this way both point forward to the climactic answer provided by Peter's confession in 9.20.

In the account of the confession itself, Peter's statement in Mark, σὺ εἶ ὁ χριστός, becomes in Luke τὸν χριστὸν τοῦ θεοῦ.[3] The phrase—which probably occurs again in Lk. 23.35 (if τοῦ θεοῦ is taken with ὁ χριστός instead of ὁ ἐκλεκτός)—recalls Lk. 2.26 (cf. Acts 3.18; 4.26), and, like that passage, emphasizes again the title's roots in the Old

1. Fitzmyer, *Luke I–IX*, pp. 763-64; Nolland, *Luke 1-9:20*, pp. 434-35, says that the feeding of the five thousand 'becomes in a special way the key to Jesus' identity...In the larger setting, the feeding now provides the culminating basis for the disciples to be able formulate an answer to the question they themselves have put in 8.25: provoked to the question by the stilling of the storm, they are to be brought to the answer by the experience of the feeding of the five thousand.' While the feeding miracle may be the 'culminating basis' for the disciples understanding, it is going too far to say it is the 'key to Jesus' identity'. No response to the miracle by the disciples is recorded by Luke and there is little in Luke's narrative to suggest such a key christological role. It is better to say that Luke sees Peter's understanding arising from the cumulative effect of Jesus' words and deeds to this point in the narrative.

2. Marshall, *Gospel of Luke*, p. 357; cf. Tannehill, *Narrative Unity*, I, pp. 214-15.

3. Luke's use of θεός instead of κύριος is not surprising since he tends to reserve κύριος for Jesus in the body of the Gospel (Nolland, *Luke 1-9.20*, p. 453).

Testament and Judaism.[1] Jesus is identified as God's chosen envoy through whom the Old Testament promises are coming to fulfillment. Luke's use of χριστός in the nativity suggests that this messianic envoy is the promised king from the line of David. Nolland writes:

> The reader knows from the infancy gospel that Peter has now rightly intuited the identity of Jesus (see 1.32-33, 69; 2.11, 26): here there is a human response which for the first time corresponds to the presentation that God has made of his envoy...*and from the infancy gospel we know as well that Davidic messianic categories are the correct ones for understanding this confession*...At the same time, already there these categories are made use of in ways that do not fit neatly into standard Jewish political messianism. Further, the dominance of Isaianic categories of thought in the eschatology that emerges in the intervening chapters... prepares us for a surprising development of these primary Davidic categories.[2] [emphasis mine]

Though Nolland does not develop his conclusions with reference to the Nazareth sermon, his comments point to a similar conclusion. Luke stays with his royal-Davidic portrait of Jesus, but expands and develops it primarily through the use of Isaianic categories.

Peter's confession, then, marks a high point in Luke's narrative[3] as Peter draws the decisive connection between the Isaianic eschatological signs which Jesus has been performing and his messianic identity. Though the multitudes are still in the dark, Peter (as the representative of the disciples) recognizes that the words and deeds of Jesus reveal that he is God's eschatological saviour. From the perspective of Luke's Markan source, it is not clear *how* Peter has come to this realization.

1. On the basis of Lk. 23.35 and Jesus' passion prediction which follows this passage, W. Dietrich, *Das Petrusbild der lukanischen Schriften* (1972), pp. 96-103, suggests that 'Christ of God' already alludes to the suffering fate of the messiah (cf. Schürmann, *Lukasevangelium*, I, p. 531). Yet the statement in Lk. 23.35 is on the lips of Jewish rulers who do not recognize that the Christ must suffer. Nor do the disciples yet realize the messiah's suffering fate (cf. the incomprehension in 9.45 and 18.34). It is only after the resurrection that they will understand the significance of Jesus' passion as the suffering of *the Christ* (cf. Lk. 24.6-8, 25-27).

2. Nolland, *Luke 1-9:20*, pp. 452-53.

3. Nolland, *Luke 1-9:20*, p. 452, reaches a similar conclusion: 'Every bit as much as in the Gospel of Mark, Peter's confession is a watershed in the Lukan narrative'. *Contra* Fitzmyer, *Luke I–IX*, p. 771: 'the confession of Peter turns out to be no longer a climactic point in the gospel-story, as it is in Mark 8...Rather the scene functions as one of the important answers given in this chapter to Herod's question.'

There is little in Mark's narrative which, by first-century Jewish standards, would prove Jesus to be the messianic king. (Compare Matthew's account [16.16-17], where Peter's knowledge came only through *divine revelation*). Luke, on the other hand, through his use of the Nazareth sermon and the question of John the Baptist has shown that the messiah's role would be to proclaim the good news, free the oppressed and heal those with infirmities. Peter's confession, then, becomes a climax in Luke's narrative as the chief disciple recognizes that the deeds Jesus has been performing (and has empowered his disciples to perform, 9.1-6) are indeed the deeds of the Christ.

At the same time, in Luke's narrative this is only half of Jesus' messianic role. Where Peter and the other disciples' are still ignorant is in the awareness that Scripture also predicted that *the Christ must suffer*. It is only when Peter confesses Jesus to be the Christ, however, that this aspect of Jesus' role becomes a major theme in Luke's narrative. It is significant that Peter's confession (9.20) is followed immediately by the first of four Son of man passion predictions (9.22; cf. 9.44; 18.31-34; 22.22).

In his redaction of Mark in 9.21, Luke connects the command to silence directly to the statement concerning the suffering of the Son of man.[1] This suggests that the *reason* for silence is the suffering Jesus must undergo. Jesus' messiahship must not yet be publicly proclaimed because his role is not yet complete. Scripture predicted that the Christ must suffer; since Jesus has not yet suffered, he is not ready to assume the messianic throne. As elsewhere in the passion predictions, Luke does not say that *the Christ* must suffer, but rather retains the traditional Son of man sayings which he inherited from Mark. Only after the resurrection is it specifically revealed that the Christ must suffer. This creates an air of suspense and brings the Gospel narrative to a climax with Jesus' revelations in Lk. 24.26, 46-47.

In summary, the confession of Peter marks a key transition and a christological high point in Luke's narrative. From the initiation of his ministry at Nazareth to Peter's confession, the Lukan Jesus progressively reveals his identity to his disciples through his preaching, healing and wonder-working activity. Once Peter confesses him to be the Christ,

1. Whereas Mark begins a new sentence after the command to silence, Luke uses a participial phrase to connect it to the Son of man saying: 'But he charged and commanded them to tell this to no one, saying that the Son of man must suffer many things...'

there is a decisive shift in the narrative. From this point on—particularly through Jesus' passion predictions and the motif of the journey to Jerusalem—Luke builds to the other great (and unexpected) revelation concerning the Christ: that he must suffer and die before entering his glory.

b. *The Suffering Role of the Christ (Luke 4.22-30)—Climaxing in the Emmaus Account (Luke 24.13-35)*

If the first part of the Nazareth sermon confirms the messianic significance of Jesus' preaching and healing ministry, the second witnesses a dramatic turn as Jesus first predicts and then experiences rejection by his own people. Though the messianic king and eschatological prophet bringing God's end time salvation, Jesus will endure the common fate of the prophets: rejection and death. The theme of Jesus' rejection in Israel has been foreshadowed already in Lk. 2.34, and will be developed in earnest starting with Jesus' first passion prediction (9.22) and then throughout the travel narrative (9.44; 13.33-34; 18.31-34; 22.22, 37). This theme reaches its climax in ch. 24, where Jesus confirms that all along it was part of God's purpose and plan that the Christ would suffer before entering his glory.

The account of the Emmaus disciples has two climaxes, first in the christological declarations of Jesus in vv. 25-27 and second in Jesus' self-revelation at the (eucharist-like?) meal (vv. 28-32). It is the former, with its declaration that 'it was necessary for the Christ to suffer...', which is our present concern.

When Jesus questions the two disciples concerning their conversation on the road, they speak of the previous week's events in Jerusalem, describing Jesus as 'a prophet mighty in deed and word in the sight of God and all the people'. Their words suggest that there was no doubt that Jesus was a great prophet—his actions proved him to be such (v. 19; cf. Lk. 7.16). Jesus' arrest and crucifixion, however, dashed their hopes for him: 'But we were hoping that it was he who was going to redeem Israel' (v. 21). What messianic figure is intended by the description ὁ μέλλων λυτροῦσθαι τὸν 'Ισραήλ? Some suggest the eschatological prophet like Moses.[1] Evidence for this is the description of Moses in Acts 7 as a 'deliverer' (λυτρωτής, v. 35), 'mighty in words and deeds' (δυνατὸς ἐν λόγοις καί ἔργοις, v. 22), which closely parallels the description of Jesus in these verses. On the other hand,

1. Cf. G. Friedrich, *TDNT*, II, p. 846.

references to Israel's redemption (Lk. 1.68; 2.25, 38) and to Jesus as the saviour (1.69; 2.10, 30) in the birth narrative point more clearly to a royal-Davidic figure. Of course for Luke the two figures are the same (the Davidic messiah functions as eschatological prophet). Our question concerns how Luke wishes to represent the pre-resurrection expectations of these disciples. I would suggest that the emphasis on the disciple's *misunderstanding* points most naturally to a royal-messianic expectation. That this misunderstanding is central to the passage is evident from Jesus' climactic response in v. 26:[1]

> O foolish men and slow of heart to believe in all that the prophets have spoken! Was it not necessary for the Christ to suffer these things and to enter into his glory?

Luke's point is clear. The doubts of the disciples concerning Jesus' identity have come from an *incomplete reading of Scriptures*. If they had believed *all* that the prophets had spoken they would have realized the divine necessity of the suffering of the Christ. This emphasis is repeated in v. 27, where Jesus explains from Moses and all the prophets the things concerning himself in *all* the Scripture. The implication is that these 'foolish ones' and 'slow of heart' (whether the disciples prior to the resurrection or the rejecting Jews of Luke's day), while correctly discerning the messiah's role as king (disciples: Lk. 19.38; Jewish leaders: Lk. 23.2, 35ff.), have missed the scriptural teaching that the messiah must first suffer before entering his kingly glory.[2] Since kingship for Luke means primarily *Davidic* kingship (Lk. 1.32; Acts 2.30), I would go a step further and suggest that while they recognized the traditional characterization of the Davidic messiah as a conquering king, they had not linked these prophecies to those predicting his suffering (i.e. those in Isaiah and elsewhere). Again, this implies that an important part of Luke's apologetic purpose is to draw a connection between the servant/prophet figure of Isaiah and the coming Davidic king.

This royal interpretation of the disciple's expectation finds support in the semantic shift which occurs in this chapter. Whereas before the

1. Cf. Evans, *Saint Luke*, p. 909: 'This is the crux of the story as Luke conceived it.'

2. Had Jesus already entered 'his glory' even though he had not yet ascended to be enthroned at God's right hand? (cf. 24.50; Acts 1.9; 2.32-35; 5.31). Luke closely links Jesus' resurrection, ascension and exaltation since all three express God's vindication of his messiah. Individually or in combination, therefore, they may be said to represent his glorification.

resurrection, it is always the *Son of man* (Lk. 9.22, 44; 18.31-34; 22.22), or '*a prophet*' (Lk. 4.24; 13.33-34; cf. 22.37) whose suffering is inevitable, after it is the *Christ* (Lk. 24.26, 46; Acts 3.18; 17.3; 26.23).[1] In spite of Jesus' repeated predictions concerning his own death, this shift gives the narrative a sense of surprise and revelation.[2] The implied reader is meant to be surprised that thc Christ would suffer. Again, the *unexpected nature* of the Christ's suffering points more clearly to a royal than a prophetic figure. Prophets were expected to suffer (Lk. 4.24-25; 6.23; 11.49-51; 13.33-34);[3] the messiah was not.[4] Luke's primary christological assertion in these verses, then, is that—contrary to popular Jewish expectations—Scripture predicted that the eschatological king would first suffer before entering his glory.

In summary, the statements of the resurrected Christ play a similar christologically climactic role for the second half of the Gospel that Peter's confession did for the first. In the narrative leading to Peter's confession, Jesus performs the scripturally ordained deeds of the Christ (Lk. 4.18-19; 7.22). While the people recognize Jesus as no more than a prophet, Peter draws the decisive connection between the Isaianic signs of eschatological salvation and the role of the Christ.[5] Similarly, in the second half of the Gospel Jesus suffers the common fate of the prophets, raising doubts even among his followers that he is the Christ. Following the resurrection, however, Jesus reveals that all along it was part of God's plan and purpose that his Christ should suffer (Lk. 24.26-27, 46-47). Just

1. The only exception is Lk. 24.7, but here the angel is referring back to a pre-resurrection prophecy of Jesus. One reason for the angel's use of Son of man here may be Luke's desire to have Jesus first reveal that the Christ must suffer.

2. It may be significant for Luke that the Emmaus disciples are not members of the twelve. Luke may be reluctant to say that the eleven, who through Peter have confessed Jesus' messiahship, would have lost hope in that messiahship after the crucifixion. He nevertheless implies this in Lk. 24.21 (cf. v. 11)

3. See especially, O.H. Steck, *Israel und das gewaltsame Geschick der Propheten* (1967).

4. Cf. W. Grundmann, *TDNT*, IX, p. 534. Against this it might be argued that while the prophets in general were expected to suffer, the eschatological prophet (like Moses) was not. But in the Moses–Jesus typology in Acts 7, Moses is said to have been 'rejected' (ἀπωθέομαι) by the disobedient people (v. 39; cf. vv. 27-28). By analogy, the prophet like Moses (v. 37) might also be expected to face opposition—like the prophets before him (v. 52).

5. Notice Luke's redaction in 19.37, where it is 'the multitude of *the disciples*', rather than the unspecified crowd (Mk 11.9), who recognize Jesus' kingship. See the conclusions of Chapter 6 section 5d below.

as Jesus' preaching and miracle-working proved he is the Christ, so his death, resurrection and glorification prove that he has fulfilled the suffering role of the Christ predicted in Scripture. Luke demonstrates that the very fact that might seem to invalidate Jesus' messiahship in fact confirms it.

Luke's apologetic with reference to Jesus' death is thus developed in a two-fold manner. On one side it is linked to Jesus' prophetic identity. It is traditionally a prophet's fate to suffer. Since Jesus was a prophet, it should come as no surprise that he suffered and died. But Jesus' death for Luke is far more than the inevitable fate of a prophet. Thus, secondly, Luke links Jesus' death to the scripturally ordained role of the Christ. That this theme is central for Luke is clear from his twin statements in this chapter (Lk. 24.26, 46) and his repeated return to the same theme in Acts (Acts 3.18; 17.3; 26.23).[1]

5. *Conclusion*

In summary, the Nazareth sermon serves as an introduction to, and outline of, the christological perspective Luke develops in the rest of his Gospel. The two sections of the sermon serve to introduce two key Lukan themes: the significance of Jesus' ministry and the necessity of his death. Through his royal-Davidic presentation in the birth narrative (chs. 1–2) and his redaction in favour of messiahship in the context of the commencement of Jesus' ministry (chs. 3–4), Luke indicates that the anointing announced by Jesus in the Nazareth Sermon represents the inauguration of a royal-messianic ministry. Jesus' application of Isaiah 61.1-2 to himself confirms that, in his words and deeds, God's eschatological salvation is breaking in on mankind. By associating the functions of Isaiah's prophet-herald and servant with Jesus' royal messiahship,

1. Surprisingly, in these contexts Luke never explicitly states which Old Testament passages are in view. On various occasions, however, he does cite Old Testament texts with references to Jesus' suffering and death: in Acts 4.25-26 he cites Ps. 2.1-2 as a prophecy relating to the opposition to Jesus; in Acts 2.25-28 and 13.35, Psalm 16 is cited concerning Jesus' death and resurrection; in Acts 4.11 and Lk. 20.17 (Mk 12.10-11; Mt. 21.42), Ps. 118.22 is cited with reference to the 'rejected stone', and in Acts 8.32, Isa. 53.7-8 is presented as referring to his suffering and death (cf. Isa. 53.12 in Lk. 22.37). It is perhaps significant that two of these texts occur in Old Testament 'servant' contexts (Isa. 53.7-8, 12) and two in royal-Davidic ones (Ps. 16.8-10; Ps. 2.1-2)—another bit of evidence that Luke has associated the servant/prophet of Isaiah 40–55 with the royal messiah.

Luke shows that Jesus' words and deeds prove he is the Christ. This theme reaches a climax in Lk. 9.20, where Peter confesses Jesus to be the 'Christ of God'. The title χριστός, though retaining the sense of *Davidic* messiah, thus expands beyond traditional Jewish expectations concerning the coming Davidic king. In the second part of the sermon, Jesus foreshadows his own suffering fate and compares it to that of the prophets. This theme is developed following Peter's confession and reaches a climax in the account of the Emmaus disciples, where Jesus reveals that the suffering of the Christ was in fulfillment of Scripture and all along was part of God's plan and purpose.

In light of this emphasis, it is significant that Luke begins his two-volume work by presenting Jesus as the Davidic messiah, and that this portrait plays such a prominent role in the passion/resurrection narrative (see Chapter 6) and in the speeches to Jewish audiences in Acts. This may provide an important clue for Luke's christological and apologetic purpose in Luke–Acts. It has been established in Chapter 2 that in the first century Jewish hopes concerning 'the Christ' were beginning to converge toward the royal-Davidic figure which became dominant in rabbinic Judaism. Though in certain circumstances a non-Davidic figure like Bar Koseba offering hopes of deliverance could be heralded as 'king-messiah', there was widespread expectation that the messiah (or at least one of the messiahs) would be a Davidid, and that through God's power and Spirit he would bring political deliverance to Israel. This figure was not generally considered a preacher or a miracle worker, nor was he expected to suffer.[1] Luke's special interest in the messianic significance of Jesus' preaching and healing ministry, as well as his stress on the divine necessity of the suffering of the Christ, may therefore indicate that he is responding to claims against Jesus in these particular areas.

If this is the case, Luke responds to these charges by expanding his portrait of the Christ beyond those categories generally associated in Judaism with the coming Davidic king—always justifying this expansion with Scripture. Against claims that Jesus' preaching and healing ministry was un-messianic, Luke uses Jesus' citation of Isa. 61.1-2 at Nazareth and the question of the Baptist to show that the deeds Jesus performed were in fact the deeds of the messiah. Similarly, against claims that

1. See Klausner, *Messianic Idea*, pp. 502ff.; Str–B, I, pp. 593-94; Bultmann, *History*, p. 275; Hahn, *Titles*, pp. 380, 391 n. 50; and the detailed discussion in Page, 'Suffering Servant', pp. 481-97.

Jesus' death disqualified any messianic claims he may have made, Luke shows that Scripture predicted that the Christ was to suffer before his glorification and enthronement. Finally—returning to the conclusions of the previous chapter—against claims that Jesus could not be the messiah since he neither restored the Davidic dynasty nor established a kingdom, Luke asserts in Acts that, at his ascension, Jesus was exalted at God's right hand and assumed the throne of David.

While this apologetic or confirmatory interest is somewhat conjectural, Luke's special interest in the words and deeds of Jesus as proof of his identity, his repeated insistence that Scripture predicted that the 'Christ must suffer', and his strong emphasis on Jesus' ascension and exaltation, make it a likely possibility. Like Paul in Acts 9.22, Luke seeks to prove and proclaim that 'this one is the Christ'. This would also explain the seemingly paradoxical nature of Luke's messianic presentation: Though closely linking Jesus' messiahship to Old Testament and Jewish hopes, at the same time he asserts that popular Jewish expectations concerning the Christ were incomplete and inadequate.

It is probably also significant that Luke's development of these themes represents an improvement on points left unexplained in Mark. Mark's opening statement that his is a gospel of Jesus *Christ* becomes in Luke a birth narrative which defines more exactly the nature of Jesus' messiahship, linking the χριστός title to its Old Testament roots and to Jesus' Davidic descent. While Peter's confession in Mark is difficult to justify from the perspective of first-century Jewish expectations, Luke from the beginning defines Jesus' activity as the deeds of the Christ. From this point on the key emphasis in both Mark and Luke is the road to the cross and the suffering role of the Christ. Whereas in Mark it is implied that Jesus' suffering was part of the purpose and plan of God (cf. Mk 14.21), Luke makes this explicit with his redaction of the third passion prediction (Lk. 18.31; cf. 22.22),[1] with the revelations of the resurrected Christ (Lk. 24.26-27, 44-47), and with the testimony of the apostles in Acts (Acts 2.23; 3.18; 4.28; 13.27; 17.3; 26.23).

1. Only Luke's account includes the phrase '...and everything that is written of the Son of man by the prophets will be accomplished'. Compare Mk 10.33; Mt. 20.18.

Chapter 6

TO JERUSALEM AND BEYOND: THE 'EXODUS' OF THE ROYAL MESSIAH

1. *Introduction*

It was suggested in the previous chapter that the events following Peter's confession in Lk. 9.20 mark a key turning point in the Lukan narrative. From this point on, Jesus' Jerusalem goal and his suffering fate occupy a prominent place in the story. The present chapter is an examination of Luke's perspective with regard to the crucial events surrounding the climax of Jesus' ministry in Jerusalem. I will seek to show that Luke identifies Jesus in his passion especially as the messianic king whose role is that of the Isaianic servant. It was God's will that his Christ should suffer on the way to his exaltation-enthronement. If this can be confirmed, Luke's christological presentation in the passion may be seen to carry forward Jesus' identity and role as introduced in the birth narrative and the Nazareth sermon.

The first section (2) will examine the transfiguration account, where Luke's redaction focuses attention on Jesus' coming passion and subsequent glorification. The account thus serves as an introduction and preview of the events accomplished in Jerusalem. It is significant in this regard that Luke describes Jesus' Jerusalem dénouement as the 'departure' or 'exodus' (ἔξοδος) which he is about to fulfill (Lk. 9.31). A number of scholars have suggested that this reference to Jesus' ἔξοδος is an integral part of Luke's Mosaic-prophet Christology, marking off Luke's central section as a 'new exodus' which Jesus will fulfill (= 'complete') in Jerusalem. The whole of the central section is thus viewed as a kind of midrash on the book of Deuteronomy (see section 3 below). Since this view, if correct, would have major implications for the present thesis, the whole of section 4 is devoted to an examination of this 'new exodus' theme. While it is evident that Luke develops a Moses–Jesus typology at various points in his narrative (especially in Acts 7), this typology will be shown to play a relatively minor role in Luke's Christology as a whole. Further, though Luke probably draws an analogy between the first exodus and the 'new exodus' deliverance accomplished through Jesus, it will be questioned (1) whether this new exodus is linked primarily or exclusively to the book of Deuteronomy; and (2) whether it is associated primarily or exclusively with Luke's central section. It will be argued instead: (1) that Luke draws the concept of an eschatological 'new exodus' as much from Isaiah and the Prophets—where the concept of an eschatological *new* exodus was already well developed—as from the exodus account itself, and (2) that the Lukan 'new exodus' thus encompasses not just the travel narrative but the whole period of eschatological salvation inaugurated by the coming of the Christ. While the decisive climax and fulfillment of this 'new exodus' occurs with Jesus' suffering, death and vindication in Jerusalem, the whole 'way' of Jesus represents the fulfillment of the new exodus. If the *Isaianic new exodus* is Luke's primary model, this would go far in explaining why Luke—though consciously redacting in favour of a new exodus motif—continues to present Jesus in terms which recall both the Davidic king and the Isaianic servant. As we have seen, the Isaianic eschatological deliverer is at the same time prophet (like Moses), Davidic king and suffering servant of Yahweh.

In section 5 Luke's christological portrait with regard to Jesus' final approach to Jerusalem will be examined. It will be shown that Jesus approaches the city as a royal-messianic figure, the Davidic heir about to be appointed his kingship. This will further confirm the present thesis. Jesus approaches the climax of his 'exodus' as a royal as well as a prophetic figure. Finally, in section 6 the passion narrative itself is considered and two christological emphases are shown to be prominent. First, Jesus is repeatedly and ironically identified as a king. While the Jewish leaders and Romans reject and mock this royal claim, the reader knows that Jesus' kingship will be vindicated following suffering, when he is exalted and enthroned at God's right hand. Secondly, while Jesus is the Davidic king, his role is that of the Isaianic servant, who, through suffering, is 'exalted and exceedingly glorified' (Isa. 52.13 LXX). Luke's portrait of Jesus in the passion narrative will thus be shown to agree with his Gospel presentation as a whole.

2. *The Transfiguration: Preview of Messiah's Jerusalem 'Exodus'*

a. *Lukan Purpose in the Transfiguration Account*

In all three Synoptics, the heavenly voice at the transfiguration parallels the declaration of Jesus' divine sonship at the baptism and represents further divine approval of Jesus and his mission. Jesus is called 'my Son', affirming again his identity as God's chosen deliverer and his unique relationship with the Father. The presence of Moses and Elijah confirms that Jesus' message and mission is from God and is in continuity with, and fulfillment of, the Old Testament. In all three Synoptics the disciples are commanded to 'hear him', affirming the authority of Jesus' words and perhaps implying their precedence over the Law.[1]

While the transfiguration account in Mark (and Matthew) probably serves as a preview of the parousia, in Luke the emphasis seems to shift to Jesus' passion and exaltation glory.[2] Various factors point in this direction: (1) Luke alone mentions that the topic of Jesus' conversation with Moses and Elijah was 'his departure (ἔξοδος) which he was about to fulfill in Jerusalem'. (2) Only Luke says that the disciples saw Jesus' glory (v. 32)—glory which Lk. 24.26 affirms Jesus entered following his passion. (3) The title 'chosen one' occurs only in Luke's version of the divine voice. Whatever the exact significance of this title (see discussion below), Lk. 23.35 links it closely to Jesus' passion. The glory which the disciples see on the mountain thus becomes a preview not so much of the parousia as of Jesus' exaltation glory, attained through his death, resurrection, ascension and exaltation.[3] (4) This emphasis is further suggested by the preceding context, which Luke links closely to the transfiguration ('now about eight days *after these words*', v. 28, Luke only). As in Mark, the sayings which precede the transfiguration include Peter's confession (9.18-21), Jesus' first Son of man passion prediction (9.22), his call to cross-bearing discipleship (9.23-26) and his statements concerning the return of the Son of man (v. 26) and the coming of the

1. See discussion below for the probability of an allusion to Deut. 18.15 (LXX).

2. Whether Mark (or Matthew) intended a parousia interpretation is disputed. The point is that Luke seems to move away from the likelihood of understanding it in this way.

3. J.G. Davies, 'The Prefigurement of the Ascension in the Third Gospel', *JTS* 6 (1955), pp. 229ff., connects the event with the ascension. Conzelmann, *Theology*, p. 59, and others, more correctly in my view, link it with 'the whole series of events, the Passion, the Resurrection, the Ascension, and the subsequent "glory" of the Lord'.

kingdom (v. 27). In this last, Luke drops Mark's phrase, 'come with power' from the statement that 'some standing here will not taste death before they see the kingdom of God'. Whatever the exact significance of 'seeing' the kingdom (whether the transfiguration itself, the disciples' comprehension of the mysteries of the kingdom after the resurrection, the visions of martyrdom as in Acts 7.56, or something else), Luke's alteration allows for a shift from a parousia interpretation to a present manifestation of the kingdom. This is in line with Luke's indications elsewhere that Jesus begins his messianic reign already at his exaltation-enthronement (Lk. 22.29, 69; 23.42; 24.26; Acts 2.36; cf. Lk. 19.11-27).[1] While Conzelmann claims that Luke here replaces the idea of the coming of the kingdom with a timeless conception of it in order to explain the delay of the parousia,[2] Luke's intention may instead be christological and apologetic. He wishes to confirm that the messianic kingdom is a present reality through Jesus' exaltation-enthronement and present heavenly reign.[3]

b. *Christological motifs*

Luke's redaction in favour of Jesus' passion and heavenly glorification raises the question of the nature of Jesus' messianic identity. As elsewhere Luke's presentation appears to bring together royal-messianic, Isaianic servant, and Mosaic-prophet imagery.[4]

i. *Royal-Messianic and Servant Imagery*. One of Luke's most significant alterations in the transfiguration account is his introduction of ἐκλελεγμένος in place of Mark's ἀγαπητός in the words of the divine voice (Lk. 9.35). If Luke has detected an allusion to Isa. 42.1 at Jesus' baptism, then ἐκλελεγμένος almost certainly represents a further allusion to the same passage. In this case, Luke would again be identifying Jesus as the Isaianic servant, or perhaps as the 'true Israel' depicted as Yahweh's servant.[5] It is not unlikely, however, that ὁ ἐκλελεγμένος also carries royal significance for Luke:

1. Cf. George, *Etudes*, p. 218; Tannehill, *Narrative Unity*, I, p. 223.
2. Conzelmann, *Theology*, pp. 104-105.
3. See the conclusions on Lukan eschatology in Chapter 7.
4. Cf. Ellis, *Gospel of Luke*, p. 143: '...Jesus is here identified with the royal 'Son' (Ps. 2.7), the chosen Servant (Isa. 42.1), and the prophet like Moses.' Cf. also Bock, *Proclamation*, p. 115.
5. Cf. Isa. 42.1 LXX: Ἰσραὴλ ὁ ἐκλεκτός μοὺ; Isa. 43.10: ὁ παῖς, ὃν ἐξελεξάμην.

(1) While a wide variety of figures are described in the Old Testament and Judaism as chosen by God or given the title 'chosen (one)',[1] the most common Old Testament use *with reference to individuals* (Israel as a nation is frequently called God's chosen) is for the divine choice of the king (Deut. 17.15).[2] God's choice of David serves as a repeated refrain throughout the David story (1 Sam. 16.8-12; 2 Sam. 6.21; 16.18) and the period of the kings (1 Kgs 8.16; 11.34; 1 Chron. 28.4; 2 Chron. 6.5-6), and is echoed in the Psalms (Ps. 78.68-70; 89.20). In many of these passages, ἐκλεκτός/ἐκλέγω is almost equivalent to χριστός/χρίω when the latter is used figuratively. The Lord's anointed is one chosen and

1. ἐκλεκτός is used of David (Ps. 88.20 LXX; cf. Sir. 45.22) and Moses (Ps. 105.23 LXX; cf. Num. 11.28 LXX), and ἐκλέγομαι of God's choice of Abraham (Neh. 9.7; cf. *4 Ezra* 3.13; *Apoc. Abr.* 14), Moses (Sir. 45.4), Levi and Aaron (Num. 17.20 [MT: 17.5]; 1 Kgs 2.28; Ps. 104.26 LXX; Sir. 45.16), Saul (1 Kgs 10.24; 12.13), David (see discussion below), Solomon (1 Chron. 28.5, 6; Josephus, *Ant.* 7.372), Zerubbabel (Hag. 2.23) and others. The teacher of righteousness is called 'his elect' in 1QpHab 9.12 and 4QMessAr refers to what may be a messianic figure as 'the elect of God'. J. Starcky, the editor of the fragment, claimed that this Aramaic 'horoscope' referred to the birth of the final prince of the congregation, the royal messiah. Others contend that it alludes to the miraculous birth of Noah (cf. 1QapGen. 2). For full discussion see J.A. Fitzmyer, 'The Aramaic "Elect of God"', in *Essays*, pp. 127-60.

The clearest 'messianic' use of the title appears in *1 En.*, where 'elect one' is the favourite title for the pre-existent figure described variously as 'son of man', 'righteous one' and 'messiah' (or, 'anointed one') (see Chapter 2 section 2c above). Throughout the *Similitudes*, God's people are called 'elect ones' and 'righteous ones' and a favourite theme of the work is the close connection and correspondence between the elect one and the elect (see Schrenk, *TDNT*, IV, pp. 184-85). This idea may have its roots in Isaianic 'servant' imagery, which fluctuates between the individual and the corporate, or it may reflect royal imagery where Israel's king represents God before the people and the people before God. As the symbol of corporate Israel he is the elect one among the elect. These two ideas are not mutually exclusive, of course, since, as we have seen, the 'servant' of Isaiah 40–55 bears royal traits.

Other 'messianic' uses of the title: *Apocalypse of Abraham,* composed sometime after the destruction of AD 70, speaks of 'my chosen one' who in the end time will be sent by God to summon God's people and humiliate the heathen. Nothing else is said of him. *T. Benj.* 11.1-4 describes 'the beloved of the Lord' (cf. Deut. 33.12) who will rise from the lineage of Judah and Levi, enlightening all nations, bringing salvation to Israel, gathering the Gentiles and being written of in sacred books, 'both his work and his word': 'And he shall be God's chosen one forever.' As with other passages in the *Testaments*, it is difficult to evaluate this text because of the possibility of Christian interpolation.

2. See also the references to Saul and Solomon in the previous note.

approved by God to represent his chosen people. Ps. 88.20b-21 (LXX; MT 89.19b-20; cf. MT, v. 3) draws together this imagery:

> I have exalted one chosen from my people;
> I have found David my servant;
> With my holy oil I anointed him.

While these verses no doubt allude back to 1 Sam. 16.8-12, where God chooses David from among the sons of Jesse and commands Samuel to anoint him, the imagery in the psalm moves beyond the historical figure of David to encompass the future heir, or heirs to the Davidic throne. The fact that the blessings promised to David *for his seed* in 2 Sam. 7.6-16—including God's eternal lovingkindness (חסד/ἔλεος, 2 Sam. 7.13; Ps. 89.25, 29), an eternal throne (2 Sam. 7.13; Ps. 89.5, 30), and divine sonship (2 Sam. 7.14; Ps. 89.27-28)—are here applied to David himself suggests that 'David' in v. 21 should be understood as a poetic reference to David and *his seed*, through whom the promises are fulfilled, and through whom David himself receives the blessing. Likewise, the 'chosen one' of v. 20 (cf. MT, v. 5) is not just David, but also David's son and heir, i.e. the Davidic messiah.[1] ('David' is also used of the future ideal king in Jer. 30.9; Ezek 34.23-24; 37.24-25 and Hos. 3.5).

(2) Though ἐκλελεγμένος alone would seem to favour a servant interpretation, the juxtaposition of election and *sonship* which results from Luke's addition points also to the figure of the Davidic king (2 Sam. 7.14; Ps. 2.7; 89.27-28; 4QFlor 1.11-13). As we have seen, elsewhere Luke consciously redacts statements concerning Jesus' divine sonship in favour of royal-messianism.[2] Though Moses and the Isaianic servant are described in the Old Testament as 'chosen' by God, neither is depicted as God's son. While Jesus could here be identified as the 'true Israel' (both election and sonship are frequently attributed to Israel), this would complement rather than contradict a royal interpretation. The messiah's sonship serves as the ideal for the nation's relationship with Yahweh (cf. Lk. 4.1-12).

(3) The only other Lukan reference to Jesus as the 'chosen one', Lk. 23.35, also suggests a merging of (suffering) 'servant' and royal imagery. In Mark's account of the abuse of Jesus on the cross, the leaders mock him as 'the Christ, the king of Israel' (Mk 15.32). In apposition

1. This suggests that Nolland, *Luke 1-9:20*, p. 163, is not strictly correct when he claims ἐκλεκτός is never used in the LXX in relation to messianic hope.

2. See Chapter 3 section 3a.

with βασιλεύς, χριστός clearly carries royal-messianic significance. In Luke's account, the leaders call on Jesus to save himself if he is 'the Christ of God, the chosen one' (ὁ χριστὸς τοῦ θεοῦ ὁ ἐκλεκτός, Lk. 23.35).[1] This is followed by the jeers of the soldiers, 'If you are the king of the Jews, save yourself!' (v. 37; Luke only). By juxtaposing ὁ χριστὸς τοῦ θεοῦ ὁ ἐκλεκτός and ὁ βασιλεὺς τῶν Ἰουδαίων, Luke makes 'God's chosen Christ' a Jewish parallel for 'king of the Jews' (cf. 23.2-3) and so retains the royal-messianic sense present in Mark. Yet by adding what is probably an allusion to Isaiah 42.1 (ὁ ἐκλεκτός), Luke expands this royal designation with servant imagery. The heavy irony present in Mark's account is thus increased in Luke's. The Jewish leaders cry out that if Jesus' is God's chosen Christ (i.e. the royal messiah), he should save himself from death. Luke knows, however, that God's choice and anointing is for this very purpose: the messiah must first suffer and die (as servant) before entering his glory (Lk. 9.31-32; 24.26). It is likely, therefore, that both here and in the transfiguration, 'chosen one' contains royal significance, while at the same time alluding to Jesus' role as Isaianic servant.

(4) The close christological relationship between the baptism and the transfiguration also suggests a merging here of servant and royal-messianic imagery. As we have seen, in its narrative context (Lk. 1-2; 3.15, 31) and with its allusions to Ps. 2.7 and Isa. 42.1, the baptism portrays Jesus as the Davidic messiah whose role is that of the servant. The transfiguration picks up and expands this emphasis by alluding more clearly to Isa. 42.1 and to Jesus' passion in Jerusalem.

(5) Finally, the close connection Luke draws between the transfiguration and the events preceding, including Peter's confession and the first passion prediction, suggest this same emphasis. Jesus is portrayed there as the messiah (v. 20) who must first suffer (v. 22) before achieving his royal reign (implied in v. 27). The themes of messiahship and reception of kingly power are linked elsewhere by Luke to Davidic messiahship, while suffering recalls the role of the servant.[2]

1. τοῦ θεοῦ could be taken either with χριστός (as in this translation) or with ἐκλεκτός ('the Christ, the chosen one of God'). In light of Luke's redaction at 9.20 (cf. Lk. 2.26; Acts 3.18; 4.26), the former is more likely.

2. For evidence that Jesus' suffering and death is linked especially to the role of the servant, see the discussion of Luke's passion narrative below, section 6c.

ii. *Moses/Sinai Imagery*. In addition to this royal-messianic and servant imagery, there are probable allusions to the Sinai theophany in the transfiguration account.[1] While some of the allusions proposed by commentators are less likely than others,[2] the following bear closer examination:

(1) The mountain as the place of revelation (Mk 9.2; Lk. 9.28) recalls the theophany on Sinai/Horeb (Exod. 24). This imagery is not limited to the account of the exodus, however; Mount Horeb was also the place of Elijah's vision in 1 Kings 19. Elsewhere in Luke, the mountain represents

1. Many commentators point to Moses/Sinai parallels in Luke's account. See Lampe, 'Holy Spirit', pp. 174-75; Schürmann, *Lukasevangelium*, I, pp. 553-67; Franklin, *Christ the Lord*, pp. 72-73; Minear, *To Heal and to Reveal*, pp. 110-11; R.P. Martin, 'Salvation and Discipleship in Luke's Gospel, *Int* 30 (1976), p. 370; Marshall, *Gospel of Luke*, p. 383; Feiler, 'Jesus the Prophet', pp. 175-78; Moessner, *Lord of the Banquet*, pp. 60ff. Some of the allusions are taken over from Mark's account, which Lane claims already presents a new Sinai theophany with Jesus as the central figure (Lane, *Mark*, p. 317).

2. Other less likely suggestions include the following: (1) It is often said that Mark's time indication 'after six days' (v. 2) alludes to the six days referred to in Exod. 24.16. While this is possible, the reference in Exodus is to the period Yahweh's glory rests on Mt Sinai, whereas in Mark it is the period *prior* to the mountain ascent. In any case, Luke has either missed, or intentionally ignored this allusion since he alters the time reference to ὡσεὶ ἡμέραι ὀκτώ (perhaps taking Mark's reference as 'about a week'). (2) Marshall, *Gospel of Luke*, p. 382, points out that Jesus, like Moses, was accompanied by three companions (Exod. 23.1, 9). Yet Moses takes with him Aaron, Nadab, Abihu *and 70 elders*; and Joshua alone accompanies him up the mountain (v. 13). Further, Jesus' 'inner circle' of Peter, James and John is too much a part of the tradition (cf. Mk 5.37; 13.3; 14.33) to be an intentional allusion to the Exodus account. (3) Moessner, *Lord of the Banquet*, p. 60, points out that Jesus' prayer indicates that he, like Moses, speaks directly with God (cf. Deut. 34.10). Yet Jesus' prayer life is a major theme throughout Luke–Acts and is unlikely to point the reader specifically to Moses at Sinai. (4) Whereas Mark says that Jesus 'led them to a high mountain' (ἀναφέρει αὐτοὺς εἰς ὄρος ὑψηλόν), Luke has ἀνέβη εἰς τὸ ὄρος. The change in verb, the singular construction and the definite τὸ ὄρος have been said to indicate an allusion to Exod. 24.18 LXX (cf. v. 15): καὶ ἀνέβη εἰς τὸ ὄρος. These words alone, however, cannot be said to constitute an allusion. ἀναβαίνω + εἰς with articular ὄρος is the more common expression for ascending a mountain (cf. Mt. 5.1; 14.23; 15.29; Mk 3.13; καταβαίνω ἐκ [or ἀπὸ] τοῦ ὄρους: Mt. 8.1; 17.9; Mk 9.9). Luke's alteration is probably stylistic. (5) Luke, like Matthew, reverses Mark's order to 'Moses and Elijah' (Lk. 9.30). While this alteration may be meant to emphasize the figure of Moses, it could merely provide a better historical order. For other suggested allusions see Franklin, *Christ the Lord*, pp. 72-73, and Moessner, *Lord of the Banquet*, pp. 60-62.

a place of prayer and revelation where Jesus communicates with his Father (cf. Lk. 6.12; 22.39).

(2) The divine voice from the cloud (Mk 9.7; Lk. 9.35) recalls the heavenly voice at Sinai/Horeb which calls to Moses 'from the midst of the cloud' (Exod. 24.16; cf. 16.10; 19.9).[1] While the cloud as a symbol of God's presence occurs frequently in the account of the exodus and elsewhere in the Old Testament and Judaism,[2] the description of the divine voice coming from the cloud finds its closest analogy in the events of Exod. 24.15-18.

(3) The fear of the disciples (Mk 9.6; Lk. 9.34) parallels the fear of the Israelites at Sinai (Exod. 19.16; 20.18; 34.30; Deut. 5.5, 23-27). Fear, of course, is the common reaction to a heavenly visitation or an act of divine power (cf. Lk. 1.12; 2.9; 5.26; 7.16; 8.25, 35-37; Acts 5.5, 11),[3] so the question of a specific allusion must be determined in light of others in the passage.

(4) Luke omits Mark's μετεμορφώθη and speaks of the change in Jesus' face: τὸ εἶδος τοῦ προσώπου αὐτοῦ ἕτερον. This, together with Luke's reference to the disciples seeing Jesus' 'glory' (9.32), may be meant to recall Moses' appearance in Exod. 34.29 LXX: δεδόξασται ἡ ὄψις τοῦ χρώματος τοῦ προσώπου αὐτοῦ (cf. vv. 30, 35).[4] On the other hand, this description is not unique to the Sinai theophany. A brightly shining appearance is frequently ascribed to the glorified state of

1. In Deuteronomy the voice is generally said to come from the 'fire' rather than the cloud (Deut. 4.12, 33, 36; 5.24-26; cf. 8.20; 18.16). The MT of Deut. 5.22-23 refers to the voice coming from the midst of fire, cloud and gloom, but the LXX translates ענן ('cloud') with γνόφος ('darkness').

2. Exod. 16.10; 19.9; 33.9; 40.34-35; Lev. 16.2; Num. 11.25; 1 Kgs 8.10-11; 2 Chron. 5.13-14; Ps. 18.11-12; 97.2; Ezek. 1.4, 28; 10.3-4; Zech. 2.17 (LXX); 2 Macc. 2.8; cf. Schürmann, *Lukasevangelium*, I, p. 560 n. 53; Oepke, *TDNT*, IV, p. 905. A number of passages speak of clouds as a vehicle of transport. God (Isa. 19.1; Ps. 104.3; cf. Ps. 18.10), the son of man (Dan. 7.13; Lk. 21.27 //s), the messiah (*4 Ezra* 13.3; cf. the cloud apocalypse in *2 Apoc. Bar.* 53.1-12; 70.1-10), and the two prophets of Rev. 11.12 (cf. Gen. 5.24; 2 Kgs 2.1ff.) are all said to be carried on clouds. The fact that the cloud in the transfiguration 'overshadows' the scene suggests that it represents God's presence rather than a means of divine transport (cf. esp. Exod. 40.35; Isa. 4.5).

3. See Wanke, *TDNT*, IX, pp. 200-203; Balz, *TDNT*, IX, pp. 209-12.

4. Cf. Matthew's reference to Jesus' shining face, ἔλαμψεν τὸ πρόσωπον αὐτοῦ ὡς ὁ ἥλιος, which may also suggest an allusion to Moses in the Exodus account (Mt. 17.2). But see also *4 Ezra* 7.97, where the faces of the glorified righteous 'shine like the sun'.

the righteous in Jewish apocalyptic (Dan. 12.3; *4 Ezra* 7.97; *1 En*. 38.4; 104.2; *2 Apoc. Bar*. 49-51). Two points suggest that Luke's redaction here serves *primarily* to present the transfiguration as a preview to Jesus' exaltation glory, rather than to allude to Moses at Sinai.[1] First, Moses and Elijah are also said to appear 'in glory' (Luke only)—that is, in their heavenly state—suggesting that Jesus' transformation previews *his* heavenly state. Secondly, Jesus' garments are said to be white 'flashing like lightning' (λευκὸς ἐξαστράπτων), a description which corresponds to the glory of heavenly beings rather than to the appearance of Moses at Sinai.[2] It is not impossible, of course, that Luke has a two-fold purpose, to recall Moses/Sinai as well as to preview Jesus' exaltation glory. If there *is* an allusion to Moses in Exod. 34.29, it is probably one of contrast as well as comparison. While Moses had a reflected glory which faded (cf. 2 Cor. 3.7–4.6), Jesus' glory is his own (δόχα *αὐτοῦ*, v. 32; cf. 9.26; 24.26).[3] Further, the presence of Moses himself in the scene rules out the possibility of Jesus as a *Moses redivivus*. Just as Jesus the Davidic messiah is greater than his father David (cf. Lk. 21.41-44), so in his person and work the 'prophet like Moses' fulfills and exceeds the words and deeds of Moses.

Individually, the above motifs are found elsewhere in the Old Testament and Judaism and so cannot be said to point exclusively to Moses at Sinai. When viewed together, however, the overall impression does recall the Sinai theophany. Two of Luke's unique contributions further support this probability:

(5) The command to 'hear him' (ἀκούετε αὐτοῦ) in Mark's version of the divine voice may be an allusion to Deut. 18.15 LXX (αὐτοῦ ἀκούσεσθε). In Luke's version, the word order is reversed (αὐτοῦ ἀκούετε) in line with the text of Deuteronomy, making the allusion

1. Fitzmyer, *Luke I–IX*, pp. 798-99, doubts an Exod. 34.29 allusion since the only phrase common to the two verses is τοῦ προσώπου αὐτοῦ. Luke's alteration in v. 29, he asserts, is best explained as a desire to avoid the pagan mythological associations of μεταμορφόω. While Luke may indeed avoid Mark's verb for this reason, this in itself does not rule out a conceptual allusion to Moses at Sinai.

2. Cf. the descriptions of angels and heavenly beings at Lk. 24.4; Acts 1.10; Mk 16.5; Mt. 28.3; Jn 20.12; Rev. 4.4; 19.14; Dan. 10.5-6; *1 En*. 71.1, and of glorified saints at Rev. 3.4-5, 18; 6.11; 7.9, 13; *1 En*. 62.15-16

3. Cf. Evans, *Saint Luke*, p. 416; Schürmann, *Lukasevangelium*, I, pp. 556-57. Schürmann adds that since δόξα in the LXX refers to the divine nature, Luke here seeks to make a christological *Wesenaussagen*. Cf. Exod. 24.17 (LXX): τὸ εἶδος τῆς δόξης κυρίου ('the appearance of the glory of the Lord').

even more likely. This is particularly significant in light of Luke's citation of the same text in Acts 3.22 concerning Jesus the 'prophet like Moses' (cf. Acts 7.37).

(6) Perhaps most significantly, as mentioned above, Luke uses the term ἔξοδος to refer to the task Jesus is about to fulfill in Jerusalem (v. 31). The term can be used euphemistically for death,[1] and this meaning is almost certainly present here. Luke's emphasis on Jesus' resurrection and ascension elsewhere further suggests that Luke uses the term as a pun both for Jesus' death and his 'departure' to heaven.[2] Evidence for this is the parallel statement in 9.51, where Jesus prepares for his ἀνάλημψις ('taking up', 'ascension') in Jerusalem. Since ἔξοδος is also used in the LXX and elsewhere in Judaism with reference to the exodus from Egypt,[3] a second pun may be intended, designating Jesus' 'departure' as an act of deliverance after the model of the first exodus.[4] In view of the overall conceptual relationship of the scene to the events at Mount Sinai, such a reference is not unlikely.

In summary, through his redaction in the transfiguration account, Luke shifts the emphasis from Jesus' parousia to his suffering fate in Jerusalem and the glorification which follows. His christological portrait is in line with this purpose, presenting Jesus as the royal messiah who functions as the Isaianic servant and the eschatological prophet like

1. Wis. 3.2; 7.6; Philo, *Virt.* 77; Josephus, *Ant.* 4.189; *T. Naph.* 1.1; cf. 2 Pet. 1.15; BAGD, p. 276.

2. Cf. Fitzmyer, *Luke I–IX*, p. 167: 'The 'departure' has to be understood as the complex of events that forms Jesus' transit to the Father: passion, death, burial, resurrection, and ascension/exaltation'.

3. Exod. 19.1; Num. 33.38; 3 Kgs 6.1; 10.29 (cf. Judg 5.4; Exod. 23.16 B; Pss. 104.38; 113.1; Philo, *Vit. Mos.* 2.248; Josephus, *Ant.* 5.72; *idem*, *Apion* 223; *T. Sim.* 9. Cf. Heb. 11.22.

4. Many commentators suggest Luke is here recalling the first exodus. See for example J. Mánek, 'The New Exodus in the Books of Luke', *NovT* 2 (1955), pp. 8-23; W.L. Liefeld, 'Theological Motifs in the Transfiguration Account', in *New Dimensions in New Testament Study* (1974), pp. 173-74; Fitzmyer, *Luke I–IX*, pp. 794-95; Tannehill, *Narrative Unity*, I, p. 223 n. 37; Moessner, *Lord of the Banquet*, pp. 66-67 and *passim.* As we shall see, the scope of this 'new exodus' is debated. Mánek (p. 12), says it refers to Jesus' suffering, death and resurrection, while Moessner, Evans, Ringe and others refer to the travel narrative. It will be argued below that though Jesus' death, resurrection and exaltation mark the decisive culmination ('fulfillment') of the new exodus, his new exodus 'way' must be seen to encompass the whole ministry from the baptism onward; the whole period represents the inauguration of the time of eschatological salvation.

Moses. By introducing the term ἔξοδος with reference to Jesus' fate in Jerusalem, Luke implicitly presents Jesus as one about to fulfill a 'new exodus' in Jerusalem. He, like Moses, will lead God's people to their promised salvation.

3. *The Central Section*

a. *Lukan Purpose in the Central Section*

Luke's purpose in the 'travel narrative', or (more neutrally) 'central section' has been a matter of much debate.[1] The chief difficulty arises from the seeming dissonance between form and content: although in Lk. 9.51 Jesus' determination to go to Jerusalem is expressed, the material which follows does not appear to record a chronologically or geographically coherent journey to the city. Geographical references are rare, and when they do appear Jesus seems to be wandering from place to place rather than heading directly to Jerusalem. Though 'travel notices' occasionally remind the reader that Jesus is journeying (Lk. 9.57; 10.1, 38; 18.35; 19.1), or more specifically that he is heading for Jerusalem (Lk. 9.51-56; 13.22, 33; 17.11; 18.31; 19.11, 28, 41; cf. 19.45), these appear primarily near the beginning and end of the section. In fact, the bulk of the material is not a travel itinerary at all but teaching of Jesus together with a few miracle-stories.

The traditional perspective of the form critics is that the section has no significant theological purpose in Luke's work. Rather, the journey motif is simply a framework for the depository of surplus traditional material.[2] While some still hold this view, most scholars recognize that such a skilled theologian and author as Luke is unlikely to present such a large body of material without some larger purpose(s).

As in most areas of Lukan purpose and theology, the perspective of Hans Conzelmann is a good place to start. Conzelmann recognizes the seeming discrepancy between form and content, but states that this 'does not lead us to reject the journey, but helps us to discover what is

1. For a summary of the many proposals see H.L. Egelkraut, *Jesus' Mission to Jerusalem: A Redaction Critical Study of the Travel Narrative in the Gospel of Luke, Lk. 9.51–19.48* (1976), pp. 44-61.

2. See for example K.L. Schmidt, *Der Rahmen der Geschichte Jesu* (1919), p. 38 n. 1; Bultmann, *History*, p. 363; J. Blinzler, 'Die literarische Eigenart des sogenannter Reiseberichts im Lukasevangelium', in *Synoptischen Studien* (1953), pp. 33-41. See the list of other proponents in Egelkraut, *Jesus' Mission*, p. 43 n. 3.

Luke's Christology'.[1] For Conzelmann, the journey is symbolic, and expresses a changed emphasis in Jesus' ministry. From Lk. 9.51 onward, Jesus is determined to go to Jerusalem to suffer. Conzelmann writes:

> The 'journey' begins after the fact of suffering has been disclosed, but not yet understood [by the disciples]. Now the destination is fixed as the place of suffering required doctrinally. This requirement is expressed in xiii, 31ff., a passage which interprets the journey as a circumstance necessary from the Christological point of view. In other words, *Jesus' awareness that he must suffer is expressed in terms of the journey*. To begin with he does not travel in a different area from before, but he travels in a different manner...[2] [emphasis mine]

For Conzelmann, the journey notices are meant to sustain the idea of a journey as a symbol of Jesus' resolved awareness of his inevitable and necessary death. Luke thus expands the traditional notion of the necessity of the passion into an entire period of Jesus' ministry.[3] Conzelmann's perspective is not wholly original, and similar perspectives on the christological significance of the central section may be found in previous writers.[4]

Many writers accept Conzelmann's christological purpose but supplement it with other Lukan interests—especially paraenetic and didactic concerns.[5] I would agree in general with Conzelmann, but with three corrections: (1) First, the evidence suggests that the central section does not have an *exclusively* christological purpose.[6] There is far too much didactic and paraenetic material here to deny that Luke uses this section also (a) to present Jesus as an authoritative teacher, (b) to give the content of much of that teaching, and (c) to set out the requirements of true discipleship. At the same time, Jesus' determination to go to

1. Conzelmann, *Theology*, p. 62.
2. Conzelmann, *Theology*, p. 65.
3. Conzelmann, *Theology*, pp. 60-73, 197-98.
4. See for example, M.J. Lagrange, *Evangile selon Saint Luc* (2nd edn, 1921), p. xxxviii; Stonehouse, *Witness of Luke*, p. 118.
5. Cf. B. Reicke, 'Instruction and Discussion in the Travel Narrative', *SE I*, in TU 73 (1959), pp. 206-16; W. Grundmann, 'Fragen der Komposition des lukanischen "Reiseberichts"', *ZNW* 50 (1959), pp. 252-70; *idem, Evangelium nach Lukas*, pp. 198-200; D. Gill, 'Observations on the Lukan Travel Narrative and Some Related Passages', *HTR* 63 (1970), pp. 199-221; A. George, 'La construction du troisième Evangile', in *Etudes sur l'œuvre de Luc*, pp. 15-41.
6. H. Conzelmann, *Die Mitte der Zeit* (5th edn, 1964), p. 59 (not in ET) allows for some didactic significance.

Jerusalem forms the framework within which this teaching and training occurs. As the authoritative teacher, Jesus represents a challenge to the Jewish authorities and comes in frequent conflict with them—conflict resulting in his rejection. Similarly, as one submissive to God's will with respect to his Jerusalem fate, Jesus models as well as teaches the meaning of true discipleship to his followers. (2) Secondly, it is not Jesus' *awareness* of his passion, as Conzelmann suggests, but his *determination* to go to Jerusalem which is central. It is significant that the first passion prediction comes in Lk. 9.21-22 before the transfiguration and the beginning of the travel narrative. For Luke Jesus is aware of his fate even before the mountain revelation. (3) Finally, the journey itself is not a Lukan creation since it appeared already in Luke's source (Mk 10.1, 17, 32). Though Luke draws special attention to it and emphasizes its *symbolic* significance, this alone does not establish its '"secondary" character'.[1]

It will be evident that this position agrees with the conclusions reached in the previous chapter. The Nazareth sermon introduces two key christological themes in Luke's presentation: the nature of his messianic ministry and the necessity of his death. From Lk. 4.31-9.20, Jesus' proclamatory activity and his miracle working confirm his messianic identity. Peter's confession of Jesus' messiahship in Lk. 9.20 thus marks a turning point in Luke's narrative. In Lk. 9.21-22 Jesus for the first time announces his passion. The transfiguration then offers a preview of Jesus' 'exodus' in Jerusalem and the journey which follows repeatedly reminds the reader of this Jerusalem goal. While Luke almost certainly has a variety of purposes in this central section—including paraenetic, didactic, ecclesiastical—his main *christological* purpose is to demonstrate Jesus' determination to go to Jerusalem to fulfill the scripturally ordained role of the Christ.[2]

From this perspective, the travel narrative is not the decisive period during which Jesus accomplishes his 'exodus' (see discussion below) but

1. Conzelmann's description (*Theology*, p. 62).

2. Concerning the structure of this paraenetic, didactic and ecclesiastical material I would agree with those who see a topical outline at work, perhaps suggested to Luke by a chiastic parable source as proposed by C.L. Blomberg, 'Midrash, Chiasmus, and the Outline of Luke's Central Section', in *Gospel Perspectives III* (1983), pp. 237-48. The 'travel notices' are not meant to outline the section but to repeatedly remind the reader that Jesus is still on his way to Jerusalem—even if the content of his teaching does not always indicate this.

is a time of preparation and determination pointing forward to the events in Jerusalem. A number of scholars have suggested, on the contrary, that Jesus' 'exodus' begins at Lk. 9.51 and that throughout the travel narrative Jesus is portrayed as the prophet like Moses leading the new exodus of God's people. In the following discussion, this perspective, as well as the role of Moses in Luke–Acts, will be presented and critically examined.

b. *Deuteronomy Parallels: The Travel Narrative as the New Exodus*?
One of the most interesting approaches to the central section was proposed by C.F. Evans in 1955.[1] Evans suggested that in this section Luke drew from his non-Markan sources to construct a Christian Deuteronomy and so present Jesus as the prophet like Moses leading Israel to the promised land (cf. Acts 3.22; 7.37).[2] In the main body of his work, Evans sought to confirm this view by listing in parallel columns correspondences and contrasts between Luke's travel narrative and Deut. 1-26. He concluded that, considering the significant coincidence of wording, content and especially order, 'the conclusion is difficult to resist that the evangelist has selected and arranged his material in such a way as to present it in a Deuteronomic sequence'.[3]

Evans's work has received a mixed response, with a few scholars taking up and developing it along their own lines.[4] The majority of commentators, however, have been less than fully convinced. Though some of Evans's parallels bear striking similarity to their corresponding passage in Deuteronomy, many others are too general or too far-fetched to be convincing. Blomberg analyzes Evans's work and concludes that while it is possible that individual texts may have drawn on themes from Deuteronomy, the limited number of conceptual and verbal parallels

1. C.F. Evans, 'The Central Section of St Luke's Gospel', in *Studies in the Gospels* (1957), pp. 37-53.

2. According to Evans, the term ἀνάλημψις in Lk. 9.51 (the beginning of the travel narrative) refers not only to the event of the ascension, but also to the whole body of teaching in the central section which leads up to the events in Jerusalem.

3. Evans, 'Central Section', p. 50.

4. Cf. Drury, *Tradition and Design*, pp. 138-64; M.D. Goulder, *The Evangelists' Calendar* (1978); J.A. Sanders, 'The Ethic of Election in Luke's Great Banquet Parable', in *Essays in Old Testament Ethics* (1974), pp. 247-71; S.H. Ringe, 'Luke 9.28-36: The Beginning of an Exodus', *Semeia* 28 (1983), p. 94. For a good critique of both Drury and Goulder see Blomberg, 'Luke's Central Section', pp. 228-33.

renders 'the notion of Luke's use of Deuteronomy as a model for all of his central section highly unlikely'.[1]

More recently, David Moessner[2] has taken the idea of Deuteronomy parallels in a new direction. Though, like Evans, Moessner seeks to show that in the travel narrative Jesus is the prophet like Moses leading a new exodus, for him this is not a one-to-one correspondence in the chronology of episodes in Deuteronomy, but rather 'a profound correspondence in the calling, execution, and fate of...the Prophet like Moses (Deut. 18.15-19), effecting a new exodus for a renewed people of God'.[3] Moessner attempts to establish this correspondence in two directions. First, he seeks to delineate the nature of Jesus' prophetic identity.[4] From an examination of the role of prophets and prophecy in Luke's two-volume work, he concludes that the prophet is the prime character model for the narrative world of Luke–Acts and Jesus fulfills the role of eschatological prophet. By comparing Moses' career in Deuteronomy with Jesus' activity in Luke 9.1-50, he then goes further and suggests that Jesus is the prophet like Moses about to undertake a new exodus journey to the divinely promised salvation.

With this suggestion in view, secondly, Moessner turns to the travel narrative itself and seeks to show that a deuteronomistic conception of Israel's history provides the controlling framework for this section.[5] He follows four tenets of prophetic rejection proposed by O.H. Steck:[6] (1) Israel's history is one long story of a rebellious and disobedient people; (2) God sent his prophets to mediate his will and to call them to repentance lest they be judged; (3) nevertheless, Israel rejected these prophets, persecuting and killing them; (4) therefore, God brought destruction in 722 and 587 BC and will do so again if Israel does not

1. Blomberg, 'Luke's Central Section', pp. 221-28. See also the detailed critiques of Evans by M. Nola, 'Towards a Positive Understanding of the Structure of Luke–Acts' (PhD dissertation; Aberdeen, 1987), pp. 10-54; G.H. Wilms, 'Deuteronomic Traditions in St. Luke's Gospel' (PhD dissertation, Edinburgh, 1972), pp. 17-32. Cf. J.W. Wenham, 'Synoptic Independence and the Origin of Luke's Travel Narrative', *NTS* 27 (1980–81), pp. 509-10.

2. D.P. Moessner, *Lord of the Banquet*.

3. Moessner, *Lord of the Banquet*, p. 60. Moessner makes this statement specifically concerning the events of Lk. 9.1-50, which he views as a preview to the whole of the travel narrative. See discussion below.

4. Moessner, *Lord of the Banquet*, Part II, pp. 46-79.

5. Moessner, *Lord of the Banquet*, Part III, pp. 82-257.

6. O.H. Steck, *Israel und das gewaltsame Geschick der Propheten* (1967).

heed his word. 'This Deuteronomistic understanding provides the conceptual world in which the disparate traditions of the central section of Luke become coherent and present a cohesive picture of a prophet rejected by the unmitigating obduracy of Israel.'[1] To confirm that Luke is following this pattern, Moessner traces each of these themes throughout the travel narrative.

Moessner's stated purpose is to resolve the dissonance between form (ostensively a journey) and content (seemingly disorganized mix of material unrelated to a journey) in the central section.[2] This is accomplished, he suggests, because Jesus is portrayed throughout the travel narrative as the journeying-guest prophet like Moses on his way to Jerusalem, bearing with him the dynamic presence of God.[3] Though he journeys as guest, Jesus turns out to be the host, the 'Lord of the Banquet' of the kingdom of God. Yet in accordance with the pattern of prophetic rejection, Jesus is not received except by 'Wisdom's children', those few child-like repentant sinners who correspond to the second generation of Deuteronomy. The people of Israel, influenced by the leaven of the Pharisees, ultimately reject Jesus and so are destined for judgment. Moessner thus seeks to show that, in the travel narrative, the deuteronomistic pattern of prophet rejection merges with a Moses–exodus–Deuteronomy typology to form a coherent portrait of Jesus as the traveling-guest prophet like Moses accomplishing the new exodus of God's people.[4]

Moessner's detailed treatment of the central section has brought out a number of important nuances in Luke's presentation. His most important contribution may be his application of Steck's four-fold pattern of prophetic rejection to the travel narrative. Jesus is indeed presented as a prophetic figure who, like the prophets before him, faces

1. Moessner, *Lord of the Banquet*, p. 84.

2. Moessner, *Lord of the Banquet*, pp. 30-33.

3. Moessner, *Lord of the Banquet*, p. 173, says, 'An astonishing fifty-two of the seventy-three pericopes in the Central Section divulge the distinctive marks of the journeying-guest motif.' Yet Moessner's categories are so general in this regard that the validity of his conclusions must be questioned. All references to journeying, meals and meal imagery, households, stewards, servants and even the 'coming' Son of man are lumped together under the one heading 'journeying-guest'. In this way he makes a wide variety of disparate material fit his scheme and hence claims far more coherence in the central section than is reasonable. One begins to wonder if any scenes from first-century life would not fit this motif!

4. See especially, Moessner, *Lord of the Banquet,* Part IV, pp. 260-88.

rejection and ultimately death at the hands of God's stubborn and resistant people. In addition, Moessner, like others before him, has rightly pointed to the significant role of Moses in Luke–Acts. The presence of Moses/Sinai imagery in the transfiguration, the identification of Jesus as the prophet like Moses and the evidence of a Jesus/Moses typology in Acts 7, all suggest that this characterization is not merely traditional, but plays a significant role in Luke's work.

It is the move from the presence of Moses/Sinai imagery and a Moses typology to more sweeping and exclusivistic claims which represents the major weakness in this view. Rather than providing a step-by-step critique of Moessner's position, in the following discussion the key issues related to the Moses/new exodus model will be examined. While interacting primarily with Moessner, the perspective of scholars with similar views will also be introduced.

4. *The 'New Exodus' in Lukan Perspective*

a. *The Significance of Moses in Luke–Acts*

Other writers before Moessner have claimed that Jesus' role as prophet—and more specifically as prophet like Moses—represents the dominant christological perspective of the central section, and indeed, of the whole of Luke–Acts. E.L. Allen, F. Gils, P.S. Minear, P.F. Feiler and others have argued that Luke develops a strong prophet Christology which he then explicitly links to Moses in Acts 3.22 and 7.17ff.[1] It is suggested that Luke's readers, steeped in the Pentateuch and in the Jewish Moses traditions, would naturally associate the prophetic description of Jesus in the central section and elsewhere with the figure of Moses. Minear writes:

> The portraits in Luke's gallery of Jesus as prophet, revealer, teacher, servant, judge, ruler, Son of God, covenant-maker, deliverer, have too many points of contact with the portrait of Moses to be accidental. To comprehend those points fully we need, of course, to project ourselves into the midst of a community in which the emotional thrust of memories and

1. E.L. Allen, 'Jesus and Moses in the New Testament', *ExpTim* 67 (1956), pp. 104-106; F. Gils, *Jésus prophète d'après les Evangiles synoptiques* (1957), esp. pp. 28-29, 30-42; Minear, *To Heal and to Reveal*, esp. pp. 102-21; Feiler, 'Jesus the Prophet', *passim.* Cf. Zehnle, *Peter's Pentecost Discourse*, esp. pp. 47-52, 75-89; and the works cited in the introduction to Part III.

> hopes was provided in large part by reverence and gratitude for the work of Moses. For Luke, no analogy to the redemptive work of Jesus could be more evocative or more far-reaching than this comparison to Moses.[1]

Various similarities between Jesus and Moses are said to point in this direction. (1) First, Jesus' miracle-working activity has parallels with that of Moses. The portrait of Moses in Acts 7.22 as a man 'mighty in words and deeds' (δυνατὸς ἐν λόγοις καὶ ἔργοις) recalls the description of Jesus in Lk. 24.19 (δυνατὸς ἐν ἔργῳ καὶ λόγῳ).[2] A Mosaic allusion may also be detected in the Lukan Beelzelbul controversy (Lk. 11.14-23). While in Matthew, Jesus says, 'But if I cast out demons by the *Spirit of God*' (Mt. 12.27), Luke's version has '...by the *finger of God*'. This is probably an allusion to Exod. 8.19 (cf. Deut. 9.10; Exod. 31.18 [MT = v. 15]; Ps. 8.3), suggesting a comparison of Jesus' exorcisms to the miracles of Moses in Pharaoh's court. While Luke is likely to have recognized such an allusion, its significance is diminished somewhat by the likelihood that 'finger of God' appeared in Luke's source and that it was Matthew who altered 'Q'.[3] While these passages suggest a moderate Moses–Jesus typology with regard to Jesus' works of power, it is dubious to conclude from a few allusions that all of Jesus' miracles should be classified as 'Mosaic' in nature. Apart from Lk. 11.20, Luke never compares the individual deeds of Jesus to those of Moses, and a close comparison between Jesus' miracles in the gospel tradition and those of Moses in the Old Testament and in the Moses literature of

1. Minear, *To Heal and to Reveal*, p. 109.

2. Note also that both Jesus (Acts 2.22) and Moses (Acts 7.36) are described as performing 'wonders and signs'—an LXX expression frequently used of the exodus. On the other hand, the expression is not a technical term for the exodus deliverance and appears in other Old Testament contexts as well (Deut. 13.1, 2; 28.46; Ps. 104.5; Isa. 8.18; 20.3; Joel 2.30; Dan. 4.37; cf. Wis. 8.8). Since Luke uses it elsewhere for the miracles performed through God's servants in general, including the apostles (Acts 2.43; 4.30; 5.12), Stephen (6.8), and Paul and Silas (14.3; 15.12), it is unlikely that Acts 2.22 has a Moses–Jesus typology specifically in view.

3. This point is disputed. While most commentators consider Luke to have retained the 'Q' reading (so T.W. Manson, *The Teaching of Jesus* [1935; 1959], pp. 82-83; *idem, The Sayings of Jesus* [1949], 86; Marshall, *Gospel of Luke*, pp. 475-76; Ellis, *Gospel of Luke*, p. 167; Fitzmyer, *Luke X–XXIV*, p. 918; Jeremias, *Sprache*, pp. 199-202; Schweizer, *TDNT*, VI, p. 398), others argue Matthew's version is original. See Turner, 'The Spirit and the Power', pp. 143-44; Menzies, *Development*, pp. 185-89, and the literature cited there.

Hellenistic and Palestinian Judaism reveals few similarities.[1] Even the feeding of the five thousand shows little evidence of conscious redaction in favour of Moses and the wilderness feedings. As we have seen, Luke links Jesus' miracles most closely to the *Isaianic signs of eschatological salvation* (Lk. 4.18; 7.22). Though the exodus—the greatest salvation event in Israel's history—may serve as a model for God's final act of salvation accomplished through Jesus, Luke does not develop a significant Moses-Jesus typology with regard to Jesus' individual miracles.

(2) Secondly, Jesus, like Moses, is portrayed as a rejected prophet.[2] These writers point to the obvious connection between the Gospel references to prophetic rejection (Lk. 4.24; 11.48-51; 13.33-34) and the rejection of Moses described by Stephen in Acts 7.24-44. The climax to Stephen's speech draws these two together (7.51-53): 'Which one of the prophets did your fathers not persecute?' Moessner writes: 'Stephen concludes his rehearsal of the entire history of Israel by voicing *the same Deuteronomistic view* that Jesus pronounces during the New Exodus journey in Luke 11.47-51 and 13.34-35.'[3] Yet while Steck's pattern of Israel's prophetic history almost certainly has application to the central section, and indeed to Luke–Acts as a whole, this motif does not point particularly to the book of Deuteronomy nor to the figure of Moses.[4] It rather represents a pattern which occurs throughout the prophetic writings and elsewhere in Judaism.[5] That Luke knew and used this rejected-prophet motif to explain Jesus' death is evident from Lk. 4.24; 6.22-23; 11.48-51; 13.33-34. and Acts 7.52. But he does not link it

1. R.E. Watts, 'The Influence of the Isaianic New Exodus on the Gospel of Mark' (PhD dissertation, Cambridge, 1990), p. 68.

2. Minear, *To Heal and to Reveal*, pp. 109-10; Feiler, 'Jesus the Prophet', pp. 172-89; Moessner, *Lord of the Banquet, passim.*

3. Moessner, *Lord of the Banquet*, pp. 303-304.

4. Moessner, *Lord of the Banquet*, pp. 84-85, admits this (hence his independent evaluation of Jesus as prophet like Moses and the Deuteronomistic pattern in the travel narrative) but argues that 'since Deuteronomy forms the keystone for the great Deuteronomistic history with its view of the tragic "end" of the prophets, and since Moses, though distinct, stands historically at the head of this line, we will at the least have elucidated traditiohistorical trajectories in which a comparison to Moses in Deuteronomy for Jesus would be a priori the more probable.'

5. Cf. 2 Kgs 17.13-14; 2 Chron. 24.17-19; Neh. 9.26-31; *Jub.* 1.12-18; Josephus, *Ant.* 9.265-66; 10.38-39. Steck, *Israel*, pp. 201-202 n. 4, claims that the fate of Moses in Deuteronomy *did not* serve as the model for the Deuteronomistic conception of the fate of the prophets.

exclusively, nor even primarily, to Moses or to the events of Deuteronomy. (In Lk. 11.51, prophetic rejection is traced from *Abel* to Zechariah, with no mention of Moses.) Though Moses represents an important type for Jesus' prophetic rejection (Acts 7.39; see below), Luke's *primary emphasis* in the Stephen speech and elsewhere is not that Israel rejected Jesus just as it rejected Moses (though this is true) but that throughout her history Israel has rejected *all* God's messengers. It is with this assertion that the speech climaxes (Acts 7.52).[1]

(3) Thirdly, according to Moessner, Moses like Jesus died for the sins of the people.[2] Yet there is little evidence that Luke views Moses' death as vicarious. Though it is true that Deuteronomy says that God was angry with Moses 'on account of' the people (Deut. 1.37; 3.26; cf. 4.21-22), the book also affirms that Moses died before entering the land *because of his own sins* (Deut. 32.50-51). Moessner dismisses this latter passage as 'non-Deuteronomistic material, perhaps from the Priestly Writings' (cf. Num. 27.12-14).[3] But the documentary theory of the Pentateuch is unlikely to have affected Luke's reading of the text! Though Moessner finds the four-fold pattern of prophetic rejection in both Qumran and Josephus, he presents no evidence that Moses' death was viewed in Judaism as vicarious. In any case, Luke never compares Moses' *death* to the suffering and death of Jesus. Moessner says that 'Moses' necessity to suffer is disclosed upon the mountain', just as in the case of Jesus.[4] Yet while it is at Sinai that the people rebel and Moses bemoans his inability to bear them (Deut. 1.12-13) and intercedes on their behalf (Deut. 9.18-21, 25-29), his death outside the land (Deut. 1.37; 3.25-28; 4.21-22; 31.2, 14, 32.50-51; 34.4) is not connected to the mountain revelation. Moessner links these two as all part of the motif of Moses' 'suffering and death' outside the land; but this is unwarranted. As we shall see, the Lukan depiction of Jesus as the righteous sufferer is

1. Hahn, *Titles*, p. 374, claims that vv. 35-50 are traditional since they reveal no Lukan traits and since a purely typological presentation is unusual for Luke. Verses 51-53, on the other hand, are clearly Lukan as demonstrated by (1) the emphasis on Jesus' innocence, (2) the persecution and murder of all the prophets, and (3) the role of the Jews as murderers. While I would agree that vv. 51-53 represent Luke's most important interest in the speech, this is not to suggest that the Moses typology has no significance for Luke. Jesus *is* the prophet *like Moses.* See discussion below.

2. Moessner, *Lord of the Banquet*, pp. 56-70, 323-24. Cf. Minear, *To Heal and to Reveal*, p. 108.

3. Moessner, *Lord of the Banquet*, p. 78 n. 102.

4. Moessner, *Lord of the Banquet*, p. 67.

drawn primarily from the portrait of the Isaianic servant rather than the Moses of Deuteronomy. Though the servant may have some characteristics in common with Moses, he has even stronger links with the Davidic messiah. Moessner's claim that the presentation of Jesus as suffering servant in his passion is an integral part of his prophet like Moses motif cannot be sustained.

These points render doubtful the suggestion that the whole of the central section can be subsumed under the figure of the prophet like Moses. Throughout this section, Jesus is never explicitly compared to Moses, not even in passages where the traditional material provided Luke with an opportunity to do so. Luke links Jesus' role and fate to the whole prophetic tradition (cf. parallels to the deeds of Elijah, Lk. 7.11-17; 9.10-17, 38-43; and Elisha, Lk. 5.12-16; 7.2-10, etc.), not primarily or exclusively to Moses.

This is not to suggest that Jesus' role as prophet or the Moses/Jesus typology are insignificant for Luke. I would agree in general with the perspective of F. Bovon that, though this prophetic portrayal of Jesus is important for Luke, 'It is only one aspect of the Christology of Luke which elsewhere is royal, messianic and lordly; an emphasis placed on the humiliation of Jesus, on his mission for his people'.[1]

What positive role does Moses play in Luke's work? Two functions are prominent: (1) First, Moses—like Isaiah, David, Joel and others—functions as a prophet who foretold the coming of the Christ. Luke equates Moses with the Pentateuch, so that James can speak of 'Moses' being read in the synagogues (Acts 15.21) and the Old Testament Scriptures can be summed up as 'Moses and the Prophets' (Lk. 16.29, 31; 24.27; 26.22; cf. Lk. 24.44; Acts 28.23; all unique to Luke).[2]

(2) Secondly, particularly in Acts 7, but also in the transfiguration account, Lk. 11.20, and Acts 3.22, Luke develops a Moses–Jesus typology. In view of Luke's emphasis on Moses as a prophet, it is not

1. Bovon, *Luc le théologien*, p. 193. Cf. F. Bovon, 'La figure de Moïse dans l'œuvre de Luc', in *La figure de Moïse: Ecriture et relectures* (1978), pp. 47-65; Teeple, *Mosaic Prophet*, pp. 87-88. Lampe, 'Holy Spirit', pp. 175-76, notes the Moses-Jesus parallels at the transfiguration but admits, 'With the notable exception of Stephen's speech, however, St. Luke nowhere presses the comparison of Jesus with Moses very far…'

2. It is not possible in the present context to enter into the heated debate concerning the role of the Law in Luke–Acts. I would merely suggest with Bovon ('La figure de Moïse', pp. 49-52, 61-62) that Luke's *primary* interest in the Law is in its *prophetic* rather than *normative* function (cf. Lk. 24.26-27, 44-48; Acts 26.22-23).

surprising that the focus of this typology is not so much on Moses as Law-giver, but as prophet.[1] Two features are prominent. First, Jesus, like Moses, is viewed as authoritative prophet to whom Israel must listen. A narrative link may be traced between Jesus' kingdom proclamation, the divine voice at the transfiguration (9.35, αὐτοῦ ἀκούετε), and Peter's warning in Acts 3.22 to 'hear' (αὐτοῦ ἀκούσεσθε) the prophet like Moses or face destruction. Secondly, the rejection of Moses functions as a model for Jesus' rejection. As pointed out above, Acts 7 develops a Moses–Jesus typology by portraying Moses as a ruler and deliverer who, though repudiated by the nation, leads them to salvation (cf. esp. vv. 22, 25, 35, 37, 39). Moses thus becomes a model for the rejection of all the prophets. This pattern began with Abel, runs from Moses to Zechariah and reaches its climax in Jesus. Indeed, it is about to be repeated with Stephen.[2]

That Luke presents Moses as a type for Jesus is not surprising. Three of the most important Old Testament figures in post-exilic eschatological expectation were Moses, David (or his son) and Elijah.[3] As we have seen, while Jesus' miracles sometimes parallel those of Elijah—revealing his continuity with the great prophets of old—it is John the Baptist who fulfills the role of the eschatological Elijah (Lk. 1.17, 76).[4] It is not surprising, then, that Luke—the writer who most emphasizes that Jesus is the fulfillment of *all* Old Testament hopes and expectations—draws a typological correspondence between Jesus and David *and* Jesus and Moses.[5] As the one who speaks with the authoritative voice of God and suffers rejection by God's people, Jesus may be viewed as a prophet, indeed as a prophet like Moses (the greatest of the prophets, Deut. 34.10). As the eschatological king who establishes God's judgment and kingdom,

1. Bovon, 'La figure de Moïse', pp. 53-62; Minear, *To Heal and to Reveal*, p. 105.

2. Besides the Moses/Jesus typology, there is also a subtle comparison between Stephen and Moses (Acts 6.8, 15) and Stephen and Jesus (7.59, 60). This again shows that the main point of the speech is not the Moses/Jesus typology itself but the pattern of rejection which characterizes Israel's history.

3. One could add the figure of Enoch to these three; but he plays no significant role in Luke's work, appearing only in the genealogy (Lk. 3.37).

4. See Chapter 3 section 2b and Chapter 6 section 4a.

5. An interesting tradition appears in *Frag. Targ.* Exod. 12.42, where an extended haggadic interpretation affirms that 'when the world shall have completed its allotted time until the end...Moses shall go forth from the wilderness and the king messiah from Rome...and they shall proceed together'.

and reigns forever on his throne, he fulfills the role of the Davidic messiah.[1] It is evident, therefore, that this Moses typology plays a significant role in Luke–Acts. It functions as one aspect of Luke's confirmation that Jesus is the Christ who fulfills all that Moses and the prophets had spoken.

While this Moses typology is thus not insignificant, Moessner certainly goes too far in his almost complete rejection of non-Mosaic features in Jesus' messianic identity. In his view, 'Christ' for Luke means *essentially* the Mosaic prophet.[2] In a single note, he dismisses Davidic messiahship as playing a 'relatively minor role' in Luke–Acts, 'restricted to the Nativity Narrative (Luke 1–2) and to the speeches in Acts (mainly Acts 2; 13)'.[3] Yet, as we have seen, the birth narrative and the speeches in Acts 2 and 13 play key introductory and programmatic roles in Luke–Acts. To dismiss these passages as relatively unimportant is unjustified and misleading.

In subsequent discussion it will be demonstrated that Luke's redaction in relation to Jesus' approach to, and entrance into, Jerusalem has strong royal and Davidic implications. When Jesus reaches Jerusalem (the culmination of his 'new exodus' according to Evans, Moessner, *et al.*), he enters the city not primarily as a Mosaic but as a royal-Davidic figure. If this is the case, the assertion that the travel narrative portrays Jesus primarily or exclusively as a Mosaic figure must be seriously questioned. It is necessary therefore to seek a synthesis of some kind between the Mosaic and Davidic features in Luke's christological portrait. As in the Nazareth sermon, I suggest that it is Isaiah's delineation of eschatological salvation which represents the key integrating motif for Luke's work. As the Isaianic eschatological deliverer, Jesus acts as God's instrument in both announcing and bringing to fulfillment God's eschatological reign and kingdom. Empowered by the Spirit, he defeats the forces of sin and Satan and leads God's people in an eschatological new exodus.[4]

1. This two-sided Christology occurred already in the gospel tradition and is especially apparent in Matthew's Gospel. Jesus for Matthew is both the royal son of David *and* the new Moses proclaiming God's law on the mountain.

2. Moessner, *Lord of the Banquet*, esp. pp. 55-56, 315.

3. Moessner, *Lord of the Banquet*, pp. 332-33 n. 100. Jesus' Davidic genealogy and the two 'son of David' passages Luke brings over from the tradition are similarly given little attention by Moessner.

4. On the Spirit as the power of Jesus' miracles see especially Turner, 'The Spirit and the Power', pp. 124-52; *idem,* 'Jesus and the Spirit', pp. 15-18. *Contra*

Having established the basic contours of Luke's Moses/Jesus typology, it is necessary to return to the question of the Lukan 'new exodus' which is seemingly introduced in the transfiguration account. If the evidence that Jesus is portrayed throughout the central section primarily or exclusively as a Mosaic figure is inadequate, how does Luke conceive of this 'new exodus'?

b. *The Old Testament Model for the Lukan New Exodus: Deuteronomy or Isaiah*?

While Evans, Drury, Moessner and others speak of a new exodus based on the portrait of Moses in Deuteronomy, they do not take into account that the concept of an eschatological *new* exodus finds its most significant development not in the Pentateuch but in the Prophets, especially Isaiah.[1] The new exodus is not merely a New Testament concept inspired by the first exodus, but is already a major Old Testament theme in the prophetic writings. By the New Testament era, Israel's exodus memory had undergone a prophetic transformation: 'While Israel may look back to its origins in the first Exodus, it was Isaiah who had *par excellence* transformed it into a future hope.'[2] If Luke intentionally presents Jesus as leading an eschatological new exodus of God's people, he is as likely to have drawn this concept from Isaiah as from Deuteronomy.

i. *The Isaianic New Exodus*. Isaiah 40–55 is appropriately called the Book of Consolation since from its opening words the prophet announces a message of comfort and salvation for the exiles in Babylon (40.1). The nation has received just punishment for her sins (v. 2); Yahweh is about to come to her aid, triumphantly revealing himself so that all flesh will see his glory (vv. 3-5). In light of the message of triumphant return from exile, it is not surprising that imagery recalling the exodus from Egypt plays a prominent role in these chapters.[3] In

E. Schweizer, *TDNT*, VI, pp. 404-15; Rese, *Alttestamentliche Motive*, pp. 143ff.; and most recently Menzies, *Development*, esp. pp. 146-204.

1. Cf. only Moessner's brief references on pp. 242 n. 215, 295, 326 n. 13.

2. Watts, 'Isaianic New Exodus', p. 15. Cf. R.E. Nixon, *The Exodus in the New Testament* (1963), pp. 9-10; Mánek, 'New Exodus', pp. 13, 17: 'Particularly the book of the Prophet Isaiah sees salvation through the spectrum of the Exodus from Egypt.'

3. The prominence of a new exodus motif in Isaiah 40–55 is well established among scholars. J. Muilenburg, *Isaiah Chapters 40–66* (1956), p. 602, writes: 'The conception of the new exodus is the most profound and most prominent of the motifs

addition to numerous individual allusions, the theme of an eschatological 'new exodus' is the specific subject in various passages:

(1)	40.3-5	The highway in the wilderness.
(2)	41.17-20	The transformation of the wilderness.
(3)	42.14-16	Yahweh leads his people in a way they know not.
(4)	43.1-3	Passing through the waters and the fire.
(5)	43.14-21	A way in the wilderness.
(6)	48.20-21	The exodus from Babylon.
(7)	49.8-12	The new entry into the Promised Land.
(8)	51.9-10	The new victory at the sea.
(9)	52.11-12	The new exodus.
(10)	55.12-13	Israel shall go out in joy and peace.[1]

The prominence of the theme is evident in that the Book of Consolation begins and ends with its announcement (40.3-5; 55.12-13). At numerous points the events of the first exodus provide the model for a new and greater exodus. As Yahweh brought Israel out of Egypt, so he will lead them forth again (Isa. 42.16; 48.20; 49.9-10; 52.12). In the first exodus Yahweh delivered his people as a mighty warrior (51.9; cf. Exod. 15.3), defeating horse and chariot at the sea (43.16-17; cf. Exod. 14.25, 28; 15.10, 21); so again with his mighty arm (40.10; 51.9-10; 52.10) he will

in the tradition which Second Isaiah employs to portray the eschatological finale.' Cf. A. Zillessen, 'Der alte und der neue Exodus', *ARW* 30 (1903), pp. 289-304; J. Fischer, 'Das Problem des neuen Exodus in Is 40-55', *TQ* 110 (1929), pp. 313-24; B.W. Anderson, 'Exodus Typology in Second Isaiah', in *Israel's Prophetic Heritage* (1962), pp. 177-95; *idem*, 'Exodus and Covenant', pp. 339-60; W. Zimmerli, 'Der "neue Exodus" in der Verkündigung der beiden grossen Exilspropheten', in *Gottes Offenbarung* (1963), pp. 192-204; R. Beaudet, 'La typologie de l'Exode dans le Second-Isaie', *LTP* 19 (1963), pp. 12-21; J. Blenkinsopp, 'Scope and Depth of the Exodus Tradition in Deutero-Isaiah', *Concilium* 2 (1966), pp. 22-26; C. Stuhlmueller, *Creative Redemption in Deutero-Isaiah* (1970), pp. 59-98.

For a contrary view see H.M. Barstad, *A Way in the Wilderness* (1989), who denies that the return from exile is portrayed as a new exodus. The imagery is rather derived from a wide range of motifs, many unrelated to the exodus. For a response to Barstad, see Watts, 'Isaianic New Exodus', p. 33 n. 130, who says Barstad's conclusion 'fails to do justice to the paradigmatic nature of the exodus as the stereotype par excellence of Yahweh's "encroachment upon the course of history" on Israel's behalf, particularly when deliverance and return to the homeland are in view'.

1. The list is from Anderson, 'Exodus Typology', pp. 181-82. Stuhlmueller, *Creative Redemption*, pp. 59-98, provides a similar list, extending the length of some passages (40.3-11; 42.14-17; 43.1-7) and including several more: 44.1-5, 27 and 50.2. Cf. his table (p. 272) listing the views of various commentators on these passages.

'go forth like a warrior' (42.13) to defeat Israel's oppressors (cf. 49.24-26; 51.22-23). As he dried up the sea and led his people through (51.10), so again he will lead them through waters and fire (43.1-2, 16). The pillar of cloud and fire which went before the people (Exod. 13.21-22) and moved behind to protect them from the Egyptians (Exod. 14.19-20) is recalled as Yahweh becomes both front and rear guard (52.12). He not only brings them out but also sustains them in the wilderness. As he caused water to flow from the rock (48.21; cf. Exod. 17.2-7; Num. 20.8) and provided food for his people, so he will now provide streams in the desert (41.17-20; 43.19-21; 49.10), feeding and shepherding his people on the way (49.9; 40.11). Though the new exodus is described as the triumphant return of Yahweh himself and a revelation of his glory (40.3-5, 10-11), his human instrument is the pagan king Cyrus, astonishingly called Yahweh's 'anointed' and 'shepherd' (44.24; 45.7; cf. 41.1-5, 21-29; 45.9-13; 46.9-11; 48.12-16).

The Isaianic new exodus is no mere repetition of the first, but surpasses and supersedes it in many respects, 'even replacing the first Exodus as *the* saving event'.[1] There are contrasts as well as comparisons to the original: whereas in the first exodus the Israelites had to celebrate the Passover in haste (Deut. 16.3; cf Exod. 12.11), the exiles 'shall *not* go out in haste' (Isa. 52.12). They will go out in joy and be led forth in *peace* (Isa. 55.12), without the dangers and terrors which accompanied the wilderness generation.[2] In the new exodus, the glory of Yahweh will be revealed not to Israel alone but to 'all flesh' (Isa. 40.5). Repeatedly the prophet points out that this is something new and creative that Yahweh is doing: 'Do not call to mind the former things, or ponder things of the past. Behold I will do something new....I will even make a roadway in the wilderness, rivers in the desert'. (Isa. 43.18-19; cf. 42.9; 48.3, 6-7).[3]

Israel's salvation will thus be a glorious renewal. There will be a rebuilding of the country and its cities (49.8, 17-21; 54.11-14) and a new

1. R.E. Watts, 'Consolation or Confrontation? Isaiah 40–55 and the Delay of the New Exodus', *TynBul* 41.1 (1990), p. 33. Cf. H.E. von Waldow, 'The Message of Deutero-Isaiah', *Int* 22 (1968), p. 276; Anderson, 'Exodus Typology', pp. 190-92.

2. Anderson, 'Exodus Typology', p. 191.

3. For creation imagery in these chapters and its relationship to the new exodus see Stuhlmueller, *Creative Redemption, passim*; Anderson, 'Exodus Typology', pp. 184-85; von Waldow, 'Message', p. 277; Blenkinsopp, 'Scope and Depth', pp. 24-25.

apportionment of the land (49.8). Her enemies will be eliminated (41.11-12; 49.26; 54.15-17); nations will do homage (45.14; 49.7, 22-23); Jerusalem and temple will be restored more glorious than ever (44.28; 49.16-17; 54.11-12); Israel will be the envy of the world (44.5); there will be great prosperity (49.17-21; 51.3). There are clear eschatological implications in the promises of Eden-like restoration (51.3), the transformation of the wilderness into rivers, pastures and gardens (41.18-19; 43.19; 49.9) and the eternal duration of Yahweh's salvation (45.17; 54.10, 15-17). 'All these motifs combined make it clear that the returning home sketched as a second exodus inaugurated a new age of the world and a new period of salvation-history (*Heilsgeschichte*).'[1]

ii. *The 'Servant' and the New Exodus*. Though consolation and new exodus salvation clearly represent dominant themes, it should also be noted that these chapters of Isaiah contain a large amount of polemic material. In this polemic, which takes the form of 'disputations' (*Disputationsworte*) and 'trial speeches' (*Gerichtsrede*),[2] the prophet responds to the complaints of Israel that Yahweh has failed to live up to his covenant and is either unwilling or unable to help his people. Throughout the prophet affirms the absolute sovereignty of God. The exile was no victory of foreign gods over Yahweh but was wrought by Yahweh himself to punish his sinful and rebellious people.

Westermann and others have suggested that this polemic material reflects the state of disappointment and disillusionment of the exiles. The words of the prophet are meant to shake them out of their depression.[3] R. Watts admits that the message of comfort is directed to a discouraged people, but claims that there is much more at stake here. He points out that throughout chs. 40–48 there is a tone of increasing opposition between the prophet and his audience. Particularly prominent is the growing emphasis in the disputations on the nation's opposition to Yahweh's choice of Cyrus (cf. 44.24-28; 45.9-13; 46.8-11; 48.12-16)—

1. Von Waldow, 'Message', p. 277; cf. R.N. Whybray, *The Second Isaiah* (1983), p. 79; Blenkinsopp, 'Scope and Depth', p. 24.

2. See A. Schoors, *I am God Your Saviour* (1973), pp. 176-295, for a detailed analysis of these and other form critical categories in these chapters. For briefer treatments see Whybray, *Second Isaiah*, pp. 22-42; von Waldow, 'Message', pp. 266-74. Schoors presents as disputations: 40.12-31; 44.24-28; 45.9-13; 46.5-11(13); 48.1-11, 12-15 (16); 55.8-13; and trial speeches: 41.1-5, 21-29; 42.18-25; 43.8-13, 22-28; 44.6-8; 45.18-25; 50.1-3.

3. Westermann, *Isaiah 40–66*, p. 18.

opposition which reflects a rejection of God's wisdom and plan.[1] Further, the strong anti-idol polemic throughout these chapters suggests that Israel still holds the idolatrous mindset which, according to chs. 1–39, led to the exile in the first place. Watts claims that this suggests that Israel's problem is much worse than mere discouragement: 'Instead, the increasingly hostile tone reflects a growing awareness on the part of the prophet that the exile has not really changed anything. Jacob–Israel is still as blind and as deaf as ever, still committed to an idolatrous world-view that rejects Yahweh's wisdom.'[2] With this perspective in view, Watts turns from chs. 40–48 to 49–55 and notes a contrast in both tone and theme. Trials and disputations are virtually absent (with a few exceptions: 50.1-3; 55.8-13); Jacob–Israel terminology ceases, and with it, the anti-idol polemics and the references to the nation's blindness; Cyrus is no longer mentioned.

> Instead we find the enigmatic 'servant' figure in a context almost entirely comprised of [*sic*] salvation words (still using New Exodus imagery) which suggests that the two are linked...whereas chapters 40-48 declare Cyrus' exaltation and the humiliation of daughter Babylon with Jacob-Israel in view, chapters 49-55 deal with the servant's humiliation and vindication/exaltation and the deliverance of daughter Jerusalem-Zion.[3]

Watts rejects that this 'unknown' servant is to be identified either as Cyrus, as the prophet himself, or as 'servant' Jacob–Israel (41.8, 9; 44.1; 45.4). Though identified with Israel in 49.3,[4] he is also distinguished from her.[5] The best solution, therefore, is that the servant represents the

1. Watts, 'Consolation', pp. 35ff. This point is well established. Cf. Schoors, *I Am God*, p. 295: 'On the one hand, they are discouraged and they no longer believe in Yahwe's [*sic*] power to redeem them. On the other hand, they are indignant at the fact that the prophet gives such a unique place to the pagan king Cyrus, whose salvific function he underlines twice with an oracle of election (xlv 1-7; xlii 5-9).' Cf. von Waldow, 'Message', p. 278.

2. Watts, 'Consolation', pp. 48-49. Cf. the strong declarations against Israel in 42.18ff.; 45.6ff.; 48.1. The statement in 46.12 that Israel is 'far from deliverance' is particularly astonishing in light of the assertion of 40.1ff. (Watts, 'Consolation', p. 35).

3. Watts, 'Consolation', p. 49.

4. Watts, 'Consolation', p. 53, accepts the textual integrity of 'Israel' in 49.3 on the basis of its almost unanimous textual support.

5. Jacob–Israel is blind and deaf in her understanding (42.18ff.), faithless (40.27ff.) and guilty. The servant hears and obeys God's instruction (50.4ff.), trusts God to vindicate him (50.7ff.), and is innocent (50.5-9; 53.9). Indeed, he is God's

faithful 'remnant' of true Israel, a remnant which—in light of the individual traits of the servant—is now reduced to one.[1] Watts summarizes his findings:

> The scenario appears to be as follows: the prophet announces the deliverance of Jacob-Israel with Cyrus as agent. Jacob-Israel's response, however, makes it clear that she is still rebellious and obdurate and therefore incapable of fulfilling the servant role. Although Cyrus carries out the word of Yahweh and the return from Babylon takes place, the glorious hope of the return as expressed in 1-39 and 40-55 is not fulfilled as chapters 56-66 make abundantly clear. The new servant who will both deliver Jacob-Israel from its 'blindness and deafness' and execute Yahweh's purposes for the nations is thus presented.[2]

In short, Watts proposes that Israel's rejection of God's plan results in the postponement of the new exodus to an indefinite future when a figure unknown to the prophet will act as Yahweh's servant to save and deliver his people.

This proposal has much to commend it. It is well established among scholars that the disputations and even the trial scenes focus particularly on Israel's objection to God's choice of Cyrus. And if Israel has rejected Cyrus, this is indeed tantamount to a rejection of his wisdom and plan, a plan which includes the glorious return to the promised land. While most commentators place all the emphasis on God's grace (he effects his plan in spite of Israel's unrepentance), it is not impossible that the prophet himself envisioned more serious consequences of Israel's rebellion, i.e. the postponement of the glorious new exodus to an indefinite future. Support for this may be found in the significant shift in tone from chs. 40–48 to 49–55. Circumstances seem to have changed in the latter chapters, with the servant taking center stage as Yahweh's agent of deliverance. The proximity of 'servant' and new exodus passages further suggest that the servant now replaces Cyrus as Yahweh's agent of deliverance. The second servant song (Isa. 49.1-9) is preceded and followed by new exodus passages (Isa. 48.20-22; 49.8-12) and it is the servant who acts as a 'covenant of the people to restore the land, to make them inherit the desolate heritages; saying to those who are bound, "go forth!"' (vv. 8-9).[3] Similarly, the fourth servant song

instrument in restoring Israel (49.5) and bears her sins (53.4-6).

1. Watts, 'Consolation', pp. 50-56.
2. Watts, 'Consolation', pp. 57-58.
3. Westermann, *Isaiah 40–66*, pp. 212-16; Whybray, *Isaiah 40–66*, pp. 140-43,

(52.13–53.12) immediately follows the final summons to the new exodus (52.11-12), suggesting that it is through the actions depicted there that Yahweh fulfills his new exodus.[1] Unlike Cyrus, who accomplishes his task through power and military might, the servant will 'justify the many' through humiliation and suffering.

The greatest difficulty in Watt's proposal is the seeming imminence of Israel's glorious return to the land.[2] Even those passages which speak of the unknown servant as Yahweh's agent suggest that the glorious return from Babylon and the eschatological consequences are about to take place (cf. 48.20-21). Nevertheless, whether or not the prophet himself intended to present a *delayed* new exodus, it is certain that later writers interpreted the glorious return depicted in Isaiah 40–55 as pointing beyond the destruction of Babylon and the time of Cyrus. In Sir. 48.22-25 the author praises Isaiah as one who was great and faithful to his vision:

> By the spirit of might he saw the last things
> and comforted those who mourned in Zion.
> He revealed what was to occur to the end of time,
> and the hidden things before they came to pass (vv. 24-25).

These verses draw allusions from Isa. 48.5, 6; 51.3; 61.2, 3, indicating not only the unity of Isaiah in Ben Sirach's day (cf. the reference to the Hezekiah story of Isa. 38.1-8 in v. 23), but also his eschatological interpretation of events in chs. 40–55.[3] It would be evident to the reader of

and others claim the poem originally contained only vv. 1-6; vv. 7-12 originally referred to Israel but a later editor (or editors) brought the two passages together and so made vv. 7-12 refer to the servant. Our concern is with the text's final form which indicates an individual servant as the agent of the new exodus.

1. Watts, 'Consolation', p. 52; W.J. Dumbrell, 'The Purpose of the Book of Isaiah', *TynBul* 36 (1985), pp. 111-28, 126; J.F.A. Sawyer, *From Moses to Patmos* (1977), p. 155; R.J. Clifford, *Fair Spoken and Persuading: An Interpretation of Second Isaiah* (1984). On the 'servant' as the agent of the new exodus, cf. Nixon, *Exodus*, p. 10 (who sees the servant as an eschatological and messianic figure); von Waldow, 'Message', p. 284: '...as in the first exodus the key figure was Moses, in the second exodus the key figure is the Ebed-Yahweh' (whom he identifies as Deutero-Isaiah).

2. Watts, 'Consolation', p. 57, admits this difficulty, but says such an objection fails to take into account the impact of Jacob–Israel's rejection of Cyrus.

3. The probable allusion to Isa. 61.2-3 suggests that Ben Sirach considered the prophet, rather than an eschatological figure, to be the speaker in Isaiah 61—an interpretation we have seen already in the targum (but one which was not universal, as

Isaiah in post-exilic Judaism and early Christianity that the promised new exodus was not fully fulfilled in the dismal return of the exiles. It was natural, then, that God's people would look ahead to a more glorious fulfillment at some future time.[1] Yahweh's agent of deliverance in this case could be neither Cyrus nor the prophet himself, but rather the humble servant of Yahweh who through suffering would raise up and restore Israel.

iii. *The Coming Davidic King and the New Exodus*. Though the significance of the new exodus theme is well recognized in Isaiah 40–55, it is not so widely noted that the theme occurs already elsewhere in Isaiah and in other prophetic writings.[2] Isaiah 35, with its message of comfort for the discouraged, transformation of the wilderness and a highway for the returning of exiles, so closely resembles the new exodus message of the Book of Consolation that many scholars consider it to have been written by the same author[3] or by a later redactor who drew on themes from chs. 40–55.[4] Isaiah 11.11-16, too, uses 'highway' imagery to develop a new exodus motif with reference to the return of the Assyrian exiles.[5] Throughout the prophets, the exodus memory is frequently recalled to confirm Yahweh's faithfulness to his chosen people and his ability to save them again. In some of these passages, there is an implicit comparison between the exodus event and Yahweh's future salvation of Israel, and hence a 'new exodus' motif. In Hosea

the eschatological interepretation in 11Q Melch demonstrates).

1. On the eschatological interpretation of Isaiah 40 in various streams of Judaism see K.R. Snodgrass, 'Streams of Tradition Emerging from Isaiah 40.1-5 and their Adaptation in the New Testament', *JSNT* 8 (1980), pp. 24-45.

2. Anderson, 'Typology', p. 181 n. 7, points to the appeal of the exodus memory in Hos. 2.14-15 (MT 2.16-17); 11.1; 12.9, 13 (MT 12.10, 14); 13.4-5; Amos 2.9-10; 3.1-2; 9.7; Mic. 6.4; Isa. 10.24, 26; 11.15-16; Jer. 2.6-7; 7.22, 25; 11.4, 7; 23.7-8 = 16.14-15; 31.32; 32.20-22; 34.13-24; Ezek. 20.5-10. Cf. M. Fishbane, *Text and Texture: Close Readings of Selected Biblical Texts* (1979), pp. 121-40, for an analysis of the exodus motif throughout the Prophets.

3. See the list in Sweeney, *Isaiah 1–4*, p. 17 n. 17.

4. Sweeney, *Isaiah 1-4*, pp. 17-18; R.E. Clements, *Isaiah 1–39* (1980), pp. 271ff.; *idem*, 'Beyond Tradition-History', p. 98; *idem*, 'Patterns', pp. 191-92; Kaiser, *Isaiah 13–39*, pp. 361ff.

5. See the discussion of this passage below. Exodus imagery also occurs in Isa. 4.2-6; 10.24-27; 63.7-19, and see the 'reversed' exodus imagery concerning Egypt in Isa. 19.19-25 (Fishbane, *Text and Texture*, pp. 128-29, 138-40).

2.14-15 (MT = 2.16-17), Israel's (and Gomer's) restoration is described as Yahweh bringing her into the wilderness where he will speak to her heart: '...And there she shall answer as in the days of her youth, as in the day when she came up from the land of Egypt.' The theme of Israel's exile and restoration continues in the next chapter, where after remaining without king or prince 'for many days', the nation will return to her rightful husband: 'Afterward the sons of Israel will return and seek Yahweh their God and David their king' (Hos. 3.5). Eschatological new exodus deliverance is thus placed side by side with the restoration of the Davidic dynasty. Similar imagery appears elsewhere in the prophets. The exodus memory is recalled in Amos 9.7 and Micah 6.4; 7.15, where the wider contexts speak of the restoration of the Davidic dynasty (Amos 9.11-12) and a new shepherd and ruler from Bethlehem (Mic. 5.2-4 [MT = 5.1-4]). A new and greater exodus is explicitly stated in Jeremiah 23:

> 'Therefore behold the days are coming,' declares Yahweh, 'when they will no longer say, "As Yahweh lives, who brought up the sons of Israel from the land of Egypt," but, "As Yahweh lives, who brought up and led back the descendants of the household of Israel from the north land and from all the countries where I had driven them." Then they will live on their own soil' (Jer. 23.7-8; cf. Jer. 16.14-15).

The return from exile is thus portrayed as a greater salvation event than even the first exodus. Significantly, immediately prior to this statement the prophet speaks of the coming Davidic king:

> 'Behold days are coming,' declares Yahweh,
> 'When I will raise up for David a righteous branch;
> And he will reign as king and act wisely,
> And execute judgment and righteousness in the land.
> In his days Judah will be saved,
> And Israel will dwell securely;
> And this is his name by which he will be called,
> "Yahweh our Righteousness"' (Jer. 23.5-6).

Though this Davidid is not explicitly stated as Yahweh's *agent* in the new exodus, it is clear that the prophet sees restoration of a Davidic king as directly linked to the return of the exiles to the promised land.[1] The

1. Though vv. 7-8 may have been unknown to Luke since they are absent from the LXX (but cf. Jer. 16.14-15), this does not affect the point at issue, which is to establish a firm connection in the Old Testament and Judaism between the new exodus and the Davidic king.

reason for this Old Testament connection between the coming Davidic king and the new exodus is evident: whenever the restoration of the Davidic dynasty plays a part in the eschatological regathering of Israel, the way is open for a 'new exodus' in which (or, after which) the king plays a prominent role.[1] This idea is already suggested in the foundational Davidic-promise passage in 2 Samuel 7. Recollection of the exodus (v. 6) is followed by a future promise of rest and peace for Israel in the land (v. 10-11) and an eternal throne for David (vv. 13, 16).

The closest link between the coming Davidic king and the new exodus restoration is found in Isaiah 11. As elsewhere our concern is with the (first-century) canonical form of the text rather than its origin or transmission history. The chapter begins with a description of the spirit-endowed shoot from the root of Jesse who will judge the poor with righteousness and slay the wicked with the breath of his lips. Verses 6-9, with their description of paradaisical conditions, place the reign of the righteous king in an eschatological context. Verse 10 returns to the person of the king, providing a transition from vv. 1-5 to the new exodus prophecy of 11-16:

> Then it will come about in that day
> That the nations will resort to the root of Jesse,
> Who will stand as a standard (נס) for the peoples;
> And his resting place will be glorious (v. 10).

In the verses which follow the new exodus is announced. The Lord will gather with his hand 'a second time' the remnant of his people who remain. He will lift up a 'standard' (נס) for the nations and will assemble the 'banished ones of Israel' from 'the four corners of the earth' (vv. 11-12): '...And there will be a highway from Assyria for the remnant of his people who will be left; just as there was for Israel in the day that they came up out of the land of Egypt' (v. 16). The reference to a *second* return in v. 11 (the first being the first exodus), together with the exodus imagery in vv. 15-16 clearly present the eschatological regathering of Israel as a new exodus. The use of the same term 'standard' (נס) for the coming Davidic king in v. 10 and for the Lord's

1. Ezekiel bears witness to a similar tradition in chs. 36–37. Yahweh will regather his people into their own restored land (36.24, 28, 33-36; 37.12, 14); he will create them anew with a new heart and a new spirit (36.26; 37.1-14); Israel and Judah will be reunited (37.15ff.); David will be their king forever (37.24-25); Yahweh will make an everlasting covenant of peace with them and will dwell in their presence (37.26-27). New exodus imagery occurs with reference to the restoration in Ezek. 20.33-38.

rallying point in v. 12 further indicate that this 'root of Jesse' is God's agent in this new exodus deliverance.[1] In its present form,[2] the text thus witnesses a tradition in which the coming Davidic king plays a central role in the eschatological new exodus of God's people.

While it could justifiably be argued that Luke's strong interest in Isaiah and the Prophets makes it likely he was aware of these Old Testament traditions concerning a 'new exodus' led by the Davidic messiah, it would strengthen my case considerably if it could be shown that Jewish writings closer to Luke's day continued to pass on and develop similar views. In this context three texts are particularly relevant: (1) *Pss. Sol.* 11.2-5, like the closely related passage in 1 Bar. 5.5-8, draws on new exodus imagery from Isaiah 40–66 to depict the joyful return of God's people to Jerusalem. In the wider context of the psalms, it is the coming Davidic king who acts as God's instrument to gather God's holy people, purge Jerusalem, restore the nations' boundaries, distribute the land 'according to their tribes', and faithfully and righteously shepherd and lead the nation (*Pss. Sol.* 17.21-46). (2) Similarly, in the vision of the man from the sea in *4 Ezra* 13, the author draws on imagery from Isa. 11.1-16 to present the role of the Davidic messiah[3] as the destruction of the wicked (13.9-11, 37-38, 49; cf. Isa. 11.4) and the eschatological regathering of the ten tribes from the Assyrian exile (13.39-48; cf. Isa. 11.11-16)—a regathering depicted as a new exodus when 'the Most High will again stop the channels of

1. While most commentators consider the 'root of Jesse' to represent either the Davidic messiah (Duhm, Gray, Young, *et al.*), or a renewed Davidic dynasty (cf. Kaiser, *Isaiah 1–12*, pp. 262-63), others suggest the referent is the post-exilic community in Judah (so H. Barth, *Die Jesaja-Worte in der Josiazeit* [1977], p. 59; J. Vermeylen, *Du prophète Isaie à l'Apocalyptique* [1977], I, p. 277).

2. Many commentators consider the chapter to represent several distinct prophecies which have been brought together by a later editor. Clements, *Isaiah 1–39*, pp. 125-27, is representative when he says v. 10 is a clumsy attempt to bring the originally distinct prophecies in vv. 1-5 (about a future Davidic king) and 11-16 (about the post-exilic community) together. This accounts for the change in imagery from the 'shoot' in v. 1 to the 'root' itself in v. 10. Yet the change in terminology may be intended to depict the coming Davidic king as not only the offspring ('shoot') of Jesse but also the root itself, i.e. the source of a renewed Davidic line (cf. Rom. 15.12; Rev. 22.16) (cf. E.J. Young, *The Book of Isaiah* [1965], I, p. 393). In any case, even if Clements's assessment were correct, the present text would link the coming Davidic king to the new exodus motif.

3. That the 'man' from the sea is the Davidic messiah is confirmed by comparing the messianic descriptions in *4 Ezra* 7.28-29; 12.31-34 and 13.25-52.

the river, so that they may be able to pass over' (13.47; cf. Isa. 11.15; Exod. 14.21-31; Josh. 3.14-16). (3) Of less certain date, but still relevant, is the targum on Lam. 2.22, where the meturgeman beseeches the Lord for a new exodus deliverance accomplished by the king messiah:

> Mayest Thou proclaim liberty to Thy people of the house of Israel by the hand of the King Messiah, just as Thou didst by the hand of Moses and Aaron on the day of the Passover; so that my young men may gather together all around from every place to which they were scattered on the day of the mighty wrath of the Lord...[1]

As Levey points out: 'The Targum expects the advent of the Messiah to be a re-enactment of the first drama of Israel's liberation. The Messiah is expected to be the active agent of deliverance, as were Moses and Aaron.'[2]

In summary, these Old Testament and Second Temple passages witness a widespread tradition in which the coming Davidic king plays a key role in the eschatological regathering, or 'new exodus', of God's people. This new exodus theme, in turn, finds its most prominent development in the book of Isaiah.

In contrast to this emerging picture, many scholars deny that the author of Isaiah 40–55 retained any such hope in a restored Davidic dynasty and so would not have envisioned a Davidid as the agent of the Isaianic new exodus. This objection, however, is irrelevant for the present discussion since our interest is in a first-century context where the unity of Isaiah was assumed. When Isaiah is read as a unity, the roles and functions of the coming Davidic king and the 'servant' overlap in a striking way. Both are described as spirit-endowed individuals who establish Yahweh's judgment and righteousness and who act as his agent in an eschatological new exodus of his people. As suggested in the previous chapter, it seems certain that Luke has identified the two figures and so considers the Davidic messiah to fulfill the role of the servant. The Davidic messiah would thus act as God's agent in leading his people—through suffering—in an eschatological new exodus.

With this in mind, it is significant that the Book of Consolation witnesses at least one link between the eschatological new exodus and Davidic restoration. In ch. 55, it is announced that God will make a new covenant with his people, the model of which is not the Mosaic but the

1. Text from Levey, *Messiah*, p. 135.
2. Levey, *Messiah*, p. 135.

Davidic covenant:[1] 'And I will make an everlasting covenant with you, (according to) the faithful mercies shown to David' (Isa. 55.3; cf. 54.10; 61.8). This is followed immediately by a description of David as a testimony among the peoples—a description of David unique in the Old Testament—and as a leader and commander to the peoples (v. 4; cf. Ps. 18.43-44).[2] David is thus characterized as a model leader (among both Israel and the Gentiles!) in a context of eschatological renewal which speaks of unknown nations streaming to Israel to be associated with her (v. 5; cf. Ps. 18.43), and which in the following verses announces the new exodus: Israel will 'go forth with joy' and 'be led forth in peace' (vv. 12-13). Though, as we have seen, many commentators consider vv. 3-5 to represent the transfer of the Davidic covenant from the dynasty to the people in general, this is not the only possible interpretation. It may refer to a longed-for restoration of the Davidic dynasty and the blessings which the people of God subsequently receive. This would open the way for an interpretation of a Davidid leading the new exodus restoration. Whether or not this is the original intent of the passage, Luke himself takes it this way in Acts 13.34, identifying τὰ ὅσια Δαυὶδ τὰ πιστά (Isa. 55.3d LXX) as the restoration of the Davidic throne established through the resurrection of Jesus the messiah and the blessings which are henceforth poured out on God's people.[3]

c. *Conclusions: The Significance and Extent of the Lukan New Exodus*

In light of this background, it is evident that if Luke drew his 'new exodus' imagery from Isaiah and the Prophets as well as from the Pentateuch, the ἔξοδος Jesus is about to fulfill in Jerusalem (Lk. 9.31) is in line with his identification as Davidic messiah. The Isaianic eschatological saviour—though certainly 'like Moses' in that he acts as

1. On the lack of emphasis on the Mosaic covenant in Isaiah 40–55, see Anderson, 'Exodus and Covenant', pp. 339-60, who claims that the prophet's stress on Yahweh's unconditional and unilateral love caused him to turn to the everlasting covenants with Noah (Isa. 54.9-10) and David (55.3-5) rather than to the conditional Mosaic covenant. '...the torah which Israel (or the Servant) is to mediate to the world is not the Mosaic commandments but, in a broader sense, the revelation of Yahweh's purpose for all mankind and the whole creation' (p. 356).

2. Some commentators emend לאמים ('peoples') to לעמים ('for the nations') in the second clause since the repetition of the same word is unusual in a parallel couple. See Whybray, *Isaiah 55–66*, p. 192. The LXX uses ἔθνεσιν in both phrases.

3. For the validity of this interpretation of the phrase see the discussion in Chapter 4 section 3c.

Yahweh's agent of deliverance[1]—may also be viewed as Davidic king and servant (even suffering servant) of Yahweh. Is there further evidence, then, that Luke is indeed thinking in terms of an Isaianic new exodus?

ii. *Evidence for an Isaianic New Exodus in Luke–Acts.* (1) Though T. Holtz's claim that Luke did not have a copy of the Pentateuch at his disposal is highly conjectural, it seems evident that Luke had a greater interest in the prophecies of Isaiah than in the book of Deuteronomy. As demonstrated in the previous chapter, Luke's work is permeated with imagery drawn from the Isaianic portrait of eschatological salvation, including comfort and consolation, healing and release of prisoners, sight for the blind, light for the Gentiles, Spirit-anointing and the proclamation of good news. It is not surprising, then, that Luke would also pick up on the Isaianic theme of an eschatological new exodus.

(2) While the first exodus centered on Yahweh leading his people out of Egypt to the promised land, the Isaianic new exodus begins with the glorious return of Yahweh to his people (Isa. 40.3-5), after which he gathers and leads them (Isa. 40.11). The latter is closer to Luke's presentation. Like the gospel tradition before him (Mk 1.2-3), Luke begins his account of the ministry of John with the inaugural new exodus passage from Isaiah 40 (Lk. 3.4-6).[2] Luke demonstrates his special interest in the quote by omitting Mark's allusion to Mal. 3.1 (but cf. Lk. 1.76; 7.27) and by extending the citation to v. 5 (Matthew, Mark

1. Cf. von Waldow, 'Message', p. 284. Von Waldow points out that the Ebed-Yahweh, like Moses, has prophetic traits, renews the covenant with Yahweh, and leads a deliverance from Babylon: '...as in the first exodus the key figure was Moses, in the second exodus the key figure is the Ebed-Yahweh. Thus the prophetic figure, the Ebed-Yahweh, is a kind of second Moses, or as he has been called, a *Moses redivivus*.' Though there is much truth in this statement, von Waldow does not take into account that the model for the new exodus covenant is not the Mosaic but the Davidic covenant (Isa. 55.3-5), and that the coming Davidic king is also associated with new exodus restoration throughout the prophetic writings. Further, that Jesus is not a *Moses redivivus* is evident from the presence of Moses himself at the transfiguration.

2. For the relationship of Luke's text to the LXX and MT see Bock, *Proclamation*, pp. 93-99. If the omission of the first part of Isa. 40.5 LXX (καὶ ἀποκαλυφθήσεται ἡ δόξα τοῦ κυρίου) is intentional on Luke's part (rather than absent from his Old Testament text), it may reflect his perspective that Jesus' divine glory will be revealed to *all* mankind only at the parousia. While the disciples saw Jesus' glory on the mountain, this privilege has not yet been granted to all humankind.

and John cite only v. 3), probably to reach the phrase 'all flesh shall see the salvation of God'.[1] The universal emphasis thus obtained points forward to the Gentile mission following Jesus' ascension and exaltation. When Jesus has accomplished his Jerusalem 'exodus', the Gentiles will experience salvation. The same Greek phrase τὸ σωτήριον τοῦ θεοῦ (Isa. 40.5; cf. Ps. 97.3 LXX) appears in Acts 28.28 with reference to the Gentile mission (cf. Lk. 2.30-32). As we have seen, Luke frequently draws on Isaianic allusions to confirm God's plan to bring salvation to the Gentiles (Lk. 1.79; 2.32; Acts 13.47; 26.23).

The reference to a road prepared for the coming of the Lord who brings salvation recalls Lk. 1.68, 78, where Zechariah announces that the Lord has 'visited' (ἐπισκέπτομαι) and 'accomplished redemption' for his people by raising up the horn of salvation in David's house (v. 68) and through the visitation of the ἀνατολή from on high (v. 78). As noted earlier (Chapter 3 section 3b), this theme is picked up in Lk. 7.16 where, following Jesus' raising of the widow's son, the people proclaim that 'God has visited his people!' In the pericope which immediately follows, Jesus responds to John's question concerning his identity with the Isaianic signs of eschatological salvation (7.18-23). The theme of 'visitation' reaches something of a climax in 19.44, where, following the rejection of Jesus by the Pharisees at his Jerusalem approach (19.37-40), Jesus predicts the destruction of Jerusalem 'because you did not recognize the time of your visitation (ἐπισκοπή)' (vv. 41-44). Jesus' whole ministry culminating in his death in Jerusalem is thus viewed as the visitation of God to his people. This description remarkably parallels the Isaianic description of the new exodus: Yahweh himself comes to his people, delivering them through his messianic envoy.

(3) The goal of the Isaianic new exodus is Jerusalem/Zion (Isa. 35.10; 40.9; 51.11), where Yahweh's glory will be revealed (40.5; 52.10) and where he will reign as king (52.7; cf. 41.21; 43.15; 44.6).[2] In Luke, too,

1. Schürmann, *Lukasevangelium*, I, p. 161, argues that Luke received the extended text from tradition. But in light of his particular interest in Isaiah 40 (cf. Lk. 1.17, 76-79; 2.25, 30-31; 9.52) and the prominence he gives elsewhere to the themes of 'salvation' and the universality of the gospel, it is more likely that Luke is responsible for the expansion. In either case, his special interest in the extension is evident.

2. Schoors, *I Am God*, p. 243: 'The prophet thinks of this salvation as a new enthronement of Yahwe [*sic*] at Zion.' Cf. Rendtorff, 'Zur Komposition', pp. 306-307; von Waldow, 'Message', p. 277; Watts, 'Isaianic New Exodus', pp. 33-34; *idem*, 'Consolation', p. 34: 'Just as the deliverance of Israel reaches its climax at Sinai, so too here, when Sinai has been subsumed in mount Zion, the new exodus

the emphasis is on Jerusalem as Jesus' goal. It is there he fulfills his ἔξοδος, resulting in his exaltation and heavenly enthronement. Though Luke does not explicitly identify Jesus' exaltation as an enthronement in the heavenly Jerusalem/Zion, this may perhaps be implied by his presentation: (a) Luke identifies Jesus' heavenly throne as a Davidic one (Lk. 1.32; Acts 2.30-36); it was inconceivable that a Davidic king would reign from anywhere but Mt Zion. (b) Psalm 110, Luke's most important Old Testament text confirming Jesus' exaltation-enthronement (Acts 2.34b-35 = Ps. 110.1; cf. Lk. 20.42-43; Acts 5.31), identifies Zion as the location of the king's throne (Ps. 110.2). Similarly, Psalm 2, which Luke alludes to at the baptism and transfiguration and cites with reference to Jesus' opposition (vv. 1-2; Acts 4.25-26) and his resurrection (v. 7; Acts 13.33), says that Yahweh installs his king 'upon Zion, my holy mountain' (v. 6). (c) Jesus' position at the right hand of God also suggests this identification. In the Old Testament Yahweh is said to be enthroned not only in heaven (Pss. 2.4; 11.4; 103.19; Isa. 66.1; cf. Mt. 5.34; 23.22; Rev. 4.2), but also on Mt Zion (Pss. 9.11; 46.; 48.1-3; 132.13-18; cf. Ps. 74.2; Amos 1.2; Jer. 8.19; 14.19-21), where his anointed king reigns at his right hand (Ps. 110.1). In the last days, Yahweh will be enthroned in Jerusalem and on Mt Zion (Isa. 24.23; Jer. 3.17). A writer with Luke's knowledge of the LXX (especially Isaiah and the Psalms!) is unlikely to have missed these connections between the holy city and the throne of God. (d) The concept of the heavenly Jerusalem/Zion was well known in Luke's day, appearing frequently in the apocalyptic literature (*4 Ezra* 7.26; 8.52; 10.27, 42, 44, 54; 13.36; *2 Apoc. Bar.* 4.1-7; cf. *1 En.* 90.28-30). (e) Finally, both Paul and the author of Hebrews bear witness to a first-century Christian tradition which contrasted the new covenant of the heavenly Jerusalem/Zion with the old covenant established at Mt Sinai (Gal. 4.25-26; Heb. 12.22; cf. Rev. 3.12; 21.2, 10); and Paul explicitly identifies this allegorical Mt Sinai as 'the present Jerusalem' (Gal. 4.25). Both authors also allude to Ps. 110.1-2 with reference to Jesus' exaltation at God's right hand (Rom. 8.34; 1 Cor. 15.25; Eph. 1.20; Col. 3.1; Heb. 1.3, 13; 8.1; 10.12-13). It is not unlikely, therefore, that Luke was aware of such a tradition and so understands

reaches its culmination in the arrival of Yahweh in Jerusalem.' Cf. Isa. 4.2-6, where the exodus/Sinai imagery of a cloud by day and fire by night is said to cover Mt Zion at Jerusalem's eschatological restoration (see discussion of this passage below). On the fate and destiny of Jerusalem/Zion as a central theme in Isaiah see Rendtorff, 'Zur Komposition', esp. pp. 305-10, 318-20; Dumbrell, 'Purpose', *passim*.

that, following Jesus' rejection by the earthly Jerusalem (representing unrepentant Israel), he is vindicated, exalted and enthroned at God's right hand in the heavenly Jerusalem/Zion.[1]

Though the emphasis of the new exodus in Isaiah 40–55 is on the *kingship of Yahweh* rather than on that of his messianic envoy, Luke's assertion that it is Jesus who is cnthroned following the 'exodus' fits his perspective elsewhere, where Old Testament texts referring to the Lord God are applied to the Lord Jesus. In Lk. 3.4-6 John is the forerunner who heralds the new exodus coming of Jesus 'the Lord' (Isa. 40.3-5; cf. Lk. 1.17, 76-79). Similarly, in Peter's sermon in Acts 2, calling on the name of the Lord to be saved (v. 21; Joel 2.32) is interpreted with reference to 'the name of Jesus Christ' (v. 38). These references may best be understood from the dual Lukan perspectives, (1) that God himself comes to his people through Jesus his chosen agent, and (2) that, following his exaltation, Jesus sits at God's right hand, where he shares his reign and dominion. Luke's conception of Jesus' universal lordship, his administration of the Spirit and his prominent role in bringing about God's eschatological salvation certainly exceeds Jewish messianic expectations. (Its origin must therefore be sought not only in the Old Testament exegesis of the early Christians, but also in the effect of the words and deeds of Jesus and in the charismatic and worship experience of the early church.)[2] Yet some justification for his perspective may be found from the reading of Isaiah as a unity, where the Spirit-endowed (though not Spirit-directing) king of Isa. 9.6-7 and 11.1-16 acts as Yahweh's vice-regent, reigning on his throne forever, administering his righteous judgment, and leading a new exodus restoration of God's people.

(4) Finally, the eschatological nature of the transfiguration account is in line with the perspective of an Isaianic new exodus. That the transfiguration carries eschatological significance is evident from the allusions to Jesus' exaltation glory[3] and the presence of the eschatological figures of Moses and Elijah. This emphasis suggests that the exodus/Sinai

1. A similar suggestion is made by Mánek, 'New Exodus', pp. 19-23, though he does not provide support.

2. See Turner, 'Spirit of Christ', pp. 181-90.

3. Eschatological fulfillment for Luke means not just the consummation of the kingdom with the coming of the Son of man (v. 26), but its arrival already with the exaltation of Jesus the messiah (v. 27). See the conclusions on Lukan eschatology in Chapter 7.

imagery at the transfiguration also carries eschatological as well as typological significance. If it is asked where exodus imagery appears in an eschatological context in the Old Testament and Judaism, the Isaianic new exodus provides the most likely answer. In Isa. 4.2-5 the restoration of Jerusalem is described in terms recalling the first exodus: 'In that day...Yahweh will create over the whole site of Mount Zion and over her assemblies a cloud (LXX: σκιάσει νεφέλη, 'a cloud will shadow it') by day, and smoke and the shining of a flaming fire by night; for over all the glory there will be a canopy'.[1] Points in common with the transfiguration account include the reference to the mountain, the 'overshadowing' cloud and the revelation of God's glory.[2] This is not to say that at the transfiguration Luke is thinking specifically of this passage, but only that the Moses/Sinai imagery need not exclude an Isaianic new exodus interpretion. It is perhaps significant that in Isaiah 4 it is Jerusalem/Zion, rather than Sinai, which is filled with God's glory, and which becomes the place of eschatological renewal. Again, this would fit well with Luke's emphasis on Jerusalem as the center of God's salvation-historical activity.

Together the above evidence suggests that it is the prophetic concept of an eschatological ingathering or 'new exodus' of God's people rather than a desire to present the travel narrative as a 'Christian Deuteronomy', which prompted Luke to designate Jesus' task as an 'exodus' which he was about to fulfill in Jerusalem. Inasmuch as the events surrounding Jesus' life, death, resurrection and exaltation result in deliverance from the oppression of sin and Satan, they may be compared to God's greatest act of deliverance in the past—the exodus from Egypt. Inasmuch as they have cosmic and eschatological significance, they represent the fulfillment of the prophetic hope for the coming of God's reign and kingdom—the eschatological new exodus.

ii. *The Extent of the Lukan New Exodus*. This conclusion raises the question of the extent of this 'new exodus' in Luke's Gospel. If, as suggested above, the 'exodus' refers to the period of salvation

1. Cf. 2 Macc. 2.8: 'Then the glory of the Lord shall appear, and the cloud also, as it was revealed to Moses, and as when Solomon considered it worthy that the place might be greatly sanctified.'

2. The Hebrew text speaks in verse 6 of a סֻכָּה ('booth') for protection from the heat of day and from the storm and rain (cf. Peter's three σκηναί), another small point in common with the transfiguration account.

inaugurated by the coming of Jesus, it would encompass the whole 'way' of Jesus (ὁδός, Lk. 1.76; 3.4; 7.27) from the commencement of his public ministry to its climax in Jerusalem; the primary focus being on the decisive events in Jerusalem, including Jesus' death, resurrection, ascension and exaltation (cf. Lk. 9.31).

Evans, Davies, Moessner and Ringe, on the other hand, point specifically to the beginning of the travel narrative (9.51) as the commencement of the new exodus.[1] While it is certainly true that the travel narrative represents a heightened resolve on Jesus' part to proceed to his Jerusalem goal—and so signifies a critical phase in Jesus' 'way'—there is little evidence that Luke considers 9.51ff. to constitute the decisive period of this exodus:

(1) The new exodus announcement in Lk. 3.4-6 (Isa. 40.3-5) suggests rather that the time of salvation commences with the inauguration of Jesus' public ministry. Support for this may be found in gospel summaries in Acts, where the critical salvation event commences following the baptism which John proclaimed (Acts 10.37; 13.24). The 'way' of Jesus proceeds from his public εἴσοδος (Acts 13.24) to the culmination of his ἔξοδος, which he completes or fulfills (πληρόω) in Jerusalem (Lk. 9.31).[2]

(2) Jesus' actions throughout the Gospel carry saving significance, suggesting that the new exodus deliverance has already begun prior to the travel narrative. He is already releasing prisoners from spiritual bondage and accomplishing the Isaianic healings associated with eschatological salvation.

(3) Jesus has already been journeying prior to the travel narrative. 'Throughout the ministry from 4.42 onward Jesus is presented always without a home, always on a mission, always on the move.'[3]

(4) It is argued by these scholars that the Sinai allusions at the

1. Evans, 'Central Section', pp. 38-40; Moessner, *Lord of the Banquet*, pp. 46, 47, 66; J.H. Davies, 'The Purpose of the Central Section of St. Luke's Gospel', *SE* 2, TU 87 (1964), pp. 165-66; Ringe, 'Luke 9.28-36', 94.

2. Cf. Marshall, *Gospel of Luke*, pp. 384-85; Schürmann, *Lukasevangelium*, I, p. 558 n. 36.

3. Ellis, *Gospel of Luke*, p. 148; cf. Marshall, *Historian*, p. 151. I would not agree, however, with Ellis' conclusion that the central section should not be considered a 'travel narrative'. From 9.51 onward, Jesus is portrayed with a heightened resolve to reach his Jerusalem goal and so travels with a new intensity (cf. Conzelmann, *Theology*, p. 65).

transfiguration reveal that Jesus is about to commence an exodus.[1] Yet the Sinai theophany did not initiate the exodus but occurred *after* Israel's escape from Egypt. Though the whole period of the wilderness wanderings may also be referred to as 'the exodus', this would still place the mountain revelation in the middle of the exodus rather than at its beginning. Thus the Sinai allusions at the transfiguration fit better with the view that the exodus begins already with the inauguration of Jesus' public ministry.

(5) While it is argued (probably correctly) that πληρόω in 9.31 carries the sense of 'complete' and so suggests that the exodus has started prior to its 'fulfillment' in Jerusalem, this meaning would also imply that the exodus has already begun prior to the transfiguration. If Jesus was 'soon to complete' (ἤμελλον πληροῦν) his exodus when he spoke with Moses and Elijah on the mountain, then that journey must have begun already.

In conclusion, when Luke speaks of the 'exodus' Jesus is about to fulfill in Jerusalem, it is likely that he is thinking especially of the eschatological new exodus which is described in Isaiah and the Prophets. Not only does this fit well Luke's eschatological perspective and strong interest in the prophecies of Isaiah, but it is also in line with his distinctive Christology, which focuses particular attention on Jesus' role as Davidic messiah, Isaianic servant and prophet like Moses. It is significant that, when Isaiah is read as a unity, the eschatological deliverer may be viewed as Davidic king who (like Moses) leads an eschatological new exodus of God's people through suffering as the servant of Yahweh. If this is indeed Luke's understanding, he probably views the whole 'way' of Jesus as his 'exodus'. (Indeed, for the church the new exodus probably continues in Acts, where Jesus' disciples follow the new exodus 'way' of salvation established through his life, death, resurrection and ascension). The term thus becomes a metaphor for the eschatological time of salvation inaugurated with the coming of Jesus. This is not to suggest that this exodus motif is *the* controlling theme of Luke's work.[2] It is rather one of the metaphors Luke uses to describe the dawn of

1. See especially Ringe, 'Luke 9.28-36', pp. 93-94.

2. The contention of R. Watts in his Cambridge dissertation, 'The Influence of the Isaianic New Exodus on the Gospel of Mark' (1990), is that the new exodus is the controlling theme of Mark's work. Though I am less than fully convinced by Watts's conclusions concerning Mark, I am indebted to his work for alerting me to the possible influence of the Isaianic new exodus in the Gospels.

eschatological salvation (similar in kind to other Isaianic motifs like the 'favourable year of the Lord' and 'light' shining in darkness).

With this perspective in view, we turn to Jesus' final approach to Jerusalem and the decisive events of the passion. If it can be shown that Luke presents Jesus as the royal messiah who suffers as the Isaianic servant, this will provide further confirmation for the view suggested above.

5. *Jesus' Royal Approach to Jerusalem*

a. *Introduction*

In previous discussion it was suggested that though the travel narrative does not begin till 9.51, the context leading up to it (from the first passion prediction in 9.21-22 onward) forms a transitional section to the commencement of this final journey to Jerusalem. The end of the journey would seem to be equally fluid in Luke's conception. In attempting to pinpoint the end of the travel narrative scholars have suggested 18.14 (v. 15: Luke picks up Mark again); 18.30 (v. 31: the final determination to go to Jerusalem is stated), 19.10 (v. 11: Jerusalem is 'near'); 19.27 (v. 28: Jesus begins his ascent to the city); 19.40 (v. 41: Jesus 'approaches' the city), 19.44 (v. 45: Jesus enters the temple); and 19.48 (vv. 45-48: Jesus teaches daily in the temple).[1] Yet it is unlikely that Luke marks any one point as the decisive 'end' of his journey. Jerusalem is the goal of Jesus' journey and it may simply be the fact of his arrival, rather than its exact moment, which is important for Luke. From the standpoint of Luke's story, the only view that may be dismissed is the first (18.14, where Luke picks up Mark again), for this is based purely on Luke's use of his sources rather than on his narrative development. There is no travel indicator here nor any indication of Jesus' determination to go to Jerusalem. I would suggest that the whole of Lk. 18.31–19.48 marks a transition from Jesus' journeying to the period of conflict and crucifixion in Jerusalem. Every pericope in this section contains a geographical reference oriented toward Jerusalem and each carries special christological significance for Luke.

The section begins with Luke's third and final passion prediction (Lk. 18.31-34). Luke thus returns to the purpose of the journey and sets the stage for the final approach to Jerusalem. Jesus tells the disciples,

1. For description and proponents of each of these views see the discussion of Egelkraut, *Jesus' Mission*, pp. 6-11. Egelkraut opts for the last.

'Behold, we are going up to Jerusalem...' The mention of Jericho in the following pericope establishes a precise geographical location—rare in the central section—and the reader knows from the parable of the good Samaritan (Lk. 10.25-37) that Jericho is on the road to Jerusalem. Jesus is on his final approach to the city. It is significant, therefore, that it is at this point that *Luke reiterates Jesus' royal status* in three key passages—the account of the blind man outside Jericho (Lk. 18.35-43), the parable of the pounds (Lk. 19.11-27) and the triumphal entry (19.28-40). Luke drops the whole of Mk 10.35-45, perhaps to link the final passion prediction to Jesus' status as the son of David about to enter Jerusalem.

b. *The 'Son of David' Approaches Jerusalem, Luke 18.35-43*

As we have seen, in Mark's account of the healing of the blind man (Bartimaeus), the 'son of David' cry prepares the reader for the cry of the crowd at Jesus' entrance into Jerusalem: 'Blessed is the coming kingdom of our father David.'[1] While Luke's redaction does little to change the internal nature of the story,[2] he places it at Jesus' entrance to Jericho instead of at his departure (as in Mark), and adds two incidents within Jericho (the Zacchaeus story and the parable of the pounds) before relating Jesus' ascent to Jerusalem. In this way Luke breaks the Markan connection to the entry into Jerusalem and so alters the story's significance in its narrative context.

What, then, is the significance of Luke's version? Burger claims that while Mark's episode acclaims the Davidic messiah, 'In Luke the healing of the blind man outside Jericho becomes one miracle story among many. The fact that Jesus may be addressed as son of David is preserved, but it plays no special role.'[3] This statement, however, does not take enough account of Luke's own christological purpose. While it is true that Luke's inclusion of the Zacchaeus story and the parable of the pounds interrupts the progression of Mark's narrative, Luke's

1. See Chapter 2 section 3c.

2. For evidence that Luke follows Mark here and detailed analysis of his redaction see Burger, *Jesus als Davidssohn*, pp. 107-12; T. Schramm, *Der Markus-Stoff bei Lukas* (1971), pp. 143-45. Luke's alterations are primarily a smoothing out and a condensing of Mark's account.

3. Burger, *Jesus als Davidssohn*, p. 111. Cf. Conzelmann, *Theology*, p. 172 n. 1: 'Luke xviii, p. 38, reproduces a title from Mark without drawing any inference from it.'

arrangement has its own christological significance. As suggested above, Jesus' restatement of his Jerusalem goal and his final passion announcement (18.31-34), together with the reference to Jericho in 18.35, confirm to the reader that Jesus is on his final approach to Jerusalem. The blind man's cry thus reminds the reader just who is approaching Jerusalem. This is the Davidic messiah, the one promised an eternal reign on the throne of his father David (Lk. 1.32-33). For Luke, this seemingly earthly and political picture calls for immediate clarification. This is achieved by his introduction of the parable of the pounds, the Zacchaeus event, and through his redaction in relation to Jesus' entrance into Jerusalem. These events serve not to sever the son of David cry from the entry into Jerusalem (as Burger suggests) but to clarify the nature of Jesus' Davidic kingship.

Various scholars have pointed out that from the parable of the pounds onward, kingship becomes a key feature of Luke's narrative.[1] This is an important point and, as we shall see, carries great significance for Luke's Jerusalem narrative. I would suggest, however, that it is the *son of David pericope* (18.35-43) rather than the parable of the pounds (Lk. 19.11-27) which *first* returns to the question of kingship. Jesus is not approaching Jerusalem as any royal figure but as the son of David, the heir to his Father's throne (1.32) and the legitimate ruler of the nation.

c. *The Parable of the Pounds, Luke 19.12-27*

Luke's parable of the pounds presents difficult source questions stemming from two factors: (1) The similarities to Matthew's parable of the talents, and (2) the presence of two distinct strands within Luke's parable. While the number of verbal parallels to Matthew suggest a common source at some point in transmission, it seems unlikely that Matthew and Luke would have redacted the same (Q) passage so differently. The preferred solutions are either (1) that a common parable has reached Matthew and Luke in different forms through separate traditions,[2] or (2) that Jesus himself told two similar parables on separate occasions.[3] Closely related

1. Cf. Ellis, *Gospel of Luke*, p. 222; Marshall, *Gospel of Luke*, p. 704; Karris, *Luke: Artist and Theologian*, p. 83.

2. Manson, *Sayings*, p. 313; A. Weiser, *Die Knechtsgleichnisse der synoptischen Evangelien* (1971), pp. 229-58; Marshall, *Gospel of Luke*, p. 701; Evans, *Saint Luke*, p. 665; *et al.*

3. Plummer, *St. Luke*, pp. 437-38, and many older commentaries; suggested as possible by Ellis, *Gospel of Luke*, pp. 221-22; Marshall, *Gospel of Luke*, p. 701. In

to this source question is the presence of two strands of thought in Luke's version. The first strand, shared with Matthew, concerns the question of the stewardship of the servants during the nobleman's absence. The second strand, present only in Luke (vv. 12, 14, 24a, 27), is clearly allegorical. It gives the reason for the nobleman's departure as the reception of kingly power in a 'far country' (v. 12). While away, his citizens reject his right to reign over them (v. 14); so at his return he condemns them to death (v. 27). This part of the parable is clearly an allegory related to Jesus' departure, reception of a heavenly throne, rejection by unbelieving Jews, and future return in judgment.[1] Whether this allegorical strand was composed by Luke himself or was part of a separate parable which Luke (or his source) added to the stewardship parable, is difficult to determine with any certainty.[2] In either case, Luke's interest in the allegory is clear from his narrative introduction:

> And while they were listening to these things [his closing statements in the Zacchaeus episode, vv. 9-10], he went on to tell a parable, *because he was near Jerusalem, and they supposed that the kingdom of God was going to appear immediately* (v. 11).

What surprises the reader is that, at first sight, the parable does not seem to deal with this issue. Neither the question of stewardship while the king is away, nor the judgment of his enemies when he returns explains *the reason* the kingdom did not appear at Jesus' entrance into Jerusalem. Both rather *assume* a gap between Jesus' 'departure' and his 'return'.[3] The only thing in the parable that explains *why* the kingdom did not appear is the reference to the departure of the nobleman to

this case the common source would be Jesus himself whose idiosyncratic language would account for the verbal parallels. It seems to me this possibility is too quickly dismissed by modern critics. What teacher would never repeat himself in two different forms?

1. Whether the parable was originally related to the story of Archelaus (Josephus, *Ant.* 17.208-22; 17.299-320; *Bell.* 2.18; 2.80-100) is inconsequential for the present discussion since in its Lukan form it clearly allegorizes the story of Jesus.

2. The commentators are well divided. See the lists in Fitzmyer, *Luke X–XXIV*, p. 1231. It seems unlikely to suppose, with Lagrange, *Luc*, pp. 490-92, *et al.*, that Matthew has dropped the allegorical elements from a more original Lukan form.

3. Marshall, *Gospel of Luke*, pp. 702, 703, recognizes this difficulty but suggests that Luke may be facing the misunderstanding that the resurrection *was* the parousia. This solution is highly speculative. It seems better to view Luke's interest here in the departure and return of the king, which explains the delay in the appearance of the kingdom.

receive kingly power. While Luke is clearly interested in the themes of stewardship and judgment present in the parable, his primary reason for placing it *at this point in his narrative* is to explain why the kingdom did not appear when Jesus first entered Jerusalem. It did not appear because Jesus had first to ascend to heaven to receive his kingly authority, after which he would return in judgment.

It has been suggested that Luke's purpose in the parable is to explain the delay of the parousia.[1] But the parable says nothing concerning an extended delay in Luke's day.[2] Rather, it explains why the kingdom did not appear (physically on earth) at Jesus' entrance into Jerusalem. In this way, the point for Luke's audience is not on the delay but on *the nature* of the kingly authority which Jesus received (and the need for stewardship during his absence). Luke is dispelling the Jewish expectation, shared by the disciples during Jesus' life, that the messiah's reign and the consummation of the kingdom of God would occur when he entered Jerusalem.[3] Luke counters that from the beginning Jesus taught that he would assume his kingly authority in heaven, from whence he would return to reign on earth and to judge those who rejected him.

Luke thus uses the parable to clarify the *nature* of Jesus' kingly reign immediately before he enters Jerusalem as 'the king who comes in the name of the Lord' (Lk. 19.38). Though Jesus is rightly proclaimed to be the king, he is not now to establish a kingdom in Jerusalem (cf. Luke's alteration of Mark's 'coming *kingdom*' to a reference to the '*king* who comes'). Rather, as the parable suggests, Jesus will receive his kingdom

1. This is the most common interpretation of the parable. Cf. esp. Conzelmann, *Theology*, pp. 113, 121, 134 n. 1, 134 n. 2; C.H. Dodd, *The Parables of the Kingdom* (1935), pp. 147, 153; Marshall, *Gospel of Luke*, p. 702; J. Dupont, 'La parabole des Talents ou des Mines (Mt. 25, 14-30; Lc 19, 12-27)', in *Etudes sur les Evangiles Synoptiques* (1985), II, pp. 706-43. For a very different interpretation see L.T. Johnson, 'The Lukan Kingship Parable', *NovT* 24 (1982), pp. 139-59, who claims that the parable *confirms* the expectation that the kingdom is about to appear. It appears beginning with Jesus' proclamation as king in 19.38, and in his reign through his apostles in the restored Israel. For a good response to Johnson see Carroll, *Response to the End of History*, pp. 100-103.

2. Though an interval of some kind is implicit in the idea of the king's departure and return, there is no indication of a lengthy delay; and the stewardship expressed in the parable could certainly be accomplished within the first generation Christians. Since in Luke's view the reception of kingly authority occurred at Jesus' exaltation-enthronment, Jesus could return at any time.

3. Str–B, II, p. 300; Acts 1.6.

in a 'distant country' (= heaven) from whence he will return to judge those who have rejected his kingly authority. The parable has a similar function in relation to the son of David incident which precedes it. Though Jesus is rightly proclaimed 'son of David' by the blind man, his reign will not be initiated at this entrance into Jerusalem but rather at his exaltation-enthronement at God's right hand.

One potential problem with this conclusion is Luke's inclusion of the story of Zacchaeus after the son of David story. Does this not interrupt the progression just described? Luke's primary reason for including the Zacchaeus story at this point may be its traditional association with Jericho.[1] At the same time the story forms a fitting conclusion to Luke's 'Gospel to the Outcast' (chs. 15–19)[2] and provides a summary statement for Jesus' ministry. The story climaxes with two statements of Jesus: 'Today salvation[3] has come to this house, because he, too, is a son of Abraham,' and, 'for the Son of man has come to seek and to save that which was lost'. It is generally admitted that this 'Son of man' statement is traditional for Luke, and that he has intentionally introduced it at this point.[4] The statement's appropriateness as an epitome of Luke's Gospel presentation suggests that its purpose here is to provide a summary statement not just for the Zacchaeus story but for Jesus' public ministry as a whole.[5] In Lk. 18.35-43, Jesus is introduced as the son of David, a title which introduces again his royal role and status. Before moving to the account of Jesus' royal entrance into Jerusalem, Luke uses the Zacchaeus story to summarize Jesus' saving ministry to the poor and outcasts on the road to Jerusalem and to prepare the reader for his

1. Cf. Evans, *Saint Luke*, p. 660.

2. See Manson, *Sayings*, pp. 282, 291, 295, 301, 305, 309, 312; Fitzmyer, *Luke X–XXIV*, pp. 1072, 1218.

3. It may be significant that this first occurrence of σωτηρία since the birth narrative comes immediately after Jesus' acclamation as the son of David (cf. Acts 13.23ff.).

4. Marshall, *Gospel of Luke*, pp. 698-99: 'Luke does not create Son of man sayings'; cf. Fitzmyer, *Luke X–XXIV*, p. 1226; Evans, *Saint Luke*, p. 664. 1 Tim. 1.15 suggests the traditional nature of the saying.

5. Marshall, *Gospel of Luke*, p. 694, says, 'The final story in the long account of Jesus on his journey to Jerusalem is meant to be a climax in the ministry of Jesus…' Cf. Evans, *Saint Luke*, p. 664: 'This [saying] places the whole episode in a christological setting as being the outcome of the mission of the Son of man (= Jesus) to seek for and save the lost'.

salvation bringing death and resurrection in Jerusalem.[1]

In summary, Luke like Mark uses the son of David cry of the blind man outside Jericho to prepare the reader for Jesus' royal entrance into Jerusalem and his passion and death as king of the Jews. But, in contrast with Mark, Luke introduces two pericopes between these events which serve to clarify Jesus' messianic role and ministry. In the Zacchaeus story, Jesus' messianic role is seen not as the conquering son of David of contemporary Judaism (*Pss. Sol.* 17; *4 Ezra* 13; 4QpIsa[a]; 1QSb 5.24-26) dealing retribution to Israel's enemies but rather as the compassionate Son of man seeking and saving the lost (i.e. the role of the messiah as set out in Lk. 4.18-19; 7.20-23). Then, in the parable of the pounds, the nature of Jesus' kingly authority and reign is presented not as the immediate establishment of an earthly kingdom on earth but rather as a departure to receive kingly authority, followed by a still future return in judgment.

d. *The Triumphal Entry, Luke 19.28-40*[2]

While the first nine verses of Luke's account of the triumphal entry follow Mark quite closely (Lk. 19.28-36; Mk 11.1-8a), from v. 37 onwards there are significant differences. These changes may be a result of Lukan redaction or may indicate his use of an independent source.[3] In either case, the fact that Luke knew Mark's account and chose to depart from it suggests that his alterations are important.[4] The presence of Lukan vocabulary and style, and the scene's coherence with Luke's perspective elsewhere, confirms that he has worked the section over and made it his own.[5]

1. Cf. Fitzmyer, *Luke X–XXIV*, p. 1222: 'The two episodes are fitting scenes at the end of the lengthy Lucan travel account, for they prepare the reader for Jesus' approach to Jerusalem as "the Son of David" and the one who brings salvation to the "lost"'.

2. The traditional designation of this episode is used even though Luke's account is not technically an 'entry' since Jesus does not enter Jerusalem or the temple in the story.

3. The former is argued by Creed, *St. Luke*, pp. 240-41; Evans, *Saint Luke*, p. 678; the latter (in various forms) by V. Taylor, *Behind the Third Gospel* (1926), pp. 94-95; Manson, *Sayings*, p. 317; Schramm, *Markus-Stoff*, pp. 145-49; H. Patsch, 'Der Einzug Jesu in Jerusalem', *ZTK* 68 (1971), pp. 7-10; Fitzmyer, *Luke X–XXIV*, pp. 1242 (vv. 39-40 only).

4. Burger, *Jesus als Davidssohn*, p. 112.

5. See Marshall, *Gospel of Luke*, pp. 714-16, for indications of Lukan vocabulary and style. See the discussion below for the presence of Lukan themes.

In Mark's account, the messianic significance of the event is somewhat muted. Though an allusion to Zech. 9.9-10 is almost certainly present,[1] it is not explicitly stated (unlike Mt. 21.5; Jn 12.15), and it is not obvious that the crowd has understood Jesus' arrival as a messianic one. The identity of the crowd is left ambiguous; Mark says merely that 'many' (πολλοί) spread their garments on the road while 'others' (ἄλλοι) spread leafy branches in his path.[2] Those who acclaim him are described merely as 'those who went before and those who followed'. The first part of their cry, taken from Ps. 118.26, was the common greeting for pilgrims arriving in Jerusalem for the feast of Tabernacles.[3] While expressing hope of God's deliverance, it does not necessarily herald the presence of the deliverer. The second part of the cry, while reflecting eschatological expectation, does not speak of the messiah but only of 'the coming *kingdom* of our father David'. While it is clear that the people are greeting Jesus as a respected and revered prophet, they are not necessarily proclaiming him to be the messiah.[4] This, of course,

1. Mark's account contains the three basic components of Zech. 9.9-10: the entry into Jerusalem of a royal figure, the riding on the colt of an ass and the jubilation of the people. This is not to say that the account was freely created around Zech. 9.9-10 or that an originally non-messianic entrance of Jesus into Jerusalem was later interpreted messianically under the influence of this passage (cf. Bultmann, *History*, pp. 261-62). For arguments in favour of the historicity of the event and its messianic significance see Taylor, *St. Mark*, pp. 451-52; W.G. Kümmel, *Promise and Fulfillment: The Eschatological Message of Jesus* (1957), pp. 116-17; Marshall, *Gospel of Luke*, pp. 709-11.

2. The spreading of garments recalls the royal greeting to Jehu in 2 Kgs 9.13. Palm branches, praise, hymns and songs are associated with the entrance of Simon Maccabeus into Jerusalem in 1 Macc. 13.51. Both acts would thus signify homage and respect to a figure of high rank and authority (cf. Lane, *Mark*, p. 296; Taylor, *St. Mark*, p. 456; Marshall, *Gospel of Luke*, p. 714; Str–B, I, pp. 844-45).

3. The only occurrence of 'Hosanna' (הוֹשִׁיעָה־נָּא = 'save now', or 'save, we pray') in the Old Testament is at Ps. 118.25 (but cf. Ps. 20.10; 2 Sam. 14.4; 2 Kgs 6.26). Though originally a prayer for help, the term came to be used as a shout of acclamation (like 'Hallelujah!') or as a greeting for addressing pilgrims or a famous Rabbi (Taylor, *St. Mark*, p. 456; Lane, *Mark*, p. 397). As one of the Hallel Psalms (Pss. 113–18), Psalm 118 was used liturgically at the Feast of Tabernacles and at the Passover meal, though its use here by Passover *pilgrims* entering Jerusalem is unusual (Bock, *Proclamation*, p. 122).

4. Lane, *Mark*, pp. 397-98. Lane points out that the rabbis interpreted Ps. 118.25-26 with reference to David or to final redemption (*b. Pesah* 119a; *Midr. Tehillim* to Ps. 118, §22, 244a), which explains the reference to the 'kingdom of our

is not the perspective of Mark or his readers. Mark almost certainly interprets Jesus' role as 'the coming one' of Ps. 118.26 in terms of the arrival of the messianic king of Zech. 9.9-10.[1] This is confirmed by Mark's narrative both before—in the confession of Peter (Mk 8.29) and the account of blind Bartimaeus (Mk 10.27-33)—and after—throughout Jesus' passion, especially in the trial before the Sanhedrin (Mk 14.62).[2]

Luke's redaction serves to make more explicit Mark's messianic understanding. The ambiguous crowd in Mark is clarified in Luke as 'the whole multitude of *the disciples*' and they explicitly proclaim Jesus as *the king* who comes in the name of the Lord (Ps. 118.26). Significantly, Luke alone mentions that they are rejoicing and praising God 'for all the mighty works that they had seen'. All three redactional alterations fit the Lukan perspective suggested previously. While the multitudes are still in the dark, Jesus' disciples believe and confess him to be the king, the royal-messiah (cf. Peter's confession in 9.20). Luke further confirms that it is Jesus' 'mighty works'—his healings, exorcisms and other miracles—not political or military activity which confirms his messianic identity (cf. Lk. 4.18-19; 7.18-23; Acts 2.22; 10.38). It is on the basis of these actions that the disciples rejoice and praise God (also Lukan, cf. 2.13, 20; 19.37; 24.53; Acts 2.47; 3.8-9), proclaiming Jesus to be the messianic king.

While Luke follows Mark in leaving the allusion to Zech. 9.9-10 implicit, his redaction serves to emphasize the messianic oracle more clearly than in Mark.[3] Zech. 9.9 LXX reads:

> Χαῖρε σφόδρα, θύγατερ Σιών·
> κήρυσσε, θύγατερ Ἰερουσαλήμ·
> ἰδοὺ ὁ βασιλεύς σου ἔρχεταί σοι, δίκαιος καὶ σῴζων αὐτός,
> πραῢς καὶ ἐπιβεβηκὼς ἐπὶ ὑποζύγιον καὶ πῶλον νέον.

father David'. Nevertheless, it is not clear that the crowd considers the time of salvation to have arrived or sees Jesus as the messiah.

1. Zech. 9.9-10 is interpreted messianically in rabbinic thought (cf. Str–B, I, pp. 842-44). Fitzmyer, *Luke X–XXIV*, pp. 1245-46, argues that this material is late and should not be introduced as evidence for a first-century Palestinian interpretation.

2. It is also possible that Mark's reference to the 'colt tied' (vv. 2, 4) is an allusion to the Shiloh oracle in Gen. 49.10-11, where the coming ruler from Judah 'ties...his donkey's colt to the vine'. If this allusion is present, it would provide further symbolism pointing to a veiled messianic interpretation of the event.

3. *Contra* Fitzmyer, *Luke X–XXIV*, p. 1244, who says, 'Luke has not the slightest reference to it [Zech. 9.9].'

In describing Jesus' position on the colt, Luke replaces Mark's 'and he sat (ἐκάθισεν) upon it' with 'they (the disciples) mounted (ἐπεβίβασαν) Jesus upon it'. Though this change could be merely stylistic (ἐπιβαίνω is the more normal term), it is not unlikely that Luke has assimilated his text to Zech. 9.9 LXX.[1] In Luke, the disciples, like the 'daughter of Jerusalem' in Zechariah, rejoice (χαίρω) at the coming of the king and his saving activity. Perhaps most significantly, in the allusion to Ps. 118.26, Mark's phrase 'Blessed is *he* who comes...' becomes 'Blessed is *the king* who comes...', echoing Zech. 9.9: ἰδοὺ *ὁ βασιλεύς* σου ἔρχεταί σοι... Finally, Luke replaces Mark's closing anthem, 'Hosanna in the highest' with 'Peace in heaven and glory in the highest'. Like the humble king of Zech. 9.9-10 who 'will speak *peace* to the nations...', so Jesus is portrayed as one who brings peace (cf. Lk. 2.14; 1.79).[2]

By bringing out this allusion more clearly, Luke emphasizes again the nature of Jesus' messiahship. His approach to Jerusalem is not as a conquering warrior but as the humble king of Zech. 9.9, 'just and endowed with salvation'. If Luke has the overall context of Zechariah in view, he would likely see the king here as the 'branch' (Zech. 3.8; 6.12; cf. Isa. 11.1; Jer. 23.5; 33.15)—the Davidic messiah typified by the prophet in the figure of Zerubbabel (cf. 4.6-10). Whether or not Luke is thinking in these specific terms, his presentation elsewhere confirms that the title 'king' refers here to the messianic king destined to reign forever on the throne of David (Lk. 1.32; Acts 2.30; 13.23).

If Luke has a Davidic figure in view, it may be asked why he has

1. Cf. Evans, *Saint Luke*, p. 679; Marshall, *Gospel of Luke*, p. 714.

2. Navone, *Themes of St. Luke*, pp. 89-90 and George, *Etudes*, p. 275, suggest that Luke intentionally recalls the coronation of Solomon. Evidence for this are the words ἐπεβίβασαν (19.35 = 1 Kgs 1.33) and καταβάσις (19.37 = 1 Kgs 1.40), the jubilation of the people (19.37 = 1 Kgs 1.40) and the two reference to peace (19.38, 42) recalling Solomon, the king of peace. While this allusion is possible, and would further emphasize the royal Davidic significance of the event, there are significant differences between the two accounts and a direct allusion remains conjectural. The occasion in 1 Kings is Solomon's anointing, which is not suggested by Luke; the rejoicing of the people occurs *after* Solomon's descent to Gihon—they are going *up* before him; there is no reference to 'peace' in the 1 Kings context; and the LXX describes David's animal which Solomon rides as a 'a mule' (ἡμίονος, MT = פרדה, 'a she-mule'), and there is no indication of its youth. Nevertheless, I would agree that the regal contexts of Zech 9.9-10 and Solomon's coronation in 1 Kgs 1.33 are closely related (the former perhaps drawing allusions from the latter), and together they suggest a royal-Davidic significance for Luke's account.

dropped Mark's reference to the 'coming kingdom of our father David' (his only omission of a Markan reference to David). The most likely answer is that he wishes to avoid the earthly and political connotations that such a statement would give to the present context.[1] Jesus is not coming to Jerusalem to set up the messianic kingdom physically on earth. Rather, he is coming to suffer and die, after which he will 'enter his glory' (24.26) and assume his kingly authority at God's right hand (Acts 2.34-35; 5.31). Luke's omission thus serves a purpose similar to the introduction to the parable of the pounds (Lk. 19.11-27) immediately previous.[2] In both cases, Luke intentionally rejects the expectation that 'the kingdom of God was going to appear immediately' (19.11). Rather, Jesus will ascend to heaven to receive his kingship, whence he will return in judgment (19.12, 27).

Luke's redaction in the final phrase of v. 38 has a similar purpose. Instead of Mark's 'hosanna in the highest',[3] Luke concludes the refrain with 'peace in heaven, and glory in the highest'. The description of peace *in heaven* is unusual and suggests that 'the messianic peace is realized now only in heaven, that is, in the realm to which the resurrected Jesus goes. "Peace on earth" (2.14) is rejected by Jerusalem (19.42) and must await the parousia for its fulfillment.'[4] While Jesus is truly the peace-bringing king of Zech. 9.9, this peace is presently available only in the spiritual realm.

The absence of physical 'peace' coming to Jerusalem recalls Luke's

1. Cf. Conzelmann, *Theology*, p. 74; Burger, *Jesus als Davidssohn*, pp. 112-14; Fitzmyer, *Luke X–XXIV*, pp. 1245-46; *et al.* Luke's omission may also be partly stylistic. Having already introduced the title 'king' with reference to Jesus, it would be grammatically awkward to add a reference to the kingdom or to David. It is unlikely that Luke wishes to eliminate the idea of a kingdom (cf. 22.29) or to reject Jesus' Davidic heritage; rather he wants *to emphasize* that the king has arrived, even if the kingdom is not immediately to appear on earth. Maddox, *Purpose*, p. 106, goes too far when he says that Luke's omission of the reference to 'David' shows that for Luke the kingdom has nothing to do with Israel. Elsewhere, Luke ties Jesus' kingship and his kingly reign closely to Israel (cf. Lk. 1.32-33; 22.29-30).

2. Note the transition to the present story in v. 28: 'and having said these things', i.e. the parable of the pounds.

3. Mark's phrase probably either means 'save us, You who dwell in the highest' (Lane, *Mark*, p. 398; cf. Taylor, *St. Mark*, p. 456) or is a 'summons to strike up songs of praise in the heavenly heights' (E. Lohse, *TDNT*, IX, p. 683; Marshall, *Gospel of Luke*, 715).

4. Ellis, *Gospel of Luke*, p. 225.

other citation of Ps. 118.26 at 13.33ff., where Jesus predicts his rejection by Jerusalem and the judgment of the city that will follow. The positive reaction of the disciples in the present passage is thus set in contrast to the unbelief of the nation as a whole. While Jesus' disciples acknowledge his messianic identity with cries from Ps. 118.26, Jerusalem as symbolic of the nation does not, and the Jewish leaders call on him to rebuke his followers (Lk. 19.39). That this is Luke's intention in the present passage is confirmed by the episode immediately following (19.41-44). Jesus weeps over Jerusalem, lamenting that she does not know 'the things which make for *peace*' (vv. 41-42). Jerusalem already stands under the sentence of judgment (vv. 43-44); she will acknowledge her messiah only at the parousia, when he returns in judgment (Lk. 13.35).

In summary, Luke's redaction both accentuates the royal-messianic implications of Mark's account and at the same time clarifies *the nature* of Jesus' messiahship. By introducing ὁ βασιλεύς into the citation of Ps. 118.26, Luke emphasizes more clearly than Mark Jesus' royal status. The king whom Gabriel predicted in Lk. 1.32-33 would reign forever on the throne of David is at the very gates of Jerusalem. This vivid and seemingly political picture calls for immediate clarification. Luke does this first by indicating that it is Jesus' disciples who recognize his identity, an identity established not by activities traditionally associated with a conquering messiah but by Jesus' miraculous works. In addition, Luke brings out more clearly the allusion to Zech. 9.9-10 with its portrait of the humble and just king bringing peace. This peace, however, is a spiritual peace, not yet fully realized on earth. Finally, Luke precedes the scene with the parable of the pounds, further emphasizing that the kingdom is not yet about to appear (Lk. 19.11). Jesus has arrived in Jerusalem not to establish his kingdom physically on earth but to fulfill his *exodus* (9.31)—to complete his messianic task and assume his kingly reign at God's right hand.

e. *The Davidssohnfrage, Luke 20.41-44: David's son and David's Lord*

Though Jesus' question concerning the Davidic sonship of the messiah does not occur on Jesus' *approach* to Jerusalem, it is convenient to deal with the pericope here since it relates directly to Jesus' Davidic messiahship and to his Jerusalem fate. The question appears in the series of controversies which characterize Jesus' last days in the city (Lk. 20.1-47; cf. Mk 11.27-40). As we have seen, in Mark the *Davidssohnfrage* emphasizes that Jesus' essential dignity exceeds Jewish expectations concerning the Davidic messiah.[1] While Luke's version follows Mark's account with only minor changes, his presentation elsewhere gives the pericope a clearer meaning. First, Luke's repeated emphasis on Jesus' Davidic descent (Lk. 1.27, 32, 69; 2.4; 3.31) rules out the possibility that the question is meant to deny the messiah's Davidic origin. For Luke the messiah is the son of David who will reign forever on his father's throne (Lk. 1.32; 18.38, 39). Secondly, in Lk. 22.69, and especially in Peter's Pentecost sermon (Acts 2.34-35), Ps. 110.1 is taken up and applied to Jesus' exaltation-enthronement at God's right hand. For Luke, the 'son' or 'Lord' question left open during Jesus' ministry finds its answer after the resurrection. Jesus the Christ is *both* David's son and David's Lord because at his resurrection he was exalted and enthroned as Lord at the right hand of God. In the climax to his sermon, Peter cites Ps. 110.1 and proclaims that 'God has made this Jesus—whom you crucified—both Lord and Christ' (Acts 2.36).[2] While Jesus is indeed David's son and the heir to his throne, his universal dominion and authority far exceeds that of David. He is *Lord of all* (Acts 10.36).

6. *The Passion of the King as Servant*

a. *Introduction*

It would be safe to say that Luke has a variety of purposes in his passion narrative, including (among others) paraenetic, apologetic and christological ones.[3] The present section is limited to Luke's christological presentation, and seeks to show that two themes are most prominent, *Jesus' kingship and his role as Isaianic servant.* While Jesus is presented throughout as a king about to receive his kingship, his task is not one of conquest but of willing obedience to God's plan that 'his Christ

1. See Chapter 2 section 3c.

2. Cf. Burger, *Jesus als Davidssohn*, pp. 114-16. Burger claims that Luke's seemingly trivial alterations are thus theologically significant: (1) his alteration of πόθεν to πῶς brings out the question '*in what way* is David's son his Lord?' more clearly; (2) the absence of a positive response by the crowds suggests that no one, not even the disciples, can answer the question before the resurrection; and (3) Luke's alteration of Mark's 'the scribes say' to the more general 'they say' suggests that the teaching of the messiah's Davidic descent is a dogmatic question within the church.

3. On the exemplary nature of Jesus' passion see Voss, *Christologie*, pp. 121-23; G. Schneider, *Verleugnung, Verspottung und Verhör Jesu nach Lukas 22,54-71* (1969), pp. 187-90; on the possibility of a political apologetic see the references cited below.

should suffer' (Acts 3.18). It is through suffering that the king achieves his royal reign and authority. If this Lukan perspective can be demonstrated, it will provide further confirmation for the thesis set out above. Luke presents Jesus as the Isaianic eschatological saviour—the Davidic messiah who fulfills the role of the servant.

The question of sources in Luke's passion is a difficult one owing to the significant differences from Mark. While the idea that Luke's passion was a part of a Proto-Luke has not found widespread support,[1] it seems certain that Luke has made use of additional source material in compiling his account.[2] While this should caution against placing too much emphasis on alterations from Mark, it must be added that Luke almost certainly had Mark's passion account available to him and so consciously chose to depart from it—either through his own redaction or by following another source, or sources.[3] To arrive at Luke's purpose, therefore, alterations from Mark should be weighed together with clear signs of Lukan redaction, the general thrust of Luke's narrative development and the theological perspective expressed elsewhere in Luke–Acts.

b. *Jesus as King in his Passion*

As we have seen, Luke's redaction serves to emphasize Jesus' royal status in the context of his arrival in Jerusalem. This emphasis continues in the passion narrative, where Luke follows the gospel tradition in presenting Jesus especially as king at his trial and crucifixion.[4] In all four

1. For this view see especially V. Taylor, *The Passion Narrative of St Luke* (1972).

2. See especially the detailed redactional analysis of J. Green, *The Death of Jesus* (1988), pp. 24-104. Green concludes that Luke has used Mark and another unified narrative. See his appendix, 'Sources in Luke's Passion Narrative', pp. 324-30. For a different perspective (though limited to Luke 22), see M. Soards, *The Passion According to Luke* (1987), esp. pp. 115-25, who denies Luke's use of a continuous written narrative in addition to Mark. He claims Luke's alterations may be attributed to his redaction of Mark supplemented with independent units of oral tradition. It is instructive to compare Soard's reconstruction of Luke's redaction in Luke 22 (pp. 115-18) with Green's appendix.

3. Cf. Green, *Death of Jesus*, p. 102, who claims with 'virtual certainty that the Third Evangelist made use of the Markan passion account in addition to certain non-Markan source material'.

4. In all four Gospels Jesus is referred to as 'king of the Jews' by Pilate (Mk 15.2, 9, 12; Mt. 27.11; Lk. 23.3; Jn 18.33-39; 19.14, 15), in the mocking of the

Gospels Jesus is tried as a royal pretender and crucified under the *titulus* 'King of the Jews'. In all four Jesus' kingship evinces a response of incomprehension, mockery and rejection by Jews and Romans alike. Luke's own contribution to this theme is evident when his passion narrative is viewed in the context of Luke–Acts as a whole. Two emphases are prominent: (1) The titles βασιλεύς and χριστός are closely linked. This serves not only to explain the significance of χριστός for Gentiles but also to draw out the royal-messianic expectations associated with the title. (2) As elsewhere, Luke clarifies the nature of Jesus' kingship by emphasizing his *present* and *heavenly* reign rather than an earthly and political one. While Jesus is indeed 'the king who comes in the name of the Lord', he does not receive his throne at his arrival in Jerusalem nor (first) at his return in glory, but rather at his exaltation-enthronement to God's right hand, following—and directly resulting from—his suffering and death. These two emphases may be seen in the following passages.

i. *The Jewish Trial: Charges of Messianic Pretensions, Luke 22.66-71.* In contrast to the evening session in Matthew and Mark, Luke's account of Jesus' trial before the Jewish Council occurs on the following morning. The reason for this is uncertain. Luke may know of two trials, but chooses to relate only the morning session; he may have intentionally moved Mark's evening trial to the morning; or he may be following a different source which only contained a morning session.

Since Luke intentionally departs from the Markan account, we may assume his alterations are significant. His omission of the account of the false witnesses (Mk 14.55-61) may be simple condensation. More likely, by omitting other accusations against Jesus (cf. Mk 14.58) Luke intentionally emphasizes those related to his messianic identity. The Council moves immediately to the central issue: 'If you are the Christ, tell us.'

soldiers (Mk 5.18; Mt. 27.29; Lk. 23.37 [at the cross]; Jn 19.3), and on the *titulus* on the cross (Mk 15.26; Mt. 27.37, 32; Lk. 23.38; Jn 19.19, 21). In addition, in Matthew and Mark he is mocked as 'king of Israel' by the chief priests and scribes at the cross (Mk 15.32; Mt. 27.42) and in Luke is accused by the Council before Pilate of claiming to be 'Christ, a king' (Lk. 23.2) (cf. Acts 17.7: 'another king [than Caesar]'). In the three Synoptics Jesus indirectly affirms his kingship before Pilate (σὺ λέγεις, Mt. 27.53; Mk 15.2; Lk. 23.3), while in John he affirms it directly but clarifies that this kingship is not of this world (Jn 18.36-37). Cf. the purple robe and the crown of thorns in the abuse of the soldiers before the crucifixion (Mk 15.17; Mt. 27.28; Jn 19.2). Luke omits these references but records similar abuse before Herod (Lk. 23.11) and in the mocking of the soldiers at the cross (Lk. 23.37).

That this is Luke's purpose finds support from the account of the trial before Pilate which follows, where the accusation against Jesus is his claim to be χριστός, a king opposing Caesar and misleading the nation (23.1, Luke only).

Luke's other important alteration is his division of the high priest's single question (σὺ εἶ ὁ χριστὸς ὁ υἱός τοῦ εὐλογητοῦ; Mk 14.61) into two, both posed by the Council (εἰ σὺ εἶ ὁ χριστὸς εἰπὸν ἡμῖν... οὖν εἶ ὁ υἱὸς θεοῦ; vv. 67, 70). Jesus' response to the first suggests that since the Council will not accept the true role of the Christ, which includes his suffering (cf. Lk. 24.25-26), it is useless for him to answer (vv. 67b-68a). This suffering, however, will result in exaltation, and so '*from now on* the Son of man will be seated at the right hand of the power of God' (v. 68b). Luke's omission of the Markan phrase 'and coming with the clouds of heaven' could be part of a delay of the parousia theme (so Conzelmann), or may be meant merely to stress Jesus' *present* reign at God's right hand. Luke's addition of ἀπὸ τοῦ νῦν, together with his failure to omit the coming Son of man statement in Lk. 21.27 (cf. Lk. 17.24, 30), makes the latter more likely. Thus while Mark's text combined the thoughts of Dan. 7.13 and Ps. 110.1, Luke drops the former allusion (except the Son of man title)[1] and so strengthens the latter (the enthronement of the Davidic messiah, cf. Acts 2.30-36; Lk. 21.41-44).[2] It is Jesus' *present heavenly reign* which is central for Luke.

This redaction may provide a clue to Luke's division of the Council's question. The enthronement language of Ps. 110.1 in v. 68 recalls the similar imagery in Ps. 2.6-7, where Yahweh's anointed is installed on Mount Zion and declared to be God's son (Ps. 2.6-7). The close association of Jesus' resurrection, ascension and exaltation in Lukan thought suggests that the citations of Ps. 2.7 in Acts 13.33 (resurrection) and Ps. 110.1 in Acts 2.34-35 (exaltation; cf. Lk. 20.42-43; Acts 5.31) are for him closely related—both expressing divine vindication at Jesus' entrance into his 'glory' (Lk. 24.26). In the present text, then, while Jesus avoids a direct response to the question of whether he is the Christ, he does admit that he is destined for the messianic throne (v. 69).

1. By retaining the title Luke may imply the suffering of the Christ before his exaltation. It is the same Son of man who suffers who will be exalted (cf. Acts 7.56).

2. The omission of the coming Son of man statement also explains Luke's omission of the phrase 'you will see'. The unbelieving Council would not comprehend or experience Jesus' heavenly reign at God's right hand.

The leaders, determined to accuse Jesus of messianic pretensions, take up his royal enthronement language from Psalm 110 and link it to Psalm 2: if Jesus claims he will be exalted to the messianic throne (Ps. 110.1; cf. Ps. 2.7), is he consequently (οὖν) claiming the intimacy of divine sonship expressed in Ps. 2.7? They thus shift from one messianic title to the other (on the basis of this Ps. 2/Ps. 110 connection) in order to gain a confession.

This explanation fits the narrative best where the views expressed are meant to be those of the Jewish leaders who would naturally (in Luke's view) associate the exaltation of the messianic Lord to God's right hand in Ps. 110.1 with the installation of the anointed king as God's son upon Mount Zion in Ps. 2.6-7 (cf. Ps. 110.2: 'Yahweh will stretch forth your strong scepter *from Zion*'). This view also finds support both from the Council's response in v. 71 (they claim to have obtained the messianic confession they were seeking) and from the Roman trial which follows immediately, where the leaders accuse Jesus of *royal* claims (23.2).

The reason for the double question for Luke, then, is not—as some argue—to subordinate χριστός to υἱὸς θεοῦ by climaxing the narrative with the latter.[1] Elsewhere Luke intentionally *associates* divine sonship with messiahship (cf. Lk. 1.32; 4.41; Acts 9.20-22; 13.33).[2] His special interest in the χριστός title throughout Luke–Acts makes it unlikely he would here subordinate it to a title of less redactional interest to him. Indeed, in Acts 2.36 χριστός (together with κύριος) is the title of exaltation.[3] Nor can the double question be meant merely to show the

1. Cf. Creed, *St. Luke*, p. 278; Fitzmyer, *Luke X–XXIV*, pp. 1467-68; Ellis, *Luke*, p. 262; Franklin, *Christ the Lord*, p. 56; Ellis writes that 'Luke qualifies Jesus' acceptance of the "messiah" title and gives prominence to the titles Son of man and Son of God.' He says the purpose for this is to distinguish the political 'messiah' from the non-political messianic terms (p. 262). P.W. Walaskay, *'And so we Came to Rome': The Political Perspective of St. Luke* (1983), p. 39, *idem,* 'The Trial and Death of Jesus in the Gospel of Luke', *JBL* 94 (1975), p. 82, and Martin, 'Salvation and Discipleship', p. 368, make similar distinctions between 'Christ' as a political and 'Son of God' as a religious designation. None of these writers offer any background evidence for such a distinction, however, and elsewhere in Luke–Acts, Luke seems unaware of any. Divine sonship in Lk. 1.32-33 is as political sounding as any of Luke's χριστός passages, and the context of Psalm 2, which brings together χριστός and divine sonship (cf. Acts 4.25-26; 13.33), can hardly be interpreted as non-political.

2. See Chapter 3 section 3a.

3. Franklin, *Christ the Lord*, p. 56, strangely asserts that 'messiah', unlike 'Son

'fundamental identity of the christological titles'.[1] Luke's version in this case would be no improvement on Mark's, since Mark puts the titles in apposition and so identifies them more closely. Rather, if the division is intentional (and Luke is not following an independent source), the best solution is that his redaction is meant to stress Jesus' exaltation-enthronement as messianic Lord and Son of God, and his present heavenly reign.

ii. *The Roman Trial and the Crucifixion: 'Christ, a King,' Luke 23.2-3, 35, 37-38.* The royal-messianic interpretation suggested for the Jewish hearing finds support from Luke's redaction in the Roman trial which follows. Luke alone mentions the Jewish accusations brought before Pilate: 'We found this man misleading our nation and forbidding to pay taxes to Caesar and saying he himself is *Christ, a king*' (Lk. 23.2). The accusation against Jesus is one of sedition, claiming to be a king in opposition to Caesar (cf. v. 5; Acts 17.7). Similar accusations are found in the crucifixion scene, where the mocking of Jesus by the leaders as ὁ χριστὸς τοῦ θεοῦ ὁ ἐκλεκτός (v. 35) is followed by the jeers of the soldiers, 'If you are the king of the Jews, save yourself' (v. 37; perhaps adapted from the abuse of the soldiers in Mk 15.18).

As in the gospel tradition before Luke, the implication of these passages is that βασιλεύς is being misunderstood as a claim to earthly and political power in the present (cf. Acts 17.7). Does this mean Luke considers the title inappropriate for Jesus? Luke's introduction of the title at 19.38 suggests this is not quite right. It would be better to say that in the passion narrative Luke uses the title as the Gentile equivalent of χριστός and then indicates that *both* χριστός and βασιλεύς were misunderstood by Jesus' opponents—the former by the Jews and the latter by the Gentiles. For Jesus' followers, however, both titles may rightly be applied to him (Lk. 9.20; 19.38). Thus, while Luke uses these passages to affirm Jesus' innocence of wrongdoing and of sedition

of God', was inadequate for Luke since it failed to do justice to Luke's exaltation motif. Similarly, Creed, *St. Luke*, p. 278, writes, 'To Luke and his readers Son of God is the supreme title of Jesus which was capable of expressing his universal significance, whereas the use of "Christ" as a title naturally tended to become subordinate.' Neither writer seems to take into account Acts 2.36! (cf. 10.36).

1. So Conzelmann, *Theology*, pp. 84, 84-85 n. 3, pp. 140-41, 171. Conzelmann claims that by associating the title messiah with Son of God Luke interprets the former in a non-political sense. The Council are thus lying when they accuse Jesus of sedition (pp. 140-41).

(vv. 4, 14, 15, 22, 41, 47), in no way does he deny his royal status. Jesus is indeed Christ the king, the chosen one, but the nature of his kingship was misunderstood and rejected by his opponents. The irony of the crucifixion scene—present in all three Synoptics—is thus particularly striking in Luke. Jesus' opponents mock and reject his kingship and his divine election because he remains on the cross. Yet for Luke and his readers, Jesus' death is an essential part of his ascension to kingly power and authority. It is for suffering that the king has been chosen, and through suffering he assumes his heavenly throne.[1]

iii. *The King Receives a Kingdom, Luke 22.28-30.* The references to Jesus' royal status in the trial and crucifixion scenes recall Lk. 22.28-30, where Jesus refers to the kingship (βασιλεία) which the Father has appointed to him (v. 29). By virtue of this appointment, he confers on the twelve a share in that rule: 'that you may eat and drink at my table in my kingdom, and sit on thrones judging the twelve tribes of Israel' (v. 30). The parallel to v. 30b in Mt. 19.28 is quite different in form (no parallel to Lk. 22.29-30a) and occurs in a very different context.[2] It is inserted into Markan material (cf. Mk 10.26-30) and becomes part of Jesus' answer to Peter's question concerning the benefits the disciples will receive for following Jesus. Jesus' answer is *thoroughly eschatological* in its setting. The disciples are promised that 'in the new age (παλιγγενεσία), when the Son of man shall sit on his glorious throne, you who have followed me will sit on twelve thrones judging the twelve tribes of Israel'.

The Lukan setting of the last supper, together with the reference to Jesus' appointment of kingly power, indicates a marked change in emphasis. The passover meal (vv. 15-18), the institution of the Lord's supper (vv. 19-20), the passion prediction (vv. 21-23) and Jesus' discourse on servanthood (vv. 24-27) all point forward to the passion and its

1. Luke's emphasis on Jesus' present heavenly reign may also be seen in his account of the two criminals crucified with Jesus (Lk. 23.39-43). Jesus' response to the repentant criminal is probably meant not only to offer the man a place with him in Paradise but also to correct the man's assumption that Jesus will only receive his kingdom at the eschaton. Jesus assures him that his royal reign is imminent. Cf. J. Neyrey, *The Passion According to Luke* (1985), 13; E.E. Ellis, 'Present and Future Eschatology in Luke', *NTS* 12 (1965–66), pp. 35-36.

2. It has been suggested that the two sayings derive from different sources (Evans, *Saint Luke*, p. 798; Manson, *Sayings*, p. 216) or from different recensions of Q (Marshall, *Gospel of Luke*, p. 815).

consequences. In view of this context, Jesus' appointment (διατίθεμαι) to kingship must refer to his heavenly reign achieved through his death, resurrection, ascension and exaltation.[1] The reign promised to Jesus in Lk. 1.32-33 finds its fulfillment in his heavenly enthronement.

c. *The King's Role as Servant*

While Jesus is presented in the Lukan passion narrative as a king about to receive his throne, his actions and treatment by others are far from 'regal' in the normal sense of the term. A non-Christian reader of Luke's passion would almost certainly agree with Pilate that Jesus was innocent of the charges of royal pretension and sedition. The present discussion will seek to show that though Luke indeed designates Jesus as the Davidic king in his passion, he presents his role as that of the Isaianic servant. It is this role, not one of conquest or domination, which leads to his royal enthronement.

There is little doubt that Jesus is portrayed throughout Luke's passion as a suffering righteous figure, a type well established in Judaism.[2] The following discussion will attempt to demonstrate, however, that Luke moves beyond this general description to the more specific one of the Isaianic servant, the suffering righteous one *par excellence*.[3]

1. Cf. O'Toole, 'Acts 2.30', p. 253; Navone, *Themes of St. Luke*, pp. 90-91; R. Tannehill, 'A Study of the Theology of Luke-Acts', *ATR* 43 (1961), p. 202; *idem, Narrative Unity,* I, p. 269.

2. Cf. especially Wisdom 1–5. Psalms 22 and 69, both lament psalms of the innocent sufferer, are recalled in Luke's traditional references to the dividing up of Jesus' garments (Lk. 23.34; Ps. 22.19), the mocking call to save himself (23.35; Ps. 22.8-9) and the offer of sour wine (23.36; Ps. 69.21-22). Cf. Ps. 31.5 in Lk. 23.46. On Jesus as the suffering righteous one see Voss, *Christologie*, 99-130; Karris, *Luke: Artist and Theologian,* esp. pp. 79-115; *idem,* 'Luke 23.47 and the Lucan View of Jesus' Death', in *Reimaging the Death of the Lukan Jeus* (1990), pp. 68-78; and B.E. Beck, '"Imitatio Christi" and the Lucan Passion Narrative', in *Suffering and Martyrdom in the New Testament* (1981), pp. 43-47.

3. That Luke's passion narrative presents Jesus as the Isaianic servant is suggested by Seccombe, 'Luke and Isaiah', pp. 255-59; Rese, *Alttestamentliche Motive*, pp. 154ff.; Taylor, *Passion Narrative*, esp. pp. 137-38; Franklin, *Christ the Lord*, pp. 61-64; Martin, 'Salvation and Discipleship', p. 367; W.C. Larkin, 'Luke's Use of the Old Testament as a Key to his Soteriology', *JETS* 20 (1977), pp. 325-35; J. Green, 'The Death of Jesus, God's Servant', in *Reimaging the Death of the Lukan Jesus* (1990), pp. 1-28.

i. *Jesus as the Servant Elsewhere in Luke–Acts*. It has been demonstrated in previous discussion that from the start Luke describes Jesus' person and work with imagery drawn from Isaiah, and especially from the Isaianic servant songs: in the birth narrative Jesus, like the servant, is the light of revelation for the Gentiles (Lk. 1.79; 2.32; cf. Acts 13.47; Isa. 42.6-7; 49.6); at Nazareth he is the herald of Isa. 61.1-2—a figure Luke almost certainly identifies with the servant—who will be rejected by his own people (Lk. 4.16-30); at the baptism he is the one delighted in by God (Lk. 3.22; Isa. 42.1), and at the transfiguration and the cross God's 'chosen one' (Lk. 9.35; 23.35; Isa. 42.1). In his exorcisms Jesus is the servant-warrior of Yahweh who plunders Satan and distributes his spoils (Lk. 11.21-22; Isa. 49.24-25; 53.12). When these passages are viewed together with the allusions in Acts 3.13-14 (Isa. 52.13; 53.12) and the explicit citations in Lk. 22.37 (Isa. 53.12; see discussion below) and Acts 8.32-33 (Isa. 53.7-9), a convincing Lukan portrait emerges of Jesus as the Isaianic servant. As noted previously, this does not mean that Luke isolates these 'servant songs' from the rest of Isaiah, or that he considers the 'servant' to represent a distinct messianic figure. Rather, he associates Jesus with each of these Isaianic passages and identifies each as prophecies concerning 'the Christ'. They are thus related to one another (as well as to Isa. 9.1-6; 11.1ff.; 61.1ff.) as part of the total Isaianic portrait of eschatological salvation.

One problem with identifying Jesus as the servant in the passion narrative is the relative rarity of explicit references to this figure (the only citation is at Lk. 22.37). This, however, is not a decisive objection. It is characteristic of Luke to bring out the salvation-historical significance of Jesus through his narrative development rather than through repeated references to Old Testament prophecies fulfilled (as in Matthew). It is not surprising, then, that the servant portrait is found in the overall progression of Luke's narrative and in a preponderance of conceptual allusions rather than in frequent Old Testament citations. It is significant that elsewhere Luke uses Old Testament citations as summaries introducing Jesus' role which will be worked out in the subsequent narrative (Lk. 3.4-6; 4.17-19; 13.34-35).[1] As we shall see, this is exactly what he does in the passion narrative, with Lk. 22.37 introducing Jesus' role throughout. Vincent Taylor seems close to the mark when he

1. See Bock, *Proclamation*, p. 338 n. 203. Rese, *Alttestamentliche Motive*, p. 207, points out that two quotations from the lips of Jesus in Luke's Gospel summarize the mission of Christ, Isa. 61.1-2 in Lk. 4.18-19 and Isa. 53.12 in Lk. 22.37.

claims that Luke's passion narrative 'depicts Jesus as the Servant of the Lord without using the name'.[1]

Another possible problem relating to Luke's 'servant' identification is his apparent lack of interest in the atoning significance of Jesus' death. This question will be raised in the conclusions concerning Lukan soteriology in Chapter 7. Here I would merely suggest that it is the servant's pattern of suffering followed by vindication and exaltation that is Luke's most important interest. The atoning significance of his death, though not wholly absent in Luke–Acts, moves to the background.

ii. *Isaiah 53.12 in Luke 22.37*. The only citation from Isaiah 53 attributed to Jesus in the Gospels occurs at the end of Luke's farewell discourse (Luke 22.14-38). The whole of the last supper narrative points forward to Jesus' imminent passion: the last Passover meal before Jesus' suffering (vv. 15-18); the institution of the Lord's supper in remembrance of Jesus' death (vv. 19-20); the prediction of Judas' betrayal (vv. 21-23); the discourse on servant leadership epitomized in Jesus' own servanthood (vv. 24-27); the granting to the disciples of a share in Jesus' soon-to-be-realized kingly reign (vv. 28-30); the prediction of Peter's denial (vv. 31-34); and the changed conditions brought about by Jesus' imminent rejection (vv. 35-38). In this last, Jesus alters the earlier mission commands to take into account the increasingly hostile opposition the disciples will now face (vv. 35-36).[2] This new situation arises because of (γάρ) the Isaianic prophecy which must be fulfilled in Jesus: 'and he was numbered with trangressors' (καὶ μετὰ ἀνόμων ἐλογίσθη, v. 37b; Isa. 53.12). Though the citation is probably traditional,[3] it is given special prominence in Luke's narrative by its long and emphatic introductory formula, 'that which is written must be fulfilled in me' (τοῦτο τὸ γεγραμμένον δεῖ τελεσθῆναι ἐν ἐμοί), and by its climactic location in the farewell discourse.[4] The seemingly repetitious phrase which follows (καὶ γὰρ τὸ περὶ ἐμοῦ τέλος ἔχει) further emphasizes

1. Taylor, *Passion Narrative*, p. 138.

2. For various views on grammatical relationships of the purse, the bag and the sword see Marshall, *Gospel of Luke*, p. 825.

3. The citation is closer to the MT than the LXX at two points, the omission of the article and the use of μετά instead of ἐν (Jeremias, *TDNT*, V, p. 707 n. 404).

4. D.J. Moo, *The Old Testament in the Gospel Passion Narratives* (1983), pp. 132-33; Voss, *Christologie*, pp. 110-11; Larkin, 'Luke's Use', pp. 329-35; Bock, *Proclamation*, p. 138; Green, 'Death of Jesus', pp. 22-23.

that this Scripture which must be fulfilled in Jesus (δεῖ, v. 37a) is indeed now coming to fulfillment (v. 37c).[1] The Isaiah quote is thus framed on either side with statements highlighting the fulfillment of this Scripture in Jesus himself.

Minear's suggestion that being 'reckoned with transgressors' refers to the disciples is unlikely.[2] Luke may be thinking specifically of the criminals crucified with Jesus, though the quote's emphatic position in the narrative suggests a widening of the reference to the passion as a whole, throughout which Jesus is treated as a law-breaker.[3] The Isaiah quote may thus be viewed as an introductory statement *summarizing Jesus' scripturally-ordained role throughout the passion.*

It must be asked, however, whether Luke interprets the prophecy atomistically without regard to its Old Testament context or with the whole servant song (and other servant songs?) in view. If the latter, then Luke would here be placing Jesus' whole passion under the banner of the servant. The abundance of 'servant' allusions elsewhere in Luke–Acts makes this a likely possibility. If it can be shown that Luke elsewhere interprets Jesus' death with reference to the servant songs, and that his passion narrative contains conceptual parallels to the actions of the servant, this will provide further evidence for this view.

iii. *Isaiah 53.7-8 in Acts 8.32-33*. Though not part of the passion narrative, Philip's encounter with the Ethiopian eunuch in Acts 8 is particularly relevant at this point, as it provides the clearest evidence that Luke interprets Jesus' passion from the perspective of the Isaianic

1. Evans, *Saint Luke*, p. 806. Another possible meaning for the phrase is 'that which concerns me (= my life's work) is at an end' (Marshall, *Gospel of Luke*, p. 826; Manson, *Sayings*, p. 342).

2. P.S. Minear, 'A Note on Luke xxii 36', *NovT* 7 (1964), pp. 128-34; so also Wilson, *Gentiles*, p. 66; F.W. Danker, *Jesus and the New Age* (1972), p. 225. In Danker's second edition (1988), he alters his view, associating the 'transgressors' either with Barabbas and the criminals, or with the Romans as lawless men (Acts 2.23) (pp. 352-53). Fitzmyer, *Luke X–XXIV*, p. 1433, calls Minear's interpretation 'strange'; Marshall, *Gospel of Luke*, p. 826, says it 'misses the point completely'.

3. Moo, *Passion Narratives*, p. 137, points out that λογίζομαι, like its Hebrew counterpart, conveys the sense of 'being treated as' or 'classed with' (so BAGD, p. 476). His further assertion, however, that Luke cannot be here referring to the two criminals since he does not identify them as ἄνομοι, is unwarranted. Luke may have considered κακοῦργοι the best term to describe the criminals (hence his alteration of Mark's λῃσταί), but retained ἄνομοι here to stay with his Old Testament source.

servant. There can be little doubt that Luke understands the text the Ethiopian is reading (Isa. 53.7-8 LXX) as a *prophecy* concerning the suffering and death of Jesus.[1] As the messiah, Jesus fulfills the role of the Isaianic servant. This again places Jesus' whole passion under the heading of the servant. Or, to state it more correctly (i.e. in a more Lukan way), he places the whole passion under the Isaianic portrait of the suffering and vindication of the Christ.

iv. *The Passion Predictions (Luke 9.22, 43-45; 17.25; 18.31-32; 22.21-23; 24.6)*. D. Moo has argued convincingly that the repeated use of the verb παραδίδωμι in the Synoptic passion predictions is derived from Isaiah 53, where the verb occurs three times (see vv. 6, 12).[2] If the ultimate subject of the 'delivering up' in the passion predictions is God himself, as seems likely, then the fourth servant song presents itself as the natural background for this idea: 'For here, as nowhere else in the Old Testament, are the sufferings of the (Messianic) figure explicitly and consistently attributed to the activity of Yahweh.'[3] It is likely that Luke has identified these allusions in the traditional passion predictions in view of his intimate acquaintance with Isaiah LXX, his citation of Isa. 53.12c in Lk. 22.37 and his strong emphasis on the divine and scriptural necessity of the passion.

v. *Jesus on the Mount of Olives, Luke 22.39-46*. Luke's passion narrative, and especially his account of Jesus on the Mount of Olives, has often been said to portray Jesus in the role of a martyr.[4] While it is true

1. Bock's (*Proclamation*, p. 229) identification of the text as prophetic is surely correct over against Rese, *Alttestamentliche Motive*, p. 99, who claims it is merely hermeneutical.

2. Moo, *Passion Narratives*, pp. 92-96. Cf. Jeremias *TDNT*, V, pp. 710, 712-13; *idem, New Testament Theology*, pp. 286-87; Lindars, *New Testament Apologetic*, pp. 80-81; Lane, *Mark*, p. 337. The servant songs are not the only Old Testament allusions in the passion predictions. ἀποδοκιμάζω in Lk. 9.22 = Mk 8.31 and Lk. 17.25 probably alludes to the 'rejected stone' passage of Ps. 118.22 (Mk 12.10; Lk. 20.17; Mt. 21.42; 1 Pet. 2.4, 7).

3. Moo, *Passion Narratives*, pp. 95-96. Cf. Jeremias, *New Testament Theology*, p. 296.

4. That Luke's passion presents Jesus as a martyr was proposed by Dibelius, *From Tradition to Gospel*, pp. 201-202, and has been followed by Conzelmann, *Theology*, pp. 81, 83, 88-89, and others. It has been defended recently by C.H. Talbert, *Reading Luke: A Literary and Theological Commentary on the Third*

that the passion narrative contains martyrological features, it is doubtful whether this is Luke's central concern, either throughout the narrative or in Lk. 22.39-46 in particular.[1] J. Green provides a detailed redactional analysis of this passage and concludes that the point Luke most emphasizes is the divine necessity of Jesus' suffering and his unreserved submission to God's will. This emphasis, he points out, is not characteristic of the literature of martyrdom but does follow the conceptual pattern of the Isaianic servant. Five features in the text suggest this identification:[2] (1) Jesus, like the servant, fulfills his mission through suffering (Isa. 49.4; 50.5-6; 52.13–53.12). (2) More particularly, there is an emphasis on the necessity of Jesus' suffering (Isa. 52.13–53.12). (3) Jesus' response to God is that of willing obedience similar to that which characterizes the servant (Isa. 50.4-5, 7; 52.13–53.12). (4) Jesus follows the will of God as one chosen for this fate; the servant, too, is chosen to accomplish God's redemptive work (Isa. 42.1; 50.5, 6; 52.13–53.12). (5) The idea of Jesus' receiving the aid of God's messenger reflects God's strengthening of his servant (Isa. 41.10; 42.6—ἐνισχύω; 49.5; 50.7, 9). When taken individually these points are too general to be wholly convincing. However, when viewed together and in the context of Luke's passion as a whole, they can be seen to carry forward the servant idea which permeates the narrative. I would therefore agree with Green's conclusion that the final picture Luke produces in this episode 'is wholly consistent

Gospel (1982), pp. 221-24; *idem,* 'Martyrdom in Luke-Acts and the Lukan Social Ethic', in *Political Issues in Luke–Acts* (1983), pp. 99-110.

1. Cf. Seccombe, 'Luke and Isaiah', p. 257; Karris, 'Luke 23.47', pp. 71-73; D. Senior, *The Passion of Jesus in the Gospel of Luke* (1989), pp. 145-46 n. 37; F.G. Untergassmair, *Kreuzweg und Kreuzigung Jesu* (1980), pp. 156-71; and especially the balanced perspective of Beck, '"Imitatio Christi"', pp. 28-47. Beck examines the data and points out that 'if martyrdom is a theme in Luke's narrative it is not the only one. The key as he himself provides it, is to be found in the Messiahship of Jesus and the scriptural necessity that as such he must suffer (cf. 24.7, 25-7, 44-9).' Jesus' suffering is not just the obedience of one martyr among many but is the specific vocation of the messiah, the elect one (p. 36). Beck rejects the Isaianic servant as Luke's example, following instead the general model of the suffering righteous figure in Judaism. He thus finds two strands in Luke's passion, one unique and messianic and the other typical and exemplary.

2. J.B. Green, 'Jesus on the Mount of Olives (Luke 22.39-46): Tradition and Theology', *JSNT* 26 (1986), pp. 29-48, esp. 38, 41-43. On the other hand, Green overly downplays the martyrological features in Luke's text; not all of his arguments (pp. 39-41) are convincing.

with his otherwise amply attested interest in portraying Jesus as the Servant of the Lord'.[1]

vi. *The Trial and Crucifixion: Jesus as ὁ δίκαιος*. The motif of Jesus' innocence, present in all the Gospels, becomes in Luke a central theme of the trial and crucifixion.[2] Pilate four times declares that he has found no guilt (αἴτιον) in Jesus (23.4, 14, 15, 22; cf. Acts 13.28) and Herod confirms this judgment (23.15). The repentant criminal also claims Jesus has done nothing wrong (ἄτοπος, 23.41), and there are implicit declarations of Jesus' innocence in his contrast with Barabbas, who is guilty of insurrection and murder (23.25; Acts 3.14-15), and in the multitudes who 'beat their breasts' as they return home—suggesting a great injustice has been done (23.48).

In view of these references, it seems likely that the climactic cry of the centurion that Jesus is δίκαιος (23.47, contrast Mark's υἱὸς θεοῦ) carries with it the idea of political innocence. On the other hand, though δίκαιος may occasionally refer merely to the absence of guilt,[3] elsewhere

1. Green, 'Mount of Olives', p. 43; cf. W.J. Larkin, 'The Old Testament Background of Luke XXII. 43-44', *NTS* (1979), pp. 250-54, who presents a number of similar arguments for a servant identification.

2. This point is made by many commentators. See especially Cadbury, *Making of Luke–Acts*, pp. 309-10; G.D. Kilpatrick, 'A Theme of the Lucan Passion Story and Luke xxxiii.47', *JTS* 43 (1942), pp. 34-36; R.F. O'Toole, 'Luke's Position on Politics and Society', in *Political Issues in Luke–Acts* (1983), p. 6; Neyrey, *Passion*, pp. 163-64; J.T. Carroll, 'Luke's Crucifixion Scene', in *Reimaging the Death of the Lukan Jesus* (1990), pp. 116-18. On the debated question of a political apologetic in Luke-Acts and especially in the passion narrative, see R.J. Cassidy, *Jesus, Politics and Society: A Study of Luke's Gospel* (1978), esp. pp. 128-30, and the various articles in *Political Issues in Luke–Acts* (eds. R.J. Cassidy and P.J. Scharper; 1983). While the political innocence of Jesus (and of his followers) before Rome may play a part in Luke's purpose, I would agree in general with D. Schmidt, 'Luke's 'Innocent' Jesus: A Scriptural Apologetic', in *Political Issues in Luke–Acts* (1983), pp. 111-21, that Luke's interest in the 'innocence' theme arises primarily from a scriptural rather than a political apologetic. Luke seeks to prove that, though Jesus was punished as a law-breaker, he was innocent and righteous, just as the Scripture predicted the messiah would be (Isa. 53.9, 11-12).

3. See the references in Kilpatrick, 'A Theme of the Lukan Passion Story', pp. 34-36. These are disputed by R.P.C. Hanson, 'Does δίκαιος in Luke xxiii.47 Explode the Proto-Luke Hypothesis?', *Hermathena* 60 (1942), pp. 74-78; cited by Beck, '"Imitatio Christi"', p. 42.

in Luke it always carries the positive sense of 'righteous' (cf. 23.50).[1] Indeed, the reference to the centurion 'glorifying God' would be strange if he is merely recognizing Jesus' innocence. Why would he praise God for the execution of an innocent man?[2] The centurion's response almost certainly carries the sense of positive righteousness and arises from Jesus' words expressing trust in God in the face of death (Lk. 23.34, 43, 46).[3] If this is the case, it is not unlikely that Luke is here implicitly designating Jesus as the innocent and righteous servant of Yahweh of Isa. 52.13–53.12 (cf. 53.11: δίκαιος). Various factors point in this direction:

(1) In Acts 3.13-16 Peter identifies Jesus as δίκαιος in a context strongly influenced by the fourth servant song. The whole conceptual framework of the passage points in this direction, with verbal parallels present in the glorification (ἐδόξαζεν, v. 13; Isa. 52.13), the 'delivering up' (παρεδώκατε, v. 13; Isa. 53.6, 12) and the righteous suffering (δίκαιον, v. 14; Isa. 53.11) of God's 'servant' (τὸν παῖδα αὐτοῦ, v. 13; Isa. 52.13).[4]

(2) The centurion's cry implicitly contrasts Jesus with those who *are* guilty, the two criminals and Barabbas (cf. Acts 3.14). The reader would naturally be reminded of Jesus' quote from Isa. 53.12 in Lk. 22.37, that he will be 'reckoned with transgressors'. Consequently, it is as ὁ δίκαιος that Jesus fulfills the prophecy of Isa. 53.12. A similar contrast between Jesus ὁ δίκαιος and Barabbas the murderer is made in Acts 3.14-15.

(3) Jesus is ironically mocked as the 'elect one' on the cross (Lk. 23.35), a title which, as we have seen, probably alludes to Isa. 42.1 (with royal implications). Assuming that Luke associates the 'servant' figures of Isa. 42.1 and Isaiah 52.13, the close connection between Jesus as ὁ ἐκλεκτός (v. 35) and as ὁ δίκαιος (v. 47; cf. 23.4, 14, 15, 22)

1. Positive righteousness must also be intended in the statement of the repentant criminal in v. 41 since he expects Jesus' righteousness to be vindicated by God (v. 42). Cf. Larkin, 'Luke's Use', p. 334.

2. Beck, '"Imitatio Christi"', p. 42. Beck points out, that although unconscious rather than active, praise to God could perhaps be intended, this meaning is unusual for Luke and hence unlikely.

3. Though it is not certain that for Luke the centurion is making a Christian confession (he may merely be acknowledging that God is at work in this righteous man, cf. Acts 13.48), praising and glorifying God in Luke *generally* means a positive expression of faith in God's saving power (Lk. 2.20; 5.25-26; 7.16; 13.13; 17.15; 18.43; Acts 4.21; 11.18; 21.20). Cf. Karris, *Luke: Artist and Theologian*, p. 110; Senior, *Passion*, pp. 146-47; Green, 'The Death of Jesus', p. 19.

4. Cf. Green, 'The Death of Jesus', pp. 20-21.

makes a servant allusion in the latter more likely.

(4) Finally, the reference to Jesus' silence in 23.9 adds support to this view. Though Luke abbreviates the opening of the Jewish trial and so omits the reference to Jesus' silence at Mk 14.60-61, he retains the reference in Lk. 23.9 (cf. Mk 15.5). Though not a *verbal* allusion in Luke or the other Gospels, the motif of silent endurance of suffering follows the same conceptual pattern of the servant, who, though oppressed and afflicted 'did not open his mouth' (Isa. 53.7). That Luke has interpreted Jesus' silence as a fulfillment of these verses is rendered more likely by his explicit citation of Isa. 53.7-8 in Acts 8.32-33, confirming that he was both aware of this prophecy and applied it to Jesus' suffering and death.[1]

vii. *The Exalted Servant.* A final piece of evidence that Luke seeks to present Jesus in the role of the Isaianic servant in his passion (and elsewhere) is his strong emphasis on Jesus' exaltation as his decisive vindication by God. The vindication of the servant is mentioned in the second and third servant songs (49.4; 50.8-9), and is especially prominent in the fourth, where after suffering the righteous servant 'will cause many to inherit'[2] and will 'divide the spoils of the mighty' (53.11-12 LXX; cf. Lk. 11.21-22). That this vindication is central to the passage is confirmed by the fact that the song begins with it (Isa. 52.13). The servant's role is not just to suffer but also to be 'exalted' (ὑψωθήσεται) and 'exceedingly glorified' (δοξασθήσεται σφόδρα). It is significant that Luke describes Jesus' vindication as being 'glorified' (ἐδόξασεν, Acts 3.13), entering into his 'glory' (δόξα, Lk. 24.26; cf. 9.32) and being 'exalted' to the right hand of God (ὑψόω, Acts 2.34; 5.31). Though this last is of course taken from Ps. 110.1 rather than Isa. 52.13,

1. Another possible conceptual allusion to the servant occurs in Jesus' prayer in Lk. 23.34a, which may refer to Isa. 53.12 where the servant makes intercession for transgressors. The textual uncertainty of the passage in Luke, together with the allusion's dependence on the Hebrew text, makes an argument based on this text less than compelling. On the textual problem see Metzger, *Textual Commentary*, p. 180; Marshall, *Gospel of Luke*, pp. 867-68.

2. See R.R. Ottley, tr. and ed., *The Book of Isaiah According to the Septuagint* (1904; 1906), I, p. 279; II, p. 348, for this translation. The MT has, 'I will allot him a portion with the great.' The LXX may have influenced Luke, who elsewhere refers to Jesus granting the disciples their inheritance in the kingdom (Lk. 22.29-30). The LXX also speaks of the Lord justifying 'the just one who serves many well' instead of the MT's 'my just servant will justify the many' (v. 11).

the pattern of 'suffering-then-vindication' presented by Luke in all these passages follows the conceptual pattern of Isa. 52.13ff. It is not unlikely that the fourth servant song serves for Luke as an interpretive bridge to explain the relationship between Jesus' suffering and his exaltation as the Davidic king (Ps. 110.1). The king suffers as the *ebed Yahweh* on the way to exaltation-enthronement at God's right hand.

In conclusion, though not all of these allusions carry equal weight, when viewed together and in the context of Luke–Acts as a whole, a convincing portrait of Jesus as the Isaianic servant is attained. When this perspective is combined with the royal features emphasized in the narrative, it is safe to conclude that Luke presents Jesus as the Davidic heir who achieves his kingly reign through suffering as the Isaianic servant. As we have seen, these two emphases come together most clearly in the last supper narrative and in the crucifixion scene. In the former, Jesus promises the disciples that they will have a share in the kingdom he is about to be appointed by the Father (Lk. 22.28-30). This reign will be achieved, however, only when that which is written about him is fulfilled, namely, 'that he was numbered with the transgressors' (Lk. 22.37; Isa. 53.12). On the cross, then, Jesus is the Christ, the king of the Jews, who suffers as the righteous and 'elect' servant of God (Lk. 23.35-37, 47; Isa. 42.1; 53.11 LXX).

7. *Conclusion*

From the first passion prediction onwards, the suffering role of the Christ becomes a prominent theme in Luke's Gospel. This emphasis is apparent in the transfiguration account, which Luke interprets as a preview of Jesus' exaltation glory achieved through suffering. By redacting in favour of exodus imagery and describing Jesus' Jerusalem dénouement as an ἔξοδος, Luke implies that Jesus is not only the royal messiah and Isaianic servant but also a prophet like Moses about to fulfill a 'new exodus' in Jerusalem. While a number of scholars have proposed that this exodus imagery introduces the Lukan travel narrative as a kind of midrash on the book of Deuteronomy, we have found insufficient evidence to draw a convincing connection between the individual passages of the travel narrative and those of Deuteronomy. Nor can it be sustained that the portrait of Jesus in the travel narrative (or in Luke–Acts as a whole) parallels the pattern of Moses' career in Deuteronomy. A more likely background for Luke's redaction may be found in the

Old Testament prophets, and especially Isaiah, where the concept of an *eschatological new exodus* was already well developed. In the Book of Consolation (Isa. 40-55), the eschatological return of the people from exile is pictured as a new exodus to the promised land. While the early chapters (40–48) portray Cyrus as Yahweh's agent in this return, in the later ones (49–55) the enigmatic servant apparently replaces Cyrus, accomplishing God's salvation through his suffering role. When Isaiah is read as a unity, moreover, an even broader portrait of the new exodus emerges. In Isaiah 11 (and elsewhere in the Prophets) the eschatological regathering, or new exodus, is associated with the longed-for restoration of the Davidic throne (a connection which appears already in the foundational promise of 2 Sam. 7.10). In Isa. 11.1-16, the coming Davidic heir is the 'standard' to which the nations rally in the new exodus restoration. The Davidic promise tradition here encompasses the new exodus restoration of God's people (cf. *Pss. Sol.* 11.2-5; 17.21-46; *4 Ezra* 13.9-48; *Targ. Ket.* Lam. 2.22).[1]

Isaiah's depiction of eschatological salvation shows particular affinity with Luke's eschatological and christological presentations. Luke begins his Gospel by presenting Jesus as the descendant of David destined to reign forever on the throne of his father (Lk. 1.27, 32-33; cf. Isa. 7.14; 9.1-7; 11.1-10). He is Yahweh's anointed, the Lord and saviour from David's house bringing light to the Gentiles and 'consolation' to Israel (Lk. 1.69-70, 78-79; 2.4, 11, 25-26, 30-32, 38; cf. Isa. 40.1ff.; 42.6; 49.6; 52.9-10). The account of Jesus' public ministry is subsequently introduced with the inaugural new exodus announcement from Isaiah: a way is prepared in the wilderness for the new exodus return of the Lord; all humankind will see the salvation of God (Lk. 3.4-5; Isa. 40.3-5). The Isaianic new exodus, while 'fulfilled' by Jesus in the decisive events in

1. Since, throughout its various trajectories in the Old Testament and Judaism, the 'everlasting covenant' made to David always includes the promise of salvation benefits not only for the dynasty but also for God's people as a whole, and since frequently, as we have seen, these benefits are described as a new exodus restoration, it would be possible to interpret the whole 'way' of Jesus in Luke–Acts as a fulfillment of the promises made to David. Of course one can only speculate as to whether Luke would have conceived of the Davidic promise tradition so broadly. What is clear is that he views the Old Testament promises and covenants as a unity, and that, to a certain extent, he views these promises as epitomized in the Davidic promise. On the other hand, it is surely going too far to suggest that Luke—with his diverse and multi-faceted Old Testament presentation—subsumes all other Old Testament promises under this one heading.

Jerusalem, may thus be seen to encompass the whole 'way' of Jesus from his public appearance onward.

This Isaianic influence continues throughout the preparatory and inaugural stages of Jesus' ministry. In the baptism account, royal-messianic and servant allusions come together in the divine voice from heaven; in the genealogy, Jesus' legitimate Davidic descent is verified; and in the temptation, Jesus represents 'true Israel' when he overcomes the wilderness temptations to which Israel in the first exodus succumbed. Jesus' role as Isaianic eschatological deliverer is confirmed in the programmatic Nazareth sermon, where Jesus introduces his messianic ministry as that of the herald of Isaiah 61, a figure whose role parallels those of the Isaianic servant and the coming Davidic king. Jesus announces that he has been anointed by the Spirit to proclaim the arrival of the time of eschatological salvation and to accomplish the signs which accompany it: preaching good news to the poor, setting free the oppressed, healing the sick, raising the dead (Lk. 4.18-19; 7.22; cf. Isa. 61.1-2; 29.18-19; 35.5-7; 26.18-19). The subsequent Gospel narrative presents Jesus as carrying out these Isaianic signs of eschatological salvation.

Jesus' suffering role, alluded to in Lk. 2.34 and foreshadowed in the events at Nazareth (Lk. 4.24-30), is developed in earnest following Peter's confession in 9.20. At his transfiguration Jesus is portrayed as royal messiah, Isaianic servant and prophet like Moses who will fulfill a new exodus in Jerusalem. While not the decisive moment of suffering, the travel narrative which follows represents the period of Jesus' heightened resolve to proceed to his Jerusalem goal where he will suffer and die. When Jesus approaches Jerusalem, he is portrayed as the Davidic king about to achieve his royal reign. Yet Jesus' kingdom will not be established physically on earth at his entrance into Jerusalem. Rather, following his suffering, he will be exalted and enthroned at God's right hand in heaven, whence he will return to consummate the kingdom and to reward and to judge. Luke's redaction in the passion narrative carries these themes forward, emphasizing not only Jesus' royal status but also his God-ordained role as the suffering servant of Yahweh. Though Jesus is indeed the king, the rightful heir to the throne of Israel, he must first suffer on the way to his exaltation-enthronement at God's right hand.

In the past, scholars have tended to treat the Mosaic and Davidic features in Luke's Christology separately and in relative isolation from one another. While some argue that the Mosaic features are merely traditional, retained but left undeveloped by Luke,[1] others claim that a Mosaic-prophet Christology underlies and implicitly controls the Gospel presentation. Those who take this latter view generally consider the Davidic features in Luke's narrative to be traditional, and developed by Luke only with regard to Jesus' exaltation-enthronement. There has been little attempt to integrate Luke's Mosaic and Davidic christologies into a coherent whole. In the above discussion I have suggested that these features come together in Isaiah's portrait of eschatological salvation. When Isaiah is read as a unity, the eschatological saviour is at the same time Davidic king, suffering servant of Yahweh and eschatological prophet who, like Moses, speaks God's word and leads his people on a new exodus to their promised salvation. Luke's frequent description of the arrival of salvation in Isaianic terms and his explicit identification of Jesus as the eschatological saviour suggests that this Isaianic portrait provides an important interpretive key for understanding Luke's christological purpose and plan.

1. Cf. Fitzmyer, *Luke I–IX*, p. 793: 'Certainly, Jesus as a new Moses is not a strong motif in the Lucan Gospel, as it is in Matthew; if it is present here, it is inherited from the tradition and finds little development of it [*sic*] in the rest of the Lucan writings.'

Chapter 7

CONCLUSION

1. *Summary and Conclusions*

This study has examined one theme within Luke's 'proclamation from prophecy and pattern' motif, that of the coming king from the line of David. To determine the background to this theme, in Chapter 2 the Davidic promise tradition was examined in its first-century context of meaning. While the diverse writings of first-century Judaism exhibit a range of eschatological expectations and speculations, we have found evidence of widespread and growing hope for a coming Davidic deliverer. Sometimes this figure is described as a new 'David', other times as a Davidic descendant—a 'seed' or 'shoot' of David. In either case the essential hope is the same: a deliverer modelled after David, Israel's greatest king, who will restore the nation and reign with justice and righteousness. While occasionally this figure appears on the scene after God has accomplished salvation, in the later writings in particular he takes a more prominent and executive role. In the *Psalms of Solomon,* the Qumran scrolls, the apocalyptic literature and some of the early rabbinic material, the king is an active agent of deliverance, destroying the wicked, judging the nations and ruling in judgment and righteousness. Some writings place special stress on his Davidic ancestry, generally in opposition to the royal pretensions of the Hasmoneans or Herodians. Yet throughout it is the fact of God's deliverance rather than the identity of the deliverer which is of primary importance. The most widely utilized promise tradition text is Isaiah 11, where the Spirit-endowed 'shoot of Jesse'—full of wisdom, knowledge, counsel and strength—will judge the poor and afflicted with justice and destroy the wicked with the rod of his mouth and the breath of his lips. In short, a mediating position has been reached between the traditional view that messianic expectations were quite fixed by the first century, and the more recent perspective that speculation was so diverse as to render the 'messianic hope' a fiction. At the turn of the Christian era Davidic hope was widespread and *relatively* stable within a broader context of eschatological diversity.

The pre-Pauline formula in Rom. 1.3-4 confirms that from an early period Christians took up the Davidic promise tradition as an aid in explaining the salvation-historical significance of Jesus the messiah. In their case, Davidic descent, divine sonship and royal exaltation language were the most utilized aspects of the promise tradition. Jesus was the promised seed of David, now 'raised up' as Son of God in fulfillment of Scripture. Despite the importance of this theme, the evidence of the Pauline letters and the Gospel of Mark suggests that in some communities Jesus' Davidic messiahship (while probably assumed) played a subordinate role to other christological conceptions. This probably resulted from the widening rift with the synagogue, when the need to defend Jesus' messianic status was no longer pressing.

From the study of the Davidic promise tradition in its first-century setting, attention was turned to Luke's use of this theme in his two-volume work. In Chapter 3 the birth narrative was found to be thoroughly Lukan in language, style and theology, introducing themes of importance for Luke and serving as an introduction to the whole of his two-volume work. It is significant, then, that Davidic messianism plays a central role in the Christology of these two chapters. Of the nativity's five major christological sections, three are explicitly royal-Davidic and two are implicitly so. In the first direct reference to Jesus in the Gospel, Luke introduces his main character as the Son of the Most High who will reign forever on the throne of his father David (Lk. 1.32-33). He is the Lord's anointed (2.26), the horn of salvation from David's house (1.69), the Davidic ἀνατολή who will visit from on high (1.78-79) and the eschatological saviour who is Christ the Lord (2.11). Further, Luke shows particular interest in Jesus' Davidic ancestry (1.27, 32, 69; 2.4, 11; cf. 3.31), and emphasizes the Davidic connection of his Bethlehem birthplace (the 'city of David'; 2.4, 11).

Through the use of Septuagintal language and style, hymnic material recalling the Psalms, and Old Testament typological parallels, Luke grounds his narrative firmly in an Old Testament 'promise' context. Moving from the fine Greek literary style of the prologue the reader enters the Semitic world of the Greek Old Testament. Devout Jews faithfully practice their ancestral religion and anxiously await the coming of the messiah. The statements of the promise—particularly those in the hymns—retain strong nationalistic overtones characteristic of contemporary Jewish expectations (1.32-33; 50-55; 68-75). This strong promise setting would appear to serve two purposes. First, it links the Jesus event firmly to its Old Testament roots. If Jesus' coming is the fulfillment of Jewish hopes and expectations, then Christianity is the legitimate heir of the covenants and promises made to the fathers. Secondly, it implicitly raises the question of the nature of the fulfillment of the promise. If Jesus did not establish the Davidic throne in Jerusalem, how can he be the messianic king of the Jews? If many in Israel are presently rejecting the message, and if Gentiles instead are receiving the salvation benefits, how can it be that Israel's promised salvation has arrived? While solutions to these questions are hinted at in the oracles of Simeon, full answers await the subsequent narrative development.

Chapter 4 turned to the speeches in Acts, generally considered to provide special insight into Luke's christological perspective. It is significant that the keynote addresses of three of the most important characters in Acts are strongly royal-Davidic in perspective. In Peter's Pentecost speech (Acts 2.14-40)—representing for Luke the Petrine (and hence the apostolic) gospel to the Jews—the leader of the apostolic band cites Pss. 16.8-11 and 110.1 to demonstrate that Jesus' resurrection and exaltation were prophesied in Scripture and together represent the fulfillment of the 'oath' God swore to David to seat one of his descendants upon his throne (Ps. 132.11). Gabriel's prophecy of Lk. 1.32-33 finds its fulfillment in Jesus' resurrection and exaltation-enthronement at the right hand of God. A programmatic role must also be assigned to Paul's sermon at Pisidian-Antioch (Acts 13.14-48). As the inaugural sermon on Paul's first missionary journey and the only synagogue sermon recorded in Acts, this address represents Luke's version of the Pauline kerygma to Jews and God-fearers. After summarizing the history of Israel to David, Paul presents Jesus as the saviour from David's seed raised up to deliver his people. This 'raising up' probably carries a two-fold significance: In his whole life, death, resurrection and exaltation, God has raised up Jesus to be Israel's saviour—the messianic king and Son of God (Ps. 2.7). At his resurrection, then, Jesus was raised to incorruptible life (Ps. 16.10), resulting in an eternal reign and universal authority. By virtue of this status, he pours out salvation blessings upon God's people (Isa. 55.3). Finally, in James' crucial decision at the Council of Jerusalem (15.1-29)—the structural and theological centre of Acts—the leader of the Jerusalem church confirms that all along it was part of God's plan to bring Gentiles into the community of the saved. As proof of this he cites Amos 9.11-13, where the prophet predicts that the Davidic dynasty, the fallen 'hut of David', would be rebuilt, 'so that the rest of mankind may seek the Lord'. The implication is that the Gentile mission is in fulfillment of Scripture and directly proceeds from the re-establishment of the Davidic throne through Jesus the messiah.

The questions implicitly raised by the nationalistic tone of the nativity thus find their answers in Acts as the Old Testament prophecies are fulfilled: (1) Jesus receives his messianic throne not in Jerusalem but at his exaltation-enthronement at the right hand of God. (2) True to Simeon's prophecy, Jesus the messiah causes the rise and fall of many in Israel; he is a sign provoking opposition. While a remnant within Israel remains faithful and becomes the foundation of the messianic community, the majority reject their messiah and so face judgment. This does not negate the plan of God, however; it was predicted in Scripture and is in line with Israel's history as a stubborn and resistant people (Acts 13.40-41 = Hab. 1.5; Acts 28.26, 27 = Isa. 6.9-10). (3) Nor is Gentile reception of the Gospel an aberration, since it too was prophesied in Scripture. All along it was God's plan that the messiah would be a 'light to the Gentiles' (Acts 13.47 = Isa. 49.6; cf. Acts 15.16-18 = Amos 9.11-12). Luke's *apologia* with regard to the evangelization of the Gentiles flows in two directions at once. The messianic prophecies demonstrate the legitimacy of the Gentile mission and the Gentile mission in turn confirms that the prophecies have been fulfilled and that Jesus is the messiah.[1]

Together Chapters 3 and 4 achieved an important result: Luke has a tendency to introduce Davidic messianism into christological sections which are introductory and programmatic for his two-volume work. This suggests that this theme plays a central role in Luke's Old Testament Christology. Such a conclusion, however, raises an enigma for Luke–Acts as a whole. There is a growing trend in New Testament scholarship to regard Luke's Christology—especially as presented in the Gospel—as *essentially* prophetic. Not only is Jesus frequently portrayed in prophetic terms but Luke explicitly identifies him as a prophet and more specifically as the eschatological prophet like Moses. Those who emphasize this aspect of Jesus' identity often regard Davidic messianism as merely traditional (and hence unimportant) or as an exaltation category which has little to do with Jesus' earthly ministry.

With this question in view, Chapters 5 and 6 turned to the Gospel

1. So especially Dupont, *Salvation of the Gentiles*, p. 33.

narrative, which at first sight appears to give little emphasis to royal-messianic themes. In the Nazareth sermon, which serves as a programmatic introduction and outline to the rest of the Gospel, Jesus is clearly portrayed as a prophet. By reading Isa. 61.1-2 (58.6) and declaring that 'Today, this scripture is fulfilled in your hearing,' Jesus identifies himself as the eschatological herald anointed by the Spirit to preach good news to the poor, to bring release to captives and sight to the blind, and to announce the arrival of the time of salvation—the favorable year of the Lord. He then alludes to his rejection in terms of the common fate of the prophets and implicitly compares his own ministry to 'outsiders' with those of the prophets Elijah and Elisha.

While this portrayal confirms that Luke views Jesus as a prophet, it does not rule out royal-messianic categories. Indeed, there is remarkable thematic and verbal correspondence between the prophet-herald of Isaiah 61, the servant of the Isaianic servant songs and the coming Davidic king of Isaiah 9 and 11. The coming king, like the servant and/or the herald, is God's anointed envoy, endowed with the Spirit of God to establish judgment and righteousness. He will bring comfort to the poor and downtrodden and will be a light to the nations, dispelling 'darkness' by releasing prisoners and freeing the oppressed. When Isaiah is read as a unity, the eschatological deliverer is at the same time Davidic king, suffering servant of Yahweh and eschatological prophet.

Luke's christological presentation remarkably parallels this Isaianic portrait. In the birth narrative Luke introduces Jesus as the coming Davidic king; he previews his public ministry with the 'new exodus' announcement of Isa. 40.3-5 (Lk. 3.4-6), and he defines that ministry in terms of the herald of Isa. 61.1-2 (Lk. 4.18-21). Allusions to Isaiah, particularly the servant songs, permeate Luke's narrative, and in Lk. 22.37 and Acts 8.32-33 Jesus is explicitly identified with the suffering 'servant' of Isaiah 53. For Luke the Christ is at the same time messianic king, prophet (like Moses) and suffering servant of Yahweh. This christological synthesis also explains why Luke sets the Nazareth sermon—which identifies Jesus as a *prophet*—in the context of the inauguration of a royal-messianic ministry (cf. Lk. 1-2; 3.15-16, 22, 31; 4.1-12, 41). The messiah (like David and Moses before him) is both prophet and king. He is not only the herald of salvation but also its executor, announcing *and* bringing to fulfillment the eschatological 'year' of God's favour.

This christological presentation helps to explain the role of the Nazareth sermon in the Gospel narrative as a whole. In the first half of the sermon (vv. 18-21), Jesus announces the arrival of the time of salvation and the inauguration of a preaching and healing ministry. By linking Jesus' Davidic messiahship to the wider context of Isaianic eschatological salvation, Luke demonstrates that Jesus' words and deeds fulfill the scripturally ordained role of the Christ. This theme reaches a climax in the confession of Peter in Lk. 9.20, where the chief disciple recognizes that the deeds Jesus has been performing are the deeds of the Christ. In the second part of the sermon (vv. 22-30), Jesus first predicts and then experiences rejection by his own people, foreshadowing his Jerusalem fate. This theme is developed in earnest starting with Jesus' first passion prediction and then throughout the travel narrative. It reaches a climax in ch. 24 with the surprising revelation that all along it was God's plan than his *Christ* would suffer. While in all previous predictions Jesus' rejection is described in terms of a prophet or the Son of man, from this point onward it becomes the suffering of *the Christ.* This gives the narrative of ch. 24 a sense of surprise and revelation. Jesus' death does not negate the claims of the birth narrative that Jesus is the Christ but rather confirms them. The prophet-like suffering of the messianic king was prophesied in Scripture and was a necessary stage on the 'way' to his glorious enthronement at God's right hand. The convergence of christological themes implicit in the Nazareth sermon is thus openly revealed in Luke 24 and the early chapters of Acts.

In Chapter 6 the second major theme of the Gospel—Jesus' Jerusalem dénouement—was examined in more detail. Luke's transfiguration account, which contains royal-messianic, servant and Moses/Sinai imagery, serves as a preview of Jesus' 'exodus' in Jerusalem (Lk. 9.31). While some have claimed that the Lukan travel narrative is a Christian midrash on the book of Deuteronomy and that Jesus is depicted throughout as the prophet like Moses leading a new exodus, I have suggested that the *primary* Old Testament model for Luke's exodus motif is not the first exodus but the eschatological *new* exodus predicted in Isaiah and the prophets. Such a suggestion not only fits well with Luke's eschatological perspective and his particular interest in Isaiah but is also in line with his distinctive prophet-servant-king Christology. In both Luke and Isaiah the eschatological deliverer may be viewed as the Davidic king who (like Moses) leads an eschatological new exodus of God's people through suffering as the servant of Yahweh.

This christological interpretation finds support in the account of Jesus' final approach to Jerusalem and in the passion narrative. As Jesus draws near to the capital city and the climax of his 'exodus', he is portrayed as a royal-Davidic figure—the son of David hailed as 'king' by his followers. Yet this is not the conquering warrior-king of traditional expectations but the compassionate Son of man seeking and saving the lost, and the humble and righteous king of Zech. 9.9-10 speaking peace to the nations. As the parable of the pounds indicates, he will not receive his throne at his entrance into Jerusalem but in a 'distant country', from whence he will return to reward and to judge. In the passion narrative which follows, Jesus appears as both king and suffering servant. At the last supper, he speaks of the kingdom he has been granted by the Father, a kingdom which will be achieved when the scripture has been fulfilled: '...and he was numbered with transgressors' (Isa. 53.12). In the trial and crucifixion scenes Jesus is repeatedly mocked as 'king', and he dies as the righteous and innocent one. There is heavy irony here. In the eyes of his opponents, Jesus' crucifixion nullifies the claim that he is the 'Christ of God', the chosen one. Yet all along it was part of God's plan that his Christ would suffer before entering his glory. It is through suffering as the servant that Jesus fulfills the Scripture and accomplishes the messianic task. Now raised from the dead and enthroned as Lord at God's right hand, he pours out salvation blessings on all who will repent and believe.

In short, a plausible synthesis has been proposed which helps to explain the unity and diversity of Luke's Old Testament Christology. Luke links the Jesus event particularly to the Isaianic portrait of eschatological salvation, where the messianic deliverer is at the same time prophet, servant and king. In this way, he is able to show that Jesus is the Christ promised in Scripture and that though his life, death, resurrection and exaltation he has fulfilled the promises made to the fathers.

2. *Implications for Lukan Purpose and Theology and Suggestions for Further Research*

Because of the constraints of space, discussion has been limited almost exclusively to christological issues. Yet Luke's use of the Davidic promise tradition has wider implications for his theology, particularly with reference to issues of ecclesiology, eschatology and soteriology. The following discussion will first seek to relate the conclusions of the present work to Luke's wider purpose in Luke–Acts and will then draw out some further implications for Lukan theology, suggesting in turn promising areas for further research.

a. *The Davidic Messiah and Lukan Purpose*

Though Luke's main aim in writing may not be christological *per se*, his christological assertions must be seen to play a positive role in the achievement of his wider purpose(s).[1] In the following discussion I will assume: (1) the unity of Luke–Acts as a single two-volume work with a unified purpose or purposes, and (2) a predominantly Christian audience. In my opinion, these points have been sufficiently demonstrated by previous scholarship.[2]

In an article on Lukan purpose, I.H. Marshall notes various Lukan themes which must be taken into account when seeking Luke's main aim in writing:[3] (1) Most basically, Luke's theme is Jesus himself—what

1. On the general question of Lukan purpose see W.C. van Unnik, 'The "Book of Acts": The Confirmation of the Gospel', in *Sparsa Collecta* (1973), pp. 340-73; P.S. Minear, 'Dear Theo: The Kerygmatic Intention and Claim of the Book of Acts', *Int* 27 (1973), pp. 131-50; N.A. Dahl, 'The Purpose of Luke–Acts', in *Jesus in the Memory of the Early Church* (1976), pp. 87-98; G. Schneider, 'Der Zweck des lukanischen Doppelwerks', in *Lukas, Theologe der Heilsgeschichte* (1985), pp. 9-30; I.H. Marshall, 'Luke and his 'Gospel'', in *Das Evangelium und die Evangelien* (1983), pp. 289-308; F. Bovon, 'Luc: Portrait et Projet', in *L'œuvre de Luc* (1987), pp. 15-25. See also the bibliography in Schneider, *Lucas*, p. 9 n. 1, and the works cited below.

For surveys of the various proposals see C.H. Talbert, *Luke and the Gnostics*, pp. 98-110; R.F. O'Toole, 'Why Did Luke Write Acts (Lk–Acts)?' *BTB* 7 (1977), pp. 66-76; R. Maddox, *The Purpose of Luke–Acts* (1982), pp. 20-22; W. Gasque, *A History of Criticism of the Acts of the Apostles* (1975); *idem*, 'A Fruitful Field: Recent Study of the Acts of the Apostles', *Int* 42 (1988), pp. 117-31.

2. See Maddox, *Purpose*, pp. 3-6, 12-15. These assumptions render it unlikely that Luke is writing (1) to defend Paul at his trial (A.J. Mattill), (2) to defend Christianity in the eyes of the Roman government (B.S. Easton, E. Haenchen), or (3) primarily for the purpose of evangelism (F.F. Bruce, J.C. O'Neill).

3. Marshall, 'Luke and his "Gospel"', pp. 298-303. Marshall draws an important distinction between various aspects of purpose: conscious and unconscious aims, primary and secondary aims, and a concrete occasion which gave rise to the composition (pp. 290-91). While some of the suggested proposals may serve as secondary or unconscious aims, few account sufficiently for the diversity and complexity of Luke's two-volume work. In addition to the proposals listed in note 3, this would probably rule out the following as Luke's *main* purpose in writing: (1) the desire to rehabilitate Paul against Jewish Christian attacks (J. Jervell); (2) community problems related to riches and poverty (R.J. Karris *et al.*); (3) a defense against

he did and taught and subsequently what his followers taught concerning him. (2) Leading from this, Luke writes to show how these words and deeds of Jesus led to the experience of salvation and the community of the saved. (3) Luke seeks to show the truth of the Gospel by the correspondence between prophecy and fulfillment. (4) Finally, within this framework special importance is given to the theme of the conversion of individuals and the *creation of the church* which functions both as the community of believers and as the instrument of mission:

> Luke...writes to tell the members of the church in his day 'how we got here' both in terms of individual faith and of corporate union in the people of God. He is particularly concerned with showing *how the church has come together as a company of believing Jews and Gentiles and how it is related to the Jewish roots from which it sprung.*[1] [emphasis mine]

Marshall concludes that this last theme probably sums up most comprehensively what Luke is trying to do in his two-part work. This seems to be a valid conclusion. Luke's particular interest in the Jewish origin of the church, questions of promise and fulfillment, the reasons for Jewish rejection of the Gospel and the legitimacy of the Gentile mission all point to the issue of the *church's self-identity*—the questions of 'who we are and how we got here'.

As far as a concrete situation is concerned, Marshall suggests a catechetical motivation on Luke's part. Luke seeks to fill out the story of Jesus and the growth of the church left incomplete by the general catechetical instruction in the kerygma which Theophilus and other Christians had received. This would assure them of the reliability of the Christian message.

While instruction and edification (or, 'filling out the story') are almost certainly important factors in Luke's purpose in writing, the conclusions reached in the present work would suggest a more pressing and apologetically oriented motivation as well. From a christological perspective, Luke's special interest in Jesus' words and deeds as proof of his messiahship, his repeated insistence that Scripture predicted that the Christ must suffer, and his emphasis on Jesus' exaltation-enthronement as divine vindication of his messianic status, all suggest that the issue of *Jesus' messianic identity* is a critical one for Luke and his community.

Gnosticism (C.H. Talbert); or (4) a response to the delay of the parousia (H. Conzelmann *et al.*) (for other proponents and bibliography see the surveys listed in note 2).

1. Marshall, 'Luke and his "Gospel"', p. 302.

Further, from an ecclesiological perspective Luke's desire to legitimize the Gentile mission and to explain the widespread Jewish rejection of the gospel suggest that he is seeking to reassure his audience in response to Jewish accusations against the church and its message.

In his monograph on Lukan purpose, Robert Maddox postulates just such an apologetic or confirmatory purpose. Like Marshall, Maddox sees *ecclesiology* as one of Luke's central concerns: 'Luke–Acts is in every way a book devoted to clarifying the Christian self-understanding.'[1] In his view, Luke writes to Christians suffering doubts caused by the Jewish rejection of the gospel and Jewish propaganda leveled against them: '...[Luke] writes to reassure the Christians of his day that their faith in Jesus is not an aberration, but the authentic goal towards which God's ancient dealings with Israel were driving.'[2] While Maddox rightly stresses this confirmatory or legitimizing purpose, his conclusions concerning Luke's view of the church and the extent to which Luke's community has broken away from its Jewish roots must be questioned. He suggests Luke is writing in the last two decades of the first century to a predominantly Gentile Christian audience facing renewed attacks from a Judaism reorganized at Jamnia. Disputes with the Jews—confident in their ancient traditions and their status as the people of God—have shaken his church's faith.[3] Luke responds, on the one hand, by linking the Christian message firmly to its Jewish roots, and, on the other, by stressing that despite every effort by Jesus and his followers to open the way of faith, Judaism as an organized community rejected the message and so cut itself off from the people of God.[4]

Against this last point, a growing body of scholars see greater continuity between Israel and the church, and a significant Jewish-Christian influence within Luke's community.[5] Luke does not write to record how salvation blessings were transferred from the Jews to the Gentiles, but rather how the gospel went forth *from a restored Israel*. The

1. Maddox, *Purpose*, 181. According to Maddox, Luke's other main concern is eschatology.

2. Maddox, *Purpose*, p. 187.

3. Maddox, *Purpose*, p. 184.

4. Maddox, *Purpose*, ch. 2, esp. pp. 46, 54-56.

5. So with various nuances, Jervell, *Luke and the People of God*, esp. pp. 41-74; A. George, 'Israël dans l'œuvre de Luc', *RB* 75 (1968), pp. 481-525; Lohfink, *Die Sammlung Israels*; Franklin, *Christ the Lord*, pp. 77-115; Tiede, *Prophecy and History*; R.F. O'Toole, *The Unity of Luke's Theology* (1984); Fitzmyer, *Luke the Theologian*, pp. 175-202; Brawley, *Luke–Acts and the Jews*; Koet, *Five Studies*.

proclamation of Jesus and his followers divides Israel into two groups, the repentant and the unrepentant. A faithful remnant within Israel is gathered into the messianic community of faith, while those who reject the message are cut off from the people of God (cf. Acts 3.22-23[1]). As the gospel spreads in Acts, Gentiles believe and become part of this community. The regathered remnant of Israel together with believing Gentiles make up the eschatological people of God.[2]

The conclusions of the present work would tend to support this perspective. In the birth narrative, where the program for the whole of Luke–Acts is announced, the dawn of eschatological salvation is closely associated with Israel: John will turn the sons of Israel to the Lord their God (1.16-17); Jesus will reign over the house of Jacob forever (1.32-33); the Lord God accomplishes redemption for his people Israel (1.68-75; cf. 1.54-55). The coming of the Lord's anointed will result both in light for the Gentiles and the glory of Israel (2.32). 'Israel' here cannot refer merely to the Gentile church as the 'new Israel' since Simeon's second oracle predicts the *division* of Israel. While some in Israel will 'rise', others will 'fall' (2.34). The nation is not rejected but divided. This perspective continues in the apostolic proclamation in Acts, where it is repeatedly stressed that the promises are for *Israel* (Acts 2.38-39; 3.25-26; 5.31; 13.32-33); salvation belongs first to her (3.26). When these statements are placed beside references to the large numbers of Jewish converts (2.41; 4.4; 21.20), it is evident that Luke views the Jewish mission as at least a partial success. Even at Rome, where Jewish rejection of the gospel is often said to be final, the Jews are divided in their response; while some reject the message, others are persuaded by it

1. Note how the combination of Davidic and Mosaic features in the messianic portrait of previous chapters prepares well for the *Mosaic* emphasis in this passage. The prophet like Moses, in turn, is constitutive for Israel.

2. While Jervell, *Luke and the People of God*, pp. 143, 147, claims that the Gentiles remain an 'associate people' beside the restored Israel, most of these scholars assert that Gentiles become part of the restored Israel. Cf. Fitzmyer, *Luke the Theologian*, p. 194: 'The Gentiles...are given a share in that same salvation and grace *as Gentiles*, because through repentance and baptism they have been associated with the reconstituted Israel. Indeed, they have thus become part of reconstituted Israel.' Since Luke never explicitly identifies the church as the true or restored 'Israel', I prefer the designations eschatological 'people of God' or 'community of faith'—made up of the faithful remnant of Israel together with believing Gentiles. Luke does not seem to have consciously developed his ecclesiology beyond this understanding of the relationship of Israel to the church.

(28.24).[1] Luke's concern in these passages is not to demonstrate that the Jews are lost, but rather that their widespread rejection of the gospel negates neither the plan of God nor the church's claims to be the people of God. While Luke clearly considers unrepentant Israel to be under God's judgment because of their rejection, he does not view this rejection as universal nor (necessarily) final.[2]

Drawing these results together, I would suggest that Luke writes to a Christian community—probably made up of both Jews and Gentiles[3]—struggling to assert itself as the legitimate heirs of the promises made to Israel.[4] Though here one must speculate, it seems likely that an ongoing debate with unbelieving Jews—focusing especially on the legitimacy of the Gentile mission, the widespread rejection of the message by the Jews and the validity of Jesus' messianic identity—is threatening to undermine the faith of this community. Luke writes to reassure his readers that they are the eschatological people of God, the legitimate heirs to the promises made to the fathers. On the ecclesiological side, Luke seeks to show that all along it was God's plan to bring salvation to the Gentiles, and that Jewish rejection was predicted in Scripture and was part of an ongoing history of a stubborn and resistant people. On the christological side, Luke seeks to demonstrate that Jesus is the messianic deliverer

1. For evidence that πείθω here refers to conversion see Brawley, *Luke–Acts and the Jews*, pp. 141-42. Even after Paul cites Isa. 6.9-10 and announces that salvation is sent to the Gentiles, he continues to welcome all who come to him (Acts 28.30). See Dupont, 'La conclusion des Actes', *Nouvelles etudes sur les Actes des Apôtres* (1984), pp. 457-511.

2. See Brawley, *Luke–Acts and the Jews*, esp. pp. 151-59, for evidence that Luke remains conciliatory toward the Jews. There are also indications (undeveloped to be sure) that Luke may envision a still future ingathering of Israel (cf. Lk. 21.24, 28; Acts 1.6; 3.21). See A.W. Wainwright, 'Luke and the Restoration of the Kingdom to Israel', *ExpT* 89 (1977–78), pp. 76-79. However, I would not agree with Wainwright's assertion that the redemption of Israel announced in the birth narrative did not occur. Just as Luke retains both present and future aspects of the kingdom, so (perhaps) there is an 'already' and a 'not yet' with regard to Israel's redemption.

3. For evidence of a mixed community see P.F. Esler, *Community and Gospel in Luke–Acts* (1987), pp. 30-45; M.A. Moscato, 'Current Theories regarding the Audience of Luke–Acts', *CTM* 3 (1976), pp. 355-61.

4. There appears to be a growing acceptance that this idea of 'legitimization', particularly with reference to the church's relationship with Israel, is central to Luke's overall purpose. See for example Carroll, *Response to the End of History*, p. 165. For this same idea from a sociological perspective see Esler, *Community and Gospel*, esp. pp. 16-23.

promised in Scripture, the Christ spoken about by Moses and all the prophets.[1] The theme which holds these threads together is promise and fulfillment. The church is the true eschatological community of faith because it is for her and through her that God's promises are being fulfilled.

The fulfillment of thc Davidic promise thus serves as a major theme within Luke's larger purpose. By demonstrating that Jesus is the legitimate heir to the throne of Israel, the saviour raised up in David's house, and by linking this figure to the Isaianic eschatological saviour—at the same time prophet, servant and king—Luke proves that Jesus' whole life, death, resurrection and exaltation were according to Scripture and fulfilled God's promise to place one of David's descendants upon his throne forever. Israel's promised salvation has arrived. The faithful must now repent and believe in Jesus for the forgiveness of sins.

b. *Further Implications for Lukan Theology*

i. *Christology*. The suggestion that ecclesiology is the predominant Lukan concern has implications for the nature of Luke's Christology. In the past, there has been a widespread conviction that Luke's perspective is essentially subordinationistic, presenting Jesus as inferior to the Father in status and role.[2] Conzelmann is characteristic of many when he claims that in Luke 'we see a significant distinction between Father and Son, which implies the latter's subordination'.[3] The primary reason for such claims is Luke's consistent portrayal of Jesus as the agent or instrument in the salvation-historical plan accomplished *by God*.

In a recent thesis on Lukan Christology, Douglas Buckwalter[4] strongly opposes this subordinationist position, claiming that throughout his two-volume work, Luke presents a very high *implicit* Christology. Through self-manifestions to his people (especially via his name and

1. This christological feature in Luke's *apologia* argues against the view that Luke is writing primarily to respond to Jewish Christian attacks against Paul. Jesus' messianic status is unlikely to have been contested by Jewish Christians.

2. Cf. especially H. Braun, 'Zur Terminologie der Acta von der Aufstehung Jesu', *TLZ* 77 (1952), pp. 533-36; Conzelmann, *Theology*, pp. 170-84; R.P.C. Hanson, *The Acts in the Revised Standard Version* (1967), p. 39; Kränkl, *Jesus der Knecht Gottes*, pp. 120, 162-63; Wilckens, *Missionsreden*, pp. 137-40, 174, 178; Franklin, *Christ the Lord*, pp. 54, 76; Schneider, *Apostelgeschichte*, I, pp. 331-35.

3. Conzelmann, *Theology*, p. 171.

4. H.D. Buckwalter, 'The Character and Purpose of Luke's Christology' (PhD dissertation, University of Aberdeen, 1991).

christophany), the exalted Jesus in Acts appears as immanent deity, taking on characteristics attributed to God alone in the Old Testament—including invisibility (transcendence), uniqueness and personal presence and activity. Further, Jesus' relationship with the Spirit parallels that of Yahweh and the Spirit in the Old Testament. Jesus gives the Spirit (Acts 2.33), mediates salvation (Acts 2.21) and guides his people through self-manifestation (compare Lk. 12.12 with 21.15). Finally, Luke presents Jesus as Lord of world history, actively leading it to its consummation and acting as final saviour and judge. Together, these features indicate 'that Luke believed that the exalted Jesus shares a divine status equal to the Father's, a reality which, according to Luke, Jesus apparently had known even during his earthly career (cf. Luke 21.15)'.[1] While admitting that Luke 'does not explicitly expound the deity of Christ', Buckwalter repeatedly insists that these features indicate *Luke's personal belief or conviction* concerning Jesus.[2]

While perhaps going too far at various points, Buckwalter's conclusions are important and suggest a very high Christology behind Luke's presentation. Yet it must be stated that an author's christological beliefs or personal convictions are not necessarily identical with the christological emphases which are dictated by his purpose in writing. In Chapter 1 a distinction was made between Luke's personal Christology—his total conception of who Jesus is—and his christological purpose in Luke–Acts—the particular message concerning Jesus he wishes to emphasize for his readers. There is little doubt that Luke knows and believes more about Jesus than he is able to develop in detail within the constraints of space, sources and narrative structure. While there may indeed be an implicit divine Christology in Luke–Acts, reflecting the author's personal conviction, Luke's main christological purpose must be sought in those themes and motifs which he most clearly develops. If we ask where the greatest emphasis of Luke's Christology lies, it must certainly be in his claim that Jesus is the Christ promised in Scripture and that according to Scripture—but contrary to popular expectation—the Christ had to suffer before entering his glory. The resurrection, exaltation and outpouring of the Spirit are divine confirmation that the

1. Buckwalter, 'Character and Purpose', p. 343. According to Buckwalter, the apparent subordinationism found in Luke–Acts is best viewed as part of a humiliation-exaltation theme similar to that which appears in the Christ hymn of Phil. 2.5-11.

2. Buckwalter, 'Character and Purpose', pp. 211, 224-25, 232, 273, 343; quote from 227.

promises have been fulfilled and that the eschatological time of salvation has arrived.

In light of this strong promise-fulfillment motif, it may be better to explain the apparent subordinationism of Luke–Acts with reference to Luke's limited christological purpose within his wider ecclesiological aims. If Luke is writing primarily to confirm the church's status as heirs to the Old Testament promises, his primary christological concern would almost certainly be to defend the claim that Jesus is the messianic king promised in Scripture. It should come as no surprise that he devotes little space to 'higher' christological issues such as Jesus' pre-existence or his role as creator. This does not *necessarily* mean he does not know or believe them, but only that it was not his primary interest to develop them. The conclusion of E. Franklin is worth noting here. He suggests that it is the strong influence of the Old Testament upon Luke which determines his outlook upon the salvation achieved through Jesus.[1] God himself visits and saves his people through his chosen agent, raising up and empowering him to complete the messianic task prophesied in Scripture. 'It is this understanding of God, grounded completely in its Old Testament proclamation, that is ultimately responsible for the subordinationism and lack of metaphysical speculation which is rightly seen to characterize Luke's Christology.'[2] While Franklin correctly points to Luke's use of essentially Old Testament modes of expression, he assumes too quickly that this sums up Luke's total conception of who Jesus is. It would be better to speak of Luke's 'apparent subordinationism'. Luke's limited christological purpose in emphasizing *first and foremost* Jesus as the fulfillment of Old Testament hopes and expectations gives the appearance of subordinationism. Yet Jesus' status as Lord of the Spirit, mediator of salvation and judge of the world all suggest a very high Christology, perhaps even implying divine status. These suggestions are tentative and point the way to further research. The whole question of a limited christological purpose within a wider ecclesiological aim is one which bears closer investigation.

ii. *Soteriology*. Another 'theological accusation'[3] frequently hurled at Luke is that he has eliminated the soteriological significance of the death

1. Franklin, *Christ the Lord*, pp. 48-76, esp. 54, 75-76.
2. Franklin, *Christ the Lord*, p. 76.
3. See W. Kümmel, 'Current Theological Accusations against Luke', *ANQ* 16 (1975), pp. 131-45.

of Jesus, transforming the *theologia crucis* into a *theologia gloriae*.[1] While it is certainly true that Luke says little concerning the sacrificial and vicarious nature of Jesus' death, it is going too far to claim that he has intentionally eliminated, or failed to comprehend, its saving significance. It is evident from Acts 20.28 (cf. Lk. 22.19b-20[2]) that Luke knew the meaning of the atonement, even if he has chosen not to stress or develop it.

The conclusions of the present work would suggest that Luke's particular emphasis may result more from his narrative method and his christological purpose than from a deficiency in theological knowledge or ability. Luke is not writing a treatise on soteriology but narrating the story of salvation:[3] how salvation came to Israel through Jesus the messiah; how, according to Scripture, it was made available to Gentiles; and how it is now being experienced in and through the church. As a result of this narrative presentation, the emphasis falls on the fact *that* salvation has arrived in the person and work of Jesus rather than on the theological basis upon which Jesus saves. One might say that in the Lukan story soteriology is subsumed to Christology and ecclesiology. Luke writes to show that salvation has indeed come through Jesus the messiah and that it is now being experienced in the eschatological community of faith.

This suggestion helps to explain two key aspects of Luke's soteriology. The first is his emphasis on the divine necessity of the cross.[4] As we have seen, Jesus and his followers repeatedly affirm that the suffering of the Christ was predicted in Scripture and was part of the purpose and plan of God (Lk. 24.26-27, 44-47; Acts 2.23; 3.18; 4.28; 13.27; 17.3;

1. Cf. E. Käsemann, 'Ministry and Community in the New Testament', in *Essays on New Testament Themes* (1964), p. 92; Cadbury, *Making of Luke–Acts*, pp. 280-82; Creed, *St. Luke*, pp. lxxi-lxxii; Conzelmann, *Theology*, p. 201; Haenchen, *Acts*, p. 92; Wilckens, *Missionsreden*, pp. 216-17; Vielhauer, 'On the 'Paulinism' of Acts', pp. 41-42; Talbert, *Luke and the Gnostics*, pp. 71-82.

2. On the authenticity of the longer text, see Metzger, *Textual Commentary*, pp. 173-77; Green, *Death of Jesus*, pp. 35ff.

3. See especially Fitzmyer, *Luke the Theologian*, pp. 210-13. On salvation as Luke's central theme see especially Marshall, *Historian*, esp. pp. 88-102; W.C. van Unnik, 'L'usage de SOZEIN 'Sauver' et des dérivés dans les évangiles synoptiques', I, pp. 16-34, esp. 32; *idem*, '"The Book of Acts"', I, p. 49, both in *Sparsa Collecta* (1973); Martin, 'Salvation and Discipleship', pp. 366-80; O'Toole, *Unity, passim.*

4. See especially C.H. Cosgrove, 'The Divine ΔΕΙ in Luke–Acts: Investigations into the Lukan Understanding of God's Providence', *NovT* 26 (1984), pp. 168-90.

26.23). It is the apologetic and christological significance of the cross rather than its atoning value which is Luke's primary concern. This same emphasis appears in his use of Isaianic servant categories. The citations from Isaiah 53 in Lk. 22.37 and Acts 8.32-33 demonstrate the scriptural necessity of the suffering of the messiah and so confirm that Jesus is the Christ. This does not (necessarily) mean that Luke has actively suppressed the atoning significance of the servant's suffering, but only that it was not in his purpose to stress it. His interest in the Isaianic servant is *primarily* christological rather than soteriological. Luke's description of Paul's proclamation to the Jews sums up this perspective well. In Acts 17.2-3 Paul reasons with the Jews from Scripture, 'explaining and proving that the Christ had to suffer and rise from the dead, and saying, "This Jesus whom I am proclaiming to you is the Christ."' Scriptural testimony that the Christ had to suffer serves as proof that Jesus is the Christ.

This leads to a second key aspect of Luke's soteriology, namely that he gives saving significance *to the whole Jesus event*, including the life, death, resurrection and exaltation-enthronement. As the eschatological deliverer, Jesus already brings salvation during his earthly ministry through healings and the forgiveness of sins. The death, too, is an integral part of the saving event since it was predicted in Scripture and served as 'the indispensable preliminary to the exaltation'.[1] Luke's greatest soteriological emphasis, however, lies with the resurrection and (especially) the exaltation as the climax of the messianic task (Acts 2.33; 5.30-31; 10.43; 13.37-38). When Jesus has accomplished the scripturally ordained role of the Christ and is enthroned as messiah and Lord at the right hand of God, salvation blessings are poured out on mankind. Again, Luke's overriding concern is to demonstrate that God has acted through Jesus his chosen agent to save and deliver his people. It is the initiative of God—the 'that' of salvation rather than the 'how'—which is his primary concern.[2] Salvation has been achieved because Jesus is the messiah promised in Scripture and because he has fulfilled the scripturally-ordained role of the Christ.

1. Martin, 'Salvation and Discipleship', pp. 367-68: 'a *theologia crucis* is a prelude to a *theologia gloriae*'. Cf. Fitzmyer, *Luke the Theologian*, p. 212; F. Schütz, *Der leidende Christus: Die angefochtene Gemeinde und das Christus Kerygma der lukanischen Schriften* (1969), esp. pp. 86ff.

2. Bovon, *L'œuvre de Luc*, pp. 173, 179.

iii. *Eschatology*. Finally, the present study has implications for Lukan eschatology, particularly with reference to issues of present and future eschatology in Luke–Acts. According to the 'classic theory' of Hans Conzelmann, the crisis in the church caused by the delay of the parousia prompted Luke to re-interpret his sources, pushing the consummation into the indefinite future.[1] The period of Jesus (*die Mitte der Zeit*) becomes not the inauguration of the kingdom but a 'picture' or 'type' of this far-in-the-future salvation which allows the church to endure its present suffering.[2] In the church age it is only the 'message' of the kingdom, or its 'image' rather than the kingdom itself, which is present.[3]

While it is beyond the scope of this book to respond in detail to Conzelmann and to those who have taken up his perspective, our results would suggest that Luke indeed views eschatology as in some sense already fulfilled in the words and deeds of Jesus, and in his resurrection, exaltation and present heavenly reign. This is most evident in Luke's consistent linkage between Jesus and the kingdom of God,[4] and in his identification of Jesus' words and deeds with the Isaianic signs of eschatological salvation. In the birth narrative the dawn of Israel's salvation is announced; God is about to visit and redeem his people through Jesus the messiah (1.16-17, 68-69). The implication is that God's reign is about to be established through his messianic envoy. This association of Jesus with the kingdom continues in the Gospel. Through his redaction in Lk. 4.43, Luke identifies the Nazareth sermon as the example *par excellence* of Jesus' kingdom preaching. To 'preach the kingdom' is to announce that 'today' the end time reign of God—the 'favourable year of the Lord'—is breaking in through Jesus' own words and deeds. In the narrative following the sermon, Jesus accomplishes the Isaianic signs associated with the new age, sight for the blind, freedom for the oppressed, good news for the poor. Repeatedly in the Gospel, Jesus'

1. Conzelmann, *Theology, passim.*
2. Conzelmann, *Theology*, pp. 36-37, 125, 129, 132.
3. Conzelmann, *Theology*, pp. 104-105, 107, 113-19, 122-23.
4. A number of scholars have noted the close connection between the kingdom of God and the person of Jesus. Cf. especially E.E. Ellis, *Eschatology in Luke* (1972), pp. 11-20; O. Merk, 'Das Reich Gottes in den lukanischen Schriften', in *Jesus und Paulus* (1975), pp. 201-20; J. Ernst, *Herr der Geschichte: Perspectiven der lukanischen Eschatologie* (1978); A. George, 'Le règne de Dieu', in *Etudes sur l'œuvre de Luc* (1978), pp. 295ff.; R.F. O'Toole, 'The Kingdom of God in Luke–Acts', in *The Kingdom of God in 20th-Century Interpretation* (1987), pp. 148-62; Carroll, *Response to the End of History*, pp. 80-87.

words and deeds are connected with the coming of the kingdom of God (Lk. 10.1-11; 11.20; 16.16; 17.21; cf. 9.57-62; 18.16, 18-30).

Jesus' resurrection and exaltation are also viewed by Luke as eschatological events. This is made explicit in Luke's addition of ἐν ταῖς ἐσχάταις ἡμέραις in the Joel citation at Acts 2.17. It is also implicit in the identification of Jesus' resurrection and exaltation as the fulfillment of the promises to David (2.30-36). If Jesus the messiah has assumed his eternal reign on the throne of David (Lk. 1.32-33), the new age has surely dawned. Throughout its various trajectories in the Old Testament and Judaism, the establishment of the messianic kingdom is always an 'eschatological' event, that is, it represents the end of the present age and the dawn of the age to come.[1] Though Luke does not explicitly link Jesus' heavenly reign with the kingdom of God, this connection is implicit in his presentation. The parable of the pounds is told because the disciples wrongly expect the kingdom of God to appear physically on earth when Jesus enters Jerusalem. Jesus corrects this anticipation by affirming that he will depart to receive 'a kingdom for himself', after which he will return to reward and to judge. The implication is that Jesus' exaltation and reception of royal authority is the present manifestation of the kingdom which will be consummated at his return.

Such a connection is probably also implied in the general way Luke refers to the kingdom proclamation. Only in Luke does the kingdom of God become the object of the preaching (Lk. 4.43; 8.1; 9.2, 11, 60; 16.16; Acts 1.3; 8.12; 19.8; 28.23). Conzelmann claims that Luke adopts these expressions to exclude the time element found in Mark and so to push the kingdom into the distant future.[2] Yet it must be recalled that Luke has already defined the *content* of this kingdom proclamation with the Nazareth sermon. Thus, when the disciples are sent to preach the kingdom, they are essentially preaching the Nazareth message: the time of salvation has arrived and Jesus is God's eschatological agent in the accomplishment of this salvation.[3] This same emphasis appears in Acts,

1. This is the case even when the messianic kingdom is a period preceding the resurrection and the final judgment itself. The coming of the messiah sets in motion the events leading to the End.

2. Conzelmann, *Theology*, pp. 113ff.; 114 n. 3. For similar statements with reference to Acts see Wilson, *Gentiles*, pp. 78-79; P. Vielhauer, 'Das Benedictus des Zacharias', in *Aufsätze zum Neuen Testament* (1965), p. 46.

3. Cf. Merk, 'Reich Gottes', p. 220: 'Die lukanische Wendung vom "Verkündigen des Gottesreichs" ist die Predigt des Evangeliums, die im "Heute" des Heils der Gegenwart Jesus ihre bleibende Grundlage hat (vgl. Lk. 4,21).'

where the apostolic proclamation is summarized by Luke both as preaching the 'kingdom of God' and as preaching the 'things concerning Jesus' (Acts 28.23, 31; cf. Lk. 24.37; Acts 1.3; 8.12; 9.22; 19.9). If the sermons are any guide, both expressions must mean to proclaim the life, death, resurrection, ascension-exaltation and return in glory[1] of Jesus the messiah.

Our conclusions would suggest, therefore, that for Luke the kingdom is closely associated with Jesus in its past, present and future manifestions.[2] In Jesus' ministry God's reign and kingdom is revealed through his own words and deeds. In the present age it is actualized through his heavenly reign at God's right hand. In the future it will be manifested universally at the coming of the Son of man in glory. These suggestions are of course preliminary and intended to point the way forward. The whole area of the relationship between Jesus' kingship and the kingdom of God is one which bears closer investigation, both in the Lukan corpus and in the New Testament as a whole.

Another area the present study has briefly touched upon, and one which needs further investigation, is the relationship of Jesus' kingship to his reign and guidance over the church in Acts. Two issues are particularly suggestive. The first is the present activity of the risen Lord.[3] Some scholars have claimed that Luke develops an 'absentee Christology' in Acts, presenting Jesus as inactive between the ascension and the parousia.[4] Yet if Jesus presently reigns on the eternal throne of David, this would suggest a more active and executive role, guiding and directing the church and administering the kingdom of God in the present age. A second issue concerns the relationship between the Isaianic new exodus which Jesus fulfills in the Gospel and the 'way' of the church in Acts. Is the Isaianic new exodus purely a Gospel theme, or does this motif continue in Acts, where the disciples follow the way of the Lord established through Jesus' life, death, resurrection and exaltation? The wider implications of this theme for Lukan purpose and theology offer a promising area for further research.

1. Though the consummation of the kingdom moves into the background in Acts, it remains part of the apostolic proclamation: Acts 3.19; 10.42; 17.31; cf. 1.11; 14.22.

2. Cf. the suggestive remarks of Beasley-Murray, *Jesus and the Kingdom*, pp. 144-46.

3. On this issue see R.F. O'Toole, 'Activity of the Risen Jesus in Luke–Acts', *Bib* 62 (1981), pp. 471-97; and Buckwalter, 'Character and Purpose', chs. 7–10.

4. See the literature in O'Toole, 'Activity', pp. 472-73.

BIBLIOGRAPHY

Abegg, M.G. Jr, 'Messianic Hope and 4Q285: A Reassessment', *JBL* 113 (1994), pp. 81-91.

Abel, E.L. 'The Genealogies of Jesus 'O ΨΡΙΣΤΟΣ', *NTS* 20 (1974), pp. 203-10.

Abrams, M.H., *A Glossary of Literary Terms* (New York: Holt, Rhinehart and Winston, 4th edn, 1981).

Achtemeier, E., *The Community and Message of Isaiah 56–66* (Minneapolis: Augsburg, 1982).

Ackroyd, P.R., *Exile and Restoration: A Study of Hebrew Thought in the Sixth Century BC* (London: SCM, 1968).

—'Isaiah I–XII: Presentation of a Prophet', VTSup 29 (1974), pp. 16-48.

Aldrich, W.M., 'The Interpretation of Acts 15.13-18', *BSac* 111 (1954), pp. 317-23.

Allegro, J.M., 'Fragments of a Qumran Scroll of Eschatological *Midrashim', JBL* 77 (1958), pp. 350-54.

—'Further Messianic References in Qumran Literature', *JBL* 75 (1956), pp. 174-87.

Allen, E.L., 'Jesus and Moses in the New Testament', *ExpTim* 67 (1956), pp. 104-106.

Allen, L.C., 'The Old Testament Background of (Προ-ὁρίζειν in the New Testament', *NTS* 17 (1970–71), pp. 104-108.

Alt, A., 'Jesaja 8, 23-9, 6: Befreiungsnacht und Kronungstag', in *Kleine Schriften zur Geschichte des Volkes Israel* (Munich: C.H. Beck, 1959), II, pp. 206-25.

Anderson, B.W., 'Exodus and Covenant in Second Isaiah and Prophetic Tradition', in F.M. Cross, W.E. Lemke and P.D. Miller Jr (eds.), *Magnalia Dei: The Mighty Acts of God* (New York: Doubleday, 1976), pp. 339-60.

—'Exodus Typology in Second Isaiah', in B.W. Anderson and W. Harrelson (eds.), *Israel's Prophetic Heritage* (New York: Harper & Row, 1962), pp. 177-95.

Audet, J.-P., 'Autour de la théologie de Luc I-II', *ScEccl* 11 (1959), pp. 409-18.

Bachmann, M., *Jerusalem und der Tempel: Die geographisch-theologischen Elemente in der lukanischen Sicht des jüdischen Kultzentrums* (BWANT 6th series, no. 9 [= no. 109]; Stuttgart: Kohlhammer, 1980).

Baer, H. von, *Der Heilige Geist in den Lukasschriften* (Stuttgart: Kohlhammer, 1926).

Bajard, J., 'La structure de la péricope de Nazareth en Lc. IV, 16-30: Propositions pour une lecture plus cohérente', *ETL* 45 (1969), pp. 165-71.

Barstad, H.M., *A Way in the Wilderness* (JSS Monograph, 12; Manchester: Manchester University Press, 1989).

Barth, H., *Die Jesaja-Worte in der Josiazeit* (WMANT, 48; Neukirchen–Vluyn: Neukirchener Verlag, 1977).

Beasley-Murray, G.R., *Jesus and the Kingdom of God* (Grand Rapids: Eerdmans, 1986).

—'The Two Messiahs in the Testaments of Twelve Patriarchs', *JTS* 48 (1947), pp. 1-12.

Beasley-Murray, P., 'Romans 1.3-4: An Early Confession of Faith in the Lordship of Jesus', *TynBul* 31 (1980), pp. 147-54.

Beaudet, R., 'La typologie de l'Exode dans le Second-Isaie', *LTP* 19 (1963), pp. 12-21.

Beck, B.E., '"Imitatio Christi" and the Lucan Passion Narrative', in W. Horbury and B. McNeil (eds.), *Suffering and Martyrdom in the New Testament: Studies presented to G.M. Styler by the Cambridge New Testament Seminar* (Cambridge: Cambridge University Press, 1981), pp. 28-47.

Becker, J., *Messianic Expectation in the Old Testament* (trans. D.E. Green; Edinburgh: T. & T. Clark, 1980).

Berger, K., 'Die königlichen Messiastraditionen des Neuen Testament', *NTS* 20 (1973–74), pp. 1-44.

Best, E., *Mark, the Gospel as Story* (Edinburgh: T. & T. Clark, 1983).

—*The Temptation and the Passion: The Markan Soteriology* (SNTSMS, 2; Cambridge: Cambridge University Press, 1965).

Betz, O., 'The Kerygma of Luke', *Int* 22 (1968), pp. 131-46.

—*What Do we Know About Jesus?* (trans. M. Kohl; London: SCM, 1967).

Beuken, W.A.M., 'Servant and Herald of Good Tidings: Isaiah 61 as an Interpretation of Isaiah 40–55', in *The Book of Isaiah. Le Livre D'Isaïe. Les oracles et leurs relectures unité et complexité de l'ouvrage* (BETL, 81; Leuven: Leuven University Press, 1989), pp. 411-42.

Bigg, H., 'The Q Debate since 1955', *Themelios* 6 (1981), pp. 18-28.

Black, M., *The Book of Enoch or I Enoch: A New English Edition* (SVTP, 7; Leiden: Brill, 1985).

Blass, F., and A. Debrunner, *A Greek Grammar of the New Testament and Other Early Christian Literature* (trans. and revision by R.W. Funk; Chicago/London: University of Chicago, 1961).

Blenkinsopp, J., 'Scope and Depth of the Exodus Tradition in Deutero-Isaiah', *Concilium* 2 (1966), pp. 22-26.

Blinzler, J., 'Die literarische Eigenart des sogenannten Reiseberichts im Lukasevangelium', in J. Schmid and A. Vögtle (eds.), *Synoptischen Studien* (Munich: Karl Zink, 1953), pp. 33-41.

Blomberg, C.L., 'Midrash, Chiasmus, and the Outline of Luke's Central Section', in R.T. France and David Wenham (eds.), *Gospel Perspectives*. III. *Studies in Midrash and Historiography* (Sheffield: JSOT Press, 1983), pp. 217-59.

Bock, D.L., *Proclamation from Prophecy and Pattern: Lucan Old Testament Christology* (JSNTSup, 12; Sheffield: JSOT Press, 1987).

Bockmuehl, M., 'A "Slain Messiah" in 4Q Serekh Milhamah (4Q285)?', *TynBul* 43 (1992), pp. 155-69.

Borgen, P., *Bread From Heaven: An Exegetical Study of the Concept of Manna in the Gospel of John and the Writings of Philo* (NovTSup, 10; Leiden: Brill, 1965).

Bousset, W., and H. Gressmann, *Die Religion des Judentums im spät-hellenistischen Zeitalter* (HNT, 21; Tübingen: Mohr, 4th edn, 1966).

Bovon, F., *Das Evangelium nach Lukas*. I. *Lk 1,1-9,50* (Evangelisch-Katholischer Kommentar zum Neuen Testament, 3; Zürich: Benziger, 1989).

—'La figure de Moïse dans l'œuvre de Luc', in R. Martin-Achard (ed.), *La Figure de Moïse: Ecriture et relectures* (Geneva: Labor et Fides, 1978), pp. 47-65.

—*L'œuvre de Luc* (Paris: Cerf, 1987): 'Luc: Portrait et Projet', pp. 15-25; 'Le salut dans les écrits de Luc', pp. 165-79.

—*Luc le théologien: Vingt-cinq ans de recherches (1950–75)* (Neuchatel: Delachaux & Niestlé, 1978).

Bowker, J.W., 'Speeches in Acts: A Study in Proem and Yelammedenu Form', *NTS* 14 (1967–68), pp. 96-111.

Box, G., *The Virgin Birth of Jesus* (London: Williams & Norgate, 1916).

Bratcher, R.G., 'Having Loosed the Pangs of Death', *Bible Translator* 10 (1959), pp. 18-20.

Braumann, G., 'Das Mittel der Zeit', *ZNW* 54 (1963), pp. 117-45.

Braun, H., 'Zur Terminologie der Acta von der Auferstehung Jesu', *TLZ* 77 (1952), pp. 533-36.

Brawley, R.L., *Luke–Acts and the Jews: Conflict, Apology and Conciliation* (SBLMS, 33; Atlanta: Scholars, 1987).

Bretscher, P., 'Exodus 4.22-23 and the Voice from Heaven', *JBL* 87 (1968), pp. 301-11.

Brooke, G.J., *Exegesis at Qumran: 4QFlorilegium in its Jewish Context* (JSOTSup, 29; Sheffield: JSOT Press, 1985).

Brown, F., S.R. Driver and C.A. Briggs (eds.), *The New Brown, Driver, and Briggs Hebrew and English Lexicon of the Old Testament* (Boston/London: Houghton, Mifflin & Co., 1981 [1907]).

Brown, R.E., *The Birth of the Messiah: A Commentary on the Infancy Narratives in Matthew and Luke* (New York: Doubleday, 1977).

—'Gospel Infancy Research from 1976 to 1986: Part II (Luke)', *CBQ* 48 (1986),

—'J. Starcky's Theory of Qumran Messianic Development', *CBQ* 28 (1966), pp. 51-57.

Brownlee, W.H., 'Messianic Motifs of Qumran and the New Testament', *NTS* 3 (1956–57), pp. 12-30, 195-210.

Bruce, F.F., *The Acts of the Apostles: Greek Text with Introduction and Commentary* (Grand Rapids: Eerdmans, 3rd edn, 1990).

—*Biblical Exegesis in the Qumran Texts* (London: Tyndale, 1960).

—*The Book of Acts* (NICNT; Grand Rapids: Eerdmans, rev. edn, 1988).

—'The Davidic Messiah in Luke–Acts', in *Biblical and Near Eastern Studies* (Festchrift W.S. Lasor; Grand Rapids: Eerdmanns, 1978), pp. 7-17.

—'Justification by Faith in the Non-Pauline Writings of the New Testament', *EvQ* 24 (1952), pp. 66-77.

—*This Is That: The New Testament Development of Some Old Testament Themes* (Devon: Paternoster, 1968).

Buckwalter, H.D., 'The Character and Purpose of Luke's Christology' (PhD dissertation, University of Aberdeen, 1991).

Bultmann, R., *The History of the Synoptic Tradition* (trans. J. Marsh; New York: Harper & Row, 1963).

—*The Theology of the New Testament* (trans. K. Grobel; New York: Scribners; vol. I, 1951, vol. II, 1955).

Burger, C., *Jesus als Davidssohn: Eine traditionsgeschichtliche Untersuchung* (FRLANT, 98; Göttingen: Vandenhoeck & Ruprecht, 1970).

Burrows, E., *The Gospel of the Infancy and other Biblical Essays* (London, 1941).
Buss, M.F.-J., *Die Missionspredigt des Apostels Paulus im pisidischen Antiochien. Analyse von Apg 13,16-41 im Hinblick auf die literarische und thematische Einheit der Paulusrede* (FB, 38; Stuttgart: Katholisches Bibelwerk, 1980).
Busse, U., *Das Nazareth-Manifest Jesu: Eine Einführung in das lukanische Jesusbild nach Lk 4,16-30* (SBS, 91; Stuttgart: Katholisches Bibelwerk, 1977).
—*Die Wunder des Propheten Jesus* (Stuttgart: Katholisches Bibelwerk, 1977).
Cadbury, Henry J., *The Making of Luke–Acts* (London: Macmillan, 1927).
—'The Speeches of Acts', in F.J. Foakes Jackson and K. Lake (eds.), *The Beginnings of Christianity. Part I: The Acts of the Apostles* (London: Macmillan, 5 vols.: 1920–1933), V, pp. 402-24.
Cannon, W.W., 'Isaiah 6.1-3 an Ebed-Jahweh Poem', *ZAW* 47 (1929), pp. 284-88.
Caquot, A., 'Ben Sira et le Messianisme', *Semitica* 16 (1966), 43-68.
—'La prophétie de Nathan et ses échos lyriques', VTSup 9 (1963), pp. 213-24.
—'Le messianisme Qumrânien', in *Qumrân, sa piété, sa théologie et son milieu* (BETL 46; Paris/Leuven: Gembloux/University, 1978), pp. 231-47.
Carroll, J.T., 'Luke's Crucifixion Scene', in D.D. Sylva (ed.), *Reimaging the Death of the Lukan Jesus* (BBB, 73; Frankfurt am Main: Hain, 1990), pp. 108-24.
—*Response to the End of History: Eschatology and Situation in Luke–Acts* (Atlanta: Scholars Press, 1988).
Carruth, T.R., 'The Jesus-as-Prophet Motif in Luke–Acts' (PhD dissertation; Waco, Texas: Baylor, 1973).
Cassidy, R.J., *Jesus, Politics and Society: A Study of Luke's Gospel* (Maryknoll, New York: Orbis, 1978).
Cassidy, R.J., and P.J. Scharper (eds.), *Political Issues in Luke–Acts* (Maryknoll, NY: Orbis Books, 1983).
Charlesworth, J.H., 'The Concept of the Messiah in the Pseudepigrapha', *ANRW* II 19.1 (1979), pp. 188-218.
—'From Jewish Messianology to Christian Christology: Some Caveats and Perspectives', in J. Neusner, W.C. Green and E.S. Frerichs (eds.), *Judaisms and their Messiahs at the Turn of the Christian Era* (Cambridge: Cambridge University Press, 1987), pp. 225-64.
—*The O.T. Pseudepigrapha and the New Testament: Prolegomena for the Study of Christian Origins* (SNTSMS, 54; Cambridge: Cambridge University Press, 1985).
Chase, F.H., *The Credibility of the Book of the Acts of the Apostles* (London: Macmillan, 1902).
Chatman, S., *Story and Discourse: Narrative Structure in Film and Literature* (Ithaca, NY: Cornell University Press, 1978),
Chevallier, M.-A., *L'Esprit et le Messie dans le Bas-Judïsme et le Nouveau Testament* (Paris: Universitaires de France, 1958).
Childs, B.S., *Introduction to the Old Testament as Scripture* (London: SCM, 1979).
Chilton, B.D., 'Jesus *ben David:* reflections on the *Davidssohnfrage*', *JSNT* 14 (1982), pp. 88-112.
—*The Isaiah Targum: Introduction, Translation, Apparatus and Notes* (Aramaic Bible, 11; Edinburgh: T. & T. Clark, 1987).
Clarke, W.K.L., 'The Use of the Septuagint in Acts', in F.J. Foakes Jackson and K. Lake (eds.), *The Beginnings of Christianity. Part I: The Acts of the Apostles* (5 vols.; London: Macmillan, 1920–33), II, pp. 66-105.

Clements, R.E., 'Beyond Tradition-History: Deutero-Isaianic Development of First Isaiah's Themes', *JSOT* 31 (1985), pp. 95-113.

—*Isaiah 1–39* (NCB; Grand Rapids: Eerdmans; London: Marshall, Morgan & Scott, 1980).

—'Patterns in the Prophetic Canon: Healing the Blind and the Lame', in G.M. Tucker, D.L. Petersen and R.R. Wilson (eds.), *Canon, Theology and Old Testament Interpretation: Essays in honor of Brevard S. Childs* (Philadelphia: Fortress Press, 1988), pp. 189-200.

—'The Unity of the Book of Isaiah', *Int* 36 (1982), pp. 117-29.

Clifford, R.J., *Fair Spoken and Persuading: An Interpretation of Second Isaiah* (New York: Paulist Press, 1984).

Collins, J.J., 'Messianism in the Maccabean Period', in J. Neusner, W.C. Green and E.S. Frerichs (eds.), *Judaisms and their Messiahs at the Turn of the Christian Era* (Cambridge: Cambridge University Press, 1987), pp. 97-109.

—*The Apocalyptic Imagination. An Introduction to the Jewish Matrix of Christianity* (New York: Crossroad, 1984).

Conzelmann, H., *The Theology of St Luke* (trans. G. Buswell; London: Faber & Faber, 1961).

—*Die Mitte der Zeit* (Tübingen: Mohr, 5th edn, 1964).

Cosgrove, C.H., 'The Divine ΔΕΙ in Luke–Acts: Investigations into the Lukan Understanding of God's Providence', *NovT* 26 (1984), pp. 168-90.

Creed, J.M., *The Gospel according to St. Luke: The Greek Text with Introduction, Notes and Indices* (London: Macmillan, 1950).

Crook, M.B., 'A Suggested Occasion for Isaiah 9.2-7 and 11.1-9', *JBL* 68 (1949), pp. 213-24.

Cullmann, O., *The Christology of the New Testament* (trans. S. Guthrie and C. Hall; NTL; ; Philadelphia: Westminster, 2nd edn, 1963).

Dahl, N.A, *The Crucified Messiah and Other Essays* (Minneapolis: Augsburg, 1974).

—*Jesus in the Memory of the Early Church* (Minneapolis: Augsburg, 1976).

Dalman, G., *The Words of Jesus: Considered in the Light of Post-Biblical Jewish Writings and the Aramaic Language* (trans. D.M. Kay; Edinburgh: T. & T. Clark, 1902).

Danker, F.W., *Jesus and the New Age: A Commentary on St. Luke's Gospel* (Philadelphia: Fortress Press, 2nd edn, 1988).

Daube, D., *The New Testament and Rabbinic Judaism* (London: Athlone, 1956).

Davies, J.G., 'The Prefigurement of the Ascension in the Third Gospel', *JTS* 6 (1955), pp. 229-33.

Davies, J.H., 'The Purpose of the Central Section of St. Luke's Gospel', *SE* 2, TU 87 (1964), pp. 164-69.

Davies, W.D., and D.C. Allison, *A Critical and Exegetical Commentary on the Gospel according to Matthew* (Edinburgh: T. & T. Clark; vol. I, 1988).

Deichgräber, R., *Gotteshymnus und Christushymnus* (Göttingen: Vandenhoeck & Ruprecht, 1967).

de Jonge, H.J.,'Sonship, Wisdom, Infancy: Luke II.41-51a', *NTS* 24 (1978), pp. 317-54.

de Jonge, M., 'Christian Influence in the Testaments of the Twelve Patriarchs', in *idem* (ed.), *Studies on the Testaments of the Twelve Patriarchs. Text and Interpretation* (SVTP, 3; Leiden: Brill, 1975), pp. 193-246.

—*Christology in Context: The Earliest Christian Response to Jesus* (Philadelphia: Westminster Press, 1988).

—'The Earliest Christian Use of *Christos:* Some Suggestions', *NTS* 32 (1986), pp. 321-43.

—'The Use of the Word "Anointed" in the Time of Jesus', *NovT* 8 (1966), pp. 132-48.

de Jonge, M. *et al.*, *The Testaments of the Twelve Patriarchs: A Critical Edition of the Greek Text* (Leiden: Brill, 1978).

de Jonge, M., and A.S. van der Woude, '11Q Melchizedek and the New Testament', *NTS* 12 (1965–66), pp. 301-26.

Delobel, J., 'La rédaction de Lc., IV,14-16a et le "Bericht vom Anfang", in F. Neirynck (ed.), *L'Evangile de Luc. The Gospel of Luke* (BETL, 32; Leuven: Leuven University Press, 1989), pp. 113-33, 306-12.

Dibelius, M., *From Tradition to Gospel* (trans. B. Woolf; Cambridge: James Clarke, 1971).

Dietrich, W., *Das Petrusbild der lukanischen Schriften* (Stuttgart: Kohlhammer, 1972).

Di Lella, A.A., *The Hebrew Text of Sirach* (Studies in Classical Literature, 1; London: Moulton & Co., 1966).

Dillon, R.J., 'The Acts of the Apostles', in *The New Jerome Bible Commentary* (ed. R. Brown *et al.*; London: Chapman, 1968, 1989).

—*From Eyewitnesses to Ministers of the Word: Tradition and Composition in Luke 24* (AnBib, 82; Rome: Biblical Institute, 1978).

Dodd, C.H., *According to the Scriptures: The Sub-Structure of New Testament Theology* (London: Collins, 1952).

—*The Parables of the Kingdom* (London: Nisbet, 1935).

Doeve, J.W., *Jewish Hermeneutics in the Synoptic Gospels and Acts* (Assen, Netherlands: Van Gorcum, 1954).

Dömer, M., *Das Heil Gottes: Studien zur Theologie des lukanischen Doppelwerkes* (BBB, 51; Köln/Bonn: Hanstein, 1978).

Drury, J., 'Luke', in R. Alter and F. Kermode (eds.), *The Literary Guide to the Bible* (Cambridge, MA: Harvard University Press, 1987).

—*Tradition and Design in Luke's Gospel: A Study in Early Christian Historiography* (London: Darton, Longman & Todd, 1976).

Duhm, B., *Das Buch Jesaja* (Göttinger Handkommentar zum Alten Testament; Göttingen: Vandenhoeck & Ruprecht, 5th edn, 1968).

Duling, D.C., 'Solomon, Exorcism and the Son of David', *HTR* 68 (1975), pp. 235-52.

—'The Promises to David and their Entrance into Christianity—Nailing Down a Likely Hypothesis', *NTS* 19 (1973), pp. 55-77.

—'The Therapeutic Son of David: An Element in Matthew's Christological Apologetic', *NTS* 24 (1977–78), pp. 392-410.

—'Traditions of the Promises to David and his Sons in Early Judaism and Primitive Christianity' (PhD dissertation, University of Chicago, 1970).

Dumais, M., *Le langage de l'évangélisation: L'annonce missionnaire en milieu juif (Actes 13,16-41)* (Recherches 16 Théologie; Tournai: Desclée & Cie; Montreal: Bellarmin, 1976).

Dumbrell, W.J., 'The Purpose of the Book of Isaiah', *TynBul* 36 (1985), pp. 111-28.

Dunn, J.D.G., 'Jesus—Flesh and Spirit: An Exposition of Romans I.3-4', *JTS* 24 (1973), pp. 40-68.

—'Spirit-and-Fire Baptism', *NovT* 14 (1972), pp. 81-92.

Dupont, J., *Etudes sur les Actes des Apôtres* (Paris: Cerf, 1967).

—*Etudes sur les Evangiles Synoptiques* (BETL, 70; Leuven: University, 2 vols., 1985).

—'Filius meus es tu: L'interpétation de Ps II,7 dans le Nouveau Testament', *RSR* 35 (1948), pp. 522-43.

—*Nouvelles Etudes sur les Actes des Apôtres* (LD, 118; Paris: Cerf, 1984).

—*The Salvation of the Gentiles: Studies in the Acts of the Apostles* (trans. J. Keating; New York: Paulist Press, 1979).

—*The Sources of the Book of Acts: The Present Position* (trans. K. Pond; London: Darton, Longman & Todd, 1964).

—'Un peuple d'entre les nations (Acts 15.14)', *NTS* 31 (1985), pp. 321-35.

Dupont-Sommer, A., *The Essene Writings from Qumran* (trans. G. Vermes; Oxford: Blackwell, 1961).

Eaton, J., *Festal Drama in Deutero-Isaiah* (London: SPCK, 1979).

Egelkraut, H.L., *Jesus' Mission to Jerusalem: A Redaction Critical Study of the Travel Narrative in the Gospel of Luke, Lk 9.51–19.48* (Europäische Hochschulschriften XXIII, 80; Frankfurt: Peter Lang, 1976).

Eissfeldt, O., *The Old Testament: An Introduction* (trans. P.R. Ackroyd; Oxford: Blackwell, 1965).

—'The Promises of Grace to David in Isaiah 55.1-5', in *Israel's Prophetic Heritage: Essays in Honor of James Muilenburg* (London: SCM, 1962), pp. 196-207.

Ellis, E.E., *Eschatology in Luke* (Philadelphia: Fortress Press, 1972).

—*The Gospel of Luke* (NCB; Grand Rapids: Eerdmanns; London: Marshall, Morgan & Scott, rev. edn, 1974).

—'Midrashic Features in the Speeches in Acts', in *Prophecy and Hermeneutic in Early Christianity* (Tübingen: Mohr, 1978), pp. 198-208.

—'Present and Future Eschatology in Luke', *NTS* 12 (1965–66), pp. 27-41.

Engnell, I., 'The Ebed Yahweh Songs and the Suffering Messiah in "Deutero-Isaiah"', *BJRL* 31 (1948), pp. 54-93.

Ernst, J., *Herr der Geschichte: Perspektiven der lukanischen Eschatologie* (SBS, 88; Stuttgart: Verlag Katholisches Bibelwerk, 1978).

Esler, P.F., *Community and Gospel in Luke–Acts: The Social and Political Motivations of Lucan Theology* (SNTSMS, 57; Cambridge: Cambridge University Press, 1987).

Evans, C.A., 'On the Unity and Parallel Structure of Isaiah', *VT* 38 (1988), pp. 129-47.

—'The Prophetic Setting of the Pentecost Sermon', *ZNW* 74 (1983), pp. 148-50.

Evans, C.F., *Saint Luke* (TPI New Testament Commentaries; London/Philadelphia: SCM/Trinity Press International, 1990).

—'The Central Section of St. Luke's Gospel', in D.E. Nineham (eds.), *Studies in the Gospels: Essays in Memory of R.H. Lightfoot* (Oxford: Blackwell, 1957), pp. 37-53.

Farris, S., *The Hymns of Luke's Infancy Narratives: Their Origin, Meaning and Significance* (JSNTSup, 9; Sheffield: JSOT Press, 1985).

Feiler, P.F., 'Jesus the Prophet: The Lucan Portrayal of Jesus as the Prophet like Moses' (PhD dissertation, Princeton University, 1986).

Fischer, J., 'Das Problem des neuen Exodus in Isa. 40-55', *TQ* 110 (1929), pp. 313-24.

Fishbane, M., *Text and Texture: Close Readings of Selected Biblical Texts* (New York: Schocken Books, 1979).

Fisher, L.R., 'Can This Be the Son of David?', in F.T. Trotter (ed.), *Jesus and the Historian* (FS E.C. Colwell; Philadelphia: Westminster Press, 1968), pp. 82-97.

Fitzmyer, J.A., 'David, "Being Therefore a Prophet..." (Acts 2:30)', *CBQ* 34 (1972), pp. 332-39.

—'Further Light on Melchizedek from Qumran Cave 11', *JBL* 86 (1967), pp. 25-41.

—*Luke the Theologian: Aspects of his Teaching* (London: Chapman, 1989).

—'The Aramaic "Elect of God" Text from Qumran Cave 4', in *Essays on the Semitic Background of the New Testament* (London: Chapman, 1971), pp. 127-60.

—'The Contribution of Qumran Aramaic to the Study of the NT', *NTS* 20 (1973–74), pp. 382-407.

—*The Dead Sea Scrolls: Major Publications and Tools for Study* (Atlanta: Scholars Press, rev. edn, 1990).

—*The Gospel according to Luke: A New Translation with Introduction and Commentary* (AB 28, 28A; New York: Doubleday, *Luke I–IX*, 1981; *Luke X–XXIV*, 1985).

—'The Priority of Mark and the "Q" Source in Luke', in D.Y. Hadidian (ed.), *Jesus and Man's Hope* (Pittsburgh: Pickwick, 1970), I, pp. 131-70.

—'The Son of David Tradition and Matthew 22.41-46 and Parallels', *Concilium* 2, 10 (1966), pp. 40-46.

Flender, H., *St. Luke: Theologian of Redemptive History* (Philadelphia: Fortress Press, 1967).

France, R.T., *Jesus and the Old Testament: His Application of Old Testament Passages to Himself and His Mission* (London: Tyndale, 1971).

France, R.T., and D. Wenham (eds.), *Gospel Perspectives*. III. *Studies in Midrash and Historiography* (Sheffield: JSOT Press, 1983).

Franklin, E., *Christ the Lord: A Study in the Purpose and Theology of Luke–Acts* (London: SPCK, 1975).

Freedman, D.N., 'The Chronicler's Purpose', *CBQ* 23 (1961), pp. 436-42.

Friedrich, G., 'Beobachtungen zur messianischen Hohepriestererwartung in den Synoptikern', *ZTK* 53 (1956), pp. 265-311.

Fuller, R.H., *The Foundations of New Testament Christology* (New York: Scribners, 1965).

Gagg, R.P., 'Jesus und die Davidssohnfrage', *TZ* 7 (1951), pp. 18-30.

Garnet, P., *Salvation and Atonement in the Qumran Scrolls* (WUNT, 2.3; Tübingen: Mohr, 1977).

Gasque, W.W., 'A Fruitful Field: Recent Study of the Acts of the Apostles', *Int* 42 (1988), pp. 117-31.

—*A History of the Criticism of the Acts of the Apostles* (Grand Rapids: Eerdmans, 1975).

George, A., *Etudes sur l'œuvre de Luc* (SB; Paris: Gabalda, 1978).

—'Israël dans l'œuvre de Luc', *RB* 75 (1968), pp. 481-525.

Gerhardsson, B., *The Testing of God's Son. Matt. 4.1-11 Par: An Analysis of an Early Christian Midrash* (Lund: Gleerup, 1966).

Gertner, M., 'Midrashim in the New Testament', *JSS* 7 (1962), pp. 267-92.

Gibbs, J.M., 'Purpose and Pattern in Matthew's Use of the Title Son of David', *NTS* 10 (1963–64), pp. 446-64.

Gill, D., 'Observations on the Lukan Travel Narrative and some Related Passages', *HTR* 63 (1970), pp. 199-221.

Gils, F., *Jésus prophète d'après les Evangiles Synoptiques* (Louvain: Publications universitaires, 1957).

Glombitza, O., 'Akta XIII. 15-41. Analyse einer lukanischen Predigt vor Juden', *NTS* 5 (1958–59), pp. 306-17.

Goldsmith, D., 'Acts 13.33-37: A *Pesher* on II Samuel 7', *JBL* 87 (1968), pp. 321-24.

Goldstein, J.A., 'How the Authors of 1 and 2 Maccabees Treated the "Messianic" Promises', in J. Neusner, W.C. Green and E.S. Frerichs (eds.), *Judaisms and their Messiahs at the Turn of the Christian Era* (Cambridge: Cambridge University Press, 1987), pp. 69-96.

—*I Maccabees* (AB, 41; Garden City: Doubleday, 1976).

Goppelt, L., *Apostolic and Post-Apostolic Times* (trans. R.A. Guelich; London: A. & C. Black, 1970; rpt., Grand Rapids: Baker, 1980).

Goulder, M.D., *Luke: A New Paradigm* (JSNTSup, 20; 2 vols.; Sheffield: JSOT Press, 1989).

—'On Putting Q to the Test', *NTS* 24 (1978), pp. 218-34.

—*The Evangelists' Calendar* (London: SPCK, 1978).

—'The Order of a Crank', in C.M. Tuckett (eds.), *Synoptic Studies* (Sheffield: JSOT Press, 1984).

Gray, G.B., *A Critical and Exegetical Commentary on the Book of Isaiah*. I. *Chapters I–XXVII* (Edinburgh: T. & T. Clark, 1912).

—'The Psalms of Solomon', in R.H. Charles (ed.), *The Apocrypha and Pseudepigrapha of the Old Testament*. II. *Pseudepigrapha* (Oxford: Clarendon Press, 1913), pp. 625-52.

Green, G.R., 'The Portrayal of Jesus as Prophet in Luke Acts' (PhD dissertation; Louisville, KY: Southern Baptist Theological Seminary, 1975).

Green, J.B., 'Jesus on the Mount of Olives (Luke 22.39-46): Tradition and Theology', *JSNT* 26 (1986), pp. 29-48.

—*The Death of Jesus: Tradition and Interpretation in the Passion Narrative* (WUNT 2nd series, 33; Tübingen: Mohr, 1988).

—'The Death of Jesus, God's Servant', in D.D. Sylva (ed.), *Reimaging the Death of the Lukan Jesus* (BBB, 73; Frankfurt am Main: Hain, 1990), pp. 1-28.

Green, W.S., 'Messiah in Judaism: Rethinking the Question', in J. Neusner, W.C. Green and E.S. Frerichs (eds.), *Judaisms and Their Messiahs at the Turn of the Christian Era* (Cambridge: Cambridge University Press, 1987), pp. 1-13.

Gressmann, H., *Der Messias* (FRLANT, 43; Göttingen: Vandenhoeck & Ruprecht, 1929).

Grogan, G.W., 'The Light and the Stone: A Christological Study in Luke and Isaiah', in H.H. Rowdon (ed.), *Christ the Lord: Studies in Christology Presented to Donald Guthrie* (Leicester: Inter-Varsity Press, 1982), pp. 151-67.

Grundmann, W., *Das Evangelium nach Lukas* (THKNT, 3; Berlin: Evangelische Verlagsanstalt, 2nd edn, 1961).

—*Das Evangelium nach Markus* (THKNT, 2; Berlin: Evangelische Verlagsanstalt, 1971).

—'Fragen der Komposition des lukanischen "Reiseberichts"', *ZNW* 50 (1959), pp. 252-70.

Guelich, R.A., *Mark 1-8:26* (WBC, 34A; Dallas, Texas: Word Books, 1989).

Gundry, R.H., *The Use of the Old Testament in St. Matthew's Gospel: With Special Reference to the Messianic Hope* (NovTSup, 18; Leiden: Brill, 1967).

Haenchen, E., *The Acts of the Apostles* (trans. B. Nobel, G. Shinn, R. McL. Wilson; Oxford: Blackwell, 1971).

—*Der Weg Jesu: Eine Erklärung des Markus-Evangeliums und der kanonischen Parallelen* (Berlin: Töpelmann, 1966).

Hahn, F., *The Titles of Jesus in Christology: Their History in Early Christianity* (trans. H. Knight and G. Ogg; New York: World, 1969).

Hammershaimb, E., *The Book of Amos: A Commentary* (Oxford: Blackwell, 1970).

Hann, R.R., '*Christos Kyrios* in Ps Sol 17.32: "The Lord's Anointed" Reconsidered', *NTS* 31 (1985), pp. 620-27.

Hanson, R.P.C., *The Acts in the Revised Standard Version* (NCB; Oxford: Oxford University Press, 1967).

—'Does δίκαιος in Luke xxiii.47 Explode the Proto-Luke Hypothesis?', *Hermathena* 60 (1942), pp. 74-78.

Hawkins, J.C., *Horae Synopticae: Contributions to the Study of the Synoptic Problem* (Oxford: Clarendon Press, 1909).

Hartman, L., 'Davids son: A propa Acta 13,16-41', *SEÅ* 18–19 (1964), pp. 117-34.

Harvey, A.E., *Jesus and the Constraints of History* (Philadelphia: Westminster Press, 1982).

Hay, D.M., *Glory at the Right Hand. Psalm 110 in Early Christianity* (SBLMS, 18; Nashville: Abingdon, 1973).

Hayes, J.H., 'The Resurrection as Enthronement and the Earliest Church Christologies', *Int* 22 (1968), pp. 333-45.

Hellholm, D., 'The Problem of Apocalyptic Genre and the Apocalypse of John', in K.H. Richards (ed.), *Society of Biblical Literature 1982 Seminar Papers* (Chico, CA: Scholars Press, 1982), pp. 157-98.

Hengel, M., *Between Jesus and Paul: Studies in the Earliest History of Christianity* (trans. J. Bowden; Philadelphia: Fortress Press, 1983).

—*Judaism and Hellenism: Studies in their Encounter in Palestine during the Early Hellenistic Period* (trans. J. Bowden; Philadelphia: Fortress Press, 1974).

—*The Son of God: The Origin of Christology and the History of Jewish-Hellenistic Religion* (trans. J. Bowden; Philadelphia: Fortress Press, 1976).

Holtz, T., *Untersuchungen über die alttestamentlichen Zitate bei Lukas* (TU, 104; Berlin: Akademie, 1968).

Hooker, M.D. *Jesus and the Servant: The Influence of the Servant Concept of Deutero-Isaiah in the New Testament* (London: SPCK, 1959).

Horsley, R.A., 'Popular Messianic Movements around the Time of Jesus', *CBQ* 46 (1984), pp. 471-95.

Horsley, R.A., with J.S. Hanson, *Bandits, Prophets, and Messiahs: Popular Movements in the Time of Jesus* (San Francisco: Harper & Row, 1985).

Horton, F.L. Jr, *The Melchizedek Tradition: A Critical Examination of the Sources to the Fifth Century A.D. and in the Epistle to the Hebrews* (SNTSMS, 30; Cambridge: Cambridge University Press, 1976).

Houston, W.J., '"Today in Your Very Hearing": Some Comments on the Christological Use of the Old Testament', in L.D. Hurst and N.T. Wright (eds.), *The Glory of Christ in the New Testament. Studies in Christology in Memory of George Bradford Caird* (Oxford: Clarendon Press, 1987), pp. 37-47.

Hurtado, L.W., *Mark* (New International Biblical Commentary; Peabody, MA: Hendrickson, 1989).

Isaac, E., '1 (Ethiopic Apocalypse of) Enoch', in J.H. Charlesworth (ed.), *The Old Testament Pseudepigrapha* (Garden City, NY: Doubleday, vol. I, 1983; vol. II, 1985), I, pp. 5-89.

Jackson, F.J.F., and K. Lake (eds.), *The Beginnings of Christianity*. I. *The Acts of the Apostles* (5 vols.; London: Macmillan, 1920–1933).

Jeremias, J., *Die Sprache des Lukasevangeliums: Redaktion und Tradition im NichtMarkusstoff des dritten Evangeliums* (Göttingen: Vandenhoeck & Ruprecht, 1980).

—*Jerusalem in the Time of Jesus* (Philadelphia: Fortress Press, 1969).

—*Jesus' Promise to the Nations* (London: SCM Press, 1958).

—*New Testament Theology: The Proclamation of Jesus* (trans. John Bowden; New York: Scribner's, 1971).

—*The Eucharistic Words of Jesus* (trans. Norman Perrin; London: SCM, 1966).

—*The Prayers of Jesus* (SBT, II 2; London: SCM, 1967).

Jervell, J., *Luke and the People of God: A New Look at Luke–Acts* (Minneapolis: Augsburg, 1972).

Jewett, R., *Paul's Anthropological Terms: A Study of their Use in Conflict Settings* (AGJU, 10; Leiden: Brill, 1971).

Johnson, L.T., *The Literary Function of Possessions in Luke–Acts* (SBLDS, 39; Missoula: Scholars, 1977).

—'The Lukan Kingship Parable (Lk. 19.11-27)', *NovT* 24 (1982), pp. 139-59.

Johnson, M.D., *The Purpose of the Biblical Genealogies, with Special Reference to the Setting of the Genealogies of Jesus* (SNTSMS, 8; Cambridge: Cambridge University Press, 2nd edn, 1988).

Johnson, S.E., 'The Davidic-Royal Motif in the Gospels', *JBL* 87 (1968), pp. 136-50.

Jones, D.L., 'The Title *Christos* in Luke–Acts', *CBQ* 32 (1970), pp. 69-76.

—'The Title "Servant" in Luke–Acts', in C.H. Talbert (ed.), *Luke–Acts, New Perspectives from the Society of Biblical Literature Seminar* (New York: Crossroad, 1984), pp. 148-65.

Josephus, *Josephus, with an English translation* (trans. H. St. J. Thackeray, R. Marcus, A. Wikgren and L.H. Feldman; LCL; London: Heinemann, 1926-1965), 9 vols.

Justin Martyr, *The Apologies of Justin Martyr* (ed. A.W.F. Blunt; Cambridge Patristic Texts; Cambridge: Cambridge University Press, 1911).

—*The Writings of Justin Martyr and Athenagoras* (trans. M. Dods, G. Reith and B.P. Pratten; Edinburgh: T. & T. Clark, 1867).

Kaiser, O., *Isaiah 1–12* (trans. John Bowden; OTL; London: SCM, 1983).

Kaiser, W.C. Jr, 'The Blessing of David: The Charter for Humanity' in J.H. Skilton (ed.), *The Law and the Prophets: OT Studies Prepared in Honor of O.T. Allis* (Philadelphia: Presbyterian and Reformed, 1974), pp. 310-18.

—'The Davidic Promise and the Inclusion of the Gentiles (Amos 9:9-15 and Acts 15.13-18): A Test Passage for Theological Systems', *JETS* 20 (1977), pp. 97-111.

—'The Promise to David in Psalm 16 and its Application in Acts 2.25-33 and 13.32-37', *JETS* 23 (1980), pp. 219-29.

Karimattam, M., 'Jesus the Prophet: A Study of the Prophet Motif in the Christology of Luke–Acts' (PhD dissertation; Pontifical Biblical Institute, Rome, 1978).

Karrer, M., *Der Gesalbte: Die Grundlagen des Christustitels* (FRLANT, 151; Göttingen: Vandenhoeck & Ruprecht, 1990).

Karris, R.J., *Luke: Artist and Theologian. Luke's Passion Account as Literature* (New York: Paulist Press, 1985).

—'Luke 23:47 and the Lucan View of Jesus' Death', in D.D. Sylva (ed.), *Reimaging the Death of the Lukan Jesus* (BBB, 73; Frankfurt am Main: Hain, 1990), pp. 68-78 (reprinted from *JBL* 105 [1986], pp. 65-74).

Käsemann, E., 'Ministry and Community in the New Testament', in *Essays on New Testament Themes* (SBT, 41; London: SCM, 1964), pp. 63-94.

Kealy, S.P., 'A Jubilee Spirituality', *Doctrine and Life* 33 (1983), pp. 584-92.

Kee, H.C., 'Testaments of the Twelve Patriarchs', in J.H. Charlesworth (ed.), *The Old Testament Pseudepigrapha* (Garden City, NY: Doubleday, vol. I, 1983; vol. II, 1985), I, pp. 775-828.

Kelber, W.H., *The Kingdom in Mark* (Philadelphia: Fortress Press, 1974).

Kilpatrick, G.D., 'A Theme of the Lucan Passion Story and Luke xxxiii.47', *JTS* 43 (1942), pp. 34-36.

Kingsbury, J.D., *Matthew as Story* (Philadelphia: Fortress Press, 1986).

—*The Christology of Mark's Gospel* (Philadelphia: Fortress Press, 1983).

—'The Title "Son of David" in Matthew's Gospel', *JBL* 95 (1976), pp. 591-602.

Klausner, J., *Jesus of Nazareth: His Life, Times, and Teaching* (New York/London: George Allen & Unwin, 1925).

—*The Messianic Idea in Israel: From Its Beginning to the Completion of the Mishnah* (trans. W.F. Stinespring; New York: Macmillan, 1955; German original, Cracow, 1903).

Knight, G.A.F., *Deutero-Isaiah* (New York/Nashville: Abingdon, 1965).

Knox, W.L., *The Acts of the Apostles* (Cambridge: Cambridge University Press, 1948).

Koet, B.J., *Five Studies on Interpretation of Scripture in Luke–Acts* (Studiorum Novi Testamenti Auxilia 14; Leuven: University, 1989).

Kramer, W., *Christ, Lord, Son of God* (trans. B. Hardy; SBT, 50; London: SCM, 1966).

Kränkl, E., *Jesus der Knecht Gottes: Die heilsgeschichtliche Stellung Jesu in den Reden der Apostelgeschichte* (Biblische Untersuchungen, 8; Regensburg: Friedrich Pustet, 1972).

Kremer, J., *Pfingstbericht und Pfingstgeschehen: Eine exegetische Untersuchung zu Apg. 2,1-13* (SB, 63-64; Stuttgart: KBW, 1973).

Kretschmar, G., 'Himmelfahrt und Pfingsten', *ZKG* 66 (1954-55), pp. 209-53.

Kuhn, G., 'Die Geschlechtsregister Jesu bei Lukas und Matthäus nach ihrer Herkunft untersucht', *ZNW* 22 (1923), pp. 206-28.

Kuhn, K.G., 'The Two Messiahs of Aaron and Israel', in K. Stendahl (ed.), *The Scrolls and the New Testament* (London: SCM, 1958), pp. 54-64.

Kümmel, W.G., 'Current Theological Accusations against Luke', *ANQ* 16 (1975), pp. 131-45.

—'"Das Gesetz und die Propheten gehen bis Johannes"—Lukas 16,16 im Zusammenhang der heilsgeschichtlichen Theologie der Lukasschriften', in O. Böcher and K. Haacker (eds.), *Verborum Veritas* (Festchrift G. Stählin; Wuppertal: Theologischer Verlag Rolf Brockhaus, 1970), pp. 89-102.

—*Promise and Fulfillment: The Eschatological Message of Jesus* (trans. D.M. Barton; London: SCM, 1957).

Kurz, W.S., 'Narrative Approaches to Luke–Acts', *Bib* 68 (1987), pp. 195-220.

Lagrange, M.J., *Evangile selon Saint Luc* (Paris: Libr. V. Lecoffre, 2nd edn, 1921).

Lampe, G.W.H., 'The Holy Spirit in the Writings of Luke', in D.E. Nineham (ed.), *Studies in the Gospels: Essays in Memory of R.H. Lightfoot* (Oxford: Blackwell, 1957), pp. 159-200.

—'The Lucan Portrait of Christ', *NTS* 2 (1955–56), pp. 160-75.

—*The Seal of the Spirit: A Study in the Doctrine of Baptism and Confirmation in the New Testament and the Fathers* (London: SPCK, 1967).

Lane, W.L., *The Gospel according to Mark* (NICNT; Grand Rapids: Eerdmans, 1974).

Larkin, W.J., 'Luke's Use of the Old Testament as a Key to his Soteriology', *JETS* 20 (1977), pp. 325-35.

—'The Old Testament Background of Luke XXII. 43-44', *NTS* 25 (1978–79), pp. 250-54.

Laurentin, R., *Structure et Théologie de Luc I-II* (Ebib; Paris: Gabalda, 1964).

Leaney, A.R.C., *The Gospel according to St. Luke* (Black's New Testament Commentaries; London: A. & C. Black, 2nd edn, 1966).

Le Déaut, 'Pentecost and Jewish Tradition', *Doctrine and Life* 20 (1970), pp. 250-67.

Levey, S.H., *The Messiah: An Aramaic Interpretation. The Messianic Exegesis of the Targum* (HUCM, 2; Cincinnati: Hebrew Union College, 1974).

Liefeld, W.L., 'Theological Motifs in the Transfiguration Narrative', in R.N. Longenecker and M.C. Tenney (eds.), *New Dimensions in New Testament Study* (Grand Rapids: Zondervan, 1974), pp. 162-79.

Lindars, B., *New Testament Apologetic: The Doctrinal Significance of the Old Testament Quotations* (London: SCM, 1961).

Linnemann, E., 'Tradition und Interpretation in Röm. 1,3f', *EvT* 31 (1971), pp. 264-75.

Liver, J., 'The Doctrine of the Two Messiahs in Sectarian Literature in the Time of the Second Commonwealth', *HTR* 52 (1959), pp. 149-85.

Loader, W.R.G., 'Christ at the Right Hand: Ps. cx. 1 in the New Testament', *NTS* 24 (1977–78), pp. 199-217.

Lohfink, G., *Die Sammlung Israels: Eine Untersuchung zur lukanischen Ekklesiologie* (SANT, 39; Munich: Kösel, 1975).

Lohmeyer, E., *Das Evangelium des Markus* (MeyerK, I, II; Göttingen, 16th edn, 1963).

—*Gottesknecht und Davidssohn* (FRLANT, 43; Göttingen: Vandenhoeck & Ruprecht, 1953).

Lohse, E., 'Der König aus Davids Geschlecht: Bemerkungen zur messianischen Erwartung der Synagoge', in O. Betz *et al.* (eds.), *Abraham Unser Vater. Juden und Christen im Gespräch über die Bibel* (Festschrift Otto Michel; Leiden: Brill, 1963), pp. 337-45.

Loisy, A., *Les Actes des Apôtres* (Paris, 1920).

Longenecker, R.N., 'The Acts of the Apostles', in F.E. Gaebelein (ed.), *The Expositors Bible Commentary* (Grand Rapids: Zondervan; vol. IX, 1981).

Lövestam, E., 'Die Davidssohnfrage', *SEÅ* 27 (1962), pp. 72-82.

—'Jésus Fils de David chez les Synoptiques', *ST* 28 (1974), pp. 97-109.

—*Son and Saviour: A Study of Acts 13,32-37. With an Appendix: 'Son of God' in the Synoptic Gospels* (ConBNT, 18; Lund: C.W.K. Gleerup; Copenhagen: Ejnar Munksgaard, 1961).

MacRae, A., 'The Scientific Approach to the OT', *BSac* 110 (1953), pp. 309-11.

McCown, C.C., 'The Geography of Luke's Central Section', *JBL* 57 (1938), pp. 51-66.

McKenzie, J.L., 'Royal Messianism', *CBQ* 19 (1957), pp. 25-52.

—'The Dynastic Oracle: II Samuel 7', *TS* 8 (1947), pp. 187-218.

Maddox, R., *The Purpose of Luke–Acts* (FRLANT, 126; Göttingen: Vandenhoeck & Ruprecht, 1982).

Mánek, J., 'The New Exodus in the Books of Luke', *NovT* 2 (1958), pp. 8-23.

Mann, J., *The Bible as Read and Preached in the Old Synagogue* (Cincinnati; vol. I, 1940; vol. II, 1966).

Manson, T.W., *The Sayings of Jesus, as Recorded in the Gospels of St. Matthew and St Luke* (London: SCM, 1949).

—*The Teaching of Jesus: Studies in its Form and Content* (Cambridge: Cambridge University Press, 1935; 1959).

Manson, W., *The Gospel of Luke* (MNTC; London: Hodder and Stoughton, 1930).

Marshall, I.H., *Luke: Historian and Theologian* (Exeter: Paternoster, 1970).

—'Luke and His "Gospel"', in P. Stuhlmacher (ed.), *Das Evangelium und die Evangelien* (WUNT, 28; Tübingen: Mohr, 1983), pp. 289-308.

—'Palestinian and Hellenistic Christianity: Some Critical Comments', *NTS* 19 (1972–73), pp. 271-87.

—'Son of God or Servant of Yahweh?: A Reconsideration of Mark I.11', *NTS* 15 (1968–69), pp. 326-36.

—*The Acts of the Apostles* (Tyndale New Testament Commentaries; Leicester: Inter-Varsity Press, 1980).

—'The Divine Sonship of Jesus', *Int* 21 (1967), pp. 87-103.

—*The Gospel of Luke: A Commentary on the Greek Text* (NIGTC; Grand Rapids: Eerdmans, 1978).

—'The Significance of Pentecost', *SJT* 30 (1977), pp. 347-69.

Martin, R.A., *Mark: Evangelist and Theologian* (Grand Rapids: Zondervan, 1973).

—'Salvation and Discipleship in Luke's Gospel', *Int* 30 (1976), pp. 366-80.

Masson, J., *Jésus fils de David dans les généalogies de Saint Mathieu et de Saint Luc* (Paris: Téqui, 1982).

Menzies, R.P., *The Development of Early Christian Pneumatology: With Special Reference to Luke–Acts* (JSOTSup, 54; Sheffield: JSOT, 1991).

Merk, O., 'Das Reich Gottes in den lukanischen Schriften', in E.E. Ellis and E. Gräßer (eds.), *Jesus und Paulus* (Festschrift W.G. Kümmel; Göttingen: Vandenhoeck & Ruprecht, 1975), pp. 201-20.

Metzger, B.M., *A Textual Commentary on the Greek New Testament* (Stuttgart: United Bible Societies, 1975).

—'The Fourth Book of Ezra', in J.H. Charlesworth (ed.), *The Old Testament Pseudepigrapha* (Garden City, NY: Doubleday, vol. I, 1983; vol. II, 1985), I, pp. 516-59.

Michaelis, W., 'Die Davidssohnschaft Jesu als historisches und dogmatisches Problem', in H. Ristow and K. Matthiae (eds.), *Der historische Jesus und der kerygmatische Christus. Beiträge zum Christusverständnis in Forschung und Verkündigung* (Berlin: Evangelische Verlagsanstalt, 1963), pp. 317-30.

Michel, O., *Der Brief an die Römer* (Gottingen: Vandenhoeck & Ruprecht; 12th edn, 1963).

Milik, J.T., 'Problèmes de la littérature hénochique à la lumière des fragments araméens de Qumrân', *HTR* 64 (1971), pp. 333-78.

—*Ten Years of Discovery in the Wilderness of Judaea* (trans. J. Strugnell; SBT, 26; London: SCM, 1959).

Miller, M., 'The Function of Isa. 61.1-2 in 11Q Melchizedek', *JBL* 88 (1969), pp. 467-69.

Miller, P.D., 'An Exposition of Luke 4.16-21', *Int* 29 (1975), pp. 417-21.

Miller, R.J., 'Elijah, John, and Jesus in the Gospel of Luke', *NTS* 34 (1988), pp. 611-22.

Minear, P.S., 'A Note on Luke xxii 36', *NovT* 7 (1964), pp. 128-34.

—'Dear Theo: The Kerygmatic Intention and Claim of the Book of Acts', *Int* 27 (1973), pp. 131-50.

—'Luke's Use of the Birth Stories', in L.E. Keck and J.L., Martyn (eds.), *Studies in Luke–Acts* (London: SPCK, 1966), pp. 111-30.

—*To Heal and to Reveal: The Prophetic Vocation according to Luke* (New York: Seabury, 1976).

Moessner, D.P., *Lord of the Banquet: The Literary and Theological Significance of the Lukan Travel Narrative* (Minneapolis: Fortress Press, 1989).

Moo, D.J., *The Old Testament in the Gospel Passion Narratives* (Sheffield: Almond Press, 1983).

Morgenstern, J., 'The Suffering Servant, a New Solution', *VT* 11 (1961), pp. 292-320.

Morgenthaler, R., *Statistik des Neutestamentlichen Wortschatzes* (Zurich: Gotthelf, 1982).

Moscato, M.A., 'Current Theories regarding the Audience of Luke–Acts', *CTM* 3 (1976), pp. 355-61.

Moule, C.F.D., *The Birth of the New Testament* (San Francisco: Harper & Row, 3rd edn, 1982).

Mowinckel, S., *He That Cometh* (trans. G.W. Anderson; Oxford: Blackwell, 1956).

Muilenburg, J., *Isaiah Chapters 40–66* (*IB*, 5; New York and Nashville: Abingdon, 1956).

Navone, J., *Themes of St. Luke* (Rome: Gregorian University, 1970).

Nebe, G., *Prophetische Züge im Bilde Jesu bei Lukas* (BWANT, 127; Stuttgart: Kohlhammer, 1989).

Neirynck, F., 'La matière marcienne dans l'évangile de Luc', in F. Neirynck (ed.), *L'evangile de Luc. The Gospel of Luke* (BETL, 32; Leuven: Leuven University Press, 1989), pp. 67-111, 304-305.

—*The Minor Agreements of Matthew and Luke against Mark, with a Cumulative List* (BETL, 37; Gembloux: Duculot, 1974).

Neugebauer, F., 'Die Davidssohnfrage (Mark xii. 35-7 parr.) und der Menschensohn', *NTS* 21 (1974), pp. 81-108.

Neusner, J., *Messiah in Context: Israel's History and Destiny in Formative Judaism* (Philadelphia: Fortress Press, 1984).

Neusner, J., W.C. Green and E.S. Frerichs (eds.), *Judaisms and their Messiahs at the Turn of the Christian Era* (Cambridge: Cambridge University Press, 1987).

Neyrey, J., *The Passion according to Luke: A Redaction Study of Luke's Soteriology* (New York/Mahwah: Paulist Press, 1985).

Nickelsburg, G.W.E., *Jewish Literature between the Bible and the Mishnah: A Historical and Literary Introduction* (London: SCM, 1981).

—'Salvation without and with a Messiah: Developing Beliefs in Writings Ascribed to Enoch', in J. Neusner, W.C. Green and E.S. Frerichs (eds.), *Judaisms and their*

Messiahs at the Turn of the Christian Era (Cambridge: Cambridge University Press, 1987), pp. 49-68.

Nixon, R.E., *The Exodus in the New Testament* (London: Tyndale, 1963).

Noack, B., 'The Day of Pentecost in Jubilees, Qumran and Acts', *ASTI* 1 (1962), pp. 73-95.

Nola, M.F., 'Towards a Positive Understanding of the Structure of Luke–Acts' (PhD dissertation; University of Aberdeen, 1987).

Nolland, J.L., 'Classical and Rabbinic Parallels to "Physician, Heal Yourself" (Lk iv 23)', *NovT* 21 (1979), pp. 193-209.

—*Luke 1–9:20* (WBC, 35A; Dallas, Texas: Word Books, 1989).

Noorda, S.J., '"Cure Yourself Doctor!" (Luke 4, 23): Classical Parallels to an Alleged Saying of Jesus', in J. Delobel (ed.), *Logia, Les Paroles de Jésus. The Sayings of Jesus* (BETL, 59; Leuven: Leuven University Press, 1982), pp. 459-67.

North, C.R., *The Suffering Servant in Deutero-Isaiah: An Historical and Critical Study* (London: Oxford University Press, 1948).

North, R., 'Theology of the Chronicler', *JBL* 82 (1963), pp. 369-81.

Noth, M., *Gesammelte Studien zum Alten Testament* (Munich: Kaiser, 1960).

—'God, King, People in the Old Testament', *Journal for Theology and Church* 1 (1965), pp. 20-45.

O'Dell, J., 'The Religious Background of the Psalms of Solomon', *RevQ* 3 (1961–62), pp. 241-57.

O'Doherty, E., 'The Organic Development of Messianic Revelation', *CBQ* 19 (1957), pp. 16-24.

Oesterley, W.O.E., *The Jewish Background of the Christian Liturgy* (Oxford: Clarendon Press, 1921).

Oliver, H.H., 'The Lucan Birth Stories and the Purpose of Luke–Acts', *NTS* 10 (1963–64), pp. 202-26.

O'Neill, J.C., *The Theology of Acts in its Historical Setting* (London: SPCK, 1961; 2nd edn, 1970).

Origen, *Origen: Contra Celsum* (trans. and ed. H. Chadwick: Cambridge: Cambridge University Press, 1953).

O'Toole, R.F., 'Activity of the Risen Jesus in Luke–Acts', *Bib* 62 (1981), pp. 471-97.

—'Acts 2.30 and the Davidic Covenant of Pentecost', *JBL* 102 (1983), pp. 245-58.

—'Luke's Position on Politics and Society', in R.J. Cassidy and P.J. Scharper (eds.), *Political Issues in Luke–Acts* (Maryknoll, NY: Orbis Books, 1983), pp. 1-17.

—'Luke's Understanding of Jesus' Resurrection-Ascension-Exaltation', *BTB* 9 (1979), pp. 106-14.

—'The Kingdom of God in Luke–Acts', in W. Willis (ed.), *The Kingdom of God in 20th-Century Interpretation* (Peabody, MA: Hendrickson, 1987), pp. 148-62.

—*The Unity of Luke's Theology: An Analysis of Luke–Acts* (Wilmington: Glazier, 1984).

—'Why Did Luke Write Acts (Lk–Acts)?' *BTB* 7 (1977), pp. 66-76.

Ott, W., *Gebet und Heil: Die Bedeutung der Gebetsparänese in der lukanischen Theologie* (SANT, 12; Munich: Kösel, 1965).

Ottley, R.R. (trans. and ed.), *The Book of Isaiah according to the Septuagint (Codex Alexandrinus)* (Cambridge: Cambridge University Press, vol. I, 1904; vol. II, 1906).

Page, S.H.T., 'The Suffering Servant between the Testaments', *NTS* (1985), pp. 481-97.

Patsch, H., 'Der Einzug Jesu in Jerusalem', *ZTK* 68 (1971), pp. 1-26.

Paulo, P.-A., *Le problème ecclésial des Actes à la lumière de deux prophéties d'Amos* (Collection Recherches, n.s. 3; Montreal: Bellarmin; Paris: Cerf, 1985).

Perrot, C., 'Les décisions de l'assemblé de Jérusalem', *RSR* 69 (1981), pp. 195-208.

Pesch, R., *Die Apostelgeschichte.* (Evangelisch-Katholischer Kommentar zum Neuen Testament 5; 2 vols.; Zürich: Benziger Verlag, 1986).

Petersen, N.R., *Literary Criticism for New Testament Critics* (Philadelphia: Fortress Press, 1978).

Philo Judaeus (trans. F.H. Colson and G.H. Whitaker; LCL; 10 vols.; London: Heinemann, 1929–41).

Plummer, A., *A Critical and Exegetical Commentary on the Gospel according to St Luke* (ICC; Edinburgh: T. & T. Clark, 4th edn, 1901).

Pokorny, P., *The Genesis of Christology: Foundations for a Theology of the New Testament* (trans. M. Lefébure; Edinburgh: T. & T. Clark, 1987).

Potin, J., *La fête juive de la Pentecôte* (Paris: Cerf, 1971).

Potterie, I. de la, 'L'onction du Christ', *NRT* 80 (1958), pp. 225-52.

Poythress, V.S., 'Is Romans 1.3-4 a *Pauline* Confession after All?', *ExpTim* 87 (1975–76), pp. 180-83.

Prior, J.W., 'John 4.44 and the "Patris" of Jesus', *CBQ* 49 (1987), pp. 254-63.

Pritchard, J.B. (ed.), *Ancient Near Eastern Texts Relating to the Old Testament* (Princeton, NJ: Princeton University Press, 1950).

Rad, G. von, *Old Testament Theology* (trans. D.M.G. Stalker; Edinburgh and London: Oliver & Boyd; vol. I, 1962; vol. II, 1965).

—'The Royal Ritual in Judah', in *The Problem of the Hexateuch and other Essays* (trans. E.W.T. Dicken; Edinburgh: Oliver & Boyd, 1966).

Rahlfs, A. (ed.), *Septuaginta* (Stuttgart: Deutsche Bibelgesellschaft, 1935, 1979).

Reicke, B., 'Instruction and Discussion in the Travel Narrative', *SE I*, TU 73 (1959), pp. 206-16.

—'Jesus in Nazareth—Luke 4,14-30', in H. Balz and S. Schulz (eds.), *Das Wort und die Wörter* (Festschrift G. Friedrich; Stuttgart: Kohlhammer, 1973), pp. 47-55.

Rendtorff, R., *The Old Testament: An Introduction* (London: SCM, 1985).

—'Zur Komposition des Buches Jesajas', *VT* 34 (1984), pp. 295-320.

Rese, M., *Alttestamentliche Motive in der Christologie des Lukas* (SNT, 1; Gerd Mohn: Gütersloher Verlagshaus, 1969).

Rhoads, D., and D. Michie, *Mark as Story. An Introduction to the Narrative of a Gospel* (Philadelphia: Fortress Press, 1982).

Ringe, S.H., 'Luke 9.28-36: The Beginning of an Exodus', *Semeia* 28 (1983), pp. 83-99.

Ringgren, H., *The Faith of Qumran: Theology of the Dead Sea Scrolls* (trans. E.T. Sander; Philadelphia: Fortress Press, 1961).

—*The Messiah in the Old Testament* (London: SCM Press, 1956).

Roberts, J.J.M., 'Isaiah in Old Testament Theology', *Int* 30 (1982).

Robbins, V.K., 'The Healing of Blind Bartimaeus (10:46-52) in the Marcan Theology', *JBL* 92 (1973), pp. 224-43.

Robinson, J.A.T., 'The Most Primitive Christology of All?', *JTS* 7 (1956), pp. 177-89.

Robinson, W.C., *Der Weg des Herrn: Studien zur Geschichte und Eschatologie im Lukas-Evangelium: Ein Gespräch mit Hans Conzelmann* (*TF*, 36; Hamburg/Bergstedt: Herbert Reich, 1964).

Roloff, J., *Die Apostelgeschichte* (NTD, 5; Göttingen: Vandenhoeck & Ruprecht, 17th edn, 1981).

Rosscup, J.E., 'The Interpretation of Acts 15:13-18' (ThD dissertation; Dallas Theological Seminary, 1966).

Rowley, H.H., 'The Servant of the Lord in the Light of Three Decades of Criticism', in *The Servant of the Lord and other Essays on the Old Testament* (London: Lutterworth, 1952), pp. 1-57.

—'The Suffering Servant and the Davidic Messiah', in *The Servant of the Lord and other Essays on the Old Testament* (London: Lutterworth, 1952), pp. 61-88.

Ryle, H.S., and M.R. James, *ΨΑΛΜΟΙ ΣΟΛΟΜΩΝΤΟΣ, Psalms of the Pharisees: Commonly Called The Psalms of Solomon* (Cambridge: Cambridge University Press, 1891).

Sahlin, H., *Der Messias und das Gottesvolk: Studien zu protolukanischen Theologie* (ASNU, 12; Uppsala: Almqvist, 1945).

Sanders, J.A., 'From Isaiah 61 to Luke 4', in J. Neusner (ed.), *Christianity, Judaism and other Greco-Roman Cults: Studies for Morton Smith at Sixty* (SJLA, 12; Leiden: Brill, 1975), I, pp. 75-106.

—'Isaiah in Luke', *Int* 30 (1982), pp. 144-55.

—'The Ethic of Election in Luke's Great Banquet Parable', in J.L. Crenshaw and J.T. Willis (eds.), *Essays in Old Testament Ethics* (New York: Ktav, 1974), pp. 247-71.

Sanders, J.A. (ed.), *The Dead Sea Psalms Scroll* (Ithaca, NY: Cornell University Press, 1967).

Sanders, J.T., *The Jews in Luke–Acts* (Philadelphia: Fortress Press, 1987).

—'The Prophetic Use of the Scriptures in Luke–Acts', in *Early Jewish and Christian Exegesis: Studies in Memory of William Hugh Brownlee* (Atlanta, GA: Scholars Press, 1987), pp. 191-98.

Sawyer, J.F.A., *From Moses to Patmos: New Perspectives in Old Testament Study* (London: SPCK, 1977).

Schlier, H., 'Zu Röm 1,3-4', in H. Baltensweiler and B. Reicke (eds.), *Neues Testament und Geschichte: Historisches Geschehen und Deutung im Neuen Testament* (Festschrift O. Cullman; Zürich/Tübingen: Theologischer Verlag, 1972), pp. 207-18.

Schmidt, D., 'Luke's "Innocent" Jesus: A Scriptural Apologetic', in R.J. Cassidy and P.J. Scharper (eds.), *Political Issues in Luke–Acts* (Maryknoll, NY: Orbis Books, 1983), pp. 111-21.

Schmidt, K.L., *Der Rahmen der Geschichte Jesu. Literarkritische Untersuchungen zur ältesten Jesusüberlieferung* (Berlin: Trowitzsch & Sohn, 1919).

Schneider, G., *Das Evangelium nach Lukas* (Ökumenischer Taschenbuchkommentar zum Neuen Testament, 3; 2 vols.; Gütersloh; Mohn; Würzburg: Echter, 1977).

—*Die Apostelgeschichte* (HTKNT, 5; Freiburg: Herder, vol. I, 1980, vol. II, 1982).

—'Die Davidssohnfrage (Mk 12,35-37) *Biblica* 53 (1972), pp. 65-90.

—'Lk. 1,34.35 als redaktionelle Einheit', *BZ* 15 (1971), pp. 255-59.

—*Lukas, Theologe der Heilsgeschichte: Aufsätze zum lukanischen Doppelwerk* (BBB, 59; Bonn: Hanstein, 1985): 'Der Zweck des lukanischen Doppelwerks', pp. 9-30.

—*Verleugnung, Verspottung und Verhör Jesu nach Lukas 22,54-71: Studien zur lukanischen Darstellung der Passion* (SANT, 22; Munich: Kösel, 1969).

—'Zur Vorgeschichte des christologischen Prädikats "Sohn Davids"', *TTZ* 80 (1971), pp. 247-53.

Schnider, F., *Jesus der Prophet* (OBO, 2; Fribourg/Göttingen: Vandenhoeck & Ruprecht, 1973).

Schniewind, J., *Das Evangelium nach Markus* (NTD, 1; Göttingen: Vandenhoeck & Ruprecht, 10th edn, 1963).

Schoors, A., *I Am God your Saviour: A Form-Critical Study of the Main Genres of Is. XL–LV* (VTSup 24; Leiden: Brill, 1973).

Schramm, T., *Der Markus-Stoff bei Lukas: Eine literarkritische und redaktionsgeschichtliche Untersuchung* (SNTSMS, 14; Cambridge: Cambridge University Press, 1971).

Schreck, C.J., 'The Nazareth Pericope, Luke 4,16-30 in Recent Study', in *L'Evangile de Luc. The Gospel of Luke* (BETL, 32; Leuven: Leuven University Press, 1989), pp. 399-471.

Schubert, P., 'The Structure and Significance of Luke 24', in W. Eltester (ed.), *Neutestamentliche Studien für Rudolf Bultmann* (BZNW, 21; Berlin: Töpelmann, 1957), pp. 165-86.

Schulz, S., *Q: Die Spruchquelle der Evangelisten* (Zürich: Theologischer-Verlag, 1972).

Schüpphaus, J., *Die Psalmen Salomos: Ein Zeugnis jerusalemer Theologie und Frömmigkeit in der Mitte des vorchristlichen Jahrhunderts* (ALGHJ, 7; Leiden: Brill, 1977).

Schürer, E., *The History of the Jewish People in the Age of Jesus Christ (175 BC–AD 135): A New English Version Revised and Edited by Geza Vermes, Fergus Millar, Matthew Black* (Edinburgh: T. & T. Clark; I, 1973; II, 1979; III.1, 1986; III.2, 1987).

Schürmann, H., *Das Lukasevangelium I. Kommentar zu Kap. 1,1-9,50* (HTKNT, 3; Freiburg: Herder, 1969).

—'Der "Bericht vom Anfang": Ein Rekonstruktionsversuch auf Grund von Lk. 4,14-16', in *SE*, II; TU 87 (1964), pp. 242-58.

—'Zur Traditionsgeschichte der Nazareth-Perikope Lk 4,16-30', in A. Descamps and A. de Halleux (eds.), *Mélanges bibliques* (Festschrift B. Rigaux; Gembloux: Duculot, 1970), pp. 187-205.

Schütz, F., *Der leidende Christus: Die angefochtene Gemeinde und das Christus Kerygma der lukanischer Schriften* (BWANT, 9; Stuttgart: Kohlhammer, 1969).

Schweizer, E., *Erniedrigung und Erhöhung bei Jesus und seinen Nachfolgern* (ATANT, 28; Zürich: Zwingli-Verlag, 1962).

—'The Concept of the Davidic "Son of God" in Acts and its Old Testament Background', in L.E. Keck and J.L. Martyn (eds.), *Studies in Luke–Acts* (London: SPCK, 1966), pp. 208-16.

—*Jesus* (trans. D. E. Green; London: SCM, 1968).

—'Röm 1,3-4 und der Gegensatz von Fleisch und Geist vor und bei Paulus', *Neotestamentica* (Zurich-Stuttgart: Zwingli, 1963), pp. 180-89.

—*The Good News according to Luke* (trans. D.E. Green; London: SPCK, 1984).

—*The Good News according to Mark* (trans. D.H. Madvig; London: SPCK, 1971).

Seccombe, D., 'Luke and Isaiah', *NTS* 27 (1981), pp. 252-59.

Semain, E., 'Le récit de la Pentecôte, Actes 2,1-13', *La Foi et le Temps*, n.s. (1971), pp. 227-56.

Senior, D., *The Passion of Jesus in the Gospel of Luke* (Wilmington, DE: Michael Glazier, 1989).

Shin, G.K.-S., *Die Ausrufung des endgültigen Jubeljahres durch Jesus in Nazareth: Eine historisch-kritische Studie zu Lk 4,16-30* (Europäische Hochschulschriften, series 23, vol. 378; Bern: Peter Lang, 1989).

Simpson, P., 'The Drama of the City of God: Jerusalem in St. Luke's Gospel', *Scripture* 15 (1963), pp. 65-80.

Skehan, P.W., and A.A. Di Lella, *The Wisdom of Ben Sira: A New Translation and Notes* (AB, 39; New York: Doubleday, 1987).

Skinner, J., *The Book of the Prophet Isaiah* (2 vols.; Cambridge: Cambridge University Press, 2nd edn, 1917; rpt. 1929–30).

Sloan, R.B., *The Favorable Year of the Lord: A Study of Jubilary Theology in the Gospel of Luke* (Austin, Texas: Schola Press, 1977).

Snodgrass, K.R., 'Streams of Tradition Emerging from Isaiah 40.1-5 and their Adaptation in the New Testament', *JSNT* 8 (1980), pp. 24-45.

Soards, M.L., *The Passion according to Luke: The Special Material of Luke 22* (JSNTSup, 14; Sheffield: JSOT, 1987).

Songer, H.S., 'Luke's Portrayal of the Origins of Jesus', *RevExp* 64 (1967), pp. 453-63.

Staerk, W. (ed.), *Altjüdische liturgische Gebete* (Bonn: A. Marcus and E. Weber, 1910).

Stählin, G., *Die Apostelgeschichte* (NTD, 5; Göttingen: Vandenhoeck & Ruprecht, 1936; 1962).

Stanton, G.N., *A Gospel for a New People: Studies in Matthew* (Edinburgh: T. & T. Clark, 1992).

Starcky, J., 'Les quatre étapes du messianisme à Qumran', *RB* 70 (1963), pp. 481-505.

Steck, O.H., *Israel und das gewaltsame Geschick der Propheten* (Neukirchen–Vluyn: Neukirchener, 1967).

Stendahl, K., *The School of Saint Matthew and its Use of the OT* (Philadelphia: Fortress Press, 1968).

Stone, M.E., *Fourth Ezra: A Commentary on the Book of Fourth Ezra* (Hermeneia; Philadelphia: Fortress Press, 1990).

—'The Concept of the Messiah in IV Ezra', in J. Neusner (eds.), *Religions in Antiquity: Essays in Memory of Erwin Ramsdell Goodenough* (Studies in the History of Religions, 14; Leiden: Brill, 1968), pp. 295-312.

—'The Question of the Messiah in 4 Ezra', in J. Neusner, W.S. Green and E. Frerichs (eds.), *Judaisms and Their Messiahs at the Turn of the Christian Era* (Cambridge: Cambridge University Press, 1987), pp. 209-24.

Stonehouse, N.B., *The Witness of the Synoptic Gospels to Christ* (Grand Rapids: Baker, rpt. 1979 [1944]).

Streeter, B.H., *The Four Gospels* (London: Macmillan, 1953).

Strobel, A., 'Die Ausrufung des Jobeljahres in der Nazarethpredigt Jesu: zur apokalyptischen Tradition Lk 4. 16-30', in W. Eltester (ed.), *Jesus in Nazareth* (Berlin: de Gruyter, 1972), pp. 38-50.

Stuhlmacher, P., *Das paulinische Evangelium*. I. *Vorgeschichte* (FRLANT, 95; Göttingen: Vandenhoeck & Ruprecht, 1968).

Stuhlmueller, C., *Creative Redemption in Deutero-Isaiah* (AnBib, 43; Rome: Pontifical Biblical Institute, 1970).

Styler, G.M., 'The Priority of Mark', in C.F.D. Moule, *The Birth of the New Testament* (San Francisco, CA: Harper & Row, 2nd edn, 1982), pp. 285-316.

Suhl, A., 'Der Davidssohn im Matthäus-Evangelium', *ZNW* 59 (1968), pp. 57-81.

—*Die Funktion der alttestamentlichen Zitate und Anspielungen im Markusevangelium* (Gütersloh: Gerd Mohn, 1965).

Sweeney, M.A., *Isaiah 1–4 and the Post-Exilic Understanding of the Isaianic Tradition* (BZAW, 171; Berlin/New York: de Gruyter, 1988).

Talbert, C.H., *Literary Patterns, Theological Themes, and the Genre of Luke–Acts* (SBLMS, 20; Montana: Scholars Press, 1974).

—*Luke and the Gnostics: An Examination of the Lucan Purpose* (Nashville: Abingdon, 1966).

—'Martyrdom in Luke–Acts and the Lukan Social Ethic', in R.J. Cassidy and P.J. Scharper (eds.), *Political Issues in Luke–Acts* (Maryknoll, NY: Orbis Books, 1983), pp. 99-110.

—'Prophecies of Future Greatness: The Contribution of Greco-Roman Biographies to an Understanding of Luke 1.5–4.15', in *The Divine Helmsman: Studies on God's Control of Human Events* (Festschrift L.H. Silberman; New York: Ktav, 1980), pp. 129-41.

—*Reading Luke: A Literary and Theological Commentary on the Third Gospel* (New York: Crossroad, 1982).

Tannehill, R.C., 'A Study in the Theology of Luke–Acts', *ATR* 43 (1961), pp. 195-203.

—'The Mission of Jesus according to Luke IV.16-30', in W. Eltester (ed.), *Jesus in Nazareth* (Berlin/New York: de Gruyter, 1972), pp. 51-75.

—*The Narrative Unity of Luke—Acts: A Literary Interpretation*. I. *The Gospel according to Luke*; II. *The Acts of the Apostles* (Philadelphia: Fortress Press; vol. I, 1986; vol. II, 1990).

Tatum, W.B., 'The Epoch of Israel: Luke i–ii and the Theological Plan of Luke–Acts', *NTS* 13 (1966–67), pp. 184-95.

Taylor, V., *Behind the Third Gospel* (Oxford: Clarendon Press, 1926).

—*The Gospel according to St Mark: The Greek Text with Introduction, Notes and Indexes* (Grand Rapids: Baker, 2nd edn, 1966; rpt. 1981).

—*The Passion Narrative of St Luke: A Critical and Historical Investigation* (ed. O.E. Evans; Cambridge: Cambridge University Press, 1972).

Teeple, H.M., *The Mosaic Eschatological Prophet* (JBL Monograph Series, 10; Philadelphia: SBL, 1957).

Tiede, D.L., *Prophecy and History in Luke–Acts* (Philadelphia: Fortress Press, 1980).

Thyen, H., *Der Stil der jüdisch-hellenistischen Homilie* (FRLANT, 65; Göttingen: Vandenhoeck & Ruprecht, 1955).

Tuckett, C.M., 'On the Relationship between Matthew and Luke', *NTS* 30 (1984), pp. 130-42.

—*The Revival of the Griesbach Hypothesis* (Cambridge: Cambridge University Press, 1983).

Turner, C.H., 'Ο υἱός μου ὁ ἀγαπητός', *JTS* 27 (1925–26), pp. 113-29.

Turner, M.M.B., 'Holy Spirit', in J.B. Green, S. McKnight and I.H. Marshall (eds.), *Dictionary of Jesus and the Gospels* (Leicester: Inter-Varsity Press, 1992), pp. 341-51.

—'Jesus and the Spirit in Lucan Perspective', *TynBul* 32 (1981), pp. 3-42.
—'The Spirit and the Power of Jesus' Miracles in the Lucan Conception', *NovT* 33 (1991), pp. 124-52.
—'The Spirit of Christ and Christology', in H.H. Rowdon (ed.), *Christ the Lord: Studies in Christology Presented to Donald Guthrie* (Leicester: Inter-Varsity Press, 1982), pp. 168-90.
Tyson, J.B., *The Death of Jesus in Luke–Acts* (Columbia, SC: University of South Carolina, 1986).
Tyson, J.B. (ed.), *Luke–Acts and the Jewish People: Eight Critical Perspectives* (Minneapolis: Augsburg, 1988).
Unnik, W.C. van, *Sparsa Collecta* (NovTSup; Leiden: Brill, 1973): 'L'usage de SOZEIN "Sauver" et des dérivés dans les évangiles synoptiques', I, pp. 16-34; 'The "Book of Acts" the Confirmation of the Gospel', pp. 340-73.
—'Jesus the Christ', *NTS* 8 (1961–62), pp. 101-16.
Untergassmair, F.G., *Kreuzweg und Kreuzigung Jesu* (Paderborn: Schöningh, 1980).
Vanhoye, A., 'Structure du "Benedictus"', *NTS* 12 (1965–66), pp. 382-89.
van Iersel, B.M.F., 'The Finding of Jesus in the Temple: Some Observations on the Original Form of Luke ii 40-52a', *NovT* 4 (1960), pp. 161-73.
Vermes, G., *The Dead Sea Scrolls in English* (London: Penguin, 3rd edn, 1987).
—'The Oxford Forum for Qumran Research Seminar on the Rule of War from Cave 4 (4Q285)', *JJS* 43 (1992), pp. 85-90.
Vermeylen, J., *Du prophète Isaie à l'Apocalyptique. Isaie 1-35* (2 vols.; Paris: Lecoffre, 1977–78).
—'L'unité du livre d'Isaïe', in *The Book of Isaiah. Le Livre d'Isaïe: Les oracles et leurs relectures unité et complexité de l'ouvrage* (BETL, 81; Leuven: Leuven University Press, 1989), pp. 11-53.
Vielhauer, P., 'Apocalypses and Related Subjects', in E. Hennecke and W. Schneemelcher (eds.), *New Testament Apocrypha* (Philadelphia: Westminster Press, 1965), II, pp. 581-607.
—*Aufsätze zum Neuen Testament* (TBü, 31; Munich: Chr. Kaiser, 1965).
—'On the "Paulinism" of Acts', in L.E. Keck and J.L. Martyn (eds.), *Studies in Luke–Acts* (London: SPCK, 1966), pp. 33-50.
von Waldow, H.E., 'The Message of Deutero-Isaiah', *Int* 22 (1968), pp. 259-87.
Voss, G., *Die Christologie der lukanischen Schriften in Grundzügen* (StudNeot, 2; Paris: Desclée de Brouwer, 1965).
—'Die Christusverkündigung der Kindheitsgeschichte im Rahmen des Lukasevangeliums', *BK* 21 (1966), pp. 112-15.
Wainwright, A.W., 'Luke and the Restoration of the Kingdom to Israel', *ExpT* 89 (1977–78), pp. 76-79.
Walaskay, P.W., *'And so we Came to Rome': The Political perspective of St. Luke* (Cambridge: Cambridge University Press, 1983).
—'The Trial and Death of Jesus in the Gospel of Luke', *JBL* 94 (1975), pp. 81-93.
Watts, R.E., 'Consolation or Confrontation? Isaiah 40–55 and the Delay of the New Exodus', *TynBul* 41.1 (1990), pp. 31-59.
—'The Influence of the Isaianic New Exodus on the Gospel of Mark' (PhD dissertation, Cambridge, 1990).

Weiser, A., *Die Apostelgeschichte*. I. *Kapitel 1–12*; II. *Kapitel 13–28* (Ökumenischer Taschenbuchkommentar zum Neuen Testament 5; Gütersloh: Gütersloher Verlaghaus; vol. I, 1982; vol. II, 1985).
—*Die Knechtsgleichnisse der synoptischen Evangelien* (SANT, 29; Munich: Kösel, 1971).
Weiss, J., *Earliest Christianity* (2 vols.; New York: Harper & Brothers, 1959).
Wellhausen, J., *Die Pharisäer und die Sadduzäer: Eine Untersuchung zur inneren jüdischen Geschichte* (Greifswald: L. Bamberg, 1874).
Wendt, H.H., *Die Apostelgeschichte* (MeyerK; Göttingen: Vandenhoeck & Ruprecht, 1913).
Wenham, J.W., 'Synoptic Independence and the Origin of Luke's Travel Narrative', *NTS* 27 (1980–81), pp. 509-10.
Westermann, C., *Genesis 37–50: A Commentary* (trans. J.J. Scullion; London: SPCK, 1986).
—*Isaiah 40–66: A Commentary* (trans. D.M.G. Stalker; OTL; London: SCM, 1969).
Whybray, R.N., *Isaiah 40–66* (NCB; London: Marshall, Morgan & Scott, 1975).
—*The Second Isaiah* (Sheffield: JSOT Press, 1983).
Wilckens, U., *Die Missionsreden der Apostelgeschichte: Form und traditionsgeschichtliche Untersuchungen* (WMANT, 5; Neukirchen–Vluyn: Neukirchener Verlag, 3rd edn, 1974).
Wilcox, M., *The Semitisms of Acts* (Oxford: Clarendon Press, 1965).
Wilms, G.H., 'Deuteronomic Traditions in St. Luke's Gospel' (PhD dissertation, Edinburgh University, 1972).
Wilson, S.G., *The Gentiles and the Gentile Mission in Luke–Acts* (Cambridge: Cambridge University Press, 1973).
Wink, W., *John the Baptist in the Gospel Tradition* (SNTSMS, 7; Cambridge: Cambridge University Press, 1968).
Winter, P., 'Lukanische Miszellen: Lc 2 11: ΧΡΙΣΤΟΣ ΚΥΡΙΟΣ oder ΧΡΙΣΤΟΣ ΚΥΡΙΟΥ?', *ZNW* 49 (1958), pp. 65-77.
Wood, C.E., 'The Use of the Second Psalm in Jewish and Christian Traditions of Exegesis: A Study of Christian Origins' (PhD dissertation; St. Andrews, 1976).
Woude, A.S. van der, *Die messianischen Vorstellungen der Gemeinde von Qumran* (SSN, 3; Assen: Van Gorcum, 1957).
—'Melchisedek als himmlische Erlösergestalt in den neugefundenen eschatologischen Midraschim aus Qumran Höhle XI', *OTS* 14 (1965), pp. 354-73.
Wrede, W., 'Jesus als Davidssohn', in *Vorträge und Studien* (Tübingen: Mohr, 1907), pp. 147-77.
Wright, A.G., 'The Literary Genre Midrash', *CBQ* 28 (1966), pp. 105-38, 417-57.
Wright, R.B., 'The Psalms of Solomon', in J.H. Charlesworth (ed.), *The Old Testament Pseudepigrapha* (Garden City, NY: Doubleday, vol. I, 1983; vol. II, 1985), I, pp. 639-70.
Young, E.J., *The Book of Isaiah* (NICOT; Grand Rapids: Eerdmans; vol. I, 1965; vol. II, 1970).
Zahn, T. von, *Das Evangelium des Lukas ausgelegt* (Leipzig: Deichert, 4th edn, 1930).
Zehnle, R.F., *Peter's Pentecost Discourse* (SBLMS, 15; New York/Nashville: Abingdon, 1971).
Zillessen, A., 'Der alte und der neue Exodus', *ARW* 30 (1903), pp. 289-304.

Zimmerli, W., 'Das "Gnadenjahr des Herrn"', in *Archäologie und Altes Testament: Festschrift für Kurt Galling* (Tübingen: Mohr, 1970), pp. 321-32.

—'Der "neue Exodus" in der Verkündigung der beiden grossen Exilspropheten', in *Gottes Offenbarung: Gesammelte Aufsätze zum Alten Testament* (TBü, 19; Munich: Kaiser, 1963), pp. 192-204.

Zimmerman, C., 'To This Agree the Words of the Prophets', *Grace Journal* 4 (1963), pp. 28-40.

INDEXES

INDEX OF REFERENCES

OLD TESTAMENT

PSEUDEPIGRAPHA

MISHNAH AND TALMUDS

MIDRASH

OTHER ANCIENT WRITINGS

INDEX OF AUTHORS

JOURNAL FOR THE STUDY OF THE NEW TESTAMENT

Supplement Series

65 The Rhetoric of Righteousness in Romans 3.21-26
Douglas A. Campbell

66 Paul, Antioch and Jerusalem:
A Study in Relationships and Authority in Earliest Christianity
Nicholas Taylor

67 The Portrait of Philip in Acts:
A Study of Roles and Relations
F. Scott Spencer

68 Jeremiah in Matthew's Gospel:
The Rejected-Prophet Motif in Matthaean Redaction
Michael P. Knowles

69 Rhetoric and Reference in the Fourth Gospel
Margaret Davies

70 After the Thousand Years:
Resurrection and Judgment in Revelation 20
J. Webb Mealy

71 Sophia and the Johannine Jesus
Martin Scott

72 Narrative Asides in Luke–Acts
Steven M. Sheeley

73 Sacred Space:
An Approach to the Theology of the Epistle to the Hebrews
Marie E. Isaacs

74 Teaching with Authority:
Miracles and Christology in the Gospel of Mark
Edwin K. Broadhead

75 Patronage and Power:
A Study of Social Networks in Corinth
John Kin-Man Chow

76 The New Testament as Canon:
A Reader in Canonical Criticism
Robert Wall and Eugene Lemcio

77 Redemptive Almsgiving in Early Christianity
Roman Garrison

78 The Function of Suffering in Philippians
L. Gregory Bloomquist

79 The Theme of Recompense in Matthew's Gospel
Blaine Charette

80 Biblical Greek Language and Linguistics:
Open Questions in Current Research
Edited by Stanley E. Porter and D.A. Carson

81 THE LAW IN GALATIANS
In-Gyu Hong
82 ORAL TRADITION AND THE GOSPELS:
THE PROBLEM OF MARK 4
Barry W. Henaut
83 PAUL AND THE SCRIPTURES OF ISRAEL
Edited by Craig A. Evans and James A. Sanders
84 FROM JESUS TO JOHN:
ESSAYS ON JESUS AND NEW TESTAMENT CHRISTOLOGY IN HONOUR OF MARINUS DE JONGE
Edited by Martinus C. De Boer
85 RETURNING HOME:
NEW COVENANT AND SECOND EXODUS AS THE CONTEXT FOR 2 CORINTHIANS 6.14–7.1
William J. Webb
86 ORIGINS OF METHOD:
TOWARDS A NEW UNDERSTANDING OF JUDAISM AND CHRISTIANITY—ESSAYS IN HONOUR OF JOHN C. HURD
Edited by Bradley H. McLean
87 WORSHIP, THEOLOGY AND MINISTRY IN THE EARLY CHURCH:
ESSAYS IN HONOUR OF RALPH P. MARTIN
Edited by Michael Wilkins and Terence Paige
88 THE BIRTH OF THE LUKAN NARRATIVE
Mark Coleridge
89 WORD AND GLORY:
ON THE EXEGETICAL AND THEOLOGICAL BACKGROUND OF JOHN'S PROLOGUE
Craig A. Evans
90 RHETORIC IN THE NEW TESTAMENT:
ESSAYS FROM THE 1992 HEIDELBERG CONFERENCE
Edited by Stanley E. Porter and Thomas H. Olbricht
91 MATTHEW'S NARRATIVE WEB:
OVER, AND OVER, AND OVER AGAIN
Janice Capel Anderson
92 LUKE:
INTERPRETER OF PAUL, CRITIC OF MATTHEW
Eric Franklin
93 ISAIAH AND PROPHETIC TRADITIONS IN THE BOOK OF REVELATION:
VISIONARY ANTECEDENTS AND THEIR DEVELOPMENT
Jan Fekkes
94 JESUS' EXPOSITION OF THE OLD TESTAMENT IN LUKE'S GOSPEL
Charles A. Kimball
95 THE SYMBOLIC NARRATIVES OF THE FOURTH GOSPEL:
THE INTERPLAY OF FORM AND MEANING
Dorothy A. Lee

96 THE COLOSSIAN CONTROVERSY:
WISDOM IN DISPUTE AT COLOSSAE
Richard E. DeMaris

97 PROPHET, SON, MESSIAH:
NARRATIVE FORM AND FUNCTION IN MARK 14–16
Edwin K. Broadhead

98 FILLING UP THE MEASURE:
POLEMICAL HYPERBOLE IN 1 THESSALONIANS 2.14-16
Carol J. Schlueter

99 PAUL'S LANGUAGE ABOUT GOD
Neil Richardson

100 TO TELL THE MYSTERY:
ESSAYS ON NEW TESTAMENT ESCHATOLOGY IN HONOR OF ROBERT H. GUNDRY
Edited by Thomas E. Schmidt and Moisés Silva

101 NEGLECTED ENDINGS:
THE SIGNIFICANCE OF THE PAULINE LETTER CLOSINGS
Jeffrey A.D. Weima

102 OTHER FOLLOWERS OF JESUS:
MINOR CHARACTERS AS MAJOR FIGURES IN MARK'S GOSPEL
Joel F. Williams

103 HOUSEHOLDS AND DISCIPLESHIP:
A STUDY OF MATTHEW 19–20
Warren Carter

104 THE GOSPELS AND THE SCRIPTURES OF ISRAEL
Edited by Craig A. Evans and W. Richard Stegner

105 THE BIBLE, THE REFORMATION AND THE CHURCH:
ESSAYS IN HONOUR OF JAMES ATKINSON
Edited by W.P. Stephens

106 JEWISH RESPONSIBILITY FOR THE DEATH OF JESUS IN LUKE–ACTS
Jon A. Weatherly

107 PROLOGUE AND GOSPEL:
THE THEOLOGY OF THE FOURTH EVANGELIST
Elizabeth Harris

108 GOSPEL IN PAUL:
STUDIES ON CORINTHIANS, GALATIANS AND ROMANS FOR RICHARD N. LONGENECKER
Edited by L. Ann Jervis and Peter Richardson

109 THE NEW LITERARY CRITICISM AND THE NEW TESTAMENT
Edited by Elizabeth Struthers Malbon and Edgar V. McKnight

110 THE DAVIDIC MESSIAH IN LUKE–ACTS:
THE PROMISE AND ITS FULFILLMENT IN LUKAN CHRISTOLOGY
Mark L. Strauss